The
Bible Knowledge
Commentary

WISDOM

The
Bible Knowledge Commentary

WISDOM

John F. Walvoord and Roy B. Zuck
GENERAL EDITORS

DAVID **C** COOK
transforming lives together

THE BIBLE KNOWLEDGE COMMENTARY: WISDOM
Published by David C Cook
4050 Lee Vance Drive
Colorado Springs, CO 80918 U.S.A.

David C Cook U.K., Kingsway Communications
Eastbourne, East Sussex BN23 6NT, England

The graphic circle C logo is a registered trademark of David C Cook.

The website addresses recommended throughout this book are offered as a resource
to you. These websites are not intended in any way to be or imply an endorsement
on the part of David C Cook, nor do we vouch for their content.

Unless otherwise noted, all Scripture quotations are taken from the Holy Bible, New
International Version®, NIV®. Copyright © 1973, 1978 by Biblica, Inc.™ Used by
permission of Zondervan. All rights reserved worldwide. www.zondervan.com.
The authors have added italics to Scripture quotations for emphasis.

LCCN 2017955599
ISBN 978-0-8307-7264-3
eISBN 978-0-8307-7294-0

Cover Design: Nick Lee
Cover Photo: Getty Images

Printed in the United States of America
First Edition 2018

1 2 3 4 5 6 7 8 9 10

010818

CONTENTS

PREFACE

The Bible Knowledge Commentary series is an exposition of the Scriptures written and edited solely by Dallas Seminary faculty members. It is designed for pastors, laypersons, Bible teachers, serious Bible students, and others who want a comprehensive but brief and reliable commentary on the entire Bible.

Why another Bible commentary when so many commentaries are already available? Several features make this series a distinctive Bible study tool.

The Bible Knowledge Commentary series is written by faculty members of one school: Dallas Theological Seminary. This commentary interprets the Scriptures consistently from the grammatical-historical approach and from the pretribulational, premillennial perspective, for which Dallas Seminary is well known. At the same time, the authors often present various views of passages where differences of opinion exist within evangelical scholarship.

Additionally, this commentary has features that not all commentaries include. (a) In their comments on the biblical text, the writers discuss how the purpose of the book unfolds, how each part fits with the whole and with what precedes and follows it. This helps readers see why the biblical authors chose the material they did as their words were guided by the Holy Spirit's inspiration. (b) Problem passages, puzzling Bible-time customs, and alleged contradictions are carefully considered and discussed. (c) Insights from modern conservative biblical scholarship are incorporated in this series. (d) Many Hebrew, Aramaic, and Greek words, important to the understanding of certain passages, are discussed. These words are transliterated for the benefit of readers not proficient in the biblical languages. Yet those who do know these languages will also appreciate these comments. (e) Throughout the series, dozens of maps, charts, and diagrams are included; they are placed conveniently with the Bible passages being discussed, not at the end of each book. (f) Numerous cross references to related or parallel passages are included with the discussions on many passages.

The material on each Bible book includes an *Introduction* (discussion of items such as authorship, date, purpose, unity, style, unique features), *Outline, Commentary,* and *Bibliography.* In the *Commentary* section, summaries of entire sections of the text are given, followed by detailed comments on the passage verse by verse and often phrase by phrase. All words quoted from the New International Version of the Bible appear in boldface type, as do the verse numbers at the beginning of paragraphs. The *Bibliography* entries, suggested for further study, are not all endorsed in their entirety by the authors and editors. The writers and editors have listed both works they have consulted and others which would be useful to readers.

Personal pronouns referring to Deity are capitalized, which often helps make it clear that the commentator is writing about a Member of the Trinity. The word LORD is the English translation of the Hebrew YHWH, often rendered *Yahweh* in English. *Lord* translates. *'Ădōnāy.* When the two names stand together as a compound name of God, they are rendered "Sovereign LORD," as in the NIV.

The consulting editors—Dr. Kenneth L. Barker and Dr. Eugene H. Merrill on the Old Testament, and Dr. Stanley D. Toussaint on the New Testament—have added to the quality of this commentary by reading the manuscripts and offering helpful suggestions. Their work is greatly appreciated. We also express thanks to Lloyd Cory, Victor Books Reference Editor, to Barbara Williams, whose careful editing enhanced the material appreciably, to Production Coordinator Myrna Jean Hasse, to Jan Arroyo, and other people in the text editing department at Scripture

Press, who spent many long hours keyboarding and preparing pages for typesetting, and to the several manuscript typists at Dallas Theological Seminary for their diligence.

This commentary series is an exposition of the Bible, an explanation of the text of Scripture, based on careful exegesis. It is not primarily a devotional commentary, or an exegetical work giving details of lexicology, grammar, and syntax with extensive discussion of critical matters pertaining to textual and background data. May this commentary deepen your insight into the Scriptures, as you seek to have "the eyes of your heart ... enlightened" (Eph. 1:18) by the teaching ministry of the Holy Spirit.

This book is designed to enrich your understanding and appreciation of the Scriptures, God's inspired, inerrant Word, and to motivate you "not merely [to] listen to the Word" but also to "do what it says" (James 1:22) and "also ... to teach others" (2 Tim. 2:2).

John F. Walvoord
Roy B. Zuck

Editors

John F. Walvoord, B.A., M.A., TH.M., Th.D., D.D., Litt.D.
Chancellor Emeritus
Professor Emeritus of Systematic Theology

Roy B. Zuck, A.B., Th.M., Th.D.
Senior Professor Emeritus of Bible Exposition
Editor, *Bibliotheca Sacra*

Consulting Editors

Old Testament
Kenneth L. Barker, B.A., Th.M., Ph.D.
Writer, Lewisville, Texas

Eugene H. Merrill, B.A., M.A., M.Phil., Ph.D.
Distinguished Professor of Old Testament Studies

New Testament
Stanley D. Toussaint, B.A., Th.M., Th.D.
Senior Professor Emeritus of Bible Exposition

Series Contributing Authors

Walter L. Baker, B.A., Th.M., D.D.
Associate Professor Emeritus of World
Missions and Intercultural Studies
Obadiah

Craig Blaising, B.S. Th.M., Th.D., Ph.D.
Professor of Christian Theology Southern
Baptist Theological Seminary Louisville,
Kentucky
Malachi

J. Ronald Blue, B.A., Th.M.
President Emeritus CAM International
Dallas, Texas
Habakkuk

Sid S. Buzzell, B.S., Th.M., Ph.D.
Professor of Bible Exposition Colorado
Christian University Lakewood,
Colorado
Proverbs

Donald K. Campbell, B.A., Th.M., Th.D.
President Emeritus
Professor Emeritus of Bible Exposition
Joshua

**Robert B. Chisholm, Jr., B.A., M. Div.,
Th.M., Th.D.**
Professor of Old Testament Studies
Hosea, Joel

Thomas L. Constable, B.A., Th.M., Th.D.
Chairman and Senior Professor of Bible
Exposition
1 and 2 Kings

Jack S. Deere, B.A., Th.M., Th.D.
Associate Senior Pastor Trinity
Fellowship Church Amarillo, Texas
Deuteronomy, Song of Songs

Charles H. Dyer, B.A., Th.M., Th.D.
Provost and Senior Vice-President of
Education
Moody Bible Institute Chicago, Illinois
Jeremiah, Lamentations, Ezekiel

Gene A. Getz, B.A., M.A., Ph.D.
Senior Pastor
Fellowship Bible Church, North Plano,
Texas
Nehemiah

Donald R. Glenn, B.S., M.A., Th.M.
Chairman and Senior Professor of Old
Testament Studies
Ecclesiastes

John D. Hannah, B.S., Th.M., Th.D.
Chairman and Distinguished Professor
of Historical Theology
Exodus, Jonah, Zephaniah

Elliott E. Johnson, B.S., Th.M., Th.D.
Senior Professor of Bible Exposition
Nahum

F. Duane Lindsey, B.A., B.D., Th.M., Th.D.
Former Registrar, Research Librarian,
and Assistant Professor of Systematic
Theology
Leviticus, Judges, Haggai, Zechariah

John A. Martin, B.A., Th.M., Th.D.
Provost
Robert Wesleyan College
Rochester, New York
Ezra, Esther, Isaiah, Micah

Eugene H. Merrill, B.A., M.A., M.Phil., Ph.D.
Distinguished Professor of Old
Testament Studies
Numbers, 1 and 2 Samuel, 1 and 2 Chronicles

J. Dwight Pentecost, B.A., Th.M., Th.D.
Distinguished Professor Emeritus of
Bible Exposition
Daniel

John W. Reed, B.A., M.A., M.Div., Ph.D.
Director of D.Min. Studies
Senior Professor Emeritus of Pastoral
Ministries
Ruth

Allen P. Ross, B.A., M.A., M.Div., Ph.D.
Professor of Old Testament Studies
Trinity Evangelical Episcopal Seminary
Ambridge, Pennsylvania
Genesis, Psalms

Donald R. Sunukjian, B.A., Th.M., Th.D., Ph.D.
Professor of Christian Ministry and
Leadership
Talbot School of Theology La Mirada,
California
Amos

Roy B. Zuck, B.A., Th.M., Th.D.
Editor, Bibliotheca Sacra
Senior Professor of Bible Exposition
Job

*Authorial information based on original edition of the Bible Knowledge Commentary set. At the time of the commentary's first printing, each author was a faculty member of Dallas Theological Seminary.

Abbreviations

A. General

act.	active	n., nn.	note(s)
Akk.	Akkadian	n.d.	no date
Apoc.	Apocrypha	neut.	neuter
Aram.	Aramaic	n.p.	no publisher, no place of publication
ca.	*circa,* about		
cf.	*confer,* compare	no.	number
chap., chaps.	chapter(s)	NT	New Testament
comp.	compiled, compilation, compiler	OT	Old Testament
		p., pp.	page(s)
ed.	edited, edition, editor	par., pars.	paragraph(s)
eds.	editors	part.	participle
e.g.	*exempli gratia,* for example	pass.	passive
Eng.	English	perf.	perfect
et al.	*et alii,* and others	pl.	plural
fem.	feminine	pres.	present
Gr.	Greek	q.v.	*quod vide,* which see
Heb.	Hebrew	Sem.	Semitic
ibid.	*ibidem,* in the same place	sing.	singular
i.e.	*id est,* that is	s.v.	*sub verbo,* under the word
imper.	imperative	trans.	translation, translator, translated
imperf.	imperfect		
lit.	literal, literally	viz.	*videlicet,* namely
LXX	Septuagint	vol., vols.	volume(s)
marg.	margin, marginal reading	v., vv.	verse(s)
masc.	masculine	vs.	versus
ms., mss.	manuscript(s)	Vul.	Vulgate
MT	Masoretic text		

B. Abbreviations of Books of the Bible

Gen.	Ruth	Job	Lam.	Jonah
Ex.	1, 2 Sam.	Ps., Pss. (pl.)	Ezek.	Micah
Lev.	1, 2 Kings	Prov.	Dan.	Nahum
Num.	1, 2 Chron.	Ecc.	Hosea	Hab.
Deut.	Ezra	Song	Joel	Zeph.
Josh.	Neh.	Isa.	Amos	Hag.
Jud.	Es.	Jer.	Obad.	Zech.
				Mal.

Matt.	Acts	Eph.	1, 2 Tim.	James
Mark	Rom.	Phil.	Titus	1, 2 Peter
Luke	1, 2 Cor.	Col.	Phile.	1, 2, 3 John
John	Gal.	1, 2 Thes.	Heb.	Jude
				Rev.

C. Abbreviations of Bible Versions, Translations, and Paraphrases

ASV	American Standard Version
JB	Jerusalem Bible
KJV	King James Version
NASB	New American Standard Bible
NEB	New English Bible
NIV	New International Version
RSV	Revised Standard Version

Transliterations

Hebrew

Consonants

א	– ʾ	ד	– ḏ	י	– y	ס	– s	ר	– r
ב	– b	ה	– h	כ	– k	ע	– ʿ	שׂ	– ś
ב	– ḇ	ו	– w	כ	– ḵ	פ	– p	שׁ	– š
ג	– g	ז	– z	ל	– l	פ	– p	ת	– t
ג	– g	ח	– ḥ	מ	– m	צ	– ṣ	ת	– ṯ
ד	– d	ט	– ṭ	נ	– n	ק	– q		

Daghesh forte is represented by doubling the letter.

Vocalization

בָּה	– bâh	בָ	– bā	בֹ	– bo[1]	בְ	– bĕ
בוֹ	– bô	בֹ	– bō	בֻ	– bu[1]	בְ	– b
בוּ	– bû	בֻ	– bū	בֻ	– be	בָּה	– bāh
בֵי	– bê	בֵ	– bē	בִ	– bi[1]	בָּא	– bāʾ
בֶי	– bè	בִי	– bī	בַ	– bă	בָּה	– bēh
בִי	– bî	בַ	– ba	בֳ	– bŏ	בֶּה	– beh

[1] In closed syllables

Greek

α, ᾳ	– a		ξ	– x		γγ	– ng	
β	– b		ο	– o		γκ	– nk	
γ	– g		π	– p		γξ	– nx	
δ	– d		ρ	– r		γχ	– nch	
ε	– e		σ, ς	– s		αἰ	– ai	
ζ	– z		τ	– t		αὐ	– au	
η, ῃ	– ē		υ	– y		εἰ	– ei	
θ	– th		φ	– ph		εὐ	– eu	
ι	– i		χ	– ch		ηὐ	– ēu	
κ	– k		ψ	– ps		οἰ	– oi	
λ	– l		ω, ῳ	– ō		οὐ	– ou	
μ	– m		ῥ	– rh		υἱ	– hui	
ν	– n		ʽ	– h				

An Overview of Old Testament History

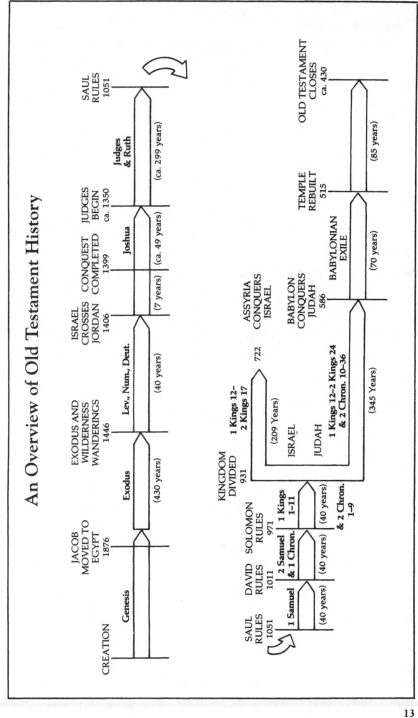

Biblical Weights and Measures

BIBLICAL UNIT		AMERICAN EQUIVALENT		METRIC EQUIVALENT	
		WEIGHT			
talent	(60 minas)	75	pounds	34	kilograms
mina	(50 shekels)	1 1/4	pounds	0.6	kilogram
shekel	(2 bekas)	2/5	ounce	11.5	grams
pim	(2/3 shekel)	1/3	ounce	7.6	grams
beka	(10 gerahs)	1/5	ounce	6	grams
gerah		1/50	ounce	0.6	gram
		LENGTH			
cubit		18	inches	0.5	meter
span		9	inches	23	centimeters
handbreadth		3	inches	7	centimeters
		CAPACITY			
		Dry Measure			
cor [homer]	(10 ephahs)	6	bushels	220	liters
lethech	(5 ephahs)	3	bushels	110	liters
ephah	(10 omers)	1/2	bushel	22	liters
seah	(1/3 ephah)	7	quarts	7.3	liters
omer	(1/10 ephah)	2	quarts	2	liters
cab	(1/18 ephah)	1/2	pint	0.3	liter
		Liquid Measure			
bath	(1 ephah)	6	gallons	22	liters
hin	(1/6 bath)	4	quarts	4	liters
log	(1/72 bath)	1/3	quart	0.3	liter

The information in this chart, while not being mathematically precise, gives approximate amounts and distances. The figures are calculated on the basis of a shekel equaling 11.5 grams, a cubit equaling 18 inches, and an ephah equaling 22 liters.

JOB

Roy B. Zuck

INTRODUCTION

Job and the Problem of Suffering. One of the best-known examples of undeserved suffering is recorded in the Book of Job. In a matter of minutes Job, a prominently wealthy and godly man, lost all his material possessions, all his children, and his health. His wife gave him no support, for she suggested he end his misery by cursing God. Then, adding anguish upon anguish, his friends condemned him rather than consoled him. Furthermore God seemed to be ignoring Job, refusing for a long time to answer him and rise to his cause.

Job's intense suffering was financial, emotional, physical, and spiritual. Everyone was against him including, it seemed, even God, whom he had served faithfully. Yet Job was a spiritually and morally upright man (1:1, 8; 2:3). Could any suffering be *more* undeserved? Should not such a righteous person be blessed, not badgered, by God? The fact that Job, an outstanding citizen and upright person, had so much and then lost so much makes him a supreme example of affliction that defies human explanation.

Many individuals can identify with Job, whose distresses were agonizingly prolonged and so seemingly unfair. Many people wonder why they should undergo affliction, why *they* should experience tragedy, heartache, and adversity. For *anyone*, suffering is hard to comprehend, but especially so when it strikes the undeserving. When pain does not seem to be punishment for wrongdoing, it is puzzling. The Book of Job addresses the mystery of unmerited misery, showing that in adversity God may have other purposes besides retribution for wrongdoing.

This book also addresses the problem of attitudes in affliction. Job's experience demonstrates that a believer, while undergoing intense agony, need not renounce God. Question Him, yes; but not deny Him. Like Job, he may long for an explanation of his experience; but being unable to comprehend the cause of his calamity, he need not curse God. Though Job came close to doing so, he did not actually denounce God as Satan had predicted.

The Book of Job also teaches that to ask why, as Job did (3:11-12, 16, 20), is not wrong. But to demand that God answer why, as Job also did (13:22; 19:7; 31:15), *is* wrong. To insist that God explain one's adversities is inappropriate for it places man above God and challenges God's sovereignty.

Literary Style. The Book of Job has been heralded as a masterpiece unequaled in all literature. Thomas Carlyle's often-quoted statement about Job bears repeating: "There is nothing written, I think, in the Bible or out of it, of equal literary merit" ("The Hero as a Prophet," *Our Heroes, Hero-Worship, and the Heroic in History*. Boston: Ginn, 1901, p. 56).

The Book of Job has a unique structure. It is a mixture of prose and poetry, and of monologue and dialogue. The prologue (chaps. 1–2) and the epilogue (42:7-17) are narrative prose; the lengthy material in between is poetry (except the opening verse in each chapter that introduces a new speech, and 32:1-6a). This prose-poetry-prose pattern, though seen in other compositions of the ancient Near East, is unique among the books of the Bible. Another way of viewing the structure of the book is seen in the chart "Parallels in the Structure of the Book of Job."

Irony is used throughout the book; some of the numerous examples are mentioned in the commentary (also see Gregory W. Parsons, "Literary Features of the Book of Job," *Bibliotheca Sacra* 138. July-September 1981:215-8; and Edwin M. Good, *Irony in the Old Testament*. Phil-

---

Parallels in the Structure of the Book of Job

  a. Opening narrative (chaps. 1–2)
   b. Job's opening soliloquy (chap. 3)
    c. The friends' disputation with Job (chaps. 4–28)
   *b*¹. Job's closing soliloquy (chaps. 29–31)
    *c*¹. Elihu's disputation with Job (chaps. 32–37)
     *c*². God's disputation with Job (38:1–42:6)
  *a*¹. Closing narrative (42:7-17)

---

adelphia: Westminster Press, 1965, pp. 196-240).

The literary form of the Book of Job is probably a composite of a lawsuit (several legal terms are frequently used by Job, his friends, and God), a controversy dialogue or wisdom disputation, and a lament. Job voiced many laments against himself, God, and his enemies (see the chart "Job's Laments," adapted from Claus Westermann, *The Structure of the Book of Job: A Form-Critical Analysis*).

Job is an outstanding literary production also because of its rich vocabulary. Dozens of words in this book occur nowhere else in the Old Testament.

Five different words are used for lions (4:10-11), six synonyms are used for traps (18:8-10), and six for darkness (3:4-6; 10:21-22). The vocabulary of the Book of Job reveals influences from several languages besides Hebrew, including Akkadian, Arabic, Aramaic, Sumerian, and Ugaritic (cf. R. Laird Harris, "The Book of Job and Its Doctrine of God," *Grace Journal* 13. Fall 1976:10-4).

The book abounds with similes and metaphors, many of them from nature. The book touches on many subjects including astronomy, geography, hunting, mining, travel, weather, zoology, and the terminology of law courts.

No wonder Alfred Tennyson labeled the book "the greatest poem of ancient or modern times" (cited by Victor E. Reichert, *Job*, p. xiii).

Author. No one knows who wrote the Book of Job, when it was written, when its events occurred, or where Job lived. These facts, shrouded in mystery, add to the book's appeal and charm.

Suggestions on who may have authored the book include Job himself, Elihu (the fourth friend, who spoke to-

ward the end of the book, chaps. 32–37), Moses, Solomon, Hezekiah, Isaiah, someone after the Babylonian Exile such as Ezra, and an anonymous author 200 years before Christ. Jewish tradition says that Moses wrote the book. Others argue for Solomon as the author because of his interest in poetic literature (e.g., Prov., Ecc., and Song) and a few similarities between Job and Proverbs (e.g., Job 28 and Prov. 8).

The details of the lengthy conversations recorded in the Book of Job give the impression that it was written by an eyewitness. Job would recall as well as other eyewitnesses what was said. In the 140 years he lived after being restored to health, he would have had ample time to compile the work. This view seems more plausible than the view that an author hundreds of years later compiled what had been handed down by oral tradition over many centuries.

In Old Testament times a person sometimes recorded events about himself in the third person. Of course, someone else may have written the last two verses (Job 42:16-17), which tell of Job's age and death. That too was not uncommon (e.g., Deut. 1–33 was written by Moses, but Deut. 34, on Moses' death, was added by someone else).

Some scholars suggest that the Book of Job was compiled over many years by several authors and editors, each of whom added small portions to the initial work. However, numerous features point to a single author (cf., e.g., Marvin H. Pope, *Job*, p. xli), and many cross-references within the book point to its unity.

Date. Views on the time when Job lived range all the way from the Patriarchal Age (Abraham, Isaac, and Jacob—ap-

Job's Laments

	Self-laments	Laments against God	Laments against "Enemies"
Job's opening soliloquy (chap. 3)	3:11-19, 24-26	3:20-23	3:3-10
Job's first speech (chaps. 6–7)	6:1-12 7:1-10	7:12-21	6:13-20
Job's second speech (chaps. 9–10)	9:25-31	9:17-23; 10:8-17	
Job's third speech (chaps. 12–14)	14:1-6, 7-15	13:3, 14-16, 23-27	
Job's fourth speech (chaps. 16–17)	17:4-10	16:9-14	
Job's fifth speech (chap. 19)		19:7-12	19:13-19
Job's sixth speech (chap. 21)			
Job's seventh speech (chaps. 23–24)	23:3-12		
Job's eighth speech (chaps. 26–31)	29:2-6, 12-20; 30:16-19, 24-31	30:20-23	30:1-15

proximately 2100 to 1900 B.C.) to the sixth century B.C. Several factors point to the time of the patriarchs:

1. Job lived 140 years after his calamities (42:16) so he may have lived to about 210. This corresponds roughly to the length of the patriarchs' lives. Terah, Abraham's father, died at the age of 205; Abraham lived to be 175; Isaac lived 180 years; and Jacob died at the age of 147.

2. Job's wealth was reckoned in livestock (1:3; 42:12), which was also true of Abraham (Gen. 12:16; 13:2), and Jacob (Gen. 30:43; 32:5).

3. The Sabeans and Chaldeans (Job 1:15, 17) were nomads in Abraham's time, but in later years they were not nomadic.

4. The Hebrew word $qᵉśîṭâh$, translated "piece of silver" (42:11), is used elsewhere only twice (Gen. 33:19; Josh. 24:32), both times in reference to Jacob.

5. Job's daughters were heirs of his estate along with their brothers (Job 42:15). This, however, was not possible later under the Mosaic Law if a daughter's brothers were still living (Num. 27:8).

6. Literary works similar in some ways to the Book of Job were written in Egypt and Mesopotamia around the time of the patriarchs.

7. The Book of Job includes no references to the Mosaic institutions (priesthood, laws, tabernacle, special religious days and feasts).

8. The name $šadday$ is used of God 31 times in Job (compared with only 17 times elsewhere in the OT) and was a name familiar to the patriarchs (see comments on Gen. 17:1; also cf. Ex. 6:3).

9. Several personal and place names in the book were also associated with the patriarchal period. Examples include (a) Sheba, a grandson of Abraham (Gen. 25:3), and the Sabeans from Sheba (Job 1:15; 6:19); (b) Tema, another grandson of Abraham (Gen. 25:15), and Tema, a location in Arabia (Job 6:19); (c) Eliphaz, a son of Esau (Gen. 36:4), and Eliphaz, one of Job's companions (Job 2:11; these two Eliphazes, however, are not necessarily the same person); (d) Uz, a nephew of Abraham (Gen. 22:21), and Uz, where Job lived (Job 1:1). Though it cannot be stated with certainty, possibly Job lived in Jacob's time or shortly thereafter.

Job was a common West Semitic name in the second millennium B.C. Job was also the name of a 19th-century-B.C. prince in the Egyptian Execration texts. Other occurrences of the name are found in the Tell el-Amarna letters (ca. 1400 B.C.) and in Ugaritic texts.

OUTLINE

COMMENTARY

I. Prologue (chaps. 1–2)

In this prose prologue, Job's spiritual character, his family and possessions, Satan's accusations and attacks on Job, Job's reactions, and the arrival of his friends—all are set before the reader in rapid fashion. By contrast, the pace in the following dialogue (3:1–42:6) is slow. The rapid narrative style in the prologue gets the reader quickly into Job's agonizing confrontations with his friends and God.

A. Job's character (1:1-5)

1. JOB'S PLACE AND PIETY (1:1)

1:1. The location of **the land of Uz,** where Job **lived,** is uncertain. Though often identified with Edom, southeast of the Dead Sea, Uz was distinguished from it in Jeremiah's time, if not before (Jer. 25:20-21). Uz was then a "daughter" of Edom, that is, a possession or neighbor of Edom (Lam. 4:21). Some scholars suggest that Uz was in Bashan, south of Damascus; others say Uz lay east of Edom, in northern Arabia. The customs, vocabulary, and references to geography and natural history relate to northern Arabia. Whatever Uz's location, it was near a desert (Job 1:19), it was fertile for agriculture and livestock-raising (1:3, 14;

42:12), and it was probably outside Palestine.

Job was **blameless** ("without moral blemish," or "morally whole") **and upright** ("straight" in the sense of not deviating from God's standards). Also **he feared God,** that is, he was aware of, revered, and submitted to God's majesty. And he **shunned evil,** rejecting the opposite of God's character. That assessment, repeated by God to Satan (1:8; 2:3), shows that Job's friends were totally wrong in accusing him of being a willful sinner.

2. JOB'S PROSPERITY (1:2-3)

1:2-3. Job had **seven sons,** often considered evidence of divine blessing (cf. Ruth 4:15; 1 Sam. 2:5) **and three daughters.** This family size was common in those times. He was remarkably wealthy. His **7,000 sheep** provided clothing and food. The **3,000 camels** provided transportation and milk. The 1,000 **oxen (500 yoke)** provided food and milk, and the power for plowing. The **500 donkeys** also provided transportation. Such a huge livestock estate required much land and many **servants.**

As **the greatest man among all the people of the East,** Job was the wealthiest of an apparently prosperous group of people in northern Arabia. The "people of the East" are identified with Kedar, in northern Arabia (Jer. 49:28). Job was also unusually wise, for the men of the East were noted for their great wisdom, expressed in proverbs, songs, and stories.

Additional biographical facts about this patriarch are given elsewhere in the Book of Job. He was highly respected (Job 29:7-11), a fair and honest judge (29:7, 12-17), a wise counselor (29:21-24), an honest employer (31:13-15, 38-39), hospitable and generous (31:16-21, 32), and a farmer of crops (31:38-40).

3. JOB'S POSTERITY (1:4-5)

1:4-5. Each time **his** seven **sons** held a feast (possibly a birthday party) in one of **their homes** along with **their . . . sisters** (cf. v. 13) **Job** would purify (sanctify) them by 10 **burnt** offerings, one **for each** child. He was concerned that they receive forgiveness of any sins committed knowingly or unknowingly. His concern that they might have inwardly **cursed**

God anticipates, ironically, Satan's insinuation that Job would curse God (2:5).

Job was an exemplary person. His sterling qualities made his upcoming adversities, by contrast, all the more severe. No one deserved suffering less than he did, and few if any have suffered more.

B. Job's calamities (1:6–2:10)

1. JOB'S FIRST TEST (1:6-22)

Job was subjected to two tests, one on his possessions and offspring (vv. 6-22) and one on his health (2:1-10). In each test are two scenes, one in heaven and one on earth. Each scene in heaven includes an accusation by Satan against Job, and each scene on earth includes an assault by Satan against Job and Job's reaction.

a. Satan's first accusation (1:6-12)

1:6-8. When **the angels** (lit., "sons of God"; unfallen angels are God's "sons" in the sense that they are His creation; cf. 38:7) **came to present** (lit., "stationed") **themselves before** God to report on their activities, **Satan** (lit., "the accuser") was **with them.** He had and still has access to heaven (cf. Rev. 12:10). He said he was **roaming through** and walking **back and forth** on **the earth,** apparently looking for those whom he could accuse and dominate (1 Peter 5:8). Satan's **going** on the earth may also suggest his exercising dominion over it and its people. To walk on land often symbolized dominion over it (cf. Deut. 1:36; 11:24; Josh 1:3; 14:9). Satan, of course, is "the god of this Age" (2 Cor. 4:4; cf. Eph. 2:2) and "the whole world is under the control of the evil one" (1 John 5:19).

The Lord spoke of **Job** by the honorable title **My servant** (cf. Job 2:3; 42:7-8 [three times in v. 8]) and referred to him as a supreme example of piety: **There is no one on earth like him.** Satan had and has dominion over much of the world, but **God** pointed out that Satan could not dominate Job!

1:9-12. Satan responded by attacking Job's motives: **Does Job fear God for nothing?** "For nothing" (*ḥinnām*) is rendered "without any reason" in 2:3 (see comments there). Because Satan could not deny God's assessment of Job's godliness, he questioned *why* Job was pious. The accuser suggested that Job was serving God not out of love but only because of what he got from God in return. If Job's rewards were removed, out would go his reverence.

Satan's subtle suggestion that worship is basically selfish hits at the heart of man's relationship to God. The Book of Job does more than raise the question of the suffering of the righteous. It also, through Satan's words, deals with the motives for godly living. Will anyone serve the LORD if he enjoys no personal gain from it? Is worship a coin that buys a heavenly reward? Is piety part of a contract by which to gain wealth and ward off trouble?

Satan suggested that if God removed His protecting hedge around Job and removed everything he owned, then Job would curse God. Job, Satan claimed, would no longer insert his coins of worship if nothing came out of the machine. Job, in other words, was worshiping for selfish reasons. This accusation also attacked the integrity of God, for it suggested that the only way He can get people to worship Him is to promise them wealth. Perhaps this indictment against His character is one of the reasons God let Satan buffet Job. Surely God knew Job's heart, but He used Job as a demonstration to silence Satan. In addition, God wanted to deepen Job's spiritual insight.

b. Satan's first assault (1:13-19)

1:13-15. Satan began his assaults on Job when his 10 children **were feasting** in the eldest **brother's house** (vv. 13, 18; cf. v. 4). The assaults were alternately caused by human and "natural" forces: a Sabean attack (v. 15), "the fire of God" (v. 16), a Chaldean raid (v. 17), a great desert wind (v. 19). God permitted Satan to move both kinds of causes to accomplish his purposes—and to do so in rapid, precise timing. Job, while reeling in shock from the news of one loss, was stunned by another.

The Sabeans, who stole the 1,000 **oxen** and 500 **donkeys** and slaughtered **the servants,** may have been from the region of Sheba in southwest Arabia, or from a town called Sheba, near Dedan, in upper Arabia (Gen. 10:7; 25:3).

1:16-17. The fire of God, which **fell from the sky and burned up the** 7,000 **sheep and the servants,** was probably started by lightning (cf. "the fire of the

LORD" in 1 Kings 18:38).

The Chaldeans attacked in companies from **three** sides and stole the 3,000 **camels** and slaughtered **the servants.** At that time the Chaldeans were fierce, marauding inhabitants of Mesopotamia. They possibly came from the north, unlike the Sabeans who had come from the south. Apparently the raids by those two groups were surprise attacks.

1:18-19. The **mighty** desert **wind** that **struck the four corners of the house** suggests a tornado or whirling wind, building in momentum as it whipped across the desert. The wind toppled the house, causing it to fall on Job's 10 children.

All Job's livestock had been stolen; all his servants had been murdered (except perhaps four messengers who had **escaped to** report; they were either Job's servants or others who had witnessed the tragedies); and all his children had been killed. In a few minutes, Job had plummeted from wealth and prosperity to grief and pauperism. Would he also plummet from loyalty to God to disloyalty?

c. Job's response to the first test (1:20-22)

1:20-22. In response to the fierceness of Satan's rapid fourfold assault, **Job . . . tore his robe,** symbolizing inner turmoil and shock (cf. 2:12; Gen. 37:29, 34; 44:13; Jud. 11:35), **and shaved his head** (cf. Isa. 15:2; Jer. 48:37; Ezek. 7:18), depicting the loss of his personal glory. Falling **to the ground,** not in despair, but in obeisance to God, Job worshiped.

Job recognized that his loss resembled his birth and his death: he had been **naked** at birth, and he would be naked at death. Similarly, now he was figuratively naked. The words **naked I will depart** (lit., "return there") suggest that he would return to his mother's womb. But how could that be? Speaking of the womb of one's mother was sometimes a poetic way of referring to the earth (cf. Ps. 139:15; Ecc. 5:15; 12:7). The connection is obvious; for man, formed in the womb, is also made "from dust from the ground" (Gen. 2:7; cf. Gen. 3:19; Job 10:9; 34:15; Ps. 103:14), and the earth, when it yields crops, "living" things, is something like a mother giving birth to a baby.

Recognizing God's sovereign rights **(The LORD gave and the LORD has taken** away), Job **praised** the LORD. It is truly remarkable that Job followed adversity with adoration, woe with worship. Unlike so many people, he did not give in to bitterness; he refused to blame **God** for **wrongdoing** (cf. Job 2:10).

Job's amazing response showed Satan was utterly wrong in predicting that Job would curse God. Devotion *is* possible without dollars received in return; people *can* be godly apart from material gain. Job's saintly worship at the moment of extreme loss and intense grief verified God's words about Job's godly character.

2. JOB'S SECOND TEST (2:1-10)

a. Satan's second accusation (2:1-6)

2:1-4. In Satan's second test he again indicted God's words and impugned Job's motives and character (cf. 1:6-8). The Hebrew for **without any reason is** *ḥinnām*, the same word Satan had used in 1:9. Though **Satan** accused **Job** of having an ulterior motive in his worship, **God** threw this back at the accuser, saying that Satan had *no* reason to incite God against the patriarch. In this third scene, back in heaven, **Satan** implied that Job was still worshiping God because he had not yet given up his life. **Skin for skin! A man will give all he has**—possessions and children—**for his own life.** "Skin for skin" was a proverbial saying, possibly about bartering or trading animal skins. Satan insinuated that Job had willingly traded the skins (lives) of his own children because in return God had given him his own skin (life). This again implied that Job was selfish.

2:5-6. Satan suggested that if Job were made to suffer physically, he would **curse** God to His **face** (cf. 1:11) for Job would have no reason for worship. He would see that God was against him. Surprisingly **the LORD** permitted Satan to afflict Job but not to kill him. God knew that Job would not deny Him.

b. Satan's second assault (2:7)

2:7. The first test involved Job's wealth, children, and nearly all his servants; the second one involved his health. **Satan** immediately caused **Job** to have **painful sores** over all his body.

The two Hebrew words translated "painful sores" were used of the plagues of "festering boils" in Egypt (Ex. 9:8-11; Deut. 28:27) and of Hezekiah's illness

(2 Kings 20:7, "boil"). Some scholars say the disease may have been smallpox; others say it was elephantiasis. It was apparently some skin condition with scabs or scales, such as pemphigus foliaceus (cf. Rupert Hallam, "Pemphigus Foliaceus," in *The British Encyclopaedia of Medical Practice*. 2nd ed. 12 vols. London: Butterworth, 1950–52, 9:490-2).

This disease, as attested by physicians today, matches the symptoms of Job's afflictions—inflamed, ulcerous sores (Job 2:7), itching (v. 8), degenerative changes in facial skin (vv. 7, 12), loss of appetite (3:24), depression (3:24-25), loss of strength (6:11), worms in the boils (7:5), running sores (7:5), difficulty in breathing (9:18), darkness under the eyes (16:16), foul breath (19:17), loss of weight (19:20; 33:21), continual pain (30:17), restlessness (30:27), blackened skin (30:30), peeling skin (30:30), and fever (30:30).

c. Job's reaction to the second test (2:8-10)

2:8. Job . . . sat among the ashes, on or near a pile of dung ashes and garbage outside the city. Missionaries in primitive cultures have reported that pemphigus foliaceus patients have soothed their sores with ashes. How humiliating for Job! He who had sat at the city gate as a local judge (29:7) was now outside the city with beggars, scraping his itching, running sores with **a piece of broken pottery.**

2:9-10a. When Job's **wife** urged **him** to forget his **integrity** (related to the word "blameless" in 1:1), **curse God and** (as a result) **die, he** called her a **foolish** (*nābāl*, "spiritually ignorant or nondiscerning") **woman.** Unknown to her, this advice that he curse God was exactly what Satan had twice predicted Job would do (1:11; 2:5). When Job needed comfort from her, he received another terrible blow—evidence of her bitterness toward God. In calm confidence in God's ways Job pointed out that **trouble** (*rā'*, "evil, calamity") as well as **good** comes **from God** (cf. Ecc. 7:14; Lam. 3:38). This contrasts starkly with most peoples' view that trouble means God's very existence is questionable! Later Job affirmed to his friends that he would retain his integrity till death (Job 27:5).

2:10b. The affirmation, **In all this, Job did not sin in what he said,** proved wrong Satan's predictions that Job would curse God, and it vindicated God's words (cf. 1:22).

C. Job's comforters (2:11-13)

2:11. Hearing about Job's perils, **three** of his **friends—Eliphaz . . . Bildad,** and **Zophar,** apparently prominent men—**met together** and visited Job. "Eliphaz" is an Edomite name (Gen. 36:4), and as a **Temanite** he was from either Teman in Edom, known for its wisdom (Jer. 49:7; Obad. 8), or Tema in Arabia. "Bildad" is not used elsewhere in the Bible, and **Shuhite** may suggest a relationship to Shuah, Abraham's youngest son by Keturah (Gen. 25:2). The name "Zophar" is used only in Job, and his lineage as a **Naamathite** is unknown, though some have suggested that Naamah, a Canaanite town inherited by Judah (Josh. 15:41), was his hometown. Elihu, was also present though he is not mentioned till later (Job 32).

Eliphaz was probably the eldest of the three, for he is listed first (2:11; 42:9), he spoke first in each of the three rounds of speeches (chaps. 4–5; 15; 22), his speeches were longer and more mature in content, and God addressed him as the representative of the others (42:7).

The purpose of the three comforters was to **sympathize with** Job **and comfort him.** But their speeches soon became anything but comforting!

2:12-13. Job was so disfigured by the disease that **they . . . hardly** recognized **him** (cf. 6:21). Then they expressed their grief and despair in three ways; **they** wept **aloud** (in emotional shock and sorrow), **tore their robes** (in brokenheartedness; cf. 1:20), and threw **dust on their heads** (in deep grief; cf. 1 Sam. 4:12; 2 Sam. 1:2; Neh. 9:1).

Sitting down in silence with him for a week may have been their way of mourning over his deathlike condition, or it may have been an act of sympathy and comfort, or a reaction of horror. Whatever the reason, in the custom of that day they allowed the grieving person to express himself first.

II. Dialogue (3:1–42:6)

A. Job's death wish (chap. 3)

The silence of Job and his friends was broken when Job bemoaned that he had ever been born and expressed his longing to die. Perhaps this week of agony impressed on him his sense of loss and reinforced the relentless pain of his disease. Perhaps too he reflected on the injustice of his condition.

In his sad soliloquy of a death wish, Job did not curse God, as Satan had predicted (1:11; 2:5), nor did Job contemplate suicide. But he did regret his birth (3:1-10), wished he had been born dead (vv. 11-19), and longed to die (vv. 20-26).

1. JOB'S WISH THAT HE HAD NOT BEEN BORN (3:1-10)

3:1-3. Job . . . **cursed the day of his birth** (lit., "his day") but interestingly he did not curse God. He wanted his birthday to be wiped from the calendar (cf. v. 6). Job then referred to **the night** which, personified, **said, A boy is born** (lit., "conceived").

In the following verses he elaborated on his day of birth (vv. 4-5), and his night of conception (vv. 6-7a). Then he concluded this poetic unit (vv. 3-10) by mentioning the reason he longed for the removal of his birthday (v. 10).

3:4-6. That day—may it turn to darkness is an interesting reversal of God's first-day creative act: "Let there be light" (Gen. 1:3). By praying **May God above not care about it** (lit., "seek it or look for it"), Job hoped that God, by not noticing that day, would therefore not notice him.

In Job 3:4-6 Job referred to darkness five times, using four different words. He longed that the day would be (a) "darkness" ($h\bar{o}\check{s}ek$, v. 4), and he asked that **darkness** ($h\bar{o}\check{s}ek$, v. 5) **and** (b) **deep shadow** ($\d{s}alm\bar{a}we\d{t}$, v. 5, used only in Job; cf. 10:21; 24:17; 28:3; 34:22; 38:17) and (c) **blackness** ($kimr\hat{i}r$) would **overwhelm its light** (lit., "terrify it," v. 5). That word for "blackness," used only here in the Old Testament, means the blackness accompanying an eclipse, tornado, or heavy storm clouds. Then Job longed that (d) **thick darkness** would **seize** the **night** of his conception. The Hebrew word for thick darkness ($\bar{o}pel$) is used five times in Job (v. 6; 10:22 [twice]; 23:17; 28:3).

3:7. Continuing his personification of the night, Job wished that the **night** had been **barren** (lit., "stony"), meaning, of course, that his mother would have been barren (as unproductive as stony ground). Emotional Near Easterners customarily shouted when a boy was born, but Job said, **May no shout of joy be heard in** (lit., "pierce") it (the night).

3:8. Job's words, **May those who curse days curse that day, those who are ready to rouse Leviathan,** refers to a custom of enchanters who claimed to make a day unfortunate (to curse it) by raising Leviathan (cf. 41:1; Pss. 74:14; 104:26; Isa. 27:1), a seven-headed sea monster of ancient Near Eastern mythology. When aroused, the dragon would cause an eclipse by swallowing the sun or moon. So if the daytime or nighttime luminary were gone, Job's birthday would, in a sense, be missing. Job was not saying he believed in this mythology. He was probably doing nothing more than utilizing for poetic purposes a common notion his hearers would understand. (See comments on the Leviathan in Job 41.)

3:9-10. The sufferer's wish that **its** (his conceptual night's) **morning stars** would **become dark** refers to the planets Venus and Mercury, easily seen at dawn because of their brilliance (cf. 38:7). **The first rays of dawn** are literally, "eyelids of the morning," a metaphor in which the morning rays of sunlight coming over the horizon at dawn are likened to the opening eyelids of a person waking up. The same figure is used later (41:18).

By longing for his conceptual night to be shrouded in darkness (3:6), be barren (v. 7), and never to turn to day (v. 9), Job was saying he wished he had never been conceived in his mother's womb. Unfortunately, he said, **the doors** of his mother's **womb** were **not shut**; he was conceived. If her womb had been shut, he would not have seen **trouble** in this life. "Trouble" (*'āmāl*, "sorrow, labor") is also used in 4:8; 5:6-7; 7:3; 11:16; 15:35; 16:2 (lit., "comforters of trouble").

2. JOB'S WISH THAT HE HAD DIED AT BIRTH (3:11-19)

Because Job's desire to blot out his night of conception and the day of his birth could not be fulfilled, he longed to have been stillborn. That, he said, would have been better than his present condition. After cursing his birthday, he subsided into a quieter reflection on the trouble-free condition he would have enjoyed if he had been born dead.

3:11-12. A stillbirth or miscarriage (vv. 11-12) would have resulted in rest in death (vv. 13-15). He repeated that same idea: a stillbirth (v. 16) would have resulted in death (vv. 17-19).

Job asked two questions (vv. 11-12). First he wondered why he could not have died as he **came** out of **the womb.** Job voiced the same complaint again (10:18-19; cf. his death wishes in 3:20-23; 6:8-9; 7:15; 14:13). Having been born dead would have been better than his present existence of turmoil. In the second question, the receiving of the **knees** refers either to his mother's taking him in her lap soon after birth, or to the patriarchs' custom of placing a newborn child on the knees of a paternal ancestor as a symbol that the child was acknowledged as in his line (cf. Gen. 50:23). Had Job's mother not **nursed** him from her **breasts,** he would have died.

3:13-15. Death at birth would have been so much better. In death he would have **peace** and **rest** (cf. vv. 17-18), whereas in life he had turmoil. In fact he would be in an enviable position with exalted personalities, including **kings . . . counselors,** and rich **rulers.**

3:16-19. Longing to have been a miscarried, **hidden** ("buried") fetus and so be **like an infant who never saw the light of day** (cf. vv. 6-7, 9), Job again referred to the restful condition he could have had in death. **There the wicked,** Job thought, no longer are in **turmoil** ("agitation, raging"; the same Heb. word *rōgez* is used in v. 26; 14:1, "trouble"; and 37:2, "roar") in their restless sin and rebellion; **the weary . . . rest;** prisoners are at **ease** (no longer hearing their taskmasters shouting at them to work harder); **the small and the great are** together; **and the slave is freed.** Job, weary with agony, would rest at death; he would no longer be a captive to his disease; he would be free from his slavery to trouble. This picturesque language expresses the experience of rest which a dead person seemingly has, in contrast with the restless condition of the living, who suffer. All who suffer intensely as Job did can appreciate his longing for release through death.

3. JOB'S WISH THAT HE COULD DIE THEN (3:20-26)

3:20-22. For the fourth of five times in this soliloquy, Job asked, "Why?" (cf. vv. 11-12, 16, 23; also cf. 7:20; 13:24) Since he had been conceived and born, and since he was not a stillbirth, he longed to die then as an adult. That would end his suffering. And yet death did not come. Referring once again to the subject of light and darkness as indicative of life and death (cf. 3:3-9; Ecc. 11:7-8; 12:2), he asked, **Why is light given to those in misery, and life** (cf. Job 3:23) **to the bitter of soul?** To Job it seemed incongruous that people like himself who are physically miserable and inwardly bitter are "given" life (cf. v. 23) when they really don't want it. The Hebrew word for "misery" is related to the noun for "trouble" (v. 10). Neither those who wait quietly (**long for death**) nor those who **search for it** find it. **Death . . . does not come.** Like buried **treasure**, it is not found. When sufferers finally do **reach the grave,** Job said, they are glad **and rejoice** because death releases them from pain.

3:23-24. Job again asked **why** (the fifth "why" in this chapter; cf. vv. 11-12, 16, 20) **life** should be **given** (cf. v. 20) to someone who does not want it. Job's **way** ("path") was **hidden** (cf. "hidden treasure," v. 21) so that he could not see where he was going. In fact Job said **God** had **hedged** him **in.** Here for the first time Job asserted that God was the cause of his affliction. Satan had used the word "hedge" to refer to God's protection of Job (1:10). Now Job used the word to refer to God's restrictions on him. His suffering limited his freedom of movement. Therefore Job was **sighing** rather than eating; his illness had made him lose his appetite. And his groaning was unending **like** the **water** of a waterfall. The word for **groans** is used of the roaring of a lion (4:10; cf. Ps. 32:3).

3:25-26. At the beginning of Job's trials, when he heard of the loss of one blessing, he **feared** the loss of another. And hearing of the second one, he feared yet another, and so on. His restless, turbulent condition is summarized in the conclusion of this soliloquy. Though he longed for **peace** with **quietness** and **rest** (cf. vv. 13, 17-18), he experienced **only turmoil** (lit., "agitation"; cf. v. 17).

Job's desire for death, his craving for the grave, emphatically underscores the extremities of his financial, physical, intellectual, emotional, and spiritual pain. Only those godly people who have relished release from life's woes through the gate of death can fully appreciate

Job's mournful wail. Job here voiced not the injustice of his plight but the intensity of it. Later, as his agony wore on, he spoke of its injustice.

B. The first round of speeches (chaps. 4–14)

After Job broke the week-long silence (2:13) with his outcry of anguish, his three companions—Eliphaz, Bildad, and Zophar (2:11)—felt compelled to speak. Shocked at his death desire, they took on themselves the responsibility of correcting Job for his brash remarks.

Each friend spoke and was in turn answered by Job. The cycle occurs three times, with one variation in the third round: the third friend did not speak a third time.

Throughout their speeches, the friends remained adamant in their theological position. Their view was that the righteous are rewarded and the unrighteous punished (cf., e.g., 4:7-8); so Job, having willfully sinned, was in need of repentance. Their syllogistic reasoning was as follows: (a) all suffering is punishment for sin; (b) Job is suffering; (c) therefore Job is a sinner. But this contradicted what God said of Job (1:1, 8; 2:3).

The friends became more vitriolic and specific as their speeches progressed. In the first round (chaps. 4–14), the three hinted at Job's sin, urging him to repent. "But if it were I, I would appeal to God" (Eliphaz, 5:8); "if you are pure and upright" (Bildad, 8:6); "if you put away the sin that is in your hand" (Zophar, 11:14).

The second round moved from suggestion to insinuation. Eliphaz said that the wicked are endangered (chap. 15), Bildad asserted that they are ensnared and forgotten (chap. 18), and Zophar affirmed that they are short-lived and lose their wealth (chap. 20). They all hoped Job would get the point and know that they were talking about him. Yet in the second cycle they said nothing about repentance.

The third round included open accusation. Eliphaz cited several sins of which he said Job was guilty (22:5-9), and Bildad announced outrightly that man is a worm (25:5-6). Only Eliphaz repeated that Job needed to repent (22:21-23).

And yet in all this, Job affirmed his innocence (6:10; 9:21; 16:17; 27:6) while also arguing that God had afflicted him (6:4; 9:17; 13:27; 16:12; 19:11). How else could Job explain his agony? But why God was doing it was beyond his comprehension (two times in these speeches he asked God "why," 7:20; 13:24; also cf. "why" in his opening soliloquy, 3:11-12, 16, 20, 23).

Job felt that if he could get God to appear in court with him, Job could prove that God was doing him wrong (13:3; 16:21; 19:23; 23:4; 31:35).

1. ELIPHAZ'S FIRST SPEECH (CHAPS. 4–5)

a. *His rebuke of Job (4:1-6)*

4:1-2. Aware that Job's solo tirade (chap. 3) had been an impatient outburst against his troubles, **Eliphaz,** probably the eldest of the three (cf. comments on 2:11), feared that any words he could speak might be met by Job with a similar or stronger impetuosity. So he asked, **If someone ventures a word with you, will you be impatient?** Eliphaz felt he had to take the risk and speak. He could not let Job get by with such an affront to the Almighty.

4:3-5. Eliphaz commended Job for having **instructed . . . strengthened,** and **supported** others emotionally and spiritually by his **words** of counsel. But that compliment contained a rebuke, for Eliphaz suggested that Job was unable to take his own medicine. He had advised others to be patient under trial, **but now trouble** had come to him and he was **discouraged.** In fact calamity struck (the same word Satan used in 1:11 and 2:5) and Job was **dismayed** (lit., "terrified, in panic"; also used in 21:6; 22:10; 23:15-16). Job had been a great encourager, but he could not encourage himself. Eliphaz failed to realize that one who is suffering cannot easily encourage himself; Eliphaz should have been the one to encourage Job!

4:6. Eliphaz then asked, **Should not your piety** (related to the word "feared," 1:1) **be your confidence, and your blameless ways** (lit., "the integrity [cf. 'blameless,' 1:1] of your ways," NASB) **your hope?** Perhaps this was a tongue-in-cheek rebuke of Job for his lack of confidence because he was no longer fearing God. Or possibly it was a reminder that because Job had had reverence for God in the past he could also trust Him now. Later, however, Eliphaz questioned Job's

"piety" (reverence, 15:4).

b. *His reasoning about suffering (4:7-11)*

4:7-9. Eliphaz then presented his theory on suffering: the **innocent** never perish (cf. "perished," "perishes," and "perish" in vv. 7, 11, 20); the **upright** (cf. 1:1, 8; 2:3) are not **destroyed;** but **those who plow evil and . . . sow trouble** ('*āmāl*; cf. 3:10) will also harvest trouble (cf. Prov. 22:8; Hosea 8:7; 10:13), and the wicked **perish** under God's **anger.** Such a theory, however, simply does not fit all the facts. Many times the innocent *do* suffer (e.g., Luke 13:4-5; John 9:1-3; 1 Peter 2:19-20), and often the wicked seemingly have no problems. This was Job's point throughout the book; Eliphaz's view of an airtight doctrine of retribution does not jibe with reality.

Eliphaz's authority for his theory was what he himself had seen in his lifetime (**as I have observed,** Job 4:8; cf. 5:3; 15:17). Inherent in this authority base, however, is a flaw: his observations, though undoubtedly extensive, were not universal. Bildad's authority was history ("Ask the former generations," 8:8), supposedly a broader base than the observations of one man. Zophar, blunt, discourteous, and dogmatic, merely assumed that what he said was true, without trying to back his statements up with some other authority.

4:10-11. Eliphaz added that though **lions** are strong, their **teeth** can be **broken,** they can perish **for lack of** food, and their **cubs** can be **scattered** by a hunter. Similarly, this senior spokesman hinted, Job, who used to be strong (cf. vv. 3-4), was broken and his children lost. **Lions** (five different Heb. words are used for "lion" in vv. 10-11) deserve to suffer because they bring problems to people; so Job also deserved to suffer.

c. *His report of a vision (4:12-21)*

4:12-16. Eliphaz sought to add authority to his theological viewpoint by relating his experience as if it had occurred in **dreams.** Though some might challenge his limited observations, who could prove his dreams wrong? **A word was secretly** spoken in **a whisper** (cf. v. 16) to him in his dreams. In his fright his **bones** shook and his **hair . . . stood** straight up. The **spirit** (v. 15), an indistinct **form** (v. 16), must have been unusually disturbing as he saw it pass by, then stop, remain quiet, and whisper.

4:17-21. Apparently the words Eliphaz claimed he heard in his dream are given in these verses. For three reasons it is doubtful that the words were a revelation from God: (a) "a word" (v. 12), not "a word of the LORD," came to Eliphaz; (b) the word came "secretly" (i.e., in an elusive manner, v. 12); and (c) the message seemed to picture God as unconcerned about man (vv. 17-21). **Can a mortal be more righteous than God?** "Mortal" renders 'ĕnôš, "weak, mortal, man"; this word is used 30 times in Job. **Can a man** (geḇer, "strong man") **be more pure than his Maker?** ("Maker" also is used in 9:9; 32:22; 35:10; 36:3; 40:19.) Scholars differ on how to translate the Hebrew word "from" in the literal phrases "from God" and "from his Maker." One rendering makes it comparative (as in the KJV and NIV): "more righteous than God," "more pure than his Maker." Another is suggested by the NASB: "before God," "before his Maker." Either way, Eliphaz implied a negative answer: Man cannot be righteous and clean before God (and certainly not more so than God). God does not **trust . . . His servants** (angels) and **He charges His angels** (i.e., fallen angels and Satan) **with error.** Therefore man certainly cannot be trusted.

Eliphaz pictured people's mortality in several ways: They **live in** mere perishable **houses** made **of clay,** built on **dust;** they are **crushed more** easily **than a moth;** they are **broken to pieces like** a vessel and their **tent** cords are **pulled up.** People perish, dying **unnoticed** and **without wisdom** (to die without ever finding wisdom was the ultimate disaster for someone in the East). These words from the friend-turned-antagonist are a not-so-subtle attack on Job. His houses were not secure; he was scattered (materially) like a moth easily crushed between one's fingers; his life was disrupted and unsettled (like a tent toppling over with no tent cord to hold it up; cf. 5:24; 8:22; 15:34). Job obviously was not a wise person, according to Eliphaz. This dream-report was given to support his theory of suffering: Job was suffering because he was a sinner. What Eliphaz apparently failed to consider is the fact that if all people, being unjust and impure,

suffer, he would be included too!

d. His recommendation to Job (5:1-16)

5:1-7. Eliphaz denied any possibility of angels (**holy ones**) intervening on Job's behalf because the angels cannot be trusted (4:18). Eliphaz interpreted Job's lament (chap. 3) as the **resentment** of **a fool** and as a simpleton's **envy** which would kill, not heal. "Resentment" renders the word ka'aś, which suggests "vexation" (as in NASB) or "provocation to the point of anger or grief." In Job this word is used three other times; 6:2, "anguish"; 10:17, "anger"; and 17:7, "grief." Eliphaz mercilessly spoke of Job as **a fool** who had begun to prosper (**taking root**) **but** was **suddenly . . . cursed** (cf. 4:9, 19) by God and therefore lost **his children** and **his wealth**—a grim, cruel reminder of Job's calamities. According to Eliphaz, the source of those afflictions was not **the soil** or **the ground;** rather, they came from within man. **Man is born** for **trouble** ('āmāl; probably an allusion to Job's words in 3:10) as certainly **as sparks** from an open fire **fly upward.** "Sparks" is literally "sons of Rešep," perhaps a poetic allusion to the Ugaritic god of lightning, pestilence, and flames.

5:8-16. In light of his cause-and-effect view of sin, Eliphaz advised Job to **appeal to God** because He is majestic, powerful (v. 9), and benevolent, sending **rain** for crops (v. 10); He encourages and helps the downcast and sorrowing (v. 11), frustrates **the crafty** (vv. 12-14), and delivers the needy and **the poor** (vv. 15-16). To save **the needy from the sword in their mouth** means to deliver them from slander (cf. v. 21). Though that advice was not wrong in itself, Eliphaz wrongly assumed that Job had sinned deliberately.

e. His reminder of God's blessings (5:17-27)

5:17-27. Eliphaz said Job's problems were disciplinary: **God** was correcting him, so Job should welcome His discipline, **not despise** it. If Job would have the right attitude God would bless him. Though God punishes (**wounds** and **injures**), **He also** restores (**binds up**) and heals. He delivers **from six calamities** and even **seven** (following one number with the next highest expresses thoroughness or emphasizes the final item; cf. Prov. 30:15, 18, 21, 29; Amos 1:3, 6, 9,

11, 13; 2:1, 4, 6). Eliphaz then mentioned **famine,** war, slander, **destruction,** and wild **beasts.** He would have good crops (**a covenant with the stones** means the stones would not hinder his farming); security (regarding the **tent,** cf. Job 4:21; 8:22; 15:34), numerous **descendants,** health, and a long life. Going **to the grave in full vigor like** stacked **sheaves** of grain beautifully pictures a life lived to the full and ready to be ended (cf. 42:17).

Eliphaz smugly concluded his first speech by reminding Job of the authority of his observations (**we have examined** them) and urged Job to heed them.

2. JOB'S FIRST REPLY TO ELIPHAZ (CHAPS. 6–7)

a. Job's defense of his complaining (6:1-7)

6:1-3. The patriarchal sufferer said that the reason he was complaining was that his **anguish** or irritation (*ka'aś*; cf. 5:2, "resentment"; 10:17, "anger"; 17:7, "grief") was heavy. But if his complaining were compared **on the scales** with his **misery,** his misery would be heavier, in fact, heavier than wet **sand.** His **words** (chap. 3), seemingly **impetuous,** were nothing compared with his suffering.

6:4-7. God was shooting poisoned **arrows** at him (cf. 7:20; 16:12-13; Lam. 3:12-13). As **a wild donkey** does not bray and **an ox** does not **bellow** when they have food, so Job would not have complained if his situation were more normal.

Food tastes better with **salt;** the two go together. And **the white of an egg** needs some flavoring; otherwise Job refused **to touch it.** So Job's trouble and his wailing went together, and his complaining, he said, should be excused.

b. Job's despair in his suffering (6:8-13)

6:8-10. Job hoped for death; he wanted **God** to **grant** his **request** that he die (voiced in 3:20-23 and also in 7:15; 10:18-19; 14:13). His misery would end if **God would . . . crush** (cf. 4:19) him, **loose His hand** from sustaining Job's life, and **cut** him **off.** The Hebrew verb translated "loose" carries the idea of setting prisoners free (e.g., Ps. 105:20) and the Hebrew verb rendered "cut off" pictures a weaver cutting thread. The one **consolation** and **joy** in Job's pain was that he was innocent of defying God. This is the first of several of Job's affirmations of his

innocence (cf. Job 9:21; 16:17; 27:6).

6:11-13. Job had no need to **be patient** (cf. 4:2) because he had nothing to **hope** for (cf. 7:6; 14:19; 17:15). His **strength** was gone. Did Eliphaz think that Job had **the strength of stone** or that he was as insensitive as **bronze?** Job's next question (6:13) should be taken as a negative statement, introduced by a strong affirmative particle meaning "indeed." Thus Job stated that he had no **help** in himself and no resources.

c. Job's disappointment in his friends (6:14-23)

6:14-17. When a **man** is in despair (cf. v. 26) **his friends,** Job felt, ought to be loyal. Job in his pain had not turned from fearing God (cf. **the Almighty** in 5:17), but even if he had, he would still need companionship.

His friends had been like a riverbed. In the rainy season, a wadi is filled with rushing, raging water from **melting snow,** but in the summer when it is most needed it dries up. So his friends, when most needed, disappointed him (cf. v. 21).

6:18-23. Travelers in **caravans** from **Tema,** in northern Arabia, and **merchants** from **Sheba,** in southwestern Arabia, both known for their trading, had gotten lost looking **for water** in the riverbeds. So they were **distressed.** Similarly Job was **disappointed,** expecting **help** from his three fellows (**you** is pl.) but getting none. In fact seeing Job's **dreadful** condition (cf. 2:12) they were **afraid.** Perhaps he meant they were afraid of being punished by God if they sympathized too deeply with one who had supposedly offended God. Job had never asked for their help before, but why wouldn't they help him now when he needed their aid?

This expression of disappointment in his friends is the first of several themes Job repeatedly came back to in his speeches (see the chart "Repeated Themes in Job's Responses").

d. Job's plea to the three (6:24-30)

6:24-27. Having voiced his keen disappointment in his friends' lack of help, Job then pleaded with them to tell him **where** he had gone **wrong.** "Where's the evidence for your idea that I have sinned?" He could benefit from **honest**

Repeated Themes in Job's Responses

	First round of speeches		
	First speech	Second speech	Third speech
1. Disappointment in his friends	6:14-30	—	12:1-3; 13:1-12
2. Declaration of God's greatness	—	9:1-12	12:7-25
3. Disillusionment with God's ways	7:11-19	9:13–10:17	12:4-6
4. Despair with life (or desire for death)	6:8-13; 7:1-10	10:18-22	chapter 14
5. Desire for vindication with God	7:20-21	—	13:13-19
	Second round of speeches		
	First speech	Second speech	Third speech
1. Disappointment in his friends	16:1-5; 17:3-5	19:1-4	21:1-6
2. Declaration of God's greatness	—	19:28-29	21:19-22
3. Disillusionment with God's ways	16:6-17	19:5-22	21:7-18, 23-34
4. Despair with life (or desire for death)	17:6-16	—	—
5. Desire for vindication with God	16:18–17:2	19:23-27	—
	Third round of speeches		
	First speech	Second speech	
1. Disappointment in his friends	—	26:1-4	
2. Declaration of God's greatness	23:8-17	26:5–27:12; chapter 28	
3. Disillusionment with God's ways	24:1-17	—	
4. Despair with life (or desire for death)	(24:18-25)*	(27:13-23)*; chapters 29–30	
5. Desire for vindication with God	23:1-7	chapter 31	

*The wicked die.

words even though they might be **painful,** but how did *their* words help? Not only were their words of no help; they even treated *his* **words** like **wind.** The three friends seemed as opposed to him as if they were taking undue advantage of an orphan or even selling a **friend**! (**Cast lots for** can be rendered "overwhelm" or it can mean "cause [a net] to fall on.")

6:28-30. Perhaps his friends could not bear to look on his disfigured **face,** for Job asked them **to look** at him. He wanted them to note his honesty (**Would I lie?**), and to turn from making **unjust** and false accusations. He was not speaking wickedly, but he could easily **discern** (lit., "taste") **malice** on their part.

e. Job's pattern of misery (7:1-5)

7:1-5. Job said that **man** ('*ĕnôš*, "weak, mortal man"; cf. comments on 4:17) is like: (a) a soldier (**hard service**

translates *ṣābā'*, "military service"; cf. 14:14; Isa. 40:2) fulfilling his time of enlistment with its toils; (b) **a hired** hand, destined to hard labor; (c) **a slave** who works in the hot sun and longs for the end of the day; and (d) **a hired** worker **waiting** to be paid. But Job's condition was worse. For he had **months,** not just days, **of futility** (lit., "emptiness"). Instead of being able to rest in the shade at the end of the day, his **nights** were miserable. (**Misery** translates '*āmāl*, "trouble"; cf. Job 3:10; 4:8; 5:6-7.) His nights were long as he tossed and turned in pain. Who could possibly sleep with his **body** covered **with worms** (probably eating his dead flesh) and dirty **scabs**? (lit., "clods of dust") The scabs on his **skin** hardened and cracked; his sores were festered with pus.

f. Job's prayer to God (7:6-21)

7:6-10. As Job turned to God, he first

spoke of the brevity of life (cf. 9:25-26; 10:20; 14:1-2, 5; 17:1). His life was passing by more rapidly **than a weaver's shuttle** (7:6), it was as short as **a breath** (v. 7), and it was vanishing like **a cloud** (v. 9). His days were ending **without hope** (cf. 6:11; 14:19; 17:11, 15). Job sensed he would **never** again **see happiness** (in contrast with the happiness Eliphaz held out for him, 5:17-26). In fact God would no longer **see** him (cf. 7:17-19, 21; he would be **gone,** in **the grave** never to **return** (cf. v. 21).

7:11-12. After asking God to remember the brevity of his life, Job spoke without restraint in bitter complaint to Him. **Am I the sea, or the monster of the deep, that You put me under guard?** Job complained that God was watching and harassing him. This monster was an allusion either to Ugaritic mythology in which the sea god Yam was defeated by Baal or to the Babylonian myth in which Marduk overcame the sea monster Tiamat and set a guard over her. Of course Job was not giving credence to those myths (cf. comments on 3:8), but was using known stories to depict his condition. Like the sea or sea monster dominated and confined by a false god, so Job felt as if he were in a subhuman condition in which the true God was guarding him like a defeated enemy.

7:13-15. Job then accused God of frightening him **with dreams** so that he could not even escape from his problems by sleep. Job again expressed his desire to end his misery by **death** (cf. 3:20-23; 6:8-9; 10:18-19; 14:13).

7:16-19. Because he **would not live forever** in his present body, Job longed for God to leave him **alone.** Why should God hound, harass, and haunt him when his life was drawing to a close and his **days** had **no meaning** (lit., "were futile," *hebel;* cf. Ecc. 1:2). Job 7:17-18 are similar to Psalm 8:4, except that the words in the psalm express awe at God's concern, whereas Job expressed remorse that he was haunted continually by God— examined **every morning** and tested **every moment.** In frustration, Job felt that God gazed at him (cf. Job. 10:14; 13:27; 31:4) continually and would not **let him alone even for an instant** (lit., "until I swallow my saliva!" an idiom still used in Arabic).

7:20-21. Job then asked God to tell him how he had **sinned** (earlier he had asked his friends a similar question, 6:24). Why should God, the **Watcher of men,** continue to stare at Job and to hit him like a **target** (cf. 6:4). If Job were a sinner, **why** didn't God **forgive** him and be done with it? (Here again is another "why" question by Job; cf. 3:11-12, 16, 20, 23.) The time would come when God would no longer toy with and tantalize His enemy, Job. Job would **soon** be dead (cf. 7:6-10); so if God wanted to grant him forgiveness, He should do so at once. To **lie down in the dust** meant to be dead (cf. 10:9; 17:16; 20:11; 34:15).

This prayer to God (7:6-21) was a cry of bitter despair. In Job's life, which was quickly passing away, Job thought God was constantly tormenting and terrifying him. Sadly, no relief was in sight.

3. BILDAD'S FIRST SPEECH (CHAP. 8)

Bildad accused Job of impugning the justice of God (v. 3) whereas Eliphaz had accused Job of resenting God's discipline (5:17). Both of these self-appointed consultants held the view that a man's calamities are the consequences of his crimes (8:11-13; cf. 4:7-8). Bildad, like Eliphaz, invited Job to repent as the way to recovery (8:5-7; cf. 5:8).

a. Bildad's defense of God's justice (8:1-7)

8:1-2. Beginning abruptly and bluntly, **Bildad** asked two questions, one pertaining to Job's windy **words** and the other pertaining to God's upright management of the moral universe (v. 3). Accusing Job's words of being **a blustering wind,** Bildad probably was picking up on Job's own reference to wind (6:26). The Hebrew word translated "blustering" is unusual; it means strong and abundant; thus Job's words, to Bildad, were like a forceful, continuous windstorm. Perhaps Bildad also was hinting that Job's rash, wild words were destructive, like the windstorm that killed his 10 children (1:19).

8:3-4. Bildad argued that to complain against **God** meant that Job was accusing Him of injustice (cf. comments on *mišpot* in 9:19). Since God never does **pervert** ("distort," used twice in 8:3) **justice,** He certainly would not be punishing Job for nothing. If Job had *not* sinned, then his suffering would mean that God had perverted His ways. And to Bildad that was unthinkable! Obviously, then, Job had sinned.

Anyone who has **sinned against** God suffers the consequences, Bildad said. Job's **children** illustrated that fact. They died because they sinned, and now Job was dying because he sinned. Why else would Job be suffering? Bildad and his cohorts were blinded to other purposes in suffering besides retribution. Surely this cruel, heartless remark hurt Job deeply. After all, he had offered sacrifices to cover his children's sins (1:5).

8:5-7. If Job were as **pure and upright** as he claimed to be, all he needed to do was **look to God and plead with** (lit., "implore the grace of") Him (cf. 5:8). "Look" translates *šāḥar* ("to seek or search"), the same word Job had used in 7:2d. Bildad was saying Job should seek God, not expect God to search for him. Such a simple step, Bildad claimed, would result in God's restoring Job to a **place** of blessing that would make his former estate seem like nothing! However, since Job had *already* pleaded with God (7:20-21) and nothing happened, Bildad's counsel was inappropriate.

b. Bildad's proof from history (8:8-10)

8:8-10. Eliphaz had supported his viewpoints by appealing to his own experiences (4:8). Bildad tried to upstage him by introducing a supposedly greater authority, the observations made by people in past **generations.** Since Job's and his compatriots' knowledge was limited (**we . . . know nothing**) and their lives were short (**shadow** may refer back to Job's words about life's brevity, 7:6-7, 9), they could learn from their ancestors. Their **words** came **from their understanding,** and were not words merely from their mouths, as were Job's words. How could Job dare suggest that the accumulated wisdom of many others was wrong? Bildad believed that if the dead could speak they too would testify that people suffer because of their sin.

c. Bildad's illustrations from nature (8:11-19)

8:11-19. To depict this cause-and-effect principle, Job's antagonist number two gave three illustrations—two from plant life and one from the insect world. Just as **papyrus** wilts **without the water**

of a **marsh** even **more quickly than grass,** so a person who opposes **God . . . the godless** (*ḥānēp*, used eight times in Job, meaning "profane" or "irreligious") will perish. Anything such a person may depend on for hope—such as Job's alleged innocence—is as useless and inadequate as leaning on **a spider's web.**

Job's wasting away, Bildad asserted, might be likened to **a well-watered plant** (with extensive **shoots** above the ground and entwining **roots** below the ground among **rocks** and **stones**) which is then pulled up (**torn**). It is then forgotten (**that place disowns it**) and **other plants grow** in its place. The words **its life withers away** are literally, "this is the joy of its way" (cf. NIV marg.), that is, the only joy such a plant could experience is knowing that something else will replace it. Again, such virulent talk must have only compounded Job's emotional wounds. Certainly Job was not forgetting God, nor was he a godless person (cf. 1:1, 8; 2:3) relying on perishable material things.

d. Bildad's slim offer of hope (8:20-22)

8:20-22. Once again affirming God's justice (cf. v. 3), Bildad said, **Surely** (cf. v. 19) **God does not reject a blameless** (cf. 1:1, 8; 2:3) person, **or strengthen** the wicked. If Job were blameless (cf. 8:6) he would not be treated this way by God. Job, then, could experience **laughter** and **joy** once again, and any who opposed him would be shamed (ironically Job's friends became his **enemies** and were later shamed; cf. 42:7-9). Besides blessing the blameless, God punishes the unrighteous (cf. 8:4, 13) by removing their **tents** (cf. 4:21), their places of security and protection. Bildad's speech ended with the words, **no more,** the same words with which Job concluded his speech in 7:21.

Bildad's harsh words included another heartless hint at Job's losses. The antagonist's attempt to defend God's justice only intensified Job's frustration about the Lord's apparent injustice. Since the sufferer had not sinned, the counselor's words were wasted.

4. JOB'S FIRST REPLY TO BILDAD (CHAPS. 9–10)

How could a man plead with God, the majestic Sovereign? (9:1-13) Job would be overwhelmed by Him if he dared confront Him (9:14-20) because, said Job, God destroys people whether they are innocent or not (9:21-24). Even though Job's case was hopeless (9:25-35), he would speak up anyway (10:1-2) and challenge God for treating His creature cruelly (10:3-17). Job would ask God to give him a little relief before he died (10:18-22).

a. God's awesome power (9:1-13)

9:1-13. Job was aware of what Bildad had said (**I know that this is true**); he knew that the wicked perish (8:13). But that only compounded Job's problem. Why then was *he* suffering?

In Eliphaz's dream, the voice had asked, "Can a mortal (*'ĕnôš*, 'weak, mortal man'; cf. comments on 4:17) be more righteous than (or 'be righteous before') God?" Job responded to that by asking, with almost the same Hebrew words, **how can a mortal** (*'ĕnôš*, "weak, mortal man") **be righteous before God? To dispute with** God (*rîb* "bring a court litigation against Him"—one of the many legal terms in the book), as Eliphaz had suggested (5:8), would be impossible. Ironically, though Job did try to subpoena God (cf. 10:2; 13:22; 14:15; 31:35-37), he found that when God finally did speak, Job **could not answer Him!** (cf. 40:3-5)

The reason Job sensed his inadequacy to present his case to God is that God, he said, is awesome in **wisdom** and **power** (cf. 12:13). Again ironically, God displayed those same two attributes when later He spoke to Job (38:1-40:2; 40:6-41:34). It would be too risky to resist God, Job knew. God can move **mountains** (9:5), cause earthquakes (v. 6), and cloud over **the sun** and **stars** (v. 7). (God, not Leviathan, eclipses the sun; cf. 3:8.) He stretched **out the heavens** (9:8; cf. Isa. 40:22) like a tent over the earth, and He **treads on the waves,** that is, His power is evident in sea storms. In His creative power He made the starry **constellations** (Job 9:9). Also He does miraculous works (v. 10, an ironic quotation of Eliphaz's words in 5:9). Furthermore Job cowered under God's invisible nature (9:11; cf. Col. 1:15; 1 Tim. 1:17; Heb. 11:27), irreversible power (Job 9:12), and irresistible **anger** (v. 13; cf. v. 5). The reference to God's passing by (v. 11) may be Job's upstaging of Eliphaz's dream of a spirit passing by his face (4:15). **Even the cohorts of Rahab** (cf. 26:12; Isa. 51:9) submit to God. This refers to the Babylonian creation myth in which Marduk defeated Tiamat (another name for Rahab, and for Leviathan; cf. Job 7:12) and then captured her helpers. Later Rahab became a nickname for Egypt (Pss. 87:4; 89:10; Isa. 30:7).

Since God in His anger conquers all the forces of evil, both real and mythical, how could Job hope to contend with Him? Job sensed his situation was helpless and hopeless.

b. God's arbitrary power (9:14-24)

9:14-20. Since God is so great (vv. 4-13), Job again wondered **how** (cf. "how" in v. 2) he could possibly plead his cause (**dispute with** is lit., "answer"; cf. "answer" in v. 15) and win. Since he would be speechless in God's presence, all he could hope for from such a **Judge** would be **mercy.** He thought he probably would not even get **a hearing,** that God **would crush** and **overwhelm** him. In both **strength** (cf. vv. 13-19a) and **justice** (cf. vv. 19b-24) God is supreme, thus leaving Job with no hope. ("Justice" translates *mišpoṭ,* a juridical term used frequently in Job and meaning justice or legal equity, 8:3; 9:19; 19:7; 27:2; 31:13; 34:5, 12; 37:23; 40:8, litigation, 9:32; 14:3, legal charges, 22:4, or a court case, 13:3, 18; 23:4.) In fact Job was afraid he would become confused and witness in court against himself (**my mouth would condemn me;** cf. 15:6 and comments on 40:8).

9:21-24. For the sake of argument Job had said, "*If* I were innocent" and "blameless" (v. 20). Now he affirmed, **I am blameless** (cf. "blameless" in 1:1, 8; 2:3; 4:6; 8:20; 9:22; 12:4; 22:3; 31:6). Several times Job avowed his innocence (cf. 6:10; 10:7; 16:17; 27:6). But even so, Job concluded, what difference does it make? Whether **blameless** or **wicked,** God would arbitrarily destroy him. Such an indiscriminate action—like **a scourge** bringing **death** to **the innocent,** and **wicked . . . judges** ruling over a nation—enraged Job. Here, for the first of several times, Job accused God of unfairness. As Job viewed life's injustices—his and others—he protested the notion of his contenders that God never perverts justice (4:7; 8:3).

c. Job's despair (9:25-35)

Job sensed that his case was useless because (a) his days were fleeting (vv. 25-

26), (b) God held him guilty no matter what he did (vv. 27-31), and (c) no one could mediate his case (vv. 32-35).

9:25-26. Bemoaning the brevity of life (cf. 7:6-9; 10:20; 14:1-2, 5; 17:1), Job said his days were fleeting like **a runner . . . like boats of papyrus,** the Egyptian speedboats of that day, and **like eagles.** The word for "eagles" is *nešer* (also used in 39:27), a word that may include both eagles and vultures. Perhaps here Job had in mind the peregrine falcon that can speed up to 120 miles per hour as it swoops **down on its prey.** These three (runner, boats, and a falcon) depict speed on land, sea, and air.

9:27-31. Job's plight was great for even if he tried to **forget** his problem and **smile** (cf. his lack of joy, v. 25), he would still be **guilty** before God. So **why** even try? Even if he were to clean himself up (outwardly as a sign of inward purity) he thought God was so against him that He would toss him into a cesspool!

9:32-35. Again the idea of debating his situation **in court** seemed useless (cf. vv. 3, 14). After all, God **is** divine and **not a man.** Furthermore no arbiter could possibly stand above both God and man (who could be greater than God?), listen impartially to both sides (**lay his hand upon us both**), and **remove God's rod** of affliction and **His terror** (cf. 13:21; 18:11). *If* such were possible, Job would confront God fearlessly; **but,** he said in despair, I **cannot.**

d. Job's desperation (chap. 10)

(1) Job's challenge to God. **10:1-7.** Since no mediator could arbitrate Job's case, he decided to become his own defense attorney. Risk was involved. He was taking his life in his hands (**I loathe my very life**; cf. 9:21). But he would vent his **complaint** in his **bitterness** even if it killed him. Rehearsing his speech, he would give **God** an order (**Do not condemn me**; cf. 9:20; 15:6; and comments on 40:8) and would insist that God list His **charges . . . against** him. In this sudden burst of self-confidence (contrast 9:3, 14, 32), Job said he would confront God with several questions: (1) Does God get some kind of sadistic pleasure out of abusing Job, whom He had made with His very **hands**? (cf. 10:8-12; 14:15) (2) Does God have **eyes** like a man and have to investigate Job? (3) Are God's **days**

short so that He has to **probe after** Job's sins? Surely God is not like that. And yet, knowing of Job's innocence, God still seemed to oppress him.

(2) Job's reminder to God. **10:8-12.** In destroying Job with His hand (cf. v. 7), God was being inconsistent because He had previously created Job in his mother's womb by His **hands.** Like a potter, God had **molded** Job, so why should he so soon be discarded to the **dust** from which he had been made? (cf. 7:21; 34:14-15; Ps. 104:29-30; Ecc. 3:20; 12:7) Job said his intricate embryonic development was like the curdling of **milk** into **cheese,** a process in which he was given **skin and flesh and knit . . . together** (cf. Ps. 139:13, 15) **with bones and sinews.** After giving him **life** (cf. Job 12:10; 27:3; 34:14-15) and watching **over** his **spirit** (cf. 29:2; 36:7), why should God turn against him? Again Job thought God was being inconsistent (cf. 10:3).

(3) Job's blaming of God. **10:13-17.** Maybe, Job opined, God had in **mind** this affliction all along. God was **watching** him (cf. 7:19-20; 13:27; 31:4) ready to chalk up every **offense.** Yet even in his innocence Job had no boldness before God (in contrast with his spurt of confidence recorded in 10:2-7). For God was stalking him **like a lion** (cf. 16:9), ready to pounce on him with His **awesome** strength (cf. 9:4-13) and summon **witnesses against** him. (**Anger** is *ka'aś,* "an angered irritation or resentment"; cf. 5:2; 6:2, "anguish.") Job's innocence, he sensed, meant nothing to God, since the Sovereign was against him, no matter what (cf. 9:15-20).

(4) Job's request to God. **10:18-22.** Once more the complainant asked for death (cf. 3:20-23; 6:8-9; 7:15; 10:18-19; 14:13), wishing he had never been born (cf. 3:17). Had he gone, like a stillborn, directly from **the womb** to the tomb, he would have bypassed all this misery. But since he was about to die (cf. 7:6-9; 9:25-26; 14:1-2, 5; 17:1) he asked God to give him at least a brief reprieve with **a moment's joy** (cf. "joy" in 9:25). Death would be final (**no return**) and gloomy. Four Hebrew words for darkness were amassed to depict the darkness of the grave (**gloom,** *ḥōšek;* cf. 3:4, "darkness"; **deep shadow,** *ṣalmāwet;* cf. 3:5; **deepest night,** *'ēpāh,* used only here and in Amos 4:13, "darkness"; and **darkness,** *'ōpel;* cf.

Job 3:6; 23:17; 28:3). This speech, like some others of Job's ended on a doleful note about death (cf. 3:21-22; 7:21; 14:21-22).

5. ZOPHAR'S FIRST SPEECH (CHAP. 11)

Zophar retorted viciously to Job for claiming to be innocent and for accusing God of malpractice in the universe. This third friend hardly lived up to the name "friend"; he was rude, insensitive, and brash.

a. His rebuke of Job's words (11:1-6)

11:1-6. Zophar was furious because of Job's many **idle** words (vv. 2-3), his mocking of God (v. 3), and his boast that he was blameless (v. 4). In stinging sarcasm, Zophar said he wished God *would* answer Job (cf. 9:3, 16) and give him insight into **true wisdom**, which is difficult to penetrate (**has two sides** is lit., "double, folded over"). Zophar said God was letting Job off easy, giving him less punishment than he deserved! This certainly was a heartless jab.

b. His praise of God's wisdom (11:7-12)

11:7-10. Zophar's laud of God's wisdom may have been a rejoinder to Job's comments about His wisdom (9:4). Zophar pointed out that the Lord's mysterious, plummetless, unknowable wisdom exceeds the height of **the heavens . . . the depths of the grave**, the length of **the earth**, and the breadth of **the sea**. How, then, could Job possibly **oppose** God in **court**? (cf. 10:2)

11:11-12. Since God is so wise, Zophar reasoned, certainly He knows the difference between **deceitful** and honest people, though Job did not seem to think so (cf. 9:22). Zophar called Job a nitwit (**a witless man**, lit., "a man who is hollowed out," i.e., empty in the head). The chances of Job's becoming **wise** were no greater than the possibility of **a wild** donkey, considered the most stupid animal, giving birth to **a man**! This was another insensitive barb.

c. His plea for Job's repentance (11:13-20)

11:13-20. Like Eliphaz and Bildad, Zophar recommended that Job repent (vv. 13-14) and receive restoration. God would **then** remove his **shame** (cf. 10:15) and give him security and confidence. Job would be able to **forget** his **trouble**

(*'āmāl*; cf. comments on 3:10) and he would have joy (11:17; cf. 9:25; 10:20), security, **hope,** and **rest** (11:18). Fear would be gone and people would again look to him for leadership. If Job continued in his wickedness, however, he would die (his **eyes** would **fail**), he would be trapped by his sin (cf. 18:8-10), and his **hope** would die with him.

These first speeches by Job's compatriots offered no comfort. Though their generalities about God's goodness, justice, and wisdom were true, their cruel charge that Job repent of some hidden sin missed the mark. They failed to see that God sometimes has other reasons for human suffering.

6. JOB'S FIRST REPLY TO ZOPHAR (CHAPS. 12-14)

The arguments of the committee of three hardly silenced Job. In fact this speech is the longest so far. Job castigated his self-selected jurors and their view of God (12:1–13:19), and again turned to God with his case (13:20–14:22).

a. Job's repudiation of his friends (12:1–13:19)

(1) Job's retort to the three (12:1-12). **12:1-3.** Job jeered their alleged wisdom. He sarcastically responded to Zophar's snidely calling him a stupid donkey (11:12) by saying that they thought they were so smart that when they would **die** all **wisdom** would be gone! Though Job was in pain, he could still think. He was **not inferior to** them (a point he repeated in 13:2); in fact what they said about God was only common knowledge.

12:4-6. God used to respond to Job's prayers but now, even though he was still **blameless** (cf. 1:1, 8; 2:3; 9:21-22), **God** had let Job **become a laughingstock.** It seemed so unfair, Job observed, for **men at ease** (like the three advisers!) to have such an attitude toward his **misfortune** while **the tents of** the wicked were **secure**, despite what Eliphaz and Bildad had said (4:21; 8:22). To **carry their god in their hands** speaks of those who make and carry idols. Why should idolaters prosper while Job, a man of true piety, suffered?

12:7-12. Again Job responded to Zophar's comment about the son of a donkey (11:12) by telling him (**you** in 12:7-8 is sing.) he needed to learn from animals . . . birds, even the earth, and fish. Job said that all of them were smarter than Zophar, knowing that calamities come from God's hand (cf. 2:10), not necessarily from one's sin. They also knew that their very breath (like that of man; cf. 10:12; 27:3; 34:14-15) comes from God's hand. Job said he could see through the friends' faulty arguments just as his tongue tasted food (cf. 6:30). He said he was surprised that the three were not displaying wisdom which normally accompanies older people (cf. Elihu's similar words in 32:7). This refuted Bildad's assertion that wisdom comes from age (8:8-10). So in 12:1-12 Job gave responses to all three of his friends.

The word LORD (Yahweh, v. 9) occurs only here in the poetic discourses. Elsewhere in Job it occurs only in chapters 1–2; 38; 40; 42. Therefore some scholars say this occurrence in 12:9 is a later insertion. However, the name Lord is intentionally conspicuous here by its rare occurrence within the debates. In the Book of Job, this name for God is spoken only by Job (1:21; 12:9). All other instances are in prose narrative portions (in statements such as "The LORD said to Satan," 1:7). In 1:21 Job acknowledged that calamities came from the Lord and in 12:9 he affirmed that same truth.

(2) Job's recounting of God's wisdom and power (12:13-25). **12:13-16.** Job was saying, in effect, "You say God is wise and powerful (5:9-12; 11:7-10), but I know more about that than you do." **God** can reverse the fortunes of leaders and even entire nations. In His **wisdom and power** (cf. 9:4) God can control nature, tearing down what man had built, imprisoning **man** (cf. 37:6-7), and bringing **drought** and flood.

12:17-21. Also all people are under God's control. He humbles **counselors** (was Job referring to his three friends?), **judges. . . . kings. . . . priests,** well-established officials, **advisers . . . elders. . . . nobles,** and **the mighty.** By stripping away their wisdom and power, God reveals His superior wisdom and power.

12:22-25. God in His wisdom can bring to **light** things that are difficult to comprehend (in mental **darkness**), things that leaders (vv. 17-21) are supposed to do. God is sovereign over **nations,** setting them up and putting them down. He can also darken **leaders** by depriving

them **of their reason** and sending them into an intellectual **waste** (the same Heb. word is rendered "formless" in Gen. 1:2), causing them to **grope** and **stagger.**

While one would normally expect leaders to be powerful and elders to be wise (cf. Job 12:12), God sometimes reverses that; for Job's advisers, older than he, were not as wise.

(3) Job's requests to the three (13:1-19). **13:1-4.** Job had **seen** and **heard** what they were saying about God; and he was **not inferior** to them (cf. 12:3; **you** in 13:2, 4-6 in Heb. is pl.). But they were not the ones he wanted to debate. He wanted to **argue** (yāḵaḥ, "dispute, debate in court") his **case with God.** Why waste time arguing with this terrible triad who were smearing the facts **with lies** about his being a sinner and who were **worthless** medical doctors with no prescription to alleviate his pain?

13:5-12. Their words, Job complained, revealed their folly; hence their silence would show their **wisdom.** Repeatedly in this chapter he pleaded for their listening, attentive ears, not their ignorant words (cf. vv. 6, 13, 17, 19). He wanted them to **listen** to his **argument** (this Heb. noun is related to the verb "argue" in v. 3) and his **plea** to God. It would do them no good to be deceitful in accusing him of sin, for the impartial **God** would not benefit from their **partiality.** Certainly they could not be God's defense attorneys (**argue the case for** translates rîḇ, a legal term, "to bring a court litigation"). In fact if God scrutinized their lives, they could not possibly **deceive Him. He would . . . rebuke** (from yāḵaḥ, the word for "argue" in v. 3 and related to "argument" in v. 6) them and **terrify** (bāʿaṯ; also in 7:14; 9:34; 13:21) them. Later they actually were reproved by God, when He convicted them of the errors of their views (42:7-9).

These men were incompetent to counsel, for their words were **proverbs of ashes,** a fitting description in view of the pile of ashes where Job was sitting (2:8). Their arguments, behind which they hid like fortresses made **of weak clay,** failed to help Job.

13:13-19. Fearlessly Job was ready to speak out to God and to take the consequences (**let come . . . what may**) even though it meant risking his **life.** The NIV marginal reading, "He will surely slay me," is preferable to the better-known rendering, **Though He slay me.** Anticipating the jeopardy (cf. v. 14) involved in his presenting his case to God, he was determined to **defend** (*yākaḥ*; cf. v. 3) his case even though it might kill him! But he was willing to risk it because of the remote possibility that God would exonerate him. Verses 14-16 show that Job was confused in his thinking. Perhaps God would kill him, but maybe not if Job's defense was well delivered. Job's willingness to dare to confront God showed he was not **godless.** Again Job asked these self-hired attorneys, these lawless lawyers, to **listen** to his **case** (cf. vv. 5-6, 13; in vv. 6, 13, 17 in Heb. the verbs and the word **your** are pl.), for his case was **prepared** (*'ārak*, "his arguments were marshaled") and he was certain God would acquit him. Later Elihu used that same verb in telling Job that man cannot marshal or "draw up" arguments against God (37:19). This contrasts with his earlier words of despair that God would *not* acquit him (9:28); his emotions were fluctuating. If **anyone** could possibly **bring charges against** him, only then could he **be silent and die.** His own silence, then, would replace the silence he requested from his protagonists.

b. Job's presentation of his case to God (13:20-28)

13:20-28. Having stated his readiness to present his own self-defense at the risk of God's striking him dead, Job then turned to **God** with his argumentation. But first he requested that God not intimidate him (cf. **terror**[s] in 9:34; 18:11), the defendant, in court. It was only right that he be given a fair trial (cf. 9:16-19). **Then** Job offered to meet God as either defendant or plaintiff. But when he asked God to enumerate his **sins** (cf. 6:24), God did not appear in court. Job asked God why He remained silent and considered Job His **enemy** (cf. 19:11; 33:10). **To torment a . . . leaf** or **chase after . . . chaff** was to molest the worthless, to hit a frail, helpless person who was down. Why, Job wondered, should God conjure up past **sins** of his adolescence and punish him for them? There was no sin at the present that deserved such terrible affliction. Why would God treat him like a prisoner, watching him closely (cf. 7:19-20; 10:14; 31:4) and mark-

ing his **feet** so He could trace Job's steps? After this sudden dash of daring, Job quickly subsided into a feeling of despair, continuing to pine away like a **rotten** moth-eaten **garment.**

c. Job's despair of hope (chap. 14)

In a sudden shift of mood, Job turned from confidence that he could win his court case against God to a melancholy lament about life's futility and death's certainty.

(1) The brevity of life (14:1-6). **14:1-4.** Man's **few days** are troublesome (the Heb. for **trouble**—the same word *rōgez* rendered "turmoil" in 3:17, 26—means agitation), and brief (cf. 7:6, 9; 9:25-26; 10:20; 14:5; 17:1) **like a** withering **flower** and fading **shadow** (cf. 8:9; Ecc. 6:12), constantly under God's scrutiny (cf. Job 7:20), and basically **impure** (cf. 9:30-31; 25:4).

14:5-6. Not only is **man's** life short; his **days** and **months** are **determined** by God, with time **limits** beyond which **he cannot** go. Since man is so hemmed in and his days so ephemeral, the least God could do would be to turn **away from** gazing on man (cf. 7:19; 10:20) and not harass him.

(2) The futility of death (14:7-17). **14:7-12.** When **a tree** is chopped **down it will** spring up **again.** Personifying a tree as if it had a human nose, Job spoke of a tree scenting **water** and then growing. In contrast with the world of botany man has no such hope. When he **dies and is laid low** (*ḥālaš*, "to be disabled or prostrate"), he is gone. (The Heb. word for **man**, v. 10, is *geḇer*, "strong man"; cf. v. 14. Even strong men die! **He** in v. 10b is *'āḏām*, the generic term for "mankind," and **man** in v. 12 is *'îš*, "male.")

This does not teach annihilation (cf. comments on v. 14). It simply means that a person cannot relive his entire life on earth in the same physical body. Though in the ground, he is not like a tree **stump** which, with its **roots . . . in the soil,** can spring up again. But a person *is* like **water** that evaporates; when it is gone, it cannot be retrieved. Death is final. At this point Job, in his way of seeing things, denied the possibility of physical resurrection. Death, he stated, is not a **sleep** from which people can be awakened. Soon, however, Job wondered if resurrection might be possible (v. 14).

14:13-14. Even though a buried corpse cannot normally be revived (some exceptions are recorded in the Bible, of course; cf. 1 Kings 17:17-23; 2 Kings 4:18-37; John 11:43-44; Matt. 27:52-53; 28:5-7), being **in the grave** would be, for Job, a hiding place from God's **anger** (cf. God's anger in Job 16:9; 19:11). Job could endure that **time** if God would limit it and not forget to resurrect him. But is resurrection possible? Pondering that faint possibility—**If a man dies, will he live again?** —Job said he was willing to **wait** out his **hard service**—(*ṣābā'*, "military service," also trans. "hard service" in 7:1; Isa. 40:2) in this life, anticipating his "release" (NIV marg.; the Heb. for **renewal** is used of one group of soldiers relieving another group). Death, with its release from the burdens of this life, would be like an honorary discharge or a changing of the guard. A person continues to exist after death, for he is transferred from one condition to another.

14:15-17. Returning to the subject of legal court proceedings, Job affirmed his certainty that God would summon him to court, for He would be longing (cf. 7:21) to see Job, His "handwork" (cf. **hands** in 10:3, 8). Job said that when God spoke, he would **answer** Him. And yet when God *did* speak, Job could not answer even one of His questions (40:4-5). Though counting his **steps** (cf. 31:4) God would no longer record his **sin**, for his **offenses** would be hidden (**sealed up in a bag**). For Job such a prospect was wonderful. But in 14:18-22 he plummeted back into despondency.

(3) The absence of hope (14:18-22). **14:18-20.** Though Job anticipated that *death* would release him from life's woes (v. 14), still he had no hope for reprieve *before* the grave. Like a crumbling **mountain**, like **stones** worn down by **water**, and like **soil** washed **away** by rainstorms, **so the hope** of man (*'ĕnôš*, "weak, mortal man"; cf. comments on 4:17) wears away. At death God forcibly overcomes him, changes **his countenance** (i.e., a person's face, once flush with life, becomes pallid at death), and sends **him away** from all he knew and possessed in this life.

14:21-22. In death a parent cannot see **his sons . . . honored** nor can he sympathize with their problems. In his postdeath life Job thought man's **pain** is

physical (as **his** cold **body**, lit., "flesh," is devoured by worms) and mental (he **mourns** in the sadness of his loneliness and separation). Fittingly Job ended this first bout in a morose tone, for he certainly was in pain and without hope.

C. The second round of speeches (chaps. 15–21)

In this second duel of desert discourses, Eliphaz, Bildad, and Zophar persisted in their theory that suffering always stems from sin. Here they became more vicious than in the first round. Missing from these speeches is a call to repent. Added is a more hostile, hardened attitude. Underscoring the fate of the wicked, these arguers at the ash pile stressed the dangers facing the wicked (Eliphaz, chap. 15), the traps awaiting the wicked (Bildad, chap. 18), and the short-lived wealth of the wicked (Zophar, chap. 20).

1. ELIPHAZ'S SECOND SPEECH (CHAP. 15)

In his first speech Eliphaz approached Job with a degree of decorum and courtesy, but not so this time. Now he lambasted the bereaved, dejected sufferer with the notion that he was a hardened sinner, disrespectful of his elders and defiant toward God.

a. A reprimand of Job's perverse attitude (15:1-16)

15:1-3. Perturbed by Job's irreverent talk (vv. 1-6) and assumed wisdom (vv. 7-16), **Eliphaz** accused the protagonist of **empty notions.** Like **the hot east wind,** the dreaded desert sirocco, Job's **words** blew hard but were useless (cf. 8:2). "Useless" translates *sākan* ("to benefit or serve," plus the negative particle *lō'*; cf. 22:2). Job later returned the accusation by calling Eliphaz's spiels windy (16:3).

15:4-6. According to Eliphaz, Job (**you** is emphatic in Heb.) hindered the cause of reverence (cf. 6:14) before **God.** Job's words stemmed from **sin** within, and therefore were the basis of his being condemned. Job's present attempt at self-defense (apart from his past sins Eliphaz said Job was guilty of) was sufficient cause for God's prosecuting him. **Your own mouth condemns you** is a response to Job's words in 9:20 ("my mouth would condemn me") and 10:2 ("Do not condemn me"; cf. comments on 40:8).

15:7-10. Eliphaz became Job's prosecutor, not his consoler. He lambasted Job for claiming to be the wisest person alive, as if he were the oldest and had some kind of inside track to **God's council** chambers. But Job had only claimed his knowledge was equal, not superior, to theirs (cf. 12:3; 13:2). Eliphaz lashed out that Job knew nothing they did **not know** (cf. 13:2). *They* were **older**—and therefore, they implied, wiser—than Job. To contest their theology was to show disrespect for the elderly, an unthinkable insult in those days.

15:11-13. Job ought to be content, Eliphaz felt, with the assurance that God was actually consoling him through Eliphaz. His **consolations** were **spoken** of **gently** by Eliphaz (5:17-27). He said that Job, in his emotional eruptions, became irrational, venting his **rage against God.** Such an attitude, resulting in venomous **words** against man and God, could hardly go unpunished. Eliphaz probably had in mind Job's audacious words in such verses as 6:4; 7:15-20; 10:2-3, 16-17; 13:20-27.

15:14-16. No **man** (*'ĕnôš*, "weak, mortal man"; cf. comments on 4:17), **born of woman** (a pickup of Job's phrase in 14:1; cf. 25:4), can **be pure** or **righteous** before **God.** So how could Job claim innocence (9:21; 12:4) when not even angels (**holy ones**) and **the heavens** are **pure**? This repeats what Eliphaz argued earlier (4:17). Surely *Job* **is vile** (i.e., repulsive) **and corrupt** (sour like milk; cf. Pss. 14:3; 53:3) and guzzles sin as if it were **water.**

b. A reminder of the fate of the wicked (15:17-35)

15:17-20. To his own observations (**what I have seen;** cf. 4:8) Eliphaz added the authority of the ancients (as Bildad had done; 8:8). The sages of the ages, **wise men** from times before their **land** had become infested with **alien** philosophies (perhaps suggesting that Job's thinking had been thereby corrupted), could inform Job that **the wicked man suffers torment.** "Suffers torment" translates the Hebrew word *ḥôl,* which means "to writhe or whirl." Here in its intensive form it speaks of writhing or tossing about in pain or anxiety (cf. "swirling" in Jer. 23:19 and "in great distress" in Es. 4:4). **Ruthless** means "terror-striking,"

giving the idea that Job was a tyrant who struck fear into other people.

15:21-26. Eliphaz enumerated (in vv. 21-35) 17 terrible troubles that befall a sinner. This friend-turned-enemy hoped to force Job to repent of his terrible ways. (1) **Terrifying sounds** are heard by a tyrant who terrifies others (cf. "ruthless," v. 20). Job had certainly heard some terrifying news (1:14-19). (2) **Marauders attack him,** which is exactly what the Sabeans and Chaldeans had done to Job's livestock and servants (1:15, 17; cf. Job's words about marauders in 12:6). (3) **Darkness** (*ḥōšek,* also used by Eliphaz in 15:23, 30; cf. 3:4; 10:21) haunts him, possibly a reference to the darkness of death. (4) **He is marked for the sword,** that is, destined to be a victim of violence, possibly because he himself was violent against others. (5) Without food and desperate, **he wanders** aimlessly, trying to escape his attackers, sensing that any day he might be killed (he would enter **the day of darkness;** cf. vv. 22, 30). (6) **Distress and anguish** hound him **like a king** ready **to attack** (cf. Job's words about **terror** in 9:34; 13:21; also cf. 18:11; 20:25). Job had said God overpowers man (14:20), but Eliphaz pointed out that a person's own anguish, not God, destroys him.

Why such misfortunes? The reason, this verbal pugilist said, is that a sinner is defiant (**shakes his fist**) and arrogant against **God** (**vaunts himself**), attacking God head-on. This contradicted Job's words that God was attacking *him* (7:20; 13:24; cf. 19:11; 33:10).

15:27-35. The first six calamities befalling the wicked (vv. 21-24) are followed by an explanation of the reasons for such punishment (vv. 25-26). Now the order is reversed; Eliphaz first gave a reason (v. 27) for the disasters he then mentioned (vv. 28-35). Self-indulgence (a fattened **face** and bulging midline) was the reason. A chubby person represented self-absorbed luxury and spiritual insensitivity (cf. Ps. 73:7, NIV marg.; Jer. 5:28).

Eliphaz proceeded with his list: (7) The wealthy wicked will come to ruin, forced to live in ghost **towns,** abandoned **houses,** and **crumbling** residences. (8) The transgressor will lose his **wealth,** a cruel recall of Job's privation (Job 1:13-17; cf. 20:12-26). (9) **Darkness** (cf. 15:22-23) overtakes him. (10) **Fire** will blight his crops. (11) He will vanish, being blown away by the hot anger of God's **breath.** (12) A wicked person who trusts in **worthless** possessions will actually gain **nothing.** This supported Eliphaz's contention that Job was trusting in his opulence, an accusation Job later firmly denied (31:24-25). (13) Though gaining nothing materially (15:31), the rebel *will* **be paid** (i.e., he will receive from God the deserved punishment for his sin). (14) Like a **vine** without **grapes,** and a dying **olive tree,** a reprobate dies prematurely, thus losing his hoped-for affluence and security. (15) Nor, said Eliphaz, will **the godless** (cf. 8:12-13) have children. (16) And an unjust person who accepts **bribes,** thereby favoring some and mistreating others, will have his **tents** burned (cf. the burning of Job's possessions by "the fire of God," 1:16; also cf. the trio's references to tents, 4:21; 8:22; 18:15; 20:26). (17) Using the figure of conception and childbirth, he said that wicked people are characterized by **trouble** (*'āmāl;* cf. comments on 3:10; 16:2), **evil** (*'āwen,* used before by Eliphaz in 4:8 and 5:6, "hardship"; and later in 22:15), and **deceit.**

By affirming that all these mishaps come to wicked people in this life, Eliphaz did not have all the facts. His attempt to jolt Job into repentance failed.

2. JOB'S SECOND REPLY TO ELIPHAZ (CHAPS. 16-17)

a. Job's disgust (16:1-5)

16:1-5. What disappointing consolers these so-called friends turned out to be! They told **Job** nothing new (cf. 9:2), and they were **miserable comforters** (lit., "comforters of trouble," *'āmāl,* the same word Eliphaz had just used, 15:35). They compounded rather than eased his trouble. Furthermore they babbled with **long-winded speeches** and arguments (cf. "blustering wind," 8:2; and "hot east wind," 15:2), unlike good counselors who console and listen. Apparently Job was surprised that Eliphaz came back at him a second time as if something **ails** him (**you** in 16:4-5 is pl., but in v. 3b it is sing).

If they could change places, Job could fire verbal bullets at them and deride them (to **shake** one's **head** was to mock; cf. 2 Kings 19:21; Ps. 22:7). But he would not do that. Instead he would give

encouragement and **comfort** (as he had done in the past for others; Job 4:4; 29:21-23) in order to provide some **relief** to their problems. He would condole, not condemn.

b. Job's distress (16:6-17)

16:6-8. Once again Job turned to bemoan his torment at the hands of God. Whether he spoke up or not, his **pain** lingered on. **God** had **worn** him down and weakened him with all his agony; he was distressed because for one thing his offspring and servants (**household**) were killed, and for another he was physically emaciated, as his **gauntness** clearly showed (cf. 17:7).

16:9-14. Like a savage beast **God,** in His hostility, Job sensed, attacked him, tore at him **in . . . anger** (cf. 14:13; 19:11), and snarled and glared at him. Besides that, people made fun of him (cf. 30:1, 9-10), struck him, and in their opposition amassed themselves **against** him like soldiers. **God** had left him in the hands of **evil men** and **the wicked,** an obvious contradiction of Eliphaz's hints that Job was wicked (15:12-35).

Job accused God of shattering him (cf. 16:7) and, again like a beast (cf. v. 9), grabbing him **by the neck** and crushing him (cf. 9:17). Besides being like a fierce beast, God was like an archer, using Job for **target** practice (cf. 6:4; 7:20), wounding him, and causing his **gall** to spill out. Job also likened God to **a warrior** attacking him. In all this, Job was again wrong in attributing hostility to God. Yet he could see no other explanation.

16:15-17. Because of God's attacks, Job wore **sackcloth** (like burlap) as a symbol of grief (cf. Gen. 37:34; 2 Kings 19:1; Neh. 9:1; Es. 4:1; Lam. 2:10; Dan. 9:3; Joel 1:8, 13), thrust his **brow** (lit., "animal horn"), **in the dust,** the figure of a defeated animal. His tears made his **face . . . red,** and his anguish put **shadows** under his eyelids. Yet Job was **free of violence,** not ruthless as Eliphaz had suggested (15:20), and his praying was from **pure** motives, not selfish ones. So his ordeal was unexplainable. Why should he be in such torment when he was not a terrible person?

c. Job's desire (16:18-17:5)

16:18-21. Job pleaded with the **earth** that it not **cover** his **blood,** that is, that his injustice be vindicated (cf. Gen. 4:10) and that his **cry** for justice not be buried and forgotten.

Turning from earth to **heaven** Job was confident that there he had a **witness,** or an **advocate** (*śāhēḏ,* an Aram. word, used only here in the OT), one who is an **intercessor** (*mēlîṣ,* "an interpreter or ambassador"; cf. Job 33:23, "mediator"; Gen. 42:23, "interpreter"; Isa. 43:27, "spokesman"). This **friend,** Job hoped, would plead (*yāḵaḥ,* "argue, debate in court") **with God** on his **behalf.** Since no mediator could rise *above* both God and man (Job 9:33), Job wanted a spokesman, a kind of heavenly defense attorney who could speak on God's level. Job's companions had not spoken on his behalf, so he needed someone who would.

16:22–17:2. Since Job thought his life was drawing to a close (**only a few years. . . . my days are cut short;** cf. 7:6, 9; 9:25-26; 10:20; 14:1-2, 5; 17:11), with death being final (**no return;** cf. 7:9; 10:21; 14:12), he needed an intercessor's help right away. He was depressed (**my spirit is broken**), for all he could see around him with his tear-filled **eyes** (cf. 16:16, 20; 17:7) were his friends (whom he called **mockers!**) with **their hostility.**

17:3-5. Though God was against him (cf. 16:7-9, 11-14), only **God** could provide a **pledge** for him in court, a bond given to the defendant as a guarantee that no advantage would be taken against him. To **put up security** is literally, "to strike hands," a practice by which an agreement was ratified (cf. Prov. 6:1; 11:15; 17:18; 22:26). This arrangement with God was necessary since Job's cohorts were mindless of his innocence and even denounced him, hoping to gain some **reward** for supposedly defending God. Such faithless friendship meant that instead of a reward, judgment might come on their **children** in the form of blindness.

d. Job's dilemma (17:6-16)

17:6-9. Job's wish for a court spokesman and for bail from God was followed by another expression of hope and then a note of pathos. People sneered at him, speaking of him in **a byword** (lit., "a proverb"; cf. 30:9), and they spat (cf. 30:10) on his **face,** a most insulting, abhorrent act. So intense was his **grief**

(*ka'aś,* "agitation"; cf. 5:2, "resentment"; 6:2 , "anguish"; 10:17, "anger") that even his eyesight was dimmed, possibly by tears (cf. **eyes** in 16:16, 20; 17:2, 5), and he was emaciated (a **shadow;** cf. 16:8).

Anyone who was **upright** and **innocent** would be **appalled at** (cf. 18:20) such outlandish treatment of Job. By this Job implied that his disputants were *not* upright. Even so, he would **hold to** and even grow in his convictions, certain of his **righteous** position before God.

17:10-16. Job sarcastically challenged the trio to **try again** to find some wrongdoing in him, but he knew they could not, partly because they were **not . . . wise** (cf. 12:2). His life was fading and his **plans** and **desires** were unfulfilled, even though the friends had held out hope to him (by appealing for his repentance). However, such hope of restoration, saying **light** was coming (cf. Zophar's words in 11:17-18) was unrealistic. Job thought his only **hope** was **the grave** where there is **darkness** (cf. 10:21-22) and **corruption** by **the worm** (cf. 21:26; 24:20) which would be closer to him in the tomb than his dearest relatives. As Job had said three times before (6:11; 7:6; 14:19), he had no **hope** of ever recovering. The hope they held out to him would vanish with him in the grave.

3. BILDAD'S SECOND SPEECH (CHAP. 18)

Bildad repeated many themes his senior had spoken (chap. 15; see Roy B. Zuck, *Job,* pp. 81-2 for details). In describing the wicked's fate Bildad emphasized their being trapped (18:8-10). Also he spoke of their experiencing calamity (vv. 11-12); being diseased (v. 13); and losing serenity (v. 11), possessions (vv. 14-16), and fame (vv. 17-18). Such a fate, Bildad implied, awaited Job.

a. His denunciation of Job (18:1-4)

18:1-4. Indignant at Job's insolent words, **Bildad** berated him. Job had expressed surprise that Eliphaz attacked him a second time (16:3), but Bildad wondered when Job would stop talking. The first line of 18:2 is literally, "How long (cf. 'How long' in 8:2) will you hunt for words?" (cf. 18:2, NASB) Later Job came back with the same, "How long?" (19:2) Job had said Bildad and the others were not wise (17:10), but Bildad replied that *Job* was the one who was not **sensible.**

Job had said **stupid** animals had more know-how than his advisers (12:7-9), but Bildad resented such strong language. Job had said God tore at him in His anger (16:9), but Bildad responded that Job was tearing *himself* by *his* **anger.** How could Job expect God to alter reality for *his* sake? Would everything give way to him, as if he were the only man on **earth?** Would God bend His ways just for Job, removing even firm things such as **rocks?** (Cf. Job's words in 14:18 about a rock.)

b. His description of the fate of the wicked (18:5-21)

18:5-12. Bildad, with Job in mind, gave a ruthless account of the misfortunes that come on **the wicked.** His **lamp,** burning in his house and symbolizing life and prosperity (cf. 21:17; Prov. 13:9; 20:20), goes **out,** plunging him into total darkness and confusion. He is **weakened** physically, defeated by his boomeranging **schemes.** In fact dangers await him like **a net** (for catching birds; cf. Prov. 1:17) and **its mesh** (the covering over a pit), a **trap,** a **snare . . . a noose . . . on the ground,** and **a trap . . . in his path.** Here Bildad used six Hebrew words for traps, more synonyms for these objects than in any other Old Testament passage. Whatever Job would do, Bildad affirmed, would ultimately ensnare him. So Job would be terrified wherever he turned (cf. **terror[s]** in Job 9:34; 13:21), with **calamity** and **disaster . . . ready** to pounce on him **when he** fell.

18:13-21. Bildad's reference to a sinner's **skin** being eaten **away** obviously alludes to Job's skin problem. Diseases are **death's** children for they serve death; so death's **firstborn** meant the worst of those diseases. **Torn from . . . his tent,** as Job was (cf. "tent[s]" in 4:21; 8:22; 15:34; 21:28), the reprobate is **marched off to the king of terrors,** that is, death. The houses of the wicked are burned and their security is gone. (Bildad's references to **roots** and **branches** recall his comments on botany in 8:11-19; cf. Job's words in 14:8 and Eliphaz's in 15:32.) No one remembers a wicked person who is in **darkness** (cf. 12:25; 15:30; 18:5-6), **banished,** and with no **descendants** to carry on his name, a terrible fate in the Middle East.

Job had said upright people would be appalled at his condition (17:8), but Bildad retorted that people everywhere **are appalled** not so much by the grief of the wicked as by their troubles and horrible end. With a note of finality, Bildad punctuated his point: **An evil man** ('*awāl,* "an unrighteous person," used later by Job three times: 27:7; 29:17; 31:3) will get what is coming to him. Amazingly Bildad insinuated that Job did not even know **God.** Since Job refused to repent, how could he possibly be righteous?

4. JOB'S SECOND REPLY TO BILDAD (CHAP. 19)

This chapter records one of Job's lowest points, emotionally and spiritually, and also one of his highest. After bemoaning the animosity of his accusers (vv. 1-6), of God (vv. 7-12), and of his relatives and friends (vv. 13-22), Job rose to a new level of spiritual confidence, certain that he would see God and be vindicated by Him (vv. 23-29).

a. The animosity of his three friends (19:1-6)

19:1-6. Nettled by the trio's wordy assaults, with which they were tormenting, crushing, and reproaching him **10 times** (a Heb. idiom meaning "often"; cf. Gen. 31:7, 41; Num. 14:22; Dan. 1:20), **Job** threw back at Bildad his words, **How long?** (cf. 8:2; 18:2, "When . . . ?") Then Job maintained that **if** he had sinned, it was his problem, not theirs. If they were going to act superior to him, they should realize that *he* had not sinned and trapped himself as Bildad had said (18:8-10); *God* had trapped him. He said **God** had **wronged** him, perverting justice in his case (this Heb. word for "wronged" is trans. "pervert" in 8:3). Again Job placed the blame squarely on God (cf. 3:23; 6:4; 7:17-21; 9:13, 22, 31, 34; 10:2-3; 13:24-27; 16:7-14; 17:6). How else could he account for his plight?

b. The animosity of God (19:7-12)

19:7-12. In his outcry (cf. 30:28) against God's violence (**I've been wronged** paraphrases the one Heb. word *ḥāmās,* "violence"), Job was further frustrated by God's silence (cf. 30:20) and seeming indifference to **justice.** In eight hostile actions, God had flouted Job: (a) **He** obstructed Job's path (cf. 3:23) and (b) **darkened** it (cf. 12:25); (c) He **removed** Job's **crown** (i.e., his place of esteem in the community; cf. 29:7-11; 30:1, 9-10); (d)

He demolished Job like a building; (e) He uprooted Job's hope like a tree (cf. 14:7). Besides all that, (f) God was angry with Job (cf. 14:13; 16:9), (g) considered Job His enemy (cf. 13:24; 33:10; certainly Job was wrong here for Satan, God's chief enemy, was also Job's enemy). Also (h) God assaulted Job like an army building a siege ramp against a beleaguered city wall and encamping around his tent. Bildad had enumerated many disasters encountered by the wicked (18:5-21), but Job responded that such catastrophes had come to him from, of all people, God Himself. Why God should buffet one of His own is always one of the most baffling questions a believer faces.

c. The animosity of his relatives and others (19:13-22)

19:13-17. The sufferer's plaint was also nurtured by loneliness. Brothers (perhaps comrades, not blood relatives), acquaintances. . . . kinsmen . . . friends, and guests abhorred and forsook Job—including even the three men who, though with him physically, abandoned him emotionally. Speaking of his household, Job then listed maidservants, his own personal servant, and even his wife and brothers among those who rejected him. His personal attendant refused to respond to him and his wife (this is the only mention of her apart from 2:9-10) stayed away because of his disease-caused halitosis.

19:18-20. Youngsters made fun of Job instead of showing the customary respect due to elders (cf. 30:1, 9-10). Job then lumped with the children those who had been his intimate friends—probably meaning "Eliphaz and Company"—and those he loved. Job lacked even the solace that normally comes from friends and loved ones in times of affliction.

Besides all that, his physical pain did not subside. He continued to lose weight (he was only skin and bones; cf. 18:13), and he had barely eluded death (escaped with only the skin of his teeth). If, as some suggest, "the skin of my teeth" meant his gums (NIV marg.) then he was saying his body was so run down that even his teeth had fallen out and only his gums were unaffected. However, the more common interpretation seems preferable.

19:21-22. In a poignant plea Job then begged his friends, probably sarcastically, to pity him. It was enough for God to have struck him (on God's hand; cf. 1:11; 2:5; 6:9; 12:9; 13:21); why did they need to be ruthless too, like animals after his flesh?

d. The certainty of seeing God (19:23-29)

Just after Job was at his lowest ebb, he rose to his highest peak. Forlorn, wracked by pain, and maligned by both God and people, he then mounted in spirited confidence to a future vindication of his cause. This was a "magnificent burst of faith" (W.B. MacLeod, The Afflictions of the Righteous. London: Hodder & Stoughton, n.d., p. 173).

19:23-24. Job expressed his desire for a permanent written record of his words of innocence and protest, either on a scroll or engraved in rock in letters filled with lead. Then present and future generations could know of his guilelessness.

19:25. In his jubilation of faith Job affirmed his certainty that God his Redeemer lives. Though Job believed God was against him, he knew that only God could vindicate his innocence. Job would die, but God lives on as his Defender, Protector, or Vindicator (gōʾēl, "a person who defended or avenged the cause of another, or who provided protection or legal aid for a close relative who could not do so for himself"; cf. Lev. 25:23-25, 47-55; Num. 35:19-27; Prov. 23:10-11; Jer. 50:34). Job knew that in the end God would stand upon the earth and, like a witness for the defendant at a court trial, would testify that Job was innocent. In that way all would not only read of his uprightness (Job 19:23-24) but also all would hear of it—from God Himself!

19:26. After my skin has been destroyed may be rendered, "After my skin has been flayed" (or "stripped off"), that is, after he had died from the constant peeling away of his skin (another symptom of pemphigus foliaceus; cf. comments on 2:7 and see 30:30) or after worms (cf. 17:14; 24:20) in his grave had eaten away his skin (though "worms," supplied in the KJV, is not in the Heb. text).

After he was dead, Job then would see God. He would continue in a conscious existence; he would not be annihilated or sink into soul sleep. But how could he say he would see the Lord **in his flesh** after he had just said he would die? Either he meant he would receive a resurrection body (in which case the Heb. preposition *min*, here trans. "in," would be trans. "from the vantage point of"; in 36:25 *min* is used in that sense) or he meant he would see God "apart from" any physical flesh at all (*min* normally means "without"; cf. 11:15b), that is, in his conscious existence after death but before the resurrection. Favoring the first view is the point that whereas *min* normally means "without," it takes on the meaning of "from the vantage point of" when it occurs with the verb "to see" (*ḥāzâh*). Favoring the second view is the fact that since 19:26a speaks of his condition in death, one would expect that verse 26b in Hebrew parallelism would also refer to death rather than to an afterdeath resurrected condition.

19:27. So certain was Job of his seeing God that he repeated this point. The Hebrew word for **see** (*ḥāzâh*) is the same in verses 26 and 27a. Also Job twice emphasized the word **I** (vv. 25, 27)—literally, "I, even I, know," and "I, even I, will see" Him. This gazing on God for all eternity will be **with** his **own eyes** (either the eyes of his resurrected body, or figuratively the eyes of his soul). Job would no longer be like a stranger to God, for God would be on his side.

This thought so overwhelmed Job that he exclaimed, **My heart yearns** (lit., "my kidneys," considered the seat of the emotions, "waste away") **within me!** He was emotionally drained by the very thought of meeting God and having Him once and for all vindicate rather than vitiate his cause.

19:28-29. If Job's friends continued to **hound** (the same word is trans. "pursue" in v. 22) **him**—to get him to accept their view that sin had precipitated his suffering, and that **the trouble** lay within **him**—God would eventually strike them down by **the sword** (perhaps a retort to Eliphaz's word about the sword in 15:22). *Then* they would see that God punished the sin of the wicked. Rather than God punishing *Job* for being wicked, *they* would be the recipients of God's **wrath** for they had repeatedly harassed an innocent victim. Confident that they were wrong about his spiritual state and that he was right, Job was able to look beyond

death to his being acquitted by God and fellowshiping with Him.

5. ZOPHAR'S SECOND SPEECH (CHAP. 20)

This sixth speech by Job's companions is the most stinging of all the diatribes. Infuriated and insulted, Zophar blasted Job, seeking to convince him that his wealth had vanished because that is what happens to those who deprive the poor.

a. The anger of Zophar (20:1-3)

20:1-3. Like his two partners before him, **Zophar** could not remain silent; he too had to speak another time. **Troubled** and **disturbed** at Job's rude words, Zophar felt he must respond. Job had said the three had insulted him numerous times (19:3), but now Zophar volleyed the notion that Job had insulted *him.* Some comforter he turned out to be!

Job had said God "closed their minds to understanding" (17:4), but Zophar retorted that his **understanding** forced him to **reply.** He had to share his insights!

b. The brief prosperity of the wicked (20:4-11)

20:4-11. Since Job claimed to **know** so much (a false accusation, for Job did not claim that), he should be aware, Zophar argued, that from the beginning of human history any **joy** experienced by a sinner **is brief** and for **a moment.** Job may be arrogant, Zophar arrogantly affirmed (!), but he will be brought low and die. Though high as **the heavens** he will, in contrast, be brought low like **dung.** People will not know where he is, for he will have vanished **like a dream** (four men in the Book of Job spoke of dreams: Eliphaz, 4:13; Job, 7:14; Zophar, 20:8; Elihu, 33:15). He will be unseen (20:9, a retort to Job's words in 7:8), **his children** will have to pay his obligations **to the poor** (since he had oppressed them, 20:19), and he will lose all his ill-gotten **wealth.** Repeatedly in this oration, Zophar mentioned wealth (vv. 10, 15, 18, 20-22, 26) and its transience, an expansion of Eliphaz's earlier statement along that line (15:29). All this suggested that Job acquired his riches dishonestly. A wealthy man, if wicked, will find that his energy will be buried with him. Zophar here may have been responding to Job's mention of **vigor** in 18:7 (cf. 21:23 and "dust" in 10:9).

c. The impoverishment of the wicked (20:12-19)

20:12-16. A sinner may enjoy sin-gained wealth like some **sweet** delicacy that he relishes **in his mouth,** but like **sour** food he will lose it. Wealth becomes like poisonous snake **venom** (cf. v. 16) with its bitter consequences.

Riches gained by godless means are not retained, Zophar argued. In fact they are vomited **up** and they **kill** the wicked like the deadly **poison of serpents** (cf. v. 14) or the venom of an adder's **fangs.**

20:17-19. Streams with their drinking water, and **honey and cream,** symbols of prosperity, cannot be enjoyed by sinners. "Cream" may be curdled milk or a kind of yogurt, a delicacy in the Middle East. As a transgressor dies, he must **give back** (cf. v. 10) the results of his toil and profits from his business without having enjoyed them. The reason for all this is that he took advantage of **the poor,** even taking their **houses,** in order to enrich himself. Of course Zophar had Job in mind, but later the suffering saint, here badgered again by verbal blows, denied such accusations (29:12, 15; 31:16-22).

d. The anger of God against the wicked (20:20-29)

20:20-23. Though always **craving** for more wealth (another unfair charge by Zophar), a wicked person will find that it **cannot save** him for it **will not endure.** Troubles will come **upon him (misery,** *'āmāl,* was a response to the same Heb. word used by Job in 3:10, 20; 7:3; 16:2; see comments on 3:10), and just when he is enjoying his prosperity (with **his belly;** cf. 20:14, full), **God will** lash out at him in His **anger** (cf. v. 28). The one who was angry, it seemed, was Zophar, not God! Zophar's vinegar-mouthed diatribe falsely and viciously incriminated Job as a selfish profiteer, heartlessly tyrannizing the poor. Such an arraignment was totally unfounded.

20:24-29. If Job tried to escape from God's anger, one **weapon** would down him if another did not. Pulling out the **arrow** (cf. 6:4) to try to save himself would do no good (cf. 16:13). He would experience **terrors** and **darkness** (cf. 15:30; 18:18), and **fire** (cf. 18:15; 22:20) would enshroud and **devour** his wealth.

God will not let a wicked person escape, Zophar averred. **The heavens** and **the earth** would witness **against him,** an obvious rejoinder to Job's desire that the earth not hide God's injustice to him (16:18) and his longing that his witness and intercessor in heaven act on his behalf (16:19-21).

His theft of the houses of the poor (20:19) will be requited by **his** own **house** being carried off by **a flood** (cf. 22:16) in **God's wrath** (cf. 20:23). **Such is the fate,** Zophar summarized, **of the wicked.** This is what **God** has **appointed for them** as their **heritage** (cf. 27:13). How then, as Zophar saw it, could Job think that his situation was any different? Since he had lost his wealth so suddenly, how else could such a calamity be explained except that he was wicked?

Zophar, of course, in his philosophical shortsightedness, made no allowance for a person being afflicted for any reason other than retribution for sin. In his stubborn invective, he flared at Job with venomous words, like the poisonous snake he spoke about.

6. JOB'S SECOND REPLY TO ZOPHAR (CHAP. 21)

In this speech Job responded to the view of the three arguers ("you" in vv. 2, 27-29, 34 is pl., and the verbs in vv. 2-3a, 5, 29, 34 are pl.) about the destruction of the wicked. Unlike his other talks, here he said nothing directly to God. Many of his remarks in verses 7-33 are direct refutations of Zophar's words in chapter 20 (see Zuck, *Job,* p. 98, for a list of these contrasts).

a. Request for silence (21:1-6)

21:1-3. If his troublesome counselors would only **listen** to what **Job** was saying, then they would console him (**consolation** renders the same Heb. word Eliphaz used in 15:11; in both verses the Heb. is pl.). This is an important reminder that sufferers want a listening ear, not a condemning mouth. Then, he added sarcastically, Zophar could **mock on** (this verb is sing., whereas as stated earlier, the verbs in 21:2-3a are pl.).

21:4-6. Since Job was complaining to God, not to them, why did he not have the right to **be impatient?** (cf. 4:2; 6:2-3) They ought to be amazed at his terrible appearance (he wanted them to **look at** him as well as listen) as they were at first

(2:12). According to Bildad, people every-where were horrified at what happens to a wicked person (18:20), so why could they not show at least a little concern about *his* situation, since they thought he was such a sinner? In fact they should be silent, putting their hands on their mouths (cf. 29:9; 40:4). Even Job's think-ing about his own deplorable situation disturbed him emotionally (he felt **terri-fied**; cf. 4:5, "dismayed"; 22:10; 23:15-16) and physically (his **body** trembled).

b. The prosperity of the wicked (21:7-16)

21:7-16. How could the contenders' viewpoint, especially Zophar's, be right about the brevity of the wicked's enjoy-ment of life (15:29, 32-34; 18:5; 20:5, 8, 22) when Job knew that **the wicked live on** into ripe **old** age (cf. 20:10), **their chil-dren** with **them, their** houses secure (cf. 20:28), seemingly with no judgment from God? (cf. 20:23, 28-29) The livestock of many sinners prospers, the wicked enjoy **music,** and even die easily. Besides, they cynically flaunt **God,** even wondering what they would . . . **gain by praying to Him.** This is strongly redolent of Satan's accusation that Job was seeking personal gain by worshiping God (1:9-11), but of course Job knew nothing of Satan's af-front. Job, however, knew that **their prosperity** did not come, ultimately, from **their own hands;** it was provided by God, whom they scorned! Therefore Job was not about to walk in the way of **the wicked** (cf. comments on 22:16-18).

Justice then is not always meted out in this life. Often the godless prosper and the godly perish. "Stern judgment in the life to come is the only possible corrective for this apparent triumph of wickedness. Postmortem retribution is clearly taught in both Testaments—compare Psalm 9:17; Isaiah 5:14-15; 30:33; Ezekiel 32:22-25; Matthew 7:13; 2 Thessalonians 1:8-9—although more clearly in later times than in the age of Job" (Gleason L. Archer, Jr., *The Book of Job: God's Answer to the Problem of Underserved Suffering*, p. 77).

c. The death of the wicked (21:17-26)

21:17-21. To Bildad's claim that "the lamp of the wicked is snuffed out" (18:5) in death and that calamity and disaster are ready to overtake him (18:12), Job asked, **how often** (asked three times in 21:17-18) do these things really happen?

This so-called **fate** allotted by God's **an-ger** (cf. 20:28; 21:30) to **the wicked,** as Zophar asserted (20:23, 29), hardly fits the facts. Sinners are seldom blown away suddenly and easily **like straw** or **chaff.**

Suppose his associates were to re-spond to Job that punishment for people he mentioned will come on their *children.* Job objected to that attempted way out by stating that a wicked person ought to suffer for his **own** sins under God's **wrath** for once he is dead, he could not care about any judgment on his **family** (cf. 20:10).

21:22-26. God's judging of the wick-ed does not follow the limited theology of Job's friends. God does not, as they suggested, often cut off the wicked (20:5) and judge their children instead. In His inscrutable ways He may allow **one man** to live on in prosperity and good health (Job's references to **vigor,** 21:23, and **bones**, v. 24, respond to Zophar's words in 20:11) and He may allow another man to be deprived and thus bitter. And yet in death they are alike, **in the dust** con-sumed by **worms** (cf. 17:14; 24:20; also cf. Ecc. 9:2-3). Wealth or health are not ways by which to judge a person's character. One may be wicked, and die either young or old; or he may be godly, and die either young or old. These facts obvi-ously conform more to reality than did the rigid view of Job's three prattling prosecutors.

d. The death of the wicked in prosperity (21:27-34)

21:27-33. Job said he was aware of how they might try to answer him. They would ask Job to point out **where . . . wicked** wealthy people were living (cf. 8:22; 18:21; 20:28). Job answered this an-ticipated question with another question: Had the three contestants **never ques-tioned** travelers? Many people who trav-el have money and yet many of them, though **evil,** do not face **calamity** or **wrath.** No one dares denounce or con-front wicked, influential people or re-quite them. Such a popular person lives on, and even has an honorable burial, with people guarding **his tomb** after a crowd follows his casket in the funeral procession.

21:34. Their consoling (cf. v. 2), Job evaluated, was only **nonsense** (*hebel,* "empty, futile, useless"; cf. "no meaning" in 7:16 and comments on Ecc. 1:2) and were evidence of their being faithless (*mā'al*, "unfaithful, treacherous"). Job simply could not buy their explanation of suffering; in fact their viewpoint meant they were unfaithful to him, their long-time friend.

D. The third round of speeches (chaps. 22–31)

In cycle one Job's visitors implied that he was a sinner and appealed to him to repent. In the second foray they insinuated that he was guilty and stressed the terrible fate of the wicked, but voiced no challenge for repentance. In the third verbal battle they attacked him by accusing him of specific sins, and only Eliphaz again gave a call for Job to turn back to God. Job stood his ground in response during all three rounds of attack. He denied (a) the premise of their implications, (b) their assertion that the wicked always suffer, and (c) that he himself was a deliberate transgressor.

1. ELIPHAZ'S THIRD SPEECH (CHAP. 22)

Eliphaz opened this speech abruptly without even mentioning Job's wordiness. He seemed determined to bring Job to his knees, to force him to repent for his wrongdoing.

a. God's uninterest in Job (22:1-5)

22:1-3. Man's goodness is of no **benefit to God**; He would **gain** nothing if Job **were righteous** or **blameless,** as Job so vociferously affirmed. Since God is not affected by whether one person is prosperous and another poor (cf. 21:23-26), they must be that way because of their righteousness or lack of it. How else could one explain such seeming indiscriminate conditions? **Eliphaz** simply could not accept the idea that God would be responsible for any deviations from justice.

22:4-5. Therefore it was totally unreasonable, Eliphaz said, for Job to think that God would rebuke him for being righteous. Why would God bring **charges against** someone who was not guilty?

b. Job's social sins (22:6-11)

22:6-9. With no evidence, Eliphaz indicted Job for several social evils: (1) Job took **security** from others (**brothers** here, as in 19:13, means countrymen),

leaving them naked. If a debtor gave his outer garment to a creditor as a pledge of payment, the garment was to be returned at night to protect the debtor from the cold (Ex. 22:26-27; Deut. 24:10-13). Failing to return such a garment was a sin. Later Job answered this false charge specifically (Job 31:19-22).

(2) Job refused to give **water** and **food** to people in need, even **though** he was **powerful** and **honored** and could obviously afford to give occasional meals to **hungry** travelers. Job also answered this false arraignment (31:16, 22).

(3) Abuse of **widows** and orphans, an atrocious felony (Ex. 22:22; Deut. 27:19; Jer. 7:6; 22:3; Zech. 7:10), was another indictment from Eliphaz. Again Job responded to this accusation (Job 31:16, 21-22). Certainly Eliphaz's theology was wrong when he lied in order to back up his position about Job's conduct.

22:10-11. **Snares,** terrifying **peril,** darkness, and **a flood** result from mistreating others, according to Eliphaz. Such a wicked person's life is hindered ("snares" is trans. "trap" in 18:9), he is frightened (cf. 18:11; 20:25; also cf. 4:5; 21:6; 23:15-16), in darkness he is confused and frustrated (cf. 15:30; 18:18; 20:26), and he faces devastating catastrophes such as a flood (cf. 20:28). Job, of course, was experiencing all these problems, but not, as Eliphaz presumed, as consequences of sin.

c. Job's spiritual defiance (22:12-20)

22:12-14. Once again Eliphaz stressed God's distance above man (cf. 4:17-19; 5:9; 15:14-16). Since **God** is so majestic, in **heaven** beyond the distant **stars,** how could Job be so insolent with **God,** questioning His knowledge and awareness of man and His ability to **judge** since He is separated from man by the **clouds?** But Eliphaz twisted what Job had said (21:22), thus again revealing the bankruptcy of his own airtight theological system. Job had said God *does* know, and that was the very thing that frustrated Job. Job had not said God cannot see man; in fact he affirmed just the opposite (7:17-20; 14:6).

22:15-18. The senior accuser then maligned Job for being a malicious sinner following the **path** (cf. 23:11) of **evil men** who **were carried off . . . by a flood,** possibly the flood in Noah's day. They defied **God,** telling Him to **leave** them **alone** (even though He blessed them), which was now what Job was wanting. This sneering quotation of what Job had just said (21:14-16) reveals Eliphaz's hateful haughtiness. He then added, **I stand aloof from the counsel of the wicked,** an exact quotation of Job's words (21:16), mockingly belittling Job for rejecting the wicked. Eliphaz wanted it known that *he* was rejecting the ideas of the wicked, but that he was doing so by **not** agreeing with wicked Job!

22:19-20. When sinners come to **their ruin,** then **righteous** people—Eliphaz and others—**rejoice** that justice is done. Job had said they could mock him (21:3), so now Eliphaz said he would gladly **mock** sinners (including Job!). Eliphaz, at first courteous (4:2), had now become unbelievably vicious. He even sounded like Bildad and Zophar, both of whom had spoken of the wicked person's possessions being burned up (18:15; 20:26).

d. Eliphaz's appeal for repentance (22:21-30)

22:21-30. Having conjured up homemade lies about Job and having twisted Job's statements into falsehoods, Eliphaz again pleaded with Job to repent.

Eliphaz set forth what Job needed to do: (a) **Submit to God,** rather than questioning and accusing Him; (b) **be at** (make) **peace with Him;** (c) **accept** God's teachings (as if Job were not willing to do that!); (d) assimilate and live out **His words;** (e) **return to the Almighty;** (f) get rid of **wickedness** (again assuming that Job was a secret sinner); and (g) quit trusting in wealth (**assign your nuggets to the dust, your gold of Ophir,** 28:16; Isa. 13:12; on the southwestern Arabian coast, **to the rocks in the ravines**). This last point was another false insinuation. How could Eliphaz prove that Job trusted in his material things? In fact he now had no gold in which to trust!

If Job would meet those conditions, Eliphaz proposed, God would then restore him and give him these blessings: (a) **prosperity** (Job 22:21), (b) restoration (v. 23) to fellowship with God, (c) trust in God (v. 25, **the Almighty will be your gold** and **silver),** (d) **delight in the Almighty** (the fifth time Eliphaz referred to God by that title in this chapter: vv. 3, 17, 23, 25-26), (e) fellowship with **God**

(v. 26), (f) answered prayers (v. 27), (g) desire to **fulfill** his **vows** (v. 27), (h) success (v. 28), (i) help to other people who were **low** and discouraged (v. 29), (j) deliverance of others through his intercessory prayers offered from a clean life (v. 30).

Eliphaz's point seemed to be that though Job's piety would not affect God one way or the other, it would affect Job.

2. JOB'S THIRD REPLY TO ELIPHAZ (CHAPS. 23–24)

Ignoring Eliphaz's allegations till later (chap. 31), Job reflected on two problems: injustices he experienced and injustices others experienced. Job wanted to present his case to God (23:1-7), but God remained inaccessible and unfair (23:8-17), and was also strangely silent about the vices of others (chap. 24). Such inequities, accompanied by divine silence, baffled Job.

a. Job's desire to find God (23:1-9)

23:1-7. In his bitterness (the fourth of five times he spoke of it; cf. 3:20; 7:11; 10:1; 27:2) and groaning Job still sensed that God's **hand** of affliction was weighing him down (cf. 13:21; 33:7). (**Heavy in spite of my groaning** should read, as in the NIV marg., "heavy on me in my groaning.") Job certainly wanted to turn to God (as each debater had advised, 5:8; 8:5; 11:13; 22:23), but he could not **find Him** (cf. 13:24). If God could be found then Job would present his **case** (23:4, *mišpoṭ,* another court term used frequently in the Book of Job), arguing persuasively (cf. 10:2) and weighing God's reply (23:5). Faced with the facts of Job's innocence, God would no longer **oppose** Job with His awesome **power** or **press charges** (*rîḇ,* lit., "contend, or bring a court litigation") **against** him. Earlier Job had stated that it would be pointless to present his case before God (9:14-16), but now he was certain that **an upright man,** meaning himself, **could present his case** (*yāḵaḥ,* "argue, debate in court") and the **Judge** (cf. 9:15) would acquit him and his troubles would terminate.

23:8-9. If a judge does not appear in court, cases cannot be presented to him. Because of that problem, Job searched in all directions for God, but in vain. God continued to be silent, to elude Job.

b. Job's declaration of innocence (23:10-12)

23:10-12. Job felt that God was evading him, because if He did show up, He, knowing **the way** of godliness Job followed, would have to declare him not guilty. Yet the sufferer perceived that when God finished with him in court, he would **come forth** (or, in view of Ugaritic and Akk. parallels, "shine" [H.H. Rowley, *Job,* p. 202]) like **gold.** Finishing with Job's trial in court may be the meaning of verse 10, rather than the more common view that God was putting him through a test so that he would be more pure than before. Job could lay claim to gold-like purity all along—before and during the trial—because he had **followed** the Lord closely, keeping to **His way** (in contrast with Eliphaz's accusation that Job followed "the old path" of "evil men," 22:15) **without** deviating and while obeying Him (cf. 22:22) and relishing every word of **His.** This is another of Job's many affirmations of his nonguilty status.

c. Job's exacerbation with God's sovereignty (23:13-17)

23:13-14. Again Job recoiled from the idea of confronting God in a court hearing. How could he dare counter God (cf. 9:3, 14, 17) who is unique (**He stands alone** is lit., "He is in one," i.e., He is in a class by Himself) and **does** what **He** wishes (cf. Ps. 115:3), including what He had in mind for Job (cf. Job 10:13).

23:15-17. Since God was so elusive (vv. 3, 8-9) and sovereign (vv. 13-14), Job was **terrified** (*bāhal,* "disturbed, dismayed," 4:5; 21:6; 22:10; 23:15-16) and weakened (**faint**). Terror came not because of his sinful nature, as Eliphaz suggested (22:10), but because of the Lord's awesome nature. Even so, Job would **not** be **silenced by the darkness** (*ḥōšek;* cf. 3:4) or **thick darkness** (*'ōpel;* cf. 3:6) of trouble that weighed him down.

d. Job's concern over God's indifference (24:1-17)

(1) God's indifference toward judging overt sinners (24:1-12). **24:1-8.** If God would post on a universal bulletin board His schedule for judging, people would be less frustrated over His seeming lackadaisical attitude toward sin. People steal land (by moving **boundary stones** to take in part of a neighbor's field) and **flocks,**

orphans' and widows' animals (a patent reply to Eliphaz's charge that Job mistreated the needy, 22:9), and **force . . . the poor** off the road so they cannot even beg. So the victimized hide for fear and wander about **in the desert,** gleaning what little they can in **fields** and **vineyards,** while going about unclothed (cf. 24:10), **cold,** and wet.

24:9-12. Oppressors even yanked young babies from their widowed mothers to pay off debts. Again Job said **the poor** were unclothed and **hungry,** and were forced to **carry the sheaves** of grain from the fields, to **crush olives (among the terraces** may mean between the rows of olive trees), and **tread** grapes in **the winepresses** while thirsty. Even in cities, people were **wounded** and **dying . . . but God** seemed oblivious to it all. This disturbed Job because he was suffering for no specific **wrongdoing,** while others, who sinned openly and deliberately, went off scot-free.

(2) God's indifference toward judging secret sinners. **24:13-17.** Murderers, burglars, and adulterers work at **night,** thinking their crimes will go undetected. They refuse to operate in **the light** (cf. John 3:19-20); they love the **deep darkness** (*ṣalmāwet;* cf. comments on Job 3:5, "deep shadow"). God seems to be apathetic toward them too.

e. Job's certainty over the wicked's eventual punishment (24:18-25)

These verses seem to contradict what Job had just said (vv. 1-17), for here he stated that God *does* punish the wicked. Therefore some scholars assign these words (vv. 18-24) to Zophar, others to Bildad, and still others to Job in quotation marks as if he were quoting one of the three in order to rebut them (v. 25). However, these could just as well be Job's words, in which he affirmed his confidence that though the wicked live on and get away with sin, *eventually* they are punished. This would oppose Zophar's view that the wicked die young (20:5) and would confirm Job's previously stated position that "the wicked live on" (21:7). Job's position was that *both* the righteous and the wicked *suffer* and *both* prosper. This differs drastically from the insistence of the three disputers that only the wicked suffer and only the righteous prosper.

24:18-25. Oppressors, Job argued, are unstable like **foam on . . . water.** Their **land is** under a curse and therefore unproductive (**so that no one goes to the vineyards** to glean grapes; cf. Lev. 19:9-10; 23:22). When they die, even their mothers (their wombs) forget them, worms eat their bodies (cf. Job 17:14; 21:26), and they **are broken like a tree.** People who mistreat widows (cf. 24:3) will be judged by **God** in **His power.** Such sinners may **become** settled, but God is fully aware (cf. 34:21) of their **feeling of security.**

Though they are in high positions for some time, God eventually debases them and they join **others** in the grave. Once prosperous, like **heads of** full-grown **grain** of barley or wheat, **they are cut off** just as sheaves are cut. They are not destroyed immediately, as the three maintained, but eventually. Why they should even prosper at all, while nonchalantly going about their sins, was Job's enigma. But he remained unmoved in his viewpoint, for it fit the facts, whereas the opinion of his colleagues did not.

3. BILDAD'S THIRD SPEECH (CHAP. 25)

Bildad's brief lecture shows he was running out of arguments with which to answer Job. Like Eliphaz in his third speech (chap. 22) and unlike his own previous speeches (chaps. 8; 18), Bildad said nothing about Job's windy words. The majesty of God, in contrast with the insignificance and iniquity of *all* men, not just of Job and the wicked, is the theme of this speech. Possibly this was a last-ditch effort to get Job to see how useless it is for an impure human to try to schedule a court hearing with the majestic God.

25:1-3. Since **God** rules (has **dominion**) He should be respected (**awe**), and Job, **Bildad** may have hinted, was not doing that. In His greatness God **establishes order** or harmony in **heaven** (so He is just; cf. 8:3). He rules over countless **forces,** probably referring to angels (so He is omnipotent). Also **His light** (the light of the sun) pervades everything, picturing His omniscience.

25:4-6. Here Bildad, rather than responding to Job's concerns about injustice (chaps. 23–24), simply repeated Eliphaz's twice-trumped-up theme (4:17-

18; 15:14-16) that **man** ('*ĕnôš*, "weak, mortal man"; cf. 25:6 with comments on 4:17) cannot possibly be **righteous** or **pure.** (In using the phrase **one born of woman** as a synonym for weak man, Bildad intentionally picked up Job's wording in 14:1; cf. 15:4.) As Eliphaz had said (15:15), "Even the heavens" in all their brilliance "are not pure." **The moon** only reflects light, **and the stars** (cf. 22:12) lack purity before God because, in comparison with His glory, they are dim. How then could puny **man** ('*ĕnôš;* cf. 25:4) or **a son of man,** suggesting man's creation from mere dust, hope to stand before God? Man is so much smaller than the starry universe and is only **a maggot** and **a worm.** This disgusting suggestion may have intentionally harked back to Job's words about his many sores being covered with worms (7:5).

Bildad sought to humiliate Job, to awaken him to his own unworthiness. But this unkind speech accomplished nothing because Job had already admitted the facts of God's majesty and of universal sin.

A review of the speeches of Job's associates shows that they were poor counselors. They failed in several ways: (1) They did not express any sympathy for Job in their speeches. (2) They did not pray for him. (3) They seemingly ignored Job's expressions of emotional and physical agony. (4) They talked too much and did not seem to listen adequately to their advisee. (5) They became defensive and argumentative. (6) They belittled rather than encouraged Job. (7) They assumed they knew the cause of Job's problems. (8) They stubbornly persisted in their views of Job's problem, even when their ideas contradicted the facts. (9) They suggested an inappropriate solution to his problem. (10) They blamed Job and condemned him for expressing grief and frustration. Counselors today do well to be sure they do not fail in similar ways.

4. JOB'S THIRD REPLY TO BILDAD (CHAPS. 26–31)

In contrast with the shortest speech in the book (chap. 25) chapters 26–31 comprise the longest. Job replied first to Bildad ("you" in 26:2-4 is sing.) but later (in chaps. 27–31) to all three ("you" in 27:5, e.g., is pl.).

*a. Job's description of God's majesty
  in nature (chap. 26)*

Here Job sought to show Bildad that
he, Job, knew more about God's majesty
than his pugilist did. But first he sarcastically rebuked Bildad, hinting that Bildad,
not Job, was the puny one.

26:1-4. In stunning irony, **Job**
mocked Bildad's futile attempt to help
him. Bildad had treated Job as if he were
powerless . . . feeble (cf. 18:7), and
without wisdom (cf. 18:2). But Bildad,
Job asserted, had not supported him, or
strengthened him, or given him any
helpful **advice** or **insight** at all. About all
Bildad could think about was what happens to the wicked (8:8-19; 18:5-21) and
about man's debased condition (25:4-6).
No one **helped** Bildad with his **words,**
which obviously were of no value. He
and his cohorts were "worthless physicians" (13:4) and "miserable comforters"
(16:2).

26:5-6. Some commentators ascribe
verses 5-14 to Bildad, to make his third
speech longer, or to Zophar to give him a
third verbal assault. However, it was
typical of Job to outdo his disputers in
statements about God's transcendence.
Did Bildad think he knew something of
the majesty of the Almighty? (25:2-3)
Then he ought to listen to what Job knew
of the Lord's supremacy!

God is over **death** (26:5-6), outer
space and the earth (v. 7), the clouds (vv.
8-9), light and darkness (v. 10), things on
the earth (mountains and the sea, vv. 11-
12), and the sky (v. 13).

Before God **the dead** are lying in **anguish** (an indication of conscious torment; cf. Luke 16:24) **beneath the waters,**
where the dead were envisioned to be,
and in *š^e'ôl* ("sheol") or **Destruction**
("Abaddon," a synonym of sheol; cf. Job
28:22; 31:12).

The word "dead" ("departed spirits," NASB) translates the Hebrew word
r^epā'îm, which sometimes is used of a
people known as the "Rephaites" and
sometimes is used to refer to the dead.
The Rephaites were tall like the Anakim
(Deut. 2:20-21). At least four giant
Rephaites are mentioned by name in the
Old Testament: Og (Deut. 3:11; cf. Josh.
12:4; 13:12); Ishbi-Benob (a descendant of
Rapha; 2 Sam. 21:16); Saph (2 Sam. 21:18;
spelled Sippai in 1 Chron. 20:4); and Go-
liath (2 Sam. 21:19). Second Samuel 21:20

refers to another tall Rephaite, who is
unnamed. Rephaites are mentioned in
Genesis 14:5; 15:20; Deuteronomy 2:11;
3:13; and Joshua 17:15.

In Ugaritic, Rephaites were the chief
gods or aristocratic warriors, apparently
called that because both groups were
seemingly giant-like in their power.
When *r^epā'îm* in Ugaritic was used of the
dead it seemed to suggest "the elite
among the dead." In Hebrew it may suggest the elite among the dead (cf. Isa.
14:9, "those who were leaders in the
world") or it may simply be a synonym
of other common words for the dead.
R^epā'îm occurs in Psalm 88:10b, "those
who are dead"; Proverbs 2:18, "the spirits of the dead"; 9:18, "the dead"; 21:16,
"the dead"; Isaiah 14:9, "the spirits of the
departed"; 26:14, "departed spirits";
26:19c, "dead." Job's point in Job 26:5
seems to be that even the elite dead are in
anguish because God knows and sees
them.

26:7-10. God sustains the **skies** (cf.
v. 13) **over empty space** and supports **the
earth** on **nothing**—statements amazingly
in accord with facts not known or agreed
on by scientists till a few hundred years
ago. In the **clouds** in the sky God gathers
up water (evaporation), and He can cover
the . . . moon with **clouds.** At the **horizon . . . light and darkness** seem to separate. The horizon is circular, for the verb
marks out translates the word *ḥûq*, "to
draw a circle," and suggests the curva-
ture of the earth. This too accords with
the facts known by scientists only in recent times.

26:11-14. Not only is God awesome
in His control over space and the earth in
space. He also is majestic on the earth.
He causes earthquakes and **sea** storms,
which He then calms. **The pillars of the
heavens** figuratively refer to mountains
that seem to support the sky (cf. 9:6). The
raging sea is pictured as a sea god named
Rahab (cf. comments on 9:13), whom
God defeated. **The gliding serpent** may
be another description of this sea god,
also known as Leviathan (Isa. 27:1). God
is over the sea, and He is also superior to
all mythological representations of evil.

By the wind, God's **breath,** He clears
the sky of clouds after a storm. This reveals **His power** and **wisdom** (cf. Job
9:4).

All these evidences of God's power

over nature (of things below, above, and on the earth) are only meager indications (**the outer fringe**) of what He does. People are so distant from God that they **hear** only a whisper (cf. 4:12) and obviously then cannot possibly fully comprehend all God's activities in His **power**.

b. Job's description of the fate of the wicked (chap. 27)

27:1-6. Before addressing the plight of the wicked (vv. 7-23) **Job** again affirmed his innocence (vv. 1-6) perhaps in an effort to show that he was not one of the godless. Repeatedly Job had accused **God** of injustice (6:4; 7:20; 10:2-3; 13:24; 16:12-13; 19:7; 23:14) and of giving him inner **bitterness** (3:20; 7:11; 10:1; 23:2). Even so, Job again affirmed his innocence as he had done before in responses to Eliphaz (6:10, 29-30; 16:17; 23:10-12), Bildad (9:21-22; 10:7), and Zophar (12:4; 13:18-19). He said that **as long as** he lived (27:3, 6), with God's **breath** in him (cf. 10:12; 12:10; 34:14-15), he would not **admit** to wrongdoing; he simply could not accept his friends' (**you** is pl. in 27:5, 11-12) viewpoint, or **deny** (cf. **denied** in v. 2) his **integrity** which his wife had urged him to do (2:9). Even with all his friends' badgering, Job was confident that he would retain his **righteousness** and that his **conscience** would **not reproach** (ḥārap, "speak sharp, accusing things against") him.

27:7-12. Imprecating his **enemies** (did Job have in mind his fellows at the ash pile?), he then asked four questions that pointed to the hopeless condition of **the godless** person ('awāl, "an unrighteous person"; cf. 18:21; 29:17; 31:3). When dying (**when God takes away his life**; cf. God as the source of life, 10:12), he will call on **God**, but since he prays only when in **distress** God will not answer him.

Job said he, in contrast with the wicked, could even instruct his compatriots about God's **ways** (thus reversing what Eliphaz said in 22:22). Since they had **seen** evidences of God's works, they were wrong to continue their false and empty (**meaningless**, hebel, 7:16; 9:29, "in vain"; 21:34, "nonsense"; 35:16, "empty") accusations, claiming **God** was punishing an innocent person.

27:13-23. Many scholars assign these words to Zophar because this would give him a third speech and because the words seem more consistent with him than with Job. However, Job had already spoken of the fate of the wicked (24:18-24). He never denied the ultimate punishment of God's enemies, but he *did* deny their immediate judgment, contrary to Zophar's claim (20:5; 21:7). If Zophar could speak of **the fate** of **the wicked** and their **heritage** (20:29), so could Job. A vile person's family members are subject to death by warfare (**the sword**), starvation, or **the plague**. He will also lose his possessions. Though he may be "filthy rich," with vast amounts of **silver** and many **clothes,** they will pass into the hands of others. His **house** will be as empty as a deserted **cocoon**, as unstable as a temporary shelter **made by a** farmer for guarding his crops. His wealth will be **gone** suddenly, and will quickly be carried off by a storm, the strong sirocco **east wind.** It will make fun of him (clap **its hands** and hiss) while he tries to escape its merciless **power.**

c. Job's discussion of God's wisdom (chap. 28)

In this chapter Job affirmed people's inability to ascertain God's wisdom fully, in contrast with the triad of antagonists who claimed they knew what God was doing in Job's life. Though seemingly an isolated chapter (which some say was spoken by one of the three, by God, or by an unnamed spokesman), this discourse does agree with Job's earlier words about man's inability to know God's wisdom and with Job's words about God's sovereignty over death and nature (cf. 28:24-27 with 26:5-13).

28:1-11. Men search for numerous metals underground (vv. 1-2—**silver . . . gold. . . . iron . . . copper**—and precious gems such as **sapphires** (v. 6; cf. v. 16). (Though the Iron Age began ca. 1200 B.C., when tools were commonly manufactured from iron, iron was known long before that; cf., e.g., Gen. 4:22.) Miners dig shafts in **the darkness** underground and dangle from ropes to reach remote areas. Beneath its surface **the earth,** overturned by miners at work, is in rubble as if it had been burned.

Birds with keen sight and stealthy animals cannot see or walk on the underground treasure troves. In his mining operations, man hammers away at the rocks, digs **tunnels,** and even finds where **rivers** begin which he must dam up (NIV marg.). As a result he is able to bring **hidden** underground **things to light.** These verses are arranged in an interesting structure (as suggested by David J. Clark, "In Search of Wisdom: Notes on Job 28," *The Bible Translator* 33. October 1982:401-5):

a. Getting valuable metals from the earth (Job 28:1-2)
  b. Going underground (v. 3)
    c. Remoteness of the mines (unseen by people, v. 4)
a¹. Getting valuable metals and gems from the earth (vv. 5-6)
    c¹. Remoteness of the mines (unseen by birds and animals, vv. 7-8)
  b¹. Going underground (v. 9)
a². Getting valuable metals from the earth (vv. 10-11).

28:12-19. In spite of man's technological skills, he cannot find, unaided, the greatest treasure of all, **wisdom.** Its value is not fully known by man (*ĕnôš,* "weak, mortal man"; cf. comments on 4:17). He can discover other hidden treasures under the earth's surface (28:4, 10), but he **cannot** discover wisdom in the inhabited earth (**the land of the living**) or in any ocean. Nor can wisdom be purchased in a market with other precious metals and jewels man has uncovered (**gold . . . silver. . . . onyx . . . sapphires. . . . crystal. . . . coral . . . jasper . . . rubies,** or **topaz**), for **wisdom** far exceeds their value (cf. Prov. 3:13-15; 8:11; 16:16).

28:20-27. After repeating the two questions Job asked before (v. 20; cf. v. 12), he affirmed that no animal, person, or bird can see **wisdom** (just as one cannot see mountain-hidden metals, vv. 4, 7-8). And just as the sea does not know where wisdom is obtainable (v. 14), neither do **Destruction** ("Abaddon," NIV marg; cf. 26:6) nor **Death** know. The only One who knows is **God,** for **He** is omnipresent (He **sees** what animals, people, and birds are unable to see, 28:7, 21). In creating the universe, God determined the elements; **the force** (lit., "weight") **of the wind,** the amount of water, the **decree** (i.e., limit) **for the rain,** and where each **thunderstorm** would occur. In His creative genius, **He** saw and valued **wisdom** (cf. Prov. 8:27-30), in contrast

with man's inability to do so (cf. Job 28:12-13).

Verses 12-27 have an interesting arrangement:
a. Inaccessibility of wisdom (vv. 12-14)
  b. Wisdom's value beyond [gold, silver] jewels (vv. 15-19)
a¹. Inaccessibility of wisdom (vv. 20-22)
  b¹. Wisdom's value known by God (vv. 23-27).

28:28. God told **man** (*'ādām,* "mankind") that the essence of **wisdom** is to **fear** ("venerate and submit to") **the LORD,** even when man cannot understand His ways, and **to** reject **evil,** living in accord with God's standards of holiness. Honoring God (the positive) involves hating sin (the negative; Prov. 8:13). Job's accusers had insisted that he was not fearing God or eschewing sin and that therefore he was not wise. In Job 28 he argued the opposite: *he* was fearing God and hating evil (as God Himself had already said of Job, 1:1, 8; 2:3), but *they* were not! Therefore wisdom and **understanding** were his, not theirs.

This closing verse also links these words of Job with chapter 29, in which he cited evidences that he revered the Lord, and with chapter 31, in which he enumerated evidences that he was not involved in sin.

d. Job's concluding soliloquy (chaps. 29-31)

As Job spoke to God alone in these closing chapters, he was like an attorney summarizing his arguments before a jury. He discussed his past pre-affliction glory (chap. 29), delineated his present gloom (chap. 30), and delivered his final oath of innocence (chap. 31).

(1) Job's past glory (chap. 29). This chapter expands Job's earlier words, "All was well with me" (16:12). **29:1-6.** In previous **months** (thus suggesting that his disease extended over at least several months' time; cf. 7:3) **God** had **watched over** him (cf. 10:12) and **blessed** him. To have God's **lamp** over him, like a lamp suspended in a tent (cf. 18:6; Ecc. 12:6; "bowl" means "lamp") meant to be under His favor. Also God guided him **through** the **darkness** of difficulties, befriended him, and was **with** him. Job had a happy home (his **children were** with him, in contrast with their now being dead), and he was prosperous (**cream** and **olive oil** were symbols of plenty).

29:7-11. The suffering saint also enjoyed social prestige as a judge (elders held court sessions at the city **gate**; cf. Deut. 21:19; 22:15; Josh. 20:4, which may partially account for Job's use of legal terms). He was respected not only by those younger than he but, contrary to normal customs, also by older persons. The silence of his elders at the city gate, where they waited for his words of wisdom (cf. Job 29:21-23), was missing from his three gabby associates! Others had put **their hands** on **their mouths** (to gesture their silence), but not these three! (21:5; cf. 40:4) Job was then **well** spoken **of** (29:11), not maligned as his present company was doing to him (19:2-3).

29:12-17. Why was Job so highly respected? One reason is that he helped the needy (vv. 12-13, contrary to Eliphaz's charges, 22:6-7, 9), including **the poor,** orphans, the **dying,** and bereaving widows. Another reason is that he administered **justice** (29:14-17), championing the causes of and assisting **the blind,** the **lame,** the **needy,** and **the stranger,** and overturning their oppressors (**the fangs of the wicked,** '*awāl,* "an unrighteous person"; cf. 18:21; 27:7; 31:3). Ironically Job's associates failed to help *him* now that *he* was down.

29:18-20. Job had fully expected God's blessings to continue, with his living a long life (**days** like the **sand**) of stability (**roots**), prosperity (**dew**), an honorable reputation (**glory**), with perennial strength (pictured by a new **bow;** cf. 30:11).

29:21-25. Besides being blessed (vv. 2-6), helping others (vv. 7-17), and expecting his health and vigor to continue (vv. 18-20), Job's **counsel** was welcomed —contrary to the attitude of his three uninvited guests! People had eagerly welcomed his opinions, like the soil drinking in **the spring rain.** In his counseling he even encouraged others by his smile; in contrast one wonders if the three friends ever uplifted Job with warm smiles. Job's counselees had taken his advice (**I chose the way for them**), and respected him (cf. v. 11) as if he were a **chief** or **king.** Besides, he also comforted those who grieved, another area in which his assailants failed.

(2) Job's present gloom (chap. 30). **30:1-8.** Job bewailed his present misery, which contrasted so starkly with his pre-disease days. He now was disrespected socially (vv. 1-15), in pain physically (vv. 16-19), abandoned spiritually (vv. 20-23), opposed socially (vv. 24-26), and exhausted physically and emotionally (vv. 27-31).

Young people, rather than respecting Job, mocked him (cf. vv. 9-10; 12:4; 16:10; 19:18), an unthinkable discourtesy in the ancient Near East. Having enjoyed "the respect of the most respectable" he now suffered "the contempt of the most contemptible" (Francis I. Andersen, *Job: An Introduction and Commentary,* p. 235). They were urchins of no **use** to him whatever, with no physical stamina (30:2), thin, hungry, and wandering about the desert (v. 3), rummaging for **food** (v. 4, **broom tree** roots tasted bitter), chased from normal society (v. 5), living in wadis, **among the rocks . . . in holes** (v. 6), sounding like braying wild donkeys, and hiding under **bushes** (v. 7). This scum of society—a **brood** without even names—considered *Job* scum!

30:9-15. In their attitude toward the poor, afflicted sufferer, these urchins mocked (cf. 16:10) and detested him and even **spit in** his **face** (cf. 17:6). In his God-induced affliction (cf. 16:9) Job was as weak (cf. 16:7) as an **unstrung . . . bow** (cf. 29:20). Even so, they unrestrainedly attacked him like an army (cf. 16:13-14), making it impossible for him to do anything (**they broke up** his **road**). No wonder Job spoke again of being overwhelmed by **terrors** (cf. "terrors" in 6:4; 13:21; 24:17; 27:20 and "terrified" in 21:6; 23:15-16). No longer did Job feel respected or safe.

30:16-19. Job then spoke of his physical agony. As his life was vanishing, nighttime was miserable, like a sword piercing to his **bones** (cf. 33:19), causing unending **pains.** Again, for the eighth time, he mentioned God's **great power** (cf. 9:4; 10:16; 12:13; 24:22; 26:12, 14; 27:11). He felt **God** had grabbed him by his clothes (NIV marg., if this is the meaning of this difficult Heb. sentence) and thrown him **into the mud.** To be like **dust and ashes** means: (a) that he looked haggard and emaciated, ashen in color, or (b) that he actually had ashes on his sores (cf. comments on 2:8), or (c) that he felt inwardly dejected. Ironically this anticipates Job's later words about repenting in dust and ashes (42:6).

30:20-23. Added to his social rejection (vv. 1-15) and physical pain (vv. 16-19), was his feeling of being neglected by God (vv. 20-23). His **cry** to **God** was ignored (cf. 19:7; 31:35) even though God saw him (cf. 7:19-20; 10:14; 13:27; 31:4). In fact God even turned against him, Job felt, attacking him (cf. 16:12) and tossing him **about** as in a violent windstorm (as Job had said God does to the wicked, 27:21).

30:24-31. His three peers had done to Job what no one else would think of doing: they opposed him when he was **broken** and **in . . . distress.** Yet Job had sympathized and **grieved** with people in *their* **trouble.** Hoping to get some help (**good** and **light**) from his friends Job got the opposite. Certainly their antagonism was undeserved!

Then Job again elaborated on his physical and emotional pain: inner **churning** or turmoil, **days of suffering** (cf. v. 16), **blackened** skin (from his disease; cf. v. 30), crying for relief, wailing like **jackals** with their doleful howls, and like screeching **owls** (or, perhaps better, "ostriches," as in the NASB, with their weird groans; cf. Isa. 13:21; 34:13; Micah 1:8), blackened and peeling **skin** (cf. Job 19:26), and intense **fever.** Consequently his joy (harps and flutes often played joyful tunes) became grief; he was **mourning and . . .** wailing like someone in a funeral dirge. His emotional pain is expressed in 30:24-26, 29, 31; verses 27-28, 30 relate to his physical pain.

Such manifold misery, as Job voiced in this chapter, had led him down a path of great depression.

(3) Job's oath of innocence (chap. 31). This solemn oath is Job's final effort to compel God to do something about his plight. The negative form of confession, in which the accused wished on himself a curse if he were in fact guilty of the charges, is a strong form of denial. Job used the "if guilty" oath repeatedly ("if" occurs 19 times in vv. 5, 7 [3 times], 9 [twice], 13, 16-17, 19, 21, 24-26, 29, 31, 33, 38-39), sometimes followed by the imprecation "let" or "then may." Besides denying Eliphaz's charges against him (22:6-9) and other sinful actions, Job also denied infractions of attitudes and motives.

31:1-4. First, Job denied being guilty of **lustfully** desiring someone of the opposite sex. Job knew that the **heritage** God gives sinners is **ruin** (wicked translates *'awâl,* "an unrighteous person"; cf. 18:21; 27:7; 29:17) and **disaster,** as both Zophar and Job had spoken of the "heritage" (20:29; 27:13). Job therefore did not *look* on female beauty in lust because **God** *looked* on him, seeing all he did (cf. 7:19-20; 10:14; 13:27) and followed his **every step** (cf. 14:16).

31:5-8. Job then denied he had dealt dishonestly with others (cf. **deceit** in 27:4). If he had cheated in weighing out goods for others then he was willing for **God** to use **scales** in an **honest** way to judge him. Confident that he was aboveboard in business, Job knew that God would admit he was **blameless.** If he were guilty of deviation in his conduct (**steps** and **hands**) or inner motives, he was willing to starve as a result of his **crops** being ruined (cf. 31:12).

31:9-12. The third sin the defendant denied was adultery (v. 1 pertained to lustful viewing; this pertains to sexually immoral actions). **If** it could be proved that he was guilty of such a heinous crime, Job asked that his **wife** be demeaned (grinding **grain** was a menial task, Ex. 11:5) and degraded sexually by **men** (pl.). Such **a sin,** he acknowledged, is **shameful** and deserves punishment. Furthermore, like **a fire** it destroys a person's life, leading **to Destruction** ("Abaddon," a synonym of sheol; cf. Job 26:6; 28:22).

31:13-15. Job also affirmed his fair treatment of his servants. If he were unjust with them when they had some complaint, then he would be unable to face **God** now that *he* was complaining to Him. In two parallel questions, that may have startled Job's onlookers, he admitted their equality with him as objects of God's creative work **in the womb** (cf. 10:8-11).

31:16-23. In answer to Eliphaz's false allegations (22:7-9), Job **denied** oppressing **the poor** and **needy.** He was not selfish (31:17), for he shared his food with orphans and even took them in under his roof. He encouraged widows (v. 16) and counseled them against oppressing creditors (v. 18), and he gave **clothing** and even **fleece** to those who lacked it even if they were unappreciative (vv. 19-20). He never mistreated orphans **in court** (lit., "in the gate," the place of court proceedings; cf. 29:7); **if** he had, he asked that his **arm** would **fall . . . off** (cf. **hand,** 31:21). He was unusually considerate of the needy, for he feared God's punishment. He knew that his money and rank would not forestall judgment **from God.**

Job's self-defense in verses 13, 16-22 (and in 29:12-17, 25) implied that he had done a better job than the Lord in carrying out justice.

31:24-28. Materialism and idolatry were two other sins Job denounced. Eliphaz had implied that Job was trusting in his riches (22:24), but the patriarch affirmed that he never did so and was not proud of his **wealth.** Besides his heart not being **enticed** toward women (31:9), his **heart** was not even inclined to worship the sky's luminaries, a common practice in the ancient Near East. Such worship of creation would be punished by the Creator (**God on high;** cf. v. 2).

31:29-34. Other sins Job said he was not guilty of were being glad over **the trouble** of an enemy (an inner attitude) or calling on God to judge (**curse**) him (an outer action). People in his family and his workmen always had plenty to eat, and even travelers enjoyed his hospitality. Nor did he hide his **sin as men do** (or, perhaps better, "as Adam did," NIV marg.). Had he been hypocritical, the public would have found it out sooner or later and would have scorned him.

31:35-37. Job longed that **someone** would **hear** him, for his committee of accusers was not really listening to his views (cf. 13:6, 17; 21:2). So, like a defendant in court, he signed (figuratively) his statement of **defense,** ready for God to **answer** him. He was so confident of his innocence that he would proudly **wear** God's written indictments, knowing they could easily be proved false. He called God his **Accuser** (lit., "Man of my indictment"). This was a daring move, for accused people usually do not want their plaintiff's indictments, whether true or false, to be publicized. Job would refute all God's incriminations, doing so in confidence **like a prince.**

31:38-40. As a wealthy landowner, Job could have mistreated his employees, but he denied any fraud or injustice. If hired farmers had been overworked in the fields or underpaid, his **land** would have cried **out** (a personification) and their **tears** in the **furrows** (spoken in a hyperbole) would have testified **against** him. In one final denial and imprecation, Job stated that if he withheld **payment** from his tenant farmers or had disheartened them by unreasonable demands or difficult working conditions, he wished his **wheat** fields would grow thornbushes and his **barley** fields weeds. This would mean a loss of much income in retaliation for his withholding his farmers' income.

With this oath of innocence, in which **Job** denied almost a dozen sins of action or attitude, he rested his case. Ending his arguments against the belligerent team of tyrants, he hoped to *force* God to move. He apparently felt that such an ultimatum would make God break His silence. If Job were innocent, then God would be required, according to legal practice, to speak up and affirm it. If Job were guilty, then God would be expected to bring down the imprecations on him. But, as Job found out, God *still* remained silent. The sovereign God cannot be pushed into a corner, or pressured into action by anyone's demand.

E. Elihu's four speeches (chaps. 32–37)

Job had persisted in his claim to innocence and had repeatedly rejected the view of his comrades-turned-critics that suffering is only retributive. Since the three could not get him to budge, they finally gave up (32:1).

And yet, though Job silenced his babblers, he could not induce God to speak. Job hoped to coerce God to admit to unfairness and therefore to relieve him from his agony.

Since the debates stalemated and since God said nothing, a fifth person then entered the ring. Elihu, a young bystander, angered at both sides of the debate, took advantage of the silence and rose to defend God's justice and sovereignty. Elihu's sensitivity to Job's need contrasts with the harsh words of the three. His views reflect greater insight into Job's situation than the three antagonists possessed. For this reason it is wrong to call Elihu a brash, heartless, young fool, as do some commentators.

Many commentators think Elihu's four speeches (chaps. 32–37) were added to the book by an editor years (even centuries!) after the original version was written. Four arguments are used to defend that idea: (1) Elihu is mentioned nowhere else in the book. (2) Elihu's style and language differ from the rest of the book. (3) Elihu's views add nothing to the argument of the book. (4) Job did not answer Elihu.

These arguments are answerable, however: (1) Elihu need not have been mentioned earlier in the book since he was a silent onlooker not yet involved in the disputation. And Elihu was not condemned by God in 42:7-8 along with Eliphaz and his two companions probably because Elihu was closer to the truth than were the three.

(2) Admittedly Elihu's style differed from that of the other four debaters. He used *'ēl* for God more than did the others (his 19 uses of *'ēl* compare with Job's 17, Eliphaz's 8, Bildad's 6, and Zophar's 2; see Samuel Rolles Driver and George Buchanan Gray, *A Critical and Exegetical Commentary on the Book of Job*, pp. xlii-iii). Elihu also used a number of Aramaic words more than the three counselors did (ibid., pp. xlvi-vii). These differences, however, simply point up his distinctive character (Édouard Dhorme, *A Commentary on the Book of Job*, p. ciii).

(3) Elihu's view of suffering differed from that of the three. They had claimed that Job was suffering because he had sinned, but Elihu said that Job was sinning (in an attitude of pride) because he was suffering. Elihu pointed out that God can use suffering to benefit people (33:17, 28, 30; 36:16). Elihu put his finger on Job's wrong attitude of complaining against God (33:13; 34:17) and suggested that Job humble himself before God (33:27; 36:21; 37:24).

(4) True, Job did not answer Elihu. But this may be because Elihu's words silenced him. Perhaps Elihu's suggestions hit home, causing Job to reflect on his sin of questioning God's ways. Furthermore, Elihu's orations provided a bridge from Job's insistence for vindication (chap. 31) to God's speeches. If the Elihu portion is not original, then God responded immediately to Job's demand, an action which is inconsistent with God. Also the Elihu speeches create an added element of suspense, as the reader awaits God's answer.

Addressees in Elihu's Speeches

First speech
> To all four (32:6-9)
> To the three (32:10-14)
> To Job (32:15–33:33)

Second speech
> To the three (34:1-15)
> To Job (34:16-37)

Third speech
> To Job (chap. 35)

Fourth speech
> To Job (36:1–37:1)
> To the three (37:2-13)
> To Job (37:14-24)

---

1. ELIHU'S FIRST SPEECH (CHAPS. 32–33)

After Elihu is introduced in the prose section (32:1-5), he gave four speeches; (a) 32:6–33:33, (b) chapter 34, (c) chapter 35, and (d) chapters 36–37.

a. Introduction to Elihu (32:1-5)

32:1-3. Job's **three** opponents gave up the battle because they could not persuade him to deny his innocence and confess to having led a wicked life. Sensing that all four debaters were talked out (cf. vv. 5, 15-16), **Elihu** then pitched in. Elihu's father **Barakel** was a **Buzite,** probably a descendant of Abraham's nephew Buz (Gen. 22:20-21). Interestingly Uz, the older brother of Buz (!), was possibly the person after whom "the land of Uz" (Job 1:1) was named.

Elihu was **angry** (cf. 32:5) with both sides of the debate. He was incensed **with Job** because he defended **himself** against all wrongdoing while accusing **God** of doing wrong (cf. 40:2). Job was more willing to cast aspersions on God's character than to admit to any sin. Also Elihu was inflamed **with the three . . . because they** pronounced **Job** guilty but without adequate evidence (cf. 32:12). Anger seemed to characterize much of these verbal bouts. The three pugilists were mad at Job; he was mad at them and at God; and he sensed that God was angry with him. And now Elihu was infuriated too!

32:4-5. **Elihu,** however, had been patient during the lengthy controversy, deferring to their age as was the custom in the ancient Near East (cf. 29:8a, 21; 32:6-

7, 11-12a). Seeing that the three men had run out of ways to play their one string, Elihu was irritated (cf. vv. 1-2). Perhaps his anger was aroused because he felt they should have done more than merely pounce on Job repeatedly as if he were an inveterate sinner who needed to repent.

b. Elihu's introduction of himself (32:6-22)

Before Elihu actually began his argument against Job (starting in 33:1) he first took a number of sentences to justify his right to speak. Rather than these words being a sign of braggadocio, as some writers suggest, they seem to be necessary as a way for Elihu to be accepted and to gain a hearing. For him, a silent listener, to barge in without defending why he should be allowed to enter the debate, would have been obtrusive. A pushy attitude might mean he would have been turned off with no one listening. Yet Elihu was confident he had insight into Job's situation (32:10, 17; 33:33; 36:2-4).

(1) Elihu's defense of his wisdom. 32:6-9. Admitting his younger age, Elihu said he dared not interrupt and give his views (he mentioned what I know four times: vv. 6, 10, 17; 33:3), because wisdom, as was acknowledged in those days, supposedly resided with the elderly (cf. 12:12). One's advanced years gave him more experience and hence more insight. However, Elihu reasoned that younger persons are not necessarily without wisdom because it comes from God, not from years. The spirit in a man may refer to the Spirit of God (cf. NIV marg.), who is often associated with wisdom (Gen. 41:38-39; Ex. 31:3; Num.

27:18-21; Isa. 11:2; Dan. 5:11-12) as its source. Understanding, Elihu dared suggest, is not limited to the aged. (The old, Job 32:9, is lit., "many," possibly meaning those who have lived many years.)

(2) Elihu's disappointment with the three (32:10-14). 32:10. Elihu now asked that they listen to him since he had listened for so long to them. Eight times he voiced his request that the three and/or Job listen to him (v. 10; 33:1, 31, 33; 34:2, 10, 16; 37:14), apparently expressing his apprehension that they might not hear him out because of his youth. But yet Elihu believed he had some knowledge on the issue at hand that had not yet been aired (what I know; cf. 32:6, 17; 33:3).

32:11-13. He had been patiently silent while they spoke and he heard their reasoning. (Their searching for words might possibly suggest that some time [hours or even days] may have lapsed between some of the speeches.) With their arguments they had not . . . proved Job wrong in his claim to an upright life. Therefore they should not claim to be wise or claim that if they could not refute him, God would. The second line of verse 13 could be understood, however, as Elihu's own suggestion, rather than as part of his quotation of the three. If so, then his point was that they should let God defeat Job's arguments, since man could not do it.

32:14. Elihu then stated that his approach would be different. He had no need to defend himself against verbal attacks by Job, as the three had felt it necessary to do, and Elihu would not re-

---

Overview of Elihu's Speeches

Job's Complaints	Elihu's Answers
1. God is silent; He does not respond to me (13:22; cf. 33:13).	First speech: God does speak—through dreams and pain (chap. 33).
2. God is unjust; He does not relieve me of my suffering (19:6-7; 27:2; cf. 34:5-6).	Second speech: God is just (chap. 34).
3. God is unconcerned; He does not reward me for my innocence (10:7; cf. 35:3).	Third speech: God is sovereign (chap. 35).

spond to Job **with** their **arguments.**

(3) Elihu's desire to speak out (32:15-22). **32:15-19.** Since the three had run out of **words** (cf. vv. 1, 5), Elihu felt his time to speak had come. He would **tell what** he knew (cf. vv. 6, 10; 33:3), **for** he was **full of words.** And verbose he was! The verses of his speeches (32:6–37:24, excluding 34:1; 35:1; 36:1) total 157, about the same as Job's final speech (chaps. 26–31, excluding 26:1; 27:1; 29:1) of 158 verses, and longer than the combined speeches of any of the three alleged friends (cf. Eliphaz's 110 verses, Bildad's 46, and Zophar's 47).

The spirit within me may refer to Elihu's inner spirit, not the Spirit of God, in view of the following two verses. **Wineskins** (animal skins used to hold wine) expand and **burst** if they have no hole for venting the fermenting gases from the wine. Elihu said he felt that way, about to burst from being filled with ideas and not having the opportunity till then to voice them.

32:20-22. Elihu felt compelled to **speak,** to reply to the three and to Job. Yet in his responses he would not take sides (he disagreed with both sides) nor would he **flatter** either party in an effort to win its favor. He said that to be guilty of **flattery,** an unfair tactic, would mean God, who gave him life (**my Maker;** cf. 4:17; 9:9; 35:10; 36:3; 40:19), would **take** it **away.**

c. *Elihu's first answer to Job (chap. 33)*

As seen in the chart "Overview of Elihu's Speeches," this young theologue was responding to three of Job's complaints. First Elihu replied to Job's charge that God is silent.

(1) Elihu's request that Job listen (33:1-7). **33:1-4.** Three times Elihu addressed **Job** by name (vv. 1, 31; 37:14), and seven other times mentioned Job's name (32:12, 14; 34:5, 7, 35-36; 36:16). In contrast, the three older speakers never once mentioned Job's name either directly or indirectly.

Job had asked his three friends to **listen** to him (13:6, 17; 21:2); now Elihu turned that around and asked that Job hear *him* (cf. comments on 32:10). The young debater had paid attention to the three (33:12); now he asked that Job give him *his* full **attention.** Elihu's **words,** which he was **about to** speak (they were

on the tip of his **tongue),** were sincere (**from an upright heart**) and would reveal insights into Job's situation (cf. **what I know,** 32:6, 10, 17). Elihu viewed himself as an equal with Job for both, he said, were created by God. Elihu said he was **made** by God (the Holy **Spirit** is involved in creating man) and given **life** (cf. Gen. 2:7) by **the breath of the Almighty** (cf. Job 12:10; 27:3; 34:14-15); Job had also said he was made by God (31:15).

33:5. The youthful speaker, after hearing Job out, challenged him to respond if he possibly could (cf. v. 32). Job, he said, should **prepare** his response and be ready to **confront** Elihu as in verbal combat. The word *'ārak,* translated "prepare," means to arrange in order, often in the sense of marshaling military forces or weapons in battle order (cf. 1 Sam. 17:8, "line up for battle," and Job 6:4, "marshaled"), and so figuratively to arrange one's words or legal case (cf. 32:14, "marshaled"; 37:19, "draw up"; 13:18, "prepared"; 23:4, "state"). The word *yāṣaḇ,* here rendered "confront," means to take one's stand or position, sometimes in the sense of readiness for battle (1 Sam. 17:16; Jer. 46:4, 14; Job 41:10). Elihu was ready for a skirmish! Of course Job had already set forth his arguments; perhaps his numerous forays with his other so-called friends had left him battle-weary.

33:6-7. Though ready to take on Job and to show him the danger of criticizing God, Elihu did not intend to lord it over the sufferer, as the three disputants had done. He admitted to equality with Job because they were both frail human beings, made **from clay** (cf. Job's similar words in 10:9 and cf. comments on 33:4). Therefore Job need not **fear** Elihu for he would treat Job kindly. He would not terrify him as Job had said God had done (7:14; 9:34; 13:21; 23:15-16). Elihu promised that in this debating he would not pressure Job (his **hand** would not be **heavy** on him), as Job had said God had done (23:2, "His hand is heavy"; cf. 13:21, "withdraw Your hand").

Though verbose, Elihu was less arrogant and presumptuous than the other spokesmen.

(2) Elihu's summary of Job's charges against God. **33:8-11.** The junior attorney had listened carefully to Job, as evidenced by his quoting Job's **very words.**

Elihu's Quotations of Job

In Elihu's First Speech

33:9a	"I am pure" (cf. 6:10; 9:21; 10:7; 12:4; 16:17; 31:6).
33:9b	"Without sin" (cf. 13:23; 23:11).
33:9c	"I am clean and free from guilt" (cf. 9:20-21; 10:7; 27:6).
33:10a	"God has found fault with me" (cf. 10:6).
33:10b	"He considers me His enemy" (cf. 13:24; 19:11).
33:11a	"He fastens my feet in shackles" (cf. 13:27).
33:11b	"He keeps close watch on all my paths" (cf. 7:17-20; 10:14; 13:27).

In Elihu's Second Speech

34:5a	"I am innocent [righteous]" (cf. 9:15, 20; 27:6).
34:5b	"God denies me justice" (cf. 19:6-7; 27:2).
34:6a	"I am right" (cf. 27:5-6).
34:6b	"I am guiltless" (cf. 10:7; chap. 31).
34:6d	"His arrow inflicts an incurable wound" (cf. 6:4; 16:13).
34:9	"It profits a man nothing when he tries to please God" (cf. 21:15).

In Elihu's Third Speech

35:2	"I will be cleared by God" (cf. 13:18; 23:7).
35:3	"What profit is it to me, and what do I gain by not sinning?" (cf. 21:15)

In Elihu's Fourth Speech

36:23	"You [God] have done wrong" (cf. 19:6-7).

Elihu reviewed Job's position by stating that Job had criticized **God** for unfair treatment, even though Job was not guilty. Many of the words in Elihu's review accurately reflect what the sufferer had said (see the chart "Elihu's Quotations of Job").

(3) Elihu's refutation of Job's claim that God was silent (33:12-33). **33:12-13.** Elihu directly confronted Job, telling him, **in this you are not right.** "This" probably refers to Job's accusing God of injustice (vv. 10-11). The reason Job should not charge God with wrongdoing is that **God is greater than man.** Because of His sov-

ereign majesty (which Job recognized) he ought not criticize God. God, in other words, has purposes in His doings that may be beyond man's comprehension and, as God, He has the right to do as He wishes. To **complain to** God that He does not answer **man's words** is wrong, Elihu contended. The word "complain" is from *rîb*, a legal verb meaning "to present or debate an indictment in court," used by Job five times (9:3, "dispute"; 10:2, "condemn"; 13:8, "argue"; 13:19, "bring charges"; 23:6, "press charges") and by God once (40:2, "contends"). Four times Job used the noun *rîb* (13:6, "argument";

29:16, "case"; 31:13, "grievance"; 31:35, "my Accuser," lit., "man of my indictment"). Job had felt God was pressing charges against him in court (10:2) **but,** Elihu said, Job should not respond by pressing charges against God!

33:14-18. God *does* **speak,** Elihu maintained. God does so in various ways—**now one way, now another.** One means is through dreams (vv. 14-18) and another is through illness and pain (vv. 19-22). The problem is that often **man** does not sense that God is communicating.

When people **dream,** Elihu said, God **may speak in their ears** (lit., "opens or uncovers the ears of men" [*ĕnôš*, "weak, mortal man"; cf. comments on 4:17]). To open one's ears meant to reveal something to him. The words **terrify them with warnings** is one possible translation of the Hebrew. Another possible rendering is "seals their instruction" (NASB; cf. KJV) and another is "seals their discipline." If the NIV rendering is correct, Elihu's point is that dreams can terrify a person (cf. Eliphaz's similar response, 4:12-17), to warn him. If the second or third suggested rendering is right then Elihu's idea may be that God makes certain that the dreams will lead one to a more informed or disciplined life.

Such dreams, whether of a warning, instructional, or disciplinary nature, are designed to **turn** people **from wrongdoing** or **pride** (the sin Elihu believed Job was guilty of; cf. 36:9) and **to preserve** them alive (**pit,** referring to the grave, is used five times in chapter 33; vv. 18, 22, 24, 28, 30). Yet Job had said that when God terrified him with dreams (7:14), he wanted to die (7:15). Whereas in Old Testament times God often spoke in dreams as well as through other media (Heb. 1:1), He now communicates to people through Christ, the Living Word (Heb. 1:2), and the Bible, the written Word (2 Tim. 3:16).

33:19-22. Another way God gets people's attention, Elihu suggested, is by causing them **pain.** A serious illness (with **distress in** one's **bones,** i.e., intense inner pain; cf. 30:17) can steal one's appetite and cause him to lose weight (cf. Job's appetite loss and emaciation, 3:24; 6:7; 19:20) so that his **bones** protrude. Such a sickness can bring a man close to death (**the pit;** cf. comments on 33:18).

The messengers of death may refer to angels who bring (or announce) death (cf. Ps. 78:49).

33:23-24. In sickness God may send **an angel** (*mal'āk*) as a mediator (*mēlîṣ*) to: (a) remind a person of the proper conduct and attitudes he should maintain in his life (**what is right**) and to (b) intercede with God to keep him from dying (**going down to the pit**). Elihu disagreed with Eliphaz, who had said that no angels could assist Job (5:1). Elihu was also disagreeing with Job, who felt he had no intercessor to arbitrate his case (9:33). By the words **one out of a thousand** (cf. Job's use of that phrase in 9:3) Elihu meant that such intervening angels are plentiful, or, perhaps better, that they are rare (cf. Ecc. 7:28). The angel's interceding work (in contrast with angelic "messengers of death," Job 33:22) was based on his providing **a ransom for** the sick person. The "ransom," while not specified, means something that can be regarded as a consideration or reason for the sufferer to be relieved from his illness.

33:25-28. As a result of the angelic intercessor, the sufferer **is restored** to health and enjoys spiritual strength as well, including prayerful communion with **God,** acceptance by God, fellowship with God, **joy** in God's presence (cf. Eliphaz's similar words in 22:26 and Bildad's in 8:21), and restoration **to his** former **righteous** state (cf. Bildad's words in 8:6). In addition he tells others: (a) that he **sinned** but that his punishment of illness was less than his sin called for (cf. 11:6), and (b) that God diverted him from death (**the pit;** cf. comments on 33:18) and restored him to life (**to enjoy the light,** i.e., of the sun, which means to enjoy life; cf. v. 30; Ecc. 11:7). Thus out of his affliction comes a deeper walk with God and a ready witness before others.

33:29-30. According to Elihu, **God** often brings dreams and illness (both bad experiences) to **man.** The idiom **twice, even three times** means often (or perhaps, as some suggest, it refers to the three means Elihu had discussed: dreams, illness, an angel). Again Elihu stated why: negatively, to divert people from death (**the pit;** cf. comments on v. 18) and positively, to help them enjoy **life** more than before (cf. v. 28). Though illness may seem to be leading to death

(vv. 21-22), God can use it to deter a person *from* death (vv. 24, 28, 30) and to give him a more fruitful life.

33:31-33. Again the new spokesman asked **Job** to bear with him, by hearing him out. Then if Job had something **to say,** he could **speak up . . . but if not,** Elihu would continue. **Listen** and **be silent** (v. 31) are repeated in verse 33.

For Elihu, suffering, though related to sin (v. 27), was more protective than punitive. The first three speakers said God afflicts in order to punish; Elihu said God afflicts in order to teach. He emphasized that suffering can help divert one from sin and resultant death, whereas the three older men felt that unrequited sin would surely lead to death.

All four counselors were wrong about Job's case, however, for all assumed a sin-results-in-suffering viewpoint. When God spoke (chaps. 38–41), He did so directly, not through an angel. And Job's experience *did* result in his enjoying a deeper relationship with God (42:2, 5-6, 9) and he *did* enjoy a long and full life (42:10, 12, 16).

2. ELIHU'S SECOND SPEECH (CHAP. 34)

Since Job remained silent (cf. 33:32), Elihu continued. His second speech was a defense of God's justice, an answer to Job's allegation that God was unfair. The young protagonist spoke first to the three older visitors (34:1-15), as indicated by the plural "you" and "men" (vv. 2, 10) and "us" in verse 4, and then to Job (vv. 16-37) as indicated by the singular "you" (vv. 16-17, 33).

a. Elihu's desire that his elders hear him out (34:1-4)

34:1-4. Elihu again asked his elders, whom he respected (**you wise men . . . you men of learning;** cf. vv. 10, 34), to **listen to** him (cf. his uses of "listen" in 32:10; 33:1, 31, 33; 34:10, 16; 37:14). Again Elihu picked up Job's words (cf. 12:11) when he referred to the need for the debaters to test the accuracy of his **words as the tongue** can discern the quality of the **food** it **tastes.** They would need to decide the **right** thing about Job's case.

b. Elihu's denunciation of Job's claim that God was unjust (34:5-9)

34:5-9. Again Elihu quoted several of Job's statements (see the chart "Elihu's

Quotations of Job," near 33:9-11). Then siding with the three, Elihu accused **Job** of being a deliberate sinner, associating with ungodly people, and claiming that **man** gains **nothing** by worshiping **God** (cf. 9:30-31; 35:2). Drinking **scorn like water** is redolent of Eliphaz's words in 15:16. Though Elihu was certainly wrong in saying Job associated with the **wicked,** he was correct in condemning Job for pouncing on **God** in a scornful, rebellious way. To say that a person is no better off for having served God is a complaint Elihu answered later (chap. 35).

c. Elihu's defense of God's justice and impartiality (34:10-20)

34:10-15. Sounding like Bildad, Elihu rose to the defense of God's justice, affirming that **God** cannot **do evil or do wrong** (cf. v. 12; 8:3, "Does God pervert justice?"). Though Job had complained that God had denied him justice (27:2), Elihu cited several evidences in support of His unflinching justice. (1) God gives **man what** he **deserves,** meting out punishment for sin (34:11). (2) For **God** to **do wrong** (v. 10) or **pervert justice** (cf. 8:3) would be inconsistent with His character and therefore **unthinkable** (34:12). (3) Having independent authority as the world's Sovereign, no one could influence **Him** away from justice (v. 13). (4) As the Sustainer of human life God, if He wished, could withdraw **His spirit** (or "Spirit," NIV marg.) **and breath** instantly and everyone **would perish** at once (cf. 12:10; 27:3; 33:4), but in His goodness to mankind He does not do that.

34:16-20. For the third time in this speech, Elihu requested that his audience of four hear him out (**hear . . . listen;** cf. vv. 2, 10). He then continued citing evidences that God is fair in His dealings. (5) If God were unjust, how could He **govern** the world? (v. 17) To accuse the **just . . . One** of injustice is obviously wrong. (6) God does not hesitate to judge incapable and wicked **kings . . . nobles . . . princes,** and **the rich.** Partiality on God's part is out of the question because He is not influenced by men's power or money. **All** are equal under Him as **the work of His hands.** In fact God can quickly, even by surprise at midnight (cf. v. 25), bring the wicked to death and remove **the mighty** (cf. v. 24). How, then, could Job say God is unfair?

d. Elihu's discussion of the punishment of the wicked (34:21-30)

34:21-30. Elihu may have been responding here to Job's concern about God's delay in executing justice (24:1-21). As further evidences of God's justice (see comments on 34:10-20), Elihu pointed up these facts: (7) God has all the facts in every case, for in His omniscience **He sees** everything everyone does (v. 21; cf. 24:23) so sinners cannot escape His judging by hiding in the darkness. Unlike human judges, God **has no need** to investigate cases (34:23; cf. Zophar's words in 11:11). God can put down **the mighty** (cf. 34:20) and set **up others in their place,** overthrowing and crushing **them in the night** (cf. v. 20). (8) God is fair for He does not overlook **wickedness. His eyes are on the ways of men** (v. 21) recalls Job's similar words in 24:23. God punishes those who reject and disregard Him and who mistreat **the poor** and **the needy** (34:26-28). (9) God's justice is seen in that, even though He may choose for a while to do nothing about sin and to remain **silent** to Job's and others' pleas for speedy justice, **yet** He as the Sovereign Ruler **over man and nation alike will see that a godless man** (ḥānēp, "irreligious person"; cf. 8:13) does not continue indefinitely and triumph endlessly (34:29-30). Job might not see God when He chose to remain silent (cf. Job's complaint along that line, 23:8-9) but that did not give him the right to **condemn** God (cf. 19:7; 30:20).

e. Elihu's arraignment of Job's nonrepentance and rebellion (34:31-37)

34:31-33. Elihu was stunned that Job would have the audacity to speak **to God** the way he did. Job had affirmed his innocence repeatedly. But then, as if to put God on the spot, Job said that if God would show him where he had gone **wrong,** he would then stop sinning (cf. 6:24; 7:20-21; 10:2; 13:23). But Elihu felt, and rightly so, that such talk was uncalled for, that it was seeking to tell **God** what to do. Since God is sovereign, He will not stoop to man's **terms,** especially in the face of a nonrepentant attitude. Elihu then said that Job would have to **decide** whether God would **reward** him when he was unrepentant.

34:34-37. Any person who is **wise**

knows that Job's speeches (in which he criticized God for injustice) lacked **knowledge** (cf. 35:16; 38:2) and **insight.** Therefore **Job** ought to **be tested to the utmost for** speaking like the **wicked.** This statement sounds much like Zophar's words (11:5). Elihu sensed in **Job** a rebellious attitude, for Job (by the derisive gesture of clapping **his hands** to silence others) scorned others for defending God's justice.

Elihu was correct in chiding Job for rebelliously (a) questioning God's justice (34:17), and (b) demanding that God answer Him (v. 29) and show him where he had sinned (v. 32). But Elihu seemed to share something of the heartless attitude of the three elder counselors by wishing that Job would be **tested** "to the utmost," and by assuming that Job's many words (cf. 35:16) meant he was **against** God.

3. ELIHU'S THIRD SPEECH (CHAP. 35)

In this speech Elihu defended God's sovereignty in answer to Job's charge that God did not reward him for his innocence. Elihu's answer was twofold: (a) Since God is supreme, He is not affected one way or the other by man's innocence or sin, and (b) God was not answering Job's cries because of his pride.

a. Job's inconsistency (35:1-3)

35:1-3. How could Job ever hope to be vindicated **by God** (cf. 13:18) as being innocent while at the same time he insisted that his innocence was of no value before God? Such a position was inconsistent, **Elihu** argued. Elihu had earlier quoted Job as having asked **what profit** or **gain** he would receive for serving God (34:9; cf. 21:15).

b. Man's inability to affect God because of God's greatness (35:4-8)

35:4-8. Replying to both Job and to the three (**your friends with you** probably refers to the three, not to Job's supposed wicked companions), Elihu pointed out that since **the heavens** and **the clouds** are higher than man, certainly God is higher than man. Therefore God is not affected adversely by man's **sins** or benefited by man's **righteous** condition. (Cf. Eliphaz's similar words about the stars, 22:12, and God's indifference to man, 22:2-3.) A person's **wickedness** or righteousness affects only man, not God. When God shows mercy it is not because man has persuaded Him to do so, and if He inflicts judgment it is not because man has injured Him. God is sovereign and therefore self-determining. He is not bribed by man; His standards for judging people are firm, impartial, and uninfluenced. But since a person's moral conduct does affect himself, it *does* make a difference for *him* whether he sins or not (cf. 35:3).

c. Man's inability to influence God
   because of man's pride (35:9-16)

35:9-11. When people are in trouble (**under . . . oppression**) they often turn to **God** for a way out, but they do not turn to Him as their **Maker** (cf. 4:17; 9:9; 32:22; 36:3; 40:19), the One who can give joy *in* times of trouble (**songs in the night**). Nor do they express gratitude to Him for giving them more intelligence than **beasts** and **birds** possess.

35:12-15. Therefore God **does not** respond to people's **empty** (insincere) cries for help, for such prayers stem from pride (**arrogance**; cf. 36:9). If such proud prayers are not answered, certainly Job's cries of arrogance and impatience would not be heard. Job claimed that he could **not see** or find God (9:11; 23:8-9; cf. 34:29); yet he had placed his **case** in God's hands (13:18; 23:7). But Elihu sensed another inconsistency in Job (cf. comments on 35:2-3): the sufferer was willing to **wait for** God in His justice to clear him, and yet Job felt, according to Elihu, that God did nothing about sin (24:1-12). Elihu here misconstrued Job, for the patriarch did not say God *never* punishes the wicked; though not punished in this life, they *will* receive judgment from God at death.

35:16. For **Job** to talk out of both sides of his **mouth** (wanting God to clear him, and yet being concerned that God does nothing to put down sin) was to make **empty** (*hebel*; cf. comments on this word in Ecc. 1:2) **talk**, speaking many **words** (cf. Job 34:37) without wisdom (cf. 34:35).

Elihu felt that Job could not be cleared by God (35:2) as long as he questioned the value of serving Him (v. 3) and prayed from a heart of pride (v. 12), while thinking that God does nothing about wickedness (v. 15).

4. ELIHU'S FOURTH SPEECH (CHAPS. 36–37)

In his second speech (chap. 34) Elihu had defended God's justice, and in his third speech (chap. 35) he championed God's sovereignty. Now in his final speech he spoke again of both of those attributes—first, of God's justice (and power) in His dealings with man (36:1-26) and then, of His sovereignty (and benevolence) in His dealings with nature (36:27–37:24). In this way Elihu sought to answer both Job (32:2; 33:10-12) and his three elders (32:3, 12).

a. Elihu's defense of God's justice and
   power in His dealings with man (36:1-26)

(1) Elihu's confidence in his own insights. **36:1-4.** As the youthful counselor began his fourth oration (suggested by the words **Elihu continued**; cf. "Then Elihu said" in 34:1 and 35:1, which introduced his second and third speeches), he was so full of ideas to share (32:18-20) that he asked Job not to become impatient (**Bear with me**). He still had more to say in defense of God. In self-confidence Elihu said his **knowledge** (cf. 36:4) was **from afar**, that is, he had a wide range of insights, in contrast with Job who, Elihu twice said, was "without knowledge" (34:35; 35:16). Elihu's first concern, as before (34:10-12, 17) was to extol God's **justice**. Again he referred to God as **my Maker** (cf. 4:17; 9:9; 32:22; 35:10; 40:19). Not lacking self-confidence, Elihu affirmed that his words were correct and that he was **perfect in knowledge**. However, the words "one perfect in knowledge" may refer to God, as they certainly do in 37:16. This view is supported by the recently discovered Ebla tablets (Mitchell Dahood, "Are the Ebla Tablets Relevant to Biblical Research?" *Biblical Archaeology Review* 6. September-October 1980:58).

(2) God's just dealings with the wicked and the righteous. **36:5-7.** Though not translated in the NIV, the Hebrew word for "Behold" introduces four statements by Elihu about God's power (vv. 5, 22, 26, 30). Though **God** is just (vv. 6-7) He **is** also **mighty**; and though He is mighty He does not lack mercy (He **does not despise men**). Again Elihu sided with the three worn-out debaters by maintaining that God does not allow **the wicked** to live (cf. v. 14; 15:27-35; 20:5-29) in contrast with Job's insistence that many sinners do live on in prosperity to a ripe old age (21:7,

27-33). Elihu affirmed, on the other hand, that God restores **afflicted** righteous people, giving them deserved blessings, watching over them in care (though Job felt this was no longer true of him, 29:2; 10:12), and even honoring **them with kings** and exalting them. This sounds much like the arguments of the three, that God always rewards people *in this life* in accord with their conduct. Job, as seen in 27:13-23, did not question God's general practice of justice. But Job did challenge the views that God always metes out justice *before* death and that God was being just with *him*.

(3) God's design in suffering—to lead people to repent of pride (36:8-12). **36:8-10.** Sometimes righteous people (**men** is lit., "they" and probably refers to the righteous mentioned in v. 7) undergo trials (**are bound in chains**) and are subjected to **affliction** (such as being chained, **held fast by cords,** to a bed of pain). "Affliction" ('*ānî,* "being weak or poor") is also used in verse 21. "Affliction" in verse 15 translates a different Hebrew word (see comments there). When God afflicts the godly, He does not forsake them. By it, He calls to their attention their wrong conduct (**what they have done**), their transgression (**have sinned** means "have transgressed"), and their arrogance (**arrogantly** is lit., "they show themselves to be strong," a form of the verb *gābar,* "to be strong"). For a person to show himself strong before God means he vaunts himself against God (this form of the verb is rendered "vaunts himself" in 15:25). Removal of pride, as Elihu had said before (33:17), is one of God's purposes in afflicting His own. By pain God gets people's attention and teaches them (**makes them listen** is lit., "opens their ears," as in 33:16 and 36:15).

36:11-12. A godly sufferer, Elihu suggested, who will listen to God and will once again **obey and serve Him** will then prosper and enjoy **contentment.** Learning from suffering and turning from pride was Elihu's point earlier (33:23-28). This sounds like the theology of the three, but they stressed that Job was guilty of sinful *actions* whereas Elihu was concerned more with Job's sinful *attitude* of pride. But believers who in pride refuse to learn from their God-induced inflictions (**they do not listen** to His corrective instruction; cf. 36:10) **will perish by the sword** (cf. 33:18) **and die without the knowledge** (cf. 34:35; 35:16) God wanted them to have. Job should not think of his calamities as proof that he was essentially ungodly (the view of the three agitators) or as evidence that God had forsaken him (as Job maintained). Instead he should see his afflictions as a means of helping him become humble before God.

(4) The reactions of people to suffering. **36:13-15.** True sinners, **the godless** (*hānēp,* "irreligious"; cf. 8:13) **in heart** resent problems by which God may bind them (cf. 36:8). They refuse to **cry for help** or if they do, it is not in sincere repentance (27:8-9). As a result **they die** at a young age, as Zophar had asserted (20:5, 11), and are treated in judgment like hardened sinners, **male prostitutes** in pagan **shrines.** ("Male prostitutes of the shrines" translates one Heb. word *qᵉdēšîm,* which is lit., "consecrated ones," i.e., individuals [males or females] given over to depraved rites, probably in idolatrous worship; cf. Deut. 23:18; 1 Kings 15:12.)

On the other hand God delivers those who are afflicted (the word for **those who suffer** is '*ānî,* "poor, afflicted," and suggests those who are righteous; cf. comments on "affliction," Job 36:8). "He opens their ears" (a lit. trans. for **He speaks to them**) and apparently they listen and obey (cf. v. 11). **Affliction** (v. 15) translates *lahas,* "oppression or distress," from the verb *lāhas,* "to squeeze, press, or oppress." (A different Heb. word is trans. "affliction" in vv. 8, 21.) God, Elihu maintained, brings a repentant believer out of the dire straits or situations which squeeze him in. Elihu used an interesting wordplay in verse 15 in that "delivers" is the word *hālas* and "affliction" is the word *lahas.*

The result—whether death or deliverance—all depends on one's heart and his response to difficulties. If Job did not admit to pride, Elihu implied, he would be showing that he was godless. But if he turned from shaking his fist in God's face, he would demonstrate that he was one of God's own.

(5) The reactions of Job to suffering (36:16-26). **36:16-19.** God was seeking to free Job from **distress** (*sar,* "straits, a cramped situation"; also used in v. 19),

and take him into **a spacious place** (cf. Pss. 18:19; 31:8), a picture of prosperity with no obstructions, and give him rich and abundant **food**. Therefore Job should not be preoccupied with God's seeming failure to exercise **justice**. He was full (*mālē'*, **laden**) with that problem (Job 36:17), whereas he could have his **table** full of (*mālē'*, **laden** with) delightful edibles (v. 16).

Elihu's advice, then, to Job was that he be sure his longing for his former condition of prosperity did not **turn** him **aside** (cf. v. 21) from God's path. (**Bribe** may be rendered "ransom or recompense," as in 33:24. Perhaps it means here "the large price Job is paying by his suffering.") As many people have learned, money and accomplishments cannot buy a person *out of* **distress** (*ṣar*, "straits, a cramped situation"; cf. 36:16) or sustain him with peace *in* distress.

36:20-21. Nor should Job be so concerned about **the night** when **people** are involved in sin (cf. 24:13-17). Elihu's words in 36:20 are difficult in the Hebrew. Another possible meaning is that Job should not long for the night of death (KJV; cf. 3:20-23), that is, he should not anticipate death as a release from his suffering (3:13, 17). Instead he should repent of his pride. Job ought to be careful that he not turn to sin, by complaining, **which** he seemed **to prefer to** bearing his **affliction** (*ʿănî*; cf. comments on 36:8) without complaint. To find fault with God would not bring Job relief from his trials.

36:22-26. Elihu then turned Job's attention to **God** and spoke of **His power** (cf. v. 5; 37:23), instructional ability (cf. 36:9-10), independence (no one can tell God what to do by prescribing **His ways**), justice (no one can prove, as Job had tried to do, that God has ever **done wrong**; cf. 19:6-7), incomprehensible greatness (36:26), and eternality (v. 26). God's **years** are innumerable and unending in contrast with man's few years (9:25; 14:1-2, 5; 16:22). So in view of God's perfections, Job ought to refrain from the sin of reproving God and ought to praise **His** great **work,** as other godly people have done, even **in song.** Everyone (**mankind** rightly translates, *'ādām*) is aware of God's majestic work even when **men** (*'ĕnôš*, "weak, mortal man"; cf. comments on 4:17) view His awesome creation (e.g., the stars) **from** a distance. Job had frequently spoken of God's greatness (9:4-13; 10:16; 12:13; 21:22; 23:13; 24:22; 26:14; 27:11), but Elihu was seeking to point out that being aware of God's majesty and criticizing Him are inconsistent.

b. Elihu's defense of God's sovereignty and benevolence in His dealings with nature (36:27–37:24)

Having referred to God's "ways" and "work" (36:23-24), which man sees (36:25), Elihu then elaborated on God's doings in nature in the autumn storm (36:27-33), the winter (37:1-13), and the summer (37:14-18).

In his third speech (chap. 35) Elihu had spoken of God's sovereignty. Now he returned to that subject but with an added emphasis that God's control over nature involves His benevolence toward the earth, animals, and people.

(1) God's sovereignty in the autumn storm (36:27-33). **36:27-31.** God manages various aspects of nature: evaporation (v. 27a), **rain** (vv. 27b-28), **clouds** (v. 29a), thunder (v. 29b; cf. v. 33; **His pavilion** is a picturesque description of the sky), **lightning** (vv. 30, 32), and the ocean. **Bathing the depths of the sea** (v. 30) should not be understood as describing the lightning; it should be translated "and covers the depths of the ocean," meaning that God so floods the bottom of the oceans with water that people on land cannot see it.

God uses evaporation, precipitation, thunder, and lightning both to judge people (possibly a trans. to be preferred to **governs the nations**) and to bless them by giving them **food** (v. 31; cf. Acts 14:17). Sometimes God uses rain to bring calamity on individuals (cf. 37:13) besides rain's more normal purpose of nourishing the soil.

36:32-33. Referring again to the **lightning,** Elihu said God **fills His hands with** it in the sense of, speaking figuratively, shooting lightning bolts like arrows. **Thunder** precedes the storm and even **cattle** sense **its approach.** "Thunder" was mentioned in verse 29 but here it is literally, "noise." **The coming storm** is the NIV's probably correct attempt to make specific the Hebrew word "it." The difficult Hebrew in the second line of verse 33 has been rendered in many ways (cf. NIV marg.; also see H.H. Rowley, *Job*, p. 301).

(2) God's sovereignty in the winter (37:1-13). **37:1-5.** People have always been fascinated by the awesome spectacle of lightning and thunder, God's "light and sound program," and Elihu was no exception. His **heart** pounded and palpitated. Perhaps an actual storm was approaching for he urged his debating audience to **listen** ("listen" is pl.) **to the roar** (*rōgez*, "agitation," rendered "turmoil" in 3:17, 26) **of His voice.** Thunder is often referred to as God's mighty voice (37:2, 4-5). Five times Elihu mentioned the **lightning** (36:30, 32; 37:3, 11, 15), which is sent by God. How God accomplishes these awesome **things** is **beyond** human comprehension (v. 5; cf. 36:26, 29), a truth that Eliphaz had affirmed once (5:9) and that Job had spoken of twice (9:10; 26:14).

37:6-13. Many people have experienced the restraining effect of a snowfall or a heavy **downpour**—events in nature that point people to God and **His work** (cf. 36:24; Rom. 1:20). He **stops** man's activities and **animals** run for shelter and hibernate when **the tempest** (windstorm) **comes . . . from its chamber,** picturesquely describing a storm being stored in a room (cf. Job 38:22) till **God** releases it. **Cold . . . winds** blow, **ice** is formed (by God's merely breathing, as it were), and lakes and rivers freeze over. Storm **clouds,** with **lightning** (cf. 36:30, 32; 37:3, 15) throughout them, **swirl around . . . the . . . earth.** Following God's **commands,** they bring judgment on some people by ruining their crops, flooding their possessions, and drowning them (cf. comments on 36:31a). Other times the storm clouds **water** the soil and thus demonstrate **His love** (cf. 36:31b; Acts 14:17)—evidence that His power is balanced with His benevolence.

(3) God's sovereignty in the summer. **37:14-18.** Elihu then challenged **Job** to contemplate what he had been saying about **God's wonders** (cf. v. 16). In a series of questions, Elihu pointed up Job's ignorance about God's power in nature. Man does not **know how God** can possibly guide **the clouds,** cause **lightning** (cf. comments on v. 3), or even **hang** the clouds in the sky. Man is ignorant, but God **is perfect in knowledge.** Nor is man capable of doing what God does, such as **spreading out** a clear, blue,

summer sky, which seems **hard** like **a mirror of . . . bronze** (cf. Deut. 28.23), causing people to perspire in the still, hot weather.

(4) Job's inability to understand God's ways (37:19-24). **37:19-21.** If Job could not comprehend the observable actions of God in nature, how could he possibly dare **draw up** (*'ārak*, "prepare, arrange, marshal"; cf. 13:18) his **case** for a legal battle with God, as Job had said he wanted to do? Job could not succeed against God because man is in **darkness,** that is, ignorant, about God (cf. 38:2). To ask **to speak** in God's presence, as Job wanted to do (10:2; 13:3, 22), to accuse Him of wrongdoing would be like asking **to be swallowed up** or destroyed by God! Puny man cannot even **look at the sun** in its brightness without being blinded. How than could he hope to endure in God's presence?

37:22-24. Perhaps sensing God's approach in a windstorm (38:1), Elihu said that **God** was coming. In Ugaritic myths Baal was said to have left his golden palace in the northern mountains. But here the true God **comes** from **the north . . . in golden splendor,** a picture of His **awesome majesty.** As Job had said, God is **beyond** the **reach** of man's mental powers (26:14; cf. Elihu's similar words, 36:26, 29; 37:5). Then Elihu summarized the two attributes he had been defending repeatedly: God's **power** (cf. 36:22) or sovereignty, and **His justice** (cf. 34:12, 17). Elihu was sure that God's dealings with Job were **not** to **oppress** or oppose him, though Job, before Elihu spoke, could see no other explanation.

Elihu's final word was a recommendation that Job **revere** (or "fear"; cf. comments on 1:1) God, which would mean doing away with self-conceit or pride (thinking of oneself as **wise in heart;** see NIV marg.). Fearing God involves recognizing God's supremacy and man's inferiority because of his finiteness. Once again Elihu put his finger on Job's problem—**pride** before God (cf. 33:17; 36:9).

Job said nothing after Elihu's speeches, possibly because he saw some truth in what Elihu was saying. According to this youthful informant, God's justice should not be questioned or His sovereignty challenged, because His ways are beyond human understanding. According to Elihu, calamities can serve to remove pride and to protect people from more grave difficulties. God, then, is to be worshiped, not criticized; He is to be extolled, not examined.

Elihu fittingly prepared the way for God to speak. He did so: (a) by defending God; (b) by sensitizing Job to his need for humility; (c) by describing God's wonders in natural revelation, which God elaborated on; (d) by probing Job with thought-provoking questions (33:13; 34:17-19, 33; 35:2, 6-7; 36:19, 22-23, 29; 37:15-18, 20), a tactic that God continued; and (e) by targeting on Job's basic problem—justifying himself and condemning God—which God Himself later mentioned (cf. 32:2 with 40:8).

F. God's two speeches and Job's replies (38:1–42:6)

At last Job's plea that God answer him was granted. Repeatedly Job had knocked on heaven's door, longing for God to answer (13:22; 31:35). Or he wished that an arbiter (9:33) or an advocate or intercessor (16:19-20) would speak on his behalf.

But God's response was nothing like Job had anticipated. Job wanted a legal hearing, an opportunity to prove the illegality of God's onslaughts against him, the patriarchal plaintiff. But instead of answering Job's charges about the Sovereign's injustices, God asked *Job* questions! Instead of answering Job's subpoena, He issued a subpoena to Job! Rather than explaining the theory of evil or the role of suffering, God rebuked Job for presuming to challenge His ways.

In more than 70 questions—none of which Job could answer—God interrogated Job regarding numerous aspects of inanimate and animate nature. These two science examinations ranged in subject matter from the constellations to the clods, from the beasts to the birds. The wonders of God's creation are dazzlingly displayed in outer space, in the sky, and on the earth. Though Job was dumbfounded by this barrage of questions, flunking both lengthy quizzes, he *did* meet God face to face. This reassured the complainer that God had not abandoned him after all.

What was the purpose of God's rebuking response? By displaying His power and wisdom, God showed Job his ignorance and impatience. How could Job comprehend or control God's ways with man, when he could not comprehend or control God's government in nature? Since Job could not answer God on these matters how could he hope to debate with God? Since God has His own ways and designs in the sky and with animals, does He not also have His own purposes in His dealings with people? Though people cannot understand God's doings, they can trust Him. Worship should stem from an appreciation of God Himself, not a comprehension of all God's ways. Though puzzled, people should still praise.

God did not explain His ways to Job; He exhibited them, thus showing that the sovereign Creator and Sustainer of the universe does not owe puny man an explanation. Man is to report to Him, not vice versa. Yet, though God did not explain His design in man's difficulties, His purpose in pain, He *did* reveal Himself.

This divine confrontation—the Bible's longest recorded oration by God Himself—is in two parts (38:1–40:2 and 40:6–41:34) with Job's response of humility (40:3-5) following the first part, and his response of repentance (42:1-6) after the second part.

This divine discourse "reaches dazzling heights of poetic splendor" (Victor E. Reichert, *Job*, p. 195). Its exuberant exaltation of God's wonders in nature exceeds all other exclamations of His creative power. No wonder Job was silenced, humbled, and repentant!

1. GOD'S FIRST SPEECH (38:1–40:2)

a. God's opening rebuke and challenge to Job (38:1-3)

38:1. God's appearance was accompanied by a **storm,** possibly the storm Elihu may have sensed was approaching (37:22). "Storm" translates $s^e\bar{a}r\hat{a}h$, "a tempest or storm accompanied by violent wind" (also used, e.g., in 2 Kings 2:1, 11; Isa. 40:24, "whirlwind"; Ps. 107:25; Isa. 29:6, "tempest"; Ezek. 1:4, "windstorm"). Ironically "a mighty wind" caused the death of Job's 10 sons and daughters. Now a violent storm accompanied God's communication. Whereas the one was the occasion of ruin resulting in personal sorrow, this one was the occasion of revelation resulting in personal submission. Sometimes God used storms to dramatize awesome occasions (cf. Ex.

19:16-17; 1 Kings 19:11-13).

38:2-3. Opening with a rebuke, God accused Job (by means of a question) of darkening **counsel**, of beclouding God's design for the universe. Job's questioning confused rather than clarified the issues (cf. Elihu's comment about man's darkness, 37:19). For Job to suggest that God had become his enemy would only confuse others about God rather than shed light on His ways. Because of this Job, though he sometimes extolled God, did not really know whereof he spoke when he blamed God for being unfair. Job's **words** were **without knowledge** (as Elihu had twice said; 34:35; 35:16).

Then God told Job to get ready for His questions. **(Brace yourself like a man**; cf. 40:7, is lit., "gird up your loins like a man," *gebeṛ*, "strong man," that is, tuck your outer robe-like garment into your sash-belt as a man does before taking on a strenuous task such as running or fighting in a battle, Ex. 12:11; 1 Kings 18:46.) Job was to be alert so he could **answer** God intelligently. This is a striking reversal of Job's words to God, "Let the Almighty answer me" (31:35). Job the plaintiff had now become the defendant!

b. God's questioning of Job regarding inanimate nature (38:4-38)

In a series of questions on cosmology, oceanography, meteorology, and astronomy, God challenged Job's competence to judge His control of the world. God used irony to point up Job's ignorance (e.g., "Tell Me," vv. 4, 18; "Surely you know!" vv. 5, 21).

(1) Questions about the earth (38:4-21). **38:4-7.** Job was immediately confronted with his insignificance, for he was not present **when** God created the earth. Since he did not observe what had taken place then, he could not **understand** it. How could he hope to advise God now? Creating the earth is depicted like constructing a building with a **foundation. . . . dimensions. . . . a measuring line. . . . footings**, and a **cornerstone.** When God put the earth into orbit, it was similar to placing parts of a building in place.

Job was absent when **the morning stars** (possibly Venus and Mercury; "morning stars" were mentioned by Job in 3:9) **sang** and **the angels** (lit., "the sons of God"; cf. 1:6; 2:1) **shouted** with **joy**

over God's Creation of the earth. The stars' singing is a poetic personification, not a reference to the noise made by stars as detected by radio astronomy. In Psalm 148:2-3 angels and stars are together commanded to praise the Lord.

38:8-11. The origin of the earth was depicted as being like the construction of a building (vv. 4-7); the origin of the oceans was described like childbirth. Job was not in God's obstetric delivery room when He created the oceans, seas, and lakes, which were like a baby coming **from a womb** (cf. v. 29). God confined the waters, His newborn, by means of shorelines (**shut . . . behind doors . . . fixed limits for it and set its doors and bars** [as on a city gate] **in place**). The waters could no longer cover the entire globe as they had done (cf. Gen. 1:2, 9; Ps. 104:9). God separated the waters on the globe from the land; also above the earth's waters He placed **the clouds** (cf. Gen. 1:6) which like a baby's **garment** (cf. Job 38:14), shroud the earth's waters at night **in thick darkness**. In limiting the waters' **proud waves,** pounding at the shore, God may have subtly hinted at His control of Job in his proud allegations. God obviously had these cosmological elements under control.

38:12-15. God's control of the earth also includes the daily sequence of **dawn** and darkness. The dawn causes **the wicked,** who are active at night (cf. 24:14-17; John 3:19), to hide. It is as if **the morning** light were shaking them out of a blanket (Job 38:13), causing them to be **broken** in their power (**upraised arm,** v. 15; cf. 40:9). As the sun comes up the earth's contours become evident and **the wicked** no longer have darkness, which they call **their light,** in which to work. Since Job had nothing to do with establishing or controlling this aspect of Creation how could he question God's doings now?

38:16-18. God also put Job in his place by asking if he had ever explored such unseen realms as: (a) **the springs of the sea** (the Heb. word for "springs," *nēbek*, occurring only here in the OT, probably refers to springs of water pouring into oceans from the ocean floors), (b) **the recesses of the deep** (the depths of the oceans), (c) **death,** pictured as having **gates** which open for its entrants (cf. Pss. 9:13; 107:18; Isa. 38:10) and pictured as being in darkness (cf. NIV marg.), and (d) the extensive regions of the earth.

38:19-21. God personified **light** and **darkness** as living in houses. By rhetorical questions the Lord pointed up to the complainant that he, a mere human, had no way of following the light, at sunset, to see where it goes, or of pursuing the darkness, at sunrise, to see **where** it resides. Their **places** and **dwellings** are inaccessible in the sense that Job could not explain how God moves the earth around the sun. **Surely you know** (cf. v. 5), **for you were already born!** was God's ironic way of affirming that Job did *not* know since he was *not* around when God set the earth's rotation in motion. Job's years were few compared with God's eternity (cf. 36:26).

(2) Questions about the sky (38:22-30). **38:22-24.** Job had no idea how God makes **snow** or **hail,** pictured as if they were kept in **storehouses** (cf. Pss. 33:7; 135:7; Jer. 10:31) and released by God when He chooses. Causing hail in battle (cf. Josh. 10:11) is an example of what Elihu had said about God's using elements of weather to stop people from working (Job 37:6-7), or to punish people (37:13). Job could not predict where God would dispense **lightning** flashes (cf. Elihu's words along this line in 36:30, 32; 37:3, 11, 15; cf. 38:35) or where the **winds** would blow.

38:25-30. Nor can God's ways with the **rain** and **ice** (cf. Elihu's comments about them in 36:27-28; 37:6, 10) be comprehended by man. Only God **cuts a channel** (an imaginary path) in the sky through which rain and **the thunderstorm** (cf. 28:26) come. **Man** does not even see where God often makes rain to fall—in **a desert** and a **wasteland.**

Again using the figure of childbirth (cf. 38:8) God asked Job if he knew whether **the rain** and **dew** have **a father** and **the ice** and **frost** have a mother. This may possibly be an allusion to and a polemic against the Canaanite myth that viewed rain as the semen of the gods, by which "mother earth" supposedly bears her "children," the crops. Certainly no one knows completely how the earth's Master sends rain and formulates elements of cold weather, including dew, ice, frost, and **frozen** lakes and rivers.

(3) Questions about stars and clouds (38:31-38). **38:31-33.** Job knew that God made the **Pleiades . . . Orion,** and **Bear** constellations (9:9), but here God pointed out that Job had nothing to do with holding together the cluster of stars known as the Pleiades, nor could he alter the configuration of stars in the Orion **constellation,** nor cause the Bear (perhaps the Big Dipper) to appear at night. And since Job knew nothing of **the laws of the heavens,** the principles by which God regulates the stars, planets, and moon, how could he begin to criticize God's laws in His dealings with mankind? **Dominion over the earth** is **God's,** not Job's.

38:34-38. God also belittled Job by pointing to his inability to call down rain at will or to send down **lightning bolts** (cf. v. 24). In verse 36, difficult to translate, the word **heart** could perhaps be rendered "cloud layers" and the word **mind,** "celestial phenomenon" (see Rowley, *Job,* pp. 315-6). If those translations are accepted, they fit God's practice in this chapter of personifying inanimate nature. The clouds and lightning bolts seem to operate as if they have minds of their own. Or if the NIV rendering of verse 36 is correct then the thought is that God gives man wisdom; yet man in all his wisdom cannot tabulate the number of **clouds** nor can he time the "tilting" of the clouds (like animal skins that hold **water**) to moisten **the dust** and **the clods.**

c. God's questioning of Job regarding animate nature (38:39–39:30)

The 12 animals described here—six beasts, five birds, and an insect—all exhibit the creative genius and providential care of God. Fittingly the list begins with the lion, the king of the beasts, and ends with the word for eagle, the king of the birds (perhaps, however, the word for eagle refers to the griffon-vulture; see comments on 39:27). Job's incompetence and ignorance are seen in that he could not provide food for the first two animals (38:39-41), did not know of the birth of their offspring (the next two, 39:1-4), did not set them free or tame them (the two in 39:5-12), did not give them their odd ways (the two in 39:13-25), or provide them with their ability of flight (the last two, 39:26-30). One might think that animals, being under man, could be controlled and cared for by man. But God showed Job that he was in some ways inferior to even the animal kingdom.

(1) Lions and ravens. 38:39-41. For his own safety, Job stayed clear of lions, not hunting their prey for them. Nor could he even provide food for black ravens, whose young are often forgotten by their parents. Job could not be the nourisher of the world's wild kingdom. Therefore since God cares for them (Jesus said ravens are fed by God, Luke 12:24), who are of less value than humans, would He neglect His care of people?

(2) Goats and deer. 39:1-4. Job did not even know when certain animals give birth to their young or did he know their gestation periods. Totally apart from man's help or knowledge, but obviously under God's supervision, mountain goats and deer bring forth their young, who soon grow up, leave their parents, and fend for themselves (cf. references to the "young" in 38:41; 39:30). This mountain goat may be the Nubian Ibex, a goat in the wilds of the Middle East that hides when it bears its young. Even now relatively few people have ever seen these goats when they are bearing their offspring (Avinoam Danin, "Do You Know When the Ibexes Give Birth?" Biblical Archaeology Review 5. November-December 1979:50-1).

(3) Wild donkeys and wild oxen (39:5-12). 39:5-8. Even the mere act of releasing wild donkeys out in the desert where they roamed the wasteland, lived in the salt flats (perhaps around the Dead Sea), rejected the noise of civilization, and ranged the hills, was beyond Job's abililty. Only God can help such animals survive.

39:9-12. In contrast with setting wild donkeys free, Job could not tame a wild ox. This animal, perhaps the auroch, resisted domestication. It would not serve Job or stay in his barn overnight, like a domesticated cow. Nor would it submit to plowing. Though unusually strong, it would not do heavy work for man. Nor would it pull a cart with grain from a field to a threshing floor. If Job could not tame even this one wild animal, how could he hope to challenge God's ways with man?

(4) Ostriches, storks, war horses, and locusts (39:13-25). 39:13-18. The ostrich, a bizarre bird, is odd-featured, weighing up to 300 pounds and reaching a height of seven or eight feet. It flaps its wings but it cannot fly. Unlike birds that fly, such as the stork, an ostrich lays its eggs in a nest on the ground. In fact several ostrich hens lay their eggs in one nest, but if there is no more room in the nest they deposit their eggs outside the nest in the sand. There other brooding hens, in the confusion of getting in and out of the nest, often crush these eggs. Ostriches' seeming unconcern for or even cruel treatment of their young (v. 16; cf. Lam. 4:3) evidences their lack of wisdom and good sense. Hens may desert the nest if they are overfed, or if impatient they may leave the nest before all the chicks are hatched. If a human disturbs a nest, an ostrich may trample the eggs. Or a hen may sit on eggs in another nest, forgetting her own. (For these and other examples of ostrich stupidity see George F. Howe, "Job and the Ostrich: A Case Study in Biblical Accuracy," Journal of the American Scientific Affiliation 15. December 1963:107-10.) Yet in spite of its stupidity, an ostrich can run 40 miles an hour, faster than a horse. Would Job even think of making such a peculiar bird?

39:19-25. Nor did Job have anything to do with creating the war horse, with its strength and its mane, ability to leap like a locust while snorting, pawing, and eagerly and fearlessly entering a battle. His rider's weapons on his side, he prances the ground as if eating it up, while waiting for the trumpet . . . blast to signal the charge. Snorting, he smells the scent of battle from a distance, and hears the battle commands. The spirited nature of the poetry in these verses matches the horse's vitality. Since Job was inferior to the strength of this horse, certainly he was inferior to the horse's Creator.

(5) Hawks and eagles. 39:26-30. The hawk's annual migration toward the south occurred without Job's wisdom. On the other hand the eagle soars and builds its nest at high altitudes, on a cliff or rocky crag, where with keen vision he (cf. 28:7) spies food at great distances below. Devouring carcasses and sucking blood may suggest that this bird is the griffon-vulture rather than the eagle (George Cansdale, Animals of Bible Lands. London: Paternoster Press, 1970, p. 144). The Hebrew nešer may include both eagles and vultures (cf. 9:26).

This view of a few of the world's fauna demonstrates that Job, unable to contend with creation, hardly qualified to condemn the Creator. At the same time these words point up God's delight in His creation. His stars and angels sang and shouted when He made the earth (38:7), and He apparently enjoys His animal world. Also, God *uses* creation to limit the wicked (38:15), to aid man (38:23), to water the earth (38:26, 37-38); He *controls* and *limits* creation (38:8-9, 11); He *regulates* creation (38:12, 25, 31-33). And in the animal world God *provides* for animals (38:39-41; 39:29-30), *helps* them (vv. 1-4, 26-28), *frees* them (vv. 5-12), and *strengthens* them (vv. 13-25). In contrast Job could do none of these. Obviously God's orderly creation is provided for and well cared for; yet Job thought God's cosmic plan was arbitrary and that He lacked control, provision, and care.

d. God's closing rebuke and challenge to Job (40:1-2)

40:1-2. God's first speech, which began with a rebuke and a challenge (cf. 38:2-3), also concluded with a rebuke and a challenge. The rebuke is in the form of a question. **The one who contends** refers to **Job.** Twice (10:2; 23:6) Job considered God's (10:1) contending with him (*rîb*, bringing a court case against him), but now ironically, God turned the accusation around. (Cf. Elihu's words, "Why do you complain [*rîb*] to Him?" [33:13]) How could Job now dare indict God? Since Job had accused **God** he should **answer** these questions (cf. "answer Me" in 38:3; 40:7).

2. JOB'S FIRST REPLY TO GOD (40:3-5)

40:3-5. Seeing that man is not the world's master, and that God controls and cares for His creation, Job acknowledged (a) his insignificance (**unworthy** comes from the verb *qālal*, "to be silent, trifling, small, insignificant") and (b) his inability to defend himself further. His former self-confidence ("I will say to God, Do not condemn me," 10:2; "Then summon me, and I will answer," 13:22; "You will call and I will answer You," 14:15) now was changed to humble submission ("**how can I reply to You?**"). Never again would Job approach God like a stately prince (31:37). Job admitted that he could not respond to God, as God

had challenged him to do (38:3; 40:2). His only response was silence—**I put my hand over my mouth**—a gesture he had suggested for his disputants ("clap your hand over your mouth," 21:5).

Job had spoken his piece, repeating himself before God (**I spoke once** even **twice**), but now he felt he should **say no more.** However, this response of the former plaintiff included no note of repentance. He was humbled, but not yet repentant. So God summoned him to answer more questions.

3. GOD'S SECOND SPEECH (40:6-41:34)

Like God's first speech, this one included a challenge (40:6-7), a rebuke (40:8-14), and questions about nature (40:15-41:34). God's first speech pointed to inanimate and animate creation; this oration called Job's attention to only two animals. Unlike the first speech this one did not end with a closing rebuke and challenge (cf. 40:2).

a. God's challenge and rebuke to Job (40:6-14)

40:6-8. Again speaking **out of the storm** (cf. comments on 38:1) God repeated verbatim His previous challenge (38:3) that Job **brace** himself **like a man** and that he **answer** God's questions. God then rebuked Job with a **question** (cf. the questions in 38:2; 40:2): **Would you discredit My justice?** Only here did God refer directly to Job's accusation of the Sovereign's supposed unfairness.

In the next question **Would you condemn Me to justify yourself?** the word "condemn" is the verb *rāša'*, "to act wickedly or to condemn as wicked." This is an amazing reprimand by God, for this verb has occurred several times already in the Book of Job. Job had said he would unwittingly condemn himself if God confronted him (9:20a). Then he said he would tell God not to condemn him (10:2). Eliphaz told Job that the sufferer was condemning himself by his words (15:6), and Elihu believed that the three had condemned Job (32:3) Now God said the One who was really being condemned was God Himself! Job's self-justification that *he* was not acting wickedly resulted in his saying that *God* was acting wickedly.

40:9-14. To contend with God suggests an assumed equality with God. And yet no mortal possesses that. Job did not have God's strength (**arm** symbolizes strength; cf. 38:15; Ps. 89:13; Isa. 40:10; and cf. **hand** in Job 40:14), or the ability to terrify by his **voice.** Without these resources to rule the world and rectify its wrongs how could Job rightfully criticize?

If his libels against the sovereign Lord were to be accepted as true, then Job would first have to prove his ability to govern the universe. Defaming God, as Job had done, was in essence a usurping of divine authority, an attempt to put himself in **God's** place. So, as God reasoned, if Job wanted the job of world Ruler, then he would need to prove he was qualified. Job would need to dress the part, putting on God's **glory and splendor,** His **honor and majesty.** Of course, he would be disqualified in even that. His assignment, God said, was to **unleash** his **wrath,** humiliating the godless and **proud** merely by looking at them (cf. the Leviathan's ability to look down on the haughty, 41:34), and then crushing and burying **them.** Since Job had accused God of neglecting to punish **the wicked** (21:29-31; 24:1-17), God ironically suggested He turn over the responsibility to Job to see if he could fulfill it. Only if Job could carry out such an awesome task, would God **admit to** the complainer's independence and self-sufficiency and the validity of his criticisms.

b. God's questioning about two animals (40:15–41:34)

God's first speech displayed a panorama of nature including 12 animals, but in His second speech His zoom lens focused on only 2 animals. God thereby impressed Job with his mere puniness and with God's majestic power.

Scholars differ in their views as to who these creatures were. Against the view that the behemoth (40:15-24) and Leviathan (chap. 41) are mythological, as some suggest, are these facts: (1) God told Job to "look at" the behemoth, (40:15). (2) God said He "made" the behemoth, as He had made Job (40:15). (3) The detailed descriptions of both animals' anatomies befits real not mythological beasts. (4) Animals in myths were based on real creatures, but were given exaggerated features. (5) The 12 animals in 38:39–39:30 were real, which would cause one to expect these 2 to be real also. (6) Though sometimes elsewhere in

Scripture the Leviathan may be mythological (e.g., 3:8; Ps. 74:14; Isa. 27:1), it is also spoken of elsewhere as a created being (Ps. 104:24, 26). And the plural Hebrew word for behemoth is used in Joel 1:20, where it is rendered "wild animals."

However, though they are apparently actual animals, they may *also* represent proud, wicked elements in the world. In the ancient Near East these beasts, in their brute force (Job 40:16-18; 41:12, 22, 26-29) and agitation of the waters (41:31-32), symbolized the chaotic effect of evil. (This helps explain how the crocodile then became the basis for the idea of a mythological dragon, a creature that causes extreme chaos in the waters.) In Egypt the Pharaoh, in preparation for his enthronement, ritually harpooned (with the help of others) a male hippopotamus and occasionally a crocodile, to dramatize his ability to dispel chaos and maintain order. The king could carry out this difficult harpooning task only because of his supposed superhuman, godlike strength. But God was showing Job that he did not have that ability. Since he could not conquer the animalistic symbols of evil, how could he subdue evil people?

The association of both animals with the water (40:21-23; 41:31-32) ties this speech to the first divine discourse (38:8-11, 16).

(1) The behemoth. **40:15-24.** God mentioned several things about the behemoth: its position with Job as a fellow creature (v. 15), its diet (v. 15), its physical strength (vv. 16-19), its habitat (vv. 20-23), and its fierceness (v. 24). The word **behemoth** is the plural of "beast." Since one animal is described in verses 15-24, the plural probably points up the animal's greatness. Suggestions as to the identity of this animal include an elephant, a rhinoceros, a plant-eating brontosaurus (dinosaur), a water buffalo, and a hippopotamus. The common view that this huge creature is the hippopotamus is supported by several observations: (1) The hippo is herbivorous (it **feeds on grass like an ox,** v. 15). Therefore **wild animals** do not fear being attacked by it (v. 20). (2) It has massive **strength** in its **loins,** stomach **muscles . . . tail . . . thighs,** metallike **bones** and **limbs** (vv. 16-18). Unlike the elephant, a hippopota-

mus' stomach muscles are particularly strong and thick. The rendering that his tail **sways like a cedar** (possibly meaning a cedar branch, not a cedar trunk) suggests to some that "tail" means the trunk of an elephant. However, Ugaritic parallels indicate that the verb "sways" (which occurs only here in the OT) means "stiffens." In that case the hippopotamus' tail, though small, was referred to. The tail stiffens when the animal is frightened or is running. (3) The hippopotamus was the largest of the animals known in the ancient Near East (**he ranks first among the works of God,** v. 19). The adult hippo of today weighs up to 8,000 pounds. "There may have been an especially gigantic variety that flourished in the Jordan in those days, and as such he may have outclassed even the elephant . . . " (Gleason L. Archer, Jr., *The Book of Job*, p. 107). (4) The hippo is difficult if not impossible to kill with a mere hand sword. The words **His Maker can approach him with His sword** (v. 19) suggest that *only* God dare approach the beast for hand combat. Nor can he be captured or harpooned when only his **eyes** or **nose** show above the water (v. 24). (5) As a hippopotamus **lies hidden . . . in the marsh. . . . the stream,** and **the river** (vv. 21-23), its sustenance (perhaps vegetation) floats down from **the hills** (v. 20). This huge creature is undisturbed by river turbulence for the rivers are his habitat (v. 23). An elephant or brontosaurus would hardly be described this way. A surging river would hardly reach the depth of a brontosaurus' mouth.

(2) The leviathan (chap. 41). The discussion of the leviathan is longer than God's comments on any of the other animals. That fact, coupled with the vicious nature of the leviathan, an animal that even attacks man (v. 8), makes chapter 41 climactic. This beast has been variously interpreted as the seven-headed sea monster Lotan of Ugaritic mythology, the whale, the dolphin, a marine dinosaur that survived the Flood, and, most likely, the crocodile. Archer suggests it was a giant crocodile of the Jordan River, not the Egyptian crocodile (*The Book of Job*, p. 107). Man's attempt to capture this animal and the detailed description of the monster's anatomy suggest that it was an actual creature. Calling the behemoth

and the leviathan dinosaurs wrongly dates Job's lifetime within only a few hundred years of the Flood. The crocodile fits God's description of the leviathan's back (vv. 13, 15-17, 23), teeth (v. 14), chest and undersides (vv. 24, 30), and its churning of the waters (vv. 31-32). (See comments on vv. 18-21 for answers to suggestions that this is a dragon.) The behemoth and leviathan have many similarities (see Roy B. Zuck, *Job*, p. 180), so if one is an actual animal, then the other probably is also.

As discussed earlier, in the ancient Near East both animals were symbols of chaotic evil.

God spoke of this creature's inability to be captured by fishing equipment and tamed by man (vv. 1-11), its awesome anatomy (vv. 12-25), and the leviathan's inability to be captured by hunting equipment (vv. 26-34).

41:1-11. A **fishhook . . . a rope. . . . a cord,** and **a hook** are inadequate to capture so fierce an animal (vv. 1-2). It is not so easily tamed that it would, personified like a human, plead to be released or agree to being tamed and used as **a pet** (vv. 3-5). **Merchants** cannot sell it, since it is seldom captured (v. 6). Larger fishing equipment, such as **harpoons** and **spears** (v. 7), and even **hand** combat (v. 8) are useless. Since people are afraid at even the sight of a crocodile, **no one** would dare wake it up (vv. 9-10). God then used this fierce amphibian to illustrate man's inability to oppose God (**to stand against** Him) or to **claim** He owes them something (since **everything** is His). If Job panicked at seeing a crocodile, how did he dare confront the crocodile's Maker, telling Him He had done wrong? If the beast's power exceeded Job's strength, certainly Job would be impotent before God.

41:12-17. God then reminded Job of the crocodile's anatomy (vv. 12-25). It is difficult to catch a crocodile because of its **strength** (v. 12), the protective armor of its tough hide (v. 13), jaws (**the doors of his mouth**) that man cannot pry open by hand (v. 14), sharp **teeth** that terrify (v. 14), and its **back . . . rows of shields** that weapons **cannot** penetrate (vv. 15-17).

41:18-21. The movements of a crocodile's nose, eyes, and mouth also put people in panic. A crocodile can stay completely submerged underwater for about five minutes. When it comes up for air and sneezes the water out **from** its **nostrils,** the spray looks like **flashes of light** in the sun. When this reptile emerges from the water, its small **eyes,** with slits for pupils like a cat's eyes, are seen first, **like** the dawn's **rays.** Interestingly in Egyptian hieroglyphs, the crocodile's eye represents the dawn (Victor E. Reichert, *Job,* p. 216).

Do the **firebrands** from its **mouth** and the **smoke** and **flames** from its nostrils (vv. 19-21) mean this is a mythical dragon, after all? No. These may be explained as the way God spoke of the crocodile's breath and water, which when emitted from its mouth, look in the sunlight like a stream of fire. This poetic language, probably spoken in hyperbole, accentuates this beast's frightful nature. This language also is the basis for the concept of a dragon in mythology. (See comments under "b. God's questioning about two animals [40:15–41:34].")

41:22-25. With a strong **neck,** tight (cf. v. 15) and **firm** flesh, and unusually **hard** chest, this creature causes **dismay** in people. No wonder, **when he rises up** out of the water, even **the mighty** tremble and run. The Hebrew word rendered "When he rises up" is actually a noun, "from his proud lifting up." Job had said *God's* "proud lifting up" (or "uprising" or "loftiness"; "splendor" in 31:23) had terrified him and would terrify the three controversialists (13:11). How inconsistent then for Job, terrified by God's loftiness, to suppose he could confront God.

41:26-34. Strong hunters (cf. v. 25) in those days seldom confronted fierce crocodiles because their normal weaponry—the **sword . . . spear . . . dart,** and javelin—had **no effect** on that animal's tough hide (vv. 15-17, 23). Instruments of **iron** or **bronze** were easily broken by this beast. Objects propelled through the air, such as **arrows** or **slingstones** bounced harmlessly off its hide. Nor could a crocodile be felled with **a club** or a **lance.**

The hide of this animal's **undersides** is so **jagged** that when he walks in **the mud** he leaves marks that look **like a threshing sledge** (with its sharp points) has been pulled through the mud. Swimming in a river, a crocodile so stirs the water that it looks as if it were **boiling.** Saying that his agitating the water is **like**

a pot of ointment means that it looks like foam caused by an apothecary when he boils ointment.

Another terrifying aspect of the leviathan is its speed. It moves through the water so fast that it leaves a shiny **wake,** whitecaps of waves that appear like **white hair.**

Nothing equals this **creature;** he is afraid of nothing, yet everyone is terrified of him. Even a **haughty** man crouches in fear before a crocodile. This unconquerable animal is therefore **king** over **proud** beasts and man. Whereas Job could not humble the haughty merely by looking down on them (40:11-14), the leviathan, a mere animal, could do so. God's concluding statements that the crocodile **looks down on** the "haughty" and is supreme **over** the "proud" would have reminded Job that his pride before *God,* the crocodile's Fashioner, was both precarious and dangerous.

In this second lecture (40:6–41:34) God was therefore challenging Job to subdue these monsters—a task he obviously could not do—if he wanted to maintain order in God's universe. Job had been concerned that God had not dealt with evil; so God was showing Job that he was unqualified to take over God's job of controlling and conquering evil for he could not even conquer the animal *symbols* of evil. In fact God had *made* these animals, which suggests that evil forces are not beyond God's control. He permits evil and chaos to rule for a time just as he had given Satan permission to test Job (1:12; 2:6).

Man cannot subdue singlehandedly a hippopotamus or a crocodile, his fellow creatures (40:15). Nor can man conquer evil in the world, which they symbolize. Only God can do that. Therefore Job's defiant impugning of God's ways in the moral universe—as if God were incompetent or even evil—was totally absurd and uncalled for.

4. JOB'S SECOND REPLY TO GOD (42:1-6)

42:1-2. In Job's first response (40:3-5) he admitted his finiteness in the face of God's display of numerous wonders of nature above, on, and under the earth. But he did not admit to God's sovereignty or to his own sin of pride. **Job** now confessed those two things in his second reply. Overwhelmed by the strength and fierceness of the behemoth and the leviathan, Job sensed his own inadequacy to conquer and control evil, which they represented. He therefore saw anew the greatness of God's power and sovereignty. Job's words **I know that You can do all things** point up the folly of his questioning God's ability to govern the universe. Job's efforts to thwart (lit., "cut off") God's **plan** were now seen as futile.

42:3. Job quoted God's question **Who is this that obscures My counsel without knowledge?** to infer that God was right. Job had spoken without knowledge (as Elihu had said, 34:35; 35:16); he talked about things beyond his comprehension, things **too wonderful** (cf. "wonders" in 37:14) or awesome in creation **for** him **to know.** Job now discarded his complaints about God's inability to rule the world with justice. The idea that he could boldly refute any of God's trumped-up charges (23:4-7; 31:35-36) was now abandoned.

42:4-5. Again Job quoted the Lord, this time citing God's challenge at the beginning of each of His two speeches (38:3; 40:7): **I will question you, and you shall answer Me.** This quotation implied an admission that Job was unable to answer any of the Sovereign's barrage of rhetorical questions. Job admitted to flunking God's biology examinations.

Job had only **heard of** God's doings. The complainer was not an eyewitness of the act of Creation, a fact God called to his attention near the beginning of His first speech (38:4-11). Nor could Job even view firsthand many aspects of natural Creation (38:16-24; 39:1-4). His perspective of God's total workings was therefore limited and secondhand.

But now that Job was addressed directly by God, this experience exceeded his previous knowledge, like seeing (**now my eyes have seen You**) compared with hearing. This thrilling view of God, probably spiritual insight, not physical vision, deepened his perspective and appreciation of God. What Job now knew of God was incomparable to his former ideas, which were really ignorant. This personal confrontation with God silenced his arguing and deepened his awe.

42:6. Having gained insight (v. 5) into God's ways and character—His creative power and genius, His sovereign control, and His providential care and love—Job confessed his own unworthiness and repented. **I despise myself** means he rejected his former accusations of God spoken in pride. God had already rebuked Job for indicting, faulting, and discrediting Him (40:2). Job then repented **in dust and ashes,** a way of expressing his self-deprecation (cf. Gen. 18:27). Throwing dust in the air so that it came down on one's head (cf. Job 2:12) and sitting in or near ashes or with ashes on one's body (cf. 2:8; Isa. 58:5; Dan. 9:3) were signs of a humbled condition. Having grieved over his losses, Job now grieved over his sin.

Obviously he did not repent of the sins which his three friends had conjured up. He stuck persistently to his position that his suffering was not merited by precalamity sins (Job 27:2-6). But, as Elihu had pointed out, bitterness and pride had followed his loss of wealth, family, and health (32:2; 33:17; 35:12-13; 36:9; 37:24). At first, however, Job's response was proper (1:21-22; 2:10). Job now saw, as God had challenged him (40:10), that no one can stand accusingly against Him. Realizing that God is not obligated to man, Job's questions vanished and his resentment left. He was now satisfied, for God had communicated with him about His own person, not about Job's problems. Now Job was willing to trust the Sovereign, whose ways are perfect (Ps. 18:30), even when he could not understand. Undoubtedly God forgave him of his former sin of pride.

III. Epilogue (42:7-17)

This section, like the opening (chaps. 1–2), is written in prose. God now turned to the three critics, before He restored Job's prosperity and family.

A. God's condemning of Job's friends (42:7-9)

42:7. God spoke **to Eliphaz,** probably the eldest of the three, and said He was **angry with** him and his **two** companions (similar to Elihu's reaction to the three, 32:3) for they had **not spoken of Me what is right, as My servant Job has.** They who had assumed a position of defending God were now on the defensive themselves. As Job had predicted (13:7-9) matters did not turn out well for them. They thought they knew God's ways but they did not expect this! The words, **My servant Job,** spoken by God four times in 42:7-8, point up his restored position as a trusting and obedient servant of the Lord (cf. 1:8; 2:3).

By insisting that suffering is always retributive, the three rhetoricians were limiting God's sovereign ability to use suffering for other purposes. As a result, they cruelly indicted innocent Job.

How then did Job speak "what is right"? Had he not repeatedly and proudly challenged God, accusing Him of injustice and unwarranted silence? Yes, but he had now repented of his proud accusations (42:6) and therefore he was accepted by God. Furthermore, he never cursed God, as Satan had predicted and his wife had urged (1:11; 2:5, 9), though he came close to it. Though Job continued to contend with God, he never renounced Him. Also his view of God's power and wisdom exceeded that of the three.

42:8-9. To the utter surprise and chagrin of the three critics, God told them to offer **a burnt offering** of **seven bulls and seven rams,** a large **sacrifice.** And they were to have **Job pray for** them as their mediator (cf. his earlier work as a priest, 1:5). Never once had they prayed for *him.* But now Job, whom they had condemned and badgered, and who had rejected their counsel, was to intercede for them. What an amazing irony!

They had defended God's justice in striking **Job** down. But now they saw that God is concerned with more than justice; He is also known for love and grace. Repentance, which they had recommended for Job, was now what *they* had to do. They too were silenced—and corrected—by God's direct communication. Elihu was excluded from this act of repentance because he, though not having all the truth on Job's situation, was nearer the truth than the other three.

Job had longed for a mediator between himself and God (16:19-21) since his three countrymen were not interceding for him; but ironically he himself became a mediator for *them,* even though they did *not* ask for one.

B. God's restoring of Job's prosperity and family (42:10-17)

42:10-11. Job's vision of God's transcendence and his ensuing repentance paved the way for his forgiveness of and intercessory praying for his three friends. Then his forgiving spirit toward them paved the way for God to bless him. His painful disease was cured either at this time or immediately after his repentance (v. 6).

All his brothers . . . sisters, and acquaintances (probably including the forgiven three!), who had forsaken him (19:13-14), heard of his restoration. They now dined **with him in his house. They comforted . . . him** regarding his **trouble** (*rā'âh,* "calamity"), though this was probably less consoling than if they had done so earlier. This woe, as **Job** himself had acknowledged (1:21; 2:10), was **brought** on by **the LORD** (through the instrumentality of Satan). Then, to show their kindness, they **each . . . gave him a piece of silver** (*qᵉśîṭâh,* a word used only here and in Gen. 33:19 and Josh. 24:32), **and a gold ring** (*nezem*), referring either to a nose ring (Gen. 24:22) or an earring (Gen. 35:4).

42:12. God restored to Job twice the number of livestock he had before (v. 10; cf. 1:3) so that his later years were **more** prosperous **than the first.** Perhaps he used the silver and gold received from his siblings and countrymen to purchase fresh livestock, from which the number probably grew by breeding over a period of time.

Did this outpouring of material blessing from God mean that the theory of the three self-appointed jurors was correct, after all? (They had predicted that prosperity follows repentance, 5:8, 17-26; 8:5-7, 21; 11:13-19.) No, the restoration of wealth was a token of God's grace, not an obligation of His justice. Since Job had (unknowingly) silenced Satan by not cursing God, and since he had repented of his pride, his suffering did not need to continue. The restoring of his estate demonstrated to his friends that God had restored him. Furthermore the Book of Job does not deny the general biblical principle that God blesses the righteous. Instead the Scriptures show that the principle is not invariable and airtight. God in His sovereignty can give—or hold back—blessings in accord with His purposes.

42:13-15. Job's grief over the loss of his 10 children was relieved somewhat, though probably not fully, by the birth of

10 others. The names of the **three** youngest **daughters** are given, whereas the names of Job's other 17 children are unknown. **Jemimah** means "dove," **Keziah** means "cinnamon perfume" (cassia, from *qᵉṣîʿâh*, is a cinnamon bark from which perfume is made), and **Keren-Happuch** means "horn of eyepaint" (i.e., an animal-horn bottle for holding a dye used to make eyelashes, eyelids, and eyebrows more attractive). These names speak of the girls' striking beauty, for which they were well known. Another interesting fact about the **daughters** is that they shared **with their brothers** in receiving from Job **an inheritance**—an unusual occurrence in those days. In later years a daughter received her father's inheritance only if she had no brothers (Num. 27:8).

42:16-17. Following his terrible ordeal, **Job lived 140 years.** If he was about 70 when the calamities struck, he lived to be about 210. According to Jewish tradition, his latter years (140) were exactly twice the number of his former ones (70). Job **saw his** descendants **to the fourth generation,** that is, he lived to see his great-great-grandchildren. His death came, not when he was in intense agony from his losses (as he had prayed, 3:20-26; 10:18-22), but later when he was **full of years.**

This book, probably the oldest in the Bible, deals with mankind's most pressing problems: the question of suffering and man's relationship with God. Job's experience billboards the truth that man's worship of God does not stem from a businesslike contract, whereby he earns material rewards from God. Man's relationship to God is not a juridical arrangement in which He is obligated to reward man for every good act. Instead, man is to trust God, worship Him regardless of his circumstances, and rely on the perfections of His character even when God's ways are not fully understood.

Misfortune does not mean God has forsaken His own. It does mean He has plans that the sufferer may know nothing of. A believer's unmerited tragedy may never be fully understood. Yet he can realize that God is in charge, that God still loves him and cares for him. This is what Job learned. His three denouncers said suffering's purpose is always *discipline* (punishment for wrongdoing); Job felt it was for *destruction* (thinking God was determined to destroy him); Elihu stressed that the aim is *direction* (to keep him from death). But God had two purposes: *demonstration* (that Satan's allegations were false) and *development* (of Job's spiritual insight). Therefore to attack God, to malign Him, challenge Him, accuse Him, bait Him, or try to corner Him—all of which Job did—are out of the question for a believer. To criticize God's wisdom only shows one's own ignorance. The chasm between God and man leaves no place for pride and self-sufficiency.

Job did not receive explanations regarding his problems; but he did come to a much deeper sense of the majesty and loving care of God. Thus he came to trust Him more fully, knowing that His ways should not be challenged. Though often inexplicable and mysterious, God's plans are benevolent and beneficial.

BIBLIOGRAPHY

Andersen, Francis I. *Job: An Introduction and Commentary.* The Tyndale Old Testament Commentaries. Downers Grove, Ill.: InterVarsity Press, 1976.

Archer, Gleason L., Jr. *The Book of Job: God's Answer to the Problem of Undeserved Suffering.* Grand Rapids: Baker Book House, 1982.

Baker, Wesley C. *More Than a Man Can Take: A Study of Job.* Philadelphia: Westminster Press, 1966.

Barnes, Albert. *Notes, Critical, Illustrative, and Practical, on the Book of Job.* 2 vols. Glasgow: Blackie & Son, 1847. Reprint. Grand Rapids: Baker Book House, 1950.

Davidson, A.B. *The Book of Job.* Cambridge: Cambridge University Press, 1903.

Dhorme, Édouard. *A Commentary on the Book of Job.* Translated by Harold Knight. New York: Thomas Nelson Publishers, 1967.

Driver, Samuel Rolles, and Gray, George Buchanan. *A Critical and Exegetical Commentary on the Book of Job.* The International Critical Commentary. Edinburgh: T. & T. Clark, 1921.

Ellison, H.L. *A Study of Job: From Tragedy to Triumph.* Grand Rapids: Zondervan Publishing House, 1971.

Gordis, Robert. *The Book of God and Man: A Study of Job.* Chicago: University of Chicago Press, 1965.

————. *The Book of Job: Commentary, New Translation, and Special Studies.* New York: Jewish Theological Seminary of America, 1978.

Green, William Henry. *The Argument of the Book of Job Unfolded.* 1874. Reprint. Minneapolis: James & Klock Christian Publishers, 1977.

Howard, David M. *How Come, God?* Philadelphia: A.J. Holman Co., 1972.

Johnson, L.D. *Israel's Wisdom: Learn and Live.* Nashville: Broadman Press, 1975.

————. *Out of the Whirlwind: The Major Message of the Book of Job.* Nashville: Broadman Press, 1971.

Pope, Marvin H. *Job.* 3rd ed. The Anchor Bible. Garden City, N.Y.: Doubleday & Co., 1973.

Reichert, Victor E. *Job.* London: Soncino Press, 1946.

Rowley, H.H. *Job.* The Century Bible. Greenwood, S.C.: Attic Press, 1970.

Schaper, Robert N. *Why Me, God?* Glendale, Calif.: Regal Books, 1974.

Stedman, Ray C. *Expository Studies in Job: Behind Suffering.* Waco, Tex.: Waco Books, 1981.

Thomas, David. *Book of Job: Expository and Homiletical Commentary.* 1878. Reprint. Grand Rapids: Kregel Publications, 1982.

Westermann, Claus. *The Structure of the Book of Job: A Form-Critical Analysis.* Philadelphia: Fortress Press, 1981.

Zuck, Roy B. *Job.* Everyman's Bible Commentary. Chicago: Moody Press, 1978.

PSALMS

Allen P. Ross

INTRODUCTION

Of all the books in the Old Testament the Book of Psalms most vividly represents the faith of individuals in the Lord. The Psalms are the inspired responses of human hearts to God's revelation of Himself in law, history, and prophecy. Saints of all ages have appropriated this collection of prayers and praises in their public worship and private meditations.

Title of the Psalms. The English title "Psalms" (or "Psalter") is derived from the Greek translation of the Old Testament. In the Codex Vaticanus (fourth century A.D.) the title *Psalmoi* and the subtitle *Biblos psalmôn* ("Book of Psalms") are used; in the Codex Alexandrinus (fifth century) the name *Psalterion* appears. The Greek word *psalmos*, which translates the Hebrew *mizmôr*, signifies music accompanied by stringed instruments. Under the influence of the Septuagint and of Christianity, the word *psalmos* came to designate a "song of praise" without an emphasis on accompaniment by stringed instruments (Christoph Barth, *Introduction to the Psalms*. N.Y.: Scribners and Sons, 1966, p. 1). Because *mizmôr* is used in the titles of 57 of the psalms, the Greek translators used the translation of that word for the title of the entire collection.

In the Hebrew Bible the title of the book is *sēp̄er tᵉhillîm*, "Book of Praises," referring to their content rather than form. This title is fitting for the collection of hymns used in Israel's worship, because most of the psalms contain an element of praise. Claus Westermann, in his study of the individual lament psalms, concludes that he found no psalms that do not progress beyond petition and lament to the praise of God (*The Praise of God in the Psalms*, p. 74). In the titles *tᵉhillâh* ("praise") is found only once (Ps. 145), but it is used some 28 times in the

book. *Tᵉhillîm* may be a technical term for the book, because the normal plural of *tᵉhillâh* is *tᵉhillôt̠*.

Place in the Canon. In the Hebrew Bible the Book of Psalms belongs to the third part, the Writings (after the Law and the Prophets). In the Hebrew manuscripts Psalms usually appears first in the Writings.

This arrangement of the biblical canon is not followed by the English versions, where the order is based on the Greek and Latin versions. Here the arrangement of the Prophets and the Writings seems to be topical and chronological.

Nature of the Psalms

1. Religious lyric poetry. The Psalms are the largest collection of ancient lyrical poetry in existence. Lyric poetry directly expresses the individual emotions of the poet. As part of the Old Testament, this poetry is also necessarily religious. Religious lyric poetry is the expression of these emotions and feelings as they are stirred by the thought of God and directed to Him (A.F. Kirkpatrick, *The Book of Psalms*, p. x).

Many psalms address God directly with their poetic expressions of petition and praise. They reveal all the religious feelings of the faithful—fears, doubts, and tragedies, as well as triumphs, joys, and hopes. The psalmists frequently drew on their experiences for examples of people's needs and God's goodness and mercy. Singing of past deliverances in easily remembered didactic poetry provided support and comfort for believers in their hours of trial, as well as warning them against unbelief and disobedience. In this regard the psalmists rejoiced over the Law of God as their guide for conduct and direction for prosperity. Several psalms also incorporate Israel's "wisdom" or philosophy of life. These hymns reflect the moral teachings of Proverbs and other pieces of Wisdom literature.

Because the Psalms formed the "hymnal" of the temple, they often celebrate the ordinances of the sanctuary and exult in the privilege of drawing near to God in His holy mountain. This aspect of the psalms, combined with their display of personal religious feelings, makes them the most powerful and complete expression of the worship of ancient Israel. Set in the form of lyric poetry, they became unforgettable.

The Psalms reveal that the Israelites were an intensely religious people, worshipers of God with a strong sense of right and wrong. Regarding themselves as God's covenant people, they opposed wickedness and unbelief. Their daily activities, their national celebrations, and their military activities were carried out with religious commitment. The fact that the songs reflect this commitment makes them all the more serviceable for the edification of the entire household of faith.

2. *Evocative language.* Lyric poetry differs from other literary forms in that it is a more concentrated form of discourse with more consciously artistic elements. Concentration is achieved through the use of images, symbols, figures, emotive vocabulary, and multiple meanings. The imagery used in the Psalms is earthy, for the Israelites were largely a nation of farmers and shepherds living in the countryside close to nature. It was also militaristic, because they were often involved in wars to conquer the land, and defensive wars against the ravages of empires which at times were part of God's discipline. To understand fully the poetic expressions they used, one must sense the people's cultural experiences.

Evocative language used in poetic discourse enabled the psalmists to convey several things at the same time. Because the truth was presented in word pictures, it evoked in the reader the feelings that the poet had when he wrote the lines; it excited in the reader the emotional significance of the words as well as their intellectual meanings. For example, the poet could picture the vitality and stability of a godly person through the image of a tree planted by water, or the fear of the fainthearted through the im-

age of melting wax, or the verbal attacks of the wicked through the imagery of swords and arrows. So an exposition of the Psalms must be sensitive to such images in order to appreciate both the intellectual and the emotional meanings of the poetry. In a word, the Psalms must be treated as religious lyrical poetry.

Several headings are used to designate the types of psalms in the book. *Mizmôr*, translated "psalms," heads 57 psalms. The term signified a song accompanied by stringed instruments. "Song" translates *šîr*; it is used of 32 songs. A *maśkîl* is probably "a contemplative poem." Thirteen psalms are labeled with this heading. The designation *miḳtām* is found with 6 psalms. Later it was understood to mean "epigram" or "inscribed poem," but this is disputed. Five psalms are labeled "prayers" (*t*e*pillâh*), and 1 is called a "praise" (*t*e*hillâh*, Ps. 145).

3. *Meter.* The fact that the psalms are artistic means that they display in fuller measure and with greater frequency the components of artistic form, including patterns, design, unity, balance, harmony, and variation. The psalmists were imaginative and creative; they regarded their artistry as crucial to the meaning of its content.

Basic to the pattern of poetry is meter. Hebrew poetry certainly has meter and rhythm, but it is not possible as yet to identify and determine that meter with any degree of certainty. Most commentators are satisfied to count the number of accented Hebrew words or word units in a line as the basis of their poetical analysis. Because only a few psalms consistently follow a metrical pattern of accented words, attempts to reconstruct the text according to preconceived or novel ideas of meter are unconvincing.

4. *Parallelism.* The predominant feature of Hebrew poetic structure is the repetition of meaning in parallel expressions—the so-called poetic parallelism. The biblical verse of poetry normally has two or more of these parallel units. The relationship between the parallel units must be studied to determine the emphasis of a verse as a whole. The following categories of parallelism have become standard, and may be used to articulate the relationships of the units (also see

A.A. Anderson, *The Book of Psalms*, 1:40-2; and James L. Kugel, *The Idea of Biblical Poetry: Parallelism and Its History*. New Haven, Conn.: Yale University Press, 1981).

Synonymous parallelism describes the closest similarity between each of the two consecutive lines. A term or unit of thought in one part is paralleled by an equivalent term or unit of thought in the other. In the following examples parallel elements have been divided in accord with the accented words in the Hebrew verse:

"Then Israel / entered / Egypt;//
Jacob / sojourned / in the land of Ham" (Ps. 105:23, author's trans.).

Antithetical parallelism balances the parallel elements through the opposition or contrast of thoughts:

"In the morning / it flourishes / and is renewed;//
in the evening / it fades / and it withers" (90:6, author's trans.).

Emblematic parallelism occurs when one of the parallel units is a metaphorical illumination of the other:

"As a father / pities / his children,//
so the Lord / pities / those who fear Him" (103:13, author's trans.).

The word order need not be the same in the parallel expressions in the verse. In fact sometimes the word order in the second part is inverted to form a chiasm in the poetry. Moreover, the parallelism is frequently *incomplete*. Two types may be distinguished:

Incomplete parallelism with compensation refers to a verse when only some of the terms are parallel, even though each part has the same number of terms:

"You will destroy / their offspring / from the earth,//
and their children / from among the / sons of men" (21:10, author's trans.).

This type may also appear with repeated expressions in a step-parallelism known as *climactic parallelism*:

"Ascribe / to the LORD / O heavenly beings,//
Ascribe / to the LORD / glory and strength,//
Ascribe / to the LORD / the glory of His name;//
Worship / the LORD / in holy array" (29:1-2, author's trans.).

Incomplete parallelism without compensation refers to a verse in which one of the lines has fewer terms:

"O LORD, / do not rebuke / me in Your anger,//
or discipline me / in Your wrath" (6:1).

When the second parallel expression is all compensation (i.e., when it simply continues the thought of the first), the parallelism is designated as *formal* (and thus not really parallelism at all):

"I have installed / My King//
on Zion / My holy hill" (2:6).

Some still find it helpful to use Lowth's general category of "synthetic parallelism" instead of "incomplete parallelism." In synthetic parallelism the second line develops the idea of the first.

Parallelism describes the relationship of expressions within verses (*internal parallelism*); at times it also reflects the relationships between verses (*external parallelism*).

5. Stylistic arrangements. Apart from a few psalms, the arrangement of lines of poetry into stanzas or strophes is not common. Psalm 119 is perhaps best known for this, for it is divided into 22 strophes of eight verses each. A few psalms have a refrain to mark out their strophic arrangements (e.g., 42:5, 11; 43:5; 57:5, 11; 80:3, 7, 19).

Certain psalms are alphabetically arranged as acrostics, that is, each verse begins with a different letter of the Hebrew alphabet in consecutive order (Pss. 9–10 [together these two psalms are an acrostic poem]; 25; 34; 37; 111–112; 145). This style is also used in Psalm 119 where each of the eight verses in each of the 22 sections begins with the same letter. Among other purposes, this structuring would have been an aid to memory.

6. Music and melody. In the praises of Israel mention is made of music and musical instruments. Cymbals, timbrels, wind instruments, and stringed instruments of various types are named, showing that musical accompaniment must have been on a grand scale.

Also many notices in the headings of the psalms indicate musical activities. Foremost is "to the choirmaster" (*lamnaṣṣēaḥ*, "for the director of music," NIV) occurring in 55 psalms. Though there are many speculations about this heading, it probably referred to the chief musician in charge of temple music. The psalms so designated may at one time comprised a collection of songs delivered to the temple for service.

The "sons of Korah," found with Psalms 42; 44–49; 84–85; 87–88, probably refers to musical performers from this family. Otherwise multiple authorship is required, and dual authorship would be required for Psalm 88. $Y^e\underline{d}\hat{u}\underline{t}\hat{u}n$ ("Jeduthun," Pss. 39; 62; 77) may also refer to a guild of musicians, for Jeduthun was one of David's chief musicians (1 Chron. 16:41).

Other headings also serve as musical indicators. $N^e\hat{g}\hat{i}n\hat{o}\underline{t}$ (Pss. 4; 6; 54–55; 67; 76) means "with stringed instruments." Psalm 61 has $n^e\hat{g}\hat{i}na\underline{t}$ (sing.), "with a stringed instrument," though the NIV also renders this plural. $\check{S}^em\hat{i}n\hat{i}\underline{t}$ (Pss. 6; 12) probably means "with an eight-stringed lute." $Neh\hat{i}l\hat{o}\underline{t}$ (Ps. 5) is obscure, but may refer to flutes used in expressing lamentation. $Gitt\hat{i}\underline{t}$ (Pss. 8; 81; 84) is also difficult; it may mean "wine song" or "instrument from Gath." '$\bar{A}l\bar{a}m\hat{o}\underline{t}$ (Ps. 46) probably means "maidens"; it may refer to a song sung by female voices.

Selâh, found within many psalms but not in their headings, may indicate when the worshipers were to "lift up" their voices (perhaps selâh is related to sālal, "to lift up or elevate"). It is used 71 times in the psalms. Selâh was not originally in the psalms; it was added later. Even so, it is quite ancient.

Several psalms also include melody indicators. "To the [tune of the] lily (lilies)" is found with Psalms 45, 60, 69, and 80. "To the doe of the morning" (lit. Heb.) occurs with Psalm 22. "To the silent dove of the distances" (lit. Heb.) is the heading of Psalm 56. "Do not destroy" occurs with Psalms 57–59, and 75. The meaning of 'al-mûṯ labbēn with Psalm 9 (rendered "To the tune of 'The Death of the Son'" in the NIV), of 'al-māḥǎlaṯ with Psalm 53, and of 'al-māḥǎlaṯ l^eʿannôṯ with Psalm 88 is disputed and uncertain. These notes in the superscriptions of the Hebrew psalms could refer to melodies used, or to some liturgical idea.

Authorship and Historical Notices. Commentators have long debated the translation of the lāme₫ preposition

which traditionally has been taken to designate the authorship of the psalms (e.g., l^edāwi₫, "of David"). Modern scholars have been skeptical of these notices on the basis of a number of historical, grammatical, and theological reasons. Many believe that David may have written a number of the psalms, but it is not possible to tell which ones, if any.

Scripture does attest that David was a singer of songs and the primary organizer of the musical guilds for the sanctuary (1 Chron. 15:3-28; 16:4-43; 23:1-5; 25; 2 Sam. 6:5; also cf. 1 Chron. 13:8). The traditions of Israel remember David as a writer of sacred poetry.

Moreover, the grammatical construction of the lāme₫ preposition with the name "David" (l^edāwi₫) certainly may represent authorship. The preposition can be translated "to," "for," or "of," or a number of other ways. Its use to distinguish authorship has been well attested in the Northwest Semitic inscriptions, other Semitic dialects such as Arabic, and other biblical passages such as Habakkuk 3:1 ("of Habakkuk"). Though a translator could interpret the preposition otherwise, sufficient evidence supports its usage in designating authorship.

However, each psalm must be taken individually, and headings that use the lāme₫ preposition must be translated in accord with the internal evidence of the psalms, since the preposition is used in a variety of ways. The overly negative reaction to these headings as marks of authorship is part of the general skepticism of the antiquity of the Psalms themselves. Though many critical scholars have posited dates in the postexilic and Maccabean periods for many of the psalms, evidence from the Ugaritic tablets of Ras Shamra has proved the antiquity of this kind of poetic expression. Expositors of the Psalms should therefore investigate the evidence thoroughly concerning the superscriptions that seem to indicate authorship. It must also be remembered that Christ and His apostles considered them as witnesses to the individual psalms' authorship.

If the notices of authorship stand, the following tabulation would be instructive for the study of the 90 psalms so designated: Psalm 90 is attributed to Moses; 73 of the psalms are credited to David; Psalms 50, 73–83 came from Asaph;

Heman the Ezrahite wrote Psalm 88; Ethan the Ezrahite (cf. 1 Kings 4:31) wrote Psalm 89; and Solomon is attested to be the author of Psalms 72 and 127. (Asaph, Heman, and Ethan were Levite musicians, 1 Chron. 15:17, 19; cf. 1 Chron. 6:39; 2 Chron. 5:12.)

The writing of the Psalms, then, spanned a period from Moses through the return from the Captivity, for some of the psalms, as indicated by their content, are clearly postexilic.

In addition to the *lāmed* preposition with a name to indicate the author, several psalms have short bits of information about the life of David. It is difficult to tell when these superscriptions were written, but there is no reason to doubt their antiquity. Fourteen psalms have historical notations:

Psalm 59 is connected with 1 Samuel 19:11.

Psalm 56 is connected with 1 Samuel 21:10-15.

Psalm 34 is connected with 1 Samuel 21:10–22:2.

Psalm 52 is connected with 1 Samuel 22:9.

Psalm 54 is connected with 1 Samuel 23:15-23.

Psalm 7 may be related to 1 Samuel 23:24-29 (but this is problematic).

Psalm 57 is related to the incident at Adullam (1 Sam. 22:1-2) or at En Gedi (1 Sam. 24).

Psalm 142, another passage that reports David's being in a cave, could refer to either of the above references as well.

Psalm 60 is from 2 Samuel 8:8, 13; and 1 Chronicles 18:9-12.

Psalm 18 is almost identical to 2 Samuel 22.

Psalm 51 is based on the incident of David's sin recorded in 2 Samuel 11–12.

Psalm 3 seems to be connected with 2 Samuel 15–18.

Psalm 63 may be related to 2 Samuel 15:23.

Psalm 30 may be connected with 1 Chronicles 21:1–22:1. (The contents of Ps. 30 suggest that David wrote it for the dedication of the temple after he sinned in numbering the people and he purchased the plot of ground for the temple.)

So the superscriptions attest that many of the psalms were written by David himself, and that several were connected with events while he was young.

Formation of the Psalter. Since the writing of the Psalms ranged over such an extended period, there must have been various stages in its collection. David's organization of the music for worship in the temple has already been mentioned. Psalm 72:20 has the note, "This concludes the prayers of David son of Jesse." Several psalms before Psalm 72 are not credited to David, and 17 psalms after it are. So this notice probably refers to an earlier collection of psalms.

Other kings in their reforms also reorganized the musical guilds and temple musicians. Solomon organized temple singing (2 Chron. 5:11-14; 7:6; 9:11; Ecc. 2:8). Jehoshaphat did also (2 Chron. 20:21-22) and so did Jehoiada (2 Chron. 23:18). Under Hezekiah's reform the musical guilds were reestablished (2 Chron. 29:25-28, 30; 30:21; 31:2). Hezekiah instructed the Levites to sing praises with the words of David and of Asaph (2 Chron. 29:30), suggesting that two collections of the Psalms existed. Later, Josiah reinstituted temple music and musical guilds (2 Chron. 35:15, 25).

The development of the Psalter would have been gradual, then, with frequent revisions and organizations. The first stage would have been the writing of individual psalms, some of which were collected for worship. Not all ancient Hebrew psalms found their way into this hymnbook. The songs of Moses (Ex. 15:1-18; Deut. 32:1-43), Miriam (Ex. 15:21), Deborah (Jud. 5), Jonah (Jonah 2), and even some of David's hymns (2 Sam. 1) were not included. In David's time Levites also prepared psalms for temple services (1 Chron. 16:4).

The collection of the psalms would have been the next stage. Possibly some songs of David were collected, as well as Asaph's. Other collections such as the songs "of ascents," or pilgrim songs (Pss. 120–134) may also have been gathered.

These smaller collections would then have been included in the books that now exist. Book I is made up of Psalms 1–41; Book II comprises Psalms 42–72; Book III is Psalms 73–89; Book IV is Psalms 90–106; and Book V includes Psalms 107–150. Each section concludes with a doxology, and the entire Psalter concludes with Psalm 150, a grand doxology. The earliest evidence for this fivefold division comes from the Qumran scrolls (found near the Dead Sea) copied soon after the beginning of the Christian era.

The final stage of the formation of the Psalter would then have come with the work of the final editor. The present order shows the impress of one individual's influence. Yet the collection does not seem to have one developing argument running throughout.

So by the close of the Old Testament canon the collections of songs and psalms had been united into their present form.

The Text of the Psalms. At least three text types are present in the manuscripts of the Psalms. The Hebrew Bible, that is, the Masoretic text (MT), certainly represents the superior text. The manuscripts of this family preserved the best readings, even though they were at times archaic, rare, or difficult. Such preservation demonstrates the high regard the scribes had for the text they received. Nevertheless translators and commentators have occasionally taken liberties in emending the text in an effort to resolve some of the difficulties. The changes suggested need to be evaluated carefully.

In the Greek Septuagint (LXX) text the Psalms are based on a different and inferior textual tradition than the Masoretic text. Where the Hebrew is particularly rare or difficult, and the Greek translators had some difficulty, they often smoothed out the text in their renderings. Jerome and the translators of many English Bibles depended rather heavily on the Greek.

The numbering of the Psalms in the Greek text differs from the Hebrew. This is important to remember when consulting Roman Catholic commentaries, or the Latin or Greek texts themselves. The following illustrates this:

MT	LXX
Psalms 1–8	Psalms 1–8
9–10	9
11–113	10–112
114–115	113
116:1-9	114
116:10-19	115
117–146	116–145
147:1-11	146
147:12-20	147
148–150	148–150

Moreover, the Greek and English versions do not include the superscriptions as part of the numbering of the verses as the Hebrew does. Frequently, then, the verse numbers in the Hebrew text (and references in books that refer to the Heb. text) will be one or more verses higher.

A third text type is attested in the Dead Sea Scrolls' Psalms scroll. This text is also inferior to the Masoretic text.

Trends in Studying the Psalms. Over the centuries there have been prevailing approaches to the study of this collection. Most conservatives probably rely on the old but serviceable historical commentaries, some of which come from the last century. Commentaries by J.A. Alexander, Franz Delitzsch, Alexander Maclaren, and J.J.S. Perowne provide historical and grammatical interpretations of the text. Sometimes, however, they go beyond the clear evidence in their reconstructions of the occasions of the Psalms.

The literary-analytical method of studying Scripture can be seen in the commentary by C.A. Briggs. On the basis of the Psalms' theological ideas, poetic structure, and philology, he believed that most of the psalms were written in the Maccabean period (ca. 150 B.C.).

A more profitable series of studies came from the form-critical approach to the Psalms. Hermann Gunkel pioneered this approach in his *Einleitung in die Psalmen* (*Introduction to the Psalms*, trans. by Thomas Horner. Philadelphia: Fortress Press, 1967). This method considered that the Psalms were to be sung with ritual acts in Israel's worship. First Samuel 1:24–2:10 and 1 Chronicles 16:1-37 provided evidence for this approach to psalmody. The task, then, was to determine the setting out of which each psalm grew.

Form critics also determined that the psalms which came from the same ritual activities in the temple would share common features such as vocabulary, ideas and moods, and forms of expressions. By comparing these similar features, one could then collect the different types of psalms.

From this approach, categories for the types of psalms were recognized. They include individual laments, national laments, thanksgivings by individuals, and hymns. There are also minor types such as royal psalms, pilgrim psalms, victory psalms, songs of Zion, songs of enthronement, *tôrâh* (Law) psalms, and wisdom psalms.

Many form critics assumed that they could trace the development of these types. As a result, most of the psalms were relegated to priestly compositions for liturgical purposes, not to poems of individual saints who wrote of their experiences with God. This endeavor of form criticism has caused many expositors to reject the entire approach. This is unfortunate because many helpful things have come from this method.

The following classifications of kinds of psalms have been used to great benefit in understanding the Psalms.

1. Individual laments. These psalms correspond roughly to prayers for help out of distress. They have the following parts:

a. Introductory cry to God. The psalmist turned to God immediately and poured out his heart in a short address (frequently a summary of the direction of the psalm).

b. Lament. The psalmist then gave full expression to his lamentable state. In describing his difficulty, he stated what his enemies had done, what straits he was in, and what God had or had not done.

c. Confession of trust. Turning from his complaint, the psalmist declared his full confidence in the Lord. Some of these sections are expanded into complete psalms of trust or confidence.

d. Petition. The psalmist then requested that God intervene on his behalf and rescue him.

e. Vow of praise or expression of praise. The psalmist concluded his lament with a full expression of his praise to God for answering his prayer. Because this section is part of the prayer out of distress, it has been described as a vow—it is what he would say in the midst of the congregation when the Lord answered his prayer. Being sure that the Lord would answer, he began the praising in the praying. Claus Westermann suggests that in the midst of the psalmist's praying God heard and inclined Himself to the psalmist (*The Praise of God in the Psalms*, p. 79). The sudden assur-

ance of this response led the psalmist into a full expression of praise.

2. National laments. These psalms follow the same pattern as the laments of individuals, but they are usually shorter. They include an introductory address and petition, a lament, a confession of trust, a petition, and a vow of praise. In each of these psalms the nation faced some difficulty, and together the people approached God with their lament.

3. Thanksgiving psalms. These psalms, also called psalms of declarative praise, take a different form. They include these five elements:

a. Proclamation to praise God. The psalmist normally began with an expression such as, "I will praise," because the psalm was a means by which he told others what God had done for him.

b. Introductory summary. The psalmist frequently offered a brief statement of what God had done.

c. Report of the deliverance. The psalmist then detailed his deliverance. He normally explained that he cried out to the Lord, the Lord heard, and the Lord delivered him.

d. Renewed vow of praise. The psalmist here actually gave God the praise he promised to give.

e. Praise or instruction. The psalm ended with direct praise of God, or it incorporated an extended section of instruction for others.

Samples of thanksgiving or declarative praise psalms are 21, 30, 32, 34, 40, and 66.

4. Descriptive praise psalms (hymns). These do not tell primarily of some personal deliverance; rather they offer direct praise to God. These psalms follow a slightly different arrangement.

a. Call to praise. The psalmist invited others to praise the Lord.

b. Cause for praise. The psalmist gave the reasons for the praise. This section normally included a summary and then a full development of the reason for praise. The cause was usually the greatness of God and His grace, amplified by specific illustrations.

c. Conclusion. The psalmist closed the song with a new exhortation to praise the Lord.

Samples of descriptive praise psalms are 33, 36, 105, 111, 113, 117, and 135.

Other types of psalms will be discussed in the *Commentary*. The most important of these are the wisdom psalms, pilgrim psalms, royal psalms, and enthronement psalms. The wisdom psalms are closely related in their motifs to the Wisdom literature of the Old Testament (e.g., Prov.). Among the features that may be present in them are the "better" sayings (Ps. 119:72), numerical sayings (62:11-12a), admonitions to "sons" (34:11), blessing formulas (1:1), emphasis on the Law (119), and contrasts between the righteous and the wicked (1:6; 49).

Psalms 120–134 have been called pilgrim songs. These all have the heading, "A song of ascents." Though this designation in the superscription has been given a variety of interpretations, it most likely refers to Israel's "goings up" to Jerusalem for the three festivals (cf. 1 Sam. 1:3; Ps. 122:4; Isa. 30:29; also see Ex. 23:17; Ps. 42:4). The contents of many of these psalms appear to be well suited to a visit up to Jerusalem.

Psalms in which the anointed king is in the foreground are called royal psalms. The text refers to some high point in the career of the monarch, such as his coronation (Ps. 2), his wedding (Ps. 45), or his going forth into battle (Pss. 20; 144). The Davidic Covenant is set to poetry in Psalm 89. Psalm 110 anticipates the king's coming in conquest, and Psalm 72 envisions his glorious reign. On the relationship of these psalms to *the* King, the Messiah, see the comments on those psalms.

The enthronement psalms are characterized by the expression "the LORD reigns" (Pss. 93; 96–97; 99) the Lord is "the great King" (Pss. 47; 95), or the Lord "comes to judge" (Ps. 98). Commentators interpret these expressions differently. Some say these psalms refer to an annual festival that celebrated the Lord's reign over the earth. However, there is no conclusive evidence that such an "enthronement festival" was ever held. Others have understood the phrase to refer to the Lord's reign over Israel. This would fit Psalm 99, but does not do justice to the contents of the others. It has also been taken to refer to God's universal reign (Alva J. McClain, *The Greatness of the Kingdom*. Grand Rapids: Zondervan

Publishing House, 1959, p. 22). Psalm 93 could be taken in this way, but again the ideas of the enthronement psalms anticipate something more dramatic.

Though something may be said for the enthronement psalms signifying characteristics of the reign of God at various stages (i.e., great acts of salvation by which His sovereignty is displayed), the fullest meaning of the terminology used pertains to the messianic kingdom. The language these psalms employ, language reminiscent of the epiphany at Sinai, harmonizes well with the prophetic oracles of the expected messianic kingdom. In fact the expression "God reigns" is found in Isaiah 52:7, which refers to the future reign of the Suffering Servant.

The study of the enthronement psalms has led many modern scholars to take a "cultic" approach to the Psalms. This approach is a development of the form-critical method; it argues that the annual autumnal festival was the center of the worship or "cult" of Israel. One proponent of this view was Sigmund Mowinckel (*The Psalms of Israel's Worship*). He argues that every fall Israel held a festival in which the Lord was enthroned in the temple, thereby ensuring God's reign over the universe for another year. Mowinckel's evidence is gathered from the biblical references to the Lord's reign or judging (Pss. 47; 93; 95–99), to the Lord's victory over nature, and to people at a festival rejoicing at the prospect of the Lord's reign. The material is sketchy, so he supports the idea from similar festivals of the surrounding nations of the ancient Near East, notably Babylon with its *Akitu* festival.

Others have interpreted the festival differently. Artur Weiser (*The Psalms: A Commentary*) agrees that a fall festival was central to the use of the enthronement psalms, but suggests that it was a covenant renewal rather than an actual enthronement of the Lord. He points up similarities with Joshua 24.

Hans-Joachim Kraus (*Worship in Israel*. Richmond, Va.: John Knox Press, 1966) sees a more complex picture of the fall festival. He views the festival as a remembrance of the Exodus and the wilderness wanderings, a covenant renewal celebration, and a tradition of Canaanite concepts of kingship emerging in the reigns of David and Solomon.

If such a fall festival actually existed and formed the key to the entire Psalter, it is surprising such is not mentioned anywhere in Scripture. Probably some of the psalms were used in connection with the fall festivals. But it is unlikely that the majority of the psalms were part of a festival patterned after pagan mythological ideas. This approach has also been criticized on the basis of the evidence from the ancient Near Eastern festivals (see Kenneth A. Kitchen, *Ancient Orient and Old Testament*. Downers Grove, Ill.: Intervarsity Press, 1966, p. 102).

This approach to the study of the Psalms, however, has provided a needed emphasis. Many of the psalms were probably connected with ritual and worship in David's tabernacle and/or Solomon's temple. Too often conservative commentators are oblivious to the worship setting of the tabernacle and the temple.

Besides the numerous references to worship and the temple ritual within the Psalms, liturgical indicators are given in some of the superscriptions. Psalm 30 is "For the dedication of the temple," Psalm 92 is designated "For the Sabbath Day," and Psalm 100 is a psalm to be used at the offering of the thanksgiving sacrifice (Lev. 7). "A petition" (lit., "to bring to remembrance") is the superscription of Psalms 38 and 70, apparently intended to remind the Lord of the one making the petition. The meaning of *šiggāyôn* in Psalm 7 is obscure. To these the title "A song of ascents" (Pss. 120–134) may be added. These songs were sung en route to or at the great festivals in Jerusalem.

Israel's religious calendar (see the chart "Calendar in Israel," near Ex. 12) is important in understanding the background of some of the psalms. The three great annual festivals are discussed in Exodus 23:14-19 and Leviticus 23:4-44. At Passover and Unleavened Bread in the spring, at Weeks or Pentecost (also called Firstfruits) in the early summer, and at Atonement and Tabernacles in the fall, the people were to go to Jerusalem and celebrate God's bounty in the harvests. At those gatherings the people would be involved in the ritual of the temple and in using the Psalms in praise.

The Psalms frequently refer to musical instruments, singing, and clapping in the religious activities. Psalm 5:7 speaks of entering God's house to worship. (Ps. 68:24-27 refers to the procession to the sanctuary accompanied by singers; cf. 42:4.) And Psalm 122:1 tells of the joy involved in a pilgrimage to the temple.

On many occasions Israel worshiped at the temple. Sabbath days, New Moons, Sabbath years, and Jubilees all provided occasions for praising God in the sanctuary.

Worshipers could come spontaneously as well. Freewill offerings could be brought to express thanks (*tôḏāh;* cf. Lev. 7:12-18; Ps. 50:14-15), for answers to prayer (1 Sam. 2:1-10), purification from ritual uncleanness or disease (Lev. 13–15), vindication in legal conflicts, atonement for sins (Ps. 51:13-17), or as special vows. On such occasions the worshiper brought his offering to be shared by those in attendance, and made his praise known (probably in the form of a declarative praise psalm) for the enrichment of the congregation.

No doubt the prayers in the Psalter also found widespread use by those who came to pray for forgiveness, healing, protection, deliverance, and comfort, as they have throughout the history of the church.

So individually or communally, the Psalms no doubt were frequently sung or said near the sanctuary. Their messages and how they were used are instructive for believers today, as the following exposition seeks to show. The prayers of the psalmists exhibit great confidence in the Lord, so great that many times they turned to praise before the answers actually came. A close study of the Psalms shows how such confidence was developed. In addition the praises of the psalmists show a genuine and spontaneous enjoyment of God's benefits. To receive from God and not praise Him was sin. The declaration of God's benefits was the final part of the process. It was also part of the enjoyment of God, for one naturally tells of the things he enjoys most (C.S. Lewis, *Reflections in the Psalms*. New York: Harcourt, Brace and World, 1958). Thus when the Scriptures call believers to praise God, they are calling them to enjoy God and His benefits. And when God blesses someone, that fact is to be shared in the congregation so that all may enter into the praise and enjoy God and His benefits.

In Israel this normally involved sharing the sacrifical meal of the worshiper who came to praise God. His sacrifice, a token of the bounty, would accompany his praise. God thus was enjoyed by His people who were thereby inspired to pray to and praise Him more.

Theology of the Psalms. Because the Psalms record such a vast range of religious ideas and impressions, it is difficult to discover a specific theology for the collection. Indeed, almost all the theological ideas of the Old Testament surface here. Yet one predominant emphasis does recur throughout. The psalmists assumed or expressed the belief that the Lord, who sovereignly rules the universe, will establish His just rule on the earth in and through His people. When faced with opposition from the wicked or from physical difficulties, they prayed for its realization in their lives, confident that the Judge of all the earth would bring vindication. When righteousness triumphed, they praised God for the triumph of His righteous cause among people.

The psalmists' participation in the worship and appreciation of the Law demonstrated their confidence in God's theocracy. At times they looked beyond their experiences to the Lord's actual reign of righteousness on earth at the Messiah's coming. How clear an understanding they had of the details of God's revelation is impossible to say. It is clear, however, that they confidently expected God to set things right.

The psalmists did not hesitate to avow their loyalty to God and His covenant. In their zeal to champion righteousness, their words frequently contain imprecations or curses. They prayed that God would break the arms of the wicked (Ps. 10:15), smash their teeth (58:6), and turn His wrath on them (69:22-28). It must be remembered that the psalmists were filled with zeal for God's theocracy. Thus these expressions were not indications of personal vendetta. The psalmists, in fact, protested that their kindness to such people had been betrayed by treachery (109:4-5). Their prayers represent their longing that God's cause be vindicated on earth, that sin would be judged—which God would do eventually.

Of course the New Testament believer has a different prayer life because of his understanding of the full revelation of God. Yet to pray for God's will to be done or for Christ to come quickly, is also to pray for the vindication of the righteous and the judgment of the wicked.

The psalmists also abhorred pagan ideas and customs, which they knew threatened the faith of the nation. Many aspects of foreign polytheistic beliefs are attacked in a subtle manner (less subtle than the prophetic oracles). These polemics may at times be a passing reference (such as the description of the Lord as the One "who rides on the clouds," 68:4, rather than the Canaanite Baal who is likewise described). At other times the polemics form the substance of the entire psalm (such as Ps. 29 which attributes a storm in Canaanite territory to the Lord rather than Canaan's storm god Baal).

Many scholars say these references are mythological borrowings from the Semitic world. However, though the Israelites shared a common vocabulary and imagery with their neighbors, these polemical portions show a spiritual parting of the ways. The fact that many Israelites ran after other gods made these polemics even more urgent. If the truth was to be secured and perpetuated from generation to generation, false and corrupting beliefs had to be destroyed. Therefore students of the Psalms must be aware of the polytheistic threats to Israel's faith as well as the historical struggle they brought to the righteous.

The conflict with forces of evil, whether pagan beliefs or apostate Israelites, forced genuine believers to contend for the faith vigorously, to avow their integrity and loyalty openly, and to hope for deliverance from God. The psalmists looked for that deliverance in this life. One would have expected that the psalmists, with all their persecution, suffering, and distress, would have despaired of this life and looked for contentment in the life to come. But this is not the case. They sensed that death would end their service and praise of God (though other Scripture passages, written later, indicate that this is not so). It was in this life that God's loyal love, faithfulness, and righteousness could be experienced (Pss. 6:5; 30:9; 88:4-5, 10-12; 115:17).

Nowhere in the Psalms is there a clear, unambiguous expression of hope in the resurrection, the kind of statement made in the Prophets (Isa. 26:19; Ezek. 37:1-14; Dan. 12:2). However, some passages in the Psalms do seem to break through to express a hope of continued fellowship with God after this life (Pss. 16–17; 49; 73). Yet the expressions used in such passages are used elsewhere for temporal, earthly experiences. For example the psalmists used the Hebrew $š^{e^\prime}\hat{o}l$ (sheol) to designate the realm of departed spirits, but also the grave and (figuratively) extreme danger. Psalm 49:15 expresses the hope of deliverance from sheol and of entrance into the presence of God. To the psalmist this may have meant a "hope of glory," but it may also have signified temporal deliverance and continuance in service, for Psalm 30:3 also mentions a deliverance from sheol that David experienced.

A.F. Kirkpatrick notes how easily these passages adapt themselves to a hope in the future life, as indicated by later biblical revelation. "Unquestionably these psalms (Pss. 16–17; 49; 73) do contain the germ and principle of the doctrine of eternal life. It was present to the mind of the Spirit who inspired their authors. The intimate fellowship with God of which they speak as man's highest good and truest happiness could not, in view of the nature and destiny of man and his relation to God, continue to be regarded as limited to this life and liable to sudden and final interruption. It required but a step forward to realize the truth of its permanence, but whether the psalmists took this step is doubtful" (*The Book of Psalms*, pp. xxv-xxvi). If they did take such a step, it was by faith.

The same ambiguity applies to the messianic psalms. With the knowledge of full revelation in Jesus Christ, one can look back to the Psalms, in fact to the entire Old Testament, and see that they often speak of Christ (cf. Luke 24:27). Yet to Old Testament believers, the full meanings of these passages were not often evident. On the one hand a psalmist described his own suffering or triumph, and on the other hand those expressions, which may have seemed extravagant for the psalmist's actual experience, later became true of Jesus Christ. Looking back one can say, with Delitzsch, "For as God

the Father molds the history of Jesus Christ in accordance with His own counsel, so His Spirit molds even the utterances of David concerning himself, the type of the Future One, with a view to that history" ("Psalms," in *Commentary on the Old Testament in Ten Volumes*, 5:307).

Typology is thus a form of prophetic statement. It differs from prophecy in that it may be discerned as typological only after its fulfillment is known. Once this antitype is revealed, one may look back and see that certain expressions and images have meanings besides the historical experience. The New Testament writers drew heavily on the Psalms to express many aspects of the person and work of Jesus, the Messiah. As the anointed Davidic King par excellence, Jesus is the great Antitype of the messianic psalms, those psalms that have the king in the foreground. Expositors must exercise caution, however; they must recognize that not *all* the contents of messianic psalms apply to Christ (i.e., not all the parts are typological). Therefore one must remember that these psalms had a primary meaning in the experience of the authors. The analysis of the historical, contextual, and grammatical meaning of the text should precede the analysis of the New Testament application to Jesus.

Many commentators have made some use of Delitzsch's five types of messianic psalms ("Psalms," pp. 68-71).

1. Purely prophetic psalms. This category probably applies to Psalm 110 which refers to a future Davidic King who would be the Lord. The New Testament (Matt. 22:44) identifies this King as Jesus Christ, not any other Davidic king.

2. Eschatological psalms. Psalms 96–99, the so-called enthronement psalms, among others, describe the coming of the Lord and the consummation of His kingdom. Though they do not refer to a Davidic king, Scripture intimates that they will be fulfilled in the second coming of Christ.

3. Typological-prophetic psalms. In these psalms the writer describes his own experience with language that goes beyond that experience and becomes historically true in Jesus (e.g., Ps. 22).

4. *Indirectly messianic psalms.* These psalms were written for a contemporary king or for royal activities in general. But their ultimate fulfillment is in Jesus Christ (Pss. 2; 45; 72).

5. *Typically messianic psalms.* These psalms are less obviously messianic. The psalmist in some way is a type of Christ (cf. 34:20), but other aspects of the passage do not apply. Perhaps, in this case Jesus and the apostles were applying familiar psalmic expressions to their experiences (e.g., 109:8 in Acts 1:20).

Certainly the language of the Psalms expresses the hopes and the truths of the faith in a most memorable way, not only as they point to Christ but also as they reflect the struggles of the faithful. The Psalms have served God's people down through the ages as the inspiration for and often the instrument of praise to God. But they have also brought comfort and hope to individual souls in their times of greatest needs, teaching them how to pray, and giving them the confidence of answered prayers and a renewed trust in their Lord. Often the Psalms change dramatically from the pouring out of a lament to a description of the answer, as if it had already happened. This expressed the psalmists' confidence that God would answer their prayers. So sure were they of God's answers that they praised the Lord in detail in anticipation of the victories. Only through genuine faith can a believer find assurance of answered prayer while praying. The psalmists had such assurance, for their praising accompanied their praying.

OUTLINE

COMMENTARY

I. Book I (Pss. 1–41)

Psalm 1

Psalm 1 is a fitting introduction for the Psalter in that it summarizes the two ways open to mankind, the way of the righteous and the way of the wicked. It may be classified as a wisdom psalm because of its emphasis on these two ways of life, the use of the similes, the announcement of blessing, and the centrality of the Law for fulfillment in life. The motifs in this psalm recur again and again throughout the collection.

The psalm describes the blessed man who leads an untarnished and prosperous life in accord with the Word of the Lord, and contrasts him with the ungodly who shall perish.

A. The blessed man (1:1-3)

1:1. With three trilogies of expressions the psalmist described the life of the **blessed** man: he **does not walk . . . stand** or **sit** in the **counsel . . . way** or **seat** of **the wicked** (ungodly), **sinners,** or **mockers** (scorners). With each parallel unit the expression becomes more intense. This signifies a progression from a casual influence of ungodly people to collusion with them in their scorn against the righteous. One who is **not** characterized by this evil influence is "blessed," that is, he is right with God and enjoys the spiritual peace and joy that results from that relationship.

1:2. A godly person is influenced not by unrighteous people but by his meditation on the Word of God. Such meditation necessarily involves study and retention. This is possible only if he has a desire to do so, here referred to as a **delight.** The psalmists found direction, not drudgery, from **the Law of** God.

1:3. For all who take their delight in living by God's Word, there is prosperity. Under the image of a fruitful **tree,** the psalmist declared that **whatever** the righteous do will prosper (cf. 92:12-14). Two qualifications need to be noted. First, the **fruit,** that is, the prosperity, is produced **in** its **season** and not necessarily immediately after planting. Second, what the godly person does will be controlled by the Law of God (1:2). So if a person meditates on God's Word, his actions will be godly, and his God-controlled activities will prosper, that is, come to their divinely directed fulfillment.

B. The wicked (1:4)

1:4. In strong contrast with a blessed person (v. 1) is an ungodly person. The

Hebrew word *rāšā'* is often translated **wicked** (cf. vv. 1, 5-6) but that may connote gross evil. People described by *rāšā'* are not in covenant relationship with God; they live according to their passions. They are not godly. They may do kind and charitable deeds, but God's evaluation of them is that they are without eternal merit.

The psalmist compared them to **chaff,** the worthless husks of the grain blown **away** by **the wind** in the process of winnowing. Such is the contrast with the fruitful (cf. v. 3), valuable, righteous person.

C. The judgment (1:5-6)

1:5. On the basis of the contrast between the godly and **the wicked,** the psalmist wrote that God will separate **the righteous** from the wicked **in the judgment.** The righteous are those who are related by covenant with the Lord, who live by His Word, who produce things of eternal value. God will divide the righteous and sinners as a man separates wheat from tares.

1:6. The basis for this judgment is the Lord's knowledge. The first half of the verse, **The LORD watches over** (lit., "knows") **the way of the righteous,** is best understood by the antithetical parallelism, **the way of the wicked will perish.** Salvation in the day of judgment is equated with being known by the Lord (cf. Matt. 7:23). In Psalm 1:6 "the way of the righteous" is contrasted with "the way of the wicked." "The way" means one's whole manner of life including what directs it and what it produces. The worthless life of the ungodly will not endure.

Psalm 2

This psalm is familiar to students of the New Testament by virtue of its relevance for Christ. However, the passage was a royal psalm in the Old Testament and therefore was used by the Davidic kings. (Other royal psalms are 18, 20–21, 45, 72, 89, 101, 110, 132, 144.) Its contents describe a celebration at the coronation despite opposition by rebellious people in surrounding territories. In a word, the psalmist exhorted the pagan nations to abandon their rebellious plans against the Lord and His anointed king and to submit to the authority of the Son whom

God has ordained to rule the nations with a rod of iron. (As indicated in Acts 4:25, Ps. 2 was written by David.)

A. The rebellion of the nations (2:1-3)

2:1-3. The first three verses express the psalmist's amazement at the plans of **the nations** to overthrow the Lord and **His Anointed One** (*māšîaḥ,* "Messiah," which in Gr. is *christos,* the Christ). Every king anointed by a prophet was a "messiah," an anointed one. If he obeyed God his rule had the authenticity of God's election and the support of God's power. This often made the plans of other nations futile.

Verse 1 expresses the psalmist's amazement in the form of a rhetorical question. He cannot believe "the nations" would **plot** something destined to fail. These earthly **kings** actually were taking a **stand . . . against the LORD** (v. 2) when they stood against His Anointed One.

Verse 3 records the nations' resolution: they wished to be free of the political control of this king. Their expression describes their bondage to this king as if they were tied down. This they could not tolerate.

B. The resolution of the Lord (2:4-6)

2:4. The psalmist turned from his description of the nations (vv. 1-3) to portray the Lord's response to their plan. In a bold description he envisioned God laughing at it. **The LORD** sits **enthroned** (cf. 9:11; 22:3; 29:10; 55:19; 102:12; 113:5; Isa. 6:1) high **in heaven** and discerns how foolish is their plan to oppose Him. The description is anthropomorphic; God's reaction is stated in human terms.

2:5-6. Based on His contempt for their evil plan God will speak in **His** burning **wrath** against them. Probably verse 6 summarizes what He says, for His resolution to install His **king** in Jerusalem will be the end of their rebellion. **Zion,** referred to 40 times in the Book of Psalms, was originally a Canaanite city conquered by David (2 Sam. 5:7). Later Zion referred to the temple area and then to the entire city of Jerusalem (cf. comments on Lam. 1:4; Zech. 8:3). **Holy hill** is a synonym for the temple mount (cf. Pss. 3:4; 15:1; 24:3; 78:54; Dan. 9:16, 20; Obad. 16; Zeph. 3:11).

When God establishes His king, He

also subjugates those who oppose His king. It was true with David; it will also be true at the end of the age with David's greater Descendant, Jesus Christ.

C. The declaration of the king (2:7-9)

2:7. The psalmist now spoke of God's affirmation of the king to show by what right the king rules. **The decree** refers to the Davidic Covenant in which God declared that He would be **Father** to the king, and the king would be His son. So when David became king, God described their affiliation as a Father-son relationship. So the expression "son" took on the meaning of a messianic title.

You are My son (cf. NIV marg.), quoted from the Davidic Covenant (2 Sam. 7:14), is appropriated here by the king to show his legitimate right to rule. **Today** then refers to the coronation day, and the expression "I have begotten you" (NIV marg.) refers not to physical birth but is an extended metaphor describing his becoming God's "son."

2:8. The significance of this adoption of the king as God's anointed son is seen in his **inheritance**. As a son inherits from his father, so the king inherits the kingdom from his "Father." The verse continues the quotation from the Lord's decree, extending an invitation to the king to **ask** for his inheritance, which someday will encompass the **ends of the earth**. People living in these **nations**, including the rebellious nations (v. 1), will be subjugated by the Lord's anointed.

2:9. This subjugation is expressed in harsh terms: he will smash (**dash . . . to pieces**) all rebellious people as he establishes his reign. The imagery is probably drawn from Egyptian execration customs in which the Pharaoh used his **scepter** to smash votive jars (**pottery**) that represented rebellious cities or nations. The Hebrew verbs in the verse—*ra'a'* ("break," NIV marg.) and *nāpaṣ* ("dash to pieces," shatter")—describe a crushing blow for the rebels. The NIV's and LXX's **rule** is similar to "break," but "rule" does not do justice to "shatter" or to the context. The verse describes the beginning of the rule, putting down rebellion.

D. The exhortation of the psalmist (2:10-12)

2:10-11. In view of all that the Lord had determined for His "son," the psalmist exhorted the foolish nations to submit to the king before his wrath was kindled. Many times in the Psalms God is referred to as **King** (v. 6; 10:16; 24:7-8, 10; 29:10; 44:4; 47:2, 6-7; 48:2; 68:24; 84:3; 95:3; 98:6; 99:4; 145:1; 149:2). The psalmist instructed the earthly **kings** to use wisdom and abandon their foolish rebellion (cf. 2:1). They would **be wise** to **serve the LORD with fear and rejoice with trembling.** "Serve," "rejoice," "fear," and "trembling" describe the religious responses of the righteous in worship. They are to lead lives of submission, not rebellion; lives characterized by fear and trembling, not arrogance; lives filled with exultation, not the gloom of oppression.

2:12. The image here is that of submission to a sovereign: **Kiss the son!** Unusual in the verse is the apparent use of *bar*, an Aramaic word for son. Therefore the versions translate it differently. Jerome rendered it, "Give pure (*bar* is a Heb. word for pure) worship," or "Worship in purity," rather than translating the word as "son." However, in an address to the nations an Aramaic term was not out of place. Moreover, "kiss" pictures homage (cf. 1 Kings 19:18; Hosea 13:2). At any rate it is clear that the psalmist is telling the earth's kings to submit to the Lord and to His anointed son, Israel's king.

The urgency of their submission is expressed by the suddenness of **his wrath.** It is not immediately clear whether this wrath is the Lord's or the king's. The nearest antecedent is the king (the son) who will smash opposition (Ps. 2:9). However, in the psalm the two persons are inseparable; a person serves the Lord (v. 11) by submitting to his *son* (v. 12). If the nations' kings do not submit, the king will destroy them, because the Lord in **angry** opposition to their plans has decreed that His son will have the throne.

The final note of the psalm expresses blessing for those **who take refuge in Him.** (The thought of taking refuge in God occurs many times in the Pss.) Again, to submit to the son is to take refuge in the Lord's anointed, and therefore in the Lord as well. Only in the son is there safety from the wrath of God.

The psalm is rich in New Testament application. Reflecting on how the leaders of Israel crucified Jesus, the Messiah,

Peter was quick to identify those Jewish leaders with the pagan kings of Psalm 2 (Acts 4:25-26).

The typological significance of the "son" is seen fulfilled in Hebrews 1:5. This coronation psalm is quoted here in referring to the exaltation of Christ at His resurrection (cf. Acts 13:33) and Ascension. By this He is "declared . . . to be the Son of God" (Rom. 1:4), a messianic title. When the Father instructs His Son to ask for His inheritance, then He will bring His Son again into the world (Heb. 1:6). The Second Coming will mean wrath to all who rebel against God and His anointed King, but great joy and refuge for all who by faith submit to God's plan to rule the world through David's greater Son, Jesus Christ. So the title of "son" from the Davidic Covenant (2 Sam. 7:14) ultimately becomes the designation of Jesus Christ as King.

Psalm 3

The superscription of this psalm identifies it as written by David. In Book One (Pss. 1–41) 37 of the 41 psalms (all except 1–2; 10; 33) are ascribed to David. Psalm 3 is said to have been written when he fled from his son Absalom (cf. 2 Sam. 15–18). It is a confident prayer of the king who had fled from the palace and was surrounded by enemies. In spite of innumerable adversaries who were convinced that he had no hope, God's elect, David, found God's safety and protection through the night and thereby had confidence in His ultimate deliverance.

A. Surrounded by enemies (3:1-2)

3:1-2. The psalm begins with David's lament: **many . . . foes** were surrounding him. In fact forces of the opposition had driven him from the palace and were then surrounding him. Their taunt was that he had no hope of being delivered by **God.** This arrogant remark was designed to say that God had abandoned David.

B. Sustained by God (3:3-6)

3:3. In the face of such antagonism, David found comfort in God's character. Using the metaphor of **a shield,** he said that God was the true Source of his protection (in spite of their taunts). The psalmists often spoke of God as a shield

to depict His protection (7:10; 18:2, 30; 28:7; 33:20; 59:11; 84:11; 115:9-11; 119:114; 144:2). David was confident that God would restore him to his throne. The words **lifts up my head** express restoration to dignity and position (see the same idiom in Gen. 40:13, 20; 2 Kings 25:27, KJV).

3:4-5. The reason for David's burst of confidence (v. 3) is expressed in verses 4-5. God had sustained him through the night in the midst of his enemies, and that protection was a token of the complete deliverance he expected. The Hebrew tenses in these verses are difficult to translate. Though they may be rendered by the English present tense, it is probably better to translate them as past tenses: I cried **to the LORD** and **He** answered **me.** He would have said this the morning after he prayed. (On **His holy hill** see comments on 2:6.) The answer to his prayer was then explained (again in the past tense): I lay **down, and** I slept; I awoke, **because the LORD** sustained **me.**

3:6. On the basis of this deliverance, the psalmist expressed his absence of **fear** over the **thousands** who took their stand **against** him **on every side.**

C. Saved by God (3:7-8)

3:7-8. These verses record David's confident petition for complete deliverance from his enemies. Perhaps David was saying in verse 7b that **God** had always destroyed his **enemies** and therefore he prayed that God would do it again. However, it may be better to understand the verbs as expressions of his confidence—he was so sure that God would destroy them that he wrote as if it had already happened.

The imagery of the destruction is bold. David used terms referring to crushing blows to state that God would utterly destroy his enemies.

His conclusion is didactic. **Deliverance** comes **from the LORD.** God's **people** should pray to Him under similar circumstances, so that they may share this blessing. So the psalm instructs those who are in the midst of danger to trust in the Lord for protection while they sleep (v. 5).

Psalm 4

Bible students have widely recognized that this psalm is closely connected with Psalm 3. The two psalms, based on the similarities in their expression and structure, may have stemmed from the same crisis. If so, then David may have written Psalm 4 after he spent the night in the midst of danger (cf. 3:1, 5-6). The connection between the two psalms is not certain. However, the message of Psalm 4 is as follows: having cried out to God for help, the psalmist warned his enemies not to sin against God by wronging him, because God had set him apart in protective care, a fact that caused him to rejoice in the face of opposition. (On the superscriptions or headings to this psalm and many others, see the comments under "Authorship and Historical Notices" in the *Introduction*.)

A. Call to God (4:1)

4:1. The psalm begins with an introductory cry for **God** to **hear** his prayer. **Give me relief** (an imperative in the NIV) is actually in the perfect tense. God had set the psalmist at large, that is, He had given him relief in the midst of his **distress**. To this God he directed his **prayer**.

B. Warning for the enemies (4:2-5)

4:2. In contrast with the righteous God (v. 1), David's rebels were mere mortals (**men** is lit., "sons of men"). He asked **how long** they would **turn** his **glory into shame** with their rebellion and lies ("lies" [NIV marg.] is preferable to **false gods**). The intrigue of Absalom, if this was in David's mind here, was partly an attempt to tarnish David's reputation (2 Sam. 15:3). The verbs **love** and **seek**, however, point to the desired end and not to the means.

4:3. This verse is the basis for the psalmist's amazement (v. 2) and his advice (v. 4). Because **the LORD** had **set apart** the psalmist in love, He would answer his prayer. David described himself as one of **the godly** (*ḥāsîḏ*), an object of God's covenantal loyal love. In the care of God, David was safe and God would **hear** and respond to his prayers.

4:4-5. The only recourse, then, for the wicked was to abandon their sinful plans and become worshipers of the Lord. Diligent souls searching for the Lord would be led to act properly toward David. They would desist from their opposition, that is, they would **be silent**. **Trust in the LORD** would result in

right (proper) **sacrifices,** offered with a right spirit (cf. Deut. 33:19; Ps. 51:19). If Absalom was in David's mind, then David was referring here to the empty sacrifices by which Absalom and his cohorts sought to enhance their cause (2 Sam. 15:12). A man of faith would yield in obedience to the Lord.

C. Joyous peace in God (4:6-8)

In the face of opposition, David joyfully expressed his peace and security in God.

4:6. This verse probably refers to the **many** discontented people following David. They would follow anyone who could **show** them **good** prospects. David's answer to their question was a prayer for blessing (cf. Num. 6:24-26); that God would cause His **face** to **shine** on them (i.e., bestow His favor; cf. Pss. 31:16; 44:3; 67:1; 80:3, 7, 19; 119:135). God would satisfy their complaint, as He had done so often in Israel's history.

4:7-8. The **joy** and contentment David experienced in trusting in the **LORD** was **greater** than the mirth of the harvest festivities. Even in distress and away from the visible evidence of God's goodness, he enjoyed **peace** and **safety** in his God (on **sleep**; cf. 3:5). True joy and peace depend not on circumstances but on God's protection and provisions (cf. Gal. 5:22; Rom. 14:17).

Psalm 5

This psalm is a prayer of David when he was exposed to danger by unscrupulous enemies. It has been argued that because verse 7 mentions the temple (which Solomon built), David could not have written the psalm. But the Hebrew word used here for temple (*hêḵāl*) is also used of the tabernacle (cf. 1 Sam. 1:9; 3:3). Furthermore the word "house" in Psalm 5:7 can refer to the tabernacle (cf. "house of the LORD" in 23:6; Josh. 6:24; 1 Sam. 1:24) as well as the temple.

In entreating God to hear his morning prayer, David expressed his confidence in drawing near to God (who hates iniquity) and prayed for divine leadership and blessing for the righteous, and destruction for the wicked.

A. Morning prayer (5:1-3)

5:1-3. The psalmist pleaded with God to **hear** (**Give ear. . . . Listen**) his lament as he prayed **morning by morning** (lit., "in the morning") with full **expectation.** "In the morning" is repeated in verse 3 for emphasis. It stresses that his first thoughts each day were prayer.

B. Confidence in God (5:4-7)

5:4-6. The psalmist expressed his confidence in approaching a **God** who hates iniquity (**evil**). An evil person **cannot dwell** with such a God. People who are presumptuous and boastful, who do not shrink from murder or deceit, God hates and will **destroy.** They are totally detestable to Him.

5:7. In contrast with such wickedness David did not extol his own virtues. Rather he stressed God's **mercy** (ḥeseḏ, "loyal love") toward him. **By** this he could approach the tabernacle (cf. comments on **house** and **temple** in the first paragraph under Ps. 5) to worship the Lord **in reverence.** The Hebrew word for **bow down** (often trans. "worshiped," e.g., Ex. 34:8) signifies prostrating oneself, a posture that represents the proper inner attitude toward God in worship. The wicked are arrogant; a worshiper is humble before God.

C. Prayer for guidance (5:8-12)

5:8. David's prayer for guidance is the central idea of verses 8-12. This prayer is for guidance **in . . . righteousness.** Because God is righteous, and because the enemies are wicked (vv. 4-6), David's desire was to follow the path of right conduct (**make straight Your way before me**) and not be numbered among those God hates. The word for **enemies** comes from the verb "to lie in wait."

5:9-10. In view of this present danger, David's prayer turned to a more urgent plea for God to judge his foes. He then cataloged their sins. They were untrustworthy in their words, deceitful in their flattery. They planned **destruction.** What they said (**their throat** is substituted by metonymy for "their words") brought death (**is an open grave**). Apparently their speech was flattering on the surface but vile in its intent (**they speak deceit;** cf. v. 6). For this, David called on God to hold **them guilty.**

5:11-12. The psalm closes with a note of encouragement (**be glad . . . sing for joy. . . . rejoice**) that God blesses and

protects **those who love** Him. Singing is a natural way to praise the Lord; this is the first of more than 70 references to singing in the Psalms. **The righteous** are those who love His **name.** The Lord's "name" (mentioned more than 100 times in the Pss.) refers to His character and attributes revealed to mankind. Here the manifestation of His name means **protection** and **favor as with a shield** (cf. 3:3).

Psalm 6

The servant of the Lord, being reproved by the chastening rod, petitioned God for deliverance. Finding assurance that his prayer had been heard, he warned his persecutors to depart for they were about to be put to shame.

This is one of the penitential psalms. David had been suffering from some illness that brought him near death. However, it is difficult to associate this psalm with any known event in his life.

A. Prayer for relief from suffering (6:1-3)

6:1. In his introductory cry David pleaded that God would stop chastening him in His anger. In Hebrew the words **not . . . in Your anger** precede the words **rebuke me,** and "not" **in Your wrath** comes first in the second line. The forward position of these words emphasizes the manner of the chastening. If God's wrath against David were to continue, he could not survive.

6:2. David's prayer was then expressed positively. He wanted the Lord to relieve him of his sufferings (**be merciful . . . heal me**) because he was in extreme pain. Bones denotes one's whole physical structure, the person himself. To say that one's **bones are in agony** is to say emphatically that his body is wracked with pain. This is often mentioned in the Psalms (31:10; 32:3; 38:3; 42:10; 102:3, 5).

6:3. The words in this verse are highly emotional. The question **how long?** is unfinished because of his intense frustration. (Cf. "How long?" in 13:1-2; 35:17; 74:10; 79:5; 80:4; 82:2; 89:46; 94:3; 119:84.) He longed for God's healing.

B. Prayer for deliverance (6:4-5)

6:4. In his earnest prayer for deliverance, David gave two reasons why God should answer. One is that the Lord should rescue him **because of** His **unfail-**

ing love. God had shown Himself again and again to be abundant in loyal love (ḥeseḏ), so David pleaded for deliverance on the basis of God's character.

6:5. David said the second reason the Lord should turn to him is because of the absence of **praises** (tôḏâh) in **the grave.** If he died because of his illness, he then could not praise God for delivering him from it. So David reasoned that if God desired someone to stand in the sanctuary and proclaim that God delivered him, then God would have to do so.

C. Lament over illness (6:6-7)

6:6-7. David offered his lament proper. Using hyperbolic language he called attention to the severity of his suffering. Throughout the **night** he suffered in agony. His health was wasting away and he was in **sorrow,** apparently **because of** his enemies. If God did not deliver him, he would die; then people would know that his **foes** were God's chastening rod.

D. Assurance of restoration (6:8-10)

6:8-10. Turning to his adversaries David exhorted them to depart **from** him, for he was confident that God had **heard** his prayer and would deliver him. His final prayer was that all those who persisted as his **enemies** be put to shame. He wanted the dismay and **disgrace** he felt at their hands to be turned **back** on them (cf. 40:14; 7:2).

Through the agony of suffering, the righteous can be confident that God will hear their **weeping** and answer their prayers for deliverance.

Psalm 7

In praying for deliverance from his slanderous enemies, the psalmist solemnly affirmed his innocence and appealed to the righteous Judge of the earth to vindicate him by judging the wicked.

The superscription refers to David's experience with "Cush, a Benjamite," referred to only here in the Bible. The song comes from a time David was hunted by Saul's men (1 Sam. 22:8; 24:9; 26:19). Šiggāyôn ("**shiggaion**") may mean a poem written with intense feeling.

A. Prayer for intervention (7:1-2)

7:1-2. David confidently prayed for deliverance **from** his enemies who were about to **tear** him to pieces **like a lion** (cf.

10:9; 17:12; 22:13, 21; 35:17; 57:4; 58:6). He knew that if God did not **rescue** him, **no one** could. Psalm 7:2 has the first of many occurrences in the Psalms of the word "rescue."

B. Protestation of innocence (7:3-5)

7:3-5. David solemnly affirmed that there was no iniquity in his **hands.** These verses are framed in the expressions of an oath. **If I have done this . . . if I have done evil . . . then let my enemy pursue and overtake me.** In view of his prayer for deliverance, this must be taken as a solemn assertion of his integrity.

Verse 4 seems to express his enemy's slanderous charge that he had "done evil to" one **who** was **at peace with** him, robbing him **without cause.**

So David invoked death by his enemy's hand if he were guilty as they charged. To **sleep in the dust** means to be dead and buried (cf. Dan. 12:2). It does not mean unconscious existence in death. It simply suggests that a dead person appears to be asleep (cf. 1 Thes. 4:13).

C. Appeal for vindication (7:6-9)

7:6-7. David appealed to God, the righteous Judge of all the earth, to vindicate his cause. The words **arise . . . rise up,** and **awake** are meant to prompt **God** to act in **justice** before **the assembled** congregation.

7:8-9. In verse 8 the verb **judge** means "vindicate," for David pleaded for judgment that would reveal his own **righteousness** and **integrity.** He also pleaded that the omniscient **righteous** Judge would **end the violence of the wicked and make the righteous secure.** Understandably the prayer of the righteous often is for God to set things right on earth. **Most High** is the first of 23 occurrences of this title of God in the Psalms; it occurs 3 times in this psalm (vv. 8, 10, 17), though the Hebrew words differ slightly. "Most High" speaks of God's exalted, sovereign position in heaven.

D. Description of God's justice (7:10-17)

7:10-11. David described how **God,** his **Shield** (cf. comments on 3:3), in saving **the upright in heart,** brings direct judgment on the wicked. Because **God is**

a righteous Judge (cf. 9:8), He is angry every day. Obedient believers can be comforted in the fact that people's wickedness does not go unnoticed. But they can also be advised that vengeance belongs to the Lord; He will repay (cf. Deut. 32:35; Rom. 12:19; Heb. 10:30).

7:12-13. Like a warrior God prepares His deadly weapons for the wicked. Swords, bows (v. 12), and arrows (v. 13) often provide the imagery for God's decree of judgment that will destroy the wicked.

7:14-16. Next David stated how God traps the wicked with their own plans. If someone conceives trouble, it will not produce its intended results. Rather the evil scheme will be turned back on the plotter (cf. pit in 9:15; 35:8; 57:6; Prov. 26:27). This is retribution from God, for the punishment fits the crime (an eye for an eye, a tooth for a tooth, etc., Ex. 21:24-25). Jesus said that they "who draw the sword will die by the sword" (Matt. 26:52).

7:17. The psalm ends with David's vowing to thank and praise God for His righteousness, a righteousness yet to be manifested in the psalmist's experience. So even though he was slandered and attacked, David wholeheartedly trusted in his righteous LORD (the Most High; cf. comments on v. 8) for vindication and equity.

Psalm 8

In this psalm David marveled that the glorious Lord of heaven, whose name is excellent, should graciously use people in the earth's dominion. The passage considers the dignity of mankind as God's representative on earth, without noting the Fall's consequence of chaos and rebellion.

A. The Lord's majesty (8:1)

8:1. The beginning and ending of the psalm (vv. 1, 9) give the same exclamation of God's majestic . . . name. The name, that is, the revealed character of God, is exalted above all Creation. The word majestic suggests splendor and magnificence. It is a fitting note of praise for the Lord of Creation.

The vocative O LORD, our Lord is important in this idea. Addressing God by His personal name Yahweh ("LORD"), David then identified Him as "our Lord"

('ăḏōnay), the Sovereign or Master. "Lord" stresses God's dominion over His Creation.

The Hebrew of the last part of verse 1 is difficult. Though the text has an imperative verb, most translations (including the NIV) apparently take it as an infinitive and render it as a statement about God's majesty: You have set. It describes His exaltation (glory) as being high above the heavens.

B. The Lord's strength (8:2)

8:2. David marveled that God uses strength (cf. NIV marg.) from children to silence His enemies (and the foe and the avenger). (The NIV translates 'ōz, "strength" by the word praise because "strength" here may indicate "praise for [God's] strength"; cf. Matt. 21:15-16.) The idea is that the Lord has ordained that the weakest shall confound the strong (cf. 1 Cor. 1:27). Mankind, even weak children and infants, represents the strength of God in the earth.

C. The Lord's Creation (8:3-8)

David now examined the marvelous theme that God should graciously entrust his dominion to man.

8:3-4. The psalmist first observed the great work of Creation (including the heavens . . . the moon, and the stars) as God's finger work, and then was amazed that finite man (the Heb. for man here is 'ĕnôš, "mortal, weak man") should have such a responsibility over it. The rhetorical questions in verse 4 emphasize that man is an insignificant creature in the universe (cf. 144:3). Yet God cares for him immensely. It amazed David that the Lord of the universe even thinks about man.

8:5. God's creation of man is described as one of power and dignity, for he was made . . . a little lower than God ('ĕlōhîm; cf. NIV marg.). The KJV followed the Septuagint in translating this word "angels." The NIV has chosen heavenly beings, which follows the same interpretation. Though in some cases 'ĕlōhîm may refer to angels, this is not its main meaning. Man was created as God's own representative on earth, over the Creation, but lower than God. David was amazed that God should exalt finite man to such a place of honor.

Hebrews 2:6-8 quotes this psalm to

contrast man's failure with his exalted destiny. Jesus Christ, the Son of Man, is the last Adam (1 Cor. 15:45, 47); all things will be subjected to Him when He comes to fulfill God the Father's intended plans for the Creation.

8:6-8. David reflected on man's position as God's representative in His Creation. After God made Adam and Eve, He commanded them to have dominion over all the earth (Gen. 1:28). All living creatures were to be **under** them. But because of sin that dominion has never been fully realized. In fact it was through a subordinate, the serpent, that man rebelled against God's order.

D. The Lord's majesty (8:9)

8:9. The psalm closes with the same expression of praise for God's **majestic . . . name** with which it began (cf. v. 1). God's majesty has been displayed in His care and design for finite man.

Psalm 9

Psalms 9 and 10 may have originally been one psalm, as they are in the Septuagint. They are connected by their form in the Hebrew, for nearly each stanza (approximately every other verse) begins with a successive letter of the Hebrew alphabet. Also the two psalms have similar wording. For example, "in times of trouble" is found in 9:9 and 10:18, and in only two other passages in the Psalms. Also each of the two psalms closes with an emphasis on mortal men (9:20; 10:18). Finally each psalm mentions "the nations" (9:5, 15, 17, 19-20; 10:16).

Yet there is warrant for the two psalms being separate. Psalm 9 is a triumphant song of thanksgiving, while Psalm 10 is a complaint and prayer about godless men in the nation. Because Psalm 9 is complete in itself, it is better to regard Psalm 10 as a related psalm.

Psalm 9 is a song of thanksgiving for vindication. Ascribed to David, this psalm is set "to the tune of 'The Death of the Son.' " What that means is unknown. In the psalm David praised the Lord for manifesting His righteousness in judging wicked nations, and for being a true and eternal Judge in whom the afflicted may trust. He then prayed that God would give him further cause for praise by seeing his affliction and removing it from him.

A. Praise: Manifestation of righteousness (9:1-12)

9:1-2. The first portion of the psalm (vv. 1-12) speaks of God as the true Judge and the Hope of the afflicted. In view of this, David resolved to **praise** Him wholeheartedly, to **tell of** His **wonders,** to be joyful in God, and to **sing** to Him. "Wonders" (*niplā'ôt*, "things extraordinary or surpassing") is used frequently of God's works in the Psalms.

9:3-6. The cause for David's praise is recorded in these verses. The Lord manifested His righteousness (v. 4) by vindicating David's cause. His **enemies** were turned **back** (v. 3), **rebuked,** and **destroyed** (v. 5). Even the **name** of **the nations** (also mentioned in vv. 15, 17, 19-20) was **blotted out.** Such a description vividly portrayed their defeat—not even their name would be perpetuated. **Memory of them** was destroyed after **their cities** were demolished (v. 6).

All of this, David wrote, was evidence that God **upheld** his **cause,** and rules **righteously** from His **throne** (v. 4).

9:7-10. On the basis of the deliverance spoken of in verses 3-6, David declared that **the Lord** is a true and eternal Judge and a Fortress for the afflicted. The psalmist's praise at first was directed to **the Lord** and His eternal reign over the earth (vv. 7-8). Then David applied that truth to people's needs. The afflicted and **the oppressed,** those who are most frequently ignored or abused by human judgment, are championed by the righteous Judge. The Lord God is their **Refuge** and **Stronghold in times of trouble.** The word *miśgob,* used twice in verse 9 and translated both "refuge" and "stronghold," suggests security and protection in a high, safe place of retreat. *Miśgob,* one of several words used in the Psalms to speak of security and safety in God, is translated "stronghold" in Psalms 18:2; 144:2, and "fortress" in 46:7, 11; 48:3; 59:9, 16-17; 62:2, 6; 94:22. Another Hebrew word translated "refuge" in the Psalms is *maḥseh,* "shelter from danger." It is used in 14:6; 46:1; 61:3; 62:7-8; 71:7; 73:28; 91:2, 9. Still another word translated "refuge" in the Psalms in the NIV is *mānôs* ("a place to flee to," 59:16; 142:5). Knowing of God's security and protection, His own can **trust** Him.

9:11-12. This praise section (vv. 1-12) closes with the psalmist's exhortation to the people, especially **the afflicted** whom God **does not ignore** (v. 12), to **sing praises to the** LORD (cf. v. 2) and tell **what He has done** (v. 11).

B. Prayer: Aid for the afflicted (9:13-20)

9:13-14. In view of God's past deliverances, David now called on God to respond to his affliction and give him reason to praise. The psalmist asked the LORD to notice **how** his **enemies persecute** him. In danger of dying, he called on God to rescue him **from the gates of death** (cf. Job 38:17; Ps. 107:18; Isa. 38:10). If delivered, he would then praise the Lord **in the gates of the Daughter of Zion** (i.e., the tabernacle in Jerusalem).

9:15-16. David's prayer was supported by his confident trust in **the** LORD. In verses 15-18 David rehearsed the reputation God has for destroying the wicked who afflict the needy. Verse 15 may have been written in anticipation of the enemy's destruction as is done in the "confidence" sections in various psalms. If so, David foresaw how the wicked would fall **into** their own **pit** (cf. 7:15) and **net** (cf. 35:8; 57:6). Nevertheless the Lord's **justice** is well **known**, for the evil that **the wicked** devise returns on them.

9:17-18. The destiny of **the wicked**, who **return to the grave** (šᵉʾôl, sheol), is contrasted with **the needy** and **afflicted** (cf. vv. 9, 12), who **will** see their **hope** fulfilled. The expression **forget God** is sometimes contrasted in the Psalms with the word "remember," a term that signifies faith and prayer. Those who reject and ignore the Lord have no hope.

9:19-20. The psalm closes with the prayer that the LORD would **arise** and put mortal **man** (ʾĕnôš; cf. comments on 8:4) to fear in a terrifying judgment. Such a destruction would make the wicked realize that **they are but** human (ʾĕnôš) and that they cannot oppress those who trust in the LORD.

Psalm 10

The idea of praise for righteous vindication, clearly evident in Psalm 9, is less pronounced in Psalm 10. This is a prayer for God not to delay His help for the afflicted. The psalmist described the awesome power of the wicked in their impiety toward God and their lurking against the helpless. Then he pleaded with God to arise and avenge the oppressed by breaking the wicked.

A. Description of the wicked (10:1-11)

10:1. The first part of the psalm is a forceful description of the wicked's vicious power. But at the beginning the writer turned his complaint to the Lord, who seemed to be uninterested in the plight of the oppressed. The fact that the wicked may triumph caused the psalmist to ask why the LORD was hiding Himself from the **trouble** (cf. "why" twice in v. 13). The question is a bold expression of the true feelings of oppressed people who cry out for help.

10:2-7. In these verses David delineated the character of the oppressor. Full of pride (**arrogance**, v. 2, and **boasts**, v. 3) **the wicked man** afflicts **the weak** and speaks abusively of **the** LORD (cf. v. 13). The wicked person is confident (**pride**, v. 4, **haughty**, v. 5), and has **no room for God** or God's **laws.** Such a person is convinced that he cannot be moved from his wicked ways. He thinks he can continue undisturbed in his prosperity (v. 5) and happiness (v. 6; cf. 73:3). His words are deceitful and destructive (10:7). The clause **trouble and evil are under his tongue** means that the words he speaks will cause calamity.

10:8-11. Here the psalmist described the wicked as lurking (**lies in wait** occurs three times in vv. 8-9) **in secret** places **like a lion** (cf. comments on 7:2) to attack **his** helpless (cf. 10:12) victims, and to drag **them off** as a fisherman does with **his net.** This imagery of a lion and a fisherman suggests cunning men waiting to attack. The afflicted (i.e., the righteous) **are crushed** by the wicked. Since God may not immediately rescue them, the wicked person is convinced that **God** does not care for or see the righteous.

B. Appeal for vengeance (10:12-18)

10:12-15. Making an earnest cry for vengeance, the psalmist called on **God** to **arise** (cf. 9:19) and help **the helpless** (cf. 10:9). One reason for this request is that **the wicked** should not be allowed to despise **God** (cf. v. 3) and to think he can get away with his actions (cf. **why** in v. 1). The Lord should be motivated to respond because the afflicted trust **God** who sees **trouble and grief** and is their **Helper** (v. 14). The psalmist's specific request was that God would punish the **wicked** (v. 15). Here the imagery is again graphic: to **break** one's **arm** means to destroy his power. If God so judges the wicked by such a destruction, then they would be called **to account for** their deeds. The psalmist would then no longer be able to say that God does not see his deeds (cf. v. 13) or care for the afflicted.

10:16-18. The psalm closes with an expression of confidence that the writer's prayer has been heard. Here as well as in Psalm 9 the psalmist declared that the LORD is sovereign (cf. 9:7) and that those in **the nations** (cf. 9:5, 15, 17, 19-20) who oppose Him **will perish** (cf. 9:3, 5, 15). The psalmist was sure that the LORD hears the **cry** of **the afflicted** and defends their cause, so that the wicked—who are mere mortals ('*ĕnôš*; cf. 9:20 and comments on 8:4)—will not **terrify** them anymore.

Faith that God defends the afflicted and the needy against the tyranny of the wicked was a comfort to the psalmist and the basis for his prayer.

Psalm 11

The historical setting of this psalm is unknown; apparently David was in desperate straits with his life in danger. The temptation to run from danger challenged his confidence in God. The psalm's message is as follows: faced with the temptation to flee at a time when lawful authority was being destroyed, the psalmist held fast to his faith in the Lord, who will ultimately destroy the wicked whom He hates and deliver the righteous whom He loves.

A. Temptation to flee (11:1-3)

11:1. The psalm begins with the psalmist's repudiation of the temptation to **flee** from danger. David marveled at this suggestion from the fainthearted because it defied his faith in the Lord. His initial declaration, **In the LORD I take** (or have taken) **refuge,** counteracts their suggestion.

The fainthearted advised David to flee **like a bird to** a **mountain** where he would be safe. But instead he fled to the Lord for safety.

11:2. This temptation came because **the wicked** were out to destroy the righteous, including David. The wicked **bend** their **bows** to fasten **the strings** on them, and then place **their arrows** on the strings **to shoot** in secrecy (cf. 10:8-9) **at the upright.** It may be that a literal attack is in view, but more likely the bows and arrows denote slanderous words that destroy, as is often true in the Psalms.

11:3. If **the foundations** of society are overthrown, **what can the righteous do?** These foundations refer to the Law and the order of society based on the Lord's rule. The temptation from the fainthearted, then, was based on a fear that the nation might crumble. Their view was experiential and earthward. David's view was higher.

B. Confidence in the Lord (11:4-7)

11:4. David contrasted the problem on earth with the exalted position of **the LORD** in heaven. "What can the righteous do?" the fainthearted had asked (v. 3). David responded that the righteous can trust in the real Source of secure government—**the LORD,** whose **throne** is exalted in the heavens, **His holy temple,** far from the dissimulation of the wicked. Because the Lord is sovereignly ruling over the earth, He sees and thoroughly investigates the activities of **the sons of men** (cf. 33:13-14). **He observes** is literally, "His eyes see," and **His eyes** is literally, "His eyelids." Eyelids normally contract when examining closely. This bold anthropomorphism stresses the precise omniscience of God.

11:5. God **examines** (tests, refines) **the righteous,** but He hates **the wicked and** people **who love violence.** God is opposed to all who choose wickedness and violence in opposition to His will.

11:6. The psalmist then looked to a sudden and swift judgment **on the wicked. He will rain** could also be translated, "May He rain." **Burning sulfur** is reminiscent of God's judgment on Sodom and Gomorrah (Gen. 19:24). **Fiery coals** may possibly be translated "snares." If so, the psalmist was anticipating a fitting judgment for the wicked—they would be trapped. At any rate **scorching** judgment is their destiny.

11:7. In contrast with God's judgment on the wicked (v. 6), **the LORD,** who **is righteous . . . loves justice** (lit., "righteousness"). The **upright**—those who by faith trust Him and seek to follow His ways—**will see His face.** This means that the righteous are admitted to His presence and enjoy His blessings.

Psalm 12

This psalm expresses David's confidence in the untarnished words of God that assure him He will deliver those who seek His salvation. This expression of confidence comes in the midst of a culture that oppressed the weak with deception. The setting of the psalm is unknown, but many incidents in the life of David could have prompted such a psalm (cf. 1 Sam. 23:11, 19; 26:19). But the language of the psalm is general enough to fit several situations.

A. Prayer for deliverance (12:1-4)

The psalmist cried out to God (vv. 1-4) for deliverance from the midst of a lying and arrogant people.

12:1-2. His introductory cry laments the fact that **the godly** were apparently extinct. People who showed **faithful** covenant loyalty had disappeared from the land. (The word for "faithful" is ḥāsîd, related to ḥesed, "loyal love or covenant loyalty.") In their place were those who lied and deceived. Their words were dishonest and therefore untrustworthy. The society had become altogether corrupt. There seemed to be no trustworthy, honest people on whom the psalmist could depend.

12:3-4. So the psalmist prayed that **the LORD** would **cut off . . . flattering,** lying **lips.** These people were filled with pride (they were **boastful**), assuming that through propaganda, flattery, and deception they could achieve their goals. Saying, **we will triumph with our tongues,** they assumed they could do as they pleased: **Who is our master?** David wanted God to destroy them and end their arrogant boasting.

B. Assurance of deliverance (12:5)

12:5. The psalmist received assurance that **the LORD** would **arise** and free **the weak and . . . the needy** from **oppression.** God promised to deliver those who trusted in Him **from those who** were maligning **them.**

C. Confidence in God's Word (12:6-8)

12:6. Because of assurance from God that the afflicted would be delivered (v. 5) the psalmist expressed confidence in the untarnished words of God, even though he knew the wicked were all around him.

In contrast with the wicked's words, the Lord's words are pure (**purified**) and true. Their untarnished nature is compared to the process of refining **silver**; it is as if **the words of the LORD** had been **refined . . . seven times,** the number of completeness and perfection. What God says is true (**flawless;** cf. 18:30) and reliable. His words are not tainted with deceit and false flattery (in contrast with the wicked's words, 12:2-3) but are fully dependable.

12:7-8. Therefore the psalmist trusted in God's word that He would **keep** them **safe** in the midst of proud **people** who **strut about** in smug self-confidence, placing a premium on things that are **vile** (zūllût, a word used only here in the OT, means something squandered or worthless). Verse 8 pictures worthless and ruthless **men** who exercise authority and power through deceptive words. Yet God's words, which are true, affirm that such people will be destroyed.

Psalm 13

This psalm records the cry of the afflicted and therefore harmonizes with several of the preceding psalms. Here David rested confidently on the loyal love of the Lord (v. 5), even though he found no immediate deliverance from the oppression of the adversary, God's enemy.

A. Lament over distress (13:1-2)

13:1-2. In a series of rhetorical questions designed to motivate God to answer his prayer, David asked God **how long** (four times in these two verses; cf. comments on 6:3) He would wait before answering. David felt ignored by God and forgotten. Would this continue indefinitely? Wrestling inwardly (**with my thoughts** is lit., "in my soul"), David lamented that he spent **every day** in this distressing situation, that his **heart** was filled with struggles and **sorrow.** As a result of his apparently being forsaken by God, his enemies triumphed **over** him.

B. Petition for deliverance (13:3-4)

13:3-4. David called on the Lord to **look . . . answer,** and rescue him from his situation. **Give light to my eyes** was

David's way of requesting divine wisdom or perspective on his need. He earnestly prayed this lest he **sleep in death** (cf. comments on 7:5; **fall** is lit., "die"), thus bringing triumphant joy to his **enemy**.

C. Confidence in the Lord (13:5a)

13:5a. David expressed his **trust in** the Lord's **unfailing love** (*ḥeseḏ*), the loyal love the Lord has for those who trust in Him. The enemies of David were challenging the faithfulness of God's love to one of his covenant believers.

D. Praise for salvation (13:5b-6)

13:5b-6. The psalmist, assured that his prayer had been heard, resolved to rejoice and **sing to the LORD** for giving him **salvation** and for dealing bountifully with him. (This is the first of several dozen references in the Pss. to God's being **good**.) He fully anticipated the end of his long wait.

Psalm 14

Knowing that the human race is foolish and corrupt, and that the Lord will destroy such people for their actions, the psalmist longed for the establishment of the Lord's kingdom on earth. (See comments on Ps. 53, which is almost identical to Ps. 14.)

A. Appraisal of the human race (14:1-3)

14:1. David affirmed God's indictment on the human race: they are fools. Verse 1 gives a summary description of **the fool** (*nāḇāl*, one who is morally insensitive and impious). A fool believes that **there is no God,** and leads a **corrupt** life. These two statements are related. As a practical atheist (i.e., living his life as if there were no God) he is separated from the wisdom revealed in God's Word. As a result he is corrupt, spoiling whatever he does. His actions **are vile,** that is, he does abominable things that the Lord hates. Without faith **no one** can please God, so **there** are none **who** do **good.**

14:2. The psalmist's evaluation of the human race was based on the Lord's looking **down** to examine people (**the sons of men**). Examples of the Lord's seeing how wicked the race was include Babel (Gen. 11:1-9) and Sodom (Gen. 18:21). The psalmist pictured **the LORD** looking **to see if** anyone had understanding, that is, if **any** were seeking **God.** The

beginning of wisdom is fear of the Lord (Prov. 1:7). Since the fool refuses to accept this fact, he has no understanding.

14:3. In searching for prudent people, God saw that the entire human race had **turned aside** and **become corrupt** (lit., "sour" like milk). This word *'ālaḥ,* which occurs only here and in Job 15:16 and Psalm 53:3, is used in a moral sense. (This word for corrupt differs from the word for corrupt in 14:1.) Consequently God said that not **one** solitary person **does good.** The only hope for the race, the Scriptures teach, is for individuals to turn to the Lord for salvation.

B. Punishment of the wicked (14:4-6)

14:4-6. David revealed the outcome of the struggle between these workers of iniquity and the righteous. He was amazed at the ignorance of **evildoers** who think they can freely **devour** God's **people.** Their wickedness is most pronounced in their vicious attack on His people. They are oblivious to the fact that God will overwhelm them, because in attacking the people of God they are attacking **God.** He is **present in the** midst of His people. So the psalmist foresaw that the wicked will be in great **dread** when the Lord judges them for persecuting His own. They may **frustrate** the lives of God's people (**the poor**) for a time, but those people will be vindicated because they trust in **the LORD . . . their Refuge** (*maḥseh,* "shelter from danger," a word used of the Lord nine times in the Pss: 14:6; 46:1; 61:3; 62:7-8; 71:7; 73:28; 91:2, 9).

C. Longing for the kingdom (14:7)

14:7. David yearned for the establishment of the Lord's kingdom (cf. Matt. 6:10). **The LORD,** when He delivers His nation **Israel** from the presence of the wicked (cf. Rom. 11:26-27), will bring great joy to **His people** (cf. Zeph. 3:14-16). The psalmist was clearly longing for the establishment of God's righteous rule from **Zion** (cf. comments on Ps. 2:6) and for the destruction of the wicked who persist in ungodliness.

Psalm 15

This psalm explains who is worthy to be a "guest" of the Lord. The psalmist delineated the flawless character of one who is fit to worship in the Lord's sanctuary.

A. The question: Who may abide? (15:1)

15:1. David pondered the matter of **who may dwell in** the Lord's **sanctuary** (the tabernacle), located on the **holy hill,** that is, Zion, the City of David (cf. 2 Sam. 6:10-12, 17 and comments on Ps. 2:6). The question is concerned with who was eligible to be a "guest" of the Lord and **live** in the place where His presence rested. It was a spiritual question: who can draw near to God and worship in His dwelling place?

B. The answer: The righteous may abide (15:2-5)

15:2a-b. The question in verse 1 is answered in summary fashion first (v. 2a-b) with two descriptions, and then delineated (vv. 2c-5) with an additional eight. The acceptable person is one **whose walk is** (a) **blameless.** Also his actions are (b) **righteous.** The metaphor of the "walk" is used throughout the Bible for one's pattern of life and conduct (cf. 1:1). "Blameless" (tāmîm) means complete, sincere, or perfect. A blameless person lives in obedience to God and maintains a life of integrity.

His activities are in harmony with God's standards, that is, they are righteous. David thus declared that if someone were to go into the presence of the Lord in Zion, he must be an obedient and righteous servant. The wicked and the hypocritical did not belong in the sanctuary.

15:2c-5a. After the general statement in the first two lines of verse 2, David spelled out what such a flawless person's character is like.

(1) The first characteristic of the righteous is that he **speaks . . . truth** sincerely. He is not like double-minded flatterers (cf. 12:2). (2) A righteous person does not **slander** maliciously. (3) Nor does he harm or (4) discredit **his neighbor.** A neighbor (or friend) is anyone with whom he comes in contact. A blameless individual's remarks do not harm or destroy any neighbor.

(5) Also a righteous person **despises . . . vile** people and **honors** believers **who fear the Lord.** A person who is "vile" (from mā'as, and therefore not the same word for vile in 14:1) is a reprobate, one who is worthless. But one who fears the Lord is living a life of faith and obedience.

(6) A righteous person also **keeps his oath even when it hurts.** Even if he took an oath rashly (Lev. 5:4), he would conscientiously keep his word.

(7) He does not lend **his money** for **usury** (lit., "he does not put the bite on them"). He does not take advantage of one who must borrow. Taking interest from fellow Israelites was forbidden as unbrotherly (Ex. 22:25; Lev. 25:36).

(8) A righteous person **does not** take bribes **against the innocent.** The Law of course forbade this (Deut. 27:25). Instead a righteous person champions the cause of the innocent and the needy.

15:5b. David concluded that one who follows this pattern of life **will never be shaken** (cf. 16:8; 21:7; 30:6; 62:2, 6; 112:6). Not only will he enjoy fellowship in the Lord's presence, but also he will experience divine blessing and security.

The fact that there are 10 descriptions of one who qualifies to abide with the Lord (sincere, righteous, honest, without slander, without doing wrong, without reproaching, distinguishes between good and evil, keeps his oath, does not take interest, does not accept bribes) suggests a comparison with the Ten Commandments (though the two lists do not correspond in every item). Obedience to God's revealed will is the requirement for full participation in the sanctuary.

Psalm 16

This psalm is a celebration of the joy of fellowship that David realized comes from faith in the Lord. The psalm may have been written when he faced great danger in the wilderness or opposition in his reign. Whatever its occasion, David was convinced that because he had come to know and trust the Lord as his Portion in life, he could trust Him in the face of death.

A. The Lord is his Portion in life (16:1-8)

16:1. In verses 1-8 David reviewed how he had come to know and trust in the Lord. Verse 1 seems to summarize the entire psalm: **Keep me safe, O God, for in You I take refuge.** Then David developed the idea of his having taken refuge in the Lord.

16:2. David announced his exclusive trust in **the Lord.** His statement of faith was, **You are my Lord; apart from You I have no good thing** (cf. 34:10; 84:11).

16:3-4. Based on his commitment to the Lord, the psalmist described the society of friends with whom he was identified. He delighted in godly people **(saints) in the land,** whom he considered to be the noble **(glorious) ones.** God had called His people to be a holy nation (Ex. 19:6), and God's servant recognized that such were his company. They were the faithful who served the Lord. The others, **those . . . who run after other gods,** will face **sorrows** and difficulties. David would not endorse their actions, or help them with their vain worship, or even mention the **names** of their gods. His loyalty was with righteous believers.

16:5-6. In direct address to the Lord, the psalmist extolled His blessings. David compared the LORD to a **portion** (cf. 73:26; 119:57; 142:5) allotted to him by inheritance. The Lord was all he needed to satisfy his heart in life. Besides his portion **and** his **cup,** the Lord had **assigned** him **a delightful inheritance. The boundary lines . . . in pleasant places** speak of portions of land measured by line and distributed by **lot.** In other words he compared God's blessings to the best inheritance a person could receive. The Lord had given him a wonderfully full life.

16:7-8. As a result of all this bounty, David praised **the LORD** because He counseled him **at night** (as well as in the daytime) and because He guided him safely. (**Praise** is lit., "bless," which means "to speak well of." This is the first of about two dozen times in the Pss. where the Lord is said to be "blessed," usually trans. "praised" in the NIV.) Because of this David knew that he would **not be shaken** (cf. comments on 15:5b) from his walk of integrity and enjoyment of the blessings he had in the Lord.

B. The Lord will preserve him (16:9-11)

16:9-11. David was assured that the Lord would preserve his life in the face of death. He rejoiced because God enabled his **body** to **rest** securely even when confronted with death. The reason he could rest is that God would **not abandon** him **to the grave, nor . . . let His holy one see decay.** This verse refers to David, who describes himself as God's "holy one," that is, one of God's saints (cf. v. 3). He

took comfort in the fact that God would not, at that time, allow his body to die and decay in the grave. In fact God had caused him to know **the path of life** so he anticipated experiencing further **joy in** God's **presence** (v. 11).

Verses 8-11 were cited by Peter on the day of Pentecost (Acts 2:25-28) and Psalm 16:10b was quoted by Paul at Antioch (Acts 13:35-37) in reference to Christ's resurrection. So the words of David are also typological; they transcended his own experience and became historically true in Christ. Preservation from the decaying grave is the idea behind both David's and Jesus' experiences, but with David it came through a *deliverance* from death, whereas with Jesus it came through a *resurrection* from death.

Death posed no threat to David because he enjoyed great blessing and fellowship with the Lord. God would not permit death and the grave to interrupt that marvelous fellowship. So in a fuller sense this is true of believers today, who having the full revelation about the doctrine of resurrection, can say that even when they die, God will not let death destroy that full fellowship they enjoy with the Lord (2 Cor. 5:8; Phil. 1:23). This expression of faith is possible because Christ conquered death (Luke 24:6) and rose to become the firstfruits of all who sleep (1 Cor. 15:20).

Psalm 17

In this psalm David was conscious of his own integrity while he was surrounded by enemies whose portion was in this life only. He prayed to be kept from the evil world that oppressed him as he looked to a glorious future in the Lord's presence.

The psalm is similar in many ways to Psalm 16, but there is a major difference. In Psalm 16 David was aware of danger in the background, but his faith encouraged him not to fear. In Psalm 17, however, the danger was pressing in on him, so help from the Lord was urgently needed.

A. The prayer of a righteous man (17:1-5)

17:1-2. David asked God to **hear** his **righteous plea,** to **listen to** him, to **give ear to** his **prayer.** This threefold request to God strikes a note of urgency.

This prayer did not come from someone who was unrighteous or hypocritical (one with **deceitful lips**). David avowed his integrity before God, so that God could **see** that he was **right** and would vindicate him.

17:3. In his integrity (vv. 3-5), David maintained that if he were examined (**probe . . . examine . . . test**) by God, he would be found pure. That is because he **resolved . . . not** to **sin**. To live righteously before God, one must resolve in his heart to serve and obey Him.

17:4-5. Moreover, David had **kept** himself separate **from the ways of** those who destroy. His life had been patterned after God's **Word**. He had **held to** God's **paths,** that is, he had followed the way God wished him to live. He had **not slipped** from this path.

B. Prayer for protection from the world (17:6-12)

David prayed to be kept from evil people in the world because they are full of vicious pride.

17:6-7. His prayer was based on God's loyal **love** for him. The Lord's **great** love is revealed by the fact that He saves **those who take refuge in** Him. David, at this point, was taking refuge, so he desired to be shown that great love.

17:8. David prayed that he would be kept in the center of God's watchful care. His two figures of speech in this verse have been most helpful to believers of all ages. **The apple of** the **eye** seems to refer to an eye's pupil, symbolizing one's sight. In other words the psalmist prayed for God's direct and careful attention.

The other figure, **the shadow of Your wings,** is also mentioned in 36:7; 57:1; 61:4, "shelter"; 63:7; 91:4 (cf. Ruth 2:12; Matt. 23:37). This image comes from the animal world, comparing God's protective care to that of a bird with its young. So David was praying for care and protection from the Lord.

17:9-12. The reason for the prayer's urgency is the nature of **the wicked,** which David delineated in an effort to motivate God to action. They tried to destroy David (v. 9); they spoke with callous indifference and pride (v. 10); and they relentlessly pursued him **like a lion** after its **prey** (vv. 11-12; cf. comments on 7:2).

C. The prospect of a glorious future (17:13-15)

17:13-14a. In contrast with David's present persecution by worldly men (vv. 6-12) he looked to the prospects of the future. His urgent prayer for the LORD to **rise up** and deliver him from these wicked people **whose reward** (portion) **is in this life** (v. 14) was a reminder of his present dilemma. Because they did not follow the LORD **. . . this life** was their only hope of enjoyment. They persecuted the righteous in a number of ways, physically and verbally.

In David's prayer he called on God's **sword** to **rescue** him. This may refer to the fact that God at times uses human armies, even of **the wicked,** to punish nations (cf. Isa. 10:5).

17:14b-15. In contrast with these who live for this life and face God's "sword," David anticipated a far greater blessing for himself and others, including satisfied appetites and **wealth for their children. In righteousness,** he wrote, he would **see** God's **face** (cf. 11:7); **when** he awakened, he would **be satisfied with seeing** God's **likeness.** The psalmist was not anticipating death, or an awakening in resurrection from death. Rather he was contrasting the destruction of the wicked, who live their lives without God, with his life, which was lived in God's grace.

Nevertheless the words are appropriate as a description of his enjoyment of God's presence. Though David may have thought of spiritual blessing and God's presence, the words lend themselves nicely to believers today, who with full New Testament revelation can anticipate a far more glorious prospect than they experience in this life.

Psalm 18

The superscription of this psalm credits the words to David after the Lord delivered him from the hand of all his enemies including "Saul." After reviewing all that the Lord was to him David then recorded his deliverance by the Lord and rejoiced in the mercies shown him. This psalm is a song of gratitude for victory by the warrior-king who at last was at peace. The psalm is also recorded in 2 Samuel 22 with slight variations. Perhaps some of the wording in 2 Samuel 22 was changed in this psalm for use in public worship, but this cannot be proved.

A. Description of the character of God (18:1-3)

18:1-3. In his vow to praise God, David multiplied metaphor after metaphor to describe all that the Lord was and had been to him. He expressed his **love** for **the LORD** who had shown mercy to him throughout his many struggles.

David described **the LORD** as a **Rock** (cf. vv. 31, 46) because He provided stability and security for him. About 20 times in the Psalms the Lord is said to be a Rock. David also compared God to a **fortress** (the same Heb. word [$m^e\d{s}\hat{u}\d{d}\hat{a}h$] is used of God in 31:3; 71:3; 91:2; 144:2). "Rock" and "fortress" picture a high place of refuge and defense to which one might flee for protection. To **take refuge** in the LORD is far better than hiding in a man-made fortress or behind a huge rock.

David also compared God to a **shield** (cf. 18:30 and comments on 3:3) and a **stronghold** (*miśgob*; cf. comments on 9:9), both military terms suggesting protection and deliverance from enemies. As **the Horn of** his **salvation** God gave him strength. Animal horns were symbols of strength. They later symbolized rulers (cf. 148:14; Dan. 7:8, 11, 20-21, 24; 8:21-22; Rev. 17:12).

Because the Lord had defended and delivered David from all his **enemies,** He was **worthy of** David's **praise.**

B. Report of the deliverance by God (18:4-29)

In an extended section of praise, David reiterated his sufferings and perils, and also the Lord's great supernatural deliverance.

18:4-5. In verses 4-19 David reported how God supernaturally delivered him. Being in **the cords of death** means that he was in such difficult distress that without divine intervention he would have died. **Destruction overwhelmed** him like a flood (**torrents**). The trappings **of death** were before him, and he was without human resources to save him.

18:6-15. When David **cried to** the LORD, God intervened **from His temple** to **help** him. (God's help is mentioned frequently in the Pss.) David then described this intervention as a tremendous epiphany, or appearance of the Lord. David said that **the earth trembled and quaked . . . because** of God's anger against His and David's enemies (v. 7); **smoke** and **fire came from His nostrils and mouth** (v. 8); **He . . . came down with clouds** (v. 9); **He soared on the wings of the wind** (v. 10); **dark rain clouds** accompanied Him (v. 11); **clouds,** hail, and **lightning** were with Him (v. 12); thunder (the Lord's **voice**; cf. Job 37:2, 4-5) **resounded** (Ps. 18:13); **lightning** bolts (cf. Job 36:30, 32; 37:3, 11; 38:24, 35) like **arrows . . . scattered the enemies** (Ps. 18:14); and the basins **of the sea . . . and the** earth's **foundations** were exposed at His coming (v. 15). This poetic description of God's divine intervention in battle portrays a tremendous storm in which God used many of the awesome phenomena of nature. Such terrible events were understood as expressions of God's judicial wrath (cf. v. 7).

18:16-19. In these verses David explained that by such an intervention the Lord **rescued** him. It was as if David were drowning in the midst of his **strong** enemies, and the Lord **drew** him **out. . . . because He delighted in** him (vv. 16, 19).

Such a dramatic portrayal of divine intervention suggests similarities with the giving of the Law (Ex. 19:16-18). Similar events are recorded in Joshua 10:11; Judges 5:20; and 1 Samuel 7:10. Descriptions like this are also frequent in prophetic visions of divine intervention (e.g., Isa. 29:6; 30:27; 64:1; Hab. 3:3-4).

18:20-24. After describing his deliverance by the Lord, David explained it in terms of his faith in **the LORD** his God. By faith David had kept his integrity (**righteousness,** vv. 20, 24) before God. This deliverance was because God was rewarding David for **the cleanness** (vv. 20, 24) **of** his **hands** (i.e., his life). David attested that he had not turned **from . . . God,** that he walked in God's **ways,** obeyed **His laws** and **decrees,** and **kept** himself **from sin.** God honored His obedient servant with tremendous victories.

18:25-29. By faith, David also understood the nature of the LORD and how He revealed Himself to mankind. God rewards people according to their inner character: faithfulness **to the faithful** (*ḥāsîd,* related to *ḥesed*), blamelessness **to**

the blameless, purity to the pure, but shrewdness to the crooked ('*iqqēš*, "twisted, perverse," a word also used in 101:4; Prov. 2:15; 8:8; 11:20; 17:20; 19:1; 22:5, "wicked"; 28:6). His dealings are always just.

Moreover, God saves the humble (lit., "the poor or afflicted") but defeats the arrogant (eyes that are haughty means a proud look; cf. Ps. 101:5; Prov. 6:17; 30:13). God sets right the affairs of man. For David, this meant that the Lord preserved him alive (kept his lamp burning; cf. Job 18:5-6; 21:17; Prov. 13:9; 20:20; 24:20) from the enemy. With God's help David could advance against and defeat any enemies.

C. Rejoicing in God's blessings (18:30-50)

18:30-31. In the first part (vv. 30-45) of this section of praise David rejoiced over God's character and His benefits to him. God's way, the psalmist said, is perfect and His Word . . . flawless (cf. 12:6; Prov. 30:5). Again (cf. Ps. 18:2) he said God was his Shield (cf. comments on 3:3), Refuge, and Rock (cf. 18:46). God can be trusted for safety and salvation.

18:32-45. Here David described how God prepared him for battle, giving him strength, agility, and efficiency (vv. 32-34); how God gave him victory over his enemies, pursuing, crushing, and destroying them (vv. 35-42), and how God gave him rule over other nations (vv. 43-45; cf. 2 Sam. 8). Because God is perfect (Ps. 18:30) He could make David's way perfect (v. 32). The predominant thought throughout these verses is that David attributed every ability and victory of his to the LORD. Everything he had done and everything he now enjoyed was due to the Lord's enabling.

18:46-50. Consequently David acknowledged the living God (v. 46) and promised to praise Him (v. 49). Proof that the LORD is alive is that He had rescued David from his enemies. As his Rock (v. 46; cf. vv. 2, 31) God was his source of safety and security. The LORD had given His king great victories and had shown His loyal love (*ḥeseḏ*, unfailing kindness) to His anointed servant, David. And God would also give victories to David's descendants.

Psalm 18 is a victor's song of grati-tude to God for all that had been accomplished.

Psalm 19

David was moved by observing that the heavens, under the dominating influence of the sun, declare the splendor of God's handiwork. By comparison, he then described the dominating influence of the Law of the Lord which enlightened him. Then he prayed for complete cleansing so that his life would be acceptable to God. The psalm, therefore, surveys both God's natural revelation and His specific revelation, which prompts a response of self-examination.

The Old Testament frequently joins the description of the Lord as Law-Giver and Creator. Accordingly in the first part of this psalm, '*ēl* ("God") is used (v. 1) to denote His power as the Creator, and in the second part, *Yahweh* ("the LORD") is used (vv. 7-9, 14), the personal name by which He made Himself known as Israel's covenant God.

The psalm may also be polemical against pagan belief. In polytheistic centers, the sun god was the god of justice. In this psalm, the Lord God is the Creator of the heavens, including the sun that pagans worship, and He is the Law-Giver, establishing justice in the earth.

A. Natural revelation of God's glory (19:1-6)

19:1-4b. David announced that the heavens declare the glory (splendor) of God's handiwork. Verse 1 is a summary statement: the majestic Creation is evidence of the even more majestic Creator-God.

The heavens continually (day after day . . . night after night) display the fact that there is a Creator (v. 2). Even though Creation does not speak audibly in words (cf. NIV marg.) its message (voice) goes out to the ends of the earth. The message from nature about the glory of God reaches all nations, and is equally intelligible to them all (cf. Rom. 1:18-20).

19:4c-6. Dominant in the heavens is the sun. Like a bridegroom who excitedly leaves his house on his wedding day, the sun rises; and like a champion runner racing on his course, the sun makes its circuit. These verses do more than speak of nature as a witness to God's glory; they also undermine pagan beliefs, for the same imagery was used of the sun god in ancient Near Eastern literature.

B. Specific revelation from God's Law (19:7-11)

19:7. In verses 7-9 David described the efficacious nature of the Law of the Lord. Just as the sun is the dominant feature of God's natural revelation (vv. 4c-6), so **the Law** was the dominant element in God's specific revelation in the Old Testament.

The **perfect** Law of God (cf. "flawless" in 12:6; 18:30; Prov. 30:5) can change people. It revives **the soul** and the Law's **statutes** can be trusted to make one **wise.**

19:8. The Law's **precepts** give **joy to the heart** and its **commands** enlighten one's **eyes,** that is, brighten his life and guide him. The statutes (v. 7), precepts, commands (v. 8), and ordinances (v. 9) are all specific instructions within the Law. Joy and guidance fill the soul of one who meditates on and follows God's commands.

19:9. Fear is here a synonym for the Law, for its purpose was to put fear into human hearts (Deut. 4:10, kjv). The Law is **pure. . . . sure,** and **righteous.** It was designed to cause believers to obey God and lead **righteous** lives.

19:10-11. David next disclosed his personal reaction to God's perfect Law. He found the statutes desirable and enjoyable. In extolling their value to him, he compared them to gold and honey— **they are more precious than gold,** the most valuable commodity in the ancient Near East, and **sweeter than honey,** the sweetest substance known in the ancient Near East. The Law was not a burden to believers who were trying to please God with their lives. For David, **keeping** God's statutes, which **warned** him of the dangers of folly and sin, brought **reward.**

C. Prayer for cleansing (19:12-14)

19:12-14. Contemplation of the holy Law led David to pray for complete cleansing so that he could live an upright (**blameless**) and acceptable life before God, his **Rock** (cf. 18:2, 31, 46) and **Redeemer.** (On the psalmist's request that his **meditation** be **pleasing** to God; cf. 104:34.) He prayed that he would be forgiven for **hidden faults** and preserved from sinning willfully. For sins committed in ignorance, the Law provided atonement; but for **willful sins,** sins committed with a high hand, there was no ceremonial prescription, though forgiveness was still available if the person repented and confessed (cf. Ps. 51). Therefore he needed the perfect Law and God's enabling to restrain him from such sins.

Psalm 20

This brief chapter is a royal psalm; the king was about to go to war, but before he did he stopped to pray in the sanctuary, where he was joined by the congregation who interceded for him. Having rehearsed the intercessory prayer of the people for their monarch who was praying for victory, the king expressed the assurance he had received from the Lord for an overwhelming victory.

A. The intercession of the people (20:1-5)

20:1-4. In intercessory prayer the congregation prayed in unison that God would **answer** their king's request for victory and protection (v. 1), and **send** him **help from the sanctuary** (the tabernacle), the dwelling place of God (v. 2). They prayed that his **sacrifices** which accompanied his prayer would be acceptable (v. 3), and that his heart's **desire** would be fulfilled (cf. 21:2) and his **plans** would be successful (20:4).

20:5. The assembled worshipers then voiced their confidence that **God** would answer their king's prayers. They anticipated shouting **for joy** over their triumph. Then they repeated their intercession in support of his prayers: **May the Lord grant all your requests.**

B. The assurance of the king (20:6-8)

20:6. The psalmist, who was the king, expressed the assurance he had received: because he trusted in **the Lord** he knew he would have an overwhelming victory.

On the basis of his faith he was convinced that the Lord would answer and save him, God's **anointed.** The Hebrew verb **saves** may be translated "saved." In the Psalms strong confidence is often expressed by the past tense, as if something had already happened. He was certain God would save him.

The deliverance David expected

would be majestic. It would be a triumphant victory by **the saving power of** God's **right hand**—the symbol of power (cf. Ex. 15:6, 12; Pss. 45:4; 60:5; 63:8; 89:13; 108:6).

20:7. In contrast with those who **trust in** military equipment (or in horses, 33:17), David trusted in the Lord. The verb for **trust** is actually "keep in memory or ponder" (*zākar*). Contemplation of the Lord builds confidence in Him.

The object of his faith was **the name of the LORD.** God's "name" is His nature, His reputation and character. David's faith came from meditating and pondering on the known reputation of **God.**

20:8. Because of God's character David envisioned a great defeat of the enemy. He foresaw the certainty of his army's victory.

C. Repeated intercession (20:9)

20:9. The assembled worshipers responded in unison with a prayer for the LORD to demonstrate that assured deliverance by saving **the king** in battle. The request that the Lord would **answer** is at the beginning and ending of the psalm (vv. 1, 9).

Psalm 21

Psalm 21 is closely related to Psalm 20 in its structure and contents. It may be the thanksgiving psalm after the battle for which the prayer in Psalm 20 was made. In Psalm 21 Psalmist David rejoiced in the strength of the Lord who had responded to his faith with an overwhelming victory. David also was encouraged by the faithful who anticipated future victory by the power of God.

A. Rejoicing in the strength of the Lord (21:1-7)

21:1-6. The royal psalmist praised the LORD who displayed His **strength** in battle. Referring to himself in the third person David expressed **his joy in the victories.** He praised God for giving **him the desire of his heart** (cf. 20:4); for giving him good things (cf. 21:6), including **a crown of pure gold** (possibly the crown of an Ammonite king, 2 Sam. 12:30); for answering his prayer **for life**; for **the victories** God had **granted him** along with abundant **blessings** (cf. Ps. 21:5) and **joy.**

21:7. The reason for this great deliverance in answer to prayer is that **the king** trusted in **the unfailing love** (*ḥeseḏ*) **of** the Lord **Most High.** Therefore he knew he was secure (he would **not be shaken**; cf. comments on 15:5).

B. Anticipation of further blessing (21:8-12)

21:8-10. The king was now addressed by the congregation. Because he trusted in **the LORD,** they knew he would defeat his **enemies** convincingly. (On God's **wrath** being like **fire** see 79:5; 89:46; 97:3.) David would inflict a tremendous defeat on his **foes,** the objects of God's "wrath," thus ending **their** hopes of having any **posterity.**

21:11-12. Even **though they** schemed to overthrow the king, they would **turn** in fear from before him. Thus the king, who trusted in the Lord, was assured of future victories.

C. Vow to praise (21:13)

21:13. The congregation vowed to **sing and praise** the **might** and power of the **LORD,** who alone is to **be exalted.**

Psalm 22

The psalmist apparently felt forsaken by God, as he was surrounded by his enemies' scornful persecution. He lamented his tremendous suffering and his desperate struggle with death, pleading with God to deliver him from such a horrible end. Apparently his prayer was answered, for he was able to declare to the elect and to the world that the Lord answered his prayer.

No known incident in the life of David fits the details of this psalm. The expressions describe an execution, not an illness; yet that execution is more appropriate to Jesus' crucifixion than David's experience. The Gospel writers also saw connections between some of the words in this psalm (vv. 8, 16, 18) and other events in Christ's Passion. Also Hebrews 2:12 quotes Psalm 22:22. Thus the church has understood this psalm to be typological of the death of Jesus Christ. This means that David used many poetic expressions to portray his immense sufferings, but these poetic words became literally true of the suffering of Jesus Christ at His enemies' hands. The interesting feature of this psalm is that it does not include one word of confession of sin, and no imprecation against enemies. It is primarily the account of a righteous man who was being put to death by wicked men.

A. Fervent prayer of one who is forsaken (22:1-10)

David, apparently feeling forsaken by God and scoffed at by his enemies, was confident that God would not fully abandon him. Verses 1-10 form the psalmist's general introductory cry out of distress; they include two cycles, one of lament (vv. 1-5) and one of confidence (vv. 6-10).

1. CYCLE ONE (22:1-5)

22:1-2. Though sensing that God had forsaken him (v. 1), the psalmist drew renewed confidence from the fact that God had answered his ancestors' prayers (v. 4). David's initial cry, **My God, my God, why have You forsaken me?** is an expression appropriated by Christ on the cross (Matt. 27:46; Mark 15:34). God, whom David was addressing as "my God," had seemingly forsaken him. David prayed constantly (**by day** and **by night**) but there was no **answer.**

22:3. The confidence he mustered was from the knowledge that God answers prayer. God is **holy,** distinct from all the false gods of the pagans in that He is alive and acts. In fact God is **enthroned** (cf. comments on 2:4) and therefore received **praise** from the Israelites for answered prayer.

22:4-5. David's ancestors, putting **their trust** in the Lord, prayed in their distress and were **delivered** by Him. So David was encouraged to keep on praying.

2. CYCLE TWO (22:6-10)

22:6-8. The psalmist, though **scorned by men,** was convinced that the God of his youth would not abandon him forever. David lamented the fact that men **despised** him. He felt like **a worm,** worthless, defenseless, and treated with utter contempt. **They** hurled **insults** at him (cf. Matt. 27:39, 44), mocking his faith since the LORD was not rescuing **him.** The expressions used in Psalm 22:8 were adapted by those who mocked at Jesus' cross (Mat. 27:42-43), not realizing that they were fulfilling this prophecy and that He was the suffering Messiah.

22:9-10. The psalmist's confidence was drawn from his training as a child. From the very beginning he was trained to trust in the Lord, who had **brought** him **out of the womb.** All his life the Lord had **been** his **God.**

B. Lament of the suffering king (22:11-18)

22:11. David lamented his desperate struggle with death at the hands of inhuman enemies. He summarized his lament with a quick plea that the Lord **not . . . be far** off, since **trouble** was **near** and he was helpless.

1. CYCLE ONE (22:12-15)

Again in two cycles (vv. 12-15 and 16-18; cf. the cycles in vv. 1-5 and 6-10) David described his enemies and his sufferings.

22:12-13. David compared his enemies to cruel and insensitive beasts (**bulls** and **lions**) who would destroy him and then described his agony. **Bulls of Bashan** were well-fed cattle (cf. comments on cows of Bashan in Amos 4:1) east of the Sea of Kinnereth (Galilee). Several other times David spoke of his enemies as lions (cf. Ps. 7:2; 10:9; 17:12; 22:21; 35:17; 57:4; 58:6).

22:14-15. Because of his enemies' attacks, David's strength was sapped **like** poured-out **water,** and his joints were racked. Moreover, like melted **wax** his courage (**heart**) was gone—he had lost his desire to resist. His **strength** was gone and his **mouth** was dry. In his weakness he was at the brink **of death.**

2. CYCLE TWO (22:16-18)

22:16. David again (cf. vv. 12-15) described his enemies and his agony. His enemies tortured him and watched him insensitively. He compared them to **dogs** (cf. v. 20), who in the ancient world were scavengers. Like dogs, his foes (**evil men**) **surrounded** him, waiting till he was dead so they could tear at his limbs. To compare his enemies to dogs was to say that he was almost dead. The words **they have pierced my hands and my feet** figuratively describe such a tearing as if by animals. Of course in the New Testament, these words in reference to Jesus Christ have greater significance (cf. Luke 24:39-40).

22:17-18. After speaking of his enemies (v. 16) the psalmist again described his agony. He was weak and emaciated. His enemies stared at him, considering him as good as dead, so they divided up his **garments,** his last possession (cf. Matt. 27:35).

C. Petition for deliverance from death (22:19-21)

22:19-21. David prayed that the LORD (his **Strength;** cf. 28:7-8; 46:1; 59:9, 17; 81:1; 118:14) would **help** him by saving his life **from the power of** his wicked enemies, who were like **dogs** (cf. v. 16), **lions** (cf. v. 13 and comments on 7:2), and **wild oxen** (cf. bulls, 22:12-13). In his prayer, he became confident that he had been heard. In the Hebrew the last part of verse 21 breaks off in the middle of the prayer and states, "You have heard" (cf. NIV marg.). The psalmist may have received an oracle of salvation, for in the rest of the psalm he said he would praise God for His deliverance.

D. Praise and encouragement for prayer (22:22-31)

22:22. David addressed **the congregation** of the people with his vow to **praise** the Lord. Verse 22 is quoted almost verbatim in Hebrews 2:12 as Jesus' praise for deliverance. Of course Jesus' prayer to be delivered from death (Heb. 5:7) was answered in a different way— He was raised from the dead. The psalmist was apparently rescued so that he did not die.

22:23-26. Then the psalmist called on the congregation to **praise** the LORD with him because He did **not** despise the **afflicted one** (the suffering psalmist) but **listened to his cry for help** (cf. vv. 1-2) and answered his prayer. On the basis of this **praise** David said he would **fulfill** his **vows** and he encouraged the congregation to **praise** the Lord with him. Moreover, he encouraged them to keep on praying (**may your hearts live forever** means "do not give up"; cf. "heart" in v. 14).

22:27-31. The psalmist then turned his attention to the world at large. He anticipated that the world would **turn to** and worship (**bow down before) the LORD** (v. 27) because He is the sovereign King, the One who **rules over the nations** (v. 28), including **the rich** and the dying. From generation to generation the people of the earth **will be told** that **the** LORD answered his prayer and rescued him, so therefore the Lord can be trusted. Of course applied to Jesus Christ, these words became more significant. When people would hear how God answered His prayer by raising Him from the dead (Heb. 5:7), many would turn to Him in trust and worship.

Psalm 23

Using the images of a shepherd and a gracious host, David reflected on the many benefits the Lord gave him in the dangers of life, and concluded that God's persistent, loving protection would restore him to full communion.

A. The Lord as Leader (23:1-4)

23:1. The psalmist employed the figure of a **shepherd** to recall the blessings he enjoyed from **the** LORD (cf. God as Shepherd in 28:9; 80:1). The metaphor was a natural one for David, the shepherd-king. It was also a common metaphor in the ancient Near East, as many kings compared themselves to shepherds in their leadership capacity. The prophecy of the coming Messiah incorporated the same (Isa. 40:11), and Jesus identified Himself as that expected "Good Shepherd" (John 10:14). He is also called the "Great Shepherd" (Heb. 13:20) and "the Chief Shepherd" (1 Peter 5:4). Because the Lord was David's Shepherd, his needs were met.

23:2a. The first blessing David experienced was spiritual nourishment. As a shepherd leads sheep to fresh grass for feeding, so the Lord leads His people. One who follows the Lord does not lack any spiritual nourishment. Under-shepherds (cf. Acts 20:28; 1 Peter 5:2) are expected to feed the flock (Ezek. 34:1-10; John 21:15-17) as well. Food for the soul is the Word of God (Heb. 5:12-14; 1 Peter 2:2).

23:2b-3a. A second blessing that comes from the Lord's leading is spiritual restoration. As a shepherd leads his sheep to placid **waters** for rest and cleansing, so the Lord **restores** or refreshes the **soul.** Here the spiritual lesson is clear: the Lord provides forgiveness and peace for those who follow Him.

23:3b. The third blessing that comes from the Lord's leading is guidance **in** the right way (**paths of righteousness**). A good shepherd knows the right paths on which to bring the sheep home safely. So too the Lord loses none of His sheep, but guides them in the right way. He does so partly because of His reputation (**for His name's sake**).

23:4. The fourth blessing from the Lord's leading is protection. If one finds himself in a **valley of** deep darkness (or **shadow of death**), he need not **fear**. The Lord is **with** him and will protect him. The **rod** and **staff** are the shepherd's equipment to protect the sheep in such situations. David was comforted by the Lord's presence and protection. Believers are never in situations the Lord is not aware of, for He never leaves or forsakes His people (cf. Heb. 13:5).

B. The Lord as Provider (23:5)

23:5. In this verse the scene changes to a banquet hall where a gracious host provides lavish hospitality. Under this imagery the psalmist rejoiced in the Lord's provision. What was comforting to David was that this was **in the presence of** his **enemies**. Despite impending danger, the Lord spread out **a table** for him, that is, God provided for him.

The image of anointing the **head with oil,** which was refreshing and soothing, harmonizes with the concept of a gracious host welcoming someone into his home. In view of the table and the oil David knew that his lot in life (his **cup**) was abundant blessing from the Lord.

C. The response of faith (23:6)

23:6. David realized that the Lord's good loyal **love** (ḥeseḏ) would go with him everywhere through **all his life.** God's blessings on His people remain with them no matter what their circumstance may be. (Cf. God's **goodness** in 27:13; 31:19; 69:16; 86:17; 109:21; 116:12; 142:7; 145:7.) So he concluded **I will dwell in the house of the Lord forever.** The house of the Lord referred to the sanctuary (tabernacle). For the rest of his life (lit., "length of days") he would enjoy full communion with the Lord. In fact the Hebrew verb translated "I will dwell" conveys the idea of returning; the same verb is translated "He restores" in 23:3. Perhaps the psalmist was in some way separated from the sanctuary and full enjoyment of its spiritual benefits. His meditation on the Lord's leading and provi-

sions prompted him to recall his communion with the Lord in His presence, in the sanctuary.

Psalm 24

In preparation for the entry of the great King of glory, the psalmist stated that those with clean hands and pure hearts may ascend to His holy place.

Many think this psalm was written for the occasion of David's taking the ark of the covenant to Jerusalem (2 Sam. 6), though this cannot be proved. If such were true, then the "ancient doors" (Ps. 24:7) refer to the old fortress that then received the ark, the symbol of the Lord's presence. Or perhaps the psalm speaks of some other return to Jerusalem after a victory in battle.

A. Ascent to the holy place (24:1-6)

24:1-2. David praised the Lord because **everything in . . . the world** belongs to Him who created it. This is a general acknowledgment of God's sovereignty over all things.

24:3-4. David then pondered **who** could go into the presence of such a sovereign Lord (i.e., to the tabernacle on **the hill** [cf. comments on "holy hill" in 2:6] **of the Lord** and its **holy place**). The answer, perhaps given by priests at the sanctuary, is that one whose conduct is pure and whose worship is faithful may do so (cf. Ps. 15). **Clean hands** refers to right actions, and **a pure heart** refers to a right attitude and will. Only those who do not worship an **idol** can be true worshipers, and can walk by faith in integrity.

24:5-6. The lesson is followed by the affirmation that **those who seek** after **God** will be blessed with righteousness. This may refer to worshipers seeking entry into the sanctuary.

B. Entry of the King of glory (24:7-10)

24:7. The psalmist offered an exhortation (v. 7) and then an explanation (v. 8). If **lift up your heads, O you gates** refers to the city of Jerusalem then he was calling for the ancient gates to open wide for the triumphant entry. This was a poetic way of displaying the superiority of the one entering. They should lift up their heads because **the King of glory** is about to **come in.**

24:8-10. David then gave an explanation. By question and answer he stated that **this King of glory** is the LORD, who is **mighty in battle. The** LORD had shown Himself **strong** by giving them great victories; so He is the glorious King who will enter the city. One can visualize a procession of triumphant Israelites carrrying the ark, the symbol of the Lord's presence, going up to the sanctuary to praise Him. The ideas in the exhortation (v. 7) and the explanation (v. 8) were repeated in verses 9-10. The repetition stressed the point: **The** LORD is a glorious **King** who is coming **in.** Only pure worshipers can enjoy His presence.

Psalm 25

David confidently turned to the Lord for divine instruction and forgiveness from his iniquity because of His mercies for Israel. This psalm is a meditation on the character of God that prompts the humble to respond with confession and prayer. The psalm is an acrostic, as each verse begins with a successive letter of the Hebrew alphabet.

A. Prayer for guidance and pardon (25:1-7)

The psalmist was not ashamed to turn to the Lord for instruction and forgiveness for the sins of his youth (v. 7).

25:1-3. David stressed his confidence in turning to the LORD. He lifted **up** his **soul** to the Lord without **shame,** for none who **trust** and **hope** (cf. vv. 5, 21) in the Lord **will . . . be put to shame** (cf. v. 20), that is, they will have their prayers answered and their needs met. This contrasts with their **enemies** and the **treacherous.**

25:4-7. David prayed first for instruction (vv. 4-5; cf. vv. 9, 12) and guidance (v. 5; cf. v. 9). He desired that God would **show** him His **ways,** including **truth,** and **teach** him His **paths.** Then he prayed for pardon (vv. 6-7). Based on God's **mercy and love,** which had been known for ages, he prayed that **the sins of** his **youth** not be held against him. (Three times he prayed **remember.**)

B. Reiteration of the prayer (25:8-22)

The psalmist reiterated his prayer for instruction in the true way (cf. vv. 4-5) and pardon (cf. vv. 6-7) for his afflicted soul, but now his prayer was grounded on the revealed character of the Lord.

25:8-10. David extolled the nature of God: He is **good and upright** and **loving and faithful.** On the basis of these attributes He teaches **sinners** and **guides the humble.** Sinful humans need the gracious guidance of **the** LORD.

25:11. The psalmist prayed for pardon for his great **iniquity—for the sake of** the Lord's **name** (His revealed character).

25:12-14. Here David described a person who **fears the** LORD: he is one in whom **the** LORD **confides** by revealing **His covenant** to him (v. 14) and instructing him (v. 12b; cf. vv. 4-5, 8-9). These statements remind the reader of the Wisdom literature, especially Proverbs. A person who fears the Lord (Prov. 1:7; 9:10; 15:33; 31:30) is instructed by the Lord's Word.

25:15-22. The psalm concludes with a prayer for the Lord's **gracious** deliverance. Beginning with his own affirmation that he trusts **the** LORD for deliverance (v. 15), the psalmist called on God to forgive (v. 18; cf. vv. 6-7, 11) his **afflicted** soul and deliver him from the **distress** caused by his cruel **enemies** (v. 18). Again he asked that in being rescued he **not be put to shame** (cf. v. 20), and he affirmed his **hope** in God (v. 21; cf. vv. 3, 5; hope in the Lord is mentioned more than two dozen times in the Pss.). The last request was for deliverance of **Israel . . . from** her **troubles** (v. 22).

The psalm strongly links the prayer for deliverance and guidance to confession of sin. The way of the Lord requires this.

Psalm 26

Psalm 26 is a strong affirmation of integrity and a prayer that God would recognize it. No time in the life of David clearly presents itself as an occasion for this passage. The psalm is similar in many ways to Psalm 25, but Psalm 26 does not include a prayer for pardon. The psalmist here declared that he kept separate from sinners, and identified himself with the worship of the Lord. On the basis of this, he prayed with confidence that the Lord would spare him from a fate like that of sinners.

A. Assertion of integrity (26:1-3)

26:1-3. David offered a twofold introductory petition: **the** LORD (a) should act justly toward him (v. 1) and (b) should **examine** his claim (v. 2; cf. 139:23). The LORD could discern that he had been consistent in his faith (26:1a) and in obedience to the Lord and His **truth** (v. 3).

B. Proof of integrity (26:4-8)

26:4-5. David proved his integrity by his separation from sinners (vv. 4-5) and his identification with worshipers (vv. 6-8). He in no way identified with **the wicked** and the **deceitful.** He did **not sit** (vv. 4a, 5b) with them or consult them (cf. 1:1). In fact he hated their assemblies.

26:6-8. The setting of these verses is the sanctuary (cf. **altar,** v. 6, and **house,** v. 8). David's worship was with integrity (he washed his **hands**; cf. 24:4, **in innocence**) and sincerity (he praised the Lord and told of His **deeds**). In contrast with his reaction to the assemblies of the wicked (26:5) David loved the sanctuary, where the **glory** of the LORD . . . **dwells.**

C. Prayer for the reward of integrity (26:9-12)

26:9-12. David petitioned the Lord to spare him from a common fate **with sinners** with whom he did not associate (cf. vv. 4-5). David was probably referring to premature death (**soul** in Heb. refers to one's life).

If swift judgment took the **wicked** away, it should not touch one who remained separate from them.

In expectation of the Lord's delivering him from such a fate, David said he would **praise** the LORD in the congregation (cf. vv. 7-8). Many times in the Psalms the writers prayed to be redeemed (v. 11) from trouble (pādâh, "to ransom, redeem," is used in 31:5; 44:26; 49:7; 55:18; 69:18; 78:42; 119:134). That Hebrew word was often used when referring to Israel's deliverance from Egypt (cf. Deut. 7:8; 9:26; 13:5; 15:15; 24:18; 2 Sam. 7:23; Micah 6:4).

Psalm 27

David at first expressed jubilant confidence in the Lord in spite of a host of enemies who threatened his life. But suddenly his mood changed: he anxiously prayed that the Lord would not forsake him, but would help and comfort him in his time of need. Because the Lord was his Source of comfort and hope, he strengthened himself to wait for the Lord. The psalm is one of courageous trust.

A. Confidence that dispels fear (27:1-3)

27:1. David expressed great confidence in the LORD: because the LORD was his **Light . . . Salvation,** and **Stronghold** (mā'ôz, "a strong fortified place"; cf. 37:39; 43:2; 52:7), nobody could harm him. Light signifies understanding, joy, and life (cf. 18:28) and the stronghold (cf. 18:2) signifies defense. With these provisions from the Lord, **whom shall** a believer **fear?** (cf. 27:3) Obviously the answer is no one.

27:2-3. In response to this question David spoke of the **enemies** who came **against** him. Even if they broke in on him, he would remain **confident** in the Lord, without **fear** (cf. v. 1).

B. Communion that brings security (27:4-6)

27:4. David further expressed his confidence in **the LORD** by his longing to dwell in His **house.** He would love to abide there **all** his **life,** to enjoy His **beauty** and **to seek Him** there in the **temple.** (Hêḵāl does not refer here to Solomon's temple since it was not yet built. The Heb. word means a magnificent structure, such as the tabernacle; cf. vv. 5-6; 5:7; 1 Sam. 1:9; 3:3; the temple, 2 Kings 24:13; or a palace, Pss. 45:15; 144:12; Dan. 1:4.)

27:5-6. To dwell in the presence of the Lord would add to David's security. The Lord would keep him safe **in the day of trouble** and establish him securely in danger. Consequently he would triumph (his **head** would **be exalted**) over his **enemies** and joyfully **sing** praises **to the LORD.** Perhaps the idea of safety in the sanctuary, where his enemies could not reach him, caused David here to meditate on the Lord's protection. The word for **shelter** (sēṯer) is also used in 32:7 ("hiding place"); 91:1; 109:114 ("refuge") to speak of God's protection. David certainly knew the true Source of security.

C. Earnest prayer in faith (27:7-14)

27:7-10. Apparently the Lord was not granting David protection promptly, for he prayed earnestly and with some anxiety for help. He asked the Lord **not** to **forsake** him since he was in great need. God had instructed the righteous to pray (to **seek His face**), and that is what David was doing. Therefore God ought not refuse to help him (to **hide** His **face**; cf. 102:2; 143:7). Moreover, David affirmed that he was the **servant** of the **LORD**, and that the Lord had **been** his **Helper**. On the basis of this motivation, he begged the Lord **not** to **reject** him. His prayer was strengthened by the knowledge that the Lord would not **forsake** him, even if his parents did (which of course was unlikely).

27:11-12. David asked God to **teach** him the **way** to go (cf. 25:4-5) **because** his enemies were lying in wait for him. He asked **not** to be turned **over to** his **foes**, who were **false witnesses** sworn to destroy him.

27:13-14. In the end, however, the psalmist's confidence surfaced again; he rejoiced in the prospect of waiting **for the LORD**. David was **confident** that he would survive and remain alive (**in the land of the living**) to **see** God's blessing. Therefore he strengthened himself to **wait for the** Lord's deliverance.

Psalm 28

The psalmist was convinced that the Lord would distinguish him from the wicked when He overthrows them and would preserve him from his distress. Therefore he prayed that the Lord would save and shepherd His people. This psalm is a companion to Psalm 26, but here the danger was imminent.

A. Petition to the Lord (28:1-4)

28:1. Addressing the **LORD**, the psalmist prayed to be kept separate from the wicked when they are overthrown. This was an urgent plea. If God would not respond, he would die (**pit,** *bôr,* is a synonym for grave; cf. 30:3).

28:2-4. David then asked (a) that the Lord would favor him as he cried for **mercy** and **help** (v. 2), (b) that the Lord would not **drag** him off with hypocritical sinners (v. 3), and (c) that the Lord would justly punish the wicked (v. 4).

B. Confident praise to the Lord (28:5-8)

28:5-8. In addressing the congregation, the psalmist confidently expressed his anticipation that **the LORD** would answer his prayer: the wicked will be overthrown permanently. Because the wicked disregard **the works of the LORD,** they will be destroyed. This prompted words of **praise . . . to the LORD**: (a) because **He . . . heard** David's prayer (v. 6; cf. v. 2); (b) because He was David's **Strength** (cf. v. 8; 22:19; 46:1; 59:9, 17; 81:1; 118:14) **and Shield** (cf. comments on 3:3) in that **the LORD** enabled him to escape the schemes of the wicked so that he could rejoice in the Lord (v. 7); and (c) because the Lord saves **His people** (cf. 18:2) and like **a fortress** defends His king (**His anointed one,** 28:8). The fact that the Lord showed Himself to be His people's Savior prompted praise from them.

C. Prayer for deliverance and guidance (28:9)

28:9. The psalmist returned to his prayer (v. 9) after expressing his confident anticipation of the outcome (vv. 5-8). He asked for salvation for the nation Israel (God's **inheritance;** cf. 33:12; 78:62, 71; 79:1; 94:14; Deut. 4:20; 9:26, 29; Joel 2:17; 3:2; Micah 7:14, 18) and guidance from their **Shepherd** (cf. Pss. 23:1; 80:1) **forever.** This prayer that the Lord would bear them up was a request that He sustain them through all their trials and tribulations.

Psalm 29

David witnessed an awesome thunderstorm moving across the land of the Canaanites, and attributed it to the power of the Lord. He called on the angels to glorify Him who sits as King forever over nature. Psalm 29 is a polemic against pagan beliefs in false gods who were credited with being responsible for storms.

A. Call to praise (29:1-2)

29:1-2. The psalmist called on the angels to glorify **the LORD. O mighty ones** is literally, "sons of the mighty," that is, God's angelic beings. The poetry here is climactic, repeating the expression **ascribe to the LORD** three times (with slight changes each time in the words that follow) and expanding the idea until the final line calls for **worship** in **holiness.** The angels were invoked to give God the credit for His **glory** and power (**strength**). Such praise should be accompanied by holiness (NIV marg.), using the imagery from Israel's solemn assemblies, for **the LORD** is holy.

B. Cause for praise (29:3-9)

The psalmist described the Lord's omnipotent control of nature in a terrifying storm.

29:3-4. David attributed the rise of the storm **over the** mighty **waters** (the Mediterranean Sea) to **the voice of the Lord.** Though **voice** may be a poetic designation of thunder (cf. 18:13), it probably also was meant to convey that He who created by His word (cf. Gen. 1:3, 6, 9, 14, 20, 24) also controls nature by His word so that a thunderstorm evidences His power.

29:5-7. As David witnessed **the voice of the Lord** at the height of the storm, he said it moved inland and destroyed **the** great **cedars of Lebanon,** rumbled the great mountains with earthquakes (v. 6), and scattered forked **lightning** in the skies (v. 7). **Lebanon** (v. 6) and **Sirion** are mountains in the Anti-Lebanon range.

All this was by the decree of the Lord. In fact seven times **the voice of the Lord** is mentioned in verses 3-9: the storm evidenced His complete majesty.

29:8-9. The storm (**the voice of the Lord**) shook not only the mountains (v. 6) but also **the Desert of Kadesh.** This Kadesh was a town about 75 miles north of Damascus, not Kadesh in the south. As the storm moved on, it shook the fauna and flora in the eastern wilderness. The storm made the hinds calve (as most versions translate the Heb.; cf. KJV, NASB, NIV marg.) prematurely due to fear, and stripped the leaves from the trees in **the forests.** As a result all creatures **in His temple,** perhaps angels again (cf. v. 1), shouted praises of **glory** to His power.

C. Conclusion (29:10-11)

29:10. The psalmist concluded that **the Lord** rules **as King forever** and is able to bless His people. Since **the flood** probably refers to the universal inundation in Noah's day, **sits enthroned** should be translated "sat enthroned" (cf. NIV marg.). Perhaps David recalled this incident to support his contention that the present storm was the Lord's work. If there was any doubt that the Lord controlled nature, that would settle it. He is **the Lord** of Creation.

29:11. This demonstration of power was an encouragement **to His people,** for He shares His power (**strength**) with them. The strength available to His people (v. 11) is His own strength (v. 1). The same Hebrew word ('ōz) is used in both verses. The power that can raise a storm is available to benefit those who trust in Him. Just as God can cause a storm to be still, so too can He bring **peace** to **His people.** Jesus' miracles over nature, especially calming the storm on the Sea of Galilee (Mark 4:37-39), demonstrate that all power was given to Him.

Psalm 30

The superscription says that this is "a psalm . . . for the dedication of the temple," written by David. This title may refer to David's dedication of the site of the temple (1 Chron. 21:26; 22:1) after the numbering of the people. (The Heb. word trans. "temple" is lit., "house," and could refer to the tabernacle [tent] in which David placed the ark, 2 Sam. 6:17.) A problem with this view is that the psalm mentions God's discipline of David (cf. Ps. 30:7) perhaps by some physical illness (v. 3) for his pride (v. 6). It may be that the illness was figurative, not literal, and referred to David's inner remorse (1 Chron. 21:13) for having through pride caused a plague which killed 70,000 Israelites (1 Chron. 21:2, 8, 14). Others take the title to be a liturgical designation for its use in dedicating buildings constructed later (e.g., Ezra 6:16; Neh. 12:27).

From his experience of deliverance from God's chastening for his sin, David praised the Lord because His anger is temporary, but His favor is permanent.

A. Deliverance from chastening (30:1-5)

David acknowledged the Lord's deliverance and called the congregation to praise Him.

30:1. He vowed to praise the Lord because he was **lifted** up from his distress. **The depths** (or the depths of the earth) speaks of nearness of death (cf. 71:20; 130:1). The rescue removed any opportunity for his **enemies** to **gloat.**

30:2-3. Here David described his answer to prayer **for help:** God **healed** him and **spared** his life. This is stated figuratively as well: God **brought** him **up from the grave** ("sheol"; cf. NIV marg.). He was about to die, perhaps because of a physical illness, but the **Lord** healed him. God's deliverance prevented death.

30:4-5. Because of God's deliverance

the psalmist called on the people to **sing to** and **praise** the LORD. The reason for the praise is the temporary nature of God's **anger** to him; it was but for a **moment,** only **for the night. In the morning** came deliverance and joy.

B. Chastening for independence (30:6-10)

30:6-7. David recorded his prayer for deliverance from his sin of independence of the LORD. In pride he **felt secure,** thinking he would **never be shaken** (cf. comments on 15:5). The word "secure" (*šelew*) implies a careless ease. Apparently he had forgotten his need to trust in the Lord and boasted in self-confidence.

As a result, God disciplined him (30:7). Previously when God had **favored** him, He made him secure (**mountain** is a figure for the strength of his position); **but when** God disciplined him, He **hid** His **face,** an expression that signifies the removal of blessing and protection.

30:8-10. When God brought the plague, because of David's pride (2 Sam. 24:15) David **cried** out to Him, pleading that there would be no benefit **in** his **destruction** and death (on **pit**; cf. Ps. 30:3 and comments on 28:1). If God wanted **praise** from the psalmist, then He would have to preserve him from the grave (cf. Isa. 38:18). This was the reasoning behind David's prayer for mercy and **help** (cf. Ps. 30:2).

C. Deliverance from discipline (30:11-12)

30:11-12. Using terminology from festive occasions (**dancing** and **joy**) David rehearsed how God delivered him from his lamentable state (on **sackcloth**; cf. 35:13 and comments on Gen. 37:34). As a result of this answer to prayer David sang praises to the Lord. Thus he vowed to acknowledge and thank the LORD his **God** (cf. Ps. 30:2) **forever.** Every deliverance a believer experiences should likewise prompt a full expression of praise.

Psalm 31

Psalm 31 is another "psalm of David" in a time of great need, a prayer from one who was despised, defamed, and persecuted. So much of David's life was spent in this condition that the Book of Psalms includes many of his prayers that grew out of such situations. In this passage he exhorted the afflicted to love the Lord and to be strong because the Lord would protect them from men's evil plans. David explained that he learned this truth as he committed his life into the hands of the Lord when his foes plotted to kill him.

A. Cry to be rescued (31:1-2)

31:1-2. These verses record David's introductory cry to the LORD, his **Refuge** (cf. vv. 2, 4). He prayed for the Lord to **come quickly** to his **rescue** (cf. 69:17; 70:1, 5; 71:2; 79:8; 102:2; 141:1; 143:7) and **be** his **Rock** and **Fortress** (cf. 31:3 and comments on 18:2). His only protection and safety were in the Lord.

B. Confidence in His love (31:3-8)

David confidently committed his life into the hands of the Lord, his Rock, knowing that he would rejoice in God's love (cf. vv. 16, 21).

31:3-4. The psalmist's confidence is stated strongly in these verses. The Lord his **Rock . . . Fortress** (cf. v. 2), and **Refuge** (cf. vv. 1-2; 18:2) would **lead** him out of danger.

31:5. With confidence in the Lord (vv. 3-4) he committed his **spirit** into the hands of the LORD, praying that **the God of truth** (cf. Isa. 65:16) would **redeem** him (see comments on Ps. 26:11). The same confident resting in God during the onslaught of the wicked was expressed by the Savior (Luke 23:46). A sufferer who has faith in God may pray to Him and leave the problem in His hands (1 Peter 4:19).

31:6-8. In addition to his trust, David asserted that he despised **those who cling to worthless idols. The** LORD is faithful, worthy of all **trust.** Therefore David confidently anticipated praising His loyal **love.** He wrote (v. 8) as if the deliverance had already been granted. With such genuine faith, believers can sing of triumph in anticipation of God's delivering them.

C. Lament over the danger (31:9-13)

31:9-13. The psalmist pleaded for grace from the LORD because his life was in danger (**distress**). In **sorrow . . . grief,** and **anguish** he was at the point of perishing (vv. 9-10). (On **bones** see comments on 6:2). **Because of** his **enemies** he was rejected and **forgotten** by **friends**

(31:11-12). Because **many** plotted against his **life** he faced **terror on every side** (cf. Jer. 20:10).

D. Prayer for deliverance (31:14-18)

31:14-18. Emphasizing that he trusted God and had placed himself in the Lord's **hands** (vv. 14-15a; cf. v. 5) the psalmist prayed that **God** would **save** him (vv. 15b-16) and silence his arrogant enemies (vv. 17-18). (On God's **face** shining, see comments on 4:6.) They with **their lying lips** should **be silenced** rather than he, with his praises.

E. Praise and exhortation (31:19-24)

31:19-24. David praised **the LORD** (**How great is Your goodness**) for His protection of the faithful in general (vv. 19-20), and for delivering him by His **love** (v. 21; cf. vv. 7, 16) in spite of David's unbelief (v. 22). On the basis of what he had learned about the Lord's deliverance of **the faithful,** he encouraged the **saints** to **be strong** in their faith and **hope in the LORD** (vv. 23-24).

Psalm 32

David, having experienced divine chastening and forgiveness (possibly for the sin of adultery and murder recorded in 2 Sam. 11), encouraged others to seek the Lord who deals graciously with sinners. If they refuse submission they will endure chastening.

This psalm may be a companion to Psalm 51, referring to David's sin with Bathsheba. At that time David refused for a year to acknowledge his sin. Psalm 51 was his prayer for pardon; Psalm 32 would then follow it, stressing God's forgiveness and the lesson David learned.

A. The blessing of forgiveness (32:1-2)

32:1-2. The psalmist, having received God's forgiveness for his **sins,** expressed his joy over that fact. **Blessed** is used in 1:1 of a person who leads an untarnished life. Here it is used of one who has forgiveness. God forgives fully, for He **does not count** a truly penitent person's **sin . . . against him.**

B. The chastening of the unrepentant (32:3-5)

32:3-5. The psalmist experienced forgiveness when he acknowledged his sin, but it came only after divine chastening.

When he was **silent** and did not confess his sin, he was weakened physically (on **bones** see comments on 6:2) and grieved inwardly. The **hand** (or power) of the Lord **was** heavy on him (32:4), that is, God dealt severely with him. The result was that his vitality (**strength**) **was sapped** (or dried up) **as in the** summer **heat.** This expression may refer to physical illness with burning fever, or it may describe in poetic language his remorse of conscience.

Therefore he confessed his **sin to** God. This is the way of restoration, for God **forgave** him.

C. The advice of the forgiven (32:6-11)

32:6-7. David encouraged others to seek the Lord because He deals graciously with sinners. The time to **pray** is when the Lord **may be found.** If this is done, calamities (spoken of as **mighty waters**) **will not** overwhelm. On the basis of this note of comfort, David turned to praise the Lord as his **Hiding Place** (*sēṭer*, also used in 27:5, "shelter"; 91:1, "shelter"; 119:114, "refuge"). God protects **from trouble** those who trust Him, and He gives them occasion to praise.

32:8. David also counseled others not to refuse to submit to the Lord until He forces it, but to make their confessions willingly. Some take the speaker in verse 8 to be God rather than David because of the words **watch over you** (cf. 25:8, 12; 73:24). But David seems to have assumed here the role of a teacher (cf. 34:11; 51:13).

32:9-11. The psalmist advised his readers to submit to **the LORD** rather than resist stubbornly **like a horse or . . . mule** that has to be **controlled.** Those who trust Him will experience His faithful loyal **love** (*ḥeseḏ*) and will be able to **sing** praises to Him.

Psalm 33

The psalmist called on the righteous to praise the Lord because His Word is dependable and His work righteous. Those who trust in Him are assured that He will fulfill His promises to them and consummate His work of salvation.

This psalm is a hymn of praise. It may have resulted from a national victory, but there is no evidence to specify which victory. The Hebrew has no superscription; the Septuagint, however, ascribes the psalm to David.

A. It is fitting to praise the Lord (33:1-3)

33:1-3. These verses include the psalmist's call to praise, in which he summoned the **righteous** to rejoice in the LORD because **it is fitting**. Praise is the natural response of God's people for receiving His benefits. But their praise should be spontaneous and fresh—new mercies demand new songs (cf. **a new song** in 40:3; 96:1; 98:1; 144:9; 149:1). It should also be done well or **skillfully**. The best talent that a person has should be offered in praising Him.

B. The Lord is dependable and righteous (33:4-19)

33:4-5. The reason for praise, detailed throughout this psalm, is summarized in these verses. The Lord's **Word** and work (**all He does**) are dependable, and **the LORD** is righteous and loyal (ḥesed, **unfailing love**; cf. vv. 18, 22).

33:6-11. These verses develop the thought in verse 4 that His Word and work are reliable. First the psalmist spoke of the power of **the word of the LORD** in Creation (vv. 6-9). Because God **spoke,** Creation **came** into existence. What God decrees, happens. Therefore **all** peoples **of the world** should worship **Him.**

Then the psalmist spoke of the power of **the LORD** in history (vv. 10-11). God's plans foil **the plans of the** wicked **nations** (cf. 2:1-6). His purposes are sustained, no matter what people endeavor to do. Surely a God with such powerful words and works should be praised.

33:12-19. These verses develop the idea that **the LORD** is righteous, just (cf. v. 4a), and loyal (cf. v. 5b). Verse 12 expresses the psalmist's joy over being part of God's elect **people,** recipients of His loyal love. (On Israel as God's **inheritance,** see comments on 28:9.) The psalmist then stated that God **sees all** people **from** His exalted position in **heaven** (**His dwelling place**; cf. 2 Chron. 6:21, 30, 33, 39; 30:27). He sees even their inner thoughts (Ps. 33:13-15). God does not save the self-confident (vv. 6-17). Those who look to a **king,** or human **strength,** or a **horse** cannot find **deliverance** (cf. 20:7). Rather **the LORD** saves and preserves those who trust and **hope** in Him (33:18-19; cf. "hope" in vv. 20, 22 and

unfailing love in vv. 5, 22). This is the lot of Israel, the **blessed . . . nation** (v. 12).

C. God's people trust in Him (33:20-22)

33:20-22. The conclusion of the psalm is a reassertion of faith in **the LORD.** God's people demonstrate their faith in three ways. First, they **wait in hope** (cf. 25:5, 21; 39:7; 62:5; 71:5) for deliverance from the Lord as their **Help** (cf. 30:10; 40:17; 46:1; 54:4; 63:7; 70:5; 115:9-11; 146:5) and **Shield** (cf. comments on 3:3). Second, they **rejoice in Him** whom they **trust** (33:21). Third, they pray for His **unfailing love** (ḥesed; cf. vv. 5, 18) to **rest** on them. So they are confident (**hope**) He will consummate His program of salvation.

Psalm 34

This song of praise is attributed to David when he escaped from Abimelech by feigning insanity (1 Sam. 21:11). In the psalm David called on the congregation to praise the Lord for their salvation. And after affirming that God is good to those who trust Him, he instructed the people on how to live a long life.

A. God is good to His people (34:1-10)

34:1-3. Verses 1-10 are filled with David's praise. In verses 1-3 David called the people to **praise** the LORD with him. He resolved to praise God continually so that **the afflicted** would **rejoice**. But here he called for all the people to **exalt** the LORD with him.

34:4-6. David here recorded the report of his deliverance. Because he cried and was **delivered** (cf. "delivers" in vv. 7, 17, 19), he was convinced that God's people **are never** put to **shame.** Instead they **are radiant** because God hears them (cf. vv. 15, 17) and rescues them from their **troubles** (cf. vv. 17, 19).

34:7-10. David declared that **the Angel of the LORD** (possibly the Lord Himself; cf. comments on Gen. 16:9) camps **around those who fear** (cf. Ps. 34:9, 11) the Lord. In military imagery David envisioned divine protection (cf. Gen. 32:2; 2 Kings 6:16).

Those who trust in **the LORD** experience genuine happiness—if they **taste and see.** All who **fear the LORD,** that is, all who are genuine worshipers, will lack **nothing** (cf. Ps. 23:1), or **no good thing** (cf. 16:2; 84:11).

B. God blesses the righteous with life (34:11-22)

34:11-14. Verses 11-22 include David's instructions to the people on how to achieve a full life in the Lord. He exhorted them to listen to his instruction concerning **the fear of the LORD.** The instruction was essentially that of a righteous, peaceful **life** (v. 12), shunning **evil** and treachery (v. 13), and doing **good** (v. 14). This is wisdom teaching about the way of the righteous, which produces a life of quality with God's blessing.

34:15-21. For those who live righteously in **the LORD** (cf. **righteous** in vv. 15, 17, 19, 21), several assurances are given. First, **the LORD** looks favorably **on the righteous,** a sign of protection (v. 15), but He **is against** the wicked and will **cut off** their **memory . . . from the** living (v. 16; cf. Prov. 10:7b). Second, **the LORD hears** (cf. Ps. 34:6, 15) the prayers of **the righteous** who are broken **in spirit** and are not arrogant and stubborn (vv. 17-18). Third, **the LORD . . . delivers** (cf. vv. 4, 7, 17) **the righteous** from his **troubles** (cf. v. 6) so that not one of **his bones** is **broken.** This is an expression of complete protection from cruel oppression. Verse 20, as well as Exodus 12:46b, was used by God in referring to the Savior in John 19:36.

34:22. In summary, the psalmist asserted that **the LORD redeems His servants** (cf. comments on "redeems" in 26:11); **no one who** trusts **in Him will be** lost. That this verse represents a summation of the reason for praise can be seen by the arrangement in the Hebrew text. This psalm is an acrostic: each verse begins with a different letter of the Hebrew alphabet in order, but one letter in the Hebrew alphabet is omitted (between vv. 5-6), thereby finishing the acrostic with verse 21. The last verse, then, breaks the sequence and calls attention to itself.

Psalm 35

This psalm is a combination of three laments over the opposition of David's enemies. Each lament develops the unified cry for deliverance from enemies who hated him without a cause.

A. Prayer for deliverance from destroyers (35:1-10)

The psalmist petitioned the Lord to deliver him from his enemies who wished to kill him, who hated him for no good reason.

35:1-6. David's prayer began with a plea for the LORD to act as his Champion (vv. 1-3) and to rout his enemies (vv. 4-6). Like worthless **chaff** (v. 5) blown away by **the wind** in threshing, so he wished his worthless enemies would be cast aside. His prayer, that **the Angel of the LORD** would drive **them away,** was a prayer for retributive justice, that the Lord would render to them what they had planned for him.

35:7-10. They had sought to take his life unaware as a hunter hides his **net** and digs **a pit** to catch an unwary animal. David prayed that their traps for others would ensnare **them** (cf. 7:15; 9:15; 57:6) **by surprise** and bring about **their ruin** (cf. 35:4; 38:12; 40:14; 70:2). **Then,** David said, he would praise **the LORD** with joy, wholeheartedly (**my whole being**) for rescuing those (**the poor and needy**) who are at the mercy of the mighty.

B. Lament over unjust hatred (35:11-18)

With an emphasis on the lament, the psalmist petitioned the Lord for help from those who unjustly hated him.

35:11-18. Here David described his lamentable state. Essentially he had been repaid **evil for good** (vv. 11-12). He had fasted and prayed for his enemies **when they were ill,** putting **on** sackcloth (cf. 30:11 and comments on Gen. 37:34), and **when** his **prayers** were not answered, he mourned and wept for them (Ps. 35:13-14). However, **when** *he* was in difficulty, they gleefully **mocked** (vv. 15-16). Because of this injustice he pleaded for help from **the LORD,** who up till then had not responded (v. 17). (On **how long?** see comments on 6:3, and on his enemies as **lions,** see comments on 7:2.) But when the Lord would answer, David said he would **praise** Him **in the . . . assembly** (35:18).

C. Petition for justice (35:19-28)

Here the psalmist petitioned the Lord for deliverance from the wicked by asking that He render justice against those who stir up trouble by their accusations against peaceful people. Here again the theme of the wicked's unjust treatment of the righteous forms the lamentable reason for his petition.

35:19-21. David prayed that the Lord

would not let the wicked triumph because their vicious words stirred up strife. Again he stressed that they were his **enemies without cause** (cf. v. 7). They winked at each other (cf. Prov. 6:13; 10:10; 16:30), revealing their malicious intentions. They devised **false accusations against those who** wished to **live quietly,** slanderously claiming to **have seen** them in some wrongdoing.

35:22-26. Though David's enemies falsely claimed to have seen him in sin and were vocal about it, David knew that the LORD had **seen** *them* in *their* wrongdoing. So he asked **God** to end His silence (i.e., not be inactive) and **rise to** the psalmist's **defense.** By vindicating David, the LORD would rightly **put to shame and confusion** all the foes' gloating (cf. v. 19).

35:27-28. David's final prayer was that the people **who** looked for his **vindication** would have occasion to be joyful and praise **the** LORD for it. Because his enemies hated him without a cause (cf. vv. 7, 19) he was convinced that the Lord would vindicate him, so that he could exalt and praise Him continually (**all day long**).

Psalm 36

In this psalm David received an oracle concerning the philosophy and lifestyle of unbelievers as they plotted their wicked schemes. David found relief in his experiential knowledge of the glorious nature of the Lord, who brings abundant blessings to believers. As a result, he prayed that the Lord would continue His loyal love and righteousness so that the wicked would not destroy his integrity.

A. An oracle concerning the wicked (36:1-4)

36:1. David received **an oracle** from the Lord **concerning the sinfulness** (*peša',* "transgression") **of the wicked.** So he recorded what he learned. The philosophy of the wicked is based on their absence of the **fear** (*pahad,* "dread"—not the usual word *yir'âh,* "fear") **of God.** They have **no** dread of the Lord; they sense no terror because of their actions, so they proceed in their wickedness.

36:2-4. Having no dread of the Lord, a wicked person commits evil continually. He soothes his own conscience (**flatters himself**) to hide his iniquity, because

if he saw it from God's viewpoint he would **hate** it. His speech is licentious and deceptive. His life has long **ceased** to be worthwhile, for as **he commits himself to a sinful course** of action, he has no inclination to **reject** evil. He even **plots evil** (cf. Hosea 7:15; Nahum 1:11) at night while going to sleep.

B. The appreciation of God's portion (36:5-9)

36:5-6. In contrast with the wickedness that surrounded him (vv. 1-4), David found relief by meditating on the glorious attributes of the LORD, and the abundant blessings that come to believers. His philosophy of life was based on an experiential knowledge of the Lord's loyal **love** (*hesed;* cf. vv. 7, 10), **faithfulness . . . righteousness,** and **justice.** These attributes are inexhaustible resources for believers. Through them the LORD preserves **man and beast** throughout life.

36:7-9. The result of this philosophy is blessing for believers (cf. the results of a wicked person's philosophy, vv. 2-4). God's loyal **love** (cf. vv. 5, 10) is precious, because humans can take **refuge** in the Lord like chicks taking refuge under their mother hen's **wings** (v. 7; cf. 17:8; 57:1; 61:4; 63:7; 91:4). The psalmist then used the imagery of the temple to say that believers enjoy the provisions of God's **house** (36:8). Moreover, Eden and Creation are suggested in the next blessings—**drink from** the **river of delights** ("delights" is "Eden" in Heb.), and **life** and **light** (i.e., understanding, joy, and life) come from God, their Source. So in contrast with the corruptions of the wicked, an obedient believer's life is characterized by security in the Lord, abundant provisions, life, and understanding in God's presence.

C. Preservation of integrity (36:10-12)

36:10-12. David prayed that the Lord would **continue** His protective **love** (cf. vv. 5, 7) so that his integrity would be preserved from the influence of **the proud** and **wicked** who would be destroyed.

Psalm 37

This psalm of David seems to build on the previous one. Here he instructed the righteous not to be disturbed over the prosperity of the wicked who reject God, for divine justice will yet be granted. Using a series of proverbial expressions, the psalmist exhorted the righteous to trust in the Lord continually and not fret about evil people who are about to be cast down. The message is similar to that in Psalms 49 and 73, as well as the Book of Job.

A. Trust and fret not (37:1-8)

37:1-8. In this first section of the psalm David called for trust despite the presence **of evil men.** One should not be **envious of** sinful people and their prosperity (cf. vv. 7-8; cf. Prov. 23:17; 24:1) because they will wither **like the grass** (cf. Pss. 90:5; 102:4, 11; 103:15-16; Isa. 40:6-8; 1 Peter 1:24) and **will soon die** (Ps. 37:1-2). Rather one should **trust in the LORD** who can answer prayers of the heart (vv. 3-4). The promise, **He will give you the desires of your heart,** is based on the condition, **delight yourself in the LORD.** One who delights in Him will have righteous desires. If a person trusts in **the LORD** (cf. v. 3) God will gloriously vindicate him (vv. 5-6).

Therefore the righteous should **not** envy or **fret** (cf. v. 1; Prov. 24:19) **when** the wicked **succeed.** Fretting **leads only to evil,** including **anger** (Ps. 37:7-8).

B. The wicked will be justly punished (37:9-22)

37:9-11. David described (a) the impending judgment on **the wicked**—they **will** shortly **be cut off** (vv. 9a, 10)—and (b) the contrasting truth that **the meek will inherit the land** (vv. 9b, 11). This promise of inheriting the land (cf. vv. 22, 29, 34) was reiterated and broadened by Jesus (see comments on Matt. 5:5).

37:12-22. Five contrasts form the basis of the affirmations in verses 9-11: (1) **The wicked** devise evil **against the righteous . . . but the Lord laughs at** them (vv. 12-13). (2) **The wicked** attack the meek, **but** their own violence will destroy them (vv. 14-15). **(Poor and needy** occur together here for the first of six times in the Pss.: v. 14; 40:17; 70:5; 74:21; 86:1; 109:22.) (3) It is **better** to have **little** than to be **wicked** with much, for their **wealth** will be lost (vv. 16-17). (4) **The LORD** knows and protects the way of the upright, **but the wicked will perish** (cf. 1:6) like grass (cf. 37:2) and

smoke (vv. 18-20). (5) Because **the wicked** selfishly keep what they **borrow** but the righteous are generous (cf. v. 26), **the LORD** will repay with justice (vv. 21-22), including **the righteous** inheriting **the land** (cf. vv. 9, 11, 29, 34).

C. The Lord loves and blesses the just (37:23-31)

37:23-31. In contrast with the retribution for the wicked, the psalmist delineated the blessings of the Lord for **the righteous:** (1) **The LORD** establishes and protects the ways of the righteous (vv. 23-24). (2) The Lord provides food for them (vv. 25-26). (3) He **loves** and protects **the just** who **do good** (cf. v. 3), giving them security in **the land** (vv. 27-29; cf. vv. 9, 11, 22, 34). (4) **The righteous** person speaks **wisdom** because **the Law of . . . God is in his heart** (vv. 30-31).

D. The conflict of good and evil (37:32-40)

37:32-38. The psalmist concluded his meditation by describing the struggle between the wicked and the righteous. His solution to the problem of wicked people was to contrast their evil plot to destroy the righteous with God's **power** to preserve. **The wicked lie in wait** to destroy, **but the LORD will not** forsake His own (vv. 32-33). One who waits on **the LORD** will enjoy security (v. 34; cf. vv. 9, 11, 22) and **the upright . . . man of peace** will have **a future** (or, perhaps better, will see his "posterity"; cf. NIV marg.). By contrast the **wicked** will flourish (v. 35; cf. v. 7b) **but they will be cut off** (vv. 36, 38; cf. v. 34).

37:39-40. David concluded that in a world with wicked people on every hand, **the LORD** is **the Salvation** and **Stronghold** (mā'ôz, "a strong fortified place"; cf. 27:1; 43:2; 52:7) for those who **take refuge in Him** from **the wicked.**

Psalm 38

Psalm 38 is a song of sorrow. It is titled "a petition" (lit., "to bring to remembrance"; cf. comments on the title to Ps. 70). The psalmist was severely chastened by the Lord for personal sin, and grievously plagued by his enemies. In his extreme plight he pleaded that the Lord in compassion would deliver him. His hope was in the Lord to whom he confessed his iniquity.

A. The Lord's discipline (38:1-12)

38:1-2. David pleaded that the LORD stop chastening him in His **wrath** (cf. 6:1). This **discipline** was apparently painful and harsh, as the figures of the **arrows** and the **hand** reflect.

38:3-8. David lamented his sufferings for the chastening of his sin. **Because of** his sin he had lost his **health** (cf. v. 7) and his fitness (**soundness**; on **bones,** see comments on 6:2). He had been made to **bear** his **guilt,** which had **overwhelmed** him (38:4). His illness was a festering, painful, debilitating one **brought** on by **sinful foolishness** (vv. 5-6). He was crushed in **body** (cf. v. 3) and spirit (he was **feeble . . . crushed,** and in **anguish**).

38:9-12. David then described the effect of his suffering on others. First, his pitiable state lay **open before** the LORD (vv. 9-10). God knew that he sighed at the point of death. Second, his **friends** avoided him (v. 11). Third, his enemies spoke evil of him and planned ways to deceive him and **ruin** him (v. 12; cf. 35:4, 8; 40:14; 70:2).

B. The sufferer's hope (38:13-22)

The second portion of the psalm expresses David's confidence that the Lord would have compassion on him and rescue him.

38:13-16. His hope was in the LORD alone. Negatively, **like a deaf . . . mute** he made no reply (vv. 13-14) to the wicked who plotted his destruction (cf. v. 12). Rather he waited **for** the LORD to **answer** his prayer and end their triumphant gloating.

38:17-20. David's need was great and his situation desperate. His **pain** (cf. v. 7) was constant. Moreover, he confessed his sin, recognizing that **sin** was the cause of his suffering (cf. vv. 3-4). But his **enemies** were **vigorous** and **numerous,** and thrived on **evil** and **slander.** The sufferer sensed that God must rescue him soon.

38:21-22. David's petition was urgent. He entreated the LORD . . . **not** to **forsake** him but **to help** him because He was his **God** and **Savior.**

Psalm 39

David acknowledged that God had made man's life brief. So he cast himself on the Lord as his only hope, praying that God would stop chastening him so he could enjoy his remaining days.

The psalm continues the theme of Psalm 38, but his enemies' onslaught had subsided. He seems to have suffered a prolonged illness that brought him near death.

A. Acknowledgment of life's brevity (39:1-6)

39:1-3. David submitted to the knowledge that his life was brief (vv. 1-6). First, he resolved not to **sin** by his words. He kept **silent** in the presence of his enemies, but suppressing his feelings only aggravated his suffering.

39:4-6. Second, he sought relief from his frustration by submitting to the Lord's determination of his life. He prayed that the LORD would help him know the brevity of **life** (cf. 90:10, 12). This prayer was prompted by the awareness that **life** is brief in duration—like a **handbreadth** and **a breath** (cf. Job 7:7; Pss. 39:11; 62:9; 144:4). All one's labors in which he **heaps up** his possessions are **vain,** for life is short.

B. Confidence in life's only hope (39:7-13)

39:7. Realizing that his afflictions were due to his sins, David cast himself wholly on the LORD to make his brief sojourn in life enjoyable. He expressed his commitment to the Lord in the words **My hope is in You** (cf. 25:5, 21; 33:20; 62:5; 71:5).

39:8-11. David petitioned the Lord to stop chastening him (vv. 8-9). God rebukes people for **sin** and consumes **their wealth like a moth** eating a garment (v. 11; cf. Job 13:28; Isa. 50:9; 51:8; Hosea 5:12; James 5:2). Because the psalmist was **overcome,** he prayed for God to **remove** His **scourge** (Ps. 39:10).

39:12-13. The psalmist's final prayer in this psalm was that God would hear his plea and treat him not as **a stranger** but with favor, by making his remaining days enjoyable.

Psalm 40

This psalm includes thanksgiving (vv. 1-10) and petition (vv. 11-17). In the first part David gladly offered himself as a sacrifice to God because of the great salvation granted him. In the second part he lamented the distress that had come on him and prayed for deliverance.

A. Sacrificial dedication to God (40:1-10)

40:1-4. The psalm begins with David's joyful report to the congregation about his deliverance and an encouragement to them to trust the Lord. **God** did something wonderful for him after a long period of prayerful, patient waiting. Using figurative language to describe his distress and release, he affirmed that **the Lord** saved him from his dilemma (like being in a **slimy pit** with **mud and mire**) and established him firmly **on a rock.** This deliverance gave him **a new song** for rejoicing (cf. 33:3; 96:1; 98:1; 144:9; 149:1).

On the basis of this deliverance he declared the blessedness of one who trusts in **the Lord** alone, without looking to the wicked (**the proud** and idol-worshipers).

40:5. David expressed appreciation for the Lord's innumerable and wonderful acts of deliverance (**wonders**). If he tried to **speak** of all the things God had **planned for** His own, **they would be too** numerous to tell.

40:6. Recognizing his rich benefits from God prompted the psalmist to dedicate himself. He recalled that God preferred his body to his sacrifices. Some have suggested that the words **my ears You have pierced** refer to the custom of boring a slave's ear (Ex. 21:6), meaning, "You have bound me as a slave to Yourself." However, it is more likely that this statement is a recognition that God had given him the ability to hear and obey the Word of the Lord (cf. NIV marg., "opened"). The Septuagint translated it much more generally, "a body You have prepared for me" (cf. NIV marg.), which captured the idea of the context.

40:7-8. David responded to the truth in verse 6 by yielding his life to do God's will. He presented himself willingly to the Lord, received direction from the book (**the scroll**), and expressed his **desire** to **do the will of God.** These verses present a marvelous example of what is involved in dedicating oneself to God's will in accordance with His Word.

Verses 6-8 take on a greater significance when cited in Hebrews 10:5-7 where the writer contrasted Christ's perfect obedience with the insufficiency of the Mosaic sacrifices. The words are ap-

plied to Christ's Incarnation to fulfill God's purpose for Him as prescribed in the book.

40:9-10. Part of the will of the Lord, according to David's compliance with it, is praise. So in these verses he announced that he willingly spoke to the congregation of many of the Lord's attributes, including His **righteousness . . . faithfulness . . . salvation. . . . love,** and **truth.**

B. Supplication to God for deliverance (40:11-17)

40:11-12. The tone of the psalm changes dramatically here to one of urgent prayer. David began his supplication by petitioning the Lord to continue His **mercy** (lit., "compassion"), loyal **love,** and **truth** because of the many **troubles** and **sins** that surrounded him. The troubles he was experiencing were directly related to his many sins (cf. 25:17-18; 38:2-14).

40:13-16. His prayer became more specific as he asked for a quick deliverance (**come quickly;** cf. v. 17) from his troubles. He believed that the Lord, in rescuing him, should confound all those who sought to **take** his **life** and bring him **ruin** (vv. 14-15; cf. 35:4, 8; 70:2). By His turning **back** David's enemies **in disgrace** (cf. 6:10; 70:2), the righteous would be encouraged to **rejoice** and praise **the Lord.** These would be the effects of God's answer to his prayer.

40:17. Then the psalmist, being **poor and needy** (see comments on 37:14), repeated his prayer that **the Lord. . . . not delay** (cf. 40:13) in helping him (see comments on 30:10).

Psalm 41

In this psalm David instructed the congregation that those who aided the needy would themselves obtain deliverance. In relation to this he recalled his prayer for revenge on those who did not have mercy on him but took advantage of his illness. Psalm 41 is a lesson based on a prayer for help against treachery.

A. The merciful obtain mercy (41:1-3)

41:1. The psalm begins with the general principle that **the Lord** will show mercy to one **who has regard for the weak.** This spirit wins divine approval and a corresponding reward.

41:2-3. Specific blessings given the merciful include protection and security **in the land** (cf. 37:9, 11, 22, 29). Also **the LORD** will **not** give **him** over **to . . . his** enemies, and **will sustain him** in **illness.**

B. The vengeance for treachery (41:4-10)

Still addressing the congregation, the psalmist pointed out that the Lord will justly punish those who take advantage of the afflicted. David developed this idea by reiterating his prayer in his experience.

41:4-10. His prayer had been one for healing after confessing his sin (v. 4). However, he lamented the fact that his **enemies** took advantage of his condition. Wanting him to **die** (v. 5), they feigned friendship while slandering him (v. 6), **saying** that he would **never** survive (vv. 7-8). **Even** his trusted **friend** betrayed **(lifted up his heel against)** him (v. 9). These words, of course, were quoted by Jesus concerning Judas (John 13:18). But here David had in mind the treachery of his friend Ahithophel, who betrayed him, and then hanged himself (2 Sam. 16:20–17:3, 23).

David's prayer had been motivated partly by his desire to **repay** his foes for their treachery (Ps. 41:10).

C. Deliverance for integrity (41:11-13)

41:11-12. Addressing God directly, David noted that God delivered him (cf. v. 1) from his enemies because he had **integrity.**

41:13. This doxology (cf. 106:48) concludes the first major section (Book I) of the Book of Psalms.

II. Book II (Pss. 42–72)

In Book II 7 psalms (Pss. 42; 44–49) have the headings, "of the Sons of Korah." This is probably not a designation of the authors, but a reference to the fact that these psalms were delivered to them to be performed. One psalm in Book II is by Asaph (Ps. 50), 20 are by David (Pss. 51–70), 3 are anonymous (Pss. 43; 67; 71), and 1 is by Solomon (Ps. 72).

Psalm 42

Apparently Psalms 42 and 43 belonged together at one time, many Hebrew manuscripts having them as one psalm. This is evident from the fact that the refrain is repeated twice in Psalm 42

(vv. 5, 11) and at the end of Psalm 43 (v. 5). Psalm 42 was the expression of the psalmist's yearning for God, and Psalm 43 was his praise at the prospect of full communion with God.

A. Longing for the living God (42:1-5)

In the first stanza, the psalmist wrote that he longed for the living God as he was taunted by his enemies, but was confident that he would yet praise Him.

42:1-2. The psalmist compared his yearning **for the living God** to the longing of a **deer** for **water.** The animal's need for water to sustain its life forms a fitting simile for a soul's need of the living **God** (cf. 143:6), the Source of spiritual life.

42:3-4. The writer explained that he had been yearning in **tears** while his enemies had been taunting him. They continually **(all day long;** cf. v. 10; 38:12) taunted his faith with the question, **Where is your God?** (cf. 42:10) while he was separated from the formal place of worship. He could only recall his joyful participation in the festal processions in Jerusalem.

42:5. In this refrain (cf. v. 11; 43:5) the psalmist in a rhetorical question encouraged himself, though downhearted (42:6), to **hope in God,** for he was confident that he would **yet** be able to **praise Him** as before.

B. Overwhelmed by his enemies (42:6-11)

In this second stanza, the psalmist lamented that his enemies had stormed over him like great billows, but again he had hope that he would yet praise the Lord.

42:6. The psalmist lamented his deep depression. Because his **soul** was **downcast** (cf. v. 5) he prayed to the Lord. The mountainous region in the tribe of Dan refers to the place from which he prayed. He was apparently miles north of the Sea of Kinnereth (Galilee). Yet he longed to be not on **Mount Mizar** (a peak in the Mount **Hermon** range) but on Mount Zion (cf. 43:3).

42:7. His distress is figuratively portrayed by billows and **waves.** Trouble had come over him like one wave after another, personified as if they were calling to each other to come down in the **waterfalls.** He had been overwhelmed as if by a flood.

42:8. Then the psalmist confidently called on the LORD to deliver him. He mustered confidence in the Lord—confidence that His love and His song would be with him continually (by day and by night). His prayer refers to his praise.

42:9-11. In his prayer (v. 8) he asked God why he had to continue suffering physically (on bones, see comments on 6:2) and emotionally (going about mourning) under oppression (cf. 43:2). He reminded the Lord that his enemies taunted his faith continually (cf. 42:3). In this way he hoped to motivate the Lord to answer.

In verse 11 he repeated his refrain (cf. v. 5; 43:5).

Psalm 43

This psalm completes the song begun in Psalm 42. Though Psalms 42 and 43 are one psalm in many Hebrew manuscripts, Psalm 43 is also an independent song of praise. In it the psalmist asked the Lord to lead him back to Jerusalem where he longed to serve and praise.

A. Vindication from his enemies (43:1-3)

43:1. In his petition to be brought back to Jerusalem the psalmist prayed for vindication from his enemies, who were ungodly . . . deceitful, and wicked. He asked God to plead his cause in their presence.

43:2. His prayer is based on the confidence that God was his Safety. However, since God was indeed His Stronghold (mā'ôz, "a strong fortified place"; cf. 27:1; 37:39; 52:7), he was troubled by his distress at the hands of his enemy (cf. 42:9). God had seemingly rejected him.

43:3. Vindication from his foes' taunting him would come through the psalmist's being brought safely to Jerusalem to worship. So he prayed that God's light and . . . truth would guide Him to God's dwelling place, the holy mountain (cf. 48:1; 87:1; 99:9). This refers to Jerusalem where David's tabernacle and later Solomon's temple were erected. "Light" represented understanding and life, and "truth" represented God's faithful Word by which the psalm-writer would find guidance. He awaited God's manifestations for direction.

B. Resolution to praise (43:4)

43:4. The psalmist expressed his vow to praise . . . God for his deliverance when he returned to the altar in Jerusalem. Arriving there, the longing of his soul would be satisfied with God, his joy and his delight.

C. Encouragement for the soul (43:5)

43:5. The refrain from Psalm 42:5, 11 is repeated here. The psalmist found encouragement for his downcast and disturbed soul in the hope (confidence) that he would yet praise the Lord.

Psalm 44

Psalm 44 is a lament of the nation in a time of unequaled disaster. Because of God's deliverance of the nation's ancestors, and because of the people's present faith, they prayed earnestly that God would give them victory. Their prayer was prompted by the fact that they were experiencing defeats which they did not understand. The psalm is unique as an assertion of national fidelity (contrast Lam. 3).

A. The historic faith of the nation (44:1-8)

The people asserted their confidence in the Lord, based on His past dealings with the nation and her present faith.

44:1-3. After stating that Israel knew of God's marvelous works in the past (v. 1), they recalled specifically that the Lord gave them the land under Joshua (v. 2). This was recognized as a miraculous work of God, by His hand . . . arm, favor (face shining; cf. comments on 4:6), and love, not by their own strength.

44:4-8. As a result of hearing what God had done, the nation trusted in Him as her King. Sometimes the psalmist wrote as if one person were involved (e.g., "my King"), but usually he wrote as if the entire nation were speaking (e.g., our enemies), indicating that the singular pronouns may be collective. The people experienced similar great victories. . . . through God in their lifetime, and were confident (in God each made his boast) regarding the future.

B. The humiliating defeat of the nation (44:9-16)

44:9-12. In spite of past victories (cf. vv. 3-4, 7) the nation had been subjected to a humiliating defeat. First the defeat is described literally, attributing it to the fact that the Lord **no longer** fought for them (vv. 9-10). Then the defeat was vividly described in figurative language (vv. 11-12): they were **scattered** like **sheep** (cf. v. 22) and were **sold** as slaves for trifling amounts which suggested their small worth.

44:13-16. As a result, the nation had been **made . . . a reproach.** Israel's enemies mockingly derided them, causing them inward feelings of ignominy (**disgrace**) and **shame.**

C. The protection of innocence (44:17-22)

44:17-22. Because this defeat was undeserved, the nation was perplexed. After affirming her integrity (v. 17), the nation affirmed her **covenant** loyalty to God. She had **not** gone astray after other gods and therefore did not deserve this crushing defeat (vv. 18-19). In fact **God** had not accused the nation of idolatry (vv. 20-21). Had they been involved in it, He in His omniscience certainly would have known it. **Yet for** His **sake** they faced **death** continually (**all day long**). That is, because they fought a holy war for Him, they were experiencing this disaster and were treated like **sheep to be slaughtered** (cf. v. 11).

D. The prayer for victory (44:23-26)

44:23-26. The nation asked God for help (**rouse Youself!**) for she saw no reason why He should ignore her **misery.** Moreover, the nation felt that God must rescue her (**rise up and help us**) because she was at her lowest (**brought down to the dust;** i.e., about to die). Though the nation was seemingly rejected by God and had apparently lost a battle (even though she had been faithful), she wholeheartedly trusted in the LORD to **redeem** (cf. comments on 26:11) her. This is the proper age-old response of the genuine believer to suffering (cf. Job 13:15, "Though He slay me, yet will I hope in Him").

Psalm 45

This is a royal psalm celebrating the wedding of the mighty king. The psalm begins with lavish praise to the royal groom for all his splendor, majesty, and righteousness. This is followed by a report of the counsel given to the bride before she was brought to the king's palace in all her glory. Then the psalmist predicted universal and eternal remembrance of the king's name through his progeny.

The psalm has a lengthy superscription and an extended introduction concerning its nature. The song is set "to the tune of 'Lilies' " and is called "a wedding song" (lit., "a song of loves").

A. Praise for the royal bridegroom (45:1-9)

45:1. The psalmist explained that this hymn is inspirational. His **heart** was **stirred** (lit., "boiling over") with this **noble theme.** What he would pour forth in hymnic praise was so inspired, he said, that it was like a finely written and edited work. It was not possible for him to contain himself as he wrote **for** his majesty **the king.**

45:2. The writer said the king was transcendent and **excellent** in his person. Of all humans he was the fairest. For example, his words were gracious—evidence that **God** had **blessed** him.

45:3-5. Since the king was a **mighty** man of valor, the hymnist called on him to demonstrate his valor by riding **forth** to champion **truth, humility, and** justice. Because the king was just, he prospered. As **nations** fell before him, his victories would be magnificent.

45:6-7. The king was righteous in his administration. In a surprising extravagance of language, the psalmist addressed the king as **God** (*'ĕlōhîm*). This is not entirely unique; judges in Moses' day were designated in this way as God's just representatives (cf. Ex. 21:6; 22:8-9; Ps. 82:1). As God's representative, this king would have an everlasting **throne** and a righteous reign (**a scepter of justice**). Because he loved **righteousness** and hated **wickedness,** God had blessed him with abundant **joy.**

Psalm 45:6-7 undoubtedly refers to the promise of an eternal throne for the house of David (cf. 2 Sam. 7:16) which will be fulfilled in Jesus Christ when He returns to reign forever. Hebrews 1:8-9 quotes this passage in reference to the exaltation and dominion of Christ. Whether the psalmist used the word *'ĕlōhîm* to mean God or His human representative, the writer of Hebrews dem-

127

onstrated that it points up the essential difference between the Son and the angels (cf. Heb. 1:5, 7).

45:8-9. The king was joyfully blessed on his wedding day. His **robes** (royal garb) were perfumed with several fragrances. **Myrrh** is a fragrant gum from trees in Arabia (cf. its use as a perfume in Prov. 7:17; Song 1:13). **Aloes** may come from a scented wood (cf. Num. 24:6; Prov. 7:17; Song 4:14). **Cassia** may be from the fragrant roots of a plant. **Ivory** beautified the **palaces,** joyful stringed **music** was played (probably on lyres and harps), and **daughters of kings** were **honored.** With him was his **bride** adorned in **gold** jewelry from **Ophir,** a prominent source of gold, probably in western Arabia (cf. 1 Kings 9:28; 10:11; 22:48; Job 22:24; 28:16; Isa. 13:12).

B. *Advice for the bride of the king (45:10-15)*

45:10-11. The psalmist gave his charge to the bride before she was conducted into the king's presence. He instructed her to do homage to her **lord** the king, forsaking her **people.** He explained that because **the king** desired (the Heb. means more than was **enthralled by**) her **beauty,** she should **honor him.**

45:12. Following his advice, he said that she would have blessing if she obeyed his instruction. She would receive **a gift** from **Tyre** and wealthy people would **seek** her **favor** perhaps by giving her expensive gifts.

45:13-15. The scene then shifted to the court where the bride was ushered into the king's presence. She was beautiful **(glorious)** in her **gold** (cf. v. 9) and **embroidered** gown, as the joyful procession of bridesmaids **led** her **to the king.**

C. *The benediction on the wedding (45:16-17)*

45:16-17. The writer predicted the prosperity of the marriage—their **sons** would become the **princes of the land.** So the king would be remembered and honored **throughout** the **nations.**

There can be little doubt that this psalm was in the mind of John as he wrote Revelation 19:6-21. As he looked forward to the marriage of Christ, the Lamb, in heaven, he recalled how the bride clothed herself with acts of righteousness in preparation for Him (Rev.

19:6-8). Then John described the royal groom going forth to battle in righteousness (Rev. 19:11-21). Psalm 45, then, is typological of the greater Davidic King, Jesus Christ.

Psalm 46

The psalmist magnified God as the saints' sure Defense at all times. He explained that God's presence makes Zion secure from all her enemies. Thus the psalm is incorporated in the Songs of Zion, because of the centrality of Jerusalem in its message.

A. *God is the Defense of His saints (46:1-3)*

46:1-3. The psalmist declared that **God** is the **Refuge** (*maḥseh,* "shelter from danger"; cf. comments on 14:6) **and Strength** (cf. comments on 18:1) of believers. In other words they find safety and courage by trusting in Him, who is always **present** to **help** them (see comments on 30:10) in their troubles. So the saints need **not fear,** even if many perils come against them. The language is hyperbolic, to describe how great the perils may be that could come. No matter what happens, those trusting in Him are safe.

B. *God is present in Zion (46:4-7)*

46:4-5. The psalmist observed that the peace of Jerusalem—**the city of God** with **the holy place where** God dwelt (i.e., made His presence known)—was secured by **God.** The Lord's presence was like a peaceful flowing **river** (in contrast with perilous torrents, v. 3). (Cf. Isa. 8:6; 33:21, where the Lord is compared to a river encircling His city.) Because **God** was **within her,** the city would **not fall.** (Years later, however, the city *did* fall. Because of extensive idolatry in the temple, Ezek. 8, God's presence left, Ezek. 10. Without His protective presence, Jerusalem fell to the Babylonians.)

46:6-7. The psalmist then described God's mighty power: by His powerful word God **melts** the **nations** that roar against Him (cf. 2:5). Though **kingdoms** would **fall,** Jerusalem was safe.

Thus **the LORD Almighty** is like a **fortress** (*miśgōb,* "a high safe place," trans. "fortress" in 46:11; 48:3; 59:9, 16-17; 62:2, 6; 94:22, and "stronghold" in 9:9; 18:2; 144:2) to His people (cf. 46:11).

They find safety when they trust in Him.

C. God will be exalted in the earth (46:8-11)

46:8-11. The psalmist exhorted the saints to observe the saving mighty deeds of God. These deeds portray how **God** brings peace to His people, destroying weapons throughout the earth. God Himself calls for the people to trust in Him and **know that** He is **God,** for He **will be exalted** throughout **the earth.** Verses 8-10 no doubt greatly encouraged the people of Jerusalem, as the final verse (v. 11) reiterates (cf. v. 7). Also to saints of all ages, the call for a silent trust in God's saving power, in anticipation of universal peace, has been a source of comfort and strength.

Psalm 47

This psalm is a song about the Lord, the great King (cf. vv. 2, 6-7). It has been classified as an enthronement psalm, celebrating His universal reign. Other enthronement psalms are 93, 95–99. It should be understood as prophetically portraying the coming kingdom of God, manifestations of which were enjoyed by Israel. In Psalm 47 the psalmist called on all peoples of the earth to pay homage to Israel's holy Monarch—the Lord—as He assumes His kingship over them all.

A. Homage to the sovereign King (47:1-4)

47:1-2. The psalmist called on **all the nations** (cf. vv. 3, 8-9) to rejoice in homage to **the LORD Most High,** who is **the great King** (cf. vv. 6-7) **over all the earth** (cf. v. 7). Such shouts **of joy** (cf. v. 5) could come only from willing subjects of this King.

47:3-4. The reason for giving homage to Him is expressed in verses 3-4. As stated generally in verse 2, He is the great King over the earth. Specifically, this was demonstrated by His subduing **the nations** when He **chose** Israel as His **inheritance.** This subjugation of foreign nations was experienced in a small measure in Israel's history, but will be especially true in the coming Millennial Age.

B. The reigning of the sovereign King (47:5-9)

47:5-6. The psalmist, picturing God's ascending His throne **amid shouts of** ac-

clamation and the playing **of trumpets,** called for the peoples to praise their **King** (note the fourfold occurrence of **sing praises** in v. 6).

47:7-9. The psalmist called for **praise** because the Lord **reigns** (cf. 93:1; 96:10; 99:1; 146:10) **over the nations** (cf. 47:1, 3, 9). This expression, common to this type of psalm, most likely is a prophetic statement of future certainty. So the psalmist anticipated the sure rule of God in which all **nobles** and **kings** will gather before Him as their Sovereign. In His **exalted** position the Lord will someday reign over all the earth and every knee shall bow before Him (Phil. 2:9-11). To those who believe in Him, the confidence that the truths of this psalm will be fulfilled brings comfort and encouragement during distressing times.

Psalm 48

Psalm 48 is a song about Zion, the city of God, the great King. In praising God who loves Jerusalem, the psalmist sang of the city's glory and security because the Lord delivered it from the enemy. On the basis of this, he offered praise to God.

A. Zion is the city of our God (48:1-3)

48:1. The psalm begins with a summary of the theme: **God,** whose **holy mountain** (cf. 43:3; 87:1; 99:9; note comments in 2:6 on the "holy hill"), **the city** of Jerusalem, is greatly to be praised.

48:2-3. The psalmist then described this holy city. Its lofty beauty (cf. 50:2) is **the joy of the whole earth.** It is **like the . . . heights of Zaphon,** probably a sacred mountain some miles north of Jerusalem. But the greatest feature of **Zion** (cf. comments on 2:6) is that **God is in her citadels** (cf. 48:13). Jerusalem's strength and safety ("fortress" translates *miśgob;* cf. comments on 9:9; 46:7) are because of His presence (cf. 46:5).

B. God makes Zion secure (48:4-8)

48:4-7. The psalmist now described the defeat of Zion's enemies. **Kings** were assembled against her, but they were terrified **when . . . they saw** Zion. They were **seized** with **terror** and **trembling** like **a woman in** child **labor.** God destroyed them swiftly, **like ships of Tarshish** (possibly large seagoing merchant ships on the Mediterranean) **shattered by**

an east wind. Many have taken this passage as a tribute to God's deliverance of Jerusalem from the invading Assyrian armies (cf. Isa. 10:8; 33:3, 14).

48:8. The psalmist confirmed the report that the LORD Almighty (lit., "the Lord of armies") had made Zion secure. This title of the Lord is frequently used in passages referring to military battles. His armies are both terrestrial (Israel's soldiers) and celestial (angels).

C. Zion rejoices in her God (48:9-14)

48:9-10. The psalmist offered praise to God for His unfailing love (ḥeseḏ, "loyal love") and righteousness. Praise of God fills the earth, for God's power demonstrates His faithfulness.

48:11-14. The psalmist then invited the congregation in Zion and all Judah to rejoice in God by observing the strength of the city (her unharmed towers . . . ramparts, and citadels; cf. v. 3) which He had preserved. This God who had made them secure will be the Guide for believers forever.

Psalm 49

This psalm is a wisdom poem, dealing with the age-old problem of the prosperity of the wicked (cf. Ps. 73). The poet called his work a dark saying (riddle, 49:4) that is worth analyzing. He had observed that the wicked are prosperous and rich, and filled with pride and a sense of security. But the wise psalmist stated that they are no better than the beasts of the field. In the final analysis, the hope of the righteous is better than the false security of the wicked.

A. Announcement of the dark saying (49:1-4)

49:1-4. The psalmist called the world to listen to his saying. All people, rich and poor alike (the subject of the psalm), should hear his wisdom. He explained that his words, though wise, would be dark, that is, they would be like a riddle in that discernment and understanding are necessary for perception. Indeed, many of life's difficulties require spiritual perception to forestall despair.

B. Observation of the prosperity of the wicked (49:5-12)

49:5. In verses 5-12 the wise poet reported his observation that the prosperous have a false security. He introduced his theme in verse 5 by stating that he marveled that he ever feared evil times brought on by the wicked. Their glory is only temporary.

49:6-9. He developed this idea by noting that the proud and arrogant cannot redeem (cf. comments on 26:11) another person's life. Life is too costly for a man to ransom, even by great riches. Wealth cannot prevent death.

49:10-12. The truth stated in verses 6-9 is known even among the wealthy. They—as well as the foolish—die (cf. Ecc. 2:15-16) and leave their wealth to their heirs (cf. Ecc. 2:19-21). Their new places of residence will be the grave, even though their earthly dwellings or lands may bear their names. Man's body, like the bodies of animals, dies (cf. Ecc. 3:19-20).

C. Encouragement in the abiding hope (49:13-20)

49:13-14. The wise psalmist concluded that the doom of the proud is sure, but the hope of the righteous is eternal. He introduced this contrast by marveling at the folly of proud people's lives. Death is the fate of the self-righteous and of those who follow them. They are turned into the grave (sheol) where death will feed on them. Their glory will be consumed in the grave. The psalmist was not concerned at this point with God's judgment on the wicked, other than the departure of their earthly glory.

49:15. As for the righteous, God will redeem them from the grave. Again the terminology contrasts with the ruin of the wicked, and includes in germ form the hope of the resurrection.

49:16-20. The writer said that it is foolish to be jealous of unbelieving wealthy people for their doom is sure. Though they enjoy great splendor and prosper in this life, they pass away into darkness, taking nothing with them (cf. Ecc. 5:15). The advice is clear: do not be overawed when a man grows rich. A proper perspective is necessary for spiritual discernment of life. The destiny of the righteous is far better than the fleeting glory of the wicked.

Psalm 50

This didactic psalm, written by Asaph, a leading Levite musician

(1 Chron. 16:4-5) who also wrote Psalms 73–83, deals with man's worship of God and duty to his neighbor, which are in the two portions of the Decalogue (Ten Commandments). Asaph described a scene in the heavenly courtroom in which the Lord will examine His people. Asaph then declared that the Lord had indictments against two sins of His people: formalism in worship and hypocrisy in living. To please God His people must bring sacrifices of thanksgiving from obedient, trusting hearts.

A. The Lord's appearance to judge (50:1-6)

50:1-3. Asaph described a courtroom scene in which **the Mighty One, God, the Lord**—three designations for the Lord—came to judge. Everyone on **the earth,** from east to west, was summoned before Him. **From** beautiful **Zion** (cf. comments on 2:6; also see 48:2, 11-12), the place of the temple, **God shines forth.** As He **comes** to judge, His presence is accompanied by devouring **fire** and a raging **tempest.** These phenomena, frequently accompanying theophanies, signify His consuming judgment.

50:4-6. Asaph then visualized the participants in the case. The inhabitants of the universe will be the witnesses (**the heavens** and **the earth** standing for the inhabitants of each). When He judges **His people,** all the universe will witness it. The defendants in the case will be the saints, **who** have **made a covenant with** Him. And **God** is the righteous **Judge.** With this scene envisioned, Asaph then reported the Lord's two charges against His people (vv. 7-15 and 16-23).

B. The Lord's indictment against formalism (50:7-15)

50:7-13. Asaph, announcing the Lord's first of two charges **against** His **people,** described their formalism in worship. The charge was given as a word from **God,** their **God,** so they would take heed. God did **not** reprove them, however, for their meticulous keeping of the letter of the Law in offering the prescribed **sacrifices.** But Israel failed to realize that God did not need their bulls or **goats** (v. 9; cf. v. 13), for He is the Lord of all Creation. He already owns **every animal** and knows **every bird.** He instituted the sacrifices not because He needed the animals but because the people desperately needed Him. He is not like the gods of the pagans who supposedly thrived on food sacrifices. The Lord does not depend on man's worship for survival.

50:14-15. Israel should offer their sacrifices of thanksgiving from a genuine trust in the Lord. The solution to formalism is to worship in genuine faith, which is why Asaph called on the people to **sacrifice thank offerings.** The Hebrew word for thank offerings is *tôdâh*, from the verb *yādâh,* "to acknowledge, thank." Such an offering could not be given unless the offerer had experienced God's work on his behalf. If he was in distress and called on **God,** the Lord would answer. Then the offerer would praise the Lord as a spontaneous expression of his enjoyment of God's benefits. If the people had been praising they would have enjoyed His benefits, not worshiping in an empty ritualistic form.

C. The Lord's indictment against hypocrisy (50:16-23)

50:16-17. Asaph, announcing God's second charge, decried the nation's hypocritical living. He first rebuked **the wicked** for reciting His **laws** and speaking of His **covenant** as their profession of faith, for they actually hated God's **instruction.** Though these wicked people assembled with those who loved the Lord, **God** knew their hearts.

50:18-21. The psalmist then selected several examples of their wickedness. While appearing righteous, they tolerated and took part in theft (cf. Ex. 20:15), adultery (cf. Ex. 20:14), and **slander** (cf. Ex. 20:16). He warned them not to confuse God's patience with His approval. God's silence did not mean that He agreed with their actions. Instead the Lord would **rebuke** them directly (**to your face**).

50:22-23. Asaph instructed the hypocrites to **consider** their ways before it was too late. Again he called on them to sacrifice **thank offerings** (cf. comments on v. 14) from hearts that are right with God.

So the psalm indicts God's people for formalism and hypocrisy in worship. Jesus' advice to "worship in spirit and in truth" (John 4:24) provides the proper correctives for these faults.

Psalm 51

Few psalms have found as much use as this one among the saints of all ages, a fact which bears witness to the spiritual needs of God's people. Psalm 51 stands as a paradigm of prayers for forgiveness of sins. Its superscription ascribes the occasion to David's sin of adultery with Bathsheba (2 Sam. 11), an incident in which David broke several of the Ten Commandments. Believers have been comforted by the fact that since David's sins were forgiven theirs can be too.

Poetry often develops the intensity of a moment. Such a moment with David came when he, having been confronted with his sin, confessed it (2 Sam. 12:13a). Because this psalm deals only with confession and has no word of the forgiveness (which did follow immediately in the historical narrative, 2 Sam. 12:13b), this psalm must be understood as a full meditation on the importance of confession. After a believer sins, he must obtain forgiveness if he is to enjoy full participation in the service of the Lord.

The message of this psalm is that the vilest offender among God's people can appeal to God for forgiveness, for moral restoration, and for the resumption of a joyful life of fellowship and service, if he comes with a broken spirit and bases his appeal on God's compassion and grace.

A. Introductory prayer (51:1-2)

David appealed to God's love and compassion as he petitioned the Lord to forgive him by grace and cleanse him from sin.

51:1a. God's attributes of **unfailing love** (*ḥesed*) for His servant and His **compassion** for the helpless, were the basis for David's appeal for mercy. Even the verb **have mercy** was a prayer for **God** to act in accord with His nature. It is also a recognition that David did not deserve forgiveness. God's forgiveness is by His grace alone.

51:1b-2. The three verbs David employed here are figurative. **Blot out** implies a comparison with human records that can be erased; **wash away** (*kābas*) compares forgiveness with washing clothing (often viewed as an extension of a person), **and cleanse** is drawn from the liturgical ceremonial law in which one might be purified for temple participation. These requests (cf. vv. 7, 9) stressed

David's desire for God's total forgiveness of his **transgressions . . . iniquity, and sin.**

B. Confession (51:3-6)

David confessed that he had sinned against the Lord (vv. 3-4), and then lamented his moral impotence (vv. 5-6).

51:3-4. When he said that his **sin** was constantly **before** him, it must be remembered that his confession came about a year after he had sinned (the young child died a week after the confession; cf. 2 Sam. 12:13-18). Perhaps David had so rationalized his actions that he did not sense his guilt until Nathan approached him. At any rate, he confessed that he had **sinned** against the Lord. And he submitted to the Lord's will, acknowledging that anything God decided about him would be just.

51:5-6. David then acknowledged that he was morally impotent. He was born **a sinner,** that is, at no time in his life was he without sin. This ran contrary to God's moral demands on his life. From his early days he faced **inner** tension, knowing that God desires **truth** and **wisdom,** that is, reliable and productive living.

C. Petition (51:7-12)

In connection with his confession, David petitioned God first for forgiveness (vv. 7-9), then for inner renewal (vv. 10-12).

51:7-9. In his prayer for forgiveness the psalmist made the same requests as before (cf. vv. 1b-2) but in reverse order: **cleanse . . . wash,** and **blot out.** When David spoke of God's cleansing him **with hyssop,** he was alluding to the use of hyssop at the religious ceremonies to sprinkle sacrificial blood on the altar. This represented the removal of sin through the shedding of blood (cf. Heb. 9:22). David then asked God to let him once again **rejoice** in the knowledge of being right with God. (On the association of **bones** with emotional anguish, see comments on Ps. 6:2.) The king asked God to remove his **sins** judicially.

51:10-12. As a corrective for his sinful nature, David petitioned **God** for inward renewal of his **heart** attitude (v. 10), preservation in service (v. 11), and restoration of **joy** (v. 12). He was aware that he had become indifferent in his attitudes so he needed renovation. He was also aware that Saul was removed from the kingship for his sin (signified in the OT by the departure of the **Holy Spirit**), so David asked that God not **take** away His Spirit and depose him too. In the New Testament the Spirit does not leave believers; at the moment of salvation He indwells them (cf. John 14:16; Rom. 8:9). But a Christian may be cast aside from service because of sin (cf. 1 Cor. 9:27). David was also aware that in order to experience the joy he once had in his **salvation,** he needed God's inner spiritual renewal.

D. Vow of praise (51:13-17)

David promised God that if He forgave him he would participate fully in His service. The requests in these verses are for things that result from forgiveness, and so they form indirect requests for forgiveness.

51:13. First, David said that if God forgave him, he would **teach . . . sinners** God's **ways** (i.e., how He deals with penitent sinners). Naturally, to be able to teach this he himself must first experience forgiveness.

51:14-15. Second, David said if God forgave him, he would **sing** and **praise** God. Only when delivered from his bloodguiltiness could he join in praising **God.**

51:16-17. Third, David promised that if **God** forgave his sins he would sacrifice to God. He knew that God did not desire simply an animal **sacrifice** from him (cf. 40:6). He needed to find forgiveness before he could sacrifice a peace offering to God. The sacrifice he had to bring was **a broken and contrite** (crushed) **heart**—a humbled **spirit** fully penitent for sin. That is what God desires and will receive.

In the Old Testament, anyone who sinned as David did had to receive a word from a priest or prophet indicating he was forgiven. Only then could the penitent person again take part in worship and make a peace offering. In the New Testament the word of forgiveness is forever written in God's Word—the blood of Jesus Christ cleanses from sin (1 John 1:7). Yet even in the New Testament a believer must have a spirit broken of all self-assertion; he must acknowledge his need before God to find spiritual renewal and cleansing (1 John 1:9).

E. Prayer for prosperity (51:18-19)

51:18-19. These verses have often been considered a later addition to the psalm because they do not readily relate to the psalm's theme. However, the anticipation of right **sacrifices** (v. 19) is closely related to verses 16-17. The prayer for the building up **of the walls of Jerusalem** could be a prayer for general prosperity of the city's defenses; but it could also be figurative, requesting the strengthening of the moral defenses of the nation (i.e., edifying the king). **Righteous** worship is compatible with moral prosperity.

Psalm 52

This psalm ascribed to David pertains to the occasion of Doeg's treachery (1 Sam. 21–22). The character described in this psalm portrays just such a man. David, who trusted in the Lord, contrasted his faith with the treacherous man who followed a course of iniquity.

A. The destruction of the man of treachery (52:1-7)

52:1. Addressing the evil **man** directly, David chided his treachery (vv. 1-5). David was amazed that the man could actually **boast** in his **evil** in view of the fact he was **a disgrace** to **God.**

52:2-4. The treacherous man, Doeg (see the superscription), had a **deceitful tongue** as sharp as a **razor** (cf. "swords" in 55:21), for what he said destroyed others (cf. James 3:6, 8). He thrived on a wicked and false way of life, loving words that devour.

52:5. Because of such wickedness, David predicted that **God** would pluck the wicked man out of **the land of the living,** that is, death would swiftly remove him forever.

52:6-7. David then anticipated the joy that this would bring to **the righteous.** They would **see** what happens to a person who trusts not in the Lord but in his own ill-gotten riches for strength. (**Stronghold** translates $mā'ôz$, "a strong fortified place"; cf. 27:1; 37:39; 43:2.)

B. The destiny of the man of faith (52:8-9)

52:8-9. In striking contrast with Doeg, the treacherous man (vv. 1-7), David portrayed his own blessed state in the Lord. He compared himself to a green **olive tree,** a figure of prosperity in God's presence (cf. Hosea 14:6). This contrasts with the wicked who will be rooted up (Ps. 52:5). The metaphor of a **flourishing** tree was used in Psalm 1:3.

David's flourishing was because of **God's unfailing love,** in which he said he trusted **forever.** So he vowed to go on praising God **for what** He had **done.** David would wait (**hope**) in God's **name** (which signified His attributes and actions; cf. Ex. 34:5-7) and then he would **praise** Him among the **saints.**

So the righteous, unlike people of treachery, place their confidence in God's love, for there abide justice and blessing.

Psalm 53

This passage is another version of Psalm 14, adapted for Book II (*'ĕlōhîm,* "God," is substituted for Yahweh, LORD). The psalm is David's, set to *māhălat,* possibly a well-known tune. The psalm reports that the entire human race is evil and that God will overthrow sinners. Therefore the psalmist longs for the establishment of God's kingdom.

A. Revelation of the human race (53:1-3)

53:1. David received a revelation of God's view of the human race: **they are all fools.** His summary description is in this verse: **the fool** believes **there is no God;** thus his life is **corrupt** and **vile** (i.e., abominable to God). In fact **no one . . . does good.**

53:2-3. He then reported the details of this revelation. God investigates the human race to see if there is **one** prudent person, but the search is fruitless. The entire human race has **become corrupt** (*'ālaḥ,* "soured" like milk, used only here and in 14:3; Job 15:16). This word for corrupt differs from the word for corrupt in Psalm 53:1. **Not . . . one** single person is without sin (cf. Rom. 3:10-12).

B. Anticipation of the destruction of the wicked (53:4-5)

53:4-5. David expressed his amazement at the ignorance of those who persecute the righteous. He foresaw that the wicked will be in great terror and **shame** when **God** destroys them. This judgment is so certain that the psalmist envisioned it as already accomplished.

C. Longing for God's kingdom (53:6)

53:6. David expressed a yearning for the establishment of God's kingdom when He **restores** the captives. Thus a time is coming when the wicked presence of unbelievers will end and God's people, **Israel,** will **rejoice.**

Psalm 54

This is a confident prayer of David when he, being pursued by Saul, was betrayed by "the Ziphites" (cf. 1 Sam. 23:19). Though David was being hotly pursued by ungodly men who sought his life, he confidently trusted in the Lord's abilities for complete deliverance.

A. Save me by Your name (54:1-3)

54:1-2. The first part of the psalm (vv. 1-3) records David's urgent **prayer** for deliverance. He based his petition on the **name** of **God.** His "name" (cf. v. 6) represents who He is and what He has done (cf. Ex. 34:5-7). David had come to know the mighty power of **God** who is able to **save.**

54:3. The reason for the appeal was that violent **men** were trying to destroy him. These **men** had no **regard for God.**

B. God is my Help (54:4-7)

54:4-5. The second portion of the psalm (vv. 4-7) records David's confident assertion of his trust in God. He declared that **God is** his Helper (see comments on 30:10) and Sustainer. This led him to pray that God would requite **evil . . . on those who** slandered him. He asked that God demonstrate His **faithfulness** to him.

54:6-7. In full confidence that God had heard his prayer and would deliver him **from all** the **troubles** brought on by his **foes,** David promised to **praise** God with **a freewill offering.** This refers to the fellowship offerings (Lev. 3; 7) that accompanied and expressed praises for deliverance. They were offered voluntarily by devout believers. David again (cf. Ps. 52:9) spoke of the Lord's **name** (cf. 54:1) as **good.**

Psalm 55

This psalm records David's experience of persecution through the betrayal of an intimate friend. Commentators speculate that the occasion was Ahithophel's treachery (2 Sam. 15:31), but this is far from certain.

In the psalm David called on God to enable him to escape from his terrible plight. He lamented the oppression that had come through being betrayed by his close friend. Yet David expressed his personal confidence in God who redeems.

A. David's terrifying oppression (55:1-8)

55:1-8. This first section records his **prayer** to be delivered from his terrible oppression. He cried out to **God,** pleading that God **hear** his restless complaint (vv. 1-2a). His **enemy** was staring at him and angrily reviling him, reducing him to **fear . . . trembling,** and **horror** (vv. 2b-5). So he longed to escape from the hostility (vv. 6-8), like **a dove** flying **away** to a place of refuge **in the desert,** to a **shelter** (*miplāṭ*, "a place of escape," used only here in the OT) **from** the **storm.**

B. David's painful betrayal (55:9-15)

55:9-11. The psalmist asked God to **confuse the wicked** who oppressed him. The basis of this imprecatory prayer is that **the city** (perhaps Jerusalem) was filled with **violence and strife** and **malice and abuse,** which in turn were caused by **threats and lies** by the wicked.

55:12-14. The painful part of his exposure to this destructive violence was that it came through the betrayal of a faithful **companion.** David said he could have borne the oppression of **an enemy** or could have hidden from **a foe** but far worse was the fact that he was betrayed by a **close friend.** David addressed the traitor (**it is you**), recalling how they worshiped the Lord together with the congregation (**throng**).

55:15. Thus the psalmist wished God's swift destruction (by **death**) on all his **enemies** (cf. v. 23).

C. David's personal confidence (55:16-23)

55:16-21. Expressing his confidence in the Lord, David said **the LORD saves me.** Knowing this, he would continue to call out to Him **in** his **distress,** for the Lord, who redeems (*pādâh*; cf. comments on 26:11) him in **battle,** would hear him. God, the sovereign Ruler, hears the prayers of His own; He also hears and knows about the violence of the wicked. Having **no fear of God,** they are defeated by the Lord. Included among those who

do not fear God was David's **companion,** who broke **his covenant** and became deceitfully destructive. This "friend's" talk was **smooth** and **soothing** but animosity was **in his heart.** Four times David spoke of his enemies' **words** being sharp and destructive like **swords** (cf. 57:4; 59:7; 64:3).

55:22-23. David's confidence found expression in his words to the saints to entrust (**cast**) their burdens (**cares**) onto **the LORD** (cf. 1 Peter 5:7). God will **never** forsake **the righteous** (cf. Deut. 31:6; Heb. 13:5). But He will destroy (cf. Ps. 55:15) **bloodthirsty and deceitful men** who afflict the righteous.

Psalm 56

Psalm 56 is a song of trust ascribed to the time of David's visit to Gath (see 1 Sam. 21:10; Ps. 34). The psalm is set "to the tune of 'A Dove on Distant Oaks.' " David asserted that even though his enemies waited to destroy him, he trusted confidently in the Lord who knew his sufferings. His confidence led him to anticipate praising God for deliverance from this danger.

A. Enemies conspired against David (56:1-7)

David prayed that the Lord would destroy those who conspired to kill him.

56:1-2. These verses include his introductory cry (**Be merciful to me, O God**) in his great peril. Proud **slanderers** hotly pursued (cf. 57:3) him **all day long** (cf. 56:5).

56:3-7. But because his confidence was **in God, whose word** he praised, he realized that he need **not** fear mere humans (**mortal man** translates *bāśār,* "flesh"; cf. "man" in v. 11). So again the psalmist laid his problem before the Lord and prayed that God would destroy his enemies (vv. 5-7). The problem is that his enemies were continually twisting his **words . . . plotting to** destroy him, and dogging his **steps.** He had no rest from their pursuit.

B. But God was for him (56:8-13)

David reiterated his confidence that the Lord knew about his suffering and would protect him.

56:8-9. He was confident because God knew him intimately, even recording his **tears.** The image of his tears being collected in a wineskin (NIV marg.) means that God did not forget his suffering. Because of that fact, he could say in full confidence, **God is for me.**

56:10-11. Here the psalmist reworded the refrain of verse 4 (see comments there). Trusting in God's **word,** he knew that mortal **man** (*'āḏām;* a different word for man is used in v. 4) is powerless to thwart **God.**

56:12-13. David's confidence led him to anticipate that **God** would deliver him from danger so that he might live (**walk . . . in the light of life**) obediently **before** Him. As in other psalms, David was so confident **God** would deliver him that he wrote in the past tense (**You have delivered me**). So he vowed to praise God for this with **thank offerings.**

Psalm 57

Psalm 57 resembles the preceding psalm in its message and structure, except that its mood is more triumphant. The superscription attributes the writing to David's experience of hiding from Saul in a cave (cf. the superscription to Ps. 142), but which cave is not known (cf. 1 Sam. 22; 24). The psalm consists of two sections, each ending with a refrain (Ps. 57:5, 11), in which David expressed his desire that God be exalted. David prayed for deliverance from his destructive enemies, and then sang a song of triumph for God's faithful love in expectation that the wicked would be caught in their own devices.

A. The need for divine intervention (57:1-5)

57:1-3. The first stanza (vv. 1-5) is the psalmist's cry that **God** would rescue him. He cried for **mercy** (cf. 56:1) from **God** as he took **refuge in the shadow of** God's **wings** (cf. 17:8; 36:7; 61:4; 63:7; 91:4) **until the disaster** had **passed.** He had no one else to turn to for safety. His trust was well founded, however, for it was God who sent **from heaven . . . His** love (*ḥeseḏ,* "loyal love") **and . . . faithfulness** (cf. 57:10). Because of God's attributes David knew He would deliver him from the hot pursuit (cf. 56:1-2) of the wicked.

57:4. David's confident cry to God was followed by a lament about his predicament. He compared his enemies to **lions** (cf. comments on 7:2) and other **ravenous beasts** that wanted to devour him. Their **teeth** and **tongues** were like military weapons as they slandered and blasphemed him. (On the tongue being like **swords;** cf. 55:21; 59:7; 64:3.) He deplored being surrounded by taunting, bloodthirsty men.

57:5. In this refrain (cf. v. 11) David expressed his desire that God **be exalted . . . above the heavens** and **the earth.** This will happen, of course, when God defeats His enemies and vindicates His righteousness.

B. The occasion for the song of triumph (57:6-11)

This second stanza is the psalmist's song to God for His loyal love and faithfulness in anticipation of victory.

57:6. David spoke again of his predicament but added that he expected his foes' destruction. **They spread a net. . . . they dug a pit . . . but they** had **fallen into it.** This is the fourth time David had written along that line (cf. "pit" in 7:15; and "pit" and "net" in 9:15; 35:8). Of course the language of nets and pits depicted the attempts of the wicked to catch him.

57:7-11. These verses are almost identical to 108:1-5. In light of the certain destruction of the wicked, David vowed to **sing** a song of victory. With his faith established in the LORD, he could **praise** Him early in the morning in anticipation of what **God** would do. David said he would praise the Lord's **love** (*ḥeseḏ,* "loyal love") and **faithfulness** (cf. 57:3) where others would hear him.

In the refrain in verse 11 (cf. v. 5), David again expressed his desire that God **be exalted . . . above the heavens** and **the earth.**

Psalm 58

David denounced unrighteous judges who were wickedly destructive in their work. He called on God to destroy them swiftly and irrevocably. Then the righteous would be strengthened in their cause.

A. Rebuke of unjust judges (58:1-5)

By means of questions and answers, David decried the effect of the land's unjust judges.

58:1. David questioned the leaders' integrity: **Do you rulers . . . speak just-**

ly? **Do you judge uprightly?** Because the rulers and judges were unrighteous, justice in the nation was perverted.

58:2-5. No is the answer to the question in verse 1. They did not **do** justice; they planned **injustice** and **violence.** Later Micah wrote along the same lines about the leaders in his day (cf. Micah 3:1-3, 9-11; 6:12). These **wicked** judges went **astray** from **birth,** speaking **lies.** They were like serpents that poison without concern for **the charmer.** In other words they were deliberately destructive and deaf to remonstrance. They would not listen to correction.

B. Swift judgment on the judges (58:6-9)

58:6-8. David called on God to wipe out the wicked judges. He boldly asked God to **break** their **teeth,** that is, to keep them from communicating their injustice. They were ferocious as **lions** (cf. comments on 7:2), whose teeth, like **fangs,** needed to be torn out. David also prayed that the judges would meet a sudden end, by (a) vanishing as **water** evaporates, so that **their arrows** (i.e., their words) would be ineffectual; (b) melting away as a snail perishes in a drought; and (c) dying suddenly like **a stillborn** who does **not see the sun.**

58:9. The destruction of **the wicked** will be swift. A fire that burns **thorns** or brambles dies quickly (cf. comments on Ecc. 7:6). **Before . . . pots can** be placed on the fire, it goes out. God will sweep the wicked **away** before their malicious evil, like a fire, can finish its work.

C. Encouragement for the just (58:10-11)

58:10-11. David anticipated the joy of those who will see God's justice carried out on the unjust judges. Again the language is metaphorical and hyperbolic; **the righteous** bathing **their feet in the blood of the wicked** suggests a military victory.

David also anticipated that this victory would be recognized as proof that **God** will reward righteousness and judge **the earth.** People will not be left to the decisions of unjust judges forever.

Psalm 59

This is a prayer by David for defense from bloodthirsty men. It has the familiar

motif of unshaken trust in God. David prayed that the Lord would make him safe and secure from his enemies, and humiliate them so that all would recognize God's sovereignty.

The setting of the psalm is identified as Saul's siege of "David's house" (1 Sam. 19:8-11a). Michal, however, helped David escape through a window (1 Sam. 19:11b-14).

A. Conspiracy against the innocent (59:1-5)

59:1-5. Again David prayed for deliverance from a desperate situation. He asked to be saved **from evildoers . . . bloodthirsty men** who lay **in wait** to kill him, who conspired **against** him, even though he had **done** nothing **wrong. God,** David said, should **punish all** who act so treacherously.

B. Triumph over treachery (59:6-10)

59:6-7. David compared his enemies to **snarling . . . dogs** that **prowl about** at night (cf. v. 14). By their words and deeds they showed themselves to be arrogant, thinking that not even God heard them. Their words were sharp and offensive like **swords** (cf. 55:21; 57:4; 64:3).

59:8-10. But the psalmist was confident that his enemies would not succeed. He knew that **God** mocks the pagans (cf. 2:1, 4). Therefore he would **watch for** God, His **Strength** (cf. 59:17 and comments on 18:1) and **Fortress** (miśgōḇ; cf. 59:16-17 and comments on 46:7), to rescue him and enable him to see the downfall of the wicked who slandered him.

C. Demonstration of justice (59:11-13)

59:11. David prayed that the Lord, his **Shield** (cf. comments on 3:3), would punish the wicked in a way that people would learn that He is sovereign. The wicked should **not** simply perish, because they would be forgotten. Rather, they should be made to **wander** in humiliation as outcasts and fugitives.

59:12-13. David also prayed that their proud **curses and lies** be exposed, that they be **caught in** the act and consumed so others would know **that God rules** in justice.

D. Anticipation of praise (59:14-17)

59:14-17. David was confident that despite the presence of his enemies

(whom he again compared to **snarling**
. . . **dogs**; cf. v. 6) he would praise God
for **strength** (cf. v. 9), **love,** and security
(as his **Fortress;** cf. v. 9 and comments on
46:7, and his **Refuge,** *mānôs,* also used in
142:5).

Psalm 60

Psalm 60 is a didactic psalm ("for
teaching") based on David's experiences
in military victories. It is a prayer for
victory, for when David was waging war
in the north against the Arameans, Edom
invaded Judah. The psalm may have
been written when or soon after David,
Joab, and Abishai crushed Edom (2 Sam.
8:13; 1 Kings 11:15-16; 1 Chron. 18:12).
(See comments on 1 Chron. 18:12 where
the number of Edomites said to have
been killed was 18,000, whereas this
psalm's superscription has "12,000.")

Because David knew that both victory and defeat come from the Lord, he
prayed for divine aid for victory over Israel's enemies. He was assured that God
would help him triumph.

A. Prayer for deliverance (60:1-5)

60:1-3. The psalmist turned to the
Lord to ask for restoration from Israel's
disastrous predicament—a disaster
brought on by God's anger. The Lord
had **torn . . . open** the **land** and stag-
gered David's troops. Because the disaster of defeat was brought by the Lord, He
was the only One who could bring them
victory.

60:4-5. The meaning of verse 4 is difficult to determine, but it seems to be
reproachfully sarcastic: God had mustered His people to war (**raised a banner**)
but then He led them to defeat (fleeing
before the enemy's **bow**). Israel was
championing God's cause, but God was
letting them get defeated.

Therefore David asked God to deliver by His power (His **right hand;** cf. Ex.
15:6, 12; Pss. 20:6; 45:4; 89:13; 108:6) **those**
He loves. Psalm 60:5-12 is identical to
108:6-13.

B. Assurance of triumph (60:6-8)

60:6-8. The psalmist quoted the
words of the Lord that assured them victory. God had declared that because all
tribes and lands are His, He would deliver His people and subjugate their enemies. He would **parcel out Shechem**

and . . . the Valley of Succoth, that is,
He would give the land to His people.
Twenty miles east of Shechem, in the
tribe of Ephraim, is Succoth, a city in the
tribe of Gad, near the Jordan River.
Ephraim, a centrally located and large
tribe in Israel, was strong. Like a **helmet**
she was a defense for the nation. **Judah**
was the **scepter** of the Lord, that is, David (from Judah) was God's ruler even
though he was threatened. Israel's enemies would be reduced to menial labor.
Gilead, east of the Jordan River, and **Manasseh,** a tribe on both sides of the river,
belonged to Him. **Moab** would be like a
washbasin brought to the conqueror.
Edom would be like a slave to whom
God, like a warrior, would throw his
shoe. **Philistia** would hear God's triumphant **shout** after David's victory.

C. Confidence in God (60:9-12)

60:9-12. Through three rhetorical
questions the psalmist acknowledged
that the Lord, the One who had rejected
them in the battle (cf. vv. 1-4), would
lead them to victory. But because human
effort is futile, David prayed that **God**
would **give** them **aid against the enemy,**
confident that **with God . . . victory** was
theirs.

Thus it is clear that victory or defeat
belongs to God. When disaster comes,
one's only hope is God.

Psalm 61

David, feeling faint and inadequate,
found assurance in the strength of his
Rock and encouragement in God's enduring promises. Many have suggested
that this psalm describes one of David's
narrow escapes in the rocky wilderness,
but no historical setting is given.

A. Lead me to the rock (61:1-2)

61:1-2. The psalmist petitioned the
Lord for strength and security because
his **heart** was overwhelmed. He asked
that God **lead** him **to the rock that is
higher than** he was. "Rock" denotes a
place of safety; but David wanted to be
led to a rock he could not reach by himself. If **God** did this, he would be safe.

B. I long to dwell in Your tent (61:3-7)

David expressed his confidence in
the Lord who had promised strength and
security.

61:3-4. David found comfort in the character of the Lord. As his **Refuge** (*maḥseh*, "shelter from danger"; cf. comments on 14:6) and high **Tower** God had defended him **against** his foes. Now, however, the psalmist longed **to dwell** in God's presence (**in** His **tent** and under His **wings**; cf. 17:8; 36:7; 57:1; 63:7; 91:4, like a bird protected by its mother). This is the most secure place of **refuge**.

61:5-7. Then on the basis of God's promise to him, David prayed for protection in God's presence. **God** had **heard** him and had **given** him **the heritage of those who fear** His **name**; true Israelites who feared the Lord remained loyal to David's kingship and did not rebel. Thus he prayed that God would extend **the king's** (his own) **life** and that God would continue to **protect him** by His **love** (*ḥeseḏ*, "loyal love") **and faithfulness**, or His faithful love.

C. Then I will sing praise (61:8)

61:8. The king vowed to **sing** to and **praise** the Lord for His protection over him. Once delivered, he would **fulfill** his **vows** (cf. v. 5), praising the Lord daily.

Psalm 62

This psalm reflects David's confident trust in the Lord in spite of opposition. In silence he waited for God, his Strength and Security, to deliver him from his deceitful enemies. The psalm contrasts the security of trusting God with the insecurity of relying on human devices. The psalm falls into three stanzas of four verses each.

A. Rest in God when enemies assault (62:1-4)

62:1-2. The theme of this psalm is stressed in verse 1 when David wrote that he waited in silence for God. **My soul finds rest in God alone** (cf. v. 5) is literally, "Only to God is my soul silence." Only to God did he look with complete calmness. He knew that since God was his **Rock** (cf. comments on 18:2), **Salvation,** and **Fortress** (cf. comments on 46:7), he could not **be shaken** (cf. 62:6 and comments on 15:5). As warriors used to feel at ease in an impregnable fortress, so David rested in the Lord.

62:3-4. This confidence led David to marvel at the attempt of some people to thrust **him down.** The image of a **tottering fence** suggests weakness and susceptibility. As men try to **topple** a city wall or fence, the wicked attempted to overthrow David whom they thought was vulnerable. They hoped to accomplish this through **lies.** They blessed David **with their** words, **but in their hearts they** cursed him.

B. Trust in God at all times (62:5-8)

62:5-8. Repeating that he waited in silence for the Lord, David confessed that his only **hope** was **in God** (cf. 25:5, 21; 33:20; 39:7; 71:5). Again he affirmed that God was His Source of safety (**Rock**), deliverance (**Salvation**), and security (**Fortress**; cf. 62:2) and that therefore he was secure (he **would not be shaken**; cf. comments on 15:5). God was His **Salvation** and his Glory (**Honor**). Without God's innumerable deliverances, David would have been crushed by his foes.

Therefore the psalmist instructed the saints to **pour out** their **hearts** before Him in continual **trust,** realizing He is their **Refuge** (*maḥseh*, "shelter from danger"; cf. 14:6; 46:1; 61:3; 71:7; 73:28; 91:2, 9).

C. God will reward each person (62:9-12)

62:9-10. The psalmist warned that it is foolish to trust in humans. He described how transitory life is, whether a person is of low or high position. People **are nothing** but **a breath** (*heḇel*, "a vapor"; cf. 39:5, 11; 144:4 and comments on Ecc. 1:2). They are so insignificant that, if weighed, the scales would not even move. Their might is powerless against God. Therefore one should not trust in the powerful advances of the wicked. **Riches** are not to be trusted either (cf. Prov. 11:28; 23:5; 27:24).

62:11-12. The psalmist contrasted this with the fact that **God** has declared that the power is His. David **heard** God say two things: that He is **strong** and **loving.** So justice will be meted out to everybody. How much better then to find rest in the powerful **God** than in human devices.

Psalm 63

The faith expressed in Psalms 61 and 62 reaches a climax in this marvelous hymn of David, written in the wilderness. It refers to a time when David, as

PSALMS

king, was separated from the ark, the
formal place of worship (2 Sam. 15:25).
The psalmist satisfied the longing of
his soul for worship by praising God
for His loyal love even in his distress.
As a result, he confidently anticipated a
time of joy when his enemies would be
stopped.

A. Thirsting for God (63:1-2)

63:1. David's experience in the **dry,**
waterless wilderness prompted him to
think of the thirst of his **soul** for **God.**
Because his soul thirsted for and longed
for his **God,** he wrote, **Earnestly I seek
You.** This may also be translated, "Early
will I seek You." This has prompted
many believers to read this psalm in the
mornings. To seek someone early suggests doing so earnestly.

63:2. David's longing for God came
because of his vision of God's **power**
(strength) **and . . . glory.** This awareness
of God came before his enemies had driv-
en him into the wilderness. The ark was
the symbol of the Lord's glory and
strength (cf. 1 Sam. 4:21). David had had
the joy of seeing the evidence of God's
presence **in the sanctuary,** the tabernacle
in Jerusalem.

B. Satisfying the soul with praise (63:3-8)

63:3-4. In spite of his separation from
the sanctuary, David found satisfaction
in praising God, for it brought joy and
comfort to his heart. He praised God for
his loyal **love,** which **is better than life.**
This was the **praise** of one who, when in
a dry desert (v. 1), thought more of God
than of life-sustaining water.

63:5-6. Moreover, praising God
would satisfy his **soul** as much as **the
richest of foods** would satisfy his body.
Praise to Him gave vitality to his spiritual
life. Praising God is the natural expression of a heart that meditates on God, a
heart that thinks of Him **through . . . the
night.**

63:7-8. The immediate cause of the
psalmist's meditation and praise was the
safety and support he found in God. **Because** God was his **Help** (see comments
on 30:10) and Strength (His **right hand**
upheld him), David stayed **close to** Him
in the shadow of His **wings** (cf. 17:8;
36:7; 57:1; 61:4; 91:4) and continued to
praise Him by singing.

C. Rejoicing in victory (63:9-11)

63:9-11. David turned from his
thoughts on praise as the food of the soul
to his present situation. But in view of
what he knew of God, he fully anticipated that his enemies would **be destroyed**
and suffer ignominious deaths. For this
deliverance he, **the king,** would **rejoice
in God,** as **all** who are loyal to Him have
occasion to do. **Praise,** then, is essential
for one's spiritual life. It should stem
spontaneously from God's intervention
on behalf of a believer. Praise, in other
words, is an evidence that God is at
work, meeting His people's needs.

Psalm 64

This is another of David's prayers for
God's judgment on the enemies of the
righteous. David prayed for protection
from those who conspired against him.
He then delineated their malicious plans
against the righteous. He was convinced
that God would turn these schemes on
the wicked themselves.

A. The prayer for protection (64:1-2)

64:1-2. David introduced this psalm
with a cry of **complaint** to **God.** Lamenting that a **crowd of evildoers** had conspired against him, he told God he needed His protection.

B. The problem of malicious schemes (64:3-6)

64:3-4. David described how the
wicked prepare their attack on **the innocent.** He compared their speech to
swords (cf. 55:21; 57:4; 59:7) and **arrows**—weapons that pierce and destroy.
Their slanderous attacks came **suddenly**
like an **ambush.** They were confident in
what they did; they attacked others **without fear.**

64:5-6. Moreover, the wicked encouraged **each other in** their **plans** to do
injustice. They thought they had a **perfect** crime, assuming they could sin without being discovered. This, David concluded, shows how **cunning** (cf. 83:3) a
human **heart** can be.

C. The prophecy of divine judgment (64:7-10)

64:7-8a. David predicted that God
would intervene and strike them. They
might be cunning (v. 6) **but God will
shoot them with arrows.** This is justice in

140

which the punishment fits the crime. Their **tongues,** like arrows againsf others (v. 3), will be turned **against them** by God, and their slanderous plans (cf. vv. 5-6) will actually **bring** *themselves* **to ruin.**

64:8b-10. Everyone **who** would **see them** would **scorn** them for their evil plans. Moreover, seeing the destruction of the wicked, people would **fear** (cf. "fear" in v. 4) **the LORD** and tell of His **works.** God's judgment would have a lasting effect on people. As for **the righteous,** they will have reason to **rejoice,** to renew their trust in Him as their **Refuge,** and to **praise Him.**

Psalm 65

David may have written this psalm to be sung annually when the first grain of the year's barley harvest was brought to the Lord and waved by the priest as a dedication offering (see Lev. 23:9-14 and comments there). It is a song of harvest blessing in celebration of God's goodness to His people. In this "song" David declared that God, who hears prayers, atones for sin, a provision that results in God's bounty. David also announced that God uses His supernatural power to aid His people. Based on these displays of God's good pleasure, the songwriter anticipated God's blessing on the land, which would bring the people prosperity.

A. Blessing in God's courts (65:1-4)

65:1-4. The psalmist expressed his conviction that when **God** atones for sin He blesses abundantly. The psalm begins with a mention of mankind's preparation to **praise** God because He hears **prayer** (vv. 1-2). The occasion for the prayer was apparently their overwhelming **sins,** but God **atoned for** their **transgressions** (v. 3). One who thereby is brought **near to** the presence of the Lord will experience happiness (he is **blessed;** cf. 1:1) and satisfaction (**with . . . good things,** 65:4). Atonement for sin made possible the praise of the people and their entrance on festival days into the **courts** of the tabernacle (the word for **temple** is *hêkāl,* a magnificent house; cf. comments on 5:7).

B. Awesome deeds of God's power (65:5-8)

65:5-8. The psalmist was confident that **God** answers prayer; He is **the hope** of people in the farthest regions **of the earth.**

God's answers to prayer often come by **awesome deeds;** this is natural for God. He demonstrated His **power** and **strength** by forming **the mountains** and soothing **the seas** and **their waves.** God's **wonders** bring **fear** to people and **songs of joy** throughout the world (**where morning dawns and evening fades**).

C. Abundant provision of harvest (65:9-13)

65:9-13. The psalmist was convinced that Israel would have an abundantly good year when **God** poured out His blessings on the land. Verse 9a summarizes God's **care for the land,** and verses 9b-13a develop the theme of God's blessings on the land. God's control of the **water** produces the **grain** (v. 9b); God's rain **showers** prepare the land for produce (v. 10); God's blessing produces an abundant harvest (v. 11); God causes uncultivated areas to be enriched with grass (v. 12). In a word, the **flocks** and **grain** flourish under His blessing (v. 13a).

The psalmist concluded that all of nature shouts **for joy** (v. 13b), that is, abundant fruitfulness testifies to God's blessing.

Psalm 66

This is another psalm of thanksgiving to the Lord. It too, like Psalm 65, may have been written to celebrate a festive occasion, but the precise occasion is unknown. In the first section (vv. 1-12) the psalmist (not specified as David) wrote in the first person plural ("us," "our"), and in the second section (vv. 13-20) he wrote in the first person singular ("I," "me," "my"). In the psalm the nation acknowledged God's deliverance and called on the nations to join her in praising the Lord.

A. The nation praised God (66:1-12)

Verses 1-9 are addressed to the nations, and verses 10-12 are addressed to God. The psalmist called on nations everywhere to praise the Lord for His great deliverance of Israel.

66:1-4. All the earth, that is, everyone on it, was urged to **praise** the Lord by shouting (v. 1), singing (vv. 2, 4), and speaking (vv. 3-4). They were encouraged to be jubilant because of His **awe-**

some works (cf. v. 5), which resulted in His **enemies** cringing **before** His **great . . . power.**

66:5-7. The psalmist then called on the nations to **see** that God's **awesome . . . works** (cf. v. 3) on **behalf** of man demonstrate His sovereignty. Israel's crossing the Red Sea and the Jordan River were notable acts of God's power of deliverance. Therefore people should realize that **He rules forever by His power,** putting down rebels and delivering His people.

66:8-9. Israel then called on the **peoples** of the earth to bless **God** because by these and other awesome deeds **He** had **preserved** them.

66:10-12. Here the nation acknowledged that **God** had **tested** them with all kinds of burdens and oppressions, but finally **brought** them **to** the **place of** abundant blessing. This acknowledged that it was God who led them all the way and delivered them.

B. The psalmist led their praise (66:13-20)

The psalmist, the leader of the congregation, offered animal sacrifices and declarative praise to God.

66:13-15. In these verses he addressed God and in verses 16-20 he addressed the congregation. The psalmist said he would go **to** God's **temple** and offer **burnt offerings.** This would **fulfill** a vow he made **when** he cried out of distress (**trouble**).

66:16-20. Here he addressed the congregation in praise to **God** (a declarative praise). He told them that God responded to his prayer (**I cried out to Him**) and **God** delivered him. However, it **would not have** happened that way if he had clung to **sin** (cf. Prov. 28:9; Isa. 59:2). But **God** *did* listen and answer his **prayer.** The point is clear: God's people, when in need, should purify their hearts and pray to Him. Then He will answer and not withhold **His** loyal **love,** and other believers may praise and exalt Him.

Psalm 67

Having prayed for God's mercy and blessing so that His saving ways may be known (Ps. 66), the psalmist now called on the people to praise God for His righteous judgments so that they might enjoy His bounty.

A. May God be gracious (67:1-2)

67:1-2. The writer asked for God's merciful dealings by using part of the priestly blessing (v. 1; see Num. 6:24-26). God's making **His face shine** on them refers to divine favor and approval (cf. comments on Ps. 4:6). The purpose of this prayer is that God's saving **ways** would **be known** throughout the world. For if God saved them, others would hear of it.

B. May the people praise Him (67:3-7)

67:3-7. In verses 3-4 the psalmist called on people to **praise . . . God** with **joy** because He rules **justly.** In verses 5-7 he called on them to **praise . . . God** so that He in turn would **bless** them by giving them a bountiful **harvest.** Recognizing God's blessings encourages people to **fear** and worship **Him.**

Psalm 68

This is "a song" celebrating God's triumphal ascent to Mount Zion. If the superscription of Davidic authorship is correct, then the occasion may have been David's conquering the city (2 Sam. 5:6-8), or moving the ark to Zion (2 Sam. 6), or some triumphal procession after a victory, or his victories in general. Some scholars disregard the superscription, and relate the psalm to some other occasion such as the Jews' return from the Exile, though there are no clear historical references to this in the poem. Its figurative language makes the psalm adaptable to several occasions. No doubt the psalm, if written by David, would have been used at subsequent victories. The greatest triumph to which the psalm is related is Christ's Ascension, for Psalm 68:18 was paraphrased and applied to Him by Paul (Eph. 4:8).

The psalmist reviewed the history of Israel from the wilderness wanderings to the occupation and conquest of the land. He emphasized God's choice of Zion, which resulted in Israel's taking many Canaanites as captives and the Israelites receiving gifts or spoils from the captives. This is the reason he sang praises: God was marching triumphantly on behalf of the oppressed. David called on others to join him in praising their strong Lord.

A. Fear and praise over God's triumph (68:1-6)

68:1-3. David prayed that **God** would show His awesome power. The words in verse 1 are almost the same as the words Moses said whenever the Israelites set out on their march in the wilderness (Num. 10:35). When **God** arises in power **the wicked perish** like **smoke . . . blown away by the wind** and as **wax melts before the fire. The righteous,** safe from the wicked, **rejoice** greatly (cf. Prov. 28:12; 29:2).

68:4-6. David invited the people to **praise** in song the One **who rides on the clouds** (cf. v. 33; 104:3; Isa. 19:1), a poetic description of God's exalted majesty, chosen as a polemic against a similar epithet for Baal. **God** is worthy of praise because of His triumphant work: He delivers and comforts the downtrodden (**fatherless** and **widows**) and oppressed (**prisoners**), while leaving **the rebellious** desolate in the desert.

B. Remembrance of God's triumphant conquest (68:7-18)

The psalmist now traced the development of the Lord's "movement" from the wilderness to His occupation of Zion.

68:7-10. When **God** led His **people . . . through the** wilderness **wasteland,** earthquakes and **rain** occurred (cf. 77:16-19). Weary in the desert, His people (called His **inheritance;** cf. comments on Deut. 4:20) were **refreshed** by the rainfall. And God graciously **provided for the poor.**

68:11-14. The psalmist then rehearsed the victorious occupation of **the land** of Canaan from which **kings** (vv. 12, 14) were driven out. Verse 13, though difficult to understand precisely, seems to refer to Judges 5:16 which speaks of reproval of some Israelites who were remiss in supporting the Conquest. While some Israelites were sleeping at night in the open air, refusing to engage in battle, God blessed His **dove** (i.e., Israel; cf. Ps. 74:19). Their prosperity (probably spoils taken from defeated enemies) was like **silver** and **gold** on the **wings** and **feathers** of a dove. The **snow . . . on Zalmon** may refer to a snowfall on a mountain near Shechem (cf. Jud. 9:48) which helped Israel rout the enemy. Or it may suggest that God's victory was as refreshing as freshly fallen snow.

68:15-18. These verses speak of the Lord's choosing Zion above other **mountains** and of His triumphant entry into it like a conqueror. The great **mountains** of the land of **Bashan** refer to the Hermon mountain range, only a few miles north of Bashan. Choosing Zion for His dwelling place, God entered the city with a vast company (**thousands of thousands**) of angelic hosts, pictured here as riding in **chariots.** Thus the Lord went all the way **from Sinai** (cf. v. 8) to **His sanctuary** in Zion. His entrance into Jerusalem (when David conquered it, 2 Sam. 5:6-8, or when David moved the ark to Jerusalem, 2 Sam. 6) was like a mighty conqueror ascending **on high** with **captives,** receiving tribute **from** the vanquished, **the rebellious.**

Psalm 68:18 was referred to by Paul in Ephesians 4:8 (cf. comments there). However, rather than quoting the Hebrew, Paul apparently followed the Jewish interpretation of the day (the Targum), which paraphrased this verse as follows: "You did ascend to the firmament, O Prophet Moses! You led captivity captive; you taught the words of the Law; you gave [not 'received,' as in the Heb.] gifts to the sons of men." (This interpretation saw Moses as God's representative.) Paul followed this Jewish exegesis because it explained that the conqueror *distributed* the gifts to His loyal subjects. The apostle applied that idea to Christ's victory over the forces of evil and His granting spiritual gifts (cf. Eph. 4:11) to those on His side. By this analogy (based more on the Jewish interpretation of the psalm than on the exact Heb. wording) Paul emphasized the greatness of believers' spiritual victory in Christ.

C. The effect of God's victory (68:19-31)

68:19-23. David praised **the LORD . . . God** who **bears** believers' **burdens** and **saves** them **from death.** David was convinced that God's entrance into Zion on behalf of His people would result in the complete destruction of His and her **enemies.** He would **bring** Israel **from** dangers (as those experienced in **Bashan** when she conquered Og, Num. 21:33-35) and from other awesome experiences (as when she crossed the Red Sea, suggested by the words **the depths of the sea;** cf. Isa. 51:10). God would cause Israel to be victorious over her enemies, pictured as putting her **feet in** their **blood** while **dogs** licked the blood (cf. 1 Kings 22:38).

68:24-27. God's triumphal entrance **into** Zion and **the sanctuary** is again described here, pictured like a victory parade with **singers** and other **musicians.** All who saw God's victorious entrance should **praise** Him. The tribes of **Benjamin** and Judah, one small and one large, represent the southern portion of the kingdom and **Zebulun** and **Naphtali** represent the northern portion. Perhaps the last two are mentioned because of the praise bestowed on them in Deborah and Barak's song (Jud. 5:18).

68:28-31. The writer then asked **God** to demonstrate His **power** again. Seeing His **strength** and His **temple,** pagan **kings** would pay tribute in submission to Him. **The beast among the reeds** (v. 30) is a symbolic representation of the enemy, perhaps **Egypt** (v. 31). **Bulls** suggests Egypt's strength. But **envoys** from this people and from **Cush,** her neighbor to the south, eventually would be **humbled** and scattered, and would **submit . . . to God.**

D. Call to praise (68:32-35)

68:32-35. The psalmist called the nations to **sing praise** to the Rider of **the . . . skies** (cf. v. 4), in recognition of His **power** and **majesty** displayed in **Israel** and **in the skies** and given **to His people.**

Psalm 69

David pleaded with God to rescue him from destruction because he bore reproach and rejection by his brethren for the Lord's sake. Praying that God would requite the inhumanity of his oppressors, he looked forward to universal praise and restoration.

A. David's enemies hated him without a cause (69:1-4)

69:1-4. In his troubles the psalmist turned to the Lord. He used the imagery of drowning to describe his being at the brink of death, and would have died if **God** had not rescued him. His problem was brought on by numberless **enemies** who sought **to destroy** him. They hated him for no **reason** (cf. 35:19) and **forced** him to give up his possessions (which he **did not steal**).

B. He was zealous for God's house (69:5-12)

69:5-12. David sought to motivate **God** to act on his behalf, for he was suffering because of his zeal for the Lord. Even though he was a sinner (v. 5) that was not the cause of his problem this time. Rather he was suffering **for** the Lord's **sake** (v. 7). His own relatives hated him even though he had **zeal** for the Lord (vv. 8-9). Their **insults** against God were directed to him. When he was in grief, he fasted (a sign of mourning; cf. Jud. 20:26; 1 Sam. 31:13; 2 Sam. 12:16; 1 Kings 21:27; Neh. 1:4) and wore **sackcloth** (another sign of mourning; cf. Gen. 37:34; 1 Kings 21:27; Neh. 9:1; Es. 4:1-4; Pss. 30:11; 35:13; Lam. 2:10; Dan. 9:3). Even then his enemies (including judges, those **who** sat **at the gate**) and **drunkards** sang derisively about him.

C. He prayed to the Lord (69:13-28)

69:13-18. The psalmist petitioned the LORD to save him from imminent death. In God's timing (**the time of Your favor**) and out of His **love** (ḥeseḏ, vv. 13, 16) and **mercy** He should **quickly** (cf. comments on 31:2) **rescue** (69:14, 18) and **redeem** (pāḏâh; cf. comments on 26:11) him from his misery and **trouble.** Again he used the image of miry **waters** that would drown him (cf. 69:2).

69:19-21. David found confidence in the knowledge that God knew of their reproach (cf. **scorn** in v. 10) and mistreatment of him (giving him **gall** [rō'š, possibly a poisonous plant] to eat and **vinegar** to drink). The word for **food** (bārûṯ) means a meal given "to a mourner by sympathetic friends. Its use emphasizes the hypocrisy of their conduct" (A. Cohen, *The Psalms*, p. 219).

69:22-28. In his imprecation against his enemies, David prayed that their own food would cause their downfall, that **their eyes** would **be darkened so they** could not **see,** and that **their backs** would **be bent** in grief. He asked that they would be overtaken by God's **wrath** and their residences made desolate because of their deaths. These punishments were just, because **they** persecuted God's people (v. 26).

David then prayed that God would find them guilty and blot them **out of the book of life** (cf. Rev. 20:15). In the Bible the opening of books speaks of judgment (cf. Dan. 7:10; Rev. 20:12). It is as if God "listed" **the** names of the **righteous.** But of course in His omniscience God does not need written records. The point is that the wicked have no share in God's eternal blessings.

D. The Lord hears the needy (69:29-36)

69:29-33. David again prayed in his **distress** that the LORD would be His **salvation** (cf. v. 13) and would **protect** him. Confident that God would deliver, he vowed to **praise** the Lord. David knew that **thanksgiving** was more pleasing to God than offering **an ox** or **a bull. Horns** were a sign that the animal was mature; only animals with split **hoofs** could be sacrificed (Lev. 11:3). **The poor** and **the needy** (cf. Ps. 70:5) would **see** God's rescue of David and **be glad** and encouraged. They would be assured that the Lord would hear their cry too since He **does not despise** His own.

69:34-36. David called for universal **praise** to God in anticipation of His delivering the nation, and the people's settling in the land.

In this psalm the prevailing tone is prayer for deliverance from suffering for the Lord's sake. Parts of the psalm were applied to the life of Christ: hatred against Him (v. 4; cf. John 15:25), His zeal (Ps. 69:9; cf. John 2:17), and vinegar given to Him on the cross (Ps. 69:21; cf. Matt. 27:48). So this psalm is partly typological of Christ. He is the epitome of the righteous who are persecuted for their zeal in doing God's will.

Psalm 70

This short psalm records a prayer by David for a quick rescue from his present evil plight. It also anticipates the rejoicing that will follow. The heading says it is "a petition" (lit., "to bring to remembrance"; cf. the title to Ps. 38). Perhaps this was a note that the psalm was to be used in connection with the offerings (cf. 1 Chron. 16:4), which would help "remind" the Lord of the petitioner's request.

A. Hasten to help me (70:1-3)

70:1-3. The psalmist cried out to **God** to **help** him **quickly** (cf. v. 5 and comments on 31:2). Enemies tried to bring him to **ruin** (cf. 35:4, 8; 38:12). So his plea was urgent. He prayed that **those who**

had shamed and disgraced him (69:19) would themselves be in **shame** (70:2-3; 71:13) and **turned back in disgrace** (cf. 6:10; 40:14), no longer able to scorn him (**Aha!**).

B. Let God be exalted (70:4-5)

70:4-5. The psalmist then prayed that **all who seek** the LORD and **love** His **salvation** would be **glad** and would **say, Let God be exalted!** Calling himself **poor and needy** (cf. 40:17; see comments on 37:14), he prayed for hasty deliverance (cf. 70:1). God was His only source of **help** (cf. comments on 30:10).

Psalm 71

Psalm 71 combines elements from other psalms (22; 31; 35; 40). Yet it is a unit in itself expressing the faith of an older person throughout most of his lifetime. In response to his prayer the psalmist, who is not identified, anticipated the same marvelous response the Lord had given him all his life. So, vowing to praise God as he had always done, he confidently asked to be delivered from those who sought his harm and derided him for his faith.

A. Prayer for help from the Lord (71:1-4)

71:1-4. The psalmist turned to the **LORD,** praying for deliverance from the wicked. This request is filled with expressions of his confidence in the Lord's ability to save: God was his **Refuge** (v. 1), **Rock of refuge** (v. 3; cf. 31:2), and **Fortress** (the same Heb. word is used in 18:2; 31:4; 91:2). The psalmist wanted continued safety and security (71:3) along with rescue from **wicked** people (v. 4).

B. Prayer from a lifelong trust (71:5-13)

71:5-8. The psalmist reaffirmed his **confidence** in the LORD in spite of his afflictions. God was his **Hope** (cf. 25:5, 21; 33:20; 39:7; 62:5), the One in whom he trusted from his **youth** up (cf. 71:17). Though many wondered at him (he was to them **like a portent**), he would continue to trust in the Lord, his **strong Refuge** and to **praise** Him (vv. 6, 8) and His **splendor** (cf. comments on 29:2). (The Heb. word for "refuge" here is *mahseh*, "shelter from danger," also used in 14:6; 46:1; 61:3; 62:7-8; 73:28; 91:2, 9. It differs from the verb in 71:1 trans. "I have taken refuge" [ḥāsâh, related to the noun mahseh] and from the word rendered "refuge" in v. 3 [māʻôn, "dwelling"; cf. 90:1; 91:9].)

71:9-13. The psalmist then prayed for continued care (**do not forsake me**; cf. v. 18) in his **old** age, for many sought to harm him. They thought **God** had **forsaken him**—a rather strange presumption!—and supposed they could **seize him** and kill him. So the psalmist asked that God **quickly** (cf. comments on 31:2) help him and put them to **shame** (cf. 71:24), **scorn, and disgrace** (cf. 70:2-3).

C. Continuation of a life of praise (71:14-24)

Because the aging psalmist had trusted the Lord all his life, he vowed to continue to praise God for future deliverances.

71:14-18. The writer expressed his determination to **hope** in and **praise** God for His **righteousness**, fathomless **salvation,** and **mighty** saving **acts** (cf. v. 24).

His life, from his **youth** up (cf. v. 5) had been filled with praise for God's **marvelous deeds.** Now **when** he was **old** (cf. v. 9) he still desired to praise Him, but **God** must not **forsake** him (cf. v. 9) if he was to **declare** God's **power.**

71:19-21. The psalmist rehearsed some of the great things God had done for him. In **righteousness** (cf. vv. 2, 15) God had **done** many **great things** (v. 19). Therefore He is incomparable. The rhetorical question, **Who, O God, is like You?** is asked several times in the Psalms, with slight variations in wording (cf. 35:10; 77:13; 89:6; 113:5; also note Ex. 15:11; Micah 7:18).

God had shown the aging psalmist that He, being able to deliver from **troubles,** would **restore** his **life again,** bringing him up **from the depths of the earth,** that is, from the point of death (cf. Pss. 30:1; 130:1). Therefore he was confident that God would **honor** and **comfort** him **once again.**

71:22-24. In these closing verses the psalmist vowed to **praise . . . God,** by singing, by playing musical instruments (**the harp** and **the lyre**—apparently both were stringed instruments—each mentioned a number of times in Pss.), by shouting, and by telling (cf. v. 15) of God's **acts** (cf. vv. 16-17). The title **Holy One of Israel,** used frequently in the

Book of Isaiah, occurs only three times in the Book of Psalms (71:22; 78:41; 89:18). This **praise** would last all **day long** because God would put all his enemies to **shame** (cf. 71:13).

Psalm 72

Two psalms (72; 127) are attributed to "Solomon." If Psalm 72 is his, it may describe his reign. Also it speaks of the millennial reign of the Messiah. The psalm describes the blessings that flow from the righteousness of God's theocratic ruler. The psalmist fully expected that the king would reign in righteousness and peace on behalf of the oppressed, and that his dominion would extend over many kings, from sea to sea. The psalmist prayed for the blessing of peace and prosperity, basing his appeal on the fact that the king is a savior of the oppressed and is therefore worthy of honor, power, and dominion.

A. Prayer for righteous judgments (72:1-7)

72:1-4. The psalm opens with a prayer that God would give **the king** divine ability to **judge** righteously (vv. 1-2). The psalmist anticipated that the king, ruling **in righteousness** (vv. 1-3 each include the word **righteousness**), would **bring prosperity** (cf. v. 7) and peace. Also he would judge on behalf of **the afflicted** (cf. v. 12) and **the needy** (cf. vv. 12-13) and punish those who exploit the poor.

72:5-7. Preferable to the words **He will endure** (from the LXX) is the translation, "You will be feared" (from the Heb.; cf. NIV marg.). Taken that way, the verse refers not to the human king but to God who endures **through all generations.** Or if the NIV rendering is accepted, then the thought may be that the king's name or reputation endures for generations (cf. v. 17). When a king's reign is righteous, his rule is refreshing to the people. **Like rain** on soil, an upright ruler enables **the righteous** to **flourish** and **prosperity** to **abound.**

B. Anticipation of his dominion (72:8-11)

72:8-11. The psalmist anticipated that his kingdom would extend **from sea to sea** and **from** the Euphrates **River** around the world. People who live in the wilderness would **bow before him, and his enemies** would be humiliated in subjection (**lick the dust**). **Kings** on **distant shores** would **bring tribute to him** and **bow** before **him.** These **kings** would come from faraway places, including **Tarshish** (possibly Tartessus in southwest Spain), **Sheba** (cf. v. 15; present-day Yemen in southwestern Arabia), **and Seba** (in upper Egypt; cf. Gen. 10:7).

C. Justification for dominion (72:12-14)

72:12-14. The psalmist explained that the king was worthy of such dominion (v. 8) and the honor given him (vv. 9-11) because he was a savior for the oppressed. **He will deliver the needy** (**needy** occurs three times in vv. 12-13) and the destitute (cf. v. 4) **who cry** to him. **He will take pity on the weak** and **rescue them,** considering **their blood** (i.e., their lives) **precious** to him.

D. Ascription of praise (72:15-20)

72:15-17. Because of his magnificent and righteous reign, people would respond with gifts for **him** (e.g., **gold from Sheba**; cf. the massive amount of gold brought to Solomon by the queen of Sheba, 1 Kings 10:10), with prayers on his behalf, and with blessings on **him.** The people would pray for agricultural prosperity (cf. Ps. 72:3, 6-7), with **grain** and **fruit** in abundance. **Lebanon,** with its cedar forests, was a picture of a flourishing land. The blessings of such a king's rule are reciprocal; he blesses the **nations** (perhaps through trade and peaceful alliances) and they in turn speak well of **him.**

72:18-20. Verses 18-19 record the second doxology in the book, thus ending Book II (Pss. 41-72). They include words of **praise . . . to the LORD God . . . of Israel** and the request that **His glory** be evident everywhere. Verse 20 states that **this ends the prayers of David.** However, this probably refers to an earlier collection of psalms, because 18 other psalms after this one are attributed in their superscriptions to David (Pss. 86; 101; 103; 108-110; 122; 124; 131; 133; 138-145).

III. Book III (Pss. 73-89)

Eleven of the 17 psalms in this section are attributed to Asaph (Pss. 73-83),

one to David (Ps. 86), three to the sons of Korah (Pss. 84-85; 87), one to Heman (Ps. 88), and another to Ethan (Ps. 89). Asaph, Heman, and Ethan were Levite musicians in David's day (1 Chron. 15:17, 19).

Psalm 73

This psalm strikes the same theme as Psalm 49, and thus may be classified as a wisdom psalm or at least may be studied for its wisdom motifs. In it "Asaph" told of the doubts which nearly overwhelmed him when he compared the life of a worldly man with his own. But then he confessed the sinfulness of his thoughts and explained that the contrast in their destinies enabled him to keep a proper perspective.

A. Prosperity of the wicked (73:1-14)

73:1-3. Asaph began this psalm by affirming that though **God is good to** those in **Israel** who trust Him and **are pure in heart** (cf. v. 13), he himself nearly **slipped** (cf. 94:18) in his confidence in the Lord. The psalmist emphasized his own situation by beginning four verses with the Hebrew expression translated **But as for me** (73:2, 22-23, 28). His offense was that he was envious of **the prosperity of the wicked.** Why should the people who *oppose* God be better off than those who trust Him? This problem was so overwhelming he **almost** lost faith in God's goodness.

73:4-12. Asaph explained the prosperity that troubled him. He observed that the wicked do not seem to suffer trouble as other people do (vv. 4-5). They cover **themselves** with **pride** and **violence** (v. 6). Their **evil** devices are unbounded (v. 7). Their speech is scornful, malicious, and arrogant, as if they owned **the earth** (vv. 8-9). Many **people** are carried away by their evil (they **turn to them,** v. 10) and presumptuous self-confidence, thinking **God** does not **know** of their sin (v. 11; cf. 94:7). With no cares in the world (cf. 73:4-5, 12) **wicked,** arrogant people continue to prosper.

73:13-14. Asaph said he was confused over the value of his salvation. He felt that he had cleansed himself **in vain** (cf. **pure** in v. 1) because since trusting the Lord he had been **plagued** and chastened. Like many saints before and after him, Asaph was puzzled that God seemed to prosper the wicked and punish the righteous.

B. Destiny of the wicked and the righteous (73:15-28)

73:15-20. Asaph overcame his doubts by considering the **destiny** of the wicked. First, he acknowledged the impiety of his former conclusion in view of this consideration. His words are like a confession, for he knew the treachery his words could have been to the congregation (v. 15). The entire conflict was painful (**oppressive**) to him, **till** in **the sanctuary** he **understood** what will happen to the wicked. God will set **them** in dangerous (**slippery**; cf. "slipped" in v. 2) places where they will stumble and fall, be **cast . . . down** in **ruin,** and **suddenly** be **destroyed.**

When God finally sets things right, the wicked will be like **fantasies** (a **dream**), counterfeits of reality. This was the negative aspect of the solution to Asaph's problem.

73:21-26. The positive aspect of the solution was Asaph's conviction of his own glorious destiny. He confessed that his perspective had been dulled by brutish ignorance. If he had not been so **ignorant,** he admitted, his **heart** would not have been so bitter (vv. 21-22). (**Grieved** is lit., "grew sour"; **embittered** is lit., "felt stinging pains.") His true position was in stark contrast with the wicked, for he knew God was **always with** him (v. 23) and would **guide** him wisely (**with** His **counsel**) and receive him **into glory** (v. 24). "Into glory" could also be translated "with glory," meaning that God would guide him through his troubles so that he would enjoy honor (and not shame; cf. 4:2) in this life. Since "glory" for individuals in the Old Testament seldom meant heavenly glory the psalmist was probably looking for deliverance in his lifetime. This would demonstrate that he was in God's favor. Of course believers today know from the New Testament that God's punishment of the wicked and blessing of the righteous extend beyond death.

In addition, Asaph affirmed that God was his only possession **in heaven** or **on the earth.** Though Asaph was overwhelmed, **God** was his **Strength** (cf. 18:1) and His **Portion** (cf. 16:5; 119:57; 142:5). Some wicked people prosper materially but only the spiritual "possessions" of the righteous will last.

73:27-28. Asaph concluded that **those who are far from** God and **are unfaithful** will be destroyed, but that those who are **near God** find joy and safety. Though he had nearly slipped in his confidence in God (cf. v. 2) he now was reassured that God was keeping him secure. God was his **Refuge** (*maḥseh,* "shelter from danger"; cf. 14:6; 46:1; 61:3; 62:7-8; 71:7; 91:2, 9). Nearness to God always helps believers maintain a balanced perspective on material things and on the wicked.

Psalm 74

Asaph asked God to remember His people because their enemy had devastated the sanctuary. He prayed that God, who had helped destroy their enemies in the past, would not permit their reproach.

A. Prayer for remembrance (74:1-2)

74:1-2. The psalmist asked **God** not to continue His hot **anger . . . against the sheep of** His **pasture** (i.e., God's people; cf. 79:13; 95:7; 100:3). God should **remember** (and have regard for) those He has redeemed (cf. Ex. 15:13) to be His **inheritance** (cf. comments on Deut. 4:20), and He should remember His dwelling place on **Zion.** (**The tribe** stands for the nation, as seen in Jer. 10:16.)

B. Lament over the destruction (74:3-9)

74:3. Asaph prayed that God would take note of and rescue His people for **the enemy** had ruined **the sanctuary** and jeopardized the nation. The word **ruins** and the statements in verses 4-8 suggest a complete devastation of the sanctuary (cf. Ps. 79). The historical event to which this refers is uncertain. The only occasion that matches this devastation is the invasion by the Babylonians in 586 B.C., but that is too late, if the Asaph of David's time is the author. Perhaps this Asaph is a later member of the Asaph musical guild.

74:4-8. According to this psalm, the enemy had **roared in** and demolished the place. **The carved** work was **smashed** by **axes and hatchets,** the **sanctuary (the dwelling place**; cf. 76:2; 84:1; 132:5, 7; **of** God's **name,** i.e., the place where God revealed His character; cf. "name" in

74:10, 18, 21) was **burned,** and all the assembly places in the land were also **burned.**

74:9. What troubled the psalmist was that there was **no** prophet to give spiritual counsel to the people or to explain **how long this** problem would last.

C. Appeal for help (74:10-17)

74:10-17. Since no prophet was available (v. 9) the psalmist himself appealed to **God** for help, asking **how long** (cf. v. 9 and see comments on 6:3) **the enemy** would continue to **mock** (cf. 74:22) and **revile** God (cf. v. 18). Asaph suggested that God no longer remain inactive but rather show His **right hand,** a symbol of His power, **and destroy them** (v. 11). Asaph sought to motivate **God** by reminding Him of His past help: God is the sovereign **King** and Savior (v. 12), God delivered Israel through **the sea** (the Red Sea, v. 13), He **crushed . . . Leviathan,** a seven-headed mythological monster symbolic here of Egypt's power (v. 14), and He has complete power over nature (vv. 15-17), including **rivers. . . . day** and **night, the sun and moon,** and the seasons. Because of what God had done in the past, Asaph wanted Him to act now.

D. Regard for the covenant (74:18-23)

74:18-23. The psalmist appealed to God not to forget the awful mocking by **the enemy** (cf. vv. 10, 22) and to protect His **dove,** a defenseless bird (i.e., Israel; cf. 68:13), and look on His **covenant** so that His people—**oppressed . . . poor, and needy** (see comments on 37:14)— would not suffer the **disgrace** of defeat. **God** should note, he said, that the enemies are blasphemers who **mock** Him (74:22; cf. vv. 10, 18). Therefore He should not forsake His people, but should **defend** His **cause** and defeat His loud, boisterous **enemies.**

Psalm 75

This psalm celebrates anticipated victory. The psalmist recognized that God will establish judgment at the appointed time, and that the judgment will destroy the wicked and exalt the righteous. On the basis of this he warned the wicked to submit to God who alone can deliver.

A. God appoints judgment (75:1-3)

75:1-3. On behalf of the people, Asaph praised **God** for His nearness and His wondrous works (v. 1). Notable among God's deeds is His judging (v. 2; cf. v. 7; 94:2); and even though His judging causes **the earth** to **quake,** He sustains it (75:3).

B. God is the Judge (75:4-8)

75:4-6. God warns the wicked to change their heart attitude toward Him. They should not arrogantly defy God. Lifting **up . . . horns,** a metaphor from the animal world, signifies a defiant, strutting, self-confidence. Moreover, the wicked should not speak with a stiff **neck,** that is, in stubborn rebellion against God. The wicked should realize that when He judges, no help comes from any earthly direction.

75:7-8. The psalmist warned the wicked that because **God** is the Judge (cf. v. 2) they will experience His full wrath. This is pictured as being made to drink **a cup . . . of foaming wine** (cf. Job 21:20; Isa. 51:17; Jer. 25:15). **All the wicked** will be forced to undergo a staggering judgment from God, as they **drink it** to the last **dregs.**

C. God's judgment is praiseworthy (75:9-10)

75:9-10. Asaph vowed to **sing praise to . . . God** because of the triumph of the righteous. In verse 10 God may be speaking, declaring that His cutting **off** the defiance **of all the wicked** and exalting **the righteous** will be cause for praise.

Psalm 76

This is a song of praise for the power of the God of Jacob. The psalmist declared that God made Himself known in Jerusalem by executing judgment. Describing how God destroyed the wicked and delivered the righteous led Asaph to exhort the leaders to pledge their allegiance to God.

A. God's judgment is known (76:1-3)

76:1-3. God made Himself **known** by destroying Israel's enemies. He devastated **the weapons** of those who made war against Jerusalem, or **Salem** (used elsewhere only in Gen. 14:18; Heb. 7:1-2) and **Zion.** (On God's **dwelling place** being in Jerusalem see Pss. 74:7; 84:1; 132:5, 7.)

B. God's judgment is just (76:4-10)

76:4-6. Asaph praised the Lord as the God of **light,** the One who is glorious and illuminating. His majesty exceeds even the **mountains rich with** wild **game.** This phrase, literally, "mountain of prey," may mean that **God** is more majestic than the strongholds of the enemy. The soldiers of these enemies are swiftly destroyed (v. 5) by God's **rebuke** (v. 6).

76:7-10. The psalmist then explained that **God** in wrath accomplishes His sovereign purposes over His foes. No one **can stand** in the sight of this fearsome (cf. vv. 11-12) God. When God's **judgment** issued **from heaven** to deliver the righteous **(the afflicted),** the earth stood in silence and awe. God's **wrath against** wicked **men** results in believers praising Him and deters those who are not destroyed from giving full vent to their sins.

C. God's judgment is fearful (76:11-12)

76:11-12. Believers should **fulfill** their vows to . . . **God,** bringing **to the One to be feared** (cf. v. 7) what is due Him. By their allegiance to God people can escape His fearful judgment on world **rulers.** He can cause those who arrogantly rebel against Him to fear Him.

Psalm 77

The Psalmist Asaph cried earnestly in the night from his troubled spirit, searching his soul for an answer to his distress. He found comfort in meditating on God's mighty deliverance at the Exodus. This meditation bolstered the psalmist's courage and led him to try to get God to show His mighty power again.

A. The problem (77:1-9)

77:1-3. Asaph related that he **cried** earnestly all **night** for **God to hear** him, but was disquieted and confused when he **remembered . . . God** (cf. vv. 6-7). Apparently his effort to find comfort from prayer failed.

77:4-6. Then the psalmist told how he searched his **spirit** for comfort. As God **troubled** him by keeping him awake, he **thought about the former days** when he could sing **in the night** about God's deliverances. But now he was perplexed **(mused;** cf. v. 3) because he had no occasion for praise.

77:7-9. Asaph was perplexed because he seemed to be abandoned by **the LORD.** He wondered if God had cast Israel off, by discontinuing **His favor.** . . . **love** (*ḥeseḏ,* "loyal love"), and **promise** and by withholding His mercy and **compassion** because of His **anger.**

Apparently, then, the nation was in distress. God had not answered their prayers, which greatly troubled the psalmist's soul.

B. The solution (77:10-20)

The psalmist's comfort and hope came from his musing on God's great deliverance of Israel at the Exodus.

77:10-15. Asaph decided to recall **(remember . . . meditate . . . consider,** vv. 11-12) God's **miracles** (v. 11) performed in the past by His **right hand** (v. 10, i.e., in power; cf. "arm," v. 15). Asaph based his **appeal** on those **works** and **deeds.** His immediate reflection led him to praise the incomparably **holy** and **great . . . God** as Redeemer (vv. 13-15). God is incomparable because he **performs** miraculous, **mighty** deeds, such as the redemption (deliverance) of His people from Egypt by His **arm** (i.e., strength). The question, **What god is so great as our God?** does not imply that other gods live. It indicates that God far exceeds every false god people worship (cf. similar questions in 35:10; 71:19; 89:6; 113:5; Ex. 15:11; Micah 7:18).

77:16-18. Asaph vividly described the phenomena that accompanied the display of power when God redeemed His people from Egypt. **Waters** responded to Him (at the crossing of the Red Sea), and **clouds . . . thunder . . . lightning (Your arrows),** and earthquakes revealed His power (cf. 68:7-9; 97:2-5).

77:19-20. God used **Moses and Aaron** to lead His people miraculously out of danger **through the** Red **Sea** as if they were **a flock** of sheep (cf. 78:52; 79:13; 100:3).

So the implication of this praise-filled meditation is that God will again miraculously rescue His **people,** people whom He has redeemed to Himself.

Psalm 78

Psalm 78 continues the tradition of passing on the record of God's marvelous works of old from one generation to another. Psalmist Asaph implored his generation to keep the Law and not forget God's works and rebel. They should not do as their ancestors in the wilderness did, who were slain by the Lord's anger, or as a later generation did when Shiloh was plundered before the Lord chose David. The poem is a sad recounting of how their ancestors forgot God's works, but it also recounts how the Lord graciously delivered them.

A. The tradition of instruction (78:1-8)

78:1-8. Asaph called the **people** to **hear** his instruction (v. 1) about the Lord's **deeds . . . power, and . . . wonders** (v. 4) that He would make **known** to his **generation.** These had been handed down from earlier generations as God had commanded. The LORD planned this so that the nation might **trust** Him and obey the Law (v. 7), not stumbling in unbelief and rebellion **like their** unfaithful **forefathers** (v. 8).

B. The disobedience of Ephraim (78:9-11)

78:9-11. It is difficult to know for sure which event these verses refer to. Ephraim's failure in **battle** and her disobedience to God, whenever they occurred, may have resulted in Judah's being made preeminent over Ephraim (cf. vv. 67-68).

C. The marvelous deeds that men forget (78:12-72)

In the rest of the psalm Asaph reviewed God's intervention in Israel's history. In verses 12-39 the writer recounted the marvelous things God did for Israel's ancestors at the Exodus and in the desert and their failure to obey Him. In verses 40-72 Asaph recounted the marvelous things God did for the nation from the time of the plagues to His giving them David as their king, and also the people's disobedience.

78:12-20. Asaph described God's wonders in the plagues (cf. vv. 43-51; Ex. 7–11) in **Zoan,** capital city of **the land of** Goshen **in** northeast **Egypt** (Ps. 78:12), at the crossing of **the** Red **Sea** (v. 13; cf. Ex. 14:21-22), and in the wilderness (Ps. 78:14-16; cf. Ex. 13:21; 17:6). **But** the people murmured and rebelled **against** Him (Ps. 78:17-20). Doubting God's ability (cf. v. 22), they put Him **to the test** (cf. vv. 41, 56) expecting Him to do miracles for

them when they were out of His will.

78:21-33. Asaph told how **the** LORD met the Israelites' murmuring first with **anger** in sending **fire** (vv. 21-22; cf. Num. 11:1-3), then by showering them with **manna** (Ps. 78:23-25; cf. Ex. 16:14-31), called **the bread of angels** because it was sent by God (cf. Ex. 16:4), then with the **meat** (Ps. 78:27-29) of quails (cf. Ex. 16:13) driven in by southeast winds (cf. Num. 11:31). Asaph also recalled that **God's anger** (cf. Ps. 78:21) destroyed those who craved (vv. 30-33; cf. Num. 11:33).

78:34-39. Asaph added that **whenever** the Lord punished His people, they **turned to Him** as **their Rock** and **Redeemer,** even though **their hearts were not** right. But God forgave them, repeatedly restraining **His anger,** because He **remembered . . . they were** mere humans with fleeting lives (vv. 38-39).

78:40-55. Asaph lamented **how often** the people **rebelled . . . in the desert,** forgetting the mighty works that demonstrated God's **power** (vv. 40-42). So, having briefly referred to the plagues in **Egypt** (v. 12), he now described some of them in greater detail (vv. 43-51; cf. 105:28-38). **Sycamore**-fig trees were common **in Egypt.** He also wrote about God's great deliverance of the people through the wilderness as **He led** them **like a flock** (78:52-54; cf. 79:13), and about the Conquest of the **land** (78:55).

78:56-64. Then Asaph sadly recalled how the people tested **God** (see comments on v. 18), **rebelled against** Him, and turned to false gods (vv. 56-58). Because of this the Lord was **angry** and had **Shiloh** plundered so that **the ark** was captured (vv. 59-61; cf. 1 Sam. 4:4-11). Many **people** were killed at that time (Ps. 78:62-64), including the **priests** Hophni and Phinehas.

78:65-72. Asaph then reminded the people how **the Lord awoke,** figuratively speaking, like a mighty **man** and saved His people from their **enemies.** But then **He rejected the tents of Joseph,** Manasseh and **Ephraim** (see comments on vv. 9-11), representing the Northern tribes, and **chose** Judah's **Zion** for the location of **His sanctuary,** and **David His servant** to be His king. The disbelief and disobedience that brought disaster at the Battle of Aphek (1 Sam. 4:1-11) marked the turning point to a new priesthood and a new sanctuary, and a king to lead the people, God's **inheritance** (cf. Pss. 78:62; 79:1; see comments on Deut. 4:20).

Psalm 79

Complaining that Jerusalem had been devastated, the saints slaughtered, and their enemies encouraged to scoff, the psalmist pleaded with the Lord not to remember their sins but to deliver them for His name's sake. This psalm is similar in several ways to Psalm 74.

A. Lament over the destruction of Jerusalem (79:1-4)

79:1-4. The writer lamented that **the nations** had **invaded** the land of God's people (His **inheritance**; cf. comments on Deut. 4:20), **defiled** the **temple,** and plundered the holy city. Moreover, they had slaughtered many of God's servants, leaving them unburied for predators to devour. All this had made Israel an object of **scorn** and **reproach.**

B. Plea for deliverance (79:5-12)

79:5-9. The psalmist then pleaded with the LORD not to remember their sins but to help them in their **need.** He wanted to know **how long** (cf. comments on 6:3) the Lord would **be angry** with their **sins,** with His **jealousy** burning **like fire** (cf. 89:46). God was asked to destroy their enemies and deliver His own **quickly** (cf. comments on 31:2) **for** His **glory** and **for** His **name's sake,** that is, because of His reputation.

79:10-12. Seeking to motivate the LORD to answer his plea for deliverance, the psalmist desired that He would keep the Israelite **prisoners** alive and end the nations' mockery of God's people (**Where is their God?** cf. 42:3, 10; 115:2) by turning on them **seven times** (i.e., thoroughly; cf. 12:6) and ending the nations' **reproach** against God's supposed inability to help His own.

C. Promise of praise (79:13)

79:13. After the Lord would release His **people** from bondage, the psalmist promised that then they, **the sheep of** His **pasture** (cf. 74:1; 95:7; 100:3), would be eternally grateful and would **praise** Him **forever.**

Psalm 80

In his prayer that the Lord would restore and save Israel, the psalmist la-

mented the awful calamity brought on them by their enemies. He described the blessing and cursing of the nation as a vine that flourished and was then destroyed. He repeated the refrain (vv. 3, 7, 19) that God should turn and save them.

A. Appeal to Israel's Shepherd (80:1-3)

80:1-2. The psalmist appealed to the Lord, the **Shepherd** (cf. 23:1; 28:9) of His people, the sheep, to help the tribes in their distress. The Lord is pictured sitting **enthroned** in the temple above the gold-covered **cherubim** (cf. 99:1; 1 Kings 6:23-28) over the ark of the covenant. **Joseph,** representing the Northern Kingdom, and **Benjamin,** representing the Southern Kingdom, were Rachel's two sons; **Ephraim** and **Manasseh,** Joseph's sons, were her grandsons.

80:3. The psalmist then prayed that **God** would **restore** and save His people by His grace. This refrain recurs in verses 7, 19. The concept of divine favor is expressed by the image of one's **face** shining on another, like a beaming countenance of approval (cf. Num. 6:25; and comments on Ps. 4:6).

B. Discipline from God (80:4-7)

80:4-7. The psalmist lamented the fierce discipline **God** had brought on His **people.** He cried out to God, asking **how long** (cf. comments on 6:3) His **anger** would be directed against them. The situation was as if **God** (like a Shepherd) had been feeding His people **tears.** He had brought painful calamity on them so that they wept uncontrollably (expressed in hyperbole that their tears were drunk **by the bowlful**). But the most painful aspect of God's chastening was that Israel's **enemies** mocked them (cf. 79:10).

Again the refrain expressed the desire that God would **restore** His people by His favor (cf. 80:3, 19).

C. Removal of blessing (80:8-14b)

80:8-11. The psalmist pictured Israel as **a vine** that God brought from **Egypt** and **planted** in the land. It flourished so that it spread to the **mountains** in the south, to the **cedars** of Lebanon in the north, to **the Sea** (the Mediterranean to the west) and to **the River** (the Euphrates) on the east.

80:12-14b. However, this prosperity had withered. By a rhetorical question the writer lamented that God had **broken down** the **walls** of the nation to enable others to plunder her. The Hebrew word for "walls" (also used in 89:40; Isa. 5:5) does not mean city walls but walls around vineyards. The enemies who plundered Israel are here described as **boars** and beasts.

The figure of Israel as a vine may have been prompted by Genesis 49:22. It is used also in Isaiah 5:1-7; 27:2-6; Jeremiah 2:21; 12:10; Hosea 10:1. Jesus spoke of Himself as a Vine (John 15:1, 5) for He, being the promised Seed, represented and fulfilled God's purposes for Israel. Where she failed, He succeeded.

The first two lines of Psalm 80:14 are a refrain similar (but different in wording) to verses 3, 7, 19.

D. Promise of obedience (80:14c-19)

80:14c-16. Asaph continued to speak of the **vine,** lamenting that **the root** that had been **planted** and **the son** who had grown had been destroyed (**cut down**). "Son," a literal rendering of the Hebrew, refers to the nation that sprang from "the root." So "son" could be rendered "branch" (cf. NIV marg.). Again (cf. comments on v. 12) this imagery may come from Genesis 49:22. The Hebrew term "son" is also used for the nation in Exodus 4:22 and Hosea 11:1. Again the New Testament (Matt. 2:15) applied a prophet's words (Hosea 11:1) to Christ the Seed as the Representative of Israel.

80:17-19. The psalmist prayed that God's **hand** would restore them. **The man at Your right hand** may allude to Benjamin, which means "son of the right hand." **The son of man** refers to Israel (again as a son). Asaph said that if **God** would bless His own, the people would be faithful to Him.

Once more the psalm includes the refrain which requests that God would restore His people by His favor (cf. vv. 3, 7).

Psalm 81

This song is a festive celebration in memory of the Lord's deliverance. It has been traditionally identified with the Feast of Tabernacles (Lev. 23:33-36, 39-43; Deut. 16:13-15). Some have argued, on the basis of Psalm 81:5, that the Passover was the occasion for Asaph's writing Psalm 81, since the Passover was inaugu-rated in Egypt. But the jubilation in the psalm fits the Tabernacles festival better. In the psalm Asaph summoned the people to the festival which God had ordained as a memorial to His great deliverance of them from bondage in Egypt. Using the witness of history, the writer declared that the Lord would turn their affliction away if they would obey Him.

A. Summons to the celebration (81:1-5)

81:1-2. The psalmist called the congregation to sing aloud to the Lord their **Strength** (cf. 22:19; 28:7-8; 46:1; 59:9, 17; 118:14), and to praise Him with musical accompaniment.

81:3-5. Then the psalmist exhorted them to appear at the festival because it was a statute for the nation to keep. The Law stipulated that adult males were to make pilgrimages three times a year to Jerusalem to celebrate the Feasts of Passover (in association with the **Feast** of Unleavened Bread), Weeks, and Tabernacles (Deut. 16:16). The Feast of Tabernacles began on the 15th day of the seventh month (Lev. 23:33) when the moon was full. The seventh month was September-October (see "Calendar in Israel," near Ex. 12:1). **Israel** began to hear God's commandments in **Egypt** (in His instructions to her regarding the Passover). It was like a voice they had never heard before (NIV marg.).

B. Report of God's revelation (81:6-16)

These verses record God's communication to Israel as if He spoke directly to the nation.

81:6-7. First, the psalmist wrote that God said that by the Exodus He relieved the Israelites of their **burden** (in the Egyptian bondage when they had to carry bricks in baskets), and in the wilderness He **tested** them **at . . . . Meribah** (Ex. 17:7; Num. 20:13; Pss. 95:8; 106:32). The Feast of Tabernacles reminded Israel of the wanderings.

81:8-10. The psalmist then recalled God's revelation of Himself and His Law to His **people.** He had promised if they would hold their allegiance to Him (v. 9; cf. Ex. 20:3-6), He would provide their needs bountifully since He had **brought** them **up out of Egypt** (cf. Ex. 20:2). They should not turn to any **foreign god** because only He could satisfy them abundantly.

81:11-12. Asaph then reported God's words about their disobedience. Because they did **not submit to** Him, He let them run to their own destruction.

81:13-16. The psalmist recorded God's promise that if they would obey Him He would **subdue their enemies** and give them prosperity (**wheat** and **honey**; cf. Deut. 32:13-14). The words in Psalm 81:6, 11-15 address **Israel** in the third person (**their**) whereas the words in verses 7-10, 16 are in the second person (**you**). The abrupt change in verse 16 introduces the blessings that come to God's people who obey Him (v. 13).

Psalm 82

Declaring that God judges His human judges, Asaph called for Him to act on His justice. Asaph warned that judges without understanding, who ignore God's appointment of them, will perish.

A. God judges human judges (82:1)

82:1. The psalmist envisioned **God** presiding over an **assembly** of judges. The word **gods** (*'ĕlōhîm*) is used here for authorities in Israel (cf. 45:6; Ex. 21:6; 22:8-9). Some have thought this refers to angels (e.g., the Syriac trans.) in God's heavenly court. However, the remainder of the psalm clarifies that these are God's representatives who are in authority on earth.

B. God's indictment of judges (82:2-7)

Using God's words, the psalmist warned these magistrates to do their jobs right.

82:2-5. The indictment (v. 2), given in the form of a rhetorical question, is that His people were **unjust** and partial. (On the words **how long**, see comments on 6:3.) Instead they should judge fairly and champion the cause of the **oppressed** (including **the weak . . . fatherless . . . poor,** and **needy**). This is the essence of righteous judging.

However, the human judges under God's indictment roam the earth without spiritual or intellectual understanding and in moral **darkness** so that **the foundations of the earth are shaken,** that is, law and order are undermined (cf. 11:3).

82:6-7. God warned the wicked judges that they will perish. He had appointed them as **"gods"** (cf. v. 1) and as **sons of the Most High,** His representa-

tives on earth. But despite their exalted position, they were held accountable by God. Jesus appealed to verse 6 when He was accused of blasphemy (John 10:34). Since Israel's judges were, in a sense, "sons" of God, Jesus said He was not blaspheming to call Himself the Son of God.

C. Call for judgment (82:8)

82:8. Asaph called on **God** to arise and **judge the earth,** that is, all its inhabitants, **for all** are His and therefore are responsible to Him.

Psalm 83

The psalmist lamented the great danger from the many enemies that hemmed in Judah to crush her. He prayed that God would muster His power to destroy them, as He had done in former victories.

A. Danger of destruction (83:1-8)

83:1-8. These verses record Asaph's lament over Judah's grave situation. As in many other lament psalms, the writer turned immediately to **God,** asking Him to respond (v. 1).

The psalmist delineated how Judah's enemies had taken counsel to destroy her (vv. 2-5). As God's **enemies** they plotted cunningly (cf. 64:6) **against** God's **people** (83:3) and **against** God Himself (v. 5). They conspired to **destroy** the **nation** and wipe out any remembrance of her. These foes included numerous surrounding nations: **Edom . . . Ishmaelites** (also called the **descendants of Hagar**), **Moab . . . Gebal** (Byblos), **Ammon . . . Amalek . . . Philistia** and the city of **Tyre.** Mighty **Assyria** also supported this coalition which included **the descendants of Lot,** the Moabites and Ammonites (Gen. 19:36-38).

B. Powerful deliverance (83:9-18)

Verses 9-18 of the psalm record Asaph's prayer that God would use His power to overthrow Judah's enemies.

83:9-12. The psalmist's prayer at the outset alluded to past victories over the Midianites through Gideon (Jud. 7–8) and against **Sisera** through Deborah and Barak (Jud. 4–5). **Endor** is near Taanach, mentioned in Judges 5:19. Asaph spoke again of Gideon's victory, **Oreb and Zeeb** being the leaders of the Midianite warriors (Jud. 7:25) and **Zebah and Zalmunna** the Midianite kings (Jud. 8:5-6, 12, 18).

83:13-16. The psalmist asked that God would **make them like** windblown **tumbleweed** and **chaff** (cf. 1:4), insecure and pursued, and that He would hotly pursue them **as fire consumes** a **forest** on a mountain. Asaph wanted God's wrath to be like a stormy **tempest** from which they could not escape. This defeat would **shame** them and cause many to turn to the LORD.

83:17-18. The psalm closes with a reiteration of the prayer that the wicked **be ashamed** (cf. v. 16) and disgraced. By trifling with people God cherishes, they would learn the hard way that God **alone** is the sovereign LORD.

Psalm 84

This passage is a companion to Psalms 42 and 43, because it expresses the same yearning for the formal place of worship. Technically it is a pilgrimage song, though it is not in the collection of pilgrim psalms (Pss. 120–134). In Psalm 84 the pilgrim declared the blessedness of a believer who in faith journeys to the temple to pray to the Lord. The author is unknown; it was to be sung by the Korahites.

A. The soul's longing for the Lord (84:1-4)

84:1-2. The psalm breaks out with praise for the **dwelling place** (cf. 74:7; 76:2; 132:5, 7) of the LORD **Almighty** (cf. 84:3, 8, 12; lit., "Yahweh of hosts," i.e., armies). For this place (the temple with its **courts**; cf. v. 10) the psalmist's **heart and . . . flesh** (body) longed. To yearn for the temple meant to long **for the living God** Himself (cf. 42:2). In that day people could approach God through the temple priests. The psalmist's faith was thus in the living, powerful Lord God.

84:3-4. The psalmist conveyed his intense yearning for **God** and His temple by noting the enviable position of those in the temple—nesting birds and ministering servants (priests **who dwell in** the temple rooms).

B. The pilgrimage to the temple (84:5-7)

84:5-7. The psalmist declared the blessedness (cf. v. 12; i.e., the joyous privileges and great benefits) of **those** who demonstrate their faith by going **on pilgrimage** (cf. Deut. 16:16) to appear in Jerusalem (**Zion**) **before** the Lord.

On their pilgrimage they were strengthened by God's blessings. **The Valley of Baca** ("balsam tree") was apparently a waterless place that became **a place of springs.** The rains would **cover** the arid valley **with pools** of water, a vivid picture of God's blessings on the faithful pilgrims.

C. The prayer of the pilgrim (84:8-12)

84:8-9. The pilgrim, once he arrived in God's dwelling place in Zion, prayed for the king, who was like a **shield** protecting the people, and was God's **anointed one** (cf. 2:2). As the LORD **God Almighty** (lit., "Yahweh, God of hosts") and the **God of Jacob,** He is able to intervene on behalf of His people and deliver them.

84:10-12. The pilgrim-psalmist stated why he longed to go to Zion: he was confident that God would answer his prayer. Reaffirming his intense love for the temple and its **courts** (cf. v. 2), he said that **one day** there was **better . . . than a thousand elsewhere**; to be a servant there was better than living in the lavish **tents of the wicked.** The reason, of course, was that God was at the temple and would bless and protect (be **a Sun and Shield**; cf. comments on 3:3) and bestow **favor** and **good** things (cf. 16:2; 34:10) on those who would **walk** blamelessly. Another prerequisite for receiving God's blessings is trust.

Psalm 85

The psalmist acknowledged the goodness of God in restoring His people and forgiving their sins. He then prayed that the Lord would remove His wrath from His people. The psalmist's confidence in the Lord came from God's promise of salvation.

A. Prayer to God (85:1-7)

85:1-3. The song begins with praise to God for restoring the nation. This restoration evidenced the fact that God had forgiven and **covered all their sins,** and had **set aside** His **wrath** and anger.

Some scholars say this psalm was written in the early days of the exiles' return from the Babylonian Captivity; this is hard to prove. Their view, however, does stress that the forgiveness of the nations' sins ended God's wrath and prompted His people's return.

85:4-7. The psalmist prayed that the Lord would again turn His wrath away and deliver them. He wanted the Lord to **put away** His **displeasure,** and not continue to **be angry.** Apparently the past restoration referred to in verses 1-3 inspired this prayer for another restoration. Revived, they would again be able to **rejoice** and experience His **unfailing love** (*ḥeseḏ*).

B. Promise from God (85:8-9)

85:8-9. The psalmist said he would **listen** for word from **the LORD** who **promises peace** (*šālôm,* "welfare"; cf. v. 10; Es. 10:3) **to His . . . saints.** He gives salvation so **that His glory may** be evident **in the land.** "Glory" means the manifestation of His presence (cf. Isa. 60:1-2; Zech. 2:5).

These ideas expressed in God's revelation to Israel find their ultimate fulfillment in Christ. This promise of peace and salvation through the glory of the One who dwells among men may have been in John's mind when he wrote John 1:14.

C. Faith of the psalmist (85:10-13)

85:10-13. The writer was confident that **the LORD** would cause His attributes (**love** [*ḥeseḏ*], **faithfulness,** and **righteousness**) to work together to provide **peace** (welfare; cf. v. 8), **righteousness,** and prosperity (cf. 84:11).

Psalm 86

Because God is good and forgiving, and because He is incomparably able to do great things, the psalmist petitioned Him to show His strength in the face of opposition from the proud.

The psalm is ascribed to David. It seems to be a mosaic of expressions from the other psalms. Nevertheless it has a unique emphasis in the Book of Psalms.

A. Prayer for protection (86:1-5)

86:1-5. In his prayer David earnestly requested that God **hear . . . answer. . . . guard. . . . save. . . . have mercy on,** and **bring joy** to him because of his **poor and needy** condition (see comments on 37:14). Essentially in these requests he desired that God preserve him (cf. 25:20)

by His mercy. David called himself a **servant who trusts in** the Lord, one who lifts **up** his **soul** to God (cf. 25:1).

This prayer was based on the fact that God is **kind,** ready to forgive, and **abounding in love** (cf. 86:15; Ex. 34:6).

B. Praise for power (86:6-13)

86:6-10. David repeated his call for the **LORD** to **hear** him. His confidence that **in** his **trouble** God would **answer** him was strengthened by his knowledge that the Lord is incomparable (**there is none like You**; cf. Ex. 15:11), fully able to do what he asked (**no deeds can compare with Yours**). People from **all . . . nations** will serve Him, and He **alone** is the **great . . . God.** This theme of God's incomparable greatness is also reflected in the psalm's sevenfold use of the word **Lord** ('*ăḏōnay*), which stresses His lordship and sovereignty (Ps. 86:3-5, 8-9, 12, 15).

86:11-13. The psalmist prayed for instruction so that he might be even more faithful to **God** in His greatness. He desired to know God's **way** so that he could dedicate himself to it with **undivided** loyalty. In addition he vowed to **praise** God's greatness wholeheartedly (cf. **heart,** v. 11). Because of God's love He **delivered** David from death.

C. Petition for strength (86:14-17)

86:14-17. Because the proud had risen against David, he asked **God** for **strength.** His **enemies** were ruthless men with no **regard for** the Lord. But by contrast the Lord is **compassionate** (cf. 111:4), **gracious . . . slow to anger,** loving, and faithful (cf. Ex. 34:6; Neh. 9:17; Pss. 103:8; 145:8; Joel 2:13; Jonah 4:2). David's prayer for "strength" in the face of his peril was based on the greatness of **God.** He also asked for **a sign of** God's **goodness,** that is, deliverance so that others would **see** and know it was God at work.

Psalm 87

This psalm expands on the idea in Psalm 86:9, that nations will someday worship the Lord. Psalm 87 is a song about the glorious things said about Zion, the city of God. After depicting Zion as God's glorious city, the psalmist described how the nations will gather to her as children, and how joyful are those who dwell there.

A. The glorious city of God (87:1-3)

87:1-3. The first verse stands as a single-line summary of the psalm's theme: God **has set His foundation on the holy mountain** (cf. 43:3; 48:1; 99:9), that is, **He** has chosen **Zion** as His dwelling place above **all** others.

Besides Zion being loved by the Lord, **glorious things** were **said** about it. Some of those things are mentioned in the rest of the psalm (cf. Isa. 11:10).

B. The nations gathered to Zion (87:4-6)

87:4. The psalmist listed some of the nations that will be gathered to Zion. They will be like children who were **born** there (vv. 4-6). God's purpose is to reconcile people to Himself, and these statements anticipate that five nations—**Rahab . . . Babylon . . . Philistia**, Phoenicia (represented by **Tyre**), and **Cush** (present-day southern Egypt, Sudan, and northern Ethiopia)—will be **among** the peoples **who acknowledge** Him. "Rahab," representing Egypt (cf. Isa. 30:7), was probably the name of a powerful demonic force thought to be behind that nation.

87:5-6. Zion will be enriched in that day by this acquisition of new citizens. All nations in that day will look to Zion as the "mother city." God's writing their names in a **register** figuratively describes His ensuring them a place **in Zion.**

C. Joy in Zion (87:7)

87:7. This verse is a brief glimpse of the rejoicing that the other believing nations will bring to Zion. The second line of the verse states the substance of their musical praise: **All my fountains are in You.** "Fountains" signifies that Zion will be the source of all blessing and pleasure, because of the Lord's presence there.

Psalm 88

Psalm 88, written by Heman (cf. 1 Chron. 15:19; 16:41-42; 25:1, 6) the Ezrahite (a wise person, 1 Kings 4:31), has been called one of the saddest psalms in the Psalter. It voices the diligent prayer of one who suffered constantly. The psalmist lamented the terrible and fierce affliction that had brought him to the point of death. Yet he steadfastly prayed to the Lord night and day, basing his appeal on the fact that he would be useless to the Lord in the grave.

A. His terrible affliction (88:1-9a)

88:1-2. The introduction is given in these verses: the psalmist prayed (cf. v. 13) constantly (**day and night**) to **God** for deliverance.

88:3-9a. In describing his affliction, Heman first compared himself to those who are forgotten in **the grave.** His troubled **life** was near death (v. 3), he was considered dead (v. 4, **pit** is a synonym for grave; cf. v. 6; 28:1; 30:3, 9; 69:15; 143:7). He was like **the dead,** without God's **care** (88:5).

Then in direct address Heman declared that God had brought this trouble on him. God laid him **in the lowest pit** (cf. v. 4), God's **wrath . . . overwhelmed** him like **waves,** and God had separated him **from** his **friends** by his **grief.**

B. His earnest prayer (88:9b-12)

88:9b-12. The psalmist stated that he continued to pray earnestly to the LORD. He reasoned that a **dead** person cannot **praise** God's works and attributes **in the grave.** (He wrote this from a human, physical perspective, but it does not contradict other verses that speak of conscious existence after death.) He said the Lord should deliver him so that he could declare His glory. True believers want to praise the Lord, and to Heman death seemed to be the end of that opportunity.

C. His steadfast faith (88:13-18)

88:13-18. For the third time the psalmist affirmed his faith by his **cry to** God **for help** (v. 13; cf. vv. 1-2). Then, questioning why the LORD had apparently rejected him (v. 14), he again stated that his affliction was terrible (vv. 15-18). Like Job in some ways, this psalmist **suffered** under what appeared to be God's **wrath,** separated from his friends **and loved ones,** and was almost in despair (**darkness**). Yet, knowing that God was his only Source of hope, he continued to pray.

Psalm 89

This royal psalm is a prayer that God would honor the Davidic Covenant (2 Sam. 7:5-16). The psalm is attributed to "Ethan" (a Levite, 1 Chron. 15:17-18, and a wise person, 1 Kings 4:31) but the exact occasion of its writing is unknown. Various military defeats, such as the invasion of Judah by Shishak of Egypt (1 Kings 14:25) and the Babylonian Exile, have been suggested.

Faced with the perplexing problem of the affliction and defeat of the anointed Davidic king, the psalmist implored the Lord to remember His oath and end this disaster. Ethan sought to motivate the Lord to answer his prayer by rehearsing the covenant promises and the divine attributes on which they rest. So the psalm is a study in the age-old apparent conflict between the promises of a faithful, loving God, and the catastrophes that often occur.

Several key words used repeatedly show something of the psalm's emphasis: "love" (ḥeseḏ, vv. 1-2, 14, 24, 28, 33, 49), "faithfulness" (vv. 1-2, 5, 8, 33, 49), "throne" (of David; vv. 4, 14, 29, 36, 44), "David My servant" (vv. 3, 20; cf. v. 50), "anointed" (vv. 20, 38, 51), "covenant" (vv. 3, 28, 34, 39).

This psalm, because of its several references to the Davidic Covenant (vv. 3-4, 27-29, 35-37, 49), affirms that the Messiah, a descendant of David, will sit on David's throne and rule over Israel. This, taken literally, supports the position that Christ is not *now* sitting on David's throne in heaven but *will* rule on his throne on the earth (cf. comments on 2 Sam. 7:5-16).

A. The faithfulness of God (89:1-4)

89:1-4. The psalmist vowed to praise the Lord for His **love** and **faithfulness** (repeated in vv. 1-2; cf. v. 49; 92:2). Ethan's wholehearted belief that God is faithful was the basis for his appealing to the Lord in his dilemma. Since God made **covenant** promises **to David** (cf. 2 Sam. 7:5-16), should not He, the faithful God, keep His promises?

B. The nature of the covenant God (89:5-18)

89:5-14. The psalmist praised **the LORD** for His remarkable attributes (vv. 5-8) and marvelous works (vv. 9-14). God, he said, is faithful (vv. 5, 8), incomparable (v. 6), fearful, and **mighty.** (On the question, **Who is like the LORD?** cf. 35:10; 71:19; 77:13; 89:6; 113:5; Ex. 15:11; Micah 7:18.) His great works include his ruling over the **sea,** crushing **Rahab** (see comments on Ps. 87:4) with His power (**strong arm**), creating **the heavens** and

the earth, and working with strength (His **arm . . . hand,** and **right hand**; cf. "right hand" in 17:7; 18:35; 20:6; 45:4; 60:5; 63:8; 108:6) and **righteousness.** Even the mountains (including **Tabor and Hermon**) were personified as if they rejoiced in the Lord's creative **power.**

89:15-18. In view of God's attributes (vv. 5-8) and works (vv. 9-14) the psalmist spoke of the blessings of those who trust and fellowship with this marvelous God. They enjoy the benefits of His **righteousness. . . . strength,** and protection (**shield**). Being exalted like an animal's **horn** (cf. v. 24) speaks of being favored and blessed with strength (cf. 92:10; 112:9).

C. The promises of the covenant (89:19-37)

89:19-20. The psalmist reminded the Lord that He had chosen **David,** a young **warrior,** to be His **anointed** servant.

89:21-25. Then the psalmist reminded God that He had promised to **strengthen** and protect the king from all his enemies by His strength (**hand . . . arm**; cf. v. 13), to **love** him, and to extend his influence **over the** Mediterranean **Sea** and **the rivers.**

89:26-29. Then the psalmist spoke of the special relationship the Davidic king had with **God.** It was like a **Father**-son relationship (cf. 2 Sam. 7:14). Moreover, God in His unfailing covenant had promised that David's **line** (dynasty) and **throne** would last **forever** (cf. Ps. 89:35-37; 2 Sam. 7:12-13, 16).

89:30-37. The Lord had sworn not to break His covenant even if the people disobeyed. If they disobeyed, **the rod** would be brought on them (i.e., God would punish them), but He would not remove His **love** or **faithfulness** by ending the **covenant.** His promises, including those in the Davidic Covenant (cf. vv. 27-29), stand **forever.**

D. The prayer for the Lord to remember His oath (89:38-52)

89:38-45. The psalmist now lamented the fact that the king had been afflicted and defeated in spite of God's covenantal promises. Ethan wrote that God had cast off His **servant** (vv. 38-39), **broken** his vineyard **walls** (cf. comments on 80:12) and defenses (89:40), made him weak in battle (v. 41), strengthened (**exalted the**

right hand of) his enemies (vv. 42-43), and cast down his throne in shame (vv. 44-45).

89:46-52. The psalmist petitioned the LORD (on the question How long. . . ? cf. comments on 6:3) to remember His oath and come to his aid, for his life was fleeting. He was near death and was bearing the reproach of his enemies. So the psalmist's only hope in the disaster was to pray that God in His love and faithfulness (cf. 89:1-2) would honor His word.

The doxology in verse 52 ends Book III (Pss. 73–89).

IV. Book IV (Pss. 90–106)

In this section of 17 psalms all but 3 are anonymous. Psalm 90 was written by Moses and Psalms 101 and 103 were composed by David.

Psalm 90

Contrasting God's eternity with human transitoriness, and confessing that man's days pass away in God's wrath, the psalmist prayed that the compassionate God would give His people success for their labors and joy for their sorrows.

According to the superscription the psalm is "a prayer of Moses, the man of God" (cf. Deut. 33:1). There are no compelling reasons to reject this view, though many commentators do. If it was written by Moses, the occasion of his writing it is unknown. However, the period of the wilderness wanderings, when a generation of Israelites perished in the desert, readily suggests itself as the background for the psalm. If Moses was the author this is the oldest of the 150 psalms.

A. Man's transitoriness (90:1-12)

This portion of the psalm contrasts God and man, and gives the response which that contrast prompts.

90:1-6. These verses discuss the disparity between the everlasting God and finite humans. In humility the psalmist acknowledged that God is the saints' eternal dwelling place (i.e., protecting shelter) because He is from everlasting to everlasting (vv. 1-2). In all generations people have taken refuge in Him. (The Heb. word for world, *tēbēl*, v. 2, a poetic synonym for earth, means the productive part of the earth. This word is used fre-

quently in the Book of Pss.) But the Lord, who is above the limitations of time (vv. 3-4), turns mortals (men translates *'ĕnôš*, "weak man" to destruction. The word for dust (*dakkā'*, from *dākā'*, "to crush"), used only here in the Old Testament, means something pulverized like dust.

A watch in the night (cf. 63:6) was approximately four hours (Jud. 7:19 refers to a middle watch, suggesting three periods). Such a portion of the night, when man sleeps, is brief.

Man is like the grass that withers (cf. Pss. 37:2; 102:4, 11; 103:15-16; Isa. 40:6-8) in the heat of the day—God sweeps away to death (Ps. 90:5-6). Human life is thus frail and brief, in comparison with the everlasting God.

90:7-12. Man's life is transitory because of God's wrath against sin. The psalmist said that man is consumed by God's anger, for He sees man's sins; even so-called secret sins are open to Him. Since man is a sinner, all his life is spent under God's wrath, and his life is greatly limited—to 70 years (or a few more years, for some people)—and life flies away in death like a fleeting bird (cf. Job 20:8). No one can understand God's powerful wrath (Ps. 90:11).

Because life is so brief, and because it is spent under God's wrath on sin, the psalmist, representing God's people, implored God for wisdom in numbering their days (cf. 39:4), that is, realizing how few they are (cf. 39:5-6). (Our days occurs in 90:9-10, 12, 14 and "days" in v. 15.)

B. God's compassion (90:13-17)

90:13-15. The psalmist pleaded with the Lord to have compassion on His servants (cf. v. 16). This was their only hope.

In showing compassion the Lord was asked to turn their sorrow (cf. v. 10) into joy. If God satisfied them with His loyal love (*ḥeseḏ*), they could then rejoice all their days. The psalmist asked God to let them rejoice for as long as He had given them over to trouble. Verses 14-15 seem to suggest that the nation was undergoing a particularly severe period of chastening for sin, a "night" of trouble as it were. The morning suggests a new era of joy for God's people.

90:16-17. The psalmist also asked that God would display His splendor (cf. comments on 29:2) to His servants (cf.

90:13) and extend His **favor** to them rather than consume them in His wrath. Then they would enjoy success in their labors, even though life is short.

When God rebukes one for his sin, he feels most frail and transitory. But when he is blessed by God's favor he feels most worthwhile; he shares in **the work** of the everlasting God. Weakened by God's discipline, one is keenly aware of his mortality; abiding in God's love and compassion, he is aware of being crowned with glory and honor (cf. 8:5-8).

Psalm 91

Because the psalmist was convinced that there is security in trusting in the Most High God, he encouraged himself that he would be delivered from the various frightening attacks of the wicked. He knew that the Lord had appointed His angels over him to protect him.

This psalm is a beautiful testimony about security in life. Several terms link Psalms 90–92, thus suggesting they are a unit. "Dwelling" occurs in 90:1 and 91:9; "grass" in 90:5 and 92:7; "spring(s) up" in 90:6 and 92:7; "make . . . glad" in 90:15 and 92:4; "Your deeds" in 90:16 and 92:4; "Most High" in 91:1, 9 and 92:1. Also the judgment of the wicked is mentioned in 91:8 and 92:11.

A. Security in God (91:1-2)

91:1-2. The psalmist expressed his great confidence in the fact that whoever trusts in the Most High finds security and protection. The titles of God in verse 1 (**Most High** and **the Almighty**) are significant, for they stress His power as the sovereign Ruler of the world. (On the meaning of "Almighty," *šadday*, see comments on Gen. 17:1.)

The images of **the shelter** and **the shadow** vividly portray divine protection. "Shelter" (*sēṯer*) is a hiding place (also used in Pss. 27:5; 32:7; 119:114, "refuge"). The shadow, perhaps the shadow of a bird's wing (cf. 91:4), also pictures shelter and protection as well as comfort. **God** is also the believer's **Refuge** (*maḥseh*, "shelter from danger"; cf. v. 9 and comments on 14:6) **and . . . Fortress** (*mᵉṣûḏâh*, "strong protection"; used in 18:3; 31:3; 71:3; 144:2). Psalm 91:1-2 admirably expresses the fact that safety is in **the Lord**.

B. Deliverance by angels (91:3-13)

The psalmist, encouraging himself, expanded on the theme of the Lord's protection from danger.

91:3-8. He enumerated how God delivers a believer from various frightening attacks: (1) God delivers **from the fowler's snare** (v. 3a; cf. 124:7), a figure for insidious attempts against his life. (2) God delivers **from . . . deadly pestilence** (91:3b). (3) God covers him with **His wings** (v. 4a), a figure of safety and comfort (cf. 17:8; 36:7; 57:1; 61:4; 63:7). (4) God protects with **His faithfulness** (91:4b), explained here by the metaphor of a **shield and rampart.**

As a result of God's help in these ways one who trusts in the Lord **will not fear . . . terror** at **night,** attack **by day . . . pestilence** or **plague** (vv. 5-6). Destruction that might lay thousands in defeat will not affect a trusting believer; rather, he will **see . . . the wicked** destroyed (vv. 7-8).

91:9-13. The psalmist explained that **no harm** or **disaster** can **befall** those who have made **the Lord** their **refuge** (*maḥseh*, "shelter from danger"; cf. v. 2 and comments on 14:6) because He has commissioned **angels** to care for them. Angels protect from physical harm and give believers strength to overcome difficulties, pictured here as wild lions and dangerous snakes. Satan, in tempting Christ, quoted 91:11-12 (Matt. 4:6), which shows that even God's most marvelous promises can be foolishly applied.

C. God's promise of protection (91:14-16)

91:14-16. The psalmist wrote as if God Himself spoke to confirm the psalmist's faith. In return for the psalmist's love, **the Lord** promised to **rescue him** from danger, **protect him** from harm, **be with him in trouble . . . honor him,** and **satisfy him.** All the kinds of danger mentioned in this song are ineffective against one who rests in the shadow of the Almighty.

Psalm 92

A. It is good to praise the Most High (92:1-7)

92:1-3. The psalm begins with the declaration that **it is good to praise the . . . Most High** (cf. 91:1, 9) with **music . . . to proclaim** His **love** and faithfulness (cf. 89:1-2) daily. By "good" the psalmist meant that it is fitting because of the great, praiseworthy things God has done.

92:4-7. Here the psalmist elaborated on God's praiseworthy actions. The writer sang because of the Lord's deeds . . . great works, and profound . . . thoughts. Specifically he was thinking of God's vindication of the righteous by His destroying senseless . . . evildoers who sprout like grass (cf. 90:5) and flourish for a short time (cf. Pss. 49; 73).

B. The Lord is exalted forever (92:8-15)

92:8-9. Verse 8 forms a wonderful link between verses 1-7 and 9-15. In contrast with the wicked who flourish briefly (v. 7) the Lord reigns with absolute supremacy forever. Because of this His enemies will perish.

92:10-11. In verses 10-14 the psalmist anticipated what the truth in verses 8-9 meant for himself. God would surely exalt his horn and anoint him. Here again he wrote with such confidence that he described God's work as if it had already happened. An animal horn pictures strength (cf. 89:17, 24; 112:9), and the "oil" represents festivity and restoration of vitality. So because God is exalted (cf. 92:8), He will likewise bless His people. Moreover, the righteous will see the complete destruction of the wicked (v. 11; cf. v. 7).

92:12-15. The wicked may flourish but like grass their prosperity is short-lived (v. 7). On the other hand the righteous will flourish like . . . palm trees and cedars of Lebanon. These trees picture fruitfulness and vitality (v. 14) under God's good hand (cf. 1:3). Those who are so blessed will proclaim the righteousness of the Lord, their Rock (cf. comments on 18:2).

Psalm 93

This is one of the "enthronement psalms" (or "theocratic psalms" as they are sometimes called), which celebrate the Lord's reigning on the earth. Other enthronement psalms are 47, 95-99. No doubt they were used in Israel's worship to praise God's sovereignty; but they are also prophetic pictures of the consummation of the ages when the Lord will establish His righteous millennial rule on earth through the Messiah.

In Psalm 93 the psalmist exulted over the reign of the Lord, who has established His throne on high above the oceans and dwells in His holy temple.

A. The Lord establishes His reign (93:1-2)

93:1-2. The psalmist foresaw the Lord reigning (cf. 47:8; 96:10; 97:1; 99:1; 146:10) majestically on the earth, armed with strength. Clothing in the Old Testament was considered an extension of a person; so the expression robed in majesty (cf. 104:1) describes the Lord as majestic and powerful in His reign.

Also by His rule the whole world will be firmly established (cf. 96:10). This means that all the moral and legal orders of life will be solidified under His dominion. Since His throne was established in eternity past, His reign on earth is solidly insured.

B. The Lord is mighty (93:3-4)

93:3-4. The psalmist praised the might of the Lord, which is greater than the seas with their raging waves and roaring noise. In the Old Testament the sea is sometimes an emblem of hostility (cf. Isa. 17:12-13). In pagan Canaanite mythology Baal attained a position of power (and a house that was corrupt) through struggling with and overcoming Prince Yamm, the sea (in Heb. yām means "sea"). But these two verses, a polemic against Baalism, show that the Lord, not Baal, is mightier than the . . . sea. The sea is not mythological; it is a force of nature under God's power (e.g., the Red Sea, Pss. 106:9; 114:3, 5).

C. The Lord's house is holy (93:5)

93:5. Because the house of the Lord is filled with holiness (in contrast with Baal's corrupt place; cf. comments on vv. 3-4) the Lord's commands are sure. Holiness is the quality that sets the Lord apart from all others. It is made known by His power. This psalm has praised God's power, the evidence that He is alive and active, unlike pagan gods. Because He rules in power and holiness, everyone is to follow His statutes.

Psalm 94

This psalm recognizes the fact that vengeance belongs to the Lord. The psalmist called on the Lord to wreak vengeance on proud people who insolently oppress the righteous. The writer was confident that the Lord will not forsake His people but will deliver them, for the wicked have no place in the Lord's reign.

A. Prayer for vengeance (94:1-7)

94:1-3. Verses 1-7 record a prayer that **God** would avenge the **jubilant** wicked. In verses 1-3 the psalmist affirmed that vengeance belongs to the LORD. Because God is the **Judge of the earth,** it is He who must repay the **wicked.** Here again a psalmist asked **How long?** (cf. comments on 6:3) The continuing joy of the **wicked** seems out of place since they oppose **God** (cf. 73:3-12).

94:4-7. To justify his request, the psalmist lamented the oppression that the proud insolently inflict on the righteous. The speech of the wicked is **arrogant.** They oppress God's **people,** His **inheritance** (cf. v. 14 and comments on 28:9; Deut. 4:20). The wicked destroy the needy and oppressed (the very ones righteous leaders must help; cf. Ps. 72:4, 12-14). The wicked do all this because they are convinced that **the LORD . . . pays no attention to them** (cf. 73:11).

B. Warning about judgment (94:8-15)

94:8-11. The psalmist called on the wicked to consider their ways. He was amazed that the wicked had not **become wise**—God knows their **futile** plans and efforts to oppress the righteous. The logic here is simple but forceful: **He who** created the human **ear** surely can **hear; He who formed the eye** surely can **see;** etc.

94:12-15. Here the psalmist expressed his confidence in the LORD. A person God may **discipline** is **blessed** because he is taught **from the Law.** Even though a believer is oppressed by wicked people, he can take comfort that God can use such oppression to **teach** him and that God will give him rest from adversity when **the wicked** are destroyed. The psalmist was sure that God **will not** forsake **His people . . . His inheritance** (cf. v. 5 and comments on 28:9; Deut. 4:20), but will reestablish justice.

C. Consolation from the Lord (94:16-23)

94:16-19. The psalmist's only consolation was in the LORD. After asking **who** would **stand** on behalf of his cause **against** sinners, the writer acknowledged

that his security was from **the LORD.** When he was almost defeated by despair (**when** his **foot** was **slipping;** cf. 73:2), God's **consolation** quieted his anxious heart and gave him **joy.**

94:20-23. Then the psalmist anticipated God's retribution on the wicked. The **corrupt throne** (lit., "throne of wickedness") refers to villainous rulers whose legislation would seek to destroy **the righteous.** These have no part with God. So the psalmist trusted in **the LORD,** his **Fortress** (*miśgōb;* cf. comments on 9:9; 46:7), **Rock,** and **Refuge** (cf. comments on 18:1), knowing that the Lord **will repay them for their sins** by destroying **them.**

Psalm 95

This "enthronement psalm" calls for the people to acknowledge that the Lord is a great King above the gods. (Other enthronement psalms are 47; 93; 96–99.) But having exhorted the congregation to worship their Creator, the psalmist warned them against unbelief as in the days of the wilderness wanderings when God's rest was not experienced.

A. Praise for the Lord's sovereignty (95:1-7a)

This first section of the psalm is a typical praise song.

95:1-2. The psalmist called the congregation to **sing** (cf. comments on 5:11) praises **to the LORD.** He is designated here as **the Rock of our salvation,** a figure of God's provision of security by delivering His people. Apparently the congregation had experienced some such deliverance, for which they were to give **thanksgiving.**

95:3-5. **God** is worthy of the joyful praise mentioned in verses 1-2 because of His majesty. He is **the great King** (cf. 98:6; 99:4; and comments on 5:2) over **all gods.** Mentioning these gods (idols) does not acknowledge their reality. It is a statement of God's sovereignty and superiority over every force, real and imagined. Everything in Creation—including things the pagans venerated as gods—the Lord **made,** and therefore He has power over it all.

95:6-7a. In these verses, which conclude the praise section of the psalm, the psalmist exhorted the congregation to **worship . . . the LORD . . . for He is**

their **God,** and they are His sheep (cf. 74:1; 79:13; 100:3). The title of **Maker** may refer to His formation of the nation (cf. Deut. 32:6). **The flock** suggests again that the Lord, the Shepherd of His **people** Israel, leads and provides for them.

B. Warning against unbelief (95:7b-11)

95:7b-11. In this didactic section the psalmist warned the nation not to repeat the folly of unbelief that cost their ancestors the promised **rest** in the land. This warning was prompted by the mention of the Lord's care for His people (v. 7a); in the history of the nation too often that care was reciprocated by disobedience. The incident referred to here is the people's murmuring at Rephidim (Ex. 17; Num. 20:1-13). The names given to the place reflect the incident. **Meribah** (cf. Pss. 81:7; 106:32) means "strife" and **Massah** means "testing," for the people strove with the Lord and **tested** Him. So God swore that they could not **enter** the land, but must perish in the wilderness. The younger generation would enter the Promised Land.

In exhorting his audience the psalmist began with the word **Today,** a rhetorical device to stress the immediacy of the opportunity. They must not resist God's **voice** calling them to trust and obey. In the Bible the word **hearts** often means people's wills. To **harden** one's heart meant to refuse to obey. If this psalm's hearers also disobeyed through unbelief, God would keep them from attaining rest in the land.

This passage is quoted in Hebrews 3:7-11 as a warning for Christians who through unbelief (Heb. 3:12) were in danger of not receiving the promised rest (cf. comments on Heb. 3:7-12). In its fullest sense, that rest signifies the Lord's coming kingdom on earth, when believers will experience spiritual and temporal rest in the Lord. Believers, of course, enter that rest positionally when they cease from their works and trust Him.

The warning in Psalm 95 anticipates this because it is part of a song that celebrates the Lord's kingship (v. 3), a kingship that can only be served by true worshipers.

Psalm 96

In this psalm about the reign of the Lord, the psalmist called on people ev-erywhere and all the elements of nature to praise God because He is greater than all pagan gods and because He will reign in righteousness and truth.

A. The earth is to praise His majesty (96:1-6)

96:1-3. The psalmist invited **all the earth** (i.e., people everywhere; cf. 97:1; 98:4; 100:1) to praise **the Lord.** They were to **sing** (cf. comments on 5:11) **a new song** to Him (cf. 33:3; 40:3; 98:1; 144:9; 149:1). Singing a new song suggests that new mercies had been received. The people were told to announce **His salvation** and His **deeds** throughout the world, which would bring Him **glory** (cf. "glory" in 96:6-8).

96:4-6. The Lord is **worthy of** the **praise** called for in verses 1-3 because He is greater than **all gods** (cf. comments on 95:3; also note 97:9). Those **gods,** worshiped among **the nations, are** only **idols. He** is the One who **made** everything and is therefore superior. Moreover, His temple (the **sanctuary**) is characterized by **splendor** (cf. 96:9 and comments on 29:2; also called **majesty** and **glory**) and **strength** (cf. 96:7). In other words He is glorious and strong in the midst of His people.

B. The nations must recognize His reign (96:7-10)

96:7-9. The psalmist called for the **families** (lit., "tribes") of the earth to **ascribe . . . glory and strength** (cf. v. 6) to God and **worship** Him. Someday every knee must bow (Phil. 2:10) before this sovereign **Lord,** whose **holiness** is awesome.

96:10. People everywhere should praise Him because He **reigns** (cf. 47:8; 93:1; 97:1; 99:1; 146:10). When the Lord returns to **judge** and reign on earth His reign will at last be **established** (cf. 92:1) with righteousness.

C. All nature should rejoice (96:11-13)

96:11-13. The psalmist called on nature to **rejoice** because the Lord will come to **judge the world in righteousness** (cf. 97:2; 98:9) **and . . . truth.** These bold personifications (of **the heavens . . . the earth . . . the sea . . . the fields,** and **the trees**) may indicate that all Creation will flourish when righteousness reigns on earth, when the curse is replaced by blessing. Then earth will no longer groan, waiting for the day of redemption as it is doing now (Rom. 8:20-22). Then nature will sing.

Psalms such as this must have been uplifting for the psalmists as they have been for believers of all ages. Many psalms express a longing for the Lord to destroy wickedness and establish righteousness on the earth. The laments of the psalmists will no more be uttered when the Lord reigns in righteousness and truth.

Psalm 97

This is a didactic psalm based on a vision of the Lord. The psalmist envisioned the magnificent coming of the Lord in all His splendor. Depicting the Lord coming to reign and to judge His adversaries in righteousness, the psalmist exhorted the saints to hate evil and rejoice in the Lord (cf. 2 Peter 3:10-11, 14).

A. Announcement of the Lord's reign (97:1)

97:1. The psalmist introduced the record of his vision of the Lord by calling on **the earth** (i.e., people in it; cf. 96:1; 98:4; 100:1) to **rejoice** over the establishment of the Lord's kingdom. **The LORD reigns** is also stated in 47:8; 93:1; 96:10; 99:1; 146:10.

B. The epiphany of the Lord (97:2-9)

97:2-5. The psalmist described the Lord's magnificent reigning appearance. In her worship Israel no doubt understood that these verses spoke figuratively of the presence of the Lord's glory. In their fullest meaning, however, they describe the coming of the Lord to reign over the earth.

The Lord's coming is accompanied with **clouds and thick darkness,** often a picture of awesome judgment (cf. Deut. 4:11; 5:22-23; Ps. 18:9, 11; Jer. 13:16; Ezek. 30:3, 18; 32:7-8; 34:12; Joel 2:2; Amos 5:18-20; Zeph. 1:15). God's rule is based on **righteousness** (cf. Ps. 96:13). A consuming **fire** is also a manifestation of His appearance, for by it He in His wrath destroys **His foes** (cf. 21:9; 50:3; 79:5; 89:46; Heb. 12:29; Rev. 20:9). **Lightning** flashes terrify the world. **Mountains melt like wax** (cf. Micah 1:4). The elements of nature that men fear, and the parts of

Creation considered the most solid, all announce the coming of **the LORD of all the earth** (cf. Micah 4:13; Zech. 4:14). Often in Scripture such phenomena accompany the appearance of **the LORD.**

97:6-9. The psalmist described the effects of this epiphany. **The heavens** declare **His righteousness** and **glory.** In other words His appearance to establish righteousness on earth will be announced to the world.

Pagan idol-worshipers will be **put to shame** for they will know instantly that they have been wrong. This thought prompted the psalmist to call even the **idols** to **worship** the Lord! So the people of God rejoice because of the triumphant exaltation of their righteous **LORD.** Since He is **over all the earth** (cf. v. 5), He is higher than all false **gods** (cf. 96:4-5), and deserves people's praise.

C. Call to righteousness (97:10-12)

97:10. On the basis of this prospect, the psalmist instructed **those who love the LORD** to despise evil (cf. Prov. 8:13), that is, to live in faithful obedience to His righteous standards. By being **faithful** they will be delivered from **the wicked.**

97:11-12. The righteous are called on to acknowledge and **praise** the righteous **LORD** with gladness because of their blessings of **joy** and spiritual prosperity (spoken of as **light;** cf. 27:1; 36:9).

Psalm 98

In this psalm the writer exhorted all the earth to sing and praise the Lord who reigns, because He had done marvelous things in saving Israel by His power and will judge the world in righteousness.

A. God has made His salvation known (98:1-3)

98:1-3. The psalmist invited his readers to **sing to the LORD a new song** (cf. 33:3; 40:3; 96:1; 144:9; 149:1) because in His strength (**right hand** and **arm** are symbols of power) He has provided **salvation** and **revealed His righteousness.** God's great **salvation** is possible because of His loyal love (ḥeseḏ) and **faithfulness** (these may be trans. "faithful, loyal love"). Remembering His covenant with His people Israel, **the LORD** delivered and saved them.

B. God will judge the world in righteousness (98:4-9)

98:4-8. Anticipating the Lord's final salvation of His people prompted the psalmist to call **the earth** (inhabitants in it; cf. 96:1; 97:1; 100:1) to rejoice before Him. Everyone should **shout for joy** (98:4a, 6b) and **sing** with various musical instruments **before the LORD, the King** (cf. 95:3; 99:4; and comments on 5:2). Even nature (including **the sea. . . . rivers,** and **mountains**; cf. 96:11-13) is called to resound and rejoice **together.**

98:9. Why should people praise **the LORD?** Because **He comes to judge the. . . . world in righteousness** (cf. 96:13). The psalmist was again envisioning the Lord's coming and its purpose. He will bring salvation (98:3) and justice.

Psalm 99

The psalmist encouraged everyone to exalt the Lord with praise for two reasons: because He is holy and because He mercifully answers His people's prayers.

A. The Lord who reigns is holy (99:1-5)

99:1-3. The psalmist offered praise to the holy **LORD** who reigns. The common theocratic expression again begins this psalm: **The LORD reigns** (cf. 47:8; 93:1; 96:10; 97:1; 146:10). Therefore everyone should **tremble.**

God is described as sitting **enthroned between the** gold-covered **cherubim** (cf. 80:1) over the ark of the covenant (cf. 1 Kings 6:23-28). So He is **great in Zion,** where the temple was located.

People everywhere should **praise** this **great** Sovereign. His dwelling in Zion and His righteous reign speak of His greatness and His holiness, which are the predominant reasons for praise mentioned in this psalm.

99:4-5. The power and righteousness of **the King** (cf. 95:3; 98:6; and comments on 5:2) manifest His holiness, so the psalmist praised Him for these.

Verse 5 is a refrain (cf. v. 9) in which everyone is invited to **exalt the LORD . . . and worship at His footstool** (i.e., before the temple with its ark located inside).

B. The Lord who reigns is merciful (99:6-9)

99:6-9. The psalmist spoke of the Lord's merciful dealings with his ances-

tors in spite of Israel's iniquities. **Moses . . . Aaron,** and **Samuel** prayed and were **answered.** God **spoke to them** (i.e., Israel) **from the pillar of cloud** (cf. Ex. 13:21) and they obeyed. Even after **Israel** sinned and was **punished,** the **LORD . . . answered** their prayers and forgave them. So praise is due this Monarch not only because of His holiness (Ps. 99:3, 5) but also because of His merciful dealings with His people. God's mercy prevents His own from being consumed by His righteous judgment.

Verse 9 is a refrain (cf. v. 5 with its similar wording) in which God's people are told to **exalt the LORD** with praise **and worship at His holy mountain** (cf. 43:3; 48:1; 87:1), Zion.

Psalm 100

The superscription states that this psalm (or song) is "for giving thanks." It was used in the temple with the sacrifices of praise. The expressions in this psalm reflect the preceding enthronement psalms (Pss. 47; 93; 95–99) that celebrate the Lord's rule.

The psalmist exhorted the congregation to serve the Lord with gladness because He is the Creator, and to enter His temple with much thanksgiving because He is good and faithful.

A. Serve the Lord with gladness (100:1-3)

100:1-2. Verses 1-3 include a call for praise and joyful service. People everywhere (**all the earth;** cf. 96:1; 97:1; 98:4) should **shout . . . to the LORD;** they are not to be subdued in their praise of Him. Moreover, they are to **serve** Him **with gladness.** This service, **with joyful songs,** may mean worship.

100:3. The **LORD** should be praised and worshiped joyfully because He is sovereign. He is the Creator, and those who trust Him **are His** possession. They follow Him, for they are **the sheep of His pasture** (cf. 74:1; 79:13; 95:7; also note 23:1; 80:1).

B. Enter His courts with thanksgiving (100:4-5)

100:4-5. This second part of the psalm is a call to the saints to **enter** Jerusalem (God's **gates**) and to go to the temple (**His courts**) to offer their **thanksgiving** sacrifices for His blessings to them.

The people should **praise** the Lord for His goodness, love, and **faithfulness.** These benefits endure from generation to generation. So every generation that experiences God's goodness, love, and faithfulness can join in praising Him with "The Old One-Hundredth."

Psalm 101

Speaking to the Lord, King David said he was determined to maintain purity in his empire by removing wickedness from himself, his court, and his capital. When justice prevailed, the Lord would be pleased to dwell in their midst. So in a sense this psalm is a charter by which David ruled under God.

A. God's loyal love and justice (101:1)

101:1. The psalmist sang of the Lord's qualities of **love** (*ḥeseḏ*) **and justice.** These are characteristics of the divine rule (cf. 89:14), foundational to His effective reign.

B. David's personal integrity (101:2)

101:2. David said he resolved to live **a blameless life,** with a **blameless heart** before God. His lifestyle of integrity would begin in the privacy of his own **house.** This contrasted sharply with the corrupt lives of most kings of the ancient Near East.

C. David's purity in the palace (101:3-8)

David elaborated on the path of purity he had said he would follow (v. 2). That pure life would begin with him and extend to those who served him. This was a requirement if he was to enjoy the Lord's blessing on his reign.

101:3-4. David said he would keep himself pure by not tolerating **evil.** He would not allow **vile . . . faithless,** and **perverse** people and their activities to be around him. "Vile thing" is literally, "things of Belial" (worthless and wicked). "Perverse" (*'iqqēš*) means "crooked, twisted" (cf. comments on 18:26).

101:5-6. The king also wrote that he would surround himself with faithful servants. He would **silence** (cf. v. 8) slanderers and not tolerate the arrogant. **Haughty eyes** (cf. 18:27; Prov. 6:17; 30:13) refers to **a proud** look. David would look for **faithful** people to serve him, those whose lives were **blameless** (in integrity)

as his own was at that point (cf. Ps. 101:2).

101:7-8. David also indicated he would purge the wicked from throughout the nation, not just from the palace. As he administrated justice daily (cf. Jer. 21:12), he would **cut off** deceptive people and **the wicked.** "Cut off" often implies capital punishment, but it may also mean removal from service and fellowship.

Psalm 102

The unique superscription to this psalm points to a private, meditative use for suffering saints. The ideas recall those in Psalms 22, 69, 79. Psalm 102 also has similarities to some statements in Isaiah 40–66.

Hoping that God would speedily answer him, the psalmist lamented that he was overwhelmed and was in desolate straits because of the enemy's reproach. But he found comfort in the fact that the Lord abides, and would not forsake him—a truth that has led many generations of saints to praise God.

A. Answer me quickly (102:1-2)

102:1-2. The psalmist prayed earnestly that God would **hear** him and **not hide** His face (cf. 27:9; 143:7). **In** his **distress** he urged the Lord to **answer** him **quickly** (cf. comments on 31:2).

B. I wither away (102:3-11)

102:3-7. The psalmist described his lamentable condition to the Lord. His **days** were being consumed away **like smoke,** his **bones** (cf. comments on 6:2) were burning (i.e., he felt inwardly exhausted), his **heart** was withering **like grass** (cf. 102:11; 37:2; 103:15-16; Isa. 40:6-8). Having no appetite, he was **groaning** in physical agony. Emaciated (cf. Job 19:20), he felt desolate, **like** a mournful-looking **owl** or **a bird** sitting **alone.** His strength was gone, he was inwardly depressed, and he had lost his will to live.

102:8-9. The psalmist's dilemma was intensified when he heard that his **enemies** mocked his plight. To **eat ashes** (cf. Isa. 44:20) means to have ashes on one's head as a symbol of mourning. Mourning and weeping (**tears;** cf. Ps. 80:5) were so continuous that they were like his daily diet.

102:10-11. Moreover, he was convinced that God's **wrath** had consumed him. **Because** God had allowed this to happen, he felt his life was about over, **like the evening shadow** that indicates a day is almost gone (cf. 144:4) and like the withering **grass** (cf. 102:4).

C. He will not despise the destitute (102:12-22)

102:12-13. The complaints of the psalmist (vv. 3-11) were followed by his confidence that the LORD would answer his prayers. **You** in Hebrew is emphatic, stressing the contrast between the psalmist and the LORD. The transition to praise was sudden: the Lord sits **enthroned** (cf. comments on 2:4) **forever** and He would respond, for it was **time to show favor to** His people in Jerusalem.

102:14-17. He was confident that the Lord, who had established His reign in Zion, would not forsake those who love Him. The Lord's **servants** loved even Zion's **stones** and **dust** (a figure of the servants' intense concern for the city in its calamity) partly because it was His dwelling place. Others too—**the nations** and their **kings . . . will revere. . . . the** LORD for He **will rebuild Zion.** This indicates that the psalmist had widened his thoughts from his own weakness to reflect on the Lord's sovereignty, which guaranteed that the city would be restored. Perhaps the psalm was occasioned by a calamity in the capital city. Even so the psalmist was convinced that the Lord would answer the people's **prayer.**

102:18-20. Praise for deliverance was then anticipated. **Future** generations would **praise the** LORD when they heard how He **looked down from . . . heaven** (**His sanctuary on high**) and heard **the groans of** His people in their destitute condition. The omniscient God's taking a close look at His people is mentioned often in the psalms; it shows His great concern. The Lord sometimes intervened to deliver those about to die.

102:21-22. As a result of this deliverance, **the name of the** LORD would be praised when everyone gathered **to worship** Him **in Zion.**

D. Your years will never end (102:23-28)

102:23-28. Here the psalmist returned to his personal complaint. The Lord had weakened him (cf. vv. 4-10), seemingly about to cut his **life . . . short** (cf. vv. 3, 11). So he appealed for an extension of his life, asking that he not die prematurely: **Do not take me away . . . in the midst of my days.** Since God's **years go on** (v. 24; cf. v. 27), speaking figuratively of His eternality, the writer wanted his own life to continue for at least a while longer.

Speaking of God's eternality in contrast with His Creation was an expression of the psalmist's confidence in the Lord. **The earth and the heavens. . . . will perish** (cf. 2 Peter 3:10; Rev. 21:1), wearing **out like** old clothes. By contrast God is unchanging (Mal. 3:6; Heb. 13:8) and eternal (His **years will never end**; cf. Ps. 102:27). Therefore He will be faithful to all generations (to the saints' **children** and to **their descendants**).

Verses 25-27 are applied to Christ in Hebrews 1:10-12. The psalmist was addressing the eternal Lord, and the writer of Hebrews identified Jesus Christ as the eternal One, the Creator and Sustainer of the world. This is a strong affirmation of the deity of Jesus Christ.

Psalm 103

After reviewing the mercies of God toward him, David found hope in his people's covenant relationship with the Lord, though they were sinful and frail. In this confidence the psalmist called on all creation to bless their Lord.

This psalm, a celebration of deliverance, seems to speak of the answer to the prayer in Psalm 102.

A. The mercies of God (103:1-5)

103:1-2. David told himself (**O my soul**) to **praise the** LORD with **all** his **being,** that is, to put his whole heart in his **praise** of God's **holy name** (cf. 33:21). This was certainly warranted in view of the Lord's many **benefits.**

103:3-5. David praised the Lord for His many mercies, including forgiveness of **sins** (v. 3a), healing of sicknesses (v. 3b), deliverance from death (v. 4a; **pit** is a synonym for the grave), enrichment of his life with loyal **love** (cf. vv. 8, 11, 17) and tender **compassion** (cf. vv. 8, 13; 116:5; 119:156), satisfaction (**with good things**; cf. 104:28; 107:9), and renewal. Crowning suggests bestowing blessing (as in 8:5). Like an eagle that remains strong throughout its long life, the psalmist was spiritually vigorous under God's hand (cf. Isa. 40:31).

B. The compassion of God (103:6-18)

Alluding to certain facts in Israel's history, David meditated on the covenant loyalty the Lord maintained with frail sinners.

103:6-8. First, David recalled the Lord's covenant with Moses. After a word of praise for the Lord's **righteousness,** David said that God revealed Himself **to Moses** and Moses' **people** as a **compassionate** (cf. vv. 4, 13; 86:15; 111:4; 145:8) **and gracious** God, who is therefore **slow to anger** and abounds in covenant loyalty (**love,** ḥese̱d; cf. 103:4, 11, 17). Verse 8 is based on God's words to Moses on Mount Sinai (Ex. 34:6; cf. Neh. 9:17; Pss. 86:15; 145:8; Joel 2:13; Jonah 4:2). Because of these attributes God is faithful to His people and will deliver them from oppression.

103:9-12. David then explained that the Lord mercifully forgives sins. Because God is slow to **anger** (cf. v. 8) **He** does **not always accuse** (ri̱b, "bring a court case against") a man of sin **nor** deal with him **according to** his **sins.** And because of His **great . . . love** (cf. vv. 4, 8, 17) He completely separates sins from the sinners by forgiving them.

103:13-18. In these verses David wrote that though man's life is transitory, he is established by the Lord's **covenant.** The **Lord has compassion** (cf. vv. 4, 8) on His frail people (v. 13) **for He knows how** frail the nature of **man** is (vv. 14-16). Man is made of insignificant **dust** (cf. Gen. 2:7) and his life is brief **like** the **grass** (cf. Pss. 37:2; 90:5; 102:4, 11; Isa. 40:6-8) and wild flowers. Nevertheless **from everlasting to everlasting the Lord's** covenant love (cf. Ps. 103:4, 8, 11) **is with those who** obey **Him.** Here again (cf. 102:24-27) the eternality of the Lord is seen as a comfort for frail human beings. Man's hope is not in other fragile creatures, but in the eternal God.

C. The praise of God (103:19-22)

103:19-22. David declared that the Lord's dominion is **over all** the earth. Therefore all **angels,** God's **heavenly hosts,** who are His **servants,** and all His Creation (**His works**) **everywhere** should **praise the Lord.** David closed his psalm in the way he began: by exhorting himself (**O my soul**) to **praise the Lord.**

Psalm 104

Psalm 104 begins the same way Psalm 103 begins—with the words, "Praise the Lord, O my soul." Psalm 104 is a glorious psalm in praise of God's marvelous Creation and of His sustaining of that Creation. Whereas Psalm 103 praises the Lord's compassion with His people in history, this psalm portrays the Lord's power, wisdom, and goodness to all Creation. The psalmist spoke of God's stretching out the heavens in light, His sovereign control of the deep, His adorning the earth as a dwelling place for man, His arranging night and day for life, and His preparing the sea for its life. He then praised God who gloriously reigns over Creation and renews it by His Spirit. In view of this the psalmist prayed that God would purge sinners, who are out of harmony with Creation.

A. Prologue (104:1a)

104:1a. The psalmist encouraged himself to **praise the Lord** (cf. v. 35; 103:1, 22).

B. Praise for the Creator (104:1b-23)

104:1b-4. In verses 1b-23 the psalmist praised the majesty of the **Lord** (**You are very great** and **clothed with splendor;** cf. comments on 29:2; **and majesty;** cf. 45:3) as is seen in His works. The writer began with a poetic description of the heavens. **Light,** created on the first day (Gen. 1:3-5), is appropriate to the nature of the Lord. To be clothed "in light" means to be characterized by it. In Creation the Lord spread out **the heavens like a tent** (cf. Gen. 1:6-8; Isa. 40:22), that is, the skies cover the earth as a tent covers tent dwellers. God's dwelling place is pictured figuratively as being in **upper chambers on the waters.** He was like a builder making a private room by laying the foundation **beams** above the waters of the sky.

Also the Lord formed all the heavenly elements including **clouds . . . wind,** and **fire.** (On His riding the clouds, see comments on Ps. 68:4.) Psalm 104:4 suggests that God arrays His angels (**messengers**) with physical phenomena, similar to ways He often manifested Himself.

104:5-9. The psalmist reiterated how God founded **the earth** and **covered it**

with **the waters.** In poetic imagery the earth is seen as firmly established **on . . . foundations,** and "covered" with water **(the deep) as with a garment.** The psalmist vividly portrayed the Lord's gathering **the waters** into rivers and oceans with **a boundary** (i.e., with shorelines beyond which **they cannot** go; cf. Job 38:9-10; Jer. 5:22). God's rebuking the waters suggests they were a chaotic force to be calmed and "conquered." Some of the wording in Psalm 104:7-9 sounds like the Flood account, but the psalmist was referring to Creation.

104:10-18. In adorning the earth as a place for living, God placed **springs** in the valleys to **give water** for animals (vv. 10-12), and He **makes** things **grow** that give **food** for animals and **man,** and **oil** (from olive trees) to smooth man's **face** (vv. 13-15). Also God provides dwelling places for animals and birds (vv. 16-18). In His wisdom God made the earth amazingly well suited for all forms of life.

104:19-23. The Lord made **the moon** and **the sun** to rule the times when various creatures on earth are active.

C. Praise for the Lord's dominion (104:24-32)

104:24-30. The psalmist broke forth with praise to the LORD for all of His Creation, made in His great **wisdom.** The earth's many living forms **(creatures)** are under His dominion.

Ocean **creatures** of various sizes— including the **large. . . . leviathan** (here a real animal, not a mythological creature; cf. comments on Job 41)—wait for **food** and other **good things** (cf. Pss. 103:5; 107:9) from God (cf. 104:21). But if He hides from them **they are** troubled, as He controls life and death in the oceans. He takes **away their breath** and **they die;** He sends His **Spirit** and others are born.

Water is a predominant theme in this psalm (vv. 3, 6-16, 25-26). In the minds of ancient sages, water was a powerful force. This psalm portrays the Lord's sovereignty over it.

104:31-32. The psalmist called for **the glory of the LORD** to continue since He has such powerful control over Creation.

D. Prayer for harmony in Creation (104:33-35a)

104:33-35a. The psalmist responded to the greatness of God's Creation by

doing two things. First, he vowed to **praise . . . God** with song and pleasing **meditation** (cf. 19:14). This is the proper response of a worshiper who remembers his Creator. Second, he prayed that **sinners** would **vanish from the earth** because they are out of harmony with God's Creation.

E. Epilogue (104:35b)

104:35b. The psalmist again encouraged himself **(O my soul)** to **praise the LORD** (cf. v. 1; 103:1, 22). The final "Praise the LORD" translates the Hebrew *halᵉlû-yāh* (whence the Eng. "hallelujah"), which occurs here for the first of 23 times in the Psalms (104:35; 105:45; 106:1, 48; 112:1; 113:1, 9; 115:18; 116:19; 117:2; 135:1, 3, 21; 146:1, 10; 147:1, 20; 148:1, 14; 149:1, 9; 150:1, 6).

Psalm 105

By tracing some aspects of the history of Israel (from Abraham to the wilderness wanderings)—as the Lord moved His people miraculously in fulfillment of His covenant promises—the psalmist praised the greatness of the Lord's love for His own.

A. Praise for the Lord's greatness (105:1-6)

105:1-6. The psalmist began with a call (to Israel, v. 6) to **praise** and **rejoice** because of the Lord's many **wonderful acts** and **His holy name.** His name means His attributes that are revealed to man. Israel should depend on **the LORD (look** and **seek His face),** remembering His miraculous works.

B. Praise for the Lord's faithfulness (105:7-41)

105:7-11. The psalmist turned to offer praise for the Lord's remembrance of His promises to the nation. The nation should remember Him (v. 5) because **He remembers** them! (v. 8; cf. v. 42) **The LORD . . . God,** who exercises universal rule **(His judgments are in all the earth),** remembered (i.e., fulfills) **His covenant** and His **oath.** His covenant **made with Abraham** (Gen. 12:1-3; 15:18-21) was confirmed in Isaac's presence (Gen. 22:15-18) and also given **to Jacob** (Gen. 28:13-15; 32:12). **Israel,** God said, would be a great nation and would possess **the land** He promised.

105:12-41. The psalmist then traced something of the history of Israel in which the Lord fulfilled His promise to make Israel a great nation. First, the writer stated that the Lord protected them while they sojourned in other lands (vv. 12-15). Perhaps this refers to Abraham's journey from Ur in Chaldea to Haran (Gen. 11:31), Canaan (Gen. 12:4-5), Egypt (Gen. 12:10-20), and his living in the Negev (Gen. 20:1). Second, **the Lord** sovereignly led Israelites into Egypt and exalted **Joseph** (Ps. 105:16-22; cf. Gen. 37; 39–41). Third, in **Egypt the Lord made His people very fruitful** even though they were oppressed (Ps. 105:23-25; cf. Ex. 1:6-14). Fourth, through **Moses . . . and Aaron** the Lord worked **wonders in** Egypt (**the land of Ham**; cf. Ps. 105:23). These wonders were the plagues on Egypt (vv. 26-36) that oppressed the Egyptians (cf. Ex. 7–11; Ps. 78:44-51). God rescued His people with great booty (105:37). In fact **Egypt was** relieved **when they left** (v. 38). Fifth, the Lord led the Israelites through the wilderness and provided **quail,** manna (**bread of heaven**), and **water** from **the rock** (vv. 39-41). So even during Israel's wanderings He was faithful to them.

C. Praise for the Lord's deliverance (105:42-45)

105:42-45. The psalmist spoke again of how the Lord **remembered His** word (v. 42; cf. v. 8) and **brought . . . His people** out of Egypt and led them to the Promised Land (vv. 43-44). They were redeemed from bondage **so that they might** obey His word (v. 45).

This psalm expresses joy over God's faithfulness to His word in redeeming **His Chosen** People. So those who receive His benefits should remember His works and respond with obedience. On the words **Praise the Lord** (*hal*e*lû-yāh*), see comments on 104:35.

Psalm 106

In spite of God's faithfulness to Israel (Ps. 105) her history was filled with faithlessness and ingratitude. Psalm 106, a confessional psalm, traces some of the Israelite's rebellious activities and God's judgments on them. The psalmist then prayed that the Lord would deliver His people from their captivity. A similar confession is found in Nehemiah 9. In addition, this psalm has similarities with Isaiah 63 and Ezekiel 20.

A. Praise for God's goodness (106:1-5)

106:1-5. The psalmist praised God for His incomparable goodness, loyal **love,** and power (vv. 1-2). On the words **Praise the Lord** (*hal*e*lû-yāh*), see comments on 104:35. Since all who **do what is right** are **blessed** by **the Lord** (106:3), the psalmist prayed that when God blesses His **people** He would remember him too. That way he could **enjoy . . . prosperity** and joy, and give God **praise.**

B. Confession of sin (106:6-46)

106:6. The psalmist introduced the theme of confession with a general statement that they, the Israelites in the psalmist's day, had **sinned** as their **fathers** (i.e., ancestors) had done. This prompted him to relate their ancestors' sins.

106:7-12. The psalmist then recounted the sins of the people in the wilderness. First, he wrote of their sin at the crossing of **the Red Sea** (vv. 7-12; cf. Ex. 14:11-12). **Yet** the Lord **saved them** (cf. Ex. 14:26-30) to show **His mighty power,** and **they believed** (cf. Ex. 14:31) and **sang** praises to Him (cf. Ex. 15:1-21).

106:13-33. Then the psalmist spoke of the people's sins as they traveled to the Promised Land. **They soon forgot** God's **miracles** (cf. vv. 21-22) and began to crave (cf. Num. 11:4) and **God. . . . sent** a plague (**a wasting disease**) on **them** (cf. Num. 11:33). They also murmured out of envy over **Moses and . . . Aaron,** so God destroyed **Dathan** and his **company** (Ps. 106:16-18; cf. Num. 16; 26:8-9). **At Horeb,** the ancient name for Mount Sinai (cf. Deut. 5:2; Mal. 4:4), **they made a** golden **calf** in violation of the Law. **God. . . . would** have destroyed **them** if Moses had **not** interceded (Ps. 106:19-23; cf. Ex. 32).

They murmured again (**grumbled**) so God **swore . . . with uplifted hand** (cf. comments on Ex. 6:8) **that** they would die in the wilderness (Ps. 106:24-27; cf. Num. 14:26-35). They **despised the pleasant land** by disbelieving **the Lord.**

At **Peor** they sinned again (this time in idolatry with the Moabites), and **Phinehas . . . intervened** to stop **the plague** (Ps. 106:28-31; cf. Num. 25).

At **Meribah . . . Moses** lost patience

with them when **they rebelled against . . . God** (Ps. 106:32-33; cf. 81:7; 95:8; Ex. 17:7; Num. 20:2-13). As a result of his impatience Moses also lost the privilege of entering the land of promise (Num. 20:12).

106:34-46. The psalmist then reminded the people of their failure to **destroy** the inhabitants of the land, **as the Lord had commanded them** to do (Deut. 7:1-2). Instead of obeying the Lord's command to demolish the Canaanites' **idols** (Deut. 7:5, 16, 25-26), Israel **worshiped** them (cf. Jud. 2:11-12) and even **sacrificed their sons and . . . daughters to demons** (Ps. 106:37; cf. Deut 32:17) associated with **the idols** (Ps. 106:38).

Because Israel sinned so grievously, **the Lord was angry** (cf. Jud. 2:14, 20) **with His people** and gave **them over to the** oppression of **enemies.**

Many times, however, God **delivered them** (Ps. 106:43-46). This refers to His raising up judges to deliver Israel from her oppressors (cf. Jud. 2:16) because of **His covenant** and **His** faithful love (*ḥesed*). Thus the Lord constantly brought judgment on His disobedient people, but He also constantly responded to their cries.

C. Prayer for deliverance (106:47-48)

106:47-48. After retracing the nation's sin and God's punishment, the psalmist prayed that they would be again delivered (**gather us from the nations** apparently suggests the nation was dispersed) so that they might **praise** Him.

The doxology in verse 48 closes Book IV of the Psalter. This verse is similar to the doxology that concludes Book I (see 41:13). On the words **Praise the Lord** (*halelû-yāh*), see comments on 104:35.

V. Book V (Pss. 107–150)

Of these 44 psalms, 15 are by David (108–110; 122; 124; 131; 133; 138–145), 1 is by Solomon (Ps. 127), and the other 28 are anonymous.

Psalm 107

This psalm is a call to praise addressed to the redeemed of the Lord. The psalmist motivated them to praise Him by portraying how He delivered His people out of the wilderness, broke the bonds of prisoners, restored the sick, showed His power to mariners in the sea, and providentially governs nature and human affairs.

A. Call for the redeemed to praise (107:1-3)

107:1-3. God should be thanked for His enduring loyal **love** (cf. v. 43), especially by **the redeemed** who benefit from it. The psalm may have been written during the Babylonian Exile because of the words in verses 2b-3.

B. Cause for praise: Deliverance (107:4-32)

In these verses the psalmist cited four examples of the Lord's deliverances of His people. In each case the people pleaded for the Lord to help them out of their distress and He did so (vv. 6, 13, 19, 28). Also in each case the psalmist urged the people to thank God for His unfailing love and wonderful deeds (vv. 8, 15, 21, 31).

107:4-9. First, He delivered **some** from wandering in the wilderness. Unable to find their way, **hungry . . . thirsty,** and dying, they **cried . . . to the Lord** and **He led them** to safety. So people should praise **the Lord** because He satisfied **with good things** (v. 9; cf. 104:28) those who were **thirsty** and **hungry** in the wilderness.

107:10-16. Second, the Lord released **prisoners** from bondage. Those who were chained in dark prisons because **they had rebelled against . . . God. . . . cried** out and were freed from the **darkness and chains.** The Jewish Targum suggests this refers to King Zedekiah and the nobles of Judah in exile in Babylon. So people should praise **the Lord** because He delivers from bondage.

107:17-22. Third, **the Lord** delivered the sick from death. When rebellious sinners were afflicted and **near the gates of death** (cf. Job. 38:17; Ps. 9:13; Isa. 38:10), **they cried** out **to** Him **and He** restored **them,** healing them by **His word.** So people should praise **the Lord** and **sacrifice thank offerings** (i.e., praise offerings) because of their restored health.

107:23-32. Fourth, God delivers sailors in trouble at **sea.** Mariners see His **works** as He calls up a storm (**tempest**). **Their courage** melts, and being **at their wits' end** (lit., "all their wisdom was swallowed up"), they call on Him. He calms **the storm** and delivers them from their danger, guiding them safely to their destination. So people should praise **the LORD. . . . in the assembly.**

C. Cause for praise: Dominion (107:33-43)

The psalmist spoke of the Lord's providential governing of the world as a second major reason for praise (cf. vv. 4-32).

107:33-38. The Lord has great power over nature. (The past-tense verbs in the NIV in these verses may be rendered in the pres. tense.) He can turn **a desert** into a watered area (v. 33) or conversely He can make a **fruitful land** become a wasteland (cf. Deut. 29:23). He does this **because of the wickedness of** the people in the land (cf. Deut. 29:24-28).

On the other hand God made the barren land become habitable (**a city where they could settle;** cf. Ps. 107:4, 7) and **fruitful** (vv. 35-38). This He did for the benefit of the poor and needy, so that **their numbers greatly** flourished.

107:39-43. The Lord also has power over people's experiences. He humbles and brings down the proud, but He lifts up the poor and **needy.** So the redeemed praise **the LORD (the upright see and rejoice) but . . . the wicked** are silenced. A **wise** person will **consider** these meditations carefully, noting the Lord's **great love** (ḥeseḏ; cf. vv. 1, 8, 15, 21, 31).

Psalm 108

This is a song of triumph in praise of the Lord's loyal love, given with the full expectation that all His enemies will be destroyed in their own devices. Because David was convinced that God will exult in the subjugation of the nations, he prayed for divine leadership. Verses 1-5 are almost the same as 57:7-11, and 108:6-13 are identical with 60:5-12. No doubt the parts were joined for some liturgical purpose.

A. Song of triumph (108:1-6)

108:1-6. David sang this song of triumph in praise of God's **great . . . love** and remarkable **faithfulness** (v. 4; cf. 115:1; 117:2; 138:2). The psalmist expressed his desire that God **be exalted . . . over all the earth** so that His saints might **be delivered.** His **right hand** suggests His power (cf. Ex. 15:6, 12; Pss. 20:6; 45:4; 60:5; 89:7-13).

B. Confidence of victory (108:7-13)

108:7-13. David was convinced that the Lord will subjugate the tribes of the earth to **Judah** (vv. 7-9; see comments on the identical verses in 60:6-8). Realizing his need for God's leadership, he prayed for help **against** his **enemies** in full confidence that **God** would destroy them (108:10-13; see comments on the identical verses in 60:9-12).

Psalm 109

The psalmist prayed that the Lord would take vengeance on his enemies who opposed him with evil devices. The psalmist also heaped curses on the wicked. The superscription attributes the psalm to David, but it is not clear whether the references in the psalm are to his time as king or before. The psalm is filled with imprecations (see "Theology of the Psalms" in the *Introduction*). These are the zealous prayers of the righteous who stand for God's cause on earth. Their sentiment is harsh, but the threat of the wicked against the righteous was severe.

A. Lament over deceptive enemies (109:1-5)

109:1-5. David cried out to **God,** whom he praised, **not** to be **silent** but to deliver him from the danger of **wicked . . . men.** They were **deceitful** (v. 2) and hateful (v. 3), and rewarded his **friendship** with false accusations, reciprocating his good with **evil** and **hatred.**

B. Imprecations on the wicked (109:6-20)

In an extended section of imprecations, David wished that in retribution the wicked would be made desolate and dispossessed.

109:6-15. David prayed that his enemy would be opposed (v. 6), be **found guilty** (v. 7), die (so that **his wife** would become **a widow** and **his children** vagabonds, vv. 8-10), be made poor by an extortioner and plunderers (v. 11), and be pitied by **no one** (v. 12). David also prayed that his enemy's posterity would **be cut off** (v. 13) and that the sins of his enemy's ancestors would **be remembered** by the LORD (vv. 14-15). These were the longings of David's zealous heart for retribution. On the psalmists' imprecations see "Theology of the Psalms" in the *Introduction.*

109:16-20. Reasons for the imprecations in verses 6-15 are given here. This wicked man took advantage of **the poor . . . the needy** (cf. v. 22), **and the brokenhearted** (v. 16). **He loved to** heap curses on other people (v. 17); it was a part of him like the clothing he wore and the **water** he drank (v. 18). Therefore *he* should be cursed (v. 17); cursing should envelop and confine him (v. 19). This would be God's way of paying back (cf. v. 5) **those who** accused and slandered David (v. 20).

C. Prayer for help (109:21-31)

109:21-25. David turned to his **sovereign LORD** for help and deliverance because he was in great need. He was apparently weak (**poor and needy;** cf. vv. 16, 31 and see comments on 37:14) and perishing (he was fading **away** and thin **from fasting**) under the oppression of those wicked men. Besides being in danger, they scornfully mocked him.

109:26-31. David's prayer for **help** was based on his desire that the wicked would understand that the LORD would vindicate him (vv. 26-27), and that he might **rejoice** when they were **put to shame** and **disgrace** (vv. 28-29). David vowed he would testify of (**extol**) the LORD for delivering him (**the needy one;** cf. v. 22) **from** the oppressor.

Psalm 110

The words of this psalm are addressed to the psalmist's "LORD." The expressions are those of a prophet who had received a revelation from God. The king was also a priest, a fact that looks beyond the order of Aaron, which was not a royal order. This is one reason the psalm has been classified as a prophetic psalm. Jesus quoted Psalm 110:1 in Mark 12:36 (cf. Matt. 22:44; Luke 20:42) to demonstrate that He the Messiah was to be David's Lord, not merely David's Descendant (Mark 12:35, 37). By Jesus' use of the passage one also notes that David wrote Psalm 110, that it was inspired by the Holy Spirit, and that it refers to the Messiah. Psalm 110:1 is also quoted in Acts 2:34-35 and Hebrews 1:13. Attempts to date Psalm 110 in the Maccabean times, when some priests held temporal power, are therefore futile. Those leaders were priests first and also had civil power but in Psalm 110 the King is a Priest.

The union of the offices of priest and king in the Messiah was prophesied in other passages (e.g., Zech. 6:12-13). If Psalm 110 related to some incident in David's life, it is difficult to articulate. Perhaps it was written about the time David knew that the Anointed One was to have a righteous kingdom (2 Sam. 23:2-4). At the end of his life David knew that he was not that one, but that a greater One was coming who would have dominion, power, and glory forever.

In Psalm 110, David received an oracle about the exaltation of his Lord. He then described the holy army of this King-Priest-Messiah and His defeating all nations.

A. The oracle of exaltation (110:1-2)

110:1-2. David heard a heavenly conversation between **the LORD** (*Yahweh*) and David's **Lord** (*'ăḏōnay*), that is, between God the Father and the Messiah. The verb **says** is *nᵉ'um,* a word often used to depict an oracle or a revelation. In this oracle Yahweh said that David's Lord, the Messiah, is seated at Yahweh's **right hand** (cf. v. 5), the place of authority, until the consummation of the ages (cf. 2:8-9). At that time **the LORD** will send David's Lord, the Messiah, to make his **enemies** subject to Him. A **footstool** pictures complete subjugation. With His **scepter** the Messiah **will . . . rule** over His **enemies.**

B. The dominion of the Messiah (110:3-4)

110:3. Others will accompany the Messiah, willingly offering themselves to take part in His **battle.** But this will be no ordinary battle. This will be righteous judgment poured out on the wicked. Hence holiness is the required adornment. As the Israelites of old had to consecrate themselves to the Lord before going into battle, so at the consummation of the ages must believers be **holy** (cf. 2 Peter 3:10-11, 14).

The youthful **warriors** are compared to **the dew** (NIV marg.) **of** the morning. This suggests several ideas, including their freshness, their sudden appearance, their glittering numbers, and even the time of their appearance: in the early morning (**the womb of the dawn**). Therefore Messiah's servants will have made freewill offerings to Him, will be adorned in holiness, and will appear suddenly with youthful vigor.

110:4. The LORD (Yahweh) has affirmed by oath that the Messiah will be **a Priest forever, in the order of Melchizedek.** The people of the Messiah will have an eternal High Priest. Melchizedek was the king of Salem (Jerusalem) and priest of the Most High God (Gen. 14:18; Heb. 7:1). Years after he ruled in Jerusalem, David and his descendants ruled there.

That ancient unity of priest and king in one person will be reunited in the Messiah, a fact which necessitates the end of the line of Aaron's priesthood. This is precisely the point of the writer to the Hebrews, who four times said Melchizedek is a type of Christ (Heb. 5:6; 6:20; 7:17, 21). As a Priest Jesus sacrificed Himself by His death on the cross (Heb. 7:27-28; 10:10). Not in Aaron's line (cf. Heb. 7:11-18), He is the eternal High Priest (cf. Heb. 7:21-26, 28) of the New Covenant (cf. Heb. 8:13; 9:15). Because He is also the promised Davidic King, both offices are united in one Person.

C. The victory of the Messiah (110:5-7)

110:5-7. David anticipated the glorious victory of the Messiah. David's **Lord** (the Messiah; cf. v. 1) is seated at God the Father's **right hand** (cf. Heb. 8:1; 10:12), the place of authority. When the Messiah-Priest comes He will defeat (**crush**) **kings** (cf. Rev. 16:16; 19:13-15) and **judge . . . nations** (cf. Joel 3:2, 11-14). His refreshing Himself with a **drink** along **the way** figuratively pictures His renewed vigor, and His lifting **up His head** speaks of His being exalted.

According to the New Testament Christ, accompanied by His saints, will return to judge the world and establish His kingdom on earth.

Psalm 111

The psalmist vowed to praise the Lord in the assembly for His great and marvelous works of redemption that lead people to fear Him. This psalm is similar to Psalm 112 in its structure and message. Psalm 111 praises the righteousness of the Lord; Psalm 112 extols the blessings of a person who comes to fear Him. Both draw on expressions found elsewhere in the Psalms and in Proverbs. In addition, both are alphabetical songs, or acrostics. Some ancient versions suggest that Psalm 111 was written in the time of Haggai and Zechariah.

A. Praise in the assembly (111:1-3)

111:1-3. The psalmist vowed to **extol the** LORD wholeheartedly **in the council of the . . . assembly** of the saints. He said he would **praise the** LORD for His marvelous **works** and **deeds** that are remembered by those who enjoy (**delight in;** cf. 112:1) **them** and the benefits they bring.

B. Praise for God's marvelous works (111:4-9)

111:4-9. The psalmist now enumerated the marvels of God's work. The theme is announced in verse 4: **the** LORD has made His works memorable; He **is gracious and compassionate** (86:15; 103:8; 145:8). In His grace the Lord has helped mankind and is therefore **remembered** in praise.

Examples of His works are cited in 111:5-6. He gives **food** (cf. 132:15; 136:25; 145:15; 146:7) **to those who fear Him; He remembers His covenant,** that is, He faithfully keeps His promises: in the Conquest He gave His people the **lands** He promised.

God's **works . . . are faithful** and His word is dependable (111:7). All His works are firmly established by His covenant so that He faithfully performs them (v. 8). So **He provided redemption for His people** by **His covenant** (v. 9).

Because the Lord is faithful, **His name** is therefore **holy and awesome.** This means He is holy in a way that prompts people to fear Him.

C. Fear of the awesome Lord (111:10)

111:10. The psalmist concluded that **the fear of the** LORD (cf. 112:1) **is the beginning of wisdom** (cf. Prov. 1:7). People who **follow** Him and His standards **have good understanding.** Worship and obedience will then be accompanied by **praise** that **belongs** to Him.

Psalm 112

This psalm enumerates some of the blessings enjoyed by a person who fears the Lord. Then it anticipates the exaltation of the righteous and the grievous destruction of the wicked.

A. The blessing of the one who fears the Lord (112:1)

112:1. Building on the end of the previous psalm, this verse says that one who **fears the LORD** and delights **in His** Law is **blessed** (cf. 1:1-2). On **praise the LORD** (*hal⁻lû-yāh*), see comments on 104:35.

B. The blessings of the righteous (112:2-9)

112:2-9. Five blessings that come to one who fears God are enumerated: (1) He is **blessed** with physical and material prosperity because He is **righteous** (vv. 2-3). (2) **Light** is given **even in darkness . . . for the upright** (v. 4). This could refer to prosperity (in place of disaster) or to discernment. (3) He receives goodness in return for being **generous** (cf. v. 9) and just (v. 5). (4) He will be firmly established in his faith, unshakable (cf. comments on 15:5), with **no fear** of what man might do to him (112:6-8). (5) Because he gives **to the poor** (cf. v. 5) **his horn** (cf. 89:17, 24; 92:10) **will be lifted** up, that is, he will be made strong and honorable by **the LORD.**

C. The anxiety of the wicked (112:10)

112:10. In contrast with the blessings of God-fearers, **the wicked** will be filled with anxiety over God's goodness to the righteous. **The wicked,** who are about to perish (**waste away**), will be powerless over the righteous.

Psalm 113

The psalmist called on all the Lord's servants everywhere to praise God because even though He is exalted on high He lowers Himself to exalt the oppressed. J.J. Stewart Perowne (*The Book of Psalms,* 2:322) rightly observes that this psalm is a connecting link between the song of Hannah (1 Sam. 2:1-10) and The Magnificat of Mary (Luke 1:46-55). The psalm also describes the nature of the Lord in a way that anticipates the *kenōsis,* Jesus' emptying Himself of glory when He came to earth (Phil. 2:7).

Psalms 113-118 form the *Hallel,* a collection of songs sung at the great festivals of Israel—Passover, Pentecost, and Tabernacles—as well as on other holy days. At Passover, for example, Psalms 113-114 were sung before the meal, and 115-118 after it.

A. Call to praise (113:1-3)

113:1-3. The psalm begins and ends with the words **Praise the LORD** (*hal⁻lû-yāh;* cf. v. 9; the endings of Pss. 115-117; and comments on 104:35). The psalmist summoned the **servants of the LORD** to **praise** His **name,** for it is worthy of **praise** at all times. **The name of the LORD** (His revealed attributes) deserves praise in all the world—from east to west.

B. Cause for praise (113:4-9)

Believers should praise the Lord (cf. vv. 1-3) because of His greatness (vv. 4-5) and His grace (vv. 6-9).

113:4-5. He is incomparable—no one is **like** Him (cf. 35:10; 71:19; 77:13; 89:6; Ex. 15:11; 2 Sam. 7:22) for He **sits enthroned** (cf. comments on Ps. 2:4) **on high.**

113:6-9. God's greatness (vv. 4-5) is not something He clings to; rather, He comes **down to see** what is in **the heavens and** on **the earth.** He condescends to intervene graciously in human affairs.

Two examples of God's gracious dealings are given, one in verses 7-8 and the other in verse 9. God exalts—thus sharing His nature with man—the miserable and **the poor** to places of prominence and prosperity. The poor hover near the refuse **heap** outside the city for warmth from the perpetual burning and for food from the garbage. But God exalts them, the lowest of society, to an equal portion with the highest (**with princes**). God does not do this with *every* poor person, but when He does it for some His gracious dealings are evident. In the New Testament the truth takes on a spiritual significance, for those who trust in the Lord are given an inheritance in the heavenlies, through the grace of God.

The other example is that of **the barren woman** who becomes **a happy mother.** In Israel's history several barren women were given children (e.g., Sarah, Rachel, Hannah). To the Israelites, this was a mark of God's gracious blessing.

The point of the psalm is that God by His grace does marvelous and mighty deeds for those in need and distress. That is why He is worthy of praise. The psalm concludes with the admonition to worship, **Praise the LORD** (*hal⁻lû-yāh;* cf. v. 1).

Psalm 114

This psalm celebrates the deliverance of God's people at the Exodus—a fitting song to be sung at Passover which was instituted at that time (Ex. 12). The psalmist recalled how the sea fled and the mountains trembled when Israel escaped from Egypt. In a bold poetic stroke, he interrogated the mountains and the sea concerning their reaction, and then called on the earth to tremble at the presence of the Lord who brought water from the rock.

A. The fleeing of the sea and trembling of the mountains (114:1-6)

114:1-4. The psalmist recalled the mighty power of God that was displayed in Israel's past history. He announced that **when** God brought them **out of Egypt . . . Judah became** His **sanctuary,** which meant that Judah became the tribe in which He placed the temple. When He brought them out of Egypt and into Canaan, **the Red Sea** and **the Jordan** River **turned back** and **the mountains skipped like rams** and **lambs,** that is, they quaked.

114:5-6. The psalmist interrogated the **sea** and the **mountains,** challenging them to explain why they reacted to the Lord as they did (cf. vv. 3-4). This bold personification was designed to say that all Creation recognized and obeyed the Creator's will. The Lord's presence in the Old and New Testaments is frequently evidenced by His display of power.

B. The call for the earth to tremble (114:7-8)

114:7-8. The psalmist, instead of answering his question in verses 5-6, instructed the **earth** to continue to **tremble** before **the Lord.** The reason is that the Lord had **turned the rock,** a dry solid, **into . . . water,** beneficial to His people. Fear and trembling should always be the response to God's **presence** and awesome power.

Psalm 115

The psalmist called on the Lord to vindicate His honor among the nations. After demonstrating God's sovereignty and voicing contempt against pagan idols, he invited all to trust in the Lord for He would bless them abundantly.

This psalm may have been written at a time when the nation was humiliated by idolaters. The psalm instructs people to trust in the Lord, not in worthless idols.

A. Call for vindication (115:1-2)

115:1-2. Acknowledging the unworthiness of the people in contrast with God's **glory . . . love, and faithfulness** (cf. 108:4; 117:2; 138:2), the psalmist asked the Lᴏʀᴅ to vindicate the worthiness of His great **name.** There was no reason that the idolaters of **the nations** should taunt believers with their question, **Where is their God?** (cf. 79:10)

B. Declaration of God's sovereignty (115:3-8)

115:3-8. In verse 3 the psalmist declared his theme: **God** is sovereign. He alone **is in heaven,** and **He does whatever** He desires (cf. 135:6; Job 23:13). The significance of this is seen in contrast with the pagans' **idols. Made** of metal, they are only the works of men's **hands** (Ps. 115:4) so they are totally impotent. Though idols have **mouths . . . eyes . . . ears . . . noses . . . hands . . . feet,** and **throats,** they **cannot speak . . . see . . . hear . . . smell . . . feel . . . walk,** or talk (cf. 135:15-18). People who construct idols and those who **trust in them** become **like them**—powerless before the Lord God.

C. Call to faith (115:9-11)

115:9-11. The psalmist exhorted **Israel** to **trust in the** Lᴏʀᴅ, not in idols, for only He can protect them—as **their Help** (cf. comments on 30:10) **and Shield** (cf. comments on 3:3). Everyone in Israel—including priests (**house of Aaron**) and other worshipers (those **who fear Him;** cf. 115:12-13; 118:2-4)—should **trust in** Him.

D. Promise of blessing (115:12-18)

115:12-15. God's people are encouraged to trust the living God because He will **bless** them all (vv. 12-13) including priests and other worshipers (cf. vv. 10-11). The psalmist then prayed for blessings on the people and their **children** by God. The title **Maker of heaven and earth** points to His sovereign work in Creation (this title is also used of God in Job 4:17; 32:22; 35:10; Pss. 121:2; 124:8; 134:3; 146:6; Ecc. 11:5; Jer. 10:16).

115:16-18. The psalmist concluded this psalm by extolling the LORD. Unlike the idols He owns the highest heavens and **has given the earth . . . to man.** Since **the dead do not . . . praise,** the psalmist and his fellow believers praised Him. He was confident that God would deliver them from their idolatrous enemies, so that they could continue to praise Him then **and forevermore.** The psalm ends with **Praise the LORD** (*halᵉlû-yāh*; cf. comments on 104:35).

Psalm 116

The psalmist recalled how the Lord delivered him from certain death and enabled him to have a prolonged life of service. Because of this he vowed to acknowledge the Lord in the temple. If Psalm 115 is a congregational song, Psalm 116 is a personal song of thanksgiving for deliverance from imminent death.

A. Proclamation to praise (116:1-2)

116:1-2. The beginning of this psalm is a unique expression of **love** for the **LORD,** an expression that came from someone delivered by Him. **Because** of this, the psalmist resolved to **call on Him as long as** he lived.

B. Report of the deliverance (116:3-11)

116:3. As a means of instructing others, the psalmist testified to his deliverance by the Lord (vv. 3-11). He recalled how he was in peril of death (v. 3). His words dramatically depict that he was hunted by **death** and **the grave.** He had almost died.

116:4-6. Then the psalmist cried to **the LORD** to **save** him. The deliverance he experienced prompted him to instruct the congregation about **the LORD.** God **is gracious** and compassionate, protecting and saving those **in great need,** including the psalmist.

116:7-11. He then drew lessons from his experience for others to follow. First, believers can return and **rest** because God delivers **from death** (vv. 7-8). The psalmist's suffering and anxiety had been removed so that he could lead a peaceful and tranquil life of service.

Second, God delivers those in need so that they may live obediently **before** Him (v. 9).

Third, God is the only One who is completely trustworthy (vv. 10-11). The words **I believed** refer to verse 9b, that is, he believed that he would live. This was his confidence, even though he was **greatly afflicted,** and felt that he had been deceived by **all** (who apparently had said he would not be delivered). Faced with certain death, he knew that God was trustworthy, so he cried out to Him.

C. Vow of praise (116:12-19)

116:12-14. The writer, asking what he could give **the LORD** in repayment for **His goodness** (cf. v. 7; 13:6; 142:7), vowed to praise Him in the congregation. It has been suggested that **the cup** refers to the part of the sacrifice he would give for having been given **salvation** (deliverance). This is probably correct; otherwise, the expression would be completely figurative, that is, he would praise (**lift up**) God for his lot (his "cup") which was "salvation." In either case he would praise God, which was a paying of **vows** (cf. 116:18). Others would hear him and be edified, which is one of the purposes of public praise.

116:15-19. The psalmist, knowing that **the LORD** cares intensely about **the death of His saints,** acknowledged that he was a **servant** (vv. 15-16) of **the LORD** and would praise Him publicly (vv. 17-19). The death of a saint is not something **the LORD** considers as cheap; He does not let His people die for no reason. Here the deliverance of a saint from the brink of death (vv. 3, 8) resounded to God's praise and the edification of saints for ages to come. The psalm ends with **Praise the LORD** (*halᵉlû-yāh;* cf. comments on 104:35).

Psalm 117

Psalm 117 is an invitation to people everywhere to praise the Lord for His loyal love and faithfulness.

A. Call to praise (117:1)

117:1. The psalmist called on **the nations** to **praise the LORD,** and on **peoples** everywhere to laud Him.

B. Cause for praise (117:2)

117:2. The attributes **of the LORD** are the cause for praise. His **love** (*ḥesed*) is His covenant loyalty for His people, which is **great.**

This word *ḥeseḏ* is often accompanied by the word *'emeṯ*, "truth" or **faithfulness** (cf. 108:4; 115:1; 138:2). Because the Lord's word is reliable, He is faithful. This term strengthens the concept of His covenant loyalty.

The psalm ends with the familiar words **Praise the LORD** (*halᵉlû-yāh*; cf. comments on 104:35).

Psalm 118

This psalm completes the group of *Hallel* songs (Pss. 113–118). Possibly Psalm 118 was written for the Feast of Tabernacles, perhaps even the first celebration of that Feast when the people returned from the Exile. The contents certainly suggest that God, in reestablishing His nation, triumphed over the nations and their plans. At least it can be said that the contents describe a festal procession to the sanctuary to sacrifice to and praise the Lord. Because the song was sung at the festivals, expressions in the psalm were on the lips of the people at Jesus' entry into Jerusalem at the beginning of the Passion Week (118:25-26; Matt. 21:9). Also this psalm may have been sung in the Upper Room after the Lord's Supper (Matt. 26:30).

This psalm in its Old Testament setting, however, was a song for praising the Lord's loyal love. The psalmist recounted how the Lord triumphed over all the nations surrounding Israel. Then he exulted in the fact that their salvation was God's marvelous work and that the stone which the builders rejected had become the prominent part of God's work.

A. Praise for God's loyal love (118:1-4)

118:1-4. In response to the call to acknowledge the Lord's goodness (v. 1; cf. v. 29) the nation **Israel**, the priests (**the house of Aaron**), and all the worshipers (**those who fear the LORD**; cf. 115:9-13) declared that **His** loyal **love** is everlasting. Psalm 118:2-4 suggests that the words were spoken antiphonally, in which the psalmist called for praise, and the people answered with it.

B. Acknowledgment of triumph (118:5-21)

118:5-9. In summary fashion the psalmist announced that **the LORD** delivered him from distress (v. 5). On the basis of this he reminded the people (vv. 6-9), that since **the LORD** was **with** him, he need not fear what others might **do to** him (cf. Heb. 13:6). And because **the LORD** was his **Helper** (cf. Ps. 27:9) he could be sure of **triumph.** Therefore the people too could be sure that **it is better to turn to the LORD than to trust in** human resources.

118:10-13. The psalmist then delineated how **the LORD** gave him confidence in the midst of his enemies. **Surrounded** by enemies who tried to destroy him, he was able to triumph. The threefold refrain (vv. 10-12)—**in the name of the LORD I cut them off** (lit., "circumcised them")—refers to his victory over **the nations.** They were **cut off** suddenly like dry **thorns** that burn quickly (cf. Isa. 9:18). In it all **the LORD helped** him (cf. Ps. 118:7).

118:14-21. These verses speak of the effect of the psalmist's triumph. He joyfully praised **the LORD** as his **Strength** (cf. 22:19; 28:7-8; 46:1; 59:9, 17; 81:1), **Song** (i.e., his Source of joy), and his **Salvation** (cf. 118:21). God's **right hand** speaks of His strength. Because of this the psalmist declared that he would **live** and would enter **the gates of righteousness** and **give thanks** (vv. 19, 21; cf. v. 28) to God. The references to the gates and to praising suggest that the psalmist was anticipating joining the congregation in the sanctuary to praise **the LORD** for His great **salvation** (deliverance).

C. Significance of the triumph (118:22-29)

118:22-24. The psalmist explained that **the LORD** had taken **the stone** that **the builders rejected** and had marvelously made it **the capstone** of the nation. Therefore the people should **rejoice.** In those days great empires easily set up and removed kings. Perhaps those great nations discounted Israel as a nation. Yet the Lord took that "stone" and made it "the capstone" of His rule on earth. The image of the stone may have suggested itself from the temple construction work going on in the postexilic community.

The psalmist, perhaps the congregation's leader, may have thought of his king as the stone, for in Israel kings often represented the nation. Certainly in Jesus' Parable of the Landowner and the Tenants (Matt. 21:33-44) He applied the psalm in that way. Jesus is the Stone and the Jewish leaders, the builders of the nation, had rejected Him. But God made Him the Capstone. Thus the kingdom would be taken from them and given to others (Matt. 21:43). The fact that this psalm was probably popular at the Passover festival made Jesus' use of it all the more forceful.

118:25-29. The psalmist prayed then for his people's salvation and prosperity. The words **save us** (v. 25) and **Blessed is He who comes in the name of the LORD** (v. 26) were proclaimed at Jesus' Triumphal Entry (Matt. 21:9; "Hosanna" translates the Heb. for "save"). The people believed that Jesus was the Coming Savior. In fact the phrase **with boughs in hand** (Ps. 118:27) may have prompted their putting the branches down for Jesus (Matt. 21:8). The second half of Psalm 118:27, though difficult in the Hebrew, probably refers to the custom at the Feast of Tabernacles of waving branches before the Lord. Then later, when the psalm was used in all the feasts, this part of verse 27 became simply an expression in the hymn without boughs literally being in people's hands.

But the people in Jesus' day knew that He claimed to be the Messiah, and that this psalm spoke of the Coming One. So they appropriated its message for the occasion. Fittingly Jesus identified Himself as the Stone who would bring salvation to those who prayed to Him, "Save us."

Because the psalm is typically prophetic of the Messiah, the earlier references to "cut off" (vv. 10-12) may also have a higher significance in relation to the work of Christ. In the Old Testament, circumcision was the means by which a male Israelite was identified with the covenant, but circumcision came to signify "inner circumcision" (cf. Deut. 30:6), belief that set one apart to God. Paul wrote that a true Jew is one whose heart is circumcised (Rom. 2:29).

Perhaps Psalm 118 anticipated the time when the Stone, Jesus, would turn to the nations who would receive Him (cf. John 1:12). If so, His triumph is in a sense different from its meaning when it was historically recorded in Israel. For the psalmist, Psalm 118:25-29 spoke of the procession coming to the temple to worship, and the one coming "in the name of the LORD" was the worshiper. At the altar the worshiper would **give . . . thanks** (cf. vv. 19, 21) and acknowledge the LORD God for His goodness and loyal love. In Jesus' Triumphal Entry this psalm, sung by the people as they moved in the procession to the temple, was most appropriate as He entered Jerusalem to begin His work of salvation for those who would believe.

Psalm 119

The psalmist was persecuted by men of rank and authority, who ridiculed his beliefs, seeking to put him to shame and make him give up his faith. But he strengthened himself by meditating on the Word of the Lord, which to him was his comfort, his prized possession, his rule of life, and his resource for strength—all of which drove him to desire it even more.

This psalm is written in an acrostic (alphabetical) arrangement. In each paragraph (strophe) of eight verses each line begins with the same letter of the Hebrew alphabet. (The 22 strophes correspond to the 22 letters of the alphabet.) So verses 1-8 each begin with the first Hebrew letter, verses 9-16 each begin with the second letter, and so on.

The psalm is largely a collection of prayers and meditations on the Word of God, referred to by 10 synonyms.

"Law" (*tôrâh*), occurring 25 times in the psalm, denotes direction or instruction. More often the word refers to a body of teaching, probably Deuteronomy and Leviticus, if not the whole Pentateuch. In fact in John 10:34 the corresponding Greek word for "Law" seems to include the entire Old Testament.

"Word" (*dābār*) occurs 20 times in the psalm. It is a general term for God's revelation, but the "Ten Commandments" are called "Ten Words" (literal Heb., Deut. 4:13).

"Saying" (*'imrâh*, often trans. "promise" in the NIV) occurs 19 times. It is often a poetical synonym for *dābār*.

"Commandment" (*miṣwâh*) occurs (in the Heb.) 21 times in the plural (usually trans. "commands" in the NIV) and once in the singular collectively. It signifies a definite, authoritative command. It is frequently joined with the next two words.

"Statutes" (*ḥūqqîm*) occurs 21 times.

In the Psalms it is always in the plural. Literally it means "things inscribed." So it refers to enacted Laws (and is trans. "decrees" in the NIV).

"Judgment" (*mišpoṭ*) occurs 19 times in the plural (often trans. "laws" in NIV, and 4 times in the singular. It represents a judicial decision that constitutes a precedence, a binding law. In the Pentateuch it referred to the laws after the Ten Commandments. The word can also mean God's judgmental acts on the wicked.

"Precepts" (*piqqûḏîm*) occurs 21 times. It is a poetical word for injunctions, found only in the Psalter (always in the pl.).

"Testimony" ('*ēḏâh*) occurs 22 times in the plural and once in the singular. It is a solemn attestation, a declaration of the will of God. It is a general word for ordinances that became God's standard of conduct. It is usually rendered "statutes" in the NIV.

"Way" (*derek*), used five times in the plural and six times in the singular, is a metaphorical term describing the pattern of life marked out by God's Law.

"Path" ('*ōraḥ*), used five times in Psalms, is parallel to "way."

The psalmist often spoke of several responses he had toward God and His Word: "delight" (Ps. 119:16, 24, 35, 47, 70, 77, 92, 143, 174), "love" (vv. 47-48, 97, 113, 119, 127, 132, 159, 163, 165, 167), "obey" (vv. 8, 17, 34, 44, 56-57, 60, 67, 88, 100-101, 129, 134, 145, 158, 167-168; cf. "obeyed" in vv. 4, 136 and "obeying" in v. 5), "meditate" (vv. 15, 23, 27, 48, 78, 97, 99, 148), and "rejoice" (vv. 14, 74, 162). He also wrote that he wanted God and His Word to "renew" him (vv. 25, 37, 40, 107, 149, 154, 156; cf. vv. 50, 93) and "preserve" him (vv. 88, 159). Twelve times the psalmist referred to himself as God's servant (vv. 17, 23, 38, 49, 65, 76, 84, 124-125, 135, 140, 176).

A. Blessings of obedience (119:1-8)

119:1-8. The psalmist delighted in the fact that those **who walk** in wholehearted obedience **to the Law** are **blessed** (vv. 1-3). This prompted him to wish that he were more obedient in view of God's **commands** to follow His laws (vv. 4-6). So the psalmist vowed to give thanks **as** he learned more about God's **statutes** (vv. 7-8).

B. Cleansing by God's Word (119:9-16)

119:9-16. The psalmist declared that a person cleanses **his way** (conduct) **by** obeying God's **Word** (v. 9). The psalmist testified that he had internalized and rejoiced in God's **Word** so that he might be morally pure (vv. 10-14). He continually meditated in the Law (vv. 15-16).

C. Appreciation of God's Word (119:17-24)

119:17-24. The psalmist asked God to **open** his **eyes** so that he could **see** the marvelous blessings of God in the **Word** (vv. 17-18). He hungered for the Word (vv. 19-20). Because God curses the wicked who disobey Him, he prayed that the Lord would **remove** those who reproached him. In contrast with them, he meditated on and delighted in God's **Law** (vv. 21-24). Frequently in this psalm he referred to the wicked and those who oppressed him (vv. 23, 53, 61, 69-70, 78, 85-87, 95, 110, 115, 119, 122, 134, 155, 157-158, 161).

D. Prayer for understanding (119:25-32)

119:25-32. The psalmist prayed for quickening since he was **laid low** (v. 25). He then asked God for understanding, strengthening, and keeping (vv. 26-29). When God gave him understanding, he would comply because he treasured the **Law** (vv. 20-32).

E. Loyalty to God's Word (119:33-40)

119:33-40. The psalmist declared his loyalty to the Word, which he observed with his whole **heart** (vv. 33-35). He prayed that the Lord would **turn** him away from covetousness and vanity (vv. 36-37). He desired God to confirm His ordinances to him (vv. 38-40).

F. Salvation through God's Word (119:41-48)

119:41-48. The psalmist called on God to deliver him through His **love** and His **Word** (**promise,** v. 41). **Then** he would have an **answer** for his enemy (v. 42). He prayed (and affirmed) that the **Word** would continue to be his pattern of life (vv. 43-46). He delighted in God's **commandments** and loved them (vv. 47-48).

G. Hope from God's Word (119:49-56)

119:49-56. Declaring his **hope** in the **Word** (v. 49), which **renews . . . life** (v. 50), he decried the proud (**arrogant**; cf. vv. 69, 78, 85) who scorned his faith and hated the **Law** (vv. 51-53). He sang about and meditated on the Word (vv. 54-56).

H. Obedience to God's Word (119:57-64)

119:57-64. Because God was the psalmist's **Portion** (cf. 16:5; 73:26; 142:5), he called on God for mercy (119:57-58). He had lived in accordance with the Word (vv. 58-60), and continued his devotion while he was surrounded by enemies (vv. 61-62). His companions were also believers (vv. 63-64).

I. Trust in God's Word (119:65-72)

119:65-72. The psalmist trusted that the LORD would deal with him **according to** His **Word** (v. 65). He then asked for further instruction to prevent his going **astray** (vv. 66-68). He declared his trust in the midst of slander (vv. 69-70; cf. vv. 51, 53), and admitted that through affliction he realized more of the value of **the Law** (vv. 71-72; cf. v. 127).

J. Hope in God's Word (119:73-80)

119:73-80. The psalmist believed that God created him and had given him **hope in** the **Word** (vv. 73-74; cf. v. 81). Knowing that **in faithfulness** God had **afflicted** him (cf. vv. 67, 71), he asked God to **comfort** him and put **the arrogant** (cf. vv. 51, 69, 85-122) **to shame** (vv. 75-78). He then prayed that **those who fear** the LORD would likewise **turn to** Him in accord with His Word and that he would be kept **blameless** (vv. 79-80).

K. God's Word is faithful (119:81-88)

119:81-88. The psalmist admitted that his **soul** almost fainted while waiting for God's **Word** (vv. 81-82). He was weakened much as **a wineskin in the smoke** becomes shriveled. So he asked **how long** (cf. comments on 6:3) it would be until he was vindicated (119:83-86). He asserted that though his enemies almost consumed him, he had **not forsaken** God's **Law** (vv. 87-88).

L. God's Word is sure (119:89-96)

119:89-96. God's **Word** is settled in heaven and is attested by His **faithful-**

ness (vv. 89-91). The psalmist's **delight** (cf. 1:2; 119:174) in the established **Law** had enabled him to win the victory (vv. 92-95). He concluded that God's Word is **boundless** (v. 96) in its values.

M. God's Word is sweet (119:97-104)

119:97-104. The psalmist declared his **love** and devotion to the **Law,** which gave him more **understanding** and wisdom than his **enemies . . . teachers,** and **elders** (vv. 97-100). By God's **Word** he had **kept** himself pure (vv. 101-102; cf. vv. 9, 104). He extolled the **promises** of God as **sweet** (v. 103). **Understanding** and purity (v. 104) summarize the points made in verses 98-101.

N. God's Word is a light (119:105-112)

119:105-112. Recognizing that God's **Word** was his **light** to direct him (cf. v. 130; Prov. 6:23) the psalmist vowed to **follow** it (Ps. 119:105-106). In his distress (vv. 107-110) he called for help and affirmed that he would joyfully follow God's **statutes** and **decrees** (vv. 111-112).

O. God's Word is awe-inspiring (119:113-120)

119:113-120. The psalmist stated that he hated double-mindedness, and that he loved and hoped in God's **Word** because God was his **Refuge** (*sēter,* "hiding place"; cf. comments on 27:5) and his **Shield** (cf. comments on 3:3). The writer then addressed the wicked, demanding that they leave him (119:115), and asked God to **sustain** and deliver him (vv. 116-117) because of His judgment against the wicked (vv. 118-119). The psalmist then said he trembled **in awe** at the judgments of God (v. 120; cf. v. 161).

P. Vindication from God (119:121-128)

119:121-128. The psalmist asked God to protect him from **arrogant** (cf. vv. 51, 69, 78, 85) **oppressors** and to **deal with** him in justice and **love** (vv. 121-124). He sought to motivate God to respond by explaining his loyalty as God's **servant** (vv. 125-126; cf. vv. 122, 124). He added that he loved the Lord's laws (valuing them **more than gold;** cf. v. 72) and hated false ways (vv. 127-128; cf. vv. 101, 104).

Q. God's Word is wonderful (119:129-136)

119:129-136. The psalmist declared

his delight for God's **wonderful** Word which **gives light** (vv. 129-131; cf. v. 105). He then prayed that the Lord would **turn to** him and establish him by directing, redeeming, blessing, and teaching him (vv. 132-135). (On God making His **face shine,** see comments on 4:6.) He expressed concern over those who hate God's **Law** (119:136).

R. God's Word is righteous (119:137-144)

119:137-144. The psalmist declared that because the LORD is **righteous** His Word is **righteous** (vv. 137-138). He testified of his own **zeal** for the Word, which was pure (vv. 139-142). He found comfort in God's righteous **laws** when he was in affliction (vv. 143-144; cf. v. 92).

S. God's Word is true (119:145-152)

119:145-152. The psalmist called on the LORD to deliver him because he obeyed, hoped **in,** and meditated on His **Word** (vv. 145-149). His enemies, though **near** him, were **far** removed **from** God's **Law** (v. 150). God, however, was also **near** him and His words were reliable (vv. 151-152).

T. Love for God's Word (119:153-160)

119:153-160. The psalmist called on God to **deliver** him because he had **not forgotten** His **Law** (vv. 153-154). Knowing that **salvation is** not available to **the wicked** (v. 155), the psalmist affirmed that God's **compassion** (lit., "compassions") was **great** toward him (v. 156). He lamented that he had **many** enemies who did **not obey** God's **Word** (vv. 157-158). In contrast, however, the psalmist loved God's Word, which is **true,** and therefore asked to be preserved (cf. v. 88) from his enemies (vv. 159-160).

U. Rejoicing in God's Word (119:161-168)

119:161-168. The psalmist affirmed that though princes hated him **without a cause** he trembled in awe at God's **Word** (cf. v. 120). He rejoiced in the worth of the **Law,** loved it, and praised God repeatedly for it (vv. 162-164). Those who love God's Word and hope in Him for **salvation** enjoy **great peace** (šālôm, "well-being," vv. 165-166). The writer then said he had observed the Law out of **love** for it (vv. 167-168; cf. v. 163).

V. Deliverance by God's Word (119:169-176)

119:169-176. The psalmist called on God to hear his **supplication** and **deliver** him (vv. 169-170). He desired to **praise** God for His **Word** (vv. 171-172). He asked God to enable him to **live** since he delighted in His **Law** (vv. 173-175; cf. v. 92). The psalmist concluded this lengthy but rich psalm by confessing that he had gone astray **like a lost sheep** and by asking God to rescue him by His Word (v. 176).

Psalm 120

The title "song of ascents" identifies each of Psalms 120–134 as a pilgrim song to be sung when the Israelites "ascended" (went up) to Jerusalem for the annual feasts. Four of these 15 psalms are ascribed to David (Pss. 122; 124; 131; 133), 1 to Solomon (Ps. 127), and the other 10 are anonymous.

In Psalm 120, the psalmist prayed for deliverance from treacherous people who wanted war while he was for peace.

A. Deliverance from liars (120:1-2)

120:1-2. The pilgrim prayed for deliverance from liars who would destroy him. He was sure that God would answer him.

B. Destruction of the wicked (120:3-4)

120:3-4. The pilgrim, by directing a question to the wicked, affirmed that the Lord would destroy them. **The broom tree** was used for firewood because it burned longer than many other woods. The imagery of **sharp arrows** and **coals** of fire speaks of retribution against people with **deceitful** tongues.

C. Declaration for peace (120:5-7)

120:5-7. The pilgrim lamented his having to **dwell in** the midst of **those who hate peace** (vv. 5-6). **Meshech** (Gen. 10:2) and its barbarous people lived in the far north. **Kedar** (in northern Arabia) was where some nomadic Ishmaelites lived (cf. Gen. 25:13). The psalmist was saying that these two names represented the enemies that surrounded him.

He declared that he, in contrast, was **a man of peace** (Ps. 120:7). For that reason he knew the Lord would vindicate his cause.

Psalm 121

The pilgrim, contemplating his journey through the hills to Jerusalem, found assurance that the Lord, the Keeper of Israel, would keep him at all times on his journey.

A. Contemplation of the journey (121:1-2)

121:1-2. The pilgrim-psalmist, as he contemplated his journey through the hills to Jerusalem, asked **where** his **help** came **from**. He found the answer to his question in the affirmation of his faith that **the LORD,** who created **heaven and earth**—with those **hills**—was his only Source of **help.** On the title "**Maker** of heaven and earth" see comments on 115:15.

B. Assurance of God's protection (121:3-8)

In verses 3-8 the person changes from "I" and "my" (vv. 1-2) to "you" and "your." Verses 3-8 are therefore the words of someone, perhaps a priest, accompanying the pilgrim.

121:3-4. The person speaking assured the pilgrim that he would have divine protection. God, **who watches over** (cf. vv. 5, 7-8) His own, will not **slumber** or **sleep,** that is, He will not be indifferent to or disregard them. The Lord will be alert in protecting His own.

121:5-6. The assurance was then given that **the LORD** would protect the pilgrim at all times. The Keeper of Israel (cf. v. 4) was the pilgrim's Keeper as well, protecting him as a **shade** protects one from the blazing sun. **The sun** and **the moon** stand for dangers that occur in the **day** and in the **night.**

121:7-8. The psalm closes with the psalmist's renewed affirmation that **the LORD will keep** and **watch over** (cf. vv. 3-5; i.e., protect) the pilgrim **from all harm** at all times (vv. 7-8).

Psalm 122

The pilgrim-psalmist, designated in the superscription as David, recalled his delight in going up to Jerusalem, which was the nation's spiritual and civic center. He then called for everyone to pray for the peace and security of Jerusalem for the sake of the godly and for the sake of God Himself.

A. Delight at the pilgrimage (122:1-2)

122:1-2. The psalmist recalled how he delighted at the prospect of the pilgrimage to **Jerusalem.** Then he relished the experience of actually **standing** within the city's **gates.**

B. Acclaim of the city (122:3-5)

122:3-5. The psalmist acclaimed the **city** of **Jerusalem** for its physical splendor, with its full population **closely compacted together.** He then lauded it as the spiritual center to which the nation's **tribes** went on their annual pilgrimages. He also cited it as the seat of justice (cf. Jer. 21:11-12).

C. Prayer for peace (122:6-9)

122:6-9. The psalmist asked the people to **pray for the peace** and **security** of the city and its inhabitants (vv. 6-7; cf. 125:5; 128:6). He himself then prayed for **peace. . . . for the sake of** his **brothers,** the righteous pilgrims (122:8), and for **prosperity** for **the sake of the** sanctuary, God's dwelling place (v. 9).

Psalm 123

Lifting up his eyes to God in heaven, the slave-pilgrim called for mercy because the people were filled with contempt from the scoffing of the proud.

A. Trust in the Lord (123:1-2)

123:1-2. The psalmist affirmed his trust in **the LORD** of **heaven. I lift up my eyes** means that he looked to the Lord in prayer for deliverance. He compared his trust to that of a slave waiting for a word from a **master** or a mistress. On behalf of the people, the psalmist continued to **look to . . . God** for help.

B. Relief from contempt (123:3-4)

123:3-4. The psalmist asked God for **mercy** because the people were filled with **contempt,** that is, they had **endured much ridicule from the . . . arrogant.** Despite this taunting of their faith, they would pray for God's **mercy** until He answered.

Psalm 124

Realizing that if the Lord had not been on their side the nations would have swallowed them up, the pilgrim blessed the Lord, who allowed them to escape.

A. Protection by the Lord (124:1-5)

124:1-5. In this part of the psalm the writer attested to the Lord's protection. He called for the nation to realize that her victory was due to the Lord's being **on their side** (vv. 1-2). Then he explained what would have happened **if the LORD had not been on** their side: the nations in **their anger** would have destroyed them (vv. 3-5). Here he used the imagery of swallowing (cf. Num. 16:30; Jer. 51:34), and the imagery of floodwaters (cf. Lam. 3:54). **The raging waters** (lit., "proud waters") suitably suggests the arrogance (cf. Ps. 123:4) of the enemies. This could apply to various times in Israel's history, but it may affirm the Lord's deliverance from the Babylonian Captivity. If the return from the Exile is in view, then David was not the author as the superscription, added later, states. Rather, "David" in this case would indicate a later Davidic "king" (i.e., a potential occupant of the Davidic throne).

B. Help in the name of the Lord (124:6-8)

124:6-8. The psalmist turned to **praise . . . the LORD, who** had **not** abandoned them (v. 6) but had enabled them to escape (v. 7). The enemies' devices were compared both to **teeth** and the **snare** of a fowler (cf. 9:13).

The people's escape was by **the LORD, the Maker of heaven and earth** (cf. comments on 115:15). The faith attested here is reminiscent of that expressed in Psalm 121.

Psalm 125

Righteous believers are secure in the Lord, who will not let them be tested to the point of being shaken from their integrity. However, those who turn aside in unbelief will be banished from His blessings along with the wicked.

A. Affirmation of security (125:1-3)

125:1-3. Verse 1 summarizes the psalmist's theme that believers are secure and unshakable. He compared them to **Mount Zion,** which **endures forever.**

This imagery is continued in verse 2. Observing how **the mountains surround Jerusalem,** he declared that **the LORD surrounds His people,** protecting them on all sides.

The reason for these affirmations is made clear in verse 3. Apparently foreign domination was a burden on the nation. The psalmist said that God would not permit this **scepter** (lit., "rod") of wickedness to rest on the lot of **the righteous** to the extent it would drive them into wickedness. In other words the test would be limited to what they could endure so they should not abandon their trust in **the LORD.**

B. Prayer for prosperity (125:4)

125:4. The pilgrilm-psalmist prayed that the **LORD** would bless **those who are good** and **upright in heart.**

C. Warning of insecurity (125:5)

125:5. Those who did **turn** aside to crookedness at that time would suffer the same fate as the wicked (they would be banished). So God's people should be loyal in their faith and should continue to pray for **peace** for the nation (cf. 122:6-8; 128:6).

Psalm 126

This pilgrim psalm seems to reflect the struggle of the returned exiles. The psalmist was joyful because the Lord had restored them to their land, but he prayed for a full restoration of the captives. He found comfort in the principle of sowing and reaping.

A. Praise for the restoration (126:1-3)

126:1-3. The psalmist, speaking for the returned exiles, recalled the joy that they experienced **when the LORD brought** them **back.** They were greatly comforted and **filled with laughter** and **joy.** Comfort is suggested by the words "men restored to health" (NIV marg.; these words fit the situation better than **men who dreamed;** cf. Isa. 38:16, and are well supported by various versions and the Dead Sea Scrolls). Also **the nations** realized that **the LORD** had **done** marvelous **things** for His people. It was a time of jubilation after a time of great sadness (cf. Ps. 137).

B. Petition for full restoration (126:4)

126:4. The psalmist, however, prayed that the **LORD** would complete the restoration. He compared the returning exiles to **streams in the Negev** (the desert south of Judah), which in the dry season have little or no water but which in the rainy season overflow their banks. Under God's "showers of blessings" the highways from the east would be full of returning captives.

C. Confidence in God's blessing (126:5-6)

126:5-6. The psalmist found encouragement in the principle of sowing and reaping. These verses are connected to verses 2-3 by their references to great **joy.** Also verse 4 is the connecting link because of its use of the verb "restore" (also used in the Heb. in v. 1) and because of the comparisons with nature (cf. vv. 5-6).

The setting in verses 5-6 is agricultural. After the land had been neglected for so long, it was almost impossible to work it. The planting would be difficult, but persistence would doubtless bring a harvest. The sowing with **tears** (i.e., agonizing over the work) would signify anything someone did to help advance God's theocracy (e.g., encouraging people to respond to the Lord and return to the land). The joyful harvesting (**reap**) would then refer to other people who returned to the land in faith. The psalmist was convinced that continued labor, no matter how agonizingly difficult and frustrating, would result in more people returning to the land of Israel.

The metaphors of sowing and harvesting have been widely used by believers (cf. Gal. 6:7). Jesus spoke of sowing as spreading the message of the kingdom, and spoke of the harvest as people who received Him by faith (Matt. 13:1-8, 18, 23).

Psalm 127

This pilgrim psalm is ascribed to Solomon. It records the blessing of the Lord in domestic life. The psalmist recognized that dependence on the providence of the Lord assures valuable domestic enterprises and safeguards. The writer then epitomized that bounty in the reward of children, who in those days helped defend a family.

A. Labor is vain without God's providence (127:1-2)

127:1-2. In words that reflect Ecclesiastes (a fitting relationship if Solomon was the psalmist), the author said that it is vain to attempt things without the

Lord. **Builders** work on a **house . . . in vain** unless **the Lord builds** it, **watchmen . . . guard in vain** unless **the Lord watches,** and being anxious over one's labor **for food** and working long hours is **in vain** (cf. 128:2). The point is that work done independently of God will be futile. But a person who trusts in the Lord will find rest. Without the Lord, all domestic work is in vain.

The **toiling** (127:2) should not be taken to mean that people need not be diligent, for the Scriptures elsewhere say they should. Rather, that verse stresses that to work long days without divine providence and support is futile. The thought continues from verse 1.

B. Children are evidence of God's providence (127:3-5)

127:3-5. Children, the psalmist wrote, are some of the Lord's providential blessings (see **blessed,** v. 5). They are **a reward from** the **Lord. Sons** help defend the family for they are **like** weapons (**arrows) in the hands of a** mighty man. Sons are capable of defending the family in civil cases (at **the gate** civil cases were discussed and decided).

The imagery of arrows and of defense "in the gate" was natural for a nation endangered from without and within.

Psalm 128

After declaring the blessedness of those who fear the Lord, the psalmist enumerated some of the blessings of the good life and voiced his prayer for greater blessings.

A. Statement of blessing (128:1)

128:1. The psalmist announced the heavenly bliss of people **who fear the Lord** (cf. v. 4) and obey Him (cf. 1:1-3).

B. Enumeration of blessings (128:2-4)

128:2. A righteous person will find **prosperity** as a result of his work. Laboring in anxious independence of God is vain (127:2), but working under God and in obedience to His ways is fruitful (cf. 1:3).

128:3-4. Speaking again of fruitfulness (cf. v. 2), the psalmist referred to children obtained through his **wife.** The imagery of plants (**a vine**) and trees (**olive shoots**) naturally suggested growth and fruitfulness. The person **who fears the LORD** is blessed in this way (cf. v. 1).

At the religious festivals whole families gathered in Jerusalem. So it is no surprise to see an emphasis in some of the pilgrim psalms on God's blessings in the domestic area of life.

C. Prayer for blessings (128:5-6)

128:5-6. The pilgrim prayed for further blessings from God on people who fear Him (cf. v. 1). Those blessings include seeing **Jerusalem** prosper and living long enough **to see** one's grandchildren. Then the psalmist prayed for **peace** on the nation (cf. 122:6-7; 125:5).

Psalm 129

Speaking for Israel, the psalmist declared that the Lord delivered her from the ravages of the wicked. He then prayed that the Lord would put to shame those who hate Zion.

A. Declaration of deliverance (129:1-4)

129:1-2. The psalmist encouraged Israel to testify (**let Israel say**; cf. 124:1) that the wicked who had continued to oppress them from the beginning had **not** been victorious.

129:3-4. The imagery of plowing **furrows** describes the extreme suffering that the enemies inflicted on Israel (v. 3). It is as if they had **plowed . . . long** furrows down their backs.

Deliverance from such suffering is attributed to the righteous **LORD** (v. 4). He had **cut** them loose. Perhaps the figure from verse 3 is continued here: God may have broken the plower's harness so the plowing could not continue. Or the word **cords** in verse 4 may simply refer to subjugation (cf. 2:3).

B. Prayer for punishment (129:5-8)

129:5-8. The psalmist prayed that **all** his enemies **who** hated **Zion**, the city of the Lord, would be put to **shame** (v. 5). He prayed that they would wither up so they could not be found (vv. 6-7). **Grass on the housetops** suggests that grass seeds blown by the wind sometimes fell on flat roofs and then began to grow but withered because of no depth of soil.

In greeting someone, it was normal to wish God's **blessing** on him (cf. Ruth 2:4). But the psalmist asked that people

not do this for the wicked (Ps. 129:8). They do not deserve the Lord's blessing.

Psalm 130

Psalm 130 is an earnest cry for the Lord to show His people mercy. The psalmist, sure that God forgives sins, exhorted the nation to join him in waiting in hope for the time when the Lord would redeem them from all their iniquities.

A. Prayer for mercy (130:1-2)

130:1-2. The psalmist cried **out of the depths** (cf. 30:1; 71:20), a figure of speech suggesting his insurmountable difficulty, even to the point of death. He prayed that the **LORD** would answer his **cry for mercy**. The exact problem is not specified, but it seems to be suggested in 130:8. The nation may have been in trouble because of divine punishment for her iniquities.

B. Confidence of forgiveness (130:3-4)

130:3-4. The psalmist recognized that no one could **stand** if God dealt with sinners according to what they deserved. To "mark" (keep **a record of**) **sins** means to hold one accountable for his sins.

The comfort is that with God **there is forgiveness** (sᵉlîḥâh, "pardon," also used in Neh. 9:17; Dan. 9:9 [NIV, "forgiving"]). This is the reason for the Lord's not keeping records of sins; He forgives. Believers throughout all ages have rejoiced over this fact, for apart from this, none could endure His judgment!

God forgives so that the forgiven will fear Him. This general word for fear often includes the ideas of worship and obedience. The Scriptures state that many results come from fearing the LORD; the most notable is that the person keeps himself from sin. The forgiveness of God cannot be treated lightly. It turns sinners into saints, people who follow Him in obedience.

C. Hope in the Lord (130:5-8)

130:5-6. The psalmist testified that he was patiently waiting **for the LORD**. He compared his **wait** to that of a city's **watchmen** looking for the first rays of dawn, for then they would be relieved of their duties by other guards. He eagerly looked for God's new merciful dealings with the nation.

130:7-8. The people were encouraged to **put** their **hope in the** LORD. The reason is that **with** Him **is** loyal love (*ḥesed*) and **full** pardon. Because of His loyalty to **Israel** God would **redeem** her **from all** her **sins.** This was the psalmist's hope and prayer. Apparently "the depths" (v. 1) refer to the nation's spiritual calamity. Only when God forgave the people's sins and pardoned them would they be delivered. Because they believed this, they looked for that day of redemption.

People today who have come to know Him as the God of forgiveness also look for full redemption.

Psalm 131

Asserting that he had not been proud or followed lofty endeavors, pilgrim David spoke of his childlike trust, his hope in the Lord.

A. Humility (131:1-2)

131:1. David affirmed that he had not been arrogant. Pride is essentially independence from and disobedience to God. The psalmist knew that he depended on the LORD. **Proud** ambition (**haughty** eyes; cf. 18:27; 101:5; Prov. 6:17; 30:13) and selfishly ambitious endeavors (**great matters**) had not been his pursuits.

131:2. David then testified to his humility. His **soul** was not disturbed by selfish ambition and passion. He had **stilled** and silenced his soul. **Like a weaned child,** no longer wanting his mother's milk, he was content without that which used to seem indispensable. A mature believer leaves the clamor of proud ambition and rests in the Lord.

B. Hope (131:3)

131:3. David called for **Israel** to **hope in the** LORD forever. To trust in Him is the antithesis of pride.

Psalm 132

This psalm is a prayer of the congregation that the Lord would remember David's vow concerning the dwelling place for the ark. The congregation found the answer to this prayer when they resolved to worship at the temple. They were reminded of God's promises that David's line would continue, that Zion would be His dwelling place, and that the Messiah would appear.

It is difficult to know the setting of the psalm. Perhaps it was a prayer by the returned exiles who wondered about the fulfillment of God's promises to David, primarily the promises of eternal dominion to David's family and of worship in righteousness in Zion.

A. Remember David (132:1-5)

132:1. The theme of the psalm is expressed in the opening cry to the LORD to **remember David.** David's life and work were keenly felt at the time of the restoration from Babylon, as he was the king who had centralized the nation's worship in Zion.

132:2-5. The specific aspect of this prayer was David's **oath . . . not** to rest **till** he found **a place for the** LORD to dwell. This probably refers to David's desire to build the temple (2 Sam. 7). That desire evidenced his great devotion, for which **the** LORD made a covenant with him. The Davidic Covenant was to the later community under Ezra and Nehemiah what the Abrahamic Covenant had been to Moses. This prayer in Psalm 132 calls for God to honor His promises at a time when they seemed jeopardized.

B. Let us worship (132:6-10)

Here the tone of the psalm changes, for the congregation began to feel confident that their prayer would be answered.

132:6-8. The congregation recalled Israel's hearing that the ark (v. 8) of the covenant was **in Ephrathah** and finding it. It had rested for 20 years in **Jaar** (i.e., Kiriath Jearim, 1 Sam. 7:1-2) until David moved it to Zion (2 Sam. 6). (Ephrathah, also called Ephrath, Gen. 35:16, 19; 48:7, was an older name for Bethlehem or the name of the area around Bethlehem.)

The people resolved to **worship** in the place David had designated for the ark (the **dwelling place**; cf. Pss. 74:7; 76:2; 84:1; 132:5, 13, and **footstool** of the Lord). It was God's dwelling place in the sense that it was **His** earthly throne. It was called **the ark** of God's **might** because in battle it symbolized God's strength and victory.

132:9-10. The people's prayer for the Lord to visit them was accompanied by their prayer that the **priests be clothed**

with **righteousness** (cf. v. 16; Zech. 3:1-7), that the **saints sing for joy,** and that the Lord not **reject** David, His **anointed** king. These verses were all a part of the people's prayer when **David** established Zion as the center of God's kingdom. The psalmist here appropriated the prayer for the returnees from the Exile so that God would honor His promises to David's descendants as well. As the earlier community had followed the ark to its resting place and there prayed for blessing on the priests and David, so this community prayed for the priests in their day, descendants of the covenant's earlier ministers.

C. The Lord swore an oath (132:11-18)

132:11-18. These verses record a revelation from **the LORD** confirming His earlier promises to David. The Lord reiterated His **oath to David** that **descendants** of his would sit on David's **throne forever** (vv. 11-12; cf. 89:3-4, 27-29, 35-37). **The LORD** then affirmed His choice of Mount **Zion** (132:13-14) which He would **bless . . . with abundant provisions,** including **food** (cf. 111:5; 136:25; 145:15; 146:7) for the **poor . . . salvation** for the **priests** (cf. 132:9), and **joy** for the **saints.** God also promised the appearance and crowning of His **Anointed One,** the Messiah (vv. 17-18).

The burning **lamp** is a figure from the furnishings of the tabernacle. Here it signifies the continuation of the Davidic dynasty (cf. 2 Sam. 21:17; 1 Kings 11:36). The "Anointed One," first David, then his descendants, and eventually the Messiah (Christ) will be triumphant over His enemies.

An animal **horn** symbolized strength and vigor. Appropriately it sometimes was used of powerful rulers (cf. Dan. 7:24). This horn will **grow** (*sāmaḥ,* lit., "sprout"). Zechariah may have had this passage in mind in his prayer (Luke 1:69). Related to this verb is the noun *ṣemaḥ* ("Branch"), a messianic title (Jer. 23:5; 33:15; Zech. 3:8; 6:12). The expression then signifies the messianic King, who is David's Descendant. The "Branch" is the Coming One who will unite the offices of priest and king.

Thus Psalm 132 is an encouraging confirmation that no matter what the circumstances, God's promises will be fulfilled.

Psalm 133

Here the Psalmist David described the beauty of unity that exists among brethren.

A. The goodness of unity (133:1)

133:1. In this short pilgrim psalm David exclaimed how wonderful it is for believers to dwell **together in unity.** This thought was appropriate for the religious festivals when Israelite families came together to worship their Lord.

B. The description of unity (133:2-3)

133:2. David compared the unity mentioned in verse 1 to the **oil** that consecrated Aaron (cf. Lev. 8:12). This imagery from the priesthood was appropriate because of the pilgrims being in Jerusalem. The oil poured **on Aaron's** head flowed **down** on his **beard** and shoulders, and onto the breastplate with the names of all 12 tribes. The oil thus symbolized the unity of the nation in worship under their consecrated priest. As the oil consecrated Aaron, so the unity of the worshipers in Jerusalem would consecrate the nation under God.

133:3. David then compared the unity mentioned in verse 1 to **the dew** that covers the mountains. The picture of oil running down (v. 2) no doubt suggested dew coming down from Mount **Hermon** in the north onto **Mount Zion.** The dew of Hermon was heavy; it symbolized what was freshening and invigorating. The refreshing influence of the worshiping community on the nation was similar to the dew on vegetation. This was a fitting symbol of the Lord's **blessing** on His people.

Psalm 134

Addressing the priests and the Levites who kept watch at the temple, the pilgrim asked that heavenly blessings be given them from Zion.

A. Call to praise (134:1-2)

134:1-2. The pilgrim called on the priests, the Lord's **servants** who ministered in the temple (**the house of the LORD**), to **praise** Him with uplifted **hands.**

B. Prayer for blessing (134:3)

134:3. The pilgrim then prayed that the Creator (**the Maker of heaven and**

earth; see comments on 115:15) would
bless them. The passage forms a fitting
benediction to the pilgrim psalms (Pss.
120–134).

Psalm 135

This song of praise is a mosaic of the
Law, the Prophets, and the Psalms. In it
the psalmist called on the priests to
praise the Lord, so it builds on Psalm
134. It is a song of praising the Lord's
greatness and faithfulness to His people.

A. Call to praise (135:1-3)

135:1-3. Following the introductory
Praise the LORD (*hal⁰lû-yāh*; cf. vv. 3, 21
and comments on 104:35), the psalmist
called the priests, the **servants of the
LORD** in the temple, to praise Him (cf.
134:1). The preliminary reasons are that
God **is good** and **praise . . . is pleasant.**

B. Cause for praise (135:4-18)

135:4-7. The reasons for praise given
in verses 4-18 all stress God's sovereignty. First, He chose **Israel** as **His treasured
possession** (cf. Deut. 7:6). Second, He is
greater than all the pagan gods. So He is
sovereign, doing **whatever pleases Him**
(cf. Ps. 115:3), **in the heavens and on the
earth** (cf. Jer. 10:13), including control
over **clouds . . . lightning,** and **wind.**
(On **storehouses** see comments on Job
38:22.)

135:8-12. This theme is now expanded in relationship to Israel's history. In
the Exodus (vv. 8-9) God defeated **Egypt,**
smiting their **firstborn** (the 10th plague;
cf. 136:10) after sending other **signs and
wonders** (plagues 1-9).

God destroyed **nations** and **kings** to
give Israel her land (135:10-11; cf. 136:17-
18). **Sihon** and **Og** were two powerful
kings the Lord helped **Israel** destroy just
before they entered the land (cf. 136:19-
20; Num. 21), which was their inheritance (cf. Ps. 136:21-22).

135:13-14. The sovereignty of God is
then mentioned in reference to Israel's
future history. **The LORD,** who is eternal,
will vindicate His people because of His
compassion on them.

135:15-18. If verses 8-12 correspond
with verse 4, then verses 15-18 correspond with verse 5. The psalmist gave
specific illustrations of the Lord's sovereignty over pagan gods (cf. 115:4-8).
They were, he declared created **by . . .**

men (135:15). Idols **cannot speak . . . see
. . . hear** or breathe (perhaps v. 17b
means they cannot smell). Most importantly, they cannot save (v. 18).

C. Conclusion (135:19-21)

135:19-21. The psalmist reiterated his
call for **Israel** and her priests (**house of
Aaron**) and Levites (**house of Levi**) to
praise God **from Zion.** The psalm closes
with the same words with which it began
(**Praise the LORD;** cf. vv. 1, 3 and comments on 104:35).

Psalm 136

This psalm is similar to Psalm 135,
except that it has a refrain which stresses
the theme. The theme is "praise the
LORD who performed great wonders,"
and the refrain is "because of His enduring loyal love." The structure of Psalm
136 suggests that it was used antiphonally in worship, with one part of the congregation making a statement or phrase
and the other part responding with the
refrain (cf. Ezra 3:11; 2 Chron. 7:3, 6).

The Lord's loyal love (*ḥesed*), mentioned in each of the 26 refrains, is His
covenant faithfulness to His Chosen People whom He loves. The celebration of
God's love in this liturgical psalm gave
Israel a favorite song for festivals. This
psalm is often referred to as "the Great
Hallel" (cf. Pss. 111–113; 115–117).

A. Call to praise (136:1-3)

136:1-3. The psalmist called the congregation to thank (cf. v. 26) **the LORD,**
who is **the God of gods** and **the Lord of
lords** (cf. Deut. 10:17). Between each expression here and throughout the psalm
the reason for the praise is expressed:
His loyal love endures forever.

B. Cause for praise (136:4-25)

136:4-9. Verse 4 provides the introductory summary of the cause for praise:
the marvelous acts (**wonders**) that issued
from God's loyal **love.** The first example
of His wonders for man is Creation (vv.
5-9). He **made the heavens,** stretched **out
the earth,** and **made the great lights (the
sun. . . . the moon,** and the **stars**).

136:10-25. The second example of
God's marvelous works was **His** aid to
Israel. The psalmist related that the Lord:
(a) triumphed over **Egypt** in the 10th
plague (v. 10; cf. 135:8) and in bringing

Israel. . . . with a mighty hand and outstretched arm (cf. comments on Deut. 4:34) across the Red Sea (Ps. 136:11-15); (b) led His people through the wilderness (v. 16); and (c) triumphed over the kings of the land (including Sihon and Og, vv. 17-20; cf. 135:10-12) to establish His people in the land safely (136:21-22; cf. 135:12). In all this God worked on behalf of His people who had been enslaved, freeing them from their enemies (136:23-24).

The third demonstration of His enduring love was feeding every creature (v. 25; cf. 111:5; 132:15; 145:15; 146:7).

C. Conclusion (136:26)

136:26. As the psalmist concluded this psalm, he again called for **thanks** (cf. vv. 1-3) to be given **to the God of heaven** because of **His** enduring **love**. This is the only place in the Book of Psalms where this title of God is used (cf. comments on Ezra 1:2).

Psalm 137

In pathetic but beautiful language the exiled psalmist mourned the plight of those who wept in a strange land and could not sing their songs of Zion. Opposite to his intense love for Zion was his hatred for the destroyers of Zion; so he turned to voice imprecations against Edom and Babylon who had destroyed the city of God.

Reflecting the exilic period, this psalm may have been written toward the end of the Babylonian Captivity. Perhaps the psalmist felt that the Persians' kind treatment of the Babylonians was an insufficient judgment on those who devastated Israel.

A. Mourning for Zion (137:1-4)

137:1. The psalmist recalled that the exiles in **Babylon** . . . **sat** down **and wept** over the destruction of **Zion** (Jerusalem). **The rivers** refer to the Euphrates and the canals and waterways stemming from it.

137:2-4. So great was the exiles' grief that even the singers were silent. The exiles **hung** their **harps** on poplar trees (v. 2) for they could not **sing** their **songs** about their homeland when their oppressors taunted them to **sing** of glorious **Zion** (v. 3), as the Israelites were in a hostile **foreign land** (v. 4).

B. Faithfully remembering Jerusalem (137:5-6)

137:5-6. The psalmist vowed to retain **Jerusalem** in his memory. He wished that his **right hand** would **forget its skill** and that he would become mute if he failed to **remember . . . Jerusalem,** his **highest joy.** The people's intense grief over the destruction of their city (where the tribes gathered to praise the Lord) is contrasted here with their greatest joy.

C. Imprecating Zion's destroyers (137:7-9)

The last part of this psalm must be understood in the light of the great mourning of the Jews in exile. As an imprecation (cf. comments under "Theology of the Psalms" in the *Introduction*), it is a prayer for God to exact vengeance on their captors and those who aided them.

137:7. This is a plea for God to **remember . . . the Edomites** (cf. the psalmist's remembering, v. 6) who had rejoiced while the city of **Jerusalem** was being destroyed and encouraged the destroyers (cf. Ezek. 25:12; Joel 3:19). So the psalmist wanted God to bring retribution on Edom.

137:8-9. The psalmist addressed his curse to **Babylon** directly. The Babylonians should note that the Lord would destroy them measure for measure, that is, their little ones would be dashed **against the rocks** (cf. Isa. 13:16) for the Babylonians apparently had done this to the Jerusalemites. This is perhaps the most painful imprecation in the Book of Psalms. To the exiled psalmist, those who had ravaged the Holy Land deserved no better. Great sadness and bitterness filled the hearts of the Israelites who were in captivity (cf. Lam. 1–2).

Psalm 138

David vowed to praise the Lord's loyal love and goodness for answering his prayer. He made known his wish that all kings would acknowledge the Lord's favor to the lowly, and then expressed his confidence that the Lord would also deliver him by His loyal love.

A. Praise from the psalmist (138:1-3)

138:1-3. David vowed to **praise** the LORD wholeheartedly **before the "gods,"** and to worship Him in the **temple** for His loyal **love . . . faithfulness** (cf. 108:4;

115:1; 117:2), **name,** and **Word.** "Gods" could refer to the pagan gods, in which case David was praising the true God in spite of their supposed presence. Or "gods" may refer to human leaders (as judges or kings), though pagan gods seems preferable here.

The reason David would praise the Lord is that God had **answered** his prayer, thus strengthening his faith.

B. Praise from all kings (138:4-5)

138:4-5. David prayed that **all the kings** would acknowledge and **praise** God **when they** heard of His Word and His great **glory.**

C. Deliverance by the Lord (138:6-8)

138:6-8. David explained that **the LORD** should be praised (vv. 4-5) because He does not judge by human standards. Though He **is on high** (i.e., exalted; cf. 113:4), **He looks** to **the lowly** (cf. 113:7-9), not to **the proud.**

David expressed confidence that the LORD would deliver him from his **foes** by His **right hand** (His power) and according to His loyal **love.** Even though David was confident in **the LORD,** he asked that God not let him down.

Psalm 139

God's omniscience, omnipresence, and omnipotence are the subjects of David's meditations in this beautiful psalm. In this psalm David asked God to examine him thoroughly to affirm his innocence. The psalm has four strophes of six verses each. The message progresses significantly from one subject to another. His first meditation is on God's knowledge, that every aspect of his life was searched out and controlled by what the Lord knew. He then realized it was impossible to escape from such omniscient control, no matter how far or fast he might go, for God is everywhere. David then stated that God has such control over him because in His power He created Him secretly and planned his life with great care. On the basis of these meditations, David then affirmed his loyalty to God and prayed for God to prove him by examining him.

A. The omniscience of the Lord (139:1-6)

139:1. The theme of verses 1-6 is announced in the opening verse: the LORD

knew David penetratingly. David said God's knowledge came as if He had scoured every detail of David's life and thus knew him intimately.

139:2-4. Samples of how well God knew David are stated here. The Lord (**You** is emphatic in Heb.; cf. v. 13) knew every move he made; the two opposites of sitting and rising represent all his actions (this is a figure of speech known as a merism; cf. vv. 3, 8). God knew not only David's actions; He also knew his motivations (**thoughts;** cf. v. 17). **Afar** evidently refers not to space but to time.

The daily activities of the psalmist were also thoroughly **familiar** to the Lord. The opposites of **going out** in the morning and **lying down** at night represent the whole day's activities (another merism; cf. vv. 2, 8).

But the one sample that epitomizes God's omniscience is in verse 4. Before the psalmist could frame **a word on** his **tongue,** the LORD was thoroughly familiar with what he was about to say. (The Heb. for "word" is *millâh* and the similar-sounding word for **completely** is *kŭllâh.*)

139:5-6. David's initial response to this staggering knowledge was that he was troubled. Like many who respond to the fact of God's omniscience, he thought it was confining, that God had besieged him and cupped His **hand** over him.

Moreover, this kind of **knowledge** was out of David's control—it was **too wonderful for** him. The word "wonderful" is in the emphatic position, at the beginning of the sentence. On the meaning of "wonderful" as "extraordinary or surpassing," see comments on 9:1. In other words divine omniscience is **too** high for humans to comprehend (also cf. comments on 139:14).

B. The omnipresence of the Lord (139:7-12)

139:7. The thought of such confining knowledge (vv. 1-6) may have prompted David's desire to escape, as verses 7-12 suggest. This is indicated in verse 7 by two rhetorical questions: there is absolutely no place where he could escape from the **presence** of the Lord (cf. Jer. 23:24).

139:8-10. Hypothetical examples of where David might try to escape are given here. He first asserted that the Lord is present in **the heavens** above and in sheol (NIV marg.) below. These opposites signify that all areas in between (a third merism in this psalm; cf. vv. 2-3) are also in the Lord's presence.

Moreover, if he could fly at the speed of light (the wings of the dawn) from the east across the sky to the west (far side of the Mediterranean Sea) he could not escape from the Lord.

God's presence then began to take on a new meaning for the psalmist, as if the light were dawning on him. Now, he stated, the hand of the Lord would lead and comfort him.

139:11-12. David developed the theme of light a little further. The darkness might bruise him (probably referring to the oppressive nature of darkness). (Hide is an interpretive rendering of šûp, "to crush or bruise"; cf. "crush" in Gen. 3:15; Job 9:17, its only other uses in the OT.) But David could not be concealed from God, for darkness and light are the same to Him because of His omniscience and omnipresence.

C. The omnipotence of the Lord (139:13-18)

The thought that darkness cannot conceal anyone from the Lord (vv. 11-12) brought to David's mind this meditation in verses 13-18: God knew all about him when He created him in his mother's womb. Verse 13 begins with "For," indicating that this strophe (vv. 13-18) explains the preceding two strophes (vv. 1-6, 7-12): since God can create a person, He certainly knows him intimately and is with him everywhere.

139:13-14. The theme of verses 13-18 is announced here: the Lord (You is emphatic in Heb.; cf. v. 2) created him in his mother's womb. The language is figurative in that creating and knitting describe God's sovereign superintendence over the natural process of reproduction (on knitting; cf. Job. 10:11).

This fact prompted the psalmist to break forth in praise over the thought of how marvelously he had been made. Even David's rudimentary knowledge of the marvels of the human body led him to be in awe and wonder. The words wonderfully and wonderful are mindful of God's marvelous knowledge (Ps. 139:6).

139:15-16. Then David stressed certain features of God's superintendence

over him. In the womb he was woven together (lit., "embroidered"; cf. "knit," v. 13, suggesting his veins and arteries). When he was being formed in the womb he was as remote to the human eye as the lower part of the earth (cf. comments on Job 1:21). But God saw every detail. David's frame means his skeleton and his unformed body is his embryo. Moreover, God prerecorded all the days of the psalmist before he was even born. This statement may mean that God determined how long he would live, but in view of verses 1-4, it more likely refers to everyday details. God marvelously planned out his life.

139:17-18. This thought led David to conclude that the Lord's plans (thoughts; cf. v. 2) for His people are most precious and in fact are innumerable. They are also most relevant, for each morning when he awakened, God was still with him, extending His thoughts toward him.

D. The loyalty of David (139:19-24)

The psalmist's attention then turned to the trouble he was in. So he asserted his loyalty to the Lord and took comfort from his knowledge of the Lord's presence.

139:19-22. The psalmist petitioned God to slay the wicked men who were trying to kill him. These enemies apparently were taking the name of the LORD in vain (cf. Ex. 20:7), using it for an evil purpose. Because they were God's enemies, David affirmed that they were his enemies too and that he would have nothing to do with them. To hate them meant to reject them (cf. comments on Mal. 1:3), to disavow any association with them.

139:23-24. David concluded this psalm with a prayer for God to search and test him (cf. 26:2) in order to prove his loyalty, thus showing that he was not like the wicked mentioned in 139:19-22. The verb "to search," is also used in verse 1 in a statement about God. David asked God to test him as a refiner tests metal. Since God knows everything (cf. vv. 1-6) He would also know David's anxious thoughts (the same Heb. word is rendered "anxiety" in 94:19). God would also know if the psalmist had any offensive way (lit., "way of pain," i.e., pain caused by being afflicted for wrongdoing). Such an examination David was convinced, would yield evidence of his loyalty. The Lord in His leading would then preserve his life (**everlasting,** *'ôlām,* probably means prolonged life) here as he followed the Lord.

All believers who come to understand the attributes of God discussed in this psalm find them a great source of comfort, and a great prompting to obey Him.

Psalm 140

The psalmist uttered harsh imprecations on the wicked who sought to poison and ensnare him with their vicious devices. He spoke these imprecations in full confidence that the Lord would secure justice for the afflicted against their attacks. This is the substance of his opening prayer.

A. Petition (140:1-8)

140:1-5. David called on **the LORD** to deliver him from the wicked who planned to destroy him. Verses 1-2 include his introductory cry and verses 3-5 give his lament. He wanted God to **rescue** and **protect** (cf. v. 4) him **from men of violence** (cf. vv. 4, 11), from people who think up and carry out **evil plans** (cf. v. 8) **every day.** The imagery in the lament shows that these foes were vicious. Their speech was **sharp** and destructive, like **a serpent's** venom (v. 3). **The wicked** planned **to trip** him in his actions, so he needed God's help (v. 4). Like hunters laying snares, they had **set traps for** him (v. 5; cf. 141:9-10; 142:3). His enemies, besides being dangerous and deadly (140:3), were deliberately trying to kill him (vv. 4-5).

140:6-8. David reiterated his opening **cry for** help, praying that **the wicked** would not have their way in carrying out **their** evil **plans** (cf. v. 2) and being **proud** of their success. In his prayer the psalmist described the LORD as his strong **Deliverer who shields** his **head in . . . battle.** This military figure stresses divine protection from the wicked.

B. Imprecations (140:9-11)

140:9-11. David voiced several harsh imprecations on the wicked, which were designed to match their wickedness. He hoped that their nasty words (cf. v. 3) would bring them **trouble.** He also

hoped that **burning coals** would **fall** on **them** (cf. 11:6) reminiscent of God's judgment on Sodom and Gomorrah (cf. Gen. 19:24). And he hoped that **disaster** would overtake the **slanderers** (cf. their "poison," Ps. 140:3). Again he called his enemies **men of violence** (cf. vv. 1, 4).

C. Confidence (140:12-13)

140:12-13. David was convinced **that the** LORD would maintain his **cause** as one who was **poor** and **needy** (cf. 40:17; 70:5; 86:1; 109:22) and that **praise** would be given by **the righteous** to the Lord, who champions their cause. They would dwell in His presence in peace (cf. 102:28).

Psalm 141

The superscriptions to Psalms 141–145 attribute them to David. Psalm 141 is an evening prayer for sanctification and protection. David asked that he not speak against the Lord, or fall into alluring temptations of the wicked, but that he would be kept from the devices of the wicked who would hear his song of testimony.

A. The evening prayer (141:1-2)

141:1-2. David, comparing his prayer to the evening oblation at the sanctuary, called 'on the LORD to answer him **quickly** (cf. comments on 31:2). He wanted his **prayer** to be a sweet aroma to the Lord, similar to the **incense** in **the evening sacrifice** (around 3 P.M.) which would ascend and please the Lord. In the Book of Revelation incense appropriately pictured prayer (Rev. 5:8; 8:3-4). **Lifting up** his **hands** as a gesture in prayer is also mentioned in Psalms 28:2; 63:4; 134:2.

B. The prayer for sanctification (141:3-7)

141:3-4. The substance of David's evening prayer was that the LORD would direct his words and his actions aright. He wanted God to **set a guard** at his **lips** to prevent wrong speech. Moreover, he desired that God preserve his **heart** (i.e., his willful desires) from **wicked** allurements. **Their delicacies** refers to sensual luxuries procured by wicked activities (cf. Prov. 4:17).

141:5-7. David would not resist the rebukes of the **righteous**—they in fact were like anointing **oil,** helpful and refreshing (cf. Prov. 9:8b; 15:31; 17:10; 19:25; 25:12). But his **prayer** was **against . . . the wicked**; he anticipated they would be utterly destroyed after they learned that his **words** were correct.

C. The prayer for protection (141:8-10)

141:8-10. Along with David's prayer to be preserved from the allurements of the wicked (vv. 3-7) is his request for protection. He asserted his confidence in the LORD His **Refuge** (cf. comments on 2:12) and asked that he **not** be given **over to death.** This meant, he prayed further, that God should deliver him from **the wicked** by letting their **snares . . . traps,** and **nets** (cf. 140:5; 142:3) catch them.

Psalm 142

This psalm, also attributed to David, was written "when he was in the cave," fleeing from Saul (cf. the superscription to Ps. 57). The psalmist cried to the Lord for help, for God was the only One he could depend on. David was utterly helpless before his enemies and no one seemed to care for his life.

A. Cry to the Lord (142:1-2)

142:1-2. David, possibly addressing others with him, exclaimed that he cried out **to the LORD** (cf. v. 5) **for mercy,** voicing his **complaint** and his **trouble.**

B. Lament (142:3-4)

142:3-4. Addressing the Lord, David stated that God knew his **way** (cf. 139:2-3) **when** his **spirit** weakened (cf. 77:3; 143:4, 7). Apparently under pressure he had lost his fight for his resistance was weakened. The trouble arose from a trap **(snare)** laid for him by an enemy (cf. 140:5; 141:9-10).

He then called on God to **look to** his **right** (where normally someone would be standing to guard him) because he was without **refuge** and support—**no one** cared **for** his **life!** His only hope was the Lord to whom he prayed.

C. Petition (142:5-7)

142:5. When David cried to God (cf. v. 1) he affirmed his confidence in Him: God was his safety (**Refuge;** cf. 141:8) and his life. God was his **Portion,** his allotment, all he had (cf. 16:5; 73:26; 119:57).

142:6-7. In his **desperate** situation (cf. 79:8), likened to a **prison,** he petitioned the Lord to **rescue** him **from** his **strong** enemies (cf. 18:17) so he could then **praise** God's **name** (His revealed attributes) for what He had done. Also **the righteous** could then joyfully **gather about** him (lit., "crown themselves," i.e., rejoice in triumph) **because of** the Lord's **goodness** (cf. 13:6; 116:12) in answering his prayer.

Psalm 143

In this psalm the thought of David's spirit fainting (vv. 4, 7) is developed from the previous psalm (142:3). Psalm 143 is a prayer for deliverance and guidance. When the psalmist prayed for merciful relief from the wicked who oppressed him, he acknowledged that no living man is righteous. He desired deliverance and guidance and found encouragement from remembering God's ways.

A. Complaint (143:1-6)

143:1-4. David called on the LORD for **mercy** and **relief,** based on God's **faithfulness and righteousness** (cf. v. 11). In contrast **no human is righteous** (cf. Ecc. 7:20). David was acknowledging that his sufferings were partly punishment for sins, for he desired that God **not** judge him.

His complaint is expressed in Psalm 143:3-4 specifically. **The enemy** had attacked David and driven him out, so that he was in **darkness** (cf. 88:6, i.e., in gloom emotionally) and might as well have been **dead.** His **spirit** grew weak (cf. 142:3; 143:7) from this oppression.

143:5-6. Yet David mustered confidence when he remembered the former **days.** His faith was rekindled and his spirit strengthened when he recalled the mighty **works** of the Lord in the past. So he prayed eagerly for the Lord to meet the needs of his hungry, thirsty (cf. 42:2) heart. The image of **parched land** portrays his soul's great spiritual need at that moment, that God would come to his rescue.

B. Petition (143:7-12)

143:7. His confidence (v. 5) led to his petition for deliverance; he prayed for quick (cf. comments on 31:2) deliverance lest he in his weak **spirit** (cf. 142:3; 143:4) **go down to the pit** (a synonym for grave). Asking God **not** to **hide** His **face** (cf. 27:9; 102:2) meant he did not want God to overlook him.

143:8-12. The prayer in verse 7 is detailed in verses 8-12. First, he desired that the loyal **love** (*ḥeseḏ;* cf. v. 11) of the LORD lead him in **the way** he **should go** (v. 8). Second, he wanted to be rescued **from** his **enemies** (v. 9; cf. 140:1; 142:6). Third, he wanted to be taught by the **Spirit** of **God** (143:10). And fourth, David wanted to be preserved alive by God's **righteousness** (cf. v. 1) and **love** (cf. v. 8) from his **enemies** (vv. 11-12). Each of these prayers was based solidly on his trust in the LORD. As God's **servant,** David trusted in Him. Even though he had sinned and was now in trouble, he was confident God would guide him to safety.

Psalm 144

After blessing God for glorious deliverances in past battles, and marvelling that God took note of perishing people, King David prayed for divine intervention in combat. He expressed confidence that because the Lord gives victory the nation would experience peace and prosperity.

A. Blessing for past victories (144:1-2)

144:1-2. David praised **the LORD** for having subdued people under him. In this **praise** he used several expressions to portray the fact that the Lord enabled him to win victories. The Lord had taught him how to fight, and God was his **Rock** (cf. 18:46; also note 18:2), his **Fortress** (*mᵉṣûḏâh;* cf. 18:3; 31:3; 71:3; 91:2), his **Stronghold** (*miśgōḇ;* cf. comments on 9:9), his **Deliverer** (cf. 18:2; 40:17; 70:5; 140:7), and his **Shield** (cf. comments on 3:3). These all stress the protection and deliverance given David while God was solidifying the empire under him.

B. Prayer for divine intervention (144:3-11)

144:3-4. Having praised the nature of God, David then voiced his petition for victory in battle (vv. 3-11). The thought that God would subdue anyone under him caused him to marvel at the possibility of God's intervention on man's behalf (cf. comments on 8:4). Since **man is like a vapor** (*heḇel;* cf. 39:5, 11; 62:9; and comments on Ecc. 1:2) that vanishes away

and a **shadow** that is soon gone (cf. Job 8:9; Ps. 102:11) why would God stoop to help him?

144:5-8. But since God did care for him, he prayed for divine intervention in the war. He desired that the LORD would descend in glorious power. Even God's touching **the mountains** would cause them to **smoke** (cf. 104:32) from the fires of burning trees. David asked the Lord to use **lightning** (His **arrows;** cf. 18:14) to **scatter the enemies.** By this gracious intervention he hoped to be delivered from his enemies who were as strong as **mighty waters** and who were **deceitful** (cf. 144:11).

144:9-11. David immediately broke out in a declaration of his confidence. He vowed to praise the Lord with **a new song** (cf. 33:3; 40:3; 96:1; 98:1; 149:1) for delivering **him from the deadly sword.** Then he repeated his prayer for deliverance from his enemies, whom he described in words nearly identical to those in 144:7b-8.

C. Prospect of peace and prosperity (144:12-15)

144:12-14. Because the Lord would rescue His servant the king, the land would enjoy great benefits. First, the subjects of the king would greatly prosper, **like** growing **plants** and exquisitely **carved** palace **pillars** (v. 12). Second, the nation would prosper economically—with **barns** full of crops and with numerous **sheep** and **oxen** (v. 13). Third, the people would be blessed with peace (v. 14).

144:15. So David concluded that any **people whose God is the LORD** will be **blessed.** This royal psalm shows that divine intervention in a holy war on behalf of the Lord's anointed brings peace and prosperity.

Psalm 145

This psalm of David is titled "A psalm of praise"—the only one in the Psalter with that title. Here begins the grand doxology of the entire collection, for praise plays a greater part of Psalms 145–150 than in most of the others. The word "praise" occurs 46 times in these six psalms.

In Psalm 145 David praised the Lord for His mighty acts which are told from one generation to another, for His gracious provision of an everlasting kingdom, and for the manner in which He responds to those who love Him.

A. Praise for God's mighty acts (145:1-7)

145:1-3. David vowed to **praise** the Lord His **King** (cf. 149:2) and His **name** (His revealed attributes) **every day** because He is **great.** The greatness of **the Lord** is unfathomable; **no one** has plumbed its depths.

145:4-7. David told how great God's **acts** have been, which will be declared from **generation** to generation. Believers tell of the **splendor** (cf. v. 12 and comments on 29:2) **of His majesty . . . speak of** His **works . . . meditate on** them, **sing of** them, and **celebrate** them and His **goodness.**

B. Praise for God's everlasting kingdom (145:8-16)

145:8-10. David then wrote of the marvelous nature of God, affirming that He **is gracious and compassionate** (cf. 111:4), **slow to anger, and** full of loyal **love** (the identical statement, in Heb., is given in Ex. 34:6; Neh. 9:17; Pss. 86:15; 103:8; Joel 2:13; Jonah 4:2). Because God **is good** and compassionate **to all,** all His works and His **saints** praise Him.

145:11-13a. The saints' praise (v. 10) would include their gratitude for His **kingdom.** From generation to generation people **will tell of** God's **kingdom . . . might . . . mighty acts,** and how His **kingdom . . . endures through all generations** (cf. Dan. 4:3, 34).

145:13b-16. David then instructed the congregation on the Lord's grace and mercy to man. He **is faithful to all His promises,** He uplifts **those who fall,** He provides **food** for all (cf. 111:5; 132:15; 136:25; 146:7), and He satisfies their **desires** (cf. 145:19). These are the characteristics of the One whose dominion is everlasting (v. 13), which is why He is called faithful.

C. Praise for God's acts of deliverance (145:17-21)

145:17-21. David extolled **the Lord** for being **righteous** and **loving.** (On **all He has made;** cf. vv. 9-10, 13.) Therefore God answers the prayers of the needy—**those who fear** Him and **love** Him—when they **call** to Him. Therefore all

should **praise His . . . name** (v. 21; cf. v. 1). Once again God's greatness and grace are reasons for praise.

Psalm 146

Praise for the greatness and the grace of God is the subject of this psalm as well as of Psalm 145 and others. Here the psalmist vowed to praise God all his life because the One who made the heavens and the earth is faithful and just to the oppressed of the earth.

A. Lifelong praise (146:1-4)

146:1-2. After the initial **Praise the Lord** (haleּlû-yāh; cf. v. 10 and comments on 104:35), whichs begins and ends each of Psalms 146–150, the psalmist vowed to **praise the Lord all** his **life.**

146:3-4. The psalmist instructed the congregation to **put** their **trust** in the One who is infinitely more powerful than **mortal** man, **who cannot save.** A person's **plans** die with him. At death the **spirit** of man **departs** and the body returns to dust (cf. 104:29; Ecc. 3:20). So one who trusts in man will have no reason for praising.

B. Praise for the Creator (146:5-6)

146:5-6. In contrast with the warning not to trust in man (v. 3) the psalmist **blessed** anyone who trusts in the sovereign **Lord . . . God,** his **help** (cf. comments on 30:10) and **hope.** This One, he explained, is **the Maker of heaven and earth** (cf. comments on 115:15); because He is **the Lord** of Creation He **remains faithful.**

C. Praise for the gracious Lord (146:7-10)

146:7-9. The idea of God's faithfulness (v. 6) suggested to the psalmist many ways in which the Lord is gracious and righteous to people. He helps **the oppressed . . . gives food to the hungry** (cf. 111:5; 132:15; 136:25; 145:15), releases **prisoners . . . gives sight to . . . blind** people, raises **up** the defeated, **loves the righteous,** protects the sojourner, and leads the orphan and **widow** to security. **But,** because He is just, He also leads **the** wicked away into frustration.

146:10. The psalmist concluded that **the Lord reigns** (cf. 9:7; 47:8; 93:1; 96:10; 97:1; 99:1) **forever.** As the eternal Ruler, He is sovereign (146:6), gracious (vv. 7-

9b), and just (v. 9c). So He merits the closing **Praise the LORD** (*hal⁰lû-yāh*; cf. v. 1).

Psalm 147

The psalmist praised the Lord God for His greatness in sustaining all Creation, and for His grace in healing afflicted believers and giving them His Word. He called the congregation to join him in praise for they too received His many benefits. God is to be praised for His grace (vv. 2-3, 6, 10-14, 19-20) and His greatness (vv. 4-5, 8-9, 15-18).

A. God heals the brokenhearted (147:1-6)

This psalm has three rounds of praise (vv. 1-6, 7-11, 12-20).

147:1. After exclaiming *hal⁰lû-yāh* (**Praise the LORD;** cf. v. 20 and comments on 104:35) the psalmist stated **how good it is to . . . praise** the One who is most praiseworthy. It is **pleasant** (cf. 135:3) **and fitting** (cf. 33:1).

147:2-3. In His grace **the LORD** built **up Jerusalem** again after the Exile. This rebuilding shows that He is the God who **heals the brokenhearted.** Those who repent and turn to Him are healed and restored.

147:4-6. God's greatness is seen in His sustaining power in the universe He created (cf. vv. 8-9, 15-18). He knows **each** of the myriads of **stars** (cf. Isa. 40:26). Yet the One who has so much **power** and **understanding** (cf. Isa. 40:28) **sustains the humble** in the face of opposition. This too displays His grace.

B. God delights in those who fear Him (147:7-11)

147:7-9. In a second cycle of praise, the psalmist told everyone to praise God musically. He should be praised because of His greatness in Creation (cf. vv. 4-5, 15-18). With **rain** and **food** He sustains plant and animal life (on **ravens,** see comments on Job 38:41).

147:10-11. God should be praised because even though He is so great, He **delights** not in the mighty but in anyone who trusts **Him.** This is more evidence of His grace (cf. vv. 3, 6, 12-14, 19-20).

C. God gave His Word (147:12-20)

147:12-14. In a third round of praise (vv. 12-20) the psalmist called on **Jerusa-** lem to **praise** the One who gave them security, **peace,** and **the finest of wheat,** all further evidences of His grace.

147:15-20. In His greatness **His word** operates in **the earth** (v. 15) and by **His word** He controls nature, including sending **snow . . . frost. . . . hail. . . . icy** winds, and **breezes** (vv. 16-18). The greatest display of grace from this great and powerful God **to Israel,** however, was that He gave **His Word,** His revelation, to her and to **no other nation.**

So the writer summoned praise for the gracious and great Lord of Creation who heals and reveals. The psalm closes with *hal⁰lû-yāh* (**Praise the LORD;** cf. v. 1).

Psalm 148

The psalmist called all of heaven and its hosts to praise the Lord because He has established them by decree. And he called the earth to praise His glorious name because He had exalted Israel.

A. Praise for the Creator (148:1-6)

148:1-4. After he exclaimed **Praise the LORD** (*hal⁰lû-yāh*; cf. v. 14 and comments on 104:35; 146:1) the psalmist summoned all creation above the earth to **praise the LORD. The heavens**—the sun **. . . moon . . . stars,** and elements of nature in the heavens (**waters above the skies**)—were all personified as capable of worshiping the Lord. The **angels** in the heavens were also called on to praise Him (cf. 103:20).

148:5-6. All Creation should **praise . . . the LORD** because He **created** it all by His command and has established it all by His **decree.** His word is powerful and is sure and abiding.

B. Praise for Israel's God (148:7-14)

148:7-12. The psalmist summoned all earthly hosts to **praise the LORD. Sea creatures,** elements of nature (cf. 147:15-17) **mountains . . . hills . . . trees,** animal life, **rulers,** and peoples of various ages should praise the Lord.

148:13-14. One reason they should **praise** is that **His name** is glorious. As Creator, **His** own **splendor** (cf. comments on 29:2) is greater than that of all His Creation. Also He had **raised up . . . a horn** (a strong one, i.e., a king; cf. 89:17; 132:17) for His beloved **Israel.**

So again the psalmist summoned the people's **praise** (*hal⁰lû-yāh*; cf. v. 1) for

God's word and His work in Israel.

Psalm 149

The psalmist invited Israel to sing praises to the Lord who gives salvation to the meek and enabled His people to execute vengeance on the nations.

A. Call to praise (149:1-3)

149:1-3. After exclaiming **Praise the LORD** (*hal⁹lû-yāh*; cf. v. 9 and comments on 104:35; 146:1), the psalmist called Israel to praise **the LORD** by singing **a new song** (cf. 33:3; 40:3; 96:1; 98:1; 144:9; 149:1) **in the assembly.** Rejoicing in Him, **their Maker** (cf. 95:6) and **King** (cf. 145:1), they should **praise** Him with song, **dancing** (cf. 150:4), and musical instruments. Their whole beings should enter into the praise.

B. Cause for praise (149:4-5)

149:4-5. The Lord's **people** should praise Him because He **takes** pleasure in them and gives them **salvation.** For this they should **rejoice** and **sing** even when resting.

C. Conclusion (149:6-9)

149:6-9. The psalmist then called on Israel to take **the praise of God . . . in their mouths** and a **sword in their hands** to execute God's justice on the wicked. Israel was being encouraged to put down evil antagonism against the Lord and His anointed. Then **praise** was again summoned to **the LORD** (*hal⁹lû-yāh*; cf. v. 1).

Psalm 150

Because of God's mighty excellence in His works, the psalmist called for praise to be rendered in the sanctuary with all kinds of musical instruments.

A. Call for praise (150:1)

150:1. After again exclaiming *hal⁹lû-yāh* (**Praise the LORD**; cf. v. 6 and comments on 104:35; 146:1), the psalmist called for **praise** to be given in the **sanctuary** (lit., "holy place," probably referring here to heaven, God's dwelling place; cf. 11:4, 102:19) and in God's **heavens.**

B. Cause for praise (150:2)

150:2. This **praise** (v. 1) is called for because of His mighty excellence in the things He does.

C. Renewed call for praise (150:3-5)

150:3-5. Praise is to be given with musical instruments (including trumpets, harps, lyres, tambourines, stringed instruments, flutes, and **cymbals**), and with **dancing** (cf. 149:3).

D. Concluding call for praise (150:6)

150:6. Appropriately the last verse of the Psalter includes a call for every living thing **that has breath** to **praise the LORD.** Then the Book of Psalms closes with a final *hal⁹lû-yāh* (**Praise the LORD**; cf. v. 1).

BIBLIOGRAPHY

Introductory Works

Anderson, Bernhard W. *Out of the Depths: The Psalms Speak for Us Today.* Philadelphia: Westminster Press, 1974.

Bullinger, E.W. *Figures of Speech Used in the Bible.* 1898. Reprint. Grand Rapids: Baker Book House, 1968.

Drijvers, Pius. *The Psalms: Their Structure and Meaning.* New York: Herder and Herder, 1965.

Gunkel, Hermann. *The Psalms: A Form-Critical Introduction.* Translated by Thomas M. Horner. Philadelphia: Fortress Press, 1967.

Keel, Othmar. *The Symbolism of the Biblical World: Ancient Near Eastern Iconography and the Book of Psalms.* Translated by Timothy J. Hallett. New York: Seabury Press, 1978.

Mowinckel, Sigmund. *The Psalms in Israel's Worship.* Translated by D.R. Ap-Thomas. Nashville: Abingdon Press, 1962.

Sabourin, Leopold. *The Psalms: Their Origin and Meaning.* New York: Alba House, 1974.

Westermann, Claus. *The Praise of God in the Psalms.* Translated by Keith R. Crim. Richmond, Va.: John Knox Press, 1965.

_____. *The Psalms: Structure, Content & Message.* Translated by Ralph D. Gehrke. Minneapolis: Augsburg Publishing House, 1980.

Commentaries

Allen, Leslie C. *Psalms 101–150.* Word Biblical Commentary. Vol. 21. Waco, Tex.: Word Books, 1983.

Anderson, A.A. *The Book of Psalms.* 2 vols. New Century Bible. Grand Rapids: Wm. B. Eerdmans Publishing Co., 1981.

Barnes, Albert. *Psalms.* 3 vols. In *Notes on the Old Testament, Explanatory and Practical.* Vols. 19-21. 1868. Reprint. Grand Rapids: Baker Book House, 1950.

Cohen, A. *The Psalms.* London: Soncino Press, 1945.

Craigie, Peter C. *Psalms 1–50.* Word Biblical Commentary. Vol. 19. Waco, Tex.: Word Books, 1983.

Delitzsch, Franz. "Psalms." In *Commentary on the Old Testament in Ten Volumes.* Vol. 5. Reprint (25 vols. in 10). Grand Rapids: Wm. B. Eerdmans Publishing Co., 1982.

Goldingay, John. *Songs from a Strange Land: Psalms 42–51.* Downers Grove, Ill.: InterVarsity Press, 1978.

Kidner, Derek. *Psalms 1–72.* London: InterVarsity Press, 1973.

_____. *Psalms 73–150.* London: InterVarsity Press, 1975.

Kirkpatrick, A.F. *The Book of Psalms.* Cambridge: University Press, 1902. Reprint. Grand Rapids: Baker Book House, 1982.

Perowne, J.J. Stewart. *The Book of Psalms.* 2 vols. 4th ed. London: George Bell and Sons, 1878. Reprint (2 vols. in 1). Grand Rapids: Zondervan Publishing House, 1976.

Rogerson, J.W., and McKay, J.W. *Psalms 1–50.* New York: Cambridge University Press, 1977.

_____. *Psalms 51–100.* New York: Cambridge University Press, 1977.

_____. *Psalms 101–150.* New York: Cambridge University Press, 1977.

Weiser, Artur. *The Psalms: A Commentary.* Philadelphia: Westminster Press, 1962.

Wiersbe, Warren W. *Meet Yourself in the Psalms.* Wheaton, Ill.: SP Publications, Victor Books, 1983.

PROVERBS

Sid S. Buzzell

INTRODUCTION

The Book of Proverbs is a book of moral and ethical instructions, dealing with many aspects of life. The teachings in this book guide its readers in how to lead wise, godly lives and how to avoid the pitfalls of unwise, ungodly conduct.

It has a broad, timeless appeal because of its great variety of subjects and their relevance to everyday life. Proper and improper attitudes, conduct, and characteristics are referred to repeatedly and in succinct, penetrating ways. Proverbs is God's book on "how to wise up and live." It is His treasure book of wisdom.

If the Israelites would follow God's decrees and laws, they would be considered a people of wisdom and understanding (Deut. 4:5-6). This is true for all believers because "the statutes of the LORD" make "wise the simple" (Ps. 19:7). The Book of Proverbs showed the Israelites how their faith in the Lord and His Word should affect their daily lives. And it shows how believers in all ages can be wise in God's and others' eyes.

The Book of Proverbs rounds out the Old Testament by adding an important emphasis. The Israelites were to keep the Law and to hear and obey the Prophets, but the people were also to apply the truths of the Law and the Prophets to every aspect of living. Even if an Israelite broke no commandments in the Mosaic Law and offended no prophet he still might not be leading a full life. Proverbs warns against the illegal and the immoral, but it also focuses on leading an aggressively dynamic life.

Authorship and Date. The authorship and date of Proverbs cannot be considered apart from understanding the book's structure. The book is comprised of eight sections (see the *Outline*) written at various times and including several authors or editors. The heading "The Proverbs of Solomon" in 1:1 introduces chapters 1–9 (sections I and II). Since Solomon reigned from 971 to 931, the Proverbs he wrote may be dated in the 10th century. According to 10:1, Section III (10:1–22:16) is also the work of Solomon.

Section IV (22:17–24:34) is called the "sayings of the wise" (22:17; 24:23). The identity of these wise men is uncertain so the date of their sayings is also uncertain. Perhaps they lived before Solomon's time and he compiled their sayings, adding them to his repertoire. Or they may have lived in Solomon's day and their sayings were added by an anonymous editor.

The proverbs in Section V (chaps. 25–29) were written by Solomon but were compiled by men of Hezekiah (25:1). Since Hezekiah reigned from 729 to 686 those chapters were recorded sometime in those years.

Sections VI (chap. 30) and VII (31:1-9), were written by Agur and King Lemuel, respectively. Those men were non-Israelites, perhaps Arabians; their identities and origins are obscure.

Section VIII (31:10-31) may be a continuation of the words ascribed to Lemuel (31:1) but its construction as a separate acrostic poem and its stylistic distinction from 31:1-9 mark it off as an independent piece. If it is, its authorship is not known.

The book took its final form at least as late as Hezekiah's time (because of 25:1). Whether his men compiled the entire book is uncertain. The final date of compilation is generally considered to be around 700 B.C., assuming Agur and Lemuel wrote before then. Of course the writing and compiling were done under the superintending work of the Holy Spirit, the divine Author of all Scripture (2 Tim. 3:16).

It is appropriate that Solomon authored most of the book since he, the wisest person in his day (1 Kings 4:29-31,

34), authored 3,000 proverbs (1 Kings 4:32; cf. Ecc. 12:9). The Holy Spirit guided him to select only several hundred of them for inclusion in the Scriptures.

Presumably Solomon wrote Song of Songs in his early adult years, Proverbs in his middle years, and Ecclesiastes near the end of his life as he reflected on his experiences.

Purpose. The fivefold purpose of Proverbs is given in the introduction to the book (Prov. 1:2-4, 6): (a) "for attaining wisdom and discipline," (b) "for understanding words of insight," (c) "for acquiring a disciplined and prudent life," (d) "for giving prudence to the simple," (e) "for understanding proverbs and parables, the sayings and riddles of the wise." These purposes focus on helping readers live wisely and skillfully.

Proverbs were employed by parents and teachers to impart wisdom in a manner that made learning an adventure, a challenge. The purpose in using a proverb was to help the young acquire mental skills that promote wise living. Both the content and the structure of the sayings contributed to the hearers' development. The process was a challenge and the product a reward.

Of the several words for wisdom and related synonyms used in Proverbs, the primary and most frequent one is *ḥokmâh*. It occurs 45 times in Proverbs. In the Old Testament *ḥokmâh* is used of the skill of craftsmen, sailors, singers, mourners, administrators, and counselors. These workers and others, being knowledgeable, experienced, and efficient in their areas of expertise, were considered skillful; they were therefore "wise." Similarly in the spiritual realm a person who possesses *ḥokmâh* in reference to God is one who is both knowledgeable and experienced in following God's way. So in the Bible's Wisdom literature being wise means being skilled in godly living. Having God's wisdom means having the ability to cope with life in a God-honoring way. Crawford H. Toy wrote that "wisdom is the . . . knowledge of right living in the highest sense" (*A Critical and Exegetical Commentary on the Book of Proverbs*, p. 5).

Many ancient cultures in the Near East had wisdom writings (see the section "Relationship of Proverbs to Other Ancient Wisdom Literature"). Though the Book of Proverbs is somewhat similar to that literature, the wisdom promoted in Proverbs contains an element not found in those works. Wisdom in Proverbs includes practical sagacity, mental acumen, and functional skill, but it also includes moral, upright living which stems from a right relationship to the Lord. The statement "The fear of the LORD is the beginning of wisdom" (9:10) makes the Hebrew concept of wisdom unique. (Cf. 14:16, "A wise man fears the LORD." Also note 1:7; 15:33; Job 28:28; Ps. 111:10.) To be wise in the biblical sense one must begin with a proper relationship to God. To fear the Lord means to respect Him for who He is and to respond to Him in trust, worship, obedience, and service. If God is not honored and His Word not followed, then wisdom, as the Hebrew sages defined it, can never be attained.

The purpose of the Book of Proverbs then, is to develop in others, especially the young, a wise, skillful approach to living, which begins with being properly related to the Lord.

Addressees. The frequent occurrence of the address "my son" and "my sons" in this book has raised some question about the relationship between Solomon and his "audience." The words "my son" were written by Solomon 15 times in chapters 1–7 and twice elsewhere (19:27; 27:11). They are used 5 times in the sayings of the wise men (23:15, 19; 23:26; 24:13, 21) and once by Lemuel's mother (31:2). "My sons" occurs 4 times (4:1; 5:7; 7:24; 8:32), all by Solomon. Originally these verses with "my son(s)" were addressed orally either to students of Solomon and to students of others in the royal court, or by Solomon and others to their sons in their homes. Favoring the school environment is the fact that learners were sometimes called "sons" of their teachers. Favoring the home environment is the fact that instruction was given by mothers (1:8; 6:20; also note 23:19, 22-26) as well as by fathers. Also Lemuel's mother taught her son an oracle (31:1-2). In its written form the Book of Proverbs is useful for parents in instructing their sons and daughters, as well as helpful, obviously, for personal Bible study. The fact that the book is a collection of sayings suggests that the proverbs were brought together from various situations with various intended audiences in mind. At any rate the book was—and is—an excellent primer for the young (and adults too, for that matter) on wise, godly living.

Literary Style

1. *Meaning of the word "proverb."* "Proverb" translates *māšāl*, which probably comes from a verb meaning "to be like, to be compared with." A proverb, then, is a statement that makes a comparison or summarizes a common experience (i.e., the sentence is "like" or is compared to reality). Each of the pithy sayings in much of the Book of Proverbs is a *māšāl* (cf. 1:1; 10:1; 25:1), but brief proverbial sayings are also found elsewhere in the Old Testament (e.g., Gen. 10:9; 1 Sam. 10:12; 24:13; 1 Kings 20:11; Jer. 31:29; Ezek. 12:22; 16:44; 18:2).

Māšāl also means a "byword" (e.g., Deut. 28:37, "an object of scorn"; 1 Kings 9:7; 2 Chron. 7:20; Jer. 24:9; Ezek. 14:8). The sense seems to be that the person or nation called a byword becomes an object lesson for others. *Māšāl* may also be used of a prophetic oracle (Num. 23:7, 18; 24:3, 15, 20-21, 23) or a taunt (Isa. 14:4) of several verses in length. Perhaps the idea here is that the statements point to what the speaker wished the people were like. Job's "discourse" (Job 29–31) is a *māšāl* in the sense that it summarizes what his experience was like. "Parable" is another way of rendering *māšāl* (Ezek. 20:49); here it suggests that the parabolic story resembles some life incident. This is similar to the translation *māšāl* as "allegory" (Ezek. 17:2). Proverbs are also associated with riddles (Ps. 49:4; Prov. 1:6).

The Book of Proverbs includes a few longer discourses (e.g., 6:12-14, 16-19; 7:6-23; 30:11-14, 18-19, 21-23; 31:4-5) along with its single-verse maxims.

2. *Parallelism.* Proverbs is written entirely in poetic style. The predominant structural feature of Hebrew poetry is so-called poetic parallelism. Usually the two poetic lines in a verse have a parallel relationship.

In *synonymous parallelism* the terms or units of thought in one line are paralleled by similar terms or units of thought in the second line. Sometimes every unit in one line is matched in the next line (e.g., 1:2; 2:11). This is called complete synonymous parallelism. Other times only some of the units in one line are matched in the next line (e.g., in 1:9 the words "They will be" are not matched in the second line). This is called incomplete synonymous parallelism.

In *antithetical parallelism* one line is the opposite of or contrasts with the other line (e.g., 10:1; 11:1). Most of the verses in chapters 10–15 are antithetical.

In *emblematic parallelism* one line illumines the other by a simile or a metaphor (e.g., 10:26; 25:12, 23).

In *synthetic parallelism* the second line simply continues the thought of the first line. Sometimes the second line gives a result of the first line (3:6; 16:3) and other times the second line describes something in the first line (6:12; 15:3). Sometimes one line gives a preference over what is referred to in the other line. There are 19 such "better . . . than" verses (12:9; 15:16-17; 16:8, 16, 19, 32; 17:1, 12; 19:1, 22; 21:9, 19; 22:1; 25:7, 24; 27:5, 10; 28:6). "How much worse" or "how much more" is another kind of synthetic parallelism (11:31; 15:11; 17:7; 19:7, 10; 21:27). Most of the verses in 16:1–22:16 have either synonymous or synthetic parallelism.

Not all verses in Proverbs have two lines. Some have three (e.g., 1:27; 6:13, 17; 27:22; 30:20, 32-33; 31:4), a few have four (e.g., 30:9, 14-15, 17, 19), and one verse has even six lines (30:4). In the three-line verses, usually the first and second lines are related in some way and the second and third lines are parallel in some way (e.g., in 27:27 the second line is in synthetic parallelism to the first line, completing its thought, and the third line is in synonymous parallelism with the second line). However, the three lines in 1:27 are all in synonymous parallelism. The book *Walking in Wisdom: Studying the Proverbs of Solomon*, by William E. Mouser, Jr., is a helpful discussion of how to analyze the points being made in various kinds of parallelism in the Book of Proverbs.

Usually, though not always, the second line in a two-line parallelism does more than merely repeat the words or thought of the first line. The second line may expand the first, or complete it, define it, emphasize it, be more significant than it, enlarge on it, be the opposite of it, an alternative to it, or a counterpart of it. This pattern in which the second line is underscored is what James L. Kugel calls "A, and what's more, B" (*The Idea of Biblical Poetry: Parallelism and Its History*. New Haven, Conn.: Yale University Press, 1981, pp. 7-27, esp. p. 13).

As brief maxims, the verses in Proverbs are distilled, to-the-point sentences about life. They boil down, crystallize, and condense the experiences and observations of the writers. The brief but concentrated nature of the maxims cause their readers to reflect on their meanings. They tell what life is like and how life should be lived. In a terse, no-words-wasted fashion, some statements in Proverbs *relate* what is commonly observed in life; others *recommend* or exhort how life should be lived. And when advice is given, a reason for the counsel usually follows.

Many of the proverbial maxims should be recognized as guidelines, not absolute observations; they are not ironclad promises. What is stated is generally and usually true, but exceptions are occasionally noted (e.g., cf. Prov. 10:27 with Ps. 73:12).

Subject Matter. The Book of Proverbs focuses on human character and conduct. The book's observations and admonitions about life are addressed to individuals, not to the nation Israel as such. As already stated under "Purpose," the Book of Proverbs stresses wise living. This is synonymous with godly living, for one who is godly or righteous is wise in God's eyes. By contrast a wicked or unrighteous person is foolish. The characteristics and consequences of these two paths of living are referred to repeatedly in Proverbs. They are summarized in Psalm 1:6: "For the LORD watches over the way of the righteous, but the way of the wicked will perish."

Many human emotions, attitudes, and relationships are spoken of in Proverbs, and often they are set in contrast. Some of these many topics are listed in the chart, "Positive and Negative Topics and Other Subjects in Proverbs." One common method of studying Proverbs is to compile the verses dealing with a topic and to analyze all that is said on that topic. For example, see the chart "Words

and Speaking in Proverbs," near 6:16-17. Various verses in Proverbs deal with rural life and urban life; with business ethics, social contacts, and civil justice; with family relationships, moral standards, and inner attitudes and motives. No wonder the book has such universal appeal!

Little is said in Proverbs about the afterlife. The stress is on life now. Rewards for godly living are said to be given in the present, and ungodly living results in problems in this life (cf. comments on Ecc. 2:24-26; 11:9). Life's choices, as Proverbs stresses, are clear-cut.

The Book of Proverbs also focuses on God: His character (sovereign, faithful, holy, omniscient, omnipotent, just, etc.), His works, and His blessings. The name Yahweh ("LORD") occurs 87 times in Proverbs.

Man's relationship to the Lord is also stressed in the book. A person can lead a godly, wise life only as he fears and trusts the Lord. Proverbs stresses being rightly related to God and then being rightly related to others.

Relationship of Proverbs to Other Ancient Wisdom Literature. Though Solomon's wisdom exceeded that of all others (1 Kings 4:30-31), he was not the only wise man. Egypt had wise men (Gen. 41:8; Ex. 7:11; 1 Kings 4:30; Isa. 19:11-12) and Edom was known for its wisdom (Jer. 49:7; Obad. 8). Babylon too had its wise men (Isa. 47:1, 10; Jer. 50:35; 51:57; Dan. 1:4, 20; 2:13-14; 5:8).

In Egypt's and Babylon's wisdom literature several works are collections of proverbs or include at least some proverbial sayings. Examples from Egypt are *The Instruction of the Vizier Ptah-Hotep* (ca. 2450 B.C.), with advice on how to be a successful state official; *The Instruction of Amen-em-Het* (ca. 2000 B.C.), a father's words to his son about how people he had favored disappointed him; *The Instruction of Amen-em-Ope* (ca. 1300–900 B.C.), a king's teachings to his son about life, using some words similar to those in Proverbs (e.g., "Listen, my son," "path of life," "the way"). The fact that some sayings in *The Instruction of Amen-em-Ope* parallel parts of Proverbs (e.g., Prov. 22:17–24:22) has raised the question of whether Proverbs borrowed from this

Positive and Negative Topics
and Other Subjects in Proverbs

Positive (Righteous/Wise)	Negative (Wicked/Foolish)
Wisdom, wise	Folly, fool
Righteous	Wicked
Life	Death
Knowledge	Ignorance
Work, diligence	Laziness
Orderliness	Disorderliness
Success	Failure
Self-control	Anger
Faithfulness	Unfaithfulness
Obedience	Rebellion
Honesty, integrity	Cheating, deceit
Justice, fairness, equity	Injustice, unfairness, inequity
Truth	Lying, deception
Honor	Dishonor
Commendation	Criticism
Humility	Pride
Purity	Impurity
Encouragement	Slander
Peace	Strife, jealousy
Love	Hatred
Mercy, kindness	Cruelty
Generosity	Greed
Joy	Sadness
Hope	Anxiety
Good company	Bad company
Friendliness	Animosity, enmity
Wealth	Poverty
Virtue	Shame
Soberness	Drunkenness
Friendliness	Unfriendliness
Trust	Worry
Pleasure	Misery
Quietness	Talkativeness
Contentment	Envy
Teachableness	Unteachableness

Other Subjects

Fear of the Lord
Husbands
Wives
Fathers
Mothers
Children
Kings, rulers
Masters
Slaves
Prostitutes
Orphans and the needy
Business dealings
Hypocrisy
Stealing
Rebuke
Gluttony, food

Egyptian writing, or the Egyptian writer borrowed from Proverbs, or whether both wrote independently about common concerns. On this question see the comments on 22:17–24:22.

Samples of Babylonian wisdom literature that include proverbs are *Counsels of Wisdom* (ca. 1500–1000 B.C.), *Akkadian Proverbs* (ca. 1800–1600 B.C.), and *The Words of Aḥiqar* (700–400 B.C.).

The fact that some maxims in the Book of Proverbs are similar to these Egyptian and Mesopotamian writings does not undo the divine inspiration of the Scriptures. God guided the writers of the Book of Proverbs so that their writings, inspired by the Holy Spirit, recorded exactly what God wanted included in the biblical canon. Furthermore, most of these nonbiblical writings are more secular than the Book of Proverbs and sometimes are even rather crass in their moral tone. Proverbs' emphasis on fearing God is obviously missing from these other works. In spite of certain similarities in style and content to other works, the Book of Proverbs stands unique as part of God's written revelation.

OUTLINE

COMMENTARY

I. The Preface (1:1-7)

In these verses the author introduced himself and his literary form (v. 1), gave an extended statement of why the proverbs were recorded (vv. 2-6), and stated a theological reason why his readers should become the kind of people he wanted them to be (v. 7).

A. The author and the literary form (1:1)

1:1. Scholars differ on whether this reference to **the proverbs of Solomon** includes the entire book or just the first section (1:2–9:18). Since various authors and editors are named in other sections, this phrase probably covers chapters 1–9, with the same phrase in 10:1 introducing 10:1–22:16. (See "Authorship and Date" in the *Introduction*.)

The word "proverbs" gives not only the title of the book but also designates the type of literature in the book. On the meaning of *māšāl* ("proverb") see "Literary Style" in the *Introduction*. As discussed there, though *māšāl* usually means a brief, pithy saying, it can also refer to longer discourses. The word "proverb" then refers to various forms of wise, insightful pronouncements.

B. The purpose of the book (1:2-6)

1. SUMMARY STATEMENT (1:2)

1:2. The Proverbs were written to encourage others: (a) to acquire a disciplined skill in right living (**for attaining wisdom and discipline**) and (b) to gain mental acumen (**for understanding words of insight**). The first of these is elaborated in verses 3-5 and the second in verse 6. As stated in the *Introduction* under "Purpose," this word *ḥokmâh* ("wisdom") in the Old Testament often refers to the mental and physical skills of craftsmen, sailors, singers, mourners, administrators, counselors, and others; but other times, as in Proverbs, it focuses on the application of moral and ethical principles that result in skillful, godly living. A person with this wisdom has "expertise" in godly living. Such wise, skillful living is a life of "discipline" (cf. v. 3) and order. Discipline translates *mûsār*, "moral discipline or correction." In Hebrew the word "understanding," also used in verses 5 ("discerning") and 6 ("understanding"), means insight, or the ability to see "between" issues.

2. EXPANDED STATEMENT (1:3-6)

1:3-5. These verses elaborate on the qualities of life that must be acquired for leading a wise life. **A disciplined** (cf. v. 2) **and prudent** (cf. v. 4) **life** is one with high moral standards, a life in which one does what is **right . . . just, and fair** (cf.

2:9). An immoral or unjust person can hardly be called wise in God's sight!

The simple (*peṭî*, 1:4) refers to a person who is naive and untaught. He is not an imbecile, one who cannot comprehend, or a fool who despises wisdom. Instead, he is one whose exposure to life and wisdom has been limited. Because of inexperience he is gullible and easily influenced. Therefore he needs **prudence** (cf. 1:3), that is, cleverness or sensibleness (*'ormâh*, used elsewhere only in 8:5, 12; Ex. 21:14 ["schemes"; NASB, "craftily"]; Josh. 9:4 ["a ruse"; NASB, "craftily"]). The word *peṭî* ("simple") is used 14 times in Proverbs (Prov. 1:4, 22, 32; 7:7; 8:5; 9:4, 6, 16; 14:15, 18; 19:25; 21:11; 22:3; 27:12). On words for "fool" in Proverbs see comments on 1:7.

"The simple" and **the young** need wisdom: "prudence," **knowledge, and discretion** (*mezimmâh*, "wise planning"; also used in 2:11; 3:21, "discernment"; 5:2; 8:12). In 12:2 and 14:17 *mezimmâh* is used in a negative sense to mean crafty or wicked planning. Also the experienced (**the wise,** *ḥāḳom,* and **the discerning,** 1:5; cf. v. 2) are reminded of their need to grow in wisdom (in **learning** and **guidance**). "Guidance" (*taḥbūlôt*), literally, "steerings" (like the tackle for directing a ship), suggests moving one's life in the right direction. This Hebrew word is used elsewhere only in Job 37:12 ("direction"); Proverbs 11:14; 12:5 ("plans"); 20:18; 24:6.

1:6. A person who understands "words of insight" (v. 2) understands the meaning of **proverbs . . . parables,** and **the sayings and riddles of the wise.** The word for "riddle" (*ḥîḏâh*) means an indirect, oblique, or enigmatic statement (like a figure of speech) which needs interpretation. It is used of Samson's riddle (Jud. 14:12-19) and of the "hard questions" the Queen of Sheba asked of Solomon (1 Kings 10:1; 2 Chron. 9:1).

C. The theme of the book (1:7)

1:7. Fearing the Lord, Solomon wrote, **is the beginning of knowledge.** The fear of the Lord occurs 11 times in Proverbs (and "fear the Lord" occurs 4 times). "Beginning" is the Hebrew *rē'šît* which means "the start." One cannot gain knowledge of spiritual things if he begins at the wrong point, refusing to fear the Lord (i.e., to recognize God's character and respond by revering, trusting, worshiping, obeying, and serving Him). *Rēʾšît* also means the capstone or essence. The essence of true knowledge is fearing God. Apart from Him a person is ignorant of spiritual things (Rom. 1:22; Eph. 4:18; 1 Peter 1:14). The words of Proverbs 1:7a are repeated in 9:10 near the end of the first section (also cf. Job 28:28; Ps. 111:10).

In contrast with those who fear God and have knowledge, **fools despise wisdom and discipline.** "Despise" translates the Hebrew *bûz*, "to hold in contempt, to belittle, to ridicule" (cf. Num. 15:31; Neh. 2:19). *Bûz* is also used seven other times in Proverbs: 6:30; 11:12; 13:13; 14:21; 23:9, 22; 30:17. Three Hebrew words are translated "fool" in Proverbs. One kind of fool (*kʾsîl*) is characterized by a dull and closed mind. He is thickheaded and stubborn. This word occurs more frequently in Proverbs than the other two words; it is used 49 times in this book. By his laziness and shortsightedness, this kind of fool rejects information from others (cf. 15:14). Another word for fool is *nāḇāl*. It is used only three times in Proverbs (17:7, 21; 30:22) and refers to one who lacks spiritual perception. A third kind of fool (*ʾĕwîl*) is arrogant and flippant as well as mentally dull. He is coarse and hardened in his ways. This word is used 19 times in Proverbs and only 7 times elsewhere. The "fools" in 1:7 are those who in their arrogant, coarse ways reject God and wisdom (cf. v. 29). Two kinds of people are contrasted in this verse: those who humbly fear God and thus acquire true knowledge, and the arrogant fools who by their refusal to fear God demonstrate that they hold wisdom and discipline in contempt (cf. "wisdom and discipline" in v. 2). These two kinds of people are contrasted throughout much of the book.

II. The Words of Solomon on Wisdom's Values (1:8–9:18)

This lengthy section is an introduction to the collection of terse sayings contained in the remaining chapters of the book. The purpose of this section (1:8–9:18) is to whet the appetite of the reader(s) ("my son[s]") so he will apply his heart to his parents' wise sayings. Solomon piles statement on statement to demonstrate the superiority of wisdom

over any other way of life. Besides the warnings against crime and adultery, his statements focus on a productive and meaningful existence. The material may be divided into 16 subpoints.

A. The value of wisdom in giving honor (1:8-9)

1:8. The words **my son** (and "my sons") are used frequently in the first nine chapters and four times in 22:17–24:34. They probably refer to Solomon's own son(s), not to students of a sage, because of the reference to their mother in 1:8. (For more information on this matter see "Addressees" in the *Introduction*.) **Listen** is commanded several times (4:1, 10, 20; 5:1, 7; 7:24; 8:32; 19:20; 22:17; 23:19, 22). **Teaching** renders the Hebrew word *tôrâh*, usually translated "Law." When used, as here, with a specific person (e.g., mother) it is translated "teaching" (cf. 3:1; 4:2; 6:20; 13:14). Since parents in ideal Jewish homes taught their children God's Law (cf. Deut. 6:4-7), the same word (*tôrâh*) was used both for the Law and for instruction in it.

1:9. If children heeded their parents' teachings, they were promised **a garland** (some kind of **head** ornament; cf. 4:9) and a neck **chain** (cf. 3:3, 22). That is, heeding parental instruction would give them an attractiveness of life and position. They would be honored. The implied contrast is that disobedience and rebellion lead to dishonor.

B. The value of wisdom in preserving from disaster (1:10-33)

1. THE DISASTER THAT ACCOMPANIES THE PURSUIT OF WICKEDNESS (1:10-19)

The appeal of the wicked, so attractive initially, is presented in its full scope. A foolish person is dazzled by the prospects of acquiring wealth easily and being gratified quickly by the immediate (vv. 10-14), but a wise person views the consequence of such sin and folly.

1:10-14. The pressure of peers can be strong, especially on young people. Therefore they need to avoid the invitations by the wrong kind of people (**sinners**) who invite them to take part in murder and theft. To **give in** to such influence is a downward step (cf. v. 15). **Let's lie in wait for someone's blood** (cf. 12:6) clearly spells out their murderous intentions. (Cf. comments on "lie in wait," 1:18.) These sinners are ready to take people's lives in order to take their money, to **swallow them** just as the grave (*šᵉ'ôl*, not the afterlife here) or **the pit** (a synonym of grave) "swallow" the dead. In their greed for gaining possessions (v. 13) they urge the young (here the father's **son**) to join them (v. 14), promising to divide the booty.

1:15-19. Again Solomon urged his **son . . . not** to get involved with such people (cf. v. 10). To **set foot on their paths** (cf. 4:14) is to be involved in an almost irreversible course of action that quickly involves them in **sin** and bloodshed (cf. 1:11). **Birds** are smart enough to avoid **a net** they see **spread** out to catch them. But these gangsters, more stupid than birds, not only see the trap; they even set it for themselves! They lie **in wait** to shed others' **blood,** but they **themselves** are caught in their own trap (cf. v. 32; 26:27; 28:10). The humor of this boomeranging result is evident, that **ill-gotten gain** (1:19; cf. 10:2; 28:16) cannot be enjoyed. Thieves steal money but then **it takes** their **lives!** In other words crime does not pay.

2. THE DISASTER THAT ACCOMPANIES THE NEGLECT OF WISDOM (1:20-33)

Wisdom, personified like a woman, appeals to everyone (vv. 20-23), but a fool ignores her appeal (vv. 24-28) at his own risk (vv. 29-33). Wisdom is also personified as a woman in 3:16-18; 4:3-6; 8:1-21, 32-36; 9:1-6; 14:33.

1:20-23. Whereas the sinners in verses 10-19 were probably secretive about their appeal to the young man, here **wisdom** shouts **in the street,** and other **public** places in **the city.** In two rhetorical questions she invites three groups to forsake their ways. They are those who would be more likely to refuse her appeal. They are the **simple ones** (*peṭî;* see comments on v. 4), the **mockers** (cf. Ps. 1:1), **and fools** (*kᵉsîl;* cf. comments on Prov. 1:7). By responding to wisdom's **rebuke** a foolish person can become wise (v. 23). Rebuke is mentioned frequently in Proverbs as a helpful kind of verbal correction (vv. 23, 25, 30; 3:11; 9:8 [twice]; 13:1; 15:31; 17:10; 19:25; 25:12; 27:5; 30:6).

1:24-28. To reject and ignore wisdom and not learn from its **rebuke** (cf. vv. 23, 30) has serious consequences. When **troubles** come, as they inevitably do to everyone, wisdom mockingly refuses to help sinners. Wisdom's laughing at **disaster** and **calamity** seems cruel. But this simply means that spurned advice will haunt its rejecter when calamity comes. She had called them and they had refused. Now this would be reversed with the same results; **they** would **call . . . but** she would **not answer.** When a fool who has earlier rejected wisdom attempts to start over and follow the wise path, his efforts are of no avail. Wisdom rejected cannot be reclaimed after she has withdrawn her invitation.

1:29:33. To reject "Lady Wisdom's" call is to hate **knowledge** (cf. v. 22) and to refuse to **fear the LORD** (cf. v. 7 and comments there). So fools will suffer the consequences **of their** actions (v. 31). They reap what they sow (cf. Gal. 6:7). As illustrated in Proverbs 1:19, folly (**the simple,** *peṭî,* and **fools,** *kᵉsîl,* v. 32) ultimately results in death. By contrast, heeding the way of wisdom gives **safety** (3:23) and peace.

These contrasts between the consequences of folly (1:32) and of wisdom (v. 33) set the tone for the rest of the book.

C. The moral values of wisdom (chap. 2)

In this chapter the father instructed his son ("my son"; cf. 1:8) on the efforts needed for attaining wisdom (2:1-6), the moral benefits of wisdom's attainment (vv. 7-10), and the protection of wisdom from immoral people (vv. 11-22).

1. THE PURSUIT OF WISDOM (2:1-6)

2:1-4. Eight verbs are used in these verses: **accept . . . store up** (v. 1), **turning . . . applying . . . call . . . cry** (v. 3), **look . . . search** (v. 4). The objects of these activities are the teacher's **words** and **commands** (v. 1; cf. "commands" in 7:1), **wisdom** and **understanding** (2:2), and **insight** and **understanding** (v. 3; cf. "understanding," meaning discernment, in vv. 6, 11). Effort must be expended for one to become wise. Getting wisdom involves openness, retention, hearing (with the **ear**), applying (with the **heart;** cf. v. 10), requesting, and diligent searching.

2:5-6. The three "ifs" in verses 1, 3-4 are followed by **then,** which introduces the result. Seeking and valuing wisdom lead to a person's understanding (discerning) **the fear of the LORD** and knowing **God.** This is the same truth stated in 1:7. **The LORD** is the source of that **wisdom** (cf. James 1:5). As a person fears the Lord, he gains wisdom, **knowledge** (cf. Prov. 1:4; 2:10), **and understanding** (cf. vv. 2-3, 11).

2. THE MORAL BENEFITS OF WISDOM (2:7-10)

2:7-10. Wisdom gives positive, health-inducing moral benefits. It keeps one from evil and contributes to holiness. Wisdom is a matter of the heart, and of moral conduct, not just of intellectual attainment. This is made clear by the words **upright** and **blameless** (cf. v. 21), **the just,** and **faithful ones** (from *ḥeseḏ,* those who are loyal to God). Elsewhere in Proverbs the word for **victory** is translated "sound judgment" (3:21; 8:14; 18:1). In 2:7 it means success, the *result* of sound judgment. Like **a shield** (cf. Ps. 3:3) God protects those who by His wisdom are morally upright, those who are His (cf. Prov. 1:33). Moral living enables a person to be equitable with others, to do what is **right and just and fair** (cf. 1:3). "Fair" translates the same word rendered "upright" in 2:7. One's conduct is suggested by the synonyms **walk . . . course . . . way,** and **path** (vv. 7-9; cf. vv. 12-13, 15, 18-20).

A person who strives for **wisdom** (vv. 1-4) will find that it **will enter** his **heart** (v. 10). Obtaining wisdom requires diligence on man's part in pursuing God's will; yet wisdom is a gift from God (cf. v. 6). Having such **knowledge** from God gives inner joy or pleasure.

3. THE PROTECTION OF WISDOM FROM IMMORAL PEOPLE (2:11-22)

Wisdom is valuable; therefore it should be sought after (vv. 1-4). For one thing it guards from wicked men (vv. 12-15) and wicked women (vv. 16-19) and keeps one going in the right paths (vv. 20-22).

2:11-15. A general statement about wisdom's protection (v. 11) links verses 7-8 with verses 12-15. God protects (v. 8), and the **discretion** He gives also protects (v. 11; cf. 4:6; 13:6). Verses 12-15 take on added meaning when they are related to the warning in 1:10-19. **The ways** and **words** of the **wicked . . . are perverse** (2:12). "Perverse" and **perverseness** (v. 14) are the same word in Hebrew. Coming from the verb "to turn, turn from,

overturn," they suggest something that is "turned away" from the normal. This Hebrew word occurs eight times in Proverbs (2:12, 14; 6:14, "deceit"; 10:31-32; 16:28, 30; 23:33, "confusing") and only once elewhere (Deut. 32:20, "perversity"). Such people turn away from **the straight** (lit., "upright"; cf. Prov. 2:7) **paths** to **dark** (i.e., evil) **ways.** They even enjoy their perversity, their **crooked . . . ways.** "Crooked" translates *ʿiqqēš* ("twisted") which is also used in 6:12 ("corrupt"); it is rendered "perverse" in 11:20; 17:20; 19:1; 28:6 and "wicked" in 22:5. Their deeds are distortions of morality. Ways (2:12-13, 15) and **paths** (vv. 13, 15) help relate this passage to other parts of chapter 2 (cf. "way" in v. 8, "ways" in v. 20, "path" in v. 9, and "paths" in vv. 18-20; also cf. 4:19; 7:25; 8:20).

2:16-19. Wisdom **(it)** also protects from **(will save you . . . from;** cf. v. 12) immoral women (cf. 7:4-5). **The adulteress** (*ʾiššâ zārâh*) and **the wayward wife** (*noḵrîyâh*) are synonymous terms.

The first term can mean a non-Israelite (as Ruth in Ruth 2:10) or (as in Prov. 2:16; 5:3, 20; 7:5; 22:14; 23:27) a woman who because of her immorality was outside the circle of her proper relations. In Proverbs *noḵrîyâh* is used in 2:16; 5:20; 6:24; 7:5; 23:27. Whereas wicked men use perverse words (2:12) the adulteress uses **seductive words** (cf. 5:3; 6:24; 7:5, 21). **The partner of her youth** refers to her husband (cf. "the wife of your youth," 5:18), and **the covenant** which she **ignored** is her marriage vows. Forgetting her commitment to her husband, she became promiscuous. To be involved with such a person (in **her house) leads** to **death;** adultery puts a person on an irretrievable path that eventually results in physical death (cf. 5:5; 7:27). It is fatal. **The spirits of the dead** translates *rᵉp̄āʾîm,* which occurs also in 9:18; 21:16 (see comments on Job 26:5). On **paths** (Prov. 2:18-19) see comments on verses 13, 15 (cf. 5:6).

2:20-22. A person who pursues wisdom (vv. 1-4) avoids the wrong kind of people (vv. 11-19) and can have the right kind of companions (**good men** and **the righteous**). Merely escaping immorality is insufficient for a man of wisdom; he must also progressively pursue the good. As a result God blesses him. For the Israelites, residing **in the land** (of Canaan) was a sign of God's favor (cf. Ex. 20:12; Ps. 37:3, 9, 11, 29). The contrast between the upright and the blameless (cf. Prov. 2:7), who will enjoy God's agricultural prosperity, and the wicked and the unfaithful, who will no longer be in the land because of either exile or death, recalls the contrast in Psalm 1:6 (cf. Prov. 10:30).

D. The blessings of wisdom (3:1-12)

After another strong encouragement to pursue his teaching (vv. 1-4) the father-teacher gave four commands (vv. 5-12). Each deals with a danger of misusing a gift of God. The son is told (a) to trust in God and not lean on his own understanding (vv. 5-6), (b) to fear God and not be wise in his own eyes (vv. 7-8), (c) to honor God and not fail to give to Him (vv. 9-10), and (d) to appreciate God and not misunderstand His discipline and its value (vv. 11-12). These verses follow an alternating pattern of commands and rewards: commands (v. 1), reward (v. 2), commands (v. 3), reward (v. 4), commands (vv. 5-6a), reward (v. 6b), commands (v. 7), reward (v. 8), command (v. 9), reward (v. 10), commands (v. 11), reward (v. 12). The rewards include longevity and prosperity (v. 2), favor with God and people (v. 4), fewer problems (v. 6), health (v. 8), prosperity (v. 10), and awareness of God's love (v. 12).

1. THE APPEAL TO FOLLOW THE FATHER'S TEACHING (3:1-4)

3:1-2. Again the son (cf. 1:8, 15; 2:1; 3:11, 21) is urged—both negatively (do not forget) and positively (keep)—to heed what he was being taught. As in 1:8; 4:2; and 6:20, 23 teaching translates tôrâh (see comments on 1:8). (On commands; cf. 2:1; 4:4; 6:20.) If these instructions are part of one's inner life, two benefits will be realized: longevity (cf. 3:16; 4:10; 9:11; 10:27; 14:27; 15:24), a sign of God's blessing (cf. Ex. 20:12), and prosperity. The word for prosperity, šālôm, is often translated "peace." Though it includes peace and prosperity, it is broader in meaning. It also suggests wholeness, health, and harmony.

3:3-4. Love translates ḥesed, loyalty to one's covenant or commitment. That quality along with dependability (cf. "love and faithfulness" in 14:22; 16:6; 20:28) should grace one's life like a neck

chain (cf. 3:22; 1:9; 6:21) and should be written, figuratively, on one's heart (cf. 6:21; 7:3). These statements were not intended to encourage the use of phylacteries (see comments on Deut. 6:8-9), but to encourage strong association with and adherence to the parents' teachings. The results of such adherence are favor and a good name (good reputation). "Favor" translates ḥēn, from the verb ḥānan, "to be gracious or to show favor." The noun is translated "grace" in Proverbs 3:34; "kindhearted" in 11:16; "favor" in 3:4; 13:15; 28:23; and "charm" in 31:30. "Good name" is rendered "good understanding" in 13:15. The Hebrew śēkel ṭôb includes the idea of competence and effectiveness, and therefore a reputation for prudence.

2. THE COMMAND TO TRUST IN THE LORD AND NOT LEAN ON ONE'S OWN UNDERSTANDING (3:5-6)

3:5-6. To trust in the LORD wholeheartedly means one should not rely (lean) on his understanding, for human insights are never enough. God's ways are incomprehensible (Isa. 55:8-9; Rom. 11:33-34); yet He is trustworthy. All the wisdom a person may acquire can never replace the need for full trust in God's superior ways. Heart in Hebrew refers to one's emotions (Prov. 12:25; 13:12; 14:10, 13) but more often to his intellect (such as understanding, 10:8; discernment, 15:14; reflection, 15:28), or will (5:12).

As a person trusts in the Lord and acknowledges Him (this is not a nod of recognition but an intimate knowledge of God) in all his ways (cf. all your heart, 3:5), he finds that God makes his paths straight. This means more than guidance; it means God removes the obstacles, making a smooth path or way of life, or perhaps better, bringing one to the appointed goal. (On ways and paths, cf. v. 17 and see comments on 2:13, 15.) Proverbs teaches that those who follow wisdom have an easier, less problematic life (e.g., 3:10, 16, 24-25).

3. THE COMMAND TO FEAR THE LORD AND NOT ADMIRE ONE'S WISDOM (3:7-8)

3:7-8. Young people who acquire wisdom need to remember that they did not become wise by themselves; wisdom comes from God (2:6). This reminder is similar to 3:5b. A heart awareness of and proper response to God (**fear the LORD**; cf. comments on 1:7) help prevent the **evil** of pride (cf. Rom. 12:16). (On shunning evil; cf. Prov. 8:13; 14:16; 16:6; Ps. 97:10.) As a result God gives **health** and vigor (cf. Prov. 4:22). Health in one's **bones,** mentioned several times in Proverbs (3:8; 12:4; 14:30; 15:30; 16:24; 17:22), suggests, as is well known today, that spiritual and physical health are related.

4. HONOR THE LORD AND DO NOT WITHHOLD ONE'S OFFERING (3:9-10)

3:9-10. In Israel, honoring **the LORD with . . . the firstfruits of all** one's **crops** was a way of expressing gratitude to Him for His provisions (Deut. 26:1-3, 9-11). It was a way of acknowledging God and His help (Prov. 3:6). In return, God **then** (cf. v. 4) promised to fill the **barns** (with grain) and the **vats . . . with new wine** (*tîrôš,* "freshly squeezed grape juice"). *In general* it is true that godliness results in gain, that piety brings prosperity (cf. v. 2; Deut. 28:1-14; Matt. 6:33). But this kind of generalization, common in Proverbs, does not disallow God from making exceptions. Otherwise God is invested in, rather than honored. Proverbs 3:10 is well balanced by verses 11-12, as Derek Kidner appropriately observes (*The Proverbs: An Introduction and Commentary,* p. 64).

5. APPRECIATE THE LORD AND DO NOT MISUNDERSTAND HIS DISCIPLINE (3:11-12)

3:11-12. The God who can be trusted to smooth out obstacles and bring one to his appointed goal (vv. 5-6) and to supply one's material needs (vv. 9-10) demonstrates His love by **discipline.** The warning to the **son** (cf. vv. 1, 21) is twofold: **do not despise** ("reject or take lightly") the Lord's discipline, and **do not resent** ("loathe or abhor") **His rebuke** (see comments on 1:23 and cf. Job 5:17; Heb. 12:5-6). Physical punishment and verbal correction are hard to accept but they demonstrate God's loving concern. The same is true of a parent's discipline of his children (cf. Deut. 8:15). Loathing such discipline—thinking that God **disciplines** because He enjoys causing pain—overlooks the benefits that come from such correction.

E. The high value of wisdom (3:13-20)

3:13-15. Because **wisdom** brings happiness (**blessed;** cf. v. 18 and see comments on Ps. 1:1) and because wealth often does not bring genuine happiness (Ecc. 5:10-12), wisdom's value far exceeds the worth of precious metals such as **silver . . . gold,** and also **rubies** (cf. Prov. 8:10-11, 19). The words **profitable** and **yields better returns** (lit., "brings a higher yield") are the language of a trader or investor. What wisdom returns to her possessor is of greater value than anything gold or silver can purchase.

3:16-18. Wisdom, personified as a woman, gives with both hands, that is, generously. **Her right hand** gives longevity (cf. v. 2) and from **her left hand** she gives **riches** (what silver and gold can purchase) **and** more (viz., **honor;** cf. v. 4; 4:8; 8:18; 21:21; 22:4). Besides giving a **long life** (3:16; see comments on v. 2), wisdom also provides a quality life: pleasantness and **peace** (*šālôm;* see comments on v. 2). Long life with no thought for its quality could be a curse rather than a blessing. (On **ways** and **paths;** cf. v. 6 and see comments on 2:13, 15.)

A quality kind of life is often mentioned in Proverbs: 3:22; 4:13, 22; 6:23; 8:35; 10:11, 16-17; 11:19, 30; 12:28; 13:14; 14:27; 16:22; 19:23; 21:21; 22:4. A long and fruitful life is expressed in the figure of a tree (3:18). Much as the **tree of life** was a source of life (Gen. 2:9), so wisdom is a source of life. (Prov. also refers to a tree of life in 11:30; 13:12; 15:4.)

3:19-20. When God created the world, He used **wisdom . . . understanding,** and **knowledge.** If *God* needed these, then certainly people need them. The relationship between God and wisdom in His Creation is discussed in more detail in 8:22-31.

F. The value of wisdom in building relationships with others (3:21-35)

3:21. The familiar **my son** (cf. vv. 1, 11) introduces a plea that the son embrace valued qualities. **Sound judgment** translates the Hebrew word that is rendered "victory" in 2:7 (see comments there). **Discernment** (*mezimmāh*) is translated "discretion" in 1:4. The last part of 3:21 is like the first part of 4:21.

3:22-26. These verses mention a number of benefits that come to those who heed the exhortation in verse 21. These benefits include **life** (v. 22; cf. comments on v. 18), **safety** (v. 23; cf. 1:33; 2:7-

8), avoidance of troubles (cf. 3:6), peaceful sleep (v. 24), confidence in the future (vv. 25-26a), and avoidance of traps set by the wicked (cf. 1:15-18). The long life referred to in 3:22 may be partially attributed to the peace of mind so graphically pictured in verses 23-26.

3:27-35. These verses include five sample maxims about relationships with others, with verses 27-31 each beginning with the words Do not. These are examples of what it means to be wise. They may be grouped into three relationships (vv. 27-28, 29-30, 32-32): (1) The command Do not withhold good from those who deserve it (v. 27) is literally, "Do not withhold good from its owners." The idea is, fulfill an obligation such as paying wages to a hired laborer (Lev. 19:13b; Deut. 24:15). Proverbs 3:28 seems to reinforce the point of verse 27, but it may expand the idea to being generous to the poor. This is "right and just and fair" (1:3). (2) To harm . . . a neighbor (3:29) violates his trust, and to accuse him falsely (v. 30) violates the ninth commandment (Ex. 20:16). To plot translates ḥāraš, "to plow," from which comes the idea of plans being thought up or devised as furrows in a field are plowed. The word is also used in Proverbs 6:14, 18 ("devises"); 12:20; 14:22 (twice: "plot" and "plan"). (3) Some people envy a violent man (3:31; cf. 23:17; 24:1, 19) because they see the money he has or the pleasures he supposedly enjoys. But God gives four reasons why such envy is uncalled for: (1) The LORD hates such a perverse (from lûz, "to be devious"; cf. 14:2) person, whereas the upright in contrast enjoys fellowship with God (3:32). (2) The Lord curses the wicked but . . . blesses . . . the righteous (v. 33). (3) God mocks arrogant mockers (cf. comments on 1:22), causing their actions to boomerang on them, whereas the humble receive His grace (cf. James. 4:6; 1 Peter 5:5). (4) The wise are honored (cf. Prov. 3:16) but fools (kᵉsîl; see comments on 1:7) are shamed. These verses show that the words "upright," "righteous," "the humble," and "the wise" are basically synonymous in the Book of Proverbs.

G. An exhortation to acquire wisdom (4:1-9)

This appeal to acquire wisdom is similar to several other passages in chapters 1–9 (1:8-9; 2:1-6; 3:1-2, 21-26; 4:10, 20-22; 5:1-2; 6:20-22; 7:1-3, 24; 8:32-36). Wisdom gives life (4:4), protection (v. 6), and honor (vv. 8-9). This instruction is valid because of its enduring quality, and it is valuable because of the honor it brings.

4:1-2. The father's exhortation begins with the command to listen (cf. 1:8; 4:10, 20; 5:1, 7; 7:24). Usually the words were addressed to "my son," but here and in 5:7; 7:24; 8:32 it is plural, my sons. Pay attention is also repeated in 4:20; 5:1; 7:24; 22:17. As in 1:8; 3:1; 6:20; 13:14, tôrâh, normally translated "Law," is here properly translated teaching (see comments on 1:8).

4:3-6. Solomon spoke of his boyhood when his parents David and Bathsheba taught him. He was then their only child though later he had three brothers (1 Chron. 3:5). Proverbs 4:4b-9 quote from Solomon's father David. By quoting these words Solomon was passing the instruction on to his sons. The three generations involved here illustrate Deuteronomy 6:2. David had urged young Solomon to obey his words wholeheartedly (with all your heart; cf. Prov. 3:5) so that he would live (cf. 3:1-2). Keep my commands and you will live is repeated in 7:2a.

Perhaps David's encouragement to Solomon to get wisdom helped influence Solomon to ask God for it (1 Kings 3:5-14). Wisdom was to be pursued (three times Solomon said "get"; Prov. 4:5 [twice], 7) and valued (love her; cf. 8:17, 21) because she (wisdom is again personified as a woman) protects (cf. 2:7-8, 11; 3:21-23) and guards.

4:7-9. As stated in 3:13-15 "nothing" can compare with wisdom. Therefore it is supreme, well worth all the effort and cost involved in acquiring it. As wisdom is valued and loved (cf. 4:6), she gives honor (3:16), and an attractive life, pictured as a beautiful wreath (1:9) and a crown of splendor (used in 16:31 of gray hair, or age). The opposite is also implied: a foolish, unwise life is dishonorable, unattractive, and shameful. Solomon experienced both wisdom and folly and therefore both kinds of results.

H. The value of wisdom in preserving from trouble (4:10-19)

The ways of wisdom (vv. 10-13) and of wickedness (vv. 14-17) are described and the son-learner is again urged to pursue the former and avoid the latter. The lesson is summarized in verses 18-19 by picturing the destinations of both paths.

4:10-13. Once more Solomon addressed one of his sons (**my son**; cf. v. 20), urging him to **listen** (cf. vv. 1, 20 and see comments on 1:8) because heeding his father's words would give him a longer **life** (cf. 3:2, 16; 9:11; 10:27; 14:27; 15:24). **Straight paths** (4:11) are unrestricted paths (cf. 3:6), which are easier to walk in. This thought is amplified in 4:12: one's **steps** are **not . . . hampered** (lit., "narrowed or cramped," that is, he is not in distress). The crooked, devious path of sin is the way of problems and hardships (cf. "path" and "way" in vv. 14, 18-19 and see comments on 2:12-15).

Again an eager acquiring of **wisdom** is encouraged (4:13; cf. vv. 5-7) because it gives **life** (cf. v. 10).

4:14-17. In verses 14-15 six urgent commands are given to steer clear of the path of the wicked, and verses 16-17 state the reason for the urgency in verses 14-15. **Wicked** people are so taken up with **evil** that they are unable to **sleep till they** hurt someone (cf. 1:15-16). Sin is so much a part of them that it is like their food (**bread** and **wine**).

4:18-19. The path of the righteous, which is "the way of wisdom" (v. 11), **is like the first** rays of light in the morning, which gradually increase to **the full light of** noonday. With light on his path a believer can follow "straight paths" (v. 11) and "not be hampered" or "stumble" (v. 12). By contrast the way or path of **the wicked** (cf. v. 14) is characterized by **deep darkness** (*'ăpēlâh,* intense blackness in the middle of the night; cf. 7:9; Ex. 10:22) which causes him to **stumble.**

I. The value of wisdom in producing health (4:20-27)

4:20-22. Another exhortation to hear and **pay attention to** instruction (cf. v. 1; 5:1) opens this section. The author's words (cf. 4:4; 2:1) were to be in his son's view (cf. 3:21) and in his **heart.** The major incentive was the offer of **life** (cf. 4:10, 13, 23) **and health** (cf. 3:8).

4:23. The **heart** (cf. comments on 3:5) should be guarded for out of it (a **wellspring**) come one's actions (cf. Luke 6:45). Here the word "heart" means more than mental or emotional capacity; it also

encompasses one's values (cf. Matt. 6:21).

4:24-27. These verses apply the command to guard one's heart (v. 23), including what one says (v. 24), sees (v. 25), and does (vv. 26-27). (See comments on 6:17-18.) The mention in 4:24 of **mouth** and **lips** is similar to Christ's teaching on the relationship between one's heart and his speech (Luke 6:45c). **Perversity** comes from *'iqqēš,* "crooked" (cf. Prov. 2:15). **Corrupt** or foul **talk** (cf. 6:12) should never be on the lips of one who trusts the Lord (cf. Eph. 4:29).

Each believer should focus his **eyes** (Prov. 4:25) on the wise path (cf. v. 11), concentrating on it and not being distracted. And his conduct should be upright, as he stays on **level paths** (cf. v. 11b) and does not turn aside to **evil** (cf. v. 15; 1:15). Again paths and **ways** (4:26) are used to refer to one's conduct (cf. 2:13, 15, 20; 3:6, 17; 7:25; and cf. "path" and "way" in 4:18-19; also note 8:20). "Proverbs provides both a goal and route. The goal is successful living and the route is the way of wisdom" (Robert L. Alden, *Proverbs: A Commentary on an Ancient Book of Timeless Advice,* p. 48). Though wisdom keeps one on the right path (cf., e.g., 2:12) here the encouragement is to keep oneself on the **straight** way.

J. The value of wisdom in preserving from adultery (chap. 5)

Specific instruction is given concerning the dangers of the adulteress (vv. 1-6), the final price of infidelity (vv. 7-14), and the delights of married love (vv. 15-20). Then a reminder is given that sin is ultimately an issue with the Lord (vv. 21-23). As in 1:14-19, chapter 5 portrays against the immediate pleasure of sin its long-range consequences. If a person is wise, he sees this long-range view.

5:1-6. This chapter, like other portions in Proverbs, begins with the exhortation that the **son pay attention and listen** (cf. 4:1, 10, 20; 5:7; 7:24) to his father's **words,** for doing so gives **discretion** (cf. 1:4) and **knowledge.** Speaking (**lips,** 5:2) **wisdom** helps the son ignore the words (**lips,** v. 3) **of an adulteress** (*zārâh;* see comments on 2:16). Her deceptive, seductive words are persuasive, sweet like **honey,** the sweetest substance in ancient Israel, and **smoother than** (cf. 6:24; 7:21) olive **oil,** the smoothest substance in ancient Israel. **But** what seems attractive at first becomes **bitter** and **sharp** later. Involvement in adultery is like tasting **gall,** the bitterest substance known (from a plant), or like being cut by a **double-edged sword.** The adulteress leads men **to death** (cf. 2:18; 7:27; 9:18). Her sin makes her unaware that her ways **are crooked** (lit., "staggering or unstable"), in contrast with the "straight paths" of 4:11.

5:7-8. Again Solomon urged his **sons** (cf. comments on 4:1) to **listen** (cf. 4:1, 10, 20; 5:1; 7:24) and adhere to **what** he said. He urged them **not** to **turn** . . . **from** his teachings, but to turn from the adulteress. They were **not** even to **go near** . . . **her house** (cf. 2:18) because of the danger of succumbing to her temptations.

5:9-14. Failure to keep away from the adulteress can result in many losses: loss of **strength** (which may mean losing one's health, self-respect, or both), loss of a long life (v. 9), loss of money (cf. 6:26; 29:3b)—by paying the adulteress, paying her husband, or paying child support—and loss of health (5:11). Falling prey to lust also brings remorse when a person recognizes too late that he did not heed his parents' (here called **teachers)** instructions which inevitably leads to **ruin** and disgrace before others.

5:15-18. The rewards of chastity are a further encouragement to moral purity. A **cistern . . . well . . . springs . . . streams,** and **fountain** control water, keeping it from being dissipated **in the streets.** Similarly marital love with one's **wife** (v. 18) is pictured as enjoying one's cistern or fountain (cf. Song 4:12, 15). Sexual desires should be controlled and channeled in one's marriage, not wasted as described in Proverbs 5:7-14. Some commentators say the word **them** (v. 17) refers to children; others say it continues the metaphor of streams picturing one's sexual desires. As a person would not get water from his neighbor's cistern because he had his own (2 Kings 18:31), so a man should have his physical needs met by his own wife, not someone else's.

5:19-20. The **breasts** of a man's wife are soft to the touch and **graceful** in appearance like a **deer** (cf. Song 4:5; 7:3). Therefore a husband should be **captivated** (cf. Prov. 5:20; the verb *šāgâh* means "go astray," cf. v. 21; but it may also

suggest the idea of being captured) **by her love,** not the affections of an adulteress. By two rhetorical questions (v. 20) the author pointed up the folly of being **captivated** (cf. v. 19) **by an** immoral woman and loving someone else's **wife.**

5:21-23. The dire consequences of adultery (vv. 7-14) should motivate a person to avoid it. But four even higher motivations are given in verses 21-23: (1) Since God sees **man's ways** (cf. 15:3; Job 31:1, 4; Heb. 4:13), adultery committed in secret is known by the L ORD. (2) Also God **examines** man's conduct (on ways and **paths** see comments on Prov. 4:26). Man cannot escape God's scrutinizing. (3) Sin ensnares (cf. 1:17-18), and ties a person down like ropes (5:22). Though people like to talk about being "free" to sin as they wish, **sin** actually takes away freedom. (4) Being undisciplined (cf. v. 12) in one's moral life results in death (cf. vv. 5, 11). Such living is foolish because it leads one **astray** from God's standards. "Led astray" is from the same word *šāgâh* rendered "captivated" in verses 19-20. **Folly** appears 21 times in Proverbs. To yield to sexual lust is folly.

K. The value of wisdom in preserving from poverty (6:1-11)

Solomon warned against two practices that lead to poverty: foolish financial entanglements (vv. 1-5) and laziness (vv. 6-11). In a sense both pertain to finances because the former guards against unnecessary loss of what one has earned and the latter against the inability to earn any money at all.

1. WARNING AGAINST FOOLISH FINANCIAL ENTANGLEMENTS (6:1-5)

6:1. My son occurs in verses 1, 3, 20 in chapter 6. If a person cosigned a note involving high interest rates for someone else's loan, that cosigner was urged to get out of the obligation as soon as possible ("free yourself," vv. 3, 5). In Israel lending was intended as a means of helping a fellow Israelite, not as a money-making transaction as it is today. No interest was to be charged a fellow Israelite (Ex. 22:25; Lev. 25:35-37). Interest could be applied to a loan to non-Israelites, but even then usury (unreasonably high interest rates) was illegal. Exorbitant interest often resulted in injustice (cf. 2 Kings 4:1; Neh. 5:1-11) which the Law sought to prevent. The warning in Proverbs 6:1 is not against borrowing or lending but against being held accountable for another person's high-interest loan. Putting up security is referred to frequently in Proverbs (11:15; 17:18; 20:16; 22:26-27; 27:13).

Some say the word **neighbor** here means "stranger," and that cosigning is acceptable for one's relatives but not for strangers. The parallel word **another** suggests, however, that cosigning is advised against altogether ("neighbor" probably means "anybody"). Does this exhortation, then, speak against guaranteeing payments on a loan for one's own relatives? No. The restriction seems to be against loans with exorbitant rates of interest.

Striking **hands in pledge** was a gesture something like shaking hands. It was like "signing on the dotted line."

6:2. The words **trapped** and **ensnared** (cf. v. 5) indicate that by accepting responsibility for someone's high-interest debt, the son would be placing himself in a financial situation over which he had no control (cf. v. 3). Agreeing by word of **mouth** to cosign such a debt could lead to serious trouble.

6:3-5. In intense language Solomon urged that a person who has agreed to be security for another's loan should seek to get out of that trap. To fall **into your neighbor's hands** means that the outcome of the situation is in the neighbor's control. **Humble** is a strong word meaning "to crush or tread oneself down, to demean" and **press your plea** suggests being boisterous. One should free himself from a debt agreement, even if so doing demands great humiliation and obnoxious pleading. This urgency is stressed in verses 4-5. Nothing should stand in the way; not even one night was to pass before the situation should be taken care of. Just as **a gazelle** or **a bird,** if trapped, would immediately begin struggling for its life, so a person snared by a foolish debt agreement should frantically fight to be **free** of it (cf. v. 3).

2. WARNING AGAINST LAZINESS (6:6-11)

6:6-8. A person can become financially destitute by laziness as well as by foolish dealings. Solomon was probably not calling his son a **sluggard;** he was speaking rhetorically to anyone who might hear or read the message. The He-brew word for sluggard ('*āṣēl*) occurs 14 times in Proverbs and nowhere else in the Old Testament. It refers to more than laziness. In 15:19 a sluggard is contrasted with the "upright," and in 21:25-26 a sluggard is contrasted with the "righteous." A sluggard is associated in 19:15 with the "shiftless." A lazy, irresponsible person is challenged to learn from **the ant** (also mentioned in 30:25) **and be wise.** Ants, known for being industrious, are commended here for their initiative. Apparently ants have no leader—**no commander** to direct them, **no overseer** to inspect their work, no **ruler** to prod them on. **Yet** they work better than many people under a leader! Ants also work in anticipation of future needs, storing and gathering while it is warm, before winter comes. The virtue of wisdom is not in being busy but in having a proper view of forthcoming needs that motivate one to action (cf. 10:5). Those who act only when commanded do not possess wisdom.

6:9-11. By two questions (v. 9) Solomon urged the **sluggard** to **get** out of bed and start working. Verses 10-11, repeated later in 24:33-34, point up the danger of a person continuing to nap when he ought to be working: **poverty will come on** him suddenly in the same way a robber or **an armed man** (a soldier) quickly attacks an unsuspecting victim. Poverty is mentioned frequently in Proverbs (6:11; 10:15; 11:24; 13:18; 14:23; 21:5; 22:16; 24:34; 28:19, 22; 30:8; 31:7). With his time squandered the lazy person cannot rectify his situation and has little or no money to meet his needs. Obviously such a person is unwise.

L. The value of wisdom in preserving from dissension (6:12-19)

By describing a person who deceives and stirs up strife (vv. 12-15) and the activities such a person engages in (vv. 16-19), Solomon urged his son to avoid disaster (v. 15) and God's hatred (v. 16).

6:12. The **scoundrel and villain** refer to one person, as evidenced by the use of singular verbs in verses 12-15. "Scoundrel" (cf. 16:27; 2 Sam.16:7; 1 Kings 21:10) is literally, "man of belial," someone who is worthless and wicked. Later the word belial came to be used of the devil, the most worthless, wicked person of all (2 Cor. 6:15). A scoundrel is known by his **corrupt** (lit., "twisted"; see comments on Prov. 2:15) **mouth** (cf. 4:24), his false and deceptive words.

6:13-14. By sinister body language the scoundrel's actions contradict what he says. By winking (cf. 10:10; 16:30; Ps. 35:19) and gesturing in some way **with his feet** and **fingers** he signals certain messages to his fellow conspirators. He plans (see comments on Prov. 3:29) **evil** actions (cf. 1:11-14) from a deceitful **heart** so that people are not aware of his intentions until it is too late. Though he feigns sincerity, underneath he is perverted and causes **dissension**, drawing others into discord or strife. Dissension (cf. 6:19) is caused by hatred (10:12), and uncontrolled temper (15:18), perversity (16:28), greed (28:25), and anger (29:22). (Also see these additional verses on strife: 17:1; 18:6; 20:3; 22:10; 23:29; 26:21; 30:33.)

6:15. Besides causing discord among people by his deceptive words and his sinister gestures, a scoundrel brings **disaster** on himself. It comes unexpectedly and quickly (**in an instant** and **suddenly**) with no way to offset it (**without remedy**). Whether natural consequences or more direct divine intervention is in view is not clear. But his downfall is quick, complete, and certain.

6:16. The Lord's hatred of the scoundrel's activities (vv. 12-14) is described in verses 16-19. These two sections are linked by the words "stirs up dissension" (vv. 14, 19).

The **six . . . seven** pattern is also used in Job 5:19, and a similar pattern of other numbers plus one is used in Proverbs 30:15-16, 18-19, 21-31. The purpose of this kind of numerical pattern (x and x + 1) is not to give a complete list. Instead it is to stress the final (x + 1) item, as the culmination or product of its preceding items.

6:17-19. A person with **haughty eyes** (i.e., a proud look; cf. 8:13; 30:13; Pss. 18:27; 101:5), a **lying tongue** (cf. Prov. 12:19; 21:6; 26:28), **hands that** murder (**shed innocent blood**; cf. 1:11), a **heart that** plots (see comments on 3:29) **wicked** actions (cf. 4:16; 6:14), **feet that** move quickly **into** sin (cf. 1:16), and one who **lies** against someone when witnessing in court (cf. 12:17; 14:5, 25; 19:5, 9; 21:28; 25:18) is a person who causes discord (see comments on 6:14) **among** friends. Apparently by his lies he causes friends

to be suspicious of each other. Lying, referred to twice in this list of things God hates (vv. 17, 19), is one of the many wrong uses of words that are condemned in Proverbs. (The chart "Words and Speaking in Proverbs," which lists the many wrong and right uses of one's words referred to in Prov., arranges these subjects topically. For a list of some of the many other topics in Prov. see the chart "Positive and Negative Topics and Other Subjects in Proverbs," in the *Introduction*.)

The scoundrel (v. 12) uses various parts of his body in violation of the commands in 4:23-26, as seen in thse passages: heart, mouth, lips, eyes, feet (4:23-26); mouth, eye, feet, fingers, heart (6:12-14); eyes, tongue, hands, heart, feet (vv. 17-18).

M. The value of wisdom in preserving from sexual immorality (6:20–7:27)

Five times in chapters 1–9 Solomon spoke to the problem of sexual immorality: 2:16-19; 5:3-23; 6:20-35; chapter 7; 9:13-18. (Though 9:13-18 does not mention adultery or an adulteress, Folly, personified as a woman, may suggest such a person. See comments there.) Proverbs 6:20-35 warns against adultery and chapter 7 illustrates the seductress' ways and the consequences of involvement with her.

1. WISDOM PRESERVES FROM ADULTERY (6:20-35)

6:20-21. Once again Solomon exhorted his son (cf. comments on **my son** in 1:8) to heed his **father's** and **mother's** instructions (cf. 1:8) and adhere to them inwardly (6:21a; cf. 3:1; 7:3b) and have his life graced by them (6:21b; cf. 3:3, 22; 7:3a).

6:22-23. Parental instruction provides guidance, protection (cf. 2:11), and counsel (6:22). That teaching should be given from God's Law, for the parents' **commands,** like the Word of God, should be like **a lamp** and **a light,** giving guidance to one's conduct (Ps. 119:105). **Discipline** (cf. Prov. 1:2, 7), though painful (cf. Heb. 12:11a), helps keep a person on the right path, leading him in **the way** of life.

6:24. Wisdom, acquired from God's Word taught by one's parents (vv. 20-23) helps protect **from** adultery (cf. 2:12, 16-

Words and Speaking in Proverbs

I. Wrong Uses of Words

A. Lying
6:16-17a; 10:18a; 12:19, 22a; 17:4b, 7; 19:5b, 9b, 22b; 21:6; 26:28a

B. Slandering
10:18b; 30:10

C. Gossiping
11:13; 16:28b; 17:9b; 18:8; 20:19; 26:20, 22

D. Constant talking
10:8, 10b, 19; 17:28; 18:2; 20:19b

E. False witnessing
12:17b; 14:5b, 25b; 19:5a, 28a; 21:28; 25:18

F. Mocking
13:1b; 14:6a; 15:12; 17:5a; 19:29a; 21:11a; 22:10; 24:9b; 30:17

G. Harsh talking (perverse, reckless, harsh, evil, sly words)
10:31b-32; 12:18a; 13:3b; 14:3a; 15:1b, 28b; 17:4a; 19:1, 28b

H. Boasting
17:17a; 20:14; 25:14; 27:1-2

I. Quarreling
13:10; 15:18; 17:14, 19; 19:13; 20:3; 21:9; 19; 22:10; 25:24; 26:17, 20-21; 27:15

J. Deceiving
7:19-20; 12:2; 15:4b; 25:23

K. Flattering
26:28b; 28:23; 29:5

L. Ignorant or foolish words
14:7; 15:2b, 7-14; 18:6-7

II. Right Uses of Words

A. Words that help and encourage
10:11a, 20a, 21a; 12:14a, 18b; 15:4a; 18:4, 20-21

B. Words that express wisdom
10:13a, 31a; 14:3b; 15:2a, 7a; 16:10, 21b, 23b; 20:15

C. Words that are few
10:19; 11:12b; 13:3a; 17:27a

D. Words that are fitting (kind, appropriate, pleasant)
10:32a; 12:25; 15:1a, 4a, 23; 16:24; 25:11, 15

E. Words that are true
12:17a, 19a, 22b; 14:5a, 25a

F. Words that are carefully chosen
13:3a; 15:28; 16:23a; 21:23

19). **The immoral woman** (lit., "woman of evil")—perhaps unmarried—may be the prostitute mentioned in 6:26. **The wayward wife** (cf. 2:16; 7:5; 23:27) is a sexually promiscuous married woman (cf. "another man's wife," 6:29). In verse 26 she is called an "adulteress," literally, "a wife of a man." On *nok̲rîyâh* ("wayward") see comments on 2:16. Such women have **smooth** tongues; they speak seductively (cf. 2:16; 5:3; 7:5, 21).

6:25. This verse gives a warning and verses 26-29, 32-35 speak of the reasons for the warning. Lusting **in** one's **heart** (cf. comments on 3:5; 4:23) after a physically attractive and sexually promiscuous woman, whether married or unmarried, is wrong. Jesus spoke along a similar line (Matt. 5:28). Men who have fallen into the sin of adultery have often begun with lustful looking. If a man looks at such a woman, she may seek to **captivate** him **with her** flirting **eyes.**

6:26. Immorality is costly! A **prostitute** (cf. 7:10; 23:27; 29:3) can reduce a man to utter poverty, having only **a loaf of bread,** by spending money for her services (cf. 29:3). And a wayward wife (cf. comments on 6:24) can prey on one's **very life,** that is, bring him to ruin and death (cf. 2:18-19; 5:5, 14; 7:22-23, 26-27).

6:27-29. One cost of sexual unfaithfulness is stated in verse 26, and another in verses 27-35. Dire consequences are inevitable (vv. 27-29) and severe (vv. 30-35). As it is impossible to hold **fire** on one's **lap** without burning **his clothes** or to **walk on . . . coals without** burning one's **feet,** so it is impossible to commit adultery **with another man's wife** without being harmed. Illicit sex is like playing with fire! Such a man will be punished, possibly by the woman's husband (cf. v. 34).

6:30-31. People may sympathize with (but not approve of) **a thief** if he is attempting to avoid starvation. However, he had to repay **sevenfold** even if it cost him everything (similar to the man being reduced to a loaf of bread, v. 26). The thief's punishment, though difficult, is less severe than the adulterer's. One who "steals" another's wife finds no forgiveness and no leniency.

6:32-35. Involvement in **adultery** shows one's stupidity (cf. 7:7; 9:4, 16); he goes ahead in his sin while knowing that severe consequences will follow. He **destroys himself** (cf. 6:26b; Deut. 22:22); adultery is a kind of "suicide." Also he is disgraced and shamed; in contrast with a thief (Prov. 6:30), an adulterer is despised. And the wife's husband, learning about their conduct, becomes jealous, furious (cf. 27:4), and vengeful against the adulterer (apparently blaming the guilty man more than his wife). The anger of such a husband cannot be dispelled by bribery, no matter how **great it is.** Bribery is frequently condemned in Proverbs (6:35; 15:27; 17:8), in the Law (Ex. 23:8; Deut. 16:19; 27:25), and elsewhere (e.g., Job 36:18; Ps. 15:5; Ecc. 7:7; Isa. 33:15).

2. WISDOM PRESERVES FROM THE SEDUCTRESS (CHAP. 7)

In 6:20-35 the concerned father gave words of instruction about the tragedy of adultery. In chapter 7 he stated dramatically how a simple, naive youth can be subtly trapped by a seductive woman. Solomon exhorted his son to heed the father's teaching (vv. 1-5), depicted the tactics of the adulteress (vv. 6-23), and concluded with a warning to beware of her trap (vv. 24-27).

a. The father's instruction (7:1-5)

7:1-2. Chapter 7 begins with Solomon's familiar plea for his son (on **my son** see comments on 1:8) to hear, assimilate, and live by his parents' teaching. This instruction included the father's **words** (cf. 2:1; 4:4-5, 20; 5:1), **commands** (cf. 2:1; 3:1; 4:4; 6:20, 23; 7:2), and **teachings** (cf. the sing. "teaching" in 1:8; 3:1; 4:2; 6:20, 23). Because of their help the son was to **keep** (cf. 3:1; 4:4, 21; 6:20), **store up** (cf. 2:1; 10:14), and **guard** them like a treasure. If he did so he would enjoy a full and meaningful life (cf. 3:18; 4:4c; 8:35). **Apple** ('îšôn) is literally the center of a thing; in 7:9 it denotes the center or middle of the night, that is, intense darkness. The pupil, the center of the **eye** (cf. Deut. 32:10; Ps. 17:8), is the most sensitive and carefully guarded of the human body's exposed organs.

7:3. In 3:3 the son was exhorted to bind his father's teachings around his own neck. In 7:3 he was exhorted to **bind them** like rings **on his fingers.** Also as in 3:3 he was to **write them on** his **heart** (cf. 6:21).

7:4-5. In Old Testament times one's **sister** was considered an intimate relative. Therefore "sister" was sometimes used as a synonym for one's wife (cf. Song 4:9-10, 12; 5:1-2). Similarly a person is to be familiar with **wisdom** as if it were his sister or wife. The same is true of **understanding** ("insight"; cf. Prov. 2:2), which is to be like a **kinsman** (cf. Ruth 3:2). One's closeness to understanding should be like the intimate ties between relatives. Wisdom and understanding, often seen as synonyms in Proverbs, **keep** young men **from the adulteress** and **the wayward wife** (see comments on Prov. 2:16; 6:24), who tempt with **seductive words** (cf. 6:24; 7:21). "Seductive" is related to the word "smoother" in 5:3.

b. The victim's naiveté (7:6-9)

Verses 6-23 read like an eyewitness account. The relating of the conversation in verses 14-20 may indicate that Solomon reconstructed the account from his or others' experiences or that he talked with the young man in the account after the event. Probably Solomon did not actually hear the conversation from his vantage point in the window.

7:6-9. Looking from his latticed **window** Solomon **saw** some **simple** (peţî, naive or gullible; see comments on 1:4) **young men,** and **among** them was one **who lacked judgment** (cf. 6:32; 9:4, 16;

10:13). This points up his naiveté, not his foolishness or lust. **Walking** toward **her house** probably does not imply that he was purposely going there. Yet he may well have known she lived there. **He was going** where the temptation was in the evening, **as the day was** concluding and darkness was setting in. **The dark of night** is, literally, "in the center of night, even darkness" ("center" is rendered "apple" in 7:2). As Robert L. Alden wrote, "If you want to avoid the devil, stay away from his neighborhood. If you suspect you might be vulnerable to a particular sin, take steps to avoid it" (*Proverbs: A Commentary on an Ancient Book of Timeless Advice*, p. 63).

c. The seductress' character (7:10-12)

7:10-12. The **woman,** who was married (v. 19), went **out . . . to meet** the young man, sensing that he would be an easy prey. She was (a) brazen in her attire (**dressed** seductively **like a prostitute**), (b) secretive (**crafty intent** is lit., "secretive in heart"), (c) **loud** (cf. 9:13), (d) **defiant** against God's laws and her marriage vows, (e) a gadabout, and (f) furtive (**lurks** in the streets).

d. The seductress' tactics (7:13-20)

7:13-14. Surprising him, **she** suddenly embraced **and kissed him and** then boldly (**with a brazen face**) spoke to him. By referring to her **peace offerings at home** and **vows** she probably was referring to a sacrifice she made (hypocritically, of course) with meat left over (Lev. 7:16-17). Portions of the sacrificial animal were taken home by the offerer. Without refrigeration the meat needed to be consumed; so a feast usually accompanied the sacrifice. Her religious activity, however, was a pretense, an effort to cloud any sense of wrongdoing she may have had.

7:15-18. Building his ego up by flattery (v. 15), she then sought to lure him by describing the sensuous nature of her bedroom. The **linens** on the **bed** were imported **from Egypt** (presumably exquisite and expensive) and she had **perfumed** her **bed** with three spices: **myrrh, aloes, and cinnamon** (see comments on these same spices, Song 4:14). In suggesting that all night they **drink deep of love** she was using a figure of speech that likened sexual relations to drinking from

a fountain (cf. Prov. 5:18; Song 4:12, 15).

7:19-20. The woman sought to assure the young man that they would not be caught by her **husband** (lit., "the man") for he was away on a business trip and would **not be home till the full moon** (at least several days away), so she was unfaithful to him (cf. 2:16-17).

e. The victim's response (7:21-23)

7:21-23. Unable to resist her **persuasive,** seductive, **smooth talk** (cf. v. 5; 2:16; 5:3), he suddenly (**all at once**) **followed her** to her house and bedroom. He was **like** a dumb animal (**an ox**) being led to **slaughter** while being completely unwary of his plight. He was also **like a deer stepping into a noose.** As noted in the NIV margin, "deer" is from the Syriac, whereas the Hebrew has "fool" (cf. KJV and NASB). This verse, difficult to translate, could be rendered, "like fetters for the correction (or discipline) of a fool." He was captured like a fool whose feet are put in fetters and is taken to a correctional institution. He was suddenly overtaken like an animal shot with **an arrow** or **like a bird** being caught in **a snare.** Oblivious to these dangers, he was trapped with no way to escape. He was taken in before he realized that failure to resist this temptation (as Joseph did; cf. Gen. 39:6-12) would **cost him his life** (cf. Prov. 6:32).

f. The father's closing exhortation (7:24-27)

7:24-25. The words **Now then** introduce the father's exhortation, based on the preceding verses. **My sons** (pl.) are addressed as in 4:1; 5:7 and again Solomon their father urged them to **listen to** him (cf. comments on 1:8) attentively (**pay attention;** cf. 4:1, 20; 5:1; 22:17). He advised them to steer clear of the adulteress, by **not** turning their hearts (see comments on 4:23) **to her** (in their imaginations or fantasies) and by not physically going near her (7:25). The word **turn** is *śāṭâh,* "turn aside," a word used only six times in the Old Testament, including 4:15 (and Num. 5:12, 19-20, 29, where it is rendered "goes [gone] astray"). The word **stray** *(tāʿâh)* means "to wander." Obviously the young man got himself in trouble because he strayed or wandered near the temptress' house (Prov. 7:8).

7:26-27. The reason for the exhortation in verses 24-25 is given in verses 26-27. **Many** others had been victimized by this temptation. To be in **her house** (and with her in her bed) is to place oneself on a fast **highway to the grave** and physical **death** (cf. 2:18-19; 5:5; 9:18). A young man involved in illicit sex may die from punishment meted out by an angry husband, or from poverty, or from venereal disease, or from spiritual and emotional anguish.

N. The value of wisdom demonstrated in her virtues and rewards (8:1-21)

Solomon the teacher, personifying wisdom as a woman, wrote about her invitation (vv. 1-5), her virtues (vv. 6-11), and her rewards (vv. 12-21).

1. WISDOM'S CALL (8:1-5)

8:1. Wisdom's public invitation begins with two rhetorical questions (v. 1). The adulteress went out in the streets (7:8-12) to seduce the young man. But **wisdom,** like a virtuous woman, is seen in the streets offering her services to all who will receive them (cf. her calling aloud in 1:20-22). The lack of virtue that characterized the adulteress is contrasted with wisdom's sterling attributes. Whereas the seductress' ways are secretive and deceptive, wisdom's ways are open and honest. One who succumbs to the adulteress finds shame and death, but wisdom's followers acquire prudence for wise living.

8:2-3. Wisdom's call is made where she can be heard and where people traverse: hilltops, **the way,** intersections, **the gates** (where court cases were heard and business was conducted) and **the entrances.**

8:4-5. From verses 4-31 wisdom (**I**) speaks. She invites **all mankind;** wisdom is available to anyone. But specifically she calls to the **simple** (*peṭî;* see comments on 1:4) and the **foolish** (*keṣîl;* see comments on 1:22)—those most in need of her and more likely to ignore her invitation. Both the adulteress and wisdom appeal to the naive. Wisdom urges the simple to **gain prudence** ('*ormâh;* see comments on 1:4; cf. 8:12), a sensibleness in one's approach to life, cleverness in a good sense. And fools are urged to **gain understanding** (cf. 1:2, 6), insight, or sharp discernment.

2. WISDOM'S VIRTUES (8:6-11)

8:6-9. In verses 6-11 the straightforwardness and integrity of wisdom are presented. The young men being taught by Solomon should **listen** to wisdom (v. 6, the exhortation) because what she says is right (vv. 7-9, the reason). The young should choose wisdom (v. 10, the exhortation) because of its great value (v. 11, the reason). Wisdom speaks: **lips** (v. 6b), **mouth** (v. 7a), **lips** (v. 7b), and **mouth** (v. 8a) are referred to alternately. And her words are **worthy** (lit., "noble or princely") **things.** This word could also be translated "valid" as in 2 Samuel 15:3 or "right" as in Isaiah 30:10. The idea is that wisdom's words correspond to reality; therefore they are **right** ("upright or straight"; trans. "faultless" in Prov. 8:9), **true,** and **just** (cf. 1:3; 8:15, 20). Therefore **none** of wisdom's words are **crooked** ("twisted") **or perverse** ('*iqqēš;* see comments on 2:15). They also point in the right direction. People with insight (8:9) know that what wisdom offers is **right** "straightforward or honest"), and people "in the know" find wisdom's words **faultless** (lit., "upright or straight"; trans. "right" in v. 6).

8:10-11. Wisdom urges people to receive her **instruction** and **knowledge rather** than **silver . . . choice gold** (*ḥārûṣ,* pure, refined gold; called "fine gold" in v. 19), or **rubies** (cf. 3:13-15). The idea that wisdom's value exceeds material wealth is expounded in 8:18-21, which states that wisdom provides what is needed to gain and appreciate wealth. Also wisdom contributes to a person's integrity and peace, something silver, gold, and rubies cannot do. And in Proverbs those qualities are of greater value than anything one can buy.

3. WISDOM'S REWARDS (8:12-21)

The abundance of personal pronouns (I, mine, me, my—16 occurrences in 10 verses) makes wisdom herself the focus and not her rewards.

8:12-13. If a person has **wisdom** he also has **prudence** (see comments on 1:4; cf. 8:5), **knowledge, and discretion.** All three of these nouns are in 1:4. Some scholars say 8:13 disrupts the flow of thought between verses 12 and 14. However, verse 13 is a reminder that sensible, discreet living (v. 12) is not associated in any way with the vices mentioned in verse 13. Verse 13 shows that wisdom is moral as well as mental. One who fears **the LORD** (see comments on 1:7) and therefore is wise will **hate** (reject) **evil** (cf. 3:7; 14:16; 16:6, Ps. 97:10), **pride . . . arrogance, evil behavior, and perverse** talk. The word for "perverse" (*tahpūkâh*) is used eight times in Proverbs (cf. comments on 2:12).

8:14-16. Wisdom enables people to give wise **counsel and sound judgment,** and to **have understanding** (insight) **and power** (i.e., valor). Wisdom makes a person courageous like a soldier of valor. **Kings . . . rulers . . . princes,** and **nobles who rule** well do so by God's wisdom; they **make laws that are just.** The fact that many of Israel's and Judah's kings and her neighbors did not make fair laws shows that they lacked God's wisdom.

8:17-18. Wisdom, available to all, is acquired only by those who **love** her (cf. v. 21; 4:6) and **seek** her (cf. 2:1-4). Those who are wise receive **riches and honor** (cf. 3:16), **enduring wealth** (cf. 8:21; 14:24; 15:6; 22:4), **and prosperity.** "Enduring" is literally "surpassing" or "eminent." The riches that come to the possessor of wisdom are genuine, not artificial substitutes purchased with silver or gold. Being honored in a community is a product of one's walk (conduct) rather than one's wealth by itself. "Prosperity" is literally "righteousness" (cf. v. 20). Godly living is the major benefit from having wisdom.

8:19-21. The word **yield** (v. 19) is a term used in the marketplace; the verb focuses attention on wisdom's ability to produce benefits far superior to what **fine gold** (*hārûṣ*; cf. v. 10) and **silver** provide. Wisdom goes with **righteousness** and **justice** (cf. v. 8). The form of the Hebrew verb **walk** conveys the idea of walking steadily or continuously. (On the distinction between righteousness and justice see comments on Amos 5:7.)

As in many places in Proverbs, **way**(s) and **paths** are used synonymously (see comments on Prov. 2:13). As stated in 8:18, those who love (cf. v. 17) and acquire wisdom gain wealth (cf. 3:16; 14:24; 15:6; 22:4). Like many statements in Proverbs, this one is a generalization to which exceptions should be noted. Material substance is replenishable (keeping one's **treasuries full**) because of the skill a wise person has to maintain it.

O. The value of wisdom to the Lord in Creation (8:22-36)

Wisdom's many claims (vv. 6-21) are credible because of her association with the Lord in Creation. She existed before the world was created (vv. 22-29) and she participated with the Lord in Creation, sharing His joy at its accomplishments (vv. 30-31). Because of wisdom's unique role she makes a final plea for people to acquire her (vv. 32-36).

1. WISDOM'S EXISTENCE BEFORE CREATION (8:22-26)

8:22. Wisdom's scope of expertise is broadened from her present ability to enrich individuals (vv. 12-21) to her past involvement in Creation. Wisdom is obviously in view here; **me** clearly refers back to "I, wisdom" (v. 12). Wisdom existed before the Creation of the world (**before** occurs five times in vv. 22-23, 25-26) and therefore was present when God created the universe ("when" occurs seven times, vv. 24, 27-29).

Some Bible students say that wisdom in verses 22-31 refers to Christ. Of course He does reveal God's wisdom to believers (1 Cor. 1:30) and in Him is all wisdom and knowledge (Col. 2:3), but Proverbs 8:22-31 gives no indication that it is Christ who is referred to as wisdom. If that were so, then all other references to wisdom in Proverbs should refer to Christ too, which is unlikely. It is preferable to see wisdom spoken of here figuratively as a *personification of God's attribute of wisdom.*

8:23-26. Before creating the universe, God **appointed** (or "installed," as trans. in Ps. 2:6) wisdom. Proverbs 8:23 refers to wisdom existing **before** God created **the world** (cf. Gen. 1:1-5), before the waters were separated, making clouds and **oceans** (on the second day of Creation, Gen. 1:6-8), and before the dry land appeared (on the third day of Creation, Gen. 1:9-10). Wisdom is pictured as having been born (Prov. 8:24-25).

2. WISDOM'S WORK IN CREATION (8:27-31)

8:27-29. Wisdom, then, was present **when** God **set the heavens in place** (v. 27a; cf. Gen. 1:1-5), when He separated the waters making **clouds** and oceans (Prov. 8:27b-28; on the second day of Creation, Gen. 1:6-8), and when He caused the dry land to appear (Prov. 8:29;

on the third day, Gen. 1:9-10). On the word **deep** (Prov. 8:27) see comments on Genesis 1:2.

8:30-31. Wisdom is said to have been a **craftsman** at God's side when He created the world. This attribute of God, personified as an assistant in the Lord's creative work, poetically indicates that God was wise in what He created. Being **at His side** implies intimate association. Saying that God's work is characterized by wisdom does not suggest that wisdom itself was the designer. *God* was the Designer. This is an important distinction. Wisdom's claim to be present before and during Creation and to be involved in it gives an important credibility to her claim to reward man. Wisdom, personified, rejoices **in** God's **presence** and in His created **world,** including **mankind.**

If God involved wisdom in His creative work, then certainly people need wisdom!

3. WISDOM'S PLEA AND PROMISES (8:32-36)

8:32-34. Here wisdom herself addressed the young men as **my sons,** as the father had already done three times (4:1; 5:7; 7:24). The words **Now then** relate this appeal to wisdom's preceding claims. In verses 32-34 the words **listen** and **blessed** are used alternately (listen, v. 32; blessed, v. 32; listen, v. 33; blessed, v. 34; listens, v. 34). Wisdom's threefold call to young men to **listen** is mindful of Solomon's frequent call to them to listen (see comments on 1:8). By listening to wisdom's instruction and following it, they become **wise** and are "blessed." This blessing comes from following wisdom eagerly (**watching** and **waiting**).

8:35-36. Wisdom gives **life** (cf. 3:18; 4:4, 22; 7:2; 9:11; 19:23) and the Lord's **favor** (cf. 12:2; 18:22). The word for "favor," *rāṣôn,* is used 14 times in Proverbs, and means "acceptance, goodwill, or approval." It comes from the verb *rāṣâh,* "to be pleased with." Rejecting wisdom results in harm (cf. 6:32; 7:23; 9:12b) and **death** (cf. 2:18; 5:5; 7:27). Wisdom is the way of life and folly is the way of death. These are people's two choices.

P. The value of wisdom summarized by contrasting her invitation with folly's invitation (chap. 9)

This chapter summarizes 1:8–8:36 by contrasting the invitations of wisdom

(9:1-6) and of folly (vv. 13-18). Between the two invitations a brief series of tersely stated proverbs contrasts the nature and consequences of those who respond to each invitation (vv. 7-12). Wisdom and its rival folly are portrayed as two women each preparing a feast and inviting young men to their houses. Wisdom is portrayed as a responsible woman of character and wealth preparing a banquet, while folly is portrayed as a harlot inviting young men to a sensual meal of stolen water and food eaten in secret.

1. WISDOM'S INVITATION (9:1-6)

In Proverbs wisdom is frequently personified as a dignified lady (1:20-33; 3:16-18; 4:3-6; 8:1-21, 32-36; 9:1-6). In 9:1-6 she is a builder and a homemaker preparing a banquet for those lacking wisdom.

a. Wisdom's preparation of her banquet (9:1-2)

9:1. The common Hebrew word for **wisdom** is *ḥokmâh,* but here it appears to be in the plural form (*ḥokmôt*) with a singular verb **has built** (though some construe *ḥokmôt* also as sing. in keeping with analogous forms in Canaanite dialects). This is also the case in 1:20; 24:7; Psalm 49:3. If the form is plural it may suggest wisdom's fullness. "Lady Wisdom's" activities of building **her house,** including hewing **out** for it **seven pillars,** suggest the industriousness that accompanies wisdom. Bible scholars have offered various suggestions about the meaning of these seven pillars (e.g., the six days of Creation and God's seventh day of rest; or the sun, moon, and the five planets that were known at that time). It seems preferable to say the seven pillars suggest that the house was large and spacious. This is consistent with statements in Proverbs that relate wisdom to a high station in life.

9:2. The meal that "Lady Wisdom" prepared included **meat and mixed . . . wine** (cf. v. 5). **Prepared her** meat is literally, "slaughtered her slaughter" (i.e., she butchered animals and cooked their meat). Mixing the wine may refer to diluting it, a custom in ancient Israel (cf. the apocryphal 2 Maccabees 15:39 and *The International Standard Bible Encyclopaedia.* Grand Rapids: Wm. B. Eerdmans Publishing Co., 1939, 5:3087). Undiluted wine was considered distasteful by the

Jews, and the wine for the Passover consisted of three parts water and one part wine. Or perhaps the custom of mixing spices with the wine to enhance its flavor may be in view (cf. Ps. 75:8; also note Isa. 5:22). Or possibly both are intended.

b. Wisdom's invitation to her banquet (9:3-6)

9:3. Having prepared the meal the gracious hostess **sent out her maids** to invite people to attend the banquet (cf. Matt. 22:2-3). **The highest point of the city** (cf. Prov. 8:2) was an elevated spot where many would hear the invitation being called out. "Madam Folly" also called from such a high point (9:14).

9:4-6. The words of Wisdom's invitation include at least verses 4-6 (and possibly also vv. 7-12, as indicated by the quotation marks in the NIV). Those invited to Wisdom's fare were the **simple** (*peṭî*, "naive, gullible"; see comments on 1:4; cf. 8:5; 9:16) and **those who lack judgment** (see comments on 6:32). Those most needing her attention were invited to be Wisdom's guests. They were to **come** and **eat** and **drink**, that is, people without wisdom should acquire it and benefit from it. They were to **leave** their **simple ways** (*peṭā'îm*, 9:6, the pl. of "simple" in v. 4). This could mean "simple ones." But the second part of the verse which invites the guests to **walk in the way of understanding** suggests that "simple ways," referring to the habits of the naive, is preferable. As already stated (3:18; 4:4; 7:2) the result of wisdom is life (**you will live**; cf. 9:11; 19:23).

2. CONSEQUENCES OF ACCEPTING THE INVITATIONS (9:7-12)

At first these verses seem to interrupt the flow of the passage, coming as they do between Wisdom's invitation (vv. 1-6) and Folly's invitation (vv. 13-18). However, this section's position is appropriate, for it points to the consequences of accepting the two invitations. Those who heed Wisdom respond to and learn from rebuke (v. 8b; see comments on 1:23), add to their knowledge (9:9), and enjoy life (v. 11). But those who heed Folly's call are not open to correction (vv. 7-8a) so they suffer (v. 12b). They are mockers, unwilling to be corrected. Folly's invitation only hardens them in their ways.

9:7-8a. A mocker (see comments on 1:22), who is **wicked,** is unteachable. When someone corrects him he responds in an attitude of hatred by lashing out with insulting verbal abuses (9:7-8a). **Abuse** (*mûm*) means a blotch or defect. When corrected, a wicked person hurls back the rebuke by defaming his would-be counselor. Such a mocker is hardened in his ways.

9:8b-9. On the other hand **a wise** person appreciates **rebuke** because he learns from it. Rebukes can be helpful to the one who is willing to learn from them (15:31; 17:10; 19:25; 25:12; 27:5-6). By being teachable (cf. 10:8a; 12:15b; 14:6b; 15:32b; 21:11b) one becomes **wiser** (cf. 1:5). As elsewhere in Proverbs a wise person is **a righteous** person. Godly character should underlie one's mental sagacity.

9:10-11. The theme of the book (1:7a) is restated in 9:10a, with two variations: the Hebrew word for **beginning** here differs from the word for beginning in 1:7. In 9:10 it means "prerequisite" (see comments on 1:7). And the word **wisdom** is used in 9:10 whereas "knowledge" is used in 1:7a.

Personal **knowledge of** God—called in Proverbs **the Holy One** only here and in 30:3—gives insight into life.

Wisdom (**me,** 9:11) assures a person a long **life** (cf. v. 6; 3:2, 16; 4:10; 10:27; 14:27; 15:24).

9:12. As stated frequently in Proverbs in different ways, **wisdom** brings rewards and mocking brings suffering. Some of the rewards are mentioned in verses 8a-11.

3. FOLLY'S INVITATION (9:13-18)

9:13. Folly's feast is presented in contrast with Wisdom's feast. In similar fashion Madam **Folly** (the fem. form of *keṣîl*; see comments on 1:7), portrayed as a harlot, made her wares available. She **is loud** (cf. 7:11), **undisciplined** (lit., "naive or gullible," like her guests; cf. 9:16), and ignorant. She is attractive but unruly. Here, as elsewhere, Folly offers immediate gratification whereas Wisdom offers long-term satisfaction.

9:14-15. Unlike Lady Wisdom, who prepared for (vv. 1-2) and searched out her guests (vv. 3-6), Madam Folly merely sat **at the door** and called out. But she, like Wisdom, called from **the highest**

point of the city (cf. v. 3). Folly appealed to **those who** passed by (cf. 7:8, 10). Those **who go straight on their way** could refer to those who might otherwise pass on by without stopping or those who were leading upright lives. Perhaps both ideas are involved.

9:16-17. Folly called for guests by intentionally using the same words as Lady Wisdom (cf. v. 4 and comments there). Since drinking water from one's own fountain refers to sex in marriage (5:15-16), the **stolen water** may refer to illicit sex (cf. 7:18-19). In this way Madam Folly appealed to her guests' baser desires. **Food eaten in secret** also suggests a clandestine activity.

9:18. Though her invitation may seem attractive, the end result is not life (cf. v. 11); it is death (cf. 2:18; 5:5; 7:27). Madam Folly is obviously a wayward woman. This suggests that sexual immorality is the height of folly. The two paths of Wisdom and folly resulting in life or death reach a vivid climax in chapter 9. Almost every verse in the remainder of the book points to one or both of these paths and/or their consequences.

III. The Proverbs of Solomon (10:1–22:16)

This long portion of the Book of Proverbs contains 375 sayings. The development of thought is limited to the two (or sometimes more) lines of each verse. Chapters 10–15 continue the subject matter so dominant in chapters 1–9 contrasting the righteous (or wise) with the wicked (or foolish). The remainder of the section (16:1–22:16) is more varied in subject matter.

Most of the verses in chapters 10–15 are contrasts (in antithetic parallelism); the second line in most of the verses begins with "but." Only a few of the verses in 16:1–22:16 are contrasts; most of the verses are either comparisions (in synonymous parallelism) or completions (in synthetic parallelism), with the conjunction "and" introducing the second line in many of the verses.

The frequent change of subject from one verse to another may be intentional, to force readers to grapple with and meditate on the thoughts in one verse before moving on to the next. However, occasionally two or more consecutive verses are linked by a common subject or word.

For example 10:4-5 discusses both laziness and diligence, and 10:11-14, 18-21, 31-32 refer to talking. "LORD" is mentioned in each verse in 16:1-7, the key word in each verse in 16:12-15 is "king," 15:16-17 both begin with the word "better," each verse in 12:9-11 discusses domestic scenes, and each verse in 11:9-12 begins with the same Hebrew letter.

A. Proverbs contrasting righteous and wicked living (chaps. 10–15)

10:1. On **the proverbs of Solomon,** see "Authorship and Date" in the *Introduction.* With Solomon having authored chapters 1–9 (see 1:1) and chapters 25–29 (see 25:1), along with 10:1–22:16, he wrote about 84 percent of the book, all of it of course being inspired by the divine Author, the Holy Spirit.

A **wise son** is contrasted here with "a foolish son," in 13:1 with a mocker, and in 15:20 with a foolish man. A son who has become wise, by heeding his parents' teachings (5:1-2), **brings joy to his father,** a fact stated several times in Proverbs (15:20; 23:15, 24; 27:11; 29:3). A **foolish** (*k*ᵉ*sîl*; see comments on 1:7) **son,** on the other hand, grieves **his mother.** This does not mean that a foolish son does not grieve his father, as is clearly stated in 17:21, 25; 19:13. Nor does 10:1 mean that a mother's heart is not gladdened by a son's wisdom. The use of "father" in one line and "mother" in the other is typical of proverbial literature. Both parents experience either the joy or the grief, just as both are involved in teaching (1:8; 4:3-4; 6:20).

10:2. To say that **treasures** are **of no value** seems like a startling, almost contradictory statement until one remembers that the treasures are **ill-gotten** (cf. 1:19; 28:16; Micah 6:10), gained unjustly (cf. Prov. 16:8) by theft or deceit. An example of this is addressed in 1:11-14, 18-19. Such treasures are no good because they dwindle away (13:11; 21:6) and do not forestall death (11:4). Of course money acquired dishonestly may provide some pleasure and be valuable for a while but in the long run it does not satisfy.

10:3. Verses 3-5 discuss diligence and sloth. Satisfaction of one's appetite is related to **the LORD** (v. 3); poverty and wealth result from laziness and diligence, respectively (v. 4); industry characterizes a wise son and sleep characterizes a shameful son (v. 5). **The righteous** is literally, "the soul of the righteous." Since "soul" emphasizes the whole person, God has said here that He meets all one's needs, including the needs of his body for food (cf. Ps. 37:19, 25). **The craving of the wicked** refers to their evil desires to bring about destruction and disaster. God can keep them from carrying out such plans. Like many verses in Proverbs, this verse is a generalization. It is usually true that the godly do not starve and that the wicked do not get all they desire.

10:4-5. If a person refuses to work he will be **poor** (a word used often in Prov.), whereas a hard worker eventually is rewarded. (Besides laziness other reasons for poverty are mentioned in Prov. See comments on 14:23.) One example of diligence and therefore of wisdom (**wise** is from the verb śāḵal meaning "to be prudent or to have sound judgment"; cf. 1:3; 16:20) is harvesting in the **summer** while the **crops** are ripe. An example of laziness is a son **who sleeps** rather than works **during harvest** (in contrast with the ants, 6:6-11). In fact such a person brings shame (the meaning of **disgraceful**), probably to his parents.

10:6. Whereas a **righteous** person receives **blessings,** it is different with **the wicked. Violence overwhelms** his **mouth.** The same statement is made in verse 11. Since the word for "overwhelms" can be translated "covers" (as it is in v. 12), the idea is either that his mouth conceals or deceptively hides violence (NIV marg.), or that violence characterizes what a person says. As Jesus stated, "The evil man brings evil things out of the evil stored up in his heart" (Luke 6:45).

10:7. Speaking of blessings and the righteous (v. 6), even *thinking* about **righteous** people of the past can **be a** source of spiritual **blessing.** By contrast most people want to forget **the wicked.** Like their character, even their names are corrupt, rotting like a corpse.

10:8-9. A **wise** person is teachable, willing to become wiser (cf. 1:5; 9:9). **But** a **fool** ('ĕwîl, a coarse, hardened fool; see comments on 1:7; cf. 10:21) does not quit **chattering** long enough to learn anything. In Proverbs needless talking is often associated with folly. Such a person **comes to ruin,** a phrase repeated only

two verses later (v. 10; cf. 13:3). "Ruin" is mentioned five times in chapter 10 (vv. 8, 10, 14-15, 29). An honest person (v. 9) is secure (cf. a similar thought in 3:23; 18:10; 28:18) in his walk (his conduct) **but** a person whose **paths** are **crooked** (lit., "twisted"), whose conduct is wicked, in contrast with a person **of integrity,** eventually **will be** discovered for what he truly is.

10:10. Verses 10-12 deal with interpersonal relations. Winking **maliciously** with one's cohorts suggests sinful intentions (cf. 6:13; 16:30; Ps. 35:19). No wonder this leads to **grief** on the part of the victims of their evil plans, or the victim's loved ones. Yet a talkative **fool** will himself eventually get into trouble (cf. the same line in Prov. 10:8b).

10:11. The words of a **righteous** (and wise) person are like **a fountain of life** (cf. 13:14; 14:27; 16:22; also note 18:4). His words of wisdom are free-flowing and as refreshing as a cool spring to a weary desert traveler. On the second part of 10:11; see comments on verse 6b.

10:12. Hatred results in **dissension** (cf. 6:14) because people who despise each other can hardly work or live together in peace. **Love** contributes toward peace because it **covers** or forgives the faults of others (cf. 17:9). It does not dwell on those faults (cf. 1 Cor. 13:5; James 5:20; 1 Peter 4:8). "Covers" is kāsâh, the same word rendered "overwhelms" in Proverbs 10:6, 11. A wicked one's words are covered *over* with violence, **but** a righteous person covers *up* **wrongs** by forgiving the wrongdoers.

10:13-14. These statements contrast the wise and the fool. While **the discerning** person is characterized by his wise statements, one lacking **judgment** (cf. v. 21; 6:32; 7:7; 9:4, 16; 11:12; 12:11; 15:21; 17:18; 24:30; 28:16) experiences trouble. He may be punished by **a rod** on **the back** (cf. 14:3; 26:3). A **wise** person stores **up knowledge;** he holds it in for the right occasion without spouting off his knowledge. What **a fool** says, however, causes him trouble and eventually **ruin** because he foolishly speaks the wrong things and gets himself in trouble (cf. 10:19).

10:15-16. These verses are together because they both discuss **wealth.** The first line of verse 15 is repeated in 18:11. Though wealth should not be placed above honor (28:20) and should not be trusted in (11:4; 23:5), it can provide a hedge against some disasters. **Poverty** is a continually suppressive problem to **the poor** (cf. 14:20; 18:23; 19:7; 22:7). The Hebrew word here for poor is *dal*, "feeble, weak, helpless," translated "poor" or "helpless" in 19:4, 17; 21:13; 22:16; 28:3, 8, 11, 15; 29:7, 14. Proverbs also uses several other words for "poor" and "poverty."

Wages (10:16) refers not to money but to the natural result or "return" for **righteous** living. That result is a meaningful **life** (cf. 3:18, 21-22; 4:4; 7:2a). But **the wicked** reap trouble (Gal. 6:7).

10:17. The word **life** links verses 16 and 17. A person **who** learns from **discipline** is an example to others of **the way to** a meaningful life, whereas those who refuse to learn from discipline cause **others** to go **astray.** One's conduct affects not only himself but others as well, either favorably or unfavorably.

10:18. Each of verses 18-21 refers to some aspects of talking. The subject of **hatred** was introduced in verse 12, and in verse 18 another thought is added to the subject. When a person hates someone but tries not to show it he is often forced to lie. And hatred often leads to slandering the other who is despised. The second line in verse 18 begins with **and** rather than "but," to show that the two thoughts of hatred and **slander** are not opposites. Such lying and slandering, born out of hatred, characterize **a fool.**

10:19. Constant talking will eventually lead to **sin** and get a person into trouble (cf. "chattering" in vv. 8, 10; also note James 3:2-8). This is obviously folly because the ability to keep silent **is wise** (cf. Prov. 11:12).

10:20. In contrast with the degrading talk of the wicked (lying, slandering, and gabbing, vv. 18-19) **the** words **(tongue) of the righteous** are uplifting and therefore are valued like **choice silver.** However, with **the wicked** not even their thoughts **(heart)** have **value,** let alone their **words!**

10:21. The word "tongue" links verses 19 and 20, the word **lips** unites verse 21 with verse 18, and **the righteous** ties verses 20 and 21 together. One of the reasons righteous words are valuable (v. 20) is that they **nourish** or benefit others spiritually. Death comes to those who are **fools** (*'ĕwîl;* cf. v. 8 and see comments on 1:7) because they **lack judgment** (cf. 6:32;

7:7; 9:4, 16; 10:13; 11:12; 12:11; 15:21; 24:30; 28:16). Since the first part of 10:21 refers to talking, the second part probably implies that fools lack judgment in what they say. Their wrong kind of talking does not even nourish themselves; they are left spiritually undernourished and starved.

10:22. After the word "LORD" the Hebrew adds the word "it" for emphasis. So the first line reads, **The blessing of the LORD,** *it* **brings wealth.** The second line affirms the idea that wealth given by the Lord (to the righteous and diligent) is not accompanied by **trouble,** the tragedies of ill-gotten gain (cf. v. 2).

10:23. Most of verses 23-32 contrast the righteous and the wicked. A **fool** (*kesîl,* a thickheaded person; see comments on 1:7) enjoys sinning, whereas the wise prefer **wisdom.** This contrast between **evil conduct** and wisdom shows that wisdom in the biblical sense is moral in nature.

10:24-25. By stressing repeatedly in Proverbs that disaster comes to **the wicked** and various rewards are for the righteous, Solomon sought to convince the uninitiated and naive that the long-range, not the immediate, fruits of wisdom and folly should be kept in view. Many **wicked** people dread calamity and they receive it! And **the righteous** often receive what they want, namely, blessing. God is the ultimate Source of both. A **storm** can come suddenly, bringing disaster to **the wicked** by destroying their lives and property (cf. 1:27; 6:15; 29:1), but **the righteous** are more secure (cf. 10:9, 30; 12:3).

10:26. Just **as vinegar** (made from wine) is sour tasting, and as **smoke** irritates **the eyes,** so a **sluggard** (see comments on 6:6-11) aggravates his employers, **those who send him** to do some work or go on an errand. He is aggravating because he fails to carry out his responsibilities.

10:27-30. These verses mention several blessings that come to **the righteous:** long **life . . . joy,** safety, and security. Usually **the wicked** have none of these, when seen from the perspective of eternity. Longevity for **the righteous** and the brief lives of **the wicked** are frequent themes in Proverbs (3:2, 16; 4:10; 9:11; 14:27; 15:24). On **the fear of the LORD** see comments on 1:7 (also cf. 2:5; 3:7; 8:13;

9:10; 14:26-27; 15:16, 33; 16:6; 19:23; 22:4; 23:17; 24:21). Joy comes to those who love the Lord, but the desires of the wicked for joy are not fulfilled (cf. 10:24; 11:7). By going in the way of the LORD, that is, by following His standards, the righteous have a refuge of safety (mā'ôz; cf. Ps. 31:2, 4; Nahum 1:7). They are secure in the land (cf. Prov. 10:9, 25) but the wicked are not (cf. 2:21-22).

10:31-32. These two verses also address the subject of talking (cf. vv. 11-14, 18-21). The righteous speak wise words (cf. v. 11). **Brings forth** is literally, "bears fruit." As a tree naturally brings forth fruit so wise words are a natural result of uprightness (cf. Luke 6:43-45). Thus they are fitting or appropriate (see comments on Prov. 10:14). **Perverse,** used in both verses 31 and 32, means to be turned away from what is normal (cf. 2:12).

11:1. The LORD hates **dishonest scales** (lit., "balances of deceit"), **but** is pleased with **accurate weights** (lit., "perfect stones"). Dishonesty in business was condemned and honesty commended (cf. 16:11; 20:10, 23; Lev. 19:35-36; Deut. 25:13-16; Micah 6:10-11; also note Amos 8:5). To increase their profits many merchants used two sets of stone weights when weighing merchandise. Lighter stones were placed on the scales when selling (so that a lesser quantity was sold for the stated price), and heavier ones were used when buying (so that more was obtained for the same price). With the absence of coinage, scales were used in most daily commercial transactions. The reference to "the LORD" puts commercial matters in the spiritual realm.

11:2. This verse contains an interesting combination of words. **Pride** leads to **disgrace,** its opposite, while **humility** (this Heb. noun is used only here and its verbal form is used only in Micah 6:8, "walk humbly"), which pictures a submissive, modest spirit before both God and man, leads to or is accompanied by **wisdom.** Proverbs 13:10 also contrasts pride and wisdom. The word for "pride" (zādôn, "arrogance"; cf. 13:10) is from the verb zîd, "to boil up" (cf. "cooking," Gen. 25:29) and sounds much like the Hebrew word for disgrace (qālôn).

11:3. Verses 3-8 refer to the value of righteousness in guiding and protecting from hardships. **Integrity** (trans. "blameless" in Job 1:1; Prov. 11:20) refers to

moral wholeness, being without moral blemish. When integrity is a way of life, it **guides** like a shepherd. **Duplicity** is the contrasting characteristic. The noun selep is used only here and in 15:4 ("deceitful"); the related verb sālap means "to pervert, subvert, or overturn." It is rendered "overthrows" in 13:6 and "frustrates" in 22:12.

11:4. The day of wrath (cf. "wrath" in v. 23) probably refers to **death. Wealth** cannot buy long life; only **righteousness** can aid in that (cf. 10:2b). In 10:27 fearing the Lord is said to contribute to longevity.

11:5. Righteous living results in a **straight way** (cf. 3:5-6), a life with fewer obstacles and troubles (cf. 11:8), but **wickedness** leads to a person's downfall.

11:6. Another benefit of righteous living is deliverance, escape from troubles (see comments on v. 5) or death (v. 4). But even the **evil desires** of an **unfaithful** (lit., "treacherous") person get him in trouble (cf. v. 3). He is **trapped** (1:17-18; 6:2; 7:22-23; 12:13), for his desires lead him to sin.

11:7. Death for the **wicked** puts an end to all he hoped to accomplish. Neither his wealth (v. 4) nor his **power** can divert death. Obviously it is futile to forsake righteousness to gain power.

11:8. As stated in verses 3, 5-6, **righteous** living helps avert **trouble** (cf. 12:13). As in the Book of Esther, the trouble which wicked Haman planned for Mordecai came on Haman **instead** (Es. 3–7).

11:9. Verses 9-15 discuss community relationships: one's **neighbor** (vv. 9, 12), the city (vv. 10-11), a gossip (v. 13), advisers for a nation (v. 14), and a cosigner (v. 15). A **godless** person can defame another merely by what he says (cf. comments on 10:18-19a). The Hebrew word for "godless" is ḥānēp, "profane." The verb ḥānap is translated "defiled" (Jer. 3:1), "pollute(s)" (Num. 35:33), "desecrated" (Ps. 106:38). Contrasted with a profane person, who is careless in what he says, is **the righteous** person who escapes **through knowledge.** Perhaps this means he escapes the injury of slander either because he knows it is not true or because he knows to stay away from profane people.

11:10-11. These verses refer to the beneficial effect that **righteous** people can have on public life. People of a city appreciate and take delight in the prosperity of and God's **blessing** on its **upright** citizens because they exalt **the city.** That is, such people help keep a city sound economically and morally (cf. Jer. 22:2-5). Conversely citizens are glad when **the wicked**—who lie, slander, deceive, rob, and murder—die (cf. Prov. 28:12, 28) because then the city is safer. Wicked people's words (**mouth**; cf. 11:9)—not to mention their deeds!—can destroy a city economically and morally.

11:12-13. In these community relationships (vv. 9-15), right and wrong talking is mentioned several times: in verses 9, 11-13. Anyone who **derides** (*bûz,* "to despise, belittle, hold in contempt"; cf. comments on *bûz* in 1:7b) **his neighbor** (cf. 14:21) **lacks judgment** (see comments on 6:32; 10:13). It simply makes no sense to slander (cf. 10:18) one who lives or works nearby. Since that makes for friction and dissension, it is wise to keep quiet (hold one's **tongue;** cf. 10:19) even if he does know something unpleasant about his neighbor. Divulging **a secret** by malicious **gossip** is a betrayal of trust (also stated in 20:19). "A gossip" is literally "one who goes about in slander." Gossiping is also condemned in 16:28; 18:8; 26:20, 22.

11:14. Guidance (*tahbûlôt,* also used in 1:5) is a nautical term used of steering a ship. The "steerings" or counsel of **advisers** can be helpful (cf. 15:22; 20:18; 24:6). A wise person is open to others' opinions and counsel. Without such counsel, he may make serious mistakes.

11:15. Putting **up security for** someone poses serious problems (see comments on 6:1-5; cf. 17:18; 22:26-27).

11:16. Most of the verses in 11:16-31 refer in some way to the rewards of righteous and kind living. Verse 16 contrasts the **respect** or honor acquired by a **kindhearted** (*hēn,* "gracious") **woman** (cf. a kind man, v. 17) with the **wealth** attained by **ruthless men.** Women of commendable character are also mentioned in 12:4; 14:1; 19:14; 31:10-31. The word **only** suggests that wealth is much inferior to honor (e.g., the inadequacies of wealth are mentioned in 1:19; 10:2; 11:4). The word for "ruthless" (*'ārîs*) means one who strikes terror because of his wickedness. This keeps him from enjoying honor, respect, or even peace of mind.

11:17. Verses 17-21 all contrast the outcomes of wicked and righteous living. Both kindness (**kind** translates *hesed,* "loyal love") and cruelty are reciprocal: kindness **benefits** its giver (for the kindness is returned by its recipients), and cruelty boomerangs, harming both its recipient and its giver (cf. 13:20).

11:18. Even the **wages** a sinful person earns are **deceptive,** that is, he thinks his money will help him get ahead, but he finds that it is ultimately of no benefit (v. 4). On the other hand sowing **righteousness,** leading a righteous life, **reaps** rewards that *are* beneficial and lasting. "Deceptive" in Hebrew is *šāqer* and **reward** is the similar-sounding *śeker,* an intended alliteration and assonance to call attention to those words.

11:19. **Righteous** living is rewarded with **life** (cf. 12:28) and wickedness is rewarded with **death,** a frequent theme in Proverbs. A sinner receives harm (11:17), useless money (v. 18), and eventually death (v. 19).

11:20. In Proverbs **the LORD** is said to detest many kinds of sinful attitudes and actions: crooked (**perverse,** *'iqqēš,* means crooked or distorted; see comments on 2:15) living (3:32; 11:20), lying (12:22), hypocrisy (15:8), wicked conduct (15:9), wicked thoughts (15:26), pride (16:5), injustice (17:15), and dishonesty in business (20:10, 23). Also see 6:16-19. On the other hand the Lord takes delight **in those** who are morally whole (**blameless;** cf. 11:3) and are truthful (12:22).

11:21. **Be sure of this** is a translation of the idiomatic phrase "hand to hand" (also in 16:5b). This may refer to clasping hands over an agreement on a transaction, which closed a deal. What is certain is that sinners will be punished and the **righteous will** not be.

11:22. Israelite women wore nose rings for ornamental purposes, like earrings and rings on fingers today. How incongruous to suppose a nose **ring** would beautify a pig, a notoriously unclean animal! Similarly it is incongruous to suppose that a woman's physical beauty can excuse her lack of **discretion** (moral perception). This verse has an unusual impact by comparing **a beautiful woman** to an ugly pig. Outward female beauty with indiscreet conduct is valueless and morally ugly. This is the first of many verses in Proverbs that use the word **like** or "as" to make a comparison, in what is called emblematic parallelism.

11:23. What **the righteous** long for (cf. 10:24; 13:4) **ends** in (or "is") **good.** Conversely what **the wicked** hope for (cf. 10:28b; 11:7) ends in (or "is") **wrath** (cf. 11:4). This means either that God's wrath comes on the wicked and thwarts their desires or that the wicked desire **only** to vent their wrath.

11:24-26. These verses encourage generosity. By giving **freely** a person has plenty, a seeming paradox (cf. 2 Cor. 9:6). Conversely a person who is miserly, failing to help **others** in obvious need, will himself always be in need (cf. 28:22). By being **generous** (Prov. 11:25) a person prospers and is in turn helped (cf. v. 17). **Grain** (v. 26) in a farming society was a major medium of exchange; hoarding it could drastically affect prices. But a person who sold his grain and did not hoard it was a **blessing** to others.

11:27-28. If a person pursues (**seeks** translates *šāḥar,* "to look early or eagerly for," like looking for the dawn) **good** things in and for others **he** himself in turn receives **goodwill** (*rāṣôn,* "acceptance"; see comments on 8:35, "favor"; cf. 14:9) from others. It is reciprocal, as in 11:17a, 25. If a person **searches** for **evil** (distress or tragedy) to come on others it will come on **him** (cf. 11:17b). To have money is not wrong but to trust in it is (cf. 1 Tim. 6:9-10) because it and its owners are transitory (cf. Ps. 62:10; Prov. 23:5; 27:24; James 1:11). **But the righteous,** trusting in the Lord, flourish **like a green leaf** (cf. the tree in Prov. 11:30 and Pss. 1:3-4; 92:12-15; Jer. 17:7-8).

11:29. To bring **trouble on** one's own **family** members means that such a person will be disinherited from the estate; he will receive **only wind,** or nothing. And rather than being wealthy and having servants, such a **fool** becomes a **servant!**

11:30. As a result **(fruit) of righteous** living a person becomes **a tree of life** (cf. 3:18; 13:12; 15:4), a source of a meaningful life for others (cf. the leaf in 11:28). This contrasts with a fool who troubles his family (v. 29). **Wins souls** in verse 30 does not mean soul-winning or evangelism. Since "win" is literally "attract or take," the idea may be that a righteous person attracts others to wisdom. This fits the thought in the first part of the

verse of a tree giving life to others by its fruit.

11:31. If the righteous must be punished in this life (**on earth**) when they do wrong, then certainly (**how much more**) those who are committed to sin and evil will be punished (cf. v. 21). Or the first part of the verse can mean that the righteous are blessed in this life. "How much more" also occurs in 15:11; 19:7; 21:27 and "how much worse" is in 17:7; 19:10. Verse 31 of chapter 11 is a summary of verses 29-30.

12:1. To love (i.e., willingly accept or desire) **discipline** (*mûsār,* "moral discipline or correction"; cf. 1:2, 7; 10:17) shows that a person **loves** (desires) **knowledge.** He wants to be on the right path, to be wise. To hate (reject and despise) **correction** shows that one **is stupid** (*baʿar,* "to be brutish or dull-minded" like an animal; also used in 30:2, "ignorant"). Similar thoughts are given in 12:15; 13:1, 13, 18; 15:5, 10, 12, 31-32.

12:2. Proverbs uses many words to describe the righteous and the wise, such as upright (11:3, 11), blameless (11:5), a man of understanding (11:12), trustworthy (11:13), kind (11:17), generous (11:25), prudent (12:16, 23), truthful (v. 22). In verse 2 **good** is another characteristic. Such a person is blessed with God's **favor** (*rāṣôn,* "acceptance"; see comments on 8:35). But a person who is **crafty** (cf. 14:17) or deceptively shrewd not only is not favored by God; he is also condemned ("declared guilty"; cf. Ex. 22:9) by God.

12:3. Being settled and stable in their land was valued by the Israelites. But not everyone experienced it (cf. v. 7; 10:25). A wicked person would be **uprooted** like a plant torn up by the roots, which describes exile and/or death.

12:4. A **wife of noble character** (cf. 31:10; Ruth 3:11) is like a **crown** on **her husband's** head, that is, her strength of character (*ḥayil* is lit., "strength") makes her husband proud and honored. She adds dignity to him. Conversely **a disgraceful wife** (one who is not noble or strong morally) decays **his bones** (cf. comments on Prov. 3:8); her shame gives him inner pain.

12:5. Verses 5-8 contrast the righteous and the wicked. **The righteous** have **plans** or desires for themselves and others that are fair and honest, but **the**

wicked counsel others in **deceitful** ways, with **advice** that is dishonest and self-serving (and warped, v. 8). One's thoughts and words are usually consistent with his character.

12:6. The wicked seek to destroy other people by their **words** of advice, as stated in verse 5, which is deceitful. **The upright,** however, try to rescue **them,** the victims attacked by gossipers and slanderers.

12:7. When the **wicked** try to overthrow others (v. 6) they themselves **are overthrown** (cf. 1:18) in death. Their trap traps *them.* And they **are no more;** they cease to exist. **But the house** (family) **of** a **righteous** individual is secure (cf. 12:3; 14:11).

12:8. The attitudes people have toward the righteous and the wicked are contrasted: praise is for the wise (**wisdom** here is *śēḵel,* "prudence or sound judgment"; cf. 1:3) and hatred is for those **with warped minds.** "Warped" (*'āwâh*) is one of several words in Proverbs for crooked. It means "bent or twisted." Their thinking is distorted.

12:9. Verses 9-11 pertain to domestic scenes. A contrast is presented by the words **better** and **than** instead of "but." This is the first of 19 verses in Proverbs that use the "better . . . than" formula: verse 9; 15:16-17; 16:8, 16, 19, 32; 17:1, 12; 19:1, 22; 21:9, 19; 22:1; 25:7, 24; 27:5, 10; 28:6.

It is preferable to be unknown (**be** or pretend **to be a nobody**) and yet be in an honorable position (able to hire **a servant**) than it is to boast that one is **somebody** and yet be starving (cf. 13:7). What good is such a claim if one cannot put food on the table?

12:10. A **righteous** person is concerned about more than himself or his family. His kindness extends to his animals (pets and livestock). **Cares for the needs of his animal** is literally, "knows the soul of his beast." He sympathetically understands the life-needs of his animals (cf. 27:23). By contrast **the kindest** thing a sinner does is really **cruel.** He does not know how to treat his livestock properly.

12:11. Diligent farming results in plenty of **food** (cf. 28:19a; also note 14:23). **But** chasing (an intensive verbal form meaning to pursue frantically) **fantasies** (things that are empty or worthless), either mentally or physically, does not get the farming done and so one **lacks** food (cf. 28:19b). To neglect one's work while thinking about other things shows lack of **judgment** (see comments on 6:23; 10:13).

12:12. What **wicked** people acquire by devious means is desired by other wicked people. **Plunder,** literally "net," refers to what is caught in the net. In contrast with the temporary nature of what evil men steal (cf. 1:19; 10:2-3; 11:4-5) is **the root of the righteous** which flourishes. A righteous person is like a plant whose secure root (cf. 10:30) causes it to be green (cf. 11:28) and to bear fruit (cf. 11:30).

12:13. Verses 13-20, 22-23 all refer in one way or another to right and wrong talking (cf. 10:11-14, 18-21, 31-32; 11:9, 11-13). Being **trapped** is a common figure in Proverbs (see comments on 11:6). A **righteous** person, speaking righteously or rightly, is therefore not entangled, as is **an evil** person, by what he says. He **escapes trouble** (cf. 11:8, 21; 12:21).

12:14. The fruit of one's **lips** are his words (cf. 13:2). His speaking brings **good things** to **him** (benefits himself; cf. 11:17) as well as to others. Though perhaps less obvious, these benefits are as great as the results of manual labor.

12:15-16. Two marks of **a fool** and of **a wise man** are given in these verses: the **fool** (*'ĕwîl,* "a hardened, thickheaded fool") thinks his **way** is **right** (cf. 21:2), which explains why he will not receive instruction (cf. 1:7); when he is annoyed (perhaps by an insult) he immediately shows it. A wise (**prudent;** see comments on 12:23) **man,** in contrast, is open **to advice** (cf. 10:17; 11:14; 12:1), and is not annoyed by insults. **Overlooks** means not that he ignores the **insult** but that he controls his response to it or forgives it. The same verb (*kāsâh*) in 10:12 is translated "covers." "Insult" is rendered "disgrace" in 11:2.

12:17. The correct talk of a righteous person is seen in his testifying honestly in court (**gives** is an intensive verb carrying the idea of "bursts forth" or "breaks out"), **but** an unrighteous person deliberately **tells lies** in court (cf. 6:17, 19; 14:5, 25; 19:5, 9; 21:28).

12:18-19. Reckless words, which may not be intended to hurt, can in fact be very hurtful, piercing **like a sword.** They are not thought through. Who has not spoken something thoughtlessly only to find that his careless words were harmful? But words spoken from a **wise** heart can do just the opposite; they can heal (cf. 15:4) instead of hurt. The effects of words of kindness (cf. 12:25), encouragement, and truth **endure,** but falsehood and liars will not. **Only a moment** translates an idiom, which is literally, "the blinking of the eyes" (cf. Job 20:5).

12:20. As stated so often in Proverbs **deceit** characterizes the wicked (v. 5; 6:14; 11:18; 14:8; 15:4; 26:19, 24, 26) **but joy** comes to people **who** desire and work for others' **peace** (šālôm, "well-being"). On the word **plot** see comments on 3:29.

12:21. **The righteous** experience not only joy (v. 20) but also protection. **Befalls** may be rendered "shall be allowed to happen to." Conversely, **the wicked** experience **trouble** (cf. 11:8, 21; Ps. 32:10).

12:22. Again **lying** is referred to (cf. vv. 17, 19; 21:6; 26:28); **the LORD** hates it because it so directly opposes His standard of truth (cf. Ps. 31:5). (Cf. comments on Prov. 11:20 regarding other things He **detests.**) Truthfulness is commended (cf. 12:17, 19; 14:5, 25) for it promotes justice.

12:23. **A prudent man** is not anxious to demonstrate **his knowledge;** he is not like **fools** who blurt **out folly.** "Prudent" translates 'ārûm, "shrewd" in a good sense, a word used elsewhere only in Job (5:12; 15:5) and Proverbs (12:16, 23; 13:16; 14:8, 15, 18; 22:3; 27:12).

12:24. Diligence and laziness are contrasted here and in verse 27, and in 10:4; 13:4 (also cf. 12:11). The idea that a **diligent** person **will rule** may not mean that he becomes an official, but that he is in charge of whatever his situation may be. Laziness, on the other hand, may lead a person into slavery or servanthood (cf. 11:29), in which he has to work harder.

12:25. As is well known today in the fields of medicine and psychology, anxiety can weigh **a man down** (lit., "causes a man to bow down" or depresses him). An empathetic **kind word,** however, can give an anxious, depressed person support and can cheer **him up** (cf. v. 18).

12:26. **A righteous** person does not take on just anybody as a friend; he chooses his friends carefully. **Is cautious** could be translated "searches out" (cf. Deut. 1:33) or "investigates" (cf. Ecc.

7:25). **The wicked,** however, are unconcerned about who becomes their friends. The wicked lead other wicked people **astray** for they are all on the wrong path.

12:27. **A lazy** person (cf. v. 24) refuses to **roast his game.** "Roast" (ḥārak), used only here in the Old Testament, is difficult to translate precisely. It may mean the lazy man will not even go after food. Or (as in the NIV) it may mean that he hunts some game, but is too lazy to cook it. Diligence, however, leads a hunter to value what he has acquired. This suggests that a lazy person does not value what he owns.

12:28. Righteous conduct (**way**) leads to **life,** which probably here means temporal blessing, not eternal life (see comments on 3:18). The second line of 12:28 is difficult in the Hebrew. The NIV rendering **along that path is immortality** is a commendable translation. Though some scholars object to the idea of immortality in the Old Testament, it is certainly taught in several passages (e.g., Job 19:25-27; Ps. 16:10; Isa. 25:8).

13:1. Verses 1-3 each refer to talking. **A wise son** (cf. 10:1) is receptive to parental **instruction** (cf. comments on 12:1). The word **heeds,** though not in the Hebrew, is implied. The opposite of a wise, teachable son is **a mocker** (cf. 14:6; 15:12; 17:5; 19:29; 21:11; 22:10; 24:9; 30:17) who refuses to **listen to** and profit from a **rebuke** (see comments on 1:23).

13:2. The first clause in this verse is similar to 12:14a. **The fruit of** one's **lips** is his talk, here referring obviously to a righteous person. By speaking positively and helping others with one's words (cf. 12:18b) he in turn is blessed. What he gives he receives. **The unfaithful** (lit., "treacherous") desire not to help others but to harm them, by violent words and deeds. (Cf. "craves" in 13:4.)

13:3. Being careful about what one says helps keep him out of trouble (cf. 14:3; 21:23). But speaking **rashly** (hastily and thoughtlessly; cf. 12:18) brings on trouble (cf. **ruin** in 10:8, 14) to the one who speaks and to others. By his reckless words he makes promises he can't keep, divulges private information, offends, or misrepresents. People learn not to depend on what he says and do not want to be around him. He may also suffer physically or financially.

13:4. A lazy person (on **sluggard** see

comments on 6:6) has desires (**craves** refers to a deep-seated physical drive or appetite; cf. "craving" in 13:2), but his desires are not satisfied because he is not willing to work. However, diligence (see comments on 12:24) enables a person to be **satisfied** (cf. 11:23).

13:5. As stated in 8:13, fearing the Lord involves hating what God hates. Since He hates falsehood (12:22), so do **the righteous.** Lying degrades and leads to mistrust and injustice. **The wicked,** however, by preferring falsehood, **bring shame** (lit., "cause a stink") **and disgrace** on others and themselves.

13:6. Again righteous, wise living **guards** or protects a person (cf. v. 3; 2:11; 4:6; also note 12:21). On **integrity** see comments on 11:3. Wicked, unwise living offers no protection to **the sinner.** He is easily overthrown.

13:7. Pretends refers to an adopted lifestyle rather than to playacting. A person may **be rich** in material goods but have **nothing** socially or spiritually. Conversely another person may **be poor** materially but rich spiritually.

13:8. The words **riches** and **poor** tie this verse with the previous one. A man of wealth may need to use his money to buy himself out of trouble (**ransom his life**) **but a** poor person is not threatened with kidnapping or theft. Being poor has at least one advantage.

13:9. A **light** and a **lamp,** common metaphors (cf. 6:23; 20:20; 21:4; 24:20; Job 18:5-6; Ps. 119:105), refer here to physical life. If a lamp in a Near Eastern tent went **out** at night, the surroundings were pitch dark, mindful of the darkness of death. **The righteous** will have a long life, but **the wicked** will die early.

13:10. Pride (*zādôn,* from *zîd,* "to boil"; cf. 11:2) means an unyielding arrogance. Such an inflated, know-it-all view of oneself leads to quarreling, in contrast with a humble, wise spirit that makes one willing to learn and **take advice** (cf. 12:15; see "quarreling" in the chart "Words and Speaking in Proverbs," near 6:17-19).

13:11. Dishonest money, gained illegitimately (cf. "ill-gotten treasures," 10:2), does not last (cf. 10:2; 13:22; 23:5). On the other hand **money** can **grow** by being accumulated honestly **little by little.**

13:12. It is good for a person to have **hope,** but if it is not fulfilled for a long time (**deferred** means "put off or long drawn out") then he experiences disappointment (his **heart** becomes **sick**). But when a hope is **fulfilled** (cf. vv. 4, 19), a person is refreshed. The gratification of hope gives encouragement like a tree that gives life (cf. **tree of life** in 3:18; 11:30; 15:4).

13:13. Despising parental or other **instruction** results in a person having to make a "payment" of guilt and punishment. **But** respecting such instruction to the point of following it results in the "reward" of blessing. **Scorns** translates *bûz* ("to despise, hold in contempt, or ridicule"; cf. 14:21 and see comments on 1:7).

13:14. Being taught by and heeding a **wise** person is as refreshing and life-sustaining as **a fountain of life** (10:11; 14:27; 16:22). Along with the benefit of wise teaching is another aspect: it protects **from the snares of death** (an identical statement is made in 14:27b). Wisdom may help keep a person from a premature death (cf. 1:32-33; 2:11; 4:20-22; 8:35-36), pictured here as an animal trap that ensnares suddenly. With the second line of 13:14 being a dependent clause, this verse has synthetic parallelism (see "Literary Style" in the *Introduction*) rather than the antithetic parallelism of most of the verses in chapters 10–15.

13:15. Good understanding translates *śēkel ṭôb* which the NIV renders "good name" in 3:4 (see comments there). In 3:4 and 13:15 these Hebrew words are associated with **favor** (*ḥēn,* "grace or graciousness"). By contrast, the life **of the unfaithful** (lit., "treacherous") **is hard.** The Hebrew for "hard" (*' êṭān*) means "ever-flowing" like a river (Ps. 74:15), "enduring" like a nation (Jer. 5:15), or "long established" like leaders (Job 12:19). Perhaps in Proverbs 13:15 it refers to the calloused, ongoing conduct of the wicked, who are so entrenched in their ways that they find it difficult to turn from them.

13:16. Normally a person's conduct is consistent with his character (cf. 4:23-24). One who has **knowledge** shows prudence (*'ārûm,* "shrewd" in a good sense; see comments on 12:23; cf. 12:16), **but a fool** (*kesîl;* see comments on 1:7) **exposes his folly** (cf. 12:23b) "like a peddler who openly spreads his wares before the gaze of all men" (Crawford H. Toy, *A Critical and Exegetical Commentary on the Book of Proverbs*, p. 273).

13:17. Whereas an unreliable **messenger** gets **into trouble** (perhaps by his laziness; cf. 10:26; or his foolish conduct; cf. 26:6) and is therefore disappointing, a reliable messenger **brings healing,** that is, he contributes to the welfare of those for whom he works.

13:18. Ignoring **discipline** (*mûsār*, "moral discipline or correction"; cf. 1:2) results in **poverty and shame** because a person without self-discipline is lazy and others are ashamed of him. **But** heeding **correction** (i.e., reasoning or arguing) results in honor. Openness to taking advice is mentioned frequently in Proverbs (e.g., 12:1; 13:1, 13).

13:19. The word **fools** unites verses 19 and 20 though the subject matter of these verses differs. Verse 19a, like verse 12b, speaks of the satisfaction and joy that come when a hope or dream is realized. Fools on the other hand continue on in their sin. This implies that their hopes are *not* **fulfilled.**

13:20. One way to become **wise** is to associate with **wise** people, including companions and teachers. Conversely to associate with **fools** brings problems. The Hebrew words for **companion** (*rō'eh*) and **suffers harm** (*yērôa'*) sound a bit alike. The influence of good and bad associations is a common theme in Proverbs (1:10-11; 2:12; 4:14-17; 16:29; 22:24-25; 23:20-21; 28:7).

13:21. Verses 21-23 refer to poverty and **prosperity.** Trouble comes to **the sinner** like an animal chasing him; he can't escape. One such problem is hunger, mentioned in verse 25. Righteous people, however, who in Proverbs are equated with the wise and the diligent, enjoy good things in life, another frequent theme in Proverbs (3:2; 8:18; 10:6, 22; 21:21; 28:25). These statements in 13:21 are generally true, though exceptions could be cited.

13:22. A morally **good man** is so blessed that he can help his grandchildren by including them in his will. **But** any **wealth** a sinner may acquire is lost and eventually passes into the hands of **the righteous.** Perhaps this comes about by the sinner's foolish and unwise handling of his funds.

13:23. A **poor** man **may,** by his labor, **produce** enough **food** to feed himself (cf. 12:11a), **but** without protection from **injustice** he may lose it. Verse 22 of chapter 13 speaks of a sinner losing his money; verse 23 speaks of those who suffer at the hands of such sinners.

13:24. Verses 24-25 and 14:1-4 speak of various home scenes. A loving parent inflicts temporary discomfort on his children (by spanking with a **rod**) to spare them the long-range disaster of an undisciplined life. Refusal to **discipline** one's child when he needs it shows that a parent's genuine love and concern are questionable. Other verses in Proverbs on child discipline are 19:18; 22:15; 23:13-14; 29:15, 17. God also disciplines His own (cf. 3:11-12; Heb. 12:6).

13:25. God supplies the physical needs of **the righteous.**

14:1. **The wise woman** and **the foolish** woman probably refer to individuals rather than to wisdom and folly personified as in 9:1, 13. **Builds** may not refer to constructing a physical **house** but caring for a household and causing it to flourish. Whereas a woman of wisdom builds up her household, a woman of folly lives in such a way that her household is neglected.

14:2. A person's attitude toward **the LORD**—either fearing Him (see comments on 1:7) or despising **Him**—shows up in his behavior. His conduct is either **upright** or **devious** (cf. 2:15).

14:3. The **talk** of a fool (*'ĕwîl*, one who is arrogant, hardened and thickheaded in his ways) results in his being punished with a **rod** (not the same word for rod in 13:24) on **his back** (cf. 10:13; 26:3). **Wise** words, however, **protect** a person from such punishment (cf. 13:3).

14:4. If a farmer has **no oxen** for plowing, **the manger** (animal food trough) in his barn **is empty,** that is, clean. **But** by spending time and money to feed and clean up after oxen, he will have plenty of food, **an abundant harvest,** because of the strong oxen's plowing. Meaningful results of any kind require investing time, money, and work.

14:5. The contrast between true and false testimony is also mentioned in 12:17; 14:25. False witnessing in court is denounced in 19:5, 9; 21:28; 24:28; 25:18.

14:6. It is unusual to read in Proverbs that a **mocker** (see comments on 13:1) **seeks wisdom,** but this shows that lack of desire is not his problem so much as lack of meeting the primary condition, fearing the Lord (1:7; 9:10). Apparently mockers look for wisdom in the wrong places. **Knowledge** is **easily** acquired by people who have discernment in spiritual things. They know where to look for true knowledge.

14:7. Verses 7-9 all include statements about fools. Verse 7 is the first imperative statement in the section beginning with 10:1. Also 14:7 is written in synthetic parallelism for the second line explains the first line. Since one's associations can influence him for good or bad (cf. 13:20), he ought to steer clear of being with the **foolish** ($k^es\hat{\imath}l$) for they speak without **knowledge**. They cannot offer the young anything of value.

14:8. The **prudent** ('$\bar{a}r\hat{u}m$, "shrewd" in a good sense; cf. v. 18; see comments on 12:23) think things through and therefore are not easily deceived, but **fools** find that their own **folly** (cf. 14:18, 24, 29) trips them up. They think their ways are right (12:15).

14:9. When a fool sins, he makes fun of the idea of **making amends for** it. In contrast with **fools** who refuse to change their sinful ways are **the upright** who experience **goodwill,** that is, acceptance (on $r\bar{a}s\hat{o}n$; see comments on 8:35) by God and man.

14:10. One's inner pain (**bitterness**) and **joy** cannot be fully experienced by anyone else. They are individual, private feelings in one's own soul.

14:11. Final destinies are the subject of verses 11-14. **The wicked** person's **house** (meaning either his possessions or his family members) **will be** demolished (cf. 15:25) and will not last. On the other hand the upright's **tent** (possessions or family members) **will flourish** (lit., "bud or sprout," like a tree budding with blossoms or sending out shoots). This pictures growth, prosperity, and stability.

14:12. This verse is repeated verbatim in 16:25. A path (**way** of life) may seem **right** (level or straight) to some people. **But** because **it leads to death** it is the way of sin and folly (cf. 5:5, 23; 7:27; 9:18; 11:19; 21:25). **Man** cannot get away with sin.

14:13. By his **laughter** a person may give the impression that he is enjoying life when actually in his **heart** he is hurting emotionally (cf. v. 10; 15:13b). The

words **joy may end in grief** refer either to the fluctuating nature of human emotions or to the idea that joy is seldom pure, untainted by any grief.

14:14. Both the wicked and the righteous—**the faithless** (lit., "backslider in heart") **and the good—will be** recompensed in accord with their conduct (cf. 1:31). What they sow they will reap (Gal. 6:7).

14:15. Verses 15-18 speak of the way of the fool and begin and end with a reference to the simple and the prudent. The **simple** ($pe\underline{t}\hat{\imath}$, "naive, gullible"; see comments on 1:4) are easily influenced (see, e.g., 7:7-10, 21-23), **but** the **prudent** ('$\bar{a}r\hat{u}m$; cf. 14:8, 18 and see comments on 12:23) think before they act.

14:16. The words **the LORD** are not in the Hebrew in this verse though perhaps they are implied. The verse is literally, **a wise** person **fears . . . and shuns evil** (cf. 3:7; 8:13; 16:6; Ps. 97:10). **A fool,** driven by his impetuous (**hothead**) nature, is wild (**reckless**) with regard to evil.

14:17. Quick-tempered connects this verse with the preceding one. Such a person **does foolish things** (cf. v. 29; 15:18). "Flying off the handle"—not controlling one's temper—causes a person to do and say ridiculous things, which he may later regret and be unable to undo. Even more difficult to live or work with is a person who is **crafty** (cf. 12:2) or scheming ($m^ezimm\hat{a}h$; see comments on 1:4). A person who schemes and works underhandedly to get his way and to oppose others **is hated** by others because he is untrustworthy. He goes astray (14:22).

14:18. Because of his gullibility **the simple** (cf. v. 15 and comments there) person receives **folly,** not wisdom (cf. v. 24). The opposite kind of person—**the prudent** (see comments on v. 8; cf. v. 15)—is blessed with more **knowledge.**

14:19. Evil men will bow down in the presence of . . . good men. Since this is seldom experienced now—it is usually the other way around—this verse may be speaking of the future when the wicked will be subject to the godly.

14:20-21. Verse 20 refers to people shunning their **poor . . . neighbors.** In verse 21 this is called sin. Besides the economic frustrations that come with poverty, poor people suffer socially as people often refuse to associate with them (cf. 19:4, 7). Verse 20 of chapter 14 contrasts this social problem of the poor with the fact that many people want to befriend **the rich**. Verse 21 contrasts showing hatred toward one's poor **neighbor** with giving kindness. The attitude of despising (**despises** translates *bûz*, "to hold in contempt, to belittle, to ridicule"; cf. "scorns," 13:13; see comments on 1:7) is sin, whereas being **kind to the needy** (cf. 14:31; 19:17; 28:27) brings blessing from the Lord.

14:22. This verse includes the first question in this section that begins with 10:1. A person who plots **evil** (on the word **plot** see comments on 3:29) errs from the path of upright living. Conversely a person who plans (**plan** is the same word as "plot") **good** actions for others (cf. "kind" in 14:21) is characterized by **love** (*ḥeṣeḏ*, "loyal love") **and faithfulness** (cf. 3:3; 16:6; 20:28).

14:23. Hard work pays off (cf. 10:4; 12:11, 24) whereas people who merely **talk** about work become poor (cf. 6:10-11). Other causes of poverty mentioned in Proverbs are stinginess (11:24; 28:22), haste (21:5), hedonism (21:17), oppression (22:16), favoritism (22:16).

14:24. The wise are crowned, that is, blessed with **wealth** (cf. 3:16; 8:18, 21; 15:6; 22:4) because of their diligence (14:23), **but** foolish conduct results not in blessings but in more **folly** (cf. v. 18).

14:25. Telling the truth when giving testimony in court can save **lives** from the death penalty, whereas **false** testimony, which deliberately deceives, may send the innocent to death or prison while wrongly acquitting the guilty. People who **witness** in court cases (cf. v. 5) are in a strategic position; they can have a great influence over other people's lives.

14:26-27. These two verses are linked together as both refer to the fear of **the Lord** (see comments on 1:7). In 14:26 fearing Him provides security (cf. v. 32) and protection against a life of ruin for believers **and** also **for** their **children** who are influenced by their godly parents to fear God. In verse 27 fearing **the Lord is a fountain of life** (cf. 10:11; 13:14; 16:22), that is, one's fear of the Lord assures longevity (cf. 3:2, 16; 9:10-11; 10:27; 15:24) for it protects **from the snares of death** (cf. 10:2b; 11:4b; 13:14b).

14:28. People are **a king's** greatest resource. **But** having no one over whom to rule would make his high title and position worthless. A pompous title with no meaningful responsibilities draws little respect.

14:29. Being **patient** (cf. 16:32; 19:11) under trying circumstances evidences wisdom, but an impatient person who loses control of his temper (cf. 14:16-17) reveals **folly**. The Hebrew *rûm* (**displays**) means "to exalt or lift up for show." Controlling one's temper is always wise, and losing it is never wise!

14:30. A person's emotions affect his physical condition, as it is well known today (cf. 15:13, 30; 17:22; 18:14). **A heart at peace** (or, "a mind of health," i.e., a healthy disposition) helps produce a healthy **body,** but envy, an ardent agitating desire to have or achieve what one sees in others, produces adverse effects physically (on **bones,** see comments on 3:8).

14:31. To take advantage of **poor** people is like sinning against God (cf. 17:5) since God is the **Maker** of all people (cf. Job 31:13, 15) and because He defends the cause of the poor (Prov. 22:22-23). The righteous, wise person is **kind to the poor** (14:21; 19:17; 28:27) for this **honors God.**

14:32. Problems can be disastrous for **the wicked** (cf. 6:15) because they have no hope in the Lord. When **the righteous,** on the other hand, face **death** they **have a refuge,** namely, in God.

14:33. Wisdom is everywhere present (in the hearts of the wise **and even among fools**; cf. 1:20-22; 9:1-4) but **she** (again wisdom is personified as a woman; cf. comments on 1:20-33) receives various kinds of responses.

14:34. Righteousness among a group of **people** has a beneficial effect (**exalts** means "to lift up," used here in a moral sense), **but sin** among them has an adverse effect (it **is a disgrace,** "reproach," a word used only here and in Lev. 20:17). Though people may seem to be getting away with sin, ultimately it catches up with them and shames them.

14:35. A king is pleased when his servants are prudent (the word **wise** here means "prudent"), **but** if they are not prudent they cause him shame (the meaning of **shameful;** the word is also used in that way in 10:5; 19:26; 29:15) and he becomes angry with them. **Wrath** translates *'eḇrâh,* an outburst of anger.

The same is true of employees today: prudence pays off and lack of it causes employers problems.

15:1. Verses 1-2, 4, 7, 14b, 23, and 28b refer to talking, a subject frequently addressed in Proverbs (see the chart "Words and Speaking in Proverbs," near 6:17-19).

A gentle (lit., "soft") **answer** can dispel a potentially tense situation by dissolving a person's **wrath** (*ḥēmâh*, "rage"). Being conciliatory in such a situation requires forethought, patience, self-control, and kindness, virtues commonly lauded in Proverbs. **A harsh** (lit., "hurtful") **word,** by contrast, arouses rather than dissolves **anger.**

15:2. The **tongue** (words) **of the wise commends** (lit., "does well by") **knowledge** (cf. v. 7). The wise not only possess knowledge but also their use of it makes it attractive and desirable. A **fool,** however, **gushes** (lit., "bubbles forth," also used in v. 28) his **folly.** His many words, bubbling out like water from a spring, show how foolish he is. **The mouth of** a fool also reveals his sin (v. 28) and feeds on folly (v. 14).

15:3. In His omniscience God sees and knows what everyone does (cf. 5:21; Heb. 4:13; also note **the eyes of the LORD** in 2 Chron. 16:9), **keeping watch** like a watchman guarding a city. **Wicked** people should be warned and **good** people comforted by this truth. He sees even death and destruction (Prov. 15:11). The second line of verse 3 is a participial clause that completes the thought of the first line, so this verse has synthetic parallelism (see "Literary Style" in the *Introduction*).

15:4. Words can encourage or depress an individual. Words that bring **healing,** that contribute to a person's emotional health, are like **a tree of life** (cf. 3:18; 11:30; 13:12), a source of strength and growth. Words that are **deceitful** (*selep,* "subversive"; used in the OT only here and in 11:3, "duplicity") can crush **the spirit** (cf. 15:13; 17:22; 18:14), or depress one's morale.

15:5. If a son refuses to learn from **his father's discipline** (*mûsār;* see comments on 1:3) he is **a fool** (*ʾĕwîl,* a coarse and hardened fool; see comments on 1:7). Also he is stupid (12:1), a mocker (13:1; 15:12), and self-hating (v. 32). He will die (v. 10). To follow parental **correc-**

tion is wise. **Shows prudence** translates the verb *ʿāram,* "to be shrewd" in a good sense (also used in 19:25), similar to the noun *ʿormâh* (in 1:4; 8:5, 12) and the adjective *ʿārûm* (12:23; 13:16; 14:8, 15, 18; 22:3; 27:12). Heeding the advice of one's parents brings honor. (Cf. similar concepts in 12:1; 13:1, 13, 18.)

15:6. As stated several times in Proverbs, **righteous** (and wise) living generally results in prosperity (cf. 3:16; 8:18, 21; 14:24; 22:4), though there are many exceptions, but money acquired by **the wicked** (and unwise) results in **trouble** (cf. "trouble" in 15:27; note 1:19; 10:2).

15:7. Wise people share helpful facts, but **fools** (*kᵉsîl*) do not. They spread folly (v. 2). Peoples' words (**lips**) reveal what is in their **hearts** (cf. heart and lips in 4:23-24).

15:8-9. The LORD detests (cf. 6:16-19) **the sacrifice** and **the way of the wicked,** as well as their very thoughts (15:26). (On other things the Lord detests see comments on 11:20.) God hates sacrifices offered by **wicked** people (cf. 1 Sam. 15:22; Isa. 1:11; Jer. 7:22; Amos 5:22) because those offerings are given hypocritically. Because "the way" (conduct) of the wicked is detestable, so are their sacrifices. However, **the prayer of the upright pleases Him** so He hears them (Prov. 15:29). Offering sacrifices, an external act, is no substitute for a life of **righteousness,** which obviously God **loves.**

15:10. In verses 10-12 the second line expands the thought of the first line. When a person **leaves the path** of uprightness and righteousness (cf. vv. 8-9), he will receive **stern discipline** (*mûsār,* "moral correction"); and if he refuses **correction** (vv. 5, 12; cf. 10:17; 12:1) altogether, he will pay for it (13:13) with poverty, shame (13:18), and death (15:10).

15:11. Death (*šᵉʾôl*) **and destruction** (*ʾăḇaddôn,* from *ʾāḇaḏ,* "to perish or die") may be synonyms of the grave and of the dead in it (cf. 27:20; Job 26:6; "destruction" [*ʾăḇaddôn*] is also used in Job 28:22; 31:12; Ps. 88:11). Since God can see the dead in their graves, surely He can see living people's **hearts** (cf. Prov. 15:3), that is, their motives, thoughts, and desires (cf. Ps. 38:9a). Man's heart deceives him but God knows it (Jer. 17:9-10).

15:12. Correction here is not the word usually rendered "correction" in the NIV in Proverbs. Here it is the word for rebuking or reproving (as in 9:7-8; 19:25; 25:12). **A mocker** (cf. 13:1) **resents** (lit., "does not love") such reproof and refuses to learn from **wise** people (note the contrast in 15:31). This shows that mocking is evidence of folly.

15:13. Verses 13-15 refer to **a happy heart,** a discerning heart, and a cheerful heart. Inner joy (*śāmaḥ*; see comments on v. 21) shows on a person's **face,** but inner grief (**heartache;** cf. 14:13) depresses a person's morale (**crushes the spirit;** cf. 15:4; 17:22; 18:14). Happiness and depression are issues of the heart. What a person is inwardly has more lasting impact on his emotional state than do his circumstances. Some people hold up under difficult circumstances better than others because of inner strength.

15:14. A person who has discernment **seeks** more **knowledge** (cf. 18:15; 19:25; 21:11) and it comes to him easily (14:6). **But . . . a fool feeds on** (*rā'âh,* "grazes" like cattle), and is content with, his **folly,** (cf. 15:2, 21).

15:15. In contrast with **the oppressed** (*'ānî,* lit., "those who are bowed down," the humble, afflicted; often trans. "needy" as in 14:21), who are miserable, are those who are **cheerful** (cf. 15:13) and as a result have **a continual feast;** they enjoy life in spite of adverse circumstances. Therefore people ought to encourage the oppressed by helping them.

15:16. Verses 16 and 17 are 2 of the 19 "better . . . than" verses in Proverbs (see comments on 12:9). Generally a person would choose **wealth** (abundance) over poverty. But if he has poverty (a **little;** cf. 16:8) and **the fear of the LORD** (see comments on 1:7) that combination (cf. 1 Tim. 6:6) is certainly preferable to wealth if the money brings **with** it **turmoil** (*mᵉhûmâh;* cf. Isa. 22:5, "tumult"; Deut. 7:23, "confusion"; 1 Sam. 14:20; Ezek. 7:7, "panic"; Zech. 14:13). The statement in Proverbs 15:16 suggests (a) that the wealth mentioned here is not possessed by one who fears the Lord and (b) that fearing God gives peace, not confusion.

15:17. Like verse 16, verse 17 contrasts poverty (having a mere **meal of vegetables**) with prosperity (**a fattened calf**). Normally people would choose luxury over privation, but what is more important **is love.** Many people have found that a home where material possessions

are few but love for each other is present is far better than a house of great opulence where people hate each other (cf. 17:1). Love makes one's difficult circumstances endurable, whereas **hatred** undoes all the enjoyments that good food might otherwise bring.

15:18. **A hot-tempered man** (lit., "a man of rage"; cf. similar expressions in 14:16-17, 29; note 19:19; 22:24) **stirs up dissension** (cf. 6:14, 19; 10:12; 16:28; 28:25; 29:22; see comments on 6:14). This may be one reason for the turmoil and hatred mentioned in 15:16-17. Patience (cf. 14:29; 16:32; 19:11; 25:15), however, can quiet quarrels. **A patient man** is, literally, a man "slow to anger" (cf. James 1:19).

15:19. As hatred and anger bring problems (15:17-18) so does laziness. **Thorns in the path** (cf. 22:5; 24:30-31) depict problems that keep a person from getting what he wants; his life has obstructions. **The upright,** however, are diligent and therefore have fewer problems; their lives are more like a smooth **highway** (cf. 4:26).

15:20. Verses 20 and 21 speak of the impact of wisdom and folly on one's life. Love in a home brings peace (vv. 16-17), and obedient and **wise** conduct brings **joy** (*śāmaḥ*) to the parents, **but** folly does not. In fact only a fool **despises his mother.** Here rather than stating that folly in a son grieves his mother (as in 10:1) that reaction on her part is implied and the fool's attitude toward her is stated.

15:21. Whereas a wise son brings joy (*śāmaḥ*) to his father (v. 20), a foolish person (one **who lacks judgment,** lit., "void of heart"; see comments on 6:32; 10:13) has joy (*śāmaḥ*) in his **folly** (also see comments on *śāmaḥ* in 15:13, 23, 30). A wise person has **a straight course** (cf. clear "highway," v. 19b). The implication is that a foolish person's course is crooked (and obstructed, as in v. 19a).

15:22. Four times the Book of Proverbs focuses on the importance of getting advice from others in regard to one's **plans** (11:14; 15:22; 20:18; 24:6).

15:23. In verses 23, 30, 33 the second line begins with **and,** pointing up synonymous parallelism (see "Literary Style" in the *Introduction*). Appropriately spoken words (cf. 25:11-12), saying the right thing at the right time, delights (*śāmaḥ;* see comments on 15:20) not only the hearer but also the one who says them. **Timely** words (whether of love, encouragement, rebuke, or peacemaking) are beneficial.

15:24. Each of verses 24, 26-33 refers directly or indirectly to a characteristic of the godly: **wise** (v. 24), humble (v. 33), pure (v. 26), honest (v. 27), cautious (v. 28), prayerful (v. 29), joyful (v. 30), teachable (vv. 31-32), and reverent before the Lord (v. 33). Wisdom can **keep** a person from a premature death, a point often made in Proverbs (cf. 3:2, 16; 4:10; 9:11; 10:27; 14:27).

15:25. Verses 25 and 26 both refer to the Lord's reactions to man's character. The proud (gē'eh, also used in 16:19, from the verb gā'âh, "to rise up or be lifted up") accumulate possessions, including **houses**, but **the LORD tears** them **down** (cf. 14:11), whereas He protects widows.

Land, a precious commodity to the Israelites, was marked by **boundaries** to preserve its original parameters (Deut. 19:14). Land was kept in a family and its boundaries were important (Prov. 22:28; 23:10-11). The vulnerability of widows made them easy prey to thieves who would seek to steal their land, so the Lord Himself promised to keep **widow's** boundaries from being moved.

15:26. The LORD detests not only the sacrifices and conduct of the wicked (vv. 8-9) but also even their **thoughts** (or plans; trans. "schemes" in 6:18). But the thoughts of the pure are a delight to Him. God in His omniscience knows everything.

15:27. The Hebrew word for **greedy** (bāṣa', "to cut or break off") suggests making gain unjustly or by violence. (On "a greedy man" see 28:25.) A dishonest father, providing for his **family** by unjust or violent means, will eventually cause his wife and children to suffer (cf. **trouble** in 11:29; 15:6). Accepting or giving **bribes** is a form of dishonesty or greed because they pervert justice (see comments on 6:35). So to reject bribes helps prolong one's life and prevent trouble for one's family.

15:28. A **righteous** person **weighs** (carefully muses on or considers) his **answers** before giving them rather than blurting out the first thing that comes to his mind. That way his words are more appropriate and timely (v. 23). A fool, however, **gushes** out (lit., "bubbles

forth," also used in v. 2) **evil** words like water bubbling out of a spring.

15:29. Because God detests **the wicked** (vv. 8-9, 26) He distances Himself from them, refusing to hear them. But He hears the praying of the righteous (cf. Ps. 34:15, 17; 1 Peter 3:12) because their prayers please Him (Prov. 15:8).

15:30. A positive person's encouragement, whether nonverbal (by **a cheerful look**, lit., "bright eyes") or verbal (**good news**; cf. 25:25), is helpful and uplifting. **Brings joy** translates śāmaḥ, also in 15:20-21, 23, 31. As in verse 13a, emotional health contributes to physical wellbeing (**health to the bones**; see comments on 3:8).

15:31. Verses 31-33 speak of conditions for entering the ranks of the wise: listening to (and heeding) rebuke (v. 31), heeding correction (v. 32), and fearing the Lord and being humble (v. 33). Heeding a **rebuke** (see comments on 1:23) can be **life-giving** (cf. 1:33) because such a person is impressed by it (17:10), learns from it (19:25), and is considered **wise.**

15:32. To ignore **discipline** (mûsār, "moral correction"; cf. vv. 5, 10) results in loss of life and knowledge, which shows that the ignorer actually hates **himself** (cf. "harms himself," 8:36).

15:33. The **fear of the LORD** (see comments on 1:7) is not only the beginning of knowledge, but it also **teaches . . . wisdom.** By fearing (reverencing, trusting, obeying, serving, and worshiping) the Lord a person learns wisdom. **Humility,** associated with fearing the Lord, must precede the **honor** (cf. 18:12b; 29:23) that accompanies wisdom. (The fear of the Lord and humility are also connected in 22:4.)

B. Proverbs exalting righteous living (16:1–22:16)

Most of the 191 verses in this section are either comparisons (in synonymous parallelism) or completions (in synthetic parallelism), and only a few are contrasts (antithetic parallelism). Verses 1-7, 9 of chapter 16 each speak of the Lord; verses 1, 3, 9 refer to man's plans and God's sovereignty over them. Those plans are expressed in what one says ("the tongue," v. 1) and does ("steps," v. 9). Verses 1, 5, and 9 refer to the heart and verse 2 mentions man's motives. Pride (v. 5), evil (v. 6), and injustice (v. 8) are

239

denounced. Though man is strongly encouraged in Proverbs to acquire wisdom, he is not released from dependence on the Lord.

16:1. A person may make **plans** (placing things in order, like arranging soldiers in battle lines; cf. Gen. 14:8) in his **heart** (cf. Prov. 19:21) **but** God guides what comes out of the heart in man's words **(the reply of the tongue)**. God in His sovereignty prevails over **man** (cf. 16:9). One's heart and his speech are closely related (cf. 4:23-24).

16:2. A person may think nothing is wrong with what he does; outwardly it may **seem innocent. But** God knows his heart, whether the **motives** behind his actions are pure or not. **The Lord** judges people on the basis of *why* they act (cf. 17:3; 21:2) because He sees human hearts (cf. Matt. 6:4, 8, 18).

16:3. Committing one's **plans** (vv. 1, 9) **to the Lord** is essential to success. This verse, however, does not offer divine assistance to *all* plans. The fool (1:32) and the sluggard (6:9-11) are said to come to undesirable ends. **Commit** is literally "roll" (cf. Ps. 37:5).

16:4. God **works** all things **for His** (or "its") **own ends** (cf. Rom. 8:28), including **the wicked for** destruction. Though this may be difficult to understand and accept, punishment for the unrepentant is in keeping with God's justice and is a truth frequently taught in the Scriptures (including Prov. 16:5).

16:5. God **detests** pride, or independence of **the Lord** (for other things He detests see comments on 11:20); therefore He will punish it. **Be sure of this** is literally "hand to hand" (see comments on 11:21).

16:6. Though unrepentant sin "will not go unpunished" (v. 5), God in His **love** (ḥesed, "loyal love") **and faithfulness** (cf. 3:3; 14:22; 20:28) has provided a way for **sin** to be **atoned for.** After a person's sins have been atoned for by his trust in the Lord, he is not to continue in sin. He is to avoid **evil** (cf. 16:17) by fearing **the Lord** (see comments on 1:7; cf. 3:7; 8:13).

16:7. When a person pleases **the Lord** (by, for one thing, avoiding evil, v. 6) **he** (either that person or the Lord) **makes** that person's **enemies** to be at peace with him.

16:8. This **better . . . than** verse (see comments on 12:9) is similar to 15:16 ex-

cept that here **righteousness** is substituted for "the fear of the Lord," **much gain** replaces "great wealth," and **injustice** is used instead of "turmoil." One who amasses revenue (the meaning of the Heb. word for "gain," which is also used in 10:16, "income"; and in 15:16, "great wealth") dishonestly (cf. 10:2, 16; 13:11; 15:27) eventually will be punished. So righteous living—even if it means having **little**—is certainly better.

16:9. A man makes **plans** for his actions **but the Lord determines** (or establishes) how he will go (**his steps**). The meaning here is the same as in verse 1 but "steps" are mentioned instead of "tongue."

16:10. "King," "kings," and "a king's" are mentioned in verses 10, 12-15. When **a king** of Israel spoke **an oracle,** he did so as God's representative and therefore was to be a just ruler (cf. Deut. 17:18-20).

16:11. On **scales** and **weights** see comments on 11:1 (also cf. 20:10, 23). The king established the weights and measures (see "its weight . . . by the royal standard," 2 Sam. 14:26), but here the statement is made that **the Lord** was behind those standards. Therefore they should be honored. To use dishonest weights and measures was to disobey both the king and God.

16:12-13. Kings hate **wrongdoing** (v. 12) and value honesty (v. 13); at least they should, for a righteous, honest ruler will establish (make firm or secure) a king's **throne** (cf. 20:28; 25:5; 29:14). Dishonesty and injustice will cause his reign to topple. **Kings** should **value** honesty not only in themselves but in others also.

16:14. If someone angers a king he may be executed; only wisdom can **appease** his anger (cf. Ecc. 10:4). **A king's** power is irresistible; one's only recourse is to seek to pacify it.

16:15. One way to brighten **a king's face** is given in verse 13, to be honest. **A rain cloud in spring** (the "latter rain" in March or April) was welcomed as rain was needed for a good crop. A king's **favor** signaled much better fortune than his wrath. His favor was also compared to dew (19:12).

16:16. Wisdom is more desirable **than gold,** and **understanding . . . than silver** (cf. 3:13-15; 8:10-11, 19).

16:17. The upright person seeks to

avoid **evil** (cf. v. 6; 3:7; 8:13). Guarding **his way** (i.e., maintaining upright conduct) is a means of guarding one's **soul** (inner life with its drives, appetites, and desires) from sin.

16:18-19. These verses discuss pride, humility, and disaster. **Pride** leads to one's downfall (cf. 18:12; 29:23). Pride is so despicable that a person should avoid it even if it means being economically **oppressed**. One may **share plunder** (acquired through violent or dishonest means) **with the proud** but such dishonesty will not go unpunished (cf. 15:25).

16:20. A person who **gives heed to** (lit., "is prudent" with regard to, or "ponders"; trans. "takes note of" in 21:12) **instruction** (*dābār*, "word"; also trans. "instruction" in 13:13), **prospers** (cf. 19:8), that is, has God's blessing of happiness. Such a person is also one **who trusts in the** LORD and therefore is **blessed.**

16:21. Verses 21, 23-24 refer to wise and pleasant words. A person who is **wise** is known for his discernment, his ability to see to the heart of issues. The word for **pleasant** (*meteq*, "sweetness") is used in 27:9 ("pleasantness"). A similar word (*mātôq*, "sweet") is used in 16:24; 24:13; 27:7. Sweet (i.e., attractive or helpful) **words promote instruction** in the sense that they make learning (cf. 1:5) desirable. Harsh words do the opposite.

16:22. The word for **understanding** in this verse is *śēkel*, "prudence or insight," also used in 13:15 (and in 12:8; 19:11; 23:9, where it is trans. "wisdom"). Prudence is like **a fountain of life** (cf. 10:11; 13:14; 14:27); it is refreshing, life-sustaining, and inexhaustible. **Folly** on the other hand results in **punishment. Fools** do not learn and their foolish conduct requires discipline (*mûsār*).

16:23. A **wise** person is careful about what he says (**guides his mouth** is lit., "causes his mouth to be prudent") for he wants to help, not hurt. He does not blurt out whatever comes to his mind (cf. 15:28b). As a result **his lips promote instruction** (see comments on 16:21 on "promote instruction").

16:24. Pleasant (i.e., "delightful"; this Heb. word differs from the word "pleasant" in v. 21) **words are** as **sweet** (see comments on v. 21 on *mātôq*) and therefore as desirable as honey from **a honeycomb** (cf. Ps. 19:10). Appropriately

spoken words (cf. Prov. 15:23) that encourage, soothe, or commend can be most pleasant and even uplifting to the point of helping a person feel better physically (see comments on **bones** in 3:8).

16:25. This statement is identical with 14:12 (see comments there). Apparently this was repeated for the sake of emphasis.

16:26. Hunger can motivate people, sometimes even lazy people, to work so that with their wages they can buy food. This verse has an interesting wordplay: though a person is working as a laborer for someone else, his **appetite** is "working" for himself. Diligence is encouraged in 10:4-5; 12:24; 14:23; 28:19.

16:27. Verses 27-30 refer to troublemakers of various kinds—those who plot evil (v. 27), stir up strife (v. 28), lead others into violence (v. 29), and persist in sin (v. 30). **A scoundrel,** literally, "a man of belial" (cf. 6:12), is worthless and wicked, and lives in deep moral degradation. He **plots evil** (cf. 1:10-14; 6:14; 12:20; 14:22; 24:2, 8). "Plots evil" is literally "digs a calamity," which suggests the effort he puts forth to dig a pit to trap others. One of the main ways in which he does this is by words that burn **like . . . fire** (cf. James 3:5-6).

16:28. A **perverse man** (lit., "a man of perversity"; see comments on 2:12) **stirs up dissension** (cf. 6:14, 19; 10:12; 15:18; 28:25; 29:22), causing strife between friends. And by his **gossip** (cf. 11:13; 18:8; 20:19; 26:20, 22) he causes **close friends** (cf. 17:9) to doubt and distrust each other.

16:29. A **violent man** (lit., "a man of violence"; vv. 27-29 each begin with "a man of" in Heb.) is not content to sin; he wants to lead others with him in his wicked ways (see, e.g., 1:10-14).

16:30. By winking (cf. 6:13; 10:10; Ps. 35:19) and pursing **his lips** an evil person signals to others nonverbal clues (facial gestures) to communicate his intentions to be involved in **perversity** (cf. Prov. 16:28; see comments on 2:12) and **evil** (cf. 16:27).

16:31. Young men glory (take pride) in their strength (20:29), but old men may take pride in their **gray hair,** which is like a distinguished **crown** (cf. crown **of splendor** in 4:9). Longevity is a result of **righteous** living (cf. 9:6; 10:27), but not all who are aged have lived righteously.

16:32. In this **better . . . than** proverb (see comments on 12:9) having patience and a controlled **temper** is honored above being a soldier. In a land where safety depended on might and skill in warfare, this statement may seem surprising. Yet conquering oneself (cf. 14:17, 29; 25:28; 29:11) is of greater virtue than conquering **a city.**

16:33. The results of casting lots (cf. 18:18; see comments on Es. 3:7; Acts 1:26) may seem like mere chance, but God controls even them (cf. man's efforts and God's sovereignty in Prov. 16:1-2, 9).

17:1. Each of verses 1-20 relates closely or loosely to strife or peace. As stated in the similar **better . . . than** proverbs of 15:16-17, having a peaceful **and quiet** though spartan meal (**dry crust**) is far better than having a lot to eat (**a house full of feasting,** lit., "sacrifices," i.e., full of meat from animals sacrificed to the Lord; cf. 7:14) in a house where there is **strife.** Harmony in one's relationships is to be desired over a sumptuous supply of food.

17:2. Sometimes a **servant,** because he is **wise** ("prudent"; trans. "gives heed to instruction" in 16:20), can inherit an estate or part of it and be placed by his master in a powerful position **over a disgraceful son** (who brings shame to his parents; cf. 19:26). Interestingly Jeroboam rose over Solomon's disgraceful son Rehoboam and became the leader of 10 of the 12 tribes (1 Kings 12).

17:3. As **silver and . . . gold** are purified under intense heat (cf. 27:21), so a believer's **heart** is purified by the heat of trials which the Lord brings (James 1:2-3; 1 Peter 1:7).

17:4. A **wicked** person and **a liar** both feed on what enhances their characteristics. They readily listen to gossip, **evil** talk that plots wicked schemes, lies, and slander. **Malicious** translates *hawwōṯ,* which means "engulfing ruin, destruction, as accomplished by one person against another." (Cf. "gossip" in 11:13; 16:28; 18:8; 20:19; 26:20, 22.)

17:5. One way of engulfing others by malicious talk (v. 4) is to mock those who are **poor.** Since the poor are made in God's image, as all people are, to mock them is to speak against God, **their Maker** (cf. 14:31; 18:23). Equally bad is being glad when other people experience ca-

lamities (cf. 24:17). A person who **gloats over** the misfortunes of others will himself experience misfortune (he will be punished).

17:6. A **crown** (cause for joy and dignity) of older people (cf. 16:31) is their grandchildren. Also **children** should be proud of their **parents.** These expressions of joy and **pride** depend, of course, on the family members being properly related to God (Deut. 6:2) and to each other.

17:7. Verses 7-9 refer to various forms of injustice: lying, bribing, and gossiping. **Arrogant lips** is literally, "lips of excess," and refers to one who says too much. **Fool** is *nāḇāl,* used only three times in Proverbs (vv. 7, 21; 30:22). It refers to one who lacks spiritual perception and sensitivity. A *nāḇāl* should not talk a lot because he seldom knows what he is talking about. Similarly **lying** is totally inappropriate for a **ruler** (*nāḏîḇ,* noble or official, 17:26); a ruler should be a man of integrity, honesty, and trustworthiness (cf. "noble," *nāḏîḇ,* in Isa. 32:8). A ruler who tells lies is like a fool.

17:8. This verse does not encourage bribery, which is condemned in verse 23; 15:27; Exodus 23:8; Deuteronomy 16:19; 27:25 (see comments on Prov. 6:35). Verse 8 of chapter 17 is simply speaking from the giver's perspective; **a bribe** "works like **a charm.**" To say bribes are effective (cf. 18:16; 21:14) is not to approve them; it simply states the way things are.

17:9. Covering **over** (see comments on 10:12) **an offense** is an evidence of love and therefore **promotes love.** But repeating or gossiping about others' sins can lead **friends** to be suspicious of each other (cf. 16:28).

17:10-11. Verses 10-16 each refer to some form of evil or foolish action. Verse 10 contrasts the receptivity of a discerning person with that of **a fool.** A mere **rebuke** (see comments on 1:23) helps a wise person **more than** the physical punishment of **100 lashes** given to a fool (*keṣîl;* cf. 17:12, 16; see comments on 1:7). Since no more than 40 lashes were allowed by Law (Deut. 25:2-3), this reference to 100 lashes is probably hyperbole. The wise are sensitive and learn readily, but a thickheaded fool is unresponsive even after extreme measures of correction. **An evil** person (Prov. 17:11) insists on being rebellious; he refuses to learn from correction or rebuke (v. 10). Eventually he is brought to justice and punished (cf. 11:21; 16:5) by a merciless official.

17:12. A mother **bear** whose **cubs** have been **robbed** is angry and therefore dangerous (cf. Hosea 13:8). But a worse danger is meeting a fool (*kᵉsîl*; cf. Prov. 17:10, 16; see comments on 1:7). Not all fools are equally dangerous but, as Robert L. Alden suggests, "Consider meeting a fool with a knife, or gun, or even behind the wheel of a car; a mother bear could be less dangerous" (*Proverbs: A Commentary on an Ancient Book of Timeless Advice*, p. 134).

17:13. If someone **pays back evil** when he has received **good** he shows that his heart is evil (v. 11) and foolish (v. 12). So he will experience no more "good" (blessings). Instead **evil** (calamity) **will** stay with **his house,** that is, his family.

17:14. Starting a quarrel (cf. v. 19) may seem like a minor matter. But it often grows beyond control like a small crack in **a dam** which increases in size until the dam breaks. **So** the answer is to refuse to let an issue fester; it should be dropped **before a dispute** even starts.

17:15. Injustice in a court case—whether **acquitting the guilty** or **condemning the innocent** (cf. v. 26)—is hated by **the Lᴏʀᴅ** (cf. comments on 6:16).

17:16. A fool (*kᵉsîl*; cf. vv. 10, 12; see comments on 1:7) is so simple he thinks he can buy wisdom. He comes with money in hand, but fails to realize he lacks the one resource necessary for gaining **wisdom**: a genuine, heartfelt **desire** for it.

17:17. Some Bible translations make a contrast in this verse between **a friend** and **a brother** by beginning the second line with "but." The NIV's **and** seems preferable; it conveys the idea that both the friend and the brother are valued. However, in 18:24 a friend is extolled above a brother (relative). True friends—and relatives—are faithful in times of **adversity** as well as prosperity.

17:18. Being a reliable friend in times of adversity (v. 17) is different from a foolhardy agreement to provide financial security for a high-interest loan (see comments on 6:1-5). On **lacking in judgment** see comments on 6:32; 10:13.

17:19. Friendship (v. 17) helps overcome strife, unwise financial obligations may cause strife (v. 18), and quarreling

(v. 19), perverse motives, bad morals, and deceptive words (v. 20) all contribute to strife. Quarreling (cf. v. 14) shows that its initiator **loves sin** because a quarrel inevitably leads to trouble. Building a **high gate** either refers to a literal high door which a wealthy person builds to show off his pride or it refers figuratively to his bragging. Either way pride is present, which results in a fall (11:2; 16:18; 18:12; 29:23).

17:20. Perverse (*'iqqēš*) means "twisted or distorted" (see comments on 2:15). A person whose motives and morals (**heart**) are distorted will **not prosper** (be blessed by God; cf. 16:20). From a perverse heart a person speaks deceitfully; he lies. This will result in **trouble** (*rā'āh*, "calamity," trans. "evil" in 17:13).

17:21. Parents grieve deeply over a foolish, disappointing **son** (cf. v. 25; 10:1). Two words for **fool** are used in 17:21. The first is *kᵉsîl*, one who is dull and thickheaded. The other is *nābāl*, one who lacks spiritual perception and sensitivity (cf. v. 7; 30:22).

17:22. As in 15:13, 15, 30; 18:14, one's inner life affects his physical well-being. A **cheerful heart** translates two Hebrew words that are rendered "a happy heart" in 15:13. The word for **medicine** occurs only here in the Old Testament. A **crushed spirit** refers to being depressed or saddened (cf. 18:14). An example of a crushed spirit is a father's grief over a wayward son (17:21). On **the bones** see comments on 3:8.

17:23. Verse 8 referred to the fact that bribes often help people get what they want. Verse 23 affirms the purpose of bribes: **to pervert** ("bend") **justice.** Judges who accept bribes secretly are **wicked** (i.e., guilty). This is ironic because judges should exercise justice, including punishing those who are guilty.

17:24. The first line of this verse is literally, "In front of a man of discernment (cf. v. 10) is wisdom." A wise person finds **wisdom** in obvious places whereas **a fool's eyes wander** and never discover it.

17:25. This verse, in repeating the thought of verse 21, uses a stronger word for **grief.** The Hebrew *ka'as* means sorrow (Ecc. 1:18; 7:3), provocation (Prov. 27:3), annoyance (12:16), or irritation. **Foolish** children bring **bitterness to** mothers.

17:26. This is the first of four proverbs with the words **It is not good** (cf. 18:5; 19:2; 25:27; cf. "is not good" in 24:23; 28:21). Again injustice in the courts is denounced (cf. 17:15). **To punish an innocent** person (cf. 18:5) **or to flog officials** (only kings or judges could order this to be done) who are serving with **integrity** is, like bribery (17:23), perverting the cause of justice.

17:27-28. A wise **man** is cautious in what he says; he thinks before he talks (cf. 14:8) and does not gab. This reveals that he **is even-tempered** (lit., "cool of spirit"; cf. the recent phrase "keeping one's cool"). Restraint in talking may **even** cause a **fool** (*'ĕwîl*, an arrogant, hardened fool; see comments on 1:7) to be considered **wise**.

18:1. Some people, out of selfishness, avoid friendly relations with others. Their self-centeredness makes them enemies of **sound judgment** (cf. 3:21; 8:14). **Defies** is *lā'ag*, translated "mock(s)" in 1:26; 17:5; 30:17.

18:2. The double trouble of the **fool** is his "closed mind" and "open mouth" (Derek Kidner, *The Proverbs: An Introduction and Commentary*, p. 127). He does not really want to gain knowledge; he only wants to share **his own** views. His mouth "gushes folly" (15:2). Yet if he would keep quiet people would think he is wise (17:28). Results of a fool's talkativeness are mentioned in 18:6-7.

18:3. Sinful living is accompanied by **contempt, and with shame comes disgrace.** These words of dishonor contrast with the benefits of upright, wise living, which include honor and dignity (4:7-9). In 18:3 an interesting progression is suggested: "contempt" leads to "shame" which leads to "disgrace" (cf. "disgraceful" in 10:5; 17:2).

18:4. Verses 4, 6-8, 20-21 refer to talking. **Words . . . are** like **deep waters,** possibly meaning water in a cistern, in that (as in 20:5) they are "hidden" or "of difficult access." Words spoken out **of wisdom,** however, are fresh and **bubbling** like water from a **fountain.** Unlike the fool who airs his unwise and therefore unhelpful ideas (18:2), a wise person's words are helpful and encouraging (cf. 10:11; 13:14).

18:5. Being **partial to the wicked** is an injustice condemned frequently in Proverbs (17:15, 26; 24:23; 28:21). Equally bad is depriving **the innocent of justice**

in the courts (cf. 17:23).

18:6-7. A fool finds himself in trouble because he speaks thoughtlessly (cf. v. 2) from a corrupt heart. **Lips** and **mouth** (v. 6) are mentioned in reverse order in verse 7. His words are so out of place that others whip him (cf. "beatings," 19:29). And his talk **is his** downfall; it ensnares him (cf. 5:22).

18:8. Gossip (cf. 11:13; 16:28; 26:20) is **like choice morsels** (lit., "things greedily devoured," a Heb. word used only here and in 26:22, which is identical with 18:8). Hearing gossip is like eating a delicacy (something not everyone else hears). Therefore, like food being digested, gossiped news is assimilated in one's **inmost parts** (i.e., is retained and remembered).

18:9. A person who does **his work** poorly or carelessly **is a brother** (i.e., is similar) **to one who destroys.** A poor or unfinished job differs little from a project that someone demolished; both projects are valueless.

18:10-11. Verses 10-12 discuss true and false security. The refuge of **the righteous** is stated in verse 10, and the refuge of **the rich** is mentioned in verse 11. The righteous turn to **the name of the LORD,** that is, to His revealed character. By putting their trust in Him they **are** as **safe** (cf. 29:25) as a person hiding from the enemy in **a strong tower.** Though **wealth** is more desirable than poverty and does help keep a person from disaster (cf. 10:15 where the first line is identical with the first line of 18:11), money cannot replace the Lord as a base of security. The wealthy *think* (**imagine**) that their wealth can protect them from harm as a high city **wall** used to protect from enemy troops, but the wealthy are wrong. Money simply cannot shield people from many problems.

18:12-14. It is also wrong to trust in oneself. This verse should be read with the two preceding verses. **Is proud** translates *gābāh*, "to be high, exalted, haughty"; it is related to the noun *gōbāh*, "haughtiness," in 16:18. A person who thinks he is superior to others will experience a **downfall** (cf. 11:2; 16:18; 29:23a). **Humility** on the other hand results in strength and can give a person the determination to live; it can help bring him through an illness, as physicians know. But if a person is **crushed** ("stricken or prostrated"; cf. 15:13; 17:22) inwardly, if his inner strength is gone, medicine can hardly sustain him. A physically ill person can be borne along by his spirit, but if his spirit is down too, if he is depressed, what or who can lift him out of his illness?

18:15. The discerning and the wise are eager to increase their knowledge. They desire it with their hearts (cf. 15:14) and they listen for it with their ears (cf. 23:12). "Knowledge" occurs in the Hebrew in both lines, for emphasis, though the NIV translates it only in the first line and represents knowledge in the second by the word it.

18:16. Giving a gift to buy one's way before influential people is close to bribery (cf. 17:8, 23) though it may be less blatant. Still 18:16 is not approving or encouraging the use of such gifts; it simply states that it is done.

18:17. Verses 17-19 discuss the settling of disputes. In dealing with a dispute (a lawsuit) a judge needs to hear both sides of a case before answering (cf. v. 13) or making a decision. The same is true of parents when their children argue.

18:18. One way of settling disputes in Bible times was by casting the lot (cf. 16:33; see comments on Es. 3:7; Acts 1:26). The yes-or-no decision given by lots helped avoid an ongoing conflict or litigation between strong opponents.

18:19. The reason for the caution urged in verses 17-18 is given here. When a brother (the word can mean either a friend or a blood relative) is offended in a dispute, it may be as difficult to restore his friendship as it would be to conquer a heavily fortified city. The estranged relationship is like . . . barred gates, hard to remove.

18:20-21. A person's words, figuratively called the fruit of his mouth (cf. "fruit of his lips," 12:14; 13:2) and the harvest from his lips, can benefit himself when his words are positive and uplifting. However, one's words (tongue) may bring death as well as life. A witness in a court, for example, can help determine by his words whether a defendant lives or dies. Those who love it (the tongue) refers to people who are talkative (cf. 10:19; 18:2; 20:19); they will suffer the consequences (eat the fruit; cf. 18:20) of what they say.

18:22. Matrimony is desirable because a wife is "a suitable helper" (see Gen. 2:20 and comments there). The LORD sanctions marriage for He states that finding a wife is a good thing and that God is pleased with marriage (on the noun favor, rāṣôn, see comments on 8:35; cf. 12:2).

18:23. Unfortunately a poor person's plea for mercy from a rich person is often met with harsh words. This does not excuse such a response; it simply states a fact. Arrogant treatment of less fortunate people is wrong. Indirectly this verse warns against characteristics that might lead to poverty such as laziness (6:10-11), stinginess (11:24), unteachableness (13:18), and talkativeness (14:23).

18:24. If a person has many companions, or numerous friends chosen indiscriminately, he may find himself in trouble (lit., "be broken in pieces"). A wordplay is intended here, for the Hebrew word for companion is rēʿeh and the word for break in pieces (come to ruin) is rāʿaʿ. It is better to have a true friend (lit., "one who loves"; cf. 17:17) than many less reliable companions.

19:1-2. The first line of this verse is the same as the first line of 28:6. It is better to be poor and honest (cf. 19:22b; blameless means morally whole; cf. 2:7, 21; 11:5; 28:10, 18; Job 1:1) than to be a fool (kᵉsîl, "dull, thickheaded"; cf. comments on 1:7) who speaks words that are perverse (ʿiqqēš; "twisted"; see comments on 2:15). The word for "poor" (rāš) means destitute or hungry; it is not a dishonorable term suggesting poverty from laziness. A fool may try to get rich by devious means, but honesty is still a better policy, even if it means going hungry.

Zeal (nepeš, normally trans. "soul") here means inner drive or vitality. It refers not so much to ecstatic exuberance as to ambitious drive which without adequate knowledge may lead to hasty blunders. Such haste (cf. 21:5; 29:20) may result in a person missing the way, that is, making mistakes. As the modern-day proverb puts it, "Haste makes waste."

19:3. Foolishness ruins a person's life (lit., "overturns or subverts his way"). Bringing problems on himself, a fool is responsible for his own actions. He should not blame the results of his carelessness on the will of the LORD, but he does.

19:4. Verses 4-6 speak of false friendships. The first line of verse 4 is developed in verse 6, and the second line of verse 4 is expanded in verse 7. Most wealthy persons have **many friends** (cf. 14:20b); some stay around him in the hope of getting some of his wealth. Poverty, on the other hand, though bad enough in itself, often results in loss of friends. Many people, unfortunately, want to avoid the embarrassment of associating with poor people (cf. 14:20a; 19:7).

19:5. One form of false friendship is to be **a false witness** in court (cf. v. 9; 14:25). Perjury, however, will eventually be punished (cf. 12:19; 21:28). **Pours out** is literally "breathes out or spews out" (also used in 6:19; 12:17, "tells"; 14:5).

19:6. Curry favor (lit., "stroke the face") refers to blatantly insincere flattery. Flattering **a ruler** is often done to take advantage of other people, sometimes to pervert justice. The rich, with money to buy friends, are subject to many such offers of "friendship."

19:7. In contrast with the rich (v. 6), **a poor** person often cannot find **friends** (cf. 14:20). In fact he is a nuisance even to **his relatives.** His efforts to find a friend are often unsuccessful because people **avoid him** (cf. 19:4).

19:8. Wisdom translates *lēḇ* (lit., "heart") which here means "sense" (rendered "understanding" in 15:32). Living sensibly shows that a person **loves his . . . soul.** This does not refer to vanity or narcissism but to genuine concern for one's destiny. **Cherishes** is literally, "keeps, guards, or preserves" (cf. 19:16). To keep watch over one's **understanding** results in benefits to one's soul (8:35-36); he **prospers** (cf. 16:20) spiritually and emotionally (as well as materially).

19:9. This verse is identical to verse 5, except for the last verb. Apparently this thought is repeated because of the seriousness of lying in court.

19:10. Luxury is "inappropriate" (the meaning of **not fitting**) for fools (or is honor appropriate, as stated in 26:1). But even more inappropriate is **a slave** in a position of rulership over those who ought to be ruling (cf. 17:2; Ecc. 10:7). A slave is probably unqualified to lead so his leadership position is inappropriate.

19:11. Patience, extolled several times in Proverbs (14:29a; 15:18b; 16:32; 25:15), stems from and is a mark of **wis**dom (*śēḵel*, "prudence," also used in 12:8; 13:15; 16:22, "understanding"; 23:9). In contrast is one who is hotheaded and impatient (14:17, 29b; 15:18a; 19:19; 22:24; 29:22). A prudent, patient man is not easily upset by people who offend him; in fact he overlooks offenses (cf. 12:16), knowing that to harbor resentment or attempt revenge only leads to more trouble. Overlooking them is his **glory,** that is, it is honorable.

19:12. A king may be enraged by some people (cf. 16:14; 20:2) but at the same time extend **favor** (*rāṣôn,* "goodwill, pleasure"; see comments on 8:35) to others. The contrast is as great as that between the ominous **roar of a lion** (cf. 28:15) and the refreshing **dew** (cf. rain cloud in 16:15).

19:13. A **foolish son** (cf. 10:1; 15:20; 17:21, 25) brings **ruin** (lit., "chasm") to his father; a foolish son is like an overwhelming catastrophe that sucks a person into a deep pit. Fathers with foolish sons can testify to the engulfing agony that sinks them into depression and despair.

A **quarrelsome wife** is a problem too. This is the first of five references in Proverbs to a quarrelsome wife (lit., "quarreling of a wife"; cf. 21:9, 19; 25:24; 27:15). She **is like a constant dripping** (these two words in Heb. occur only here and in 27:15) as her quarreling continues relentlessly, is irritating, and is difficult to restrain (27:16). Crawford H. Toy summarized an Arab proverb: "Three things make a house intolerable: *tak* (the leaking through of rain), *nak* (a wife's nagging), and *bak* (bugs)" (*A Critical and Exegetical Commentary on the Book of Proverbs,* p. 373). The word for quarrelsome (*māḏôn*) is used more often in Proverbs than in any other Old Testament book. It is also translated "dissension" (6:14, 19; 10:12; 15:18; 28:25; 29:22), "disputes" (18:18-19), "quarrel(s)" (17:14; 22:10; 26:20), and "strife" (23:29).

19:14. A young man may receive part or all of his parents' estate by virtue of his having been born into their family. A **prudent wife,** however, is **from the Lord** (cf. 18:22). This is a strong statement in a culture in which fathers often selected wives for their sons. Probably then 19:14b refers to God's providence in guiding fathers who selected their future daughters-in-law. Interestingly a prudent wife is seen in contrast with a quarrelsome wife (v. 13).

19:15. The words **deep sleep** refer to a heavy sleep (cf. Job 4:13; 33:15) sometimes induced by God (Gen. 2:21; 15:12; 1 Sam. 26:12). **Laziness** can cause a person to be so inactive that he easily falls into a deep sleep, totally oblivious to the precious time he is losing (cf. Prov. 20:13). A **shiftless man** is literally, "a soul (or person) of laxness" (*rᵉmiyyâh* is used four times in Prov. and once elsewhere, Jer. 48:10, "lax"). Laziness leading to hunger is also seen in Proverbs 6:9-11.

19:16. The words **obeys** and **guards** are the same in Hebrew, and may be rendered "keeps" (cf. comments on v. 8). To keep, that is, to obey **instructions** (cf. v. 20) is self-preserving; to do the opposite is self-destructive (1:32; 6:32; also see "ruin" in 10:8, 10, 14, 29; 13:3). To be **contemptuous of** (*bāzâh*, "to despise or disregard with contempt") **his ways** refers to either the ways of Solomon the father-teacher, or to God's ways, or to the learner's ways. In view of 19:8 the third option may be preferable.

19:17. Being **kind to the poor** (*dal,* "feeble, weak, helpless"; see comments on 10:15) refers to a concern that goes beyond "pity." It refers to giving a helping hand, to meeting their needs. Benevolence to the poor is encouraged in the Law (Deut. 15:7-11) and in Proverbs (Prov. 14:21b, 31b; 22:9; 28:27). Lack of such kindness is condemned (14:31a; 21:13; 22:16; 28:3, 27b). Giving to the poor is like lending **to the Lord** as it is an investment God will **reward.** God blesses people's generosity with His generosity.

19:18. This verse is an imperative, unlike most of the verses in Proverbs which are declarative sentences. The command, **discipline your son,** is a strong warning against parental passivity. It is consistent with 13:24; 22:15; 23:13-14. A child guilty of wrongdoings should be chastised in his early years while **there is hope** for him. To neglect such needed discipline may contribute to the child's **death.** Death refers either to capital punishment under the Law (Deut. 21:18-21) or to the danger of natural consequences accompanying the child's foolish behavior, in which he destroys himself. Death is often the lot of the fool (Prov. 1:32), the wicked (10:27), and the sluggard (21:25).

19:19. A **hot-tempered** person (cf. 15:18; 22:24; 29:22) repeatedly gets himself in trouble and has to **pay** for it. If a self-controlled person would **rescue him** from his penalty, the hot-tempered person would probably take advantage of that help so that the kindness would **have to** be repeated. A hot-tempered person, in other words, does not learn. Like many undisciplined sons, he is incorrigible.

19:20. Listening (see comments on 1:8) to counsel and accepting (cf. 2:1; 4:10; 10:8) **instruction** (*mûsār,* "moral correction and discipline") will make a person **wise. In the end** (cf. 5:4; 14:12) could mean the end of one's life but more likely it refers to some time after the instruction is given.

19:21. A person may and should make **plans** (cf. 16:1, 9) **but** God can sovereignly overrule and accomplish His **purpose** through what one seemingly plans on his own.

19:22. Loyalty (*ḥeseḏ,* **unfailing love**) is a virtue people desire in others. But lying, an evidence of the absence of loyalty, is so despicable that poverty is preferred to it (cf. v. 1).

19:23. One who fears **the Lord** (see comments on 1:7) has **life** (cf. 11:19; 12:28) and is secure and at peace with himself and others (cf. 3:26).

19:24. The **sluggard** (cf. 6:6, 9; 10:26; 13:4; 15:19; 20:4; 22:13; 24:30; 26:13-16) is so lazy that, comically, he does not even have the strength to lift **his hand** from his **dish . . . to his mouth** to satisfy his hunger. This idea is repeated in almost the same words in 26:15.

19:25. Suffering and mistreating others are the subjects of verses 25-29. When **a mocker** is flogged (cf. v. 29), **the simple** (*peṭî;* see comments on 1:4) **learn prudence** (*'ārûm;* see comments on 15:5). But mockers do not learn (cf. 9:8; 13:1; 21:11). "The simple" are the untaught, uninitiated, open-minded, who here are warned by the public punishment of another. Whereas flogging is needed for mockers, a mere verbal **rebuke** (see comments on 1:23) is enough for **a discerning** person.

19:26. A grown **son** who **robs** (assaults or mistreats) **his father** (cf. 28:24) **and drives . . . his mother** off their property, **brings shame and disgrace** to himself and his society. To disregard the instruction of one's parents is bad enough, but to abuse them physically (or to curse them, 20:20) is despicable.

19:27. When a person stops **listening to instruction** he is not learning (cf. v. 20). Being wise is not a static state. This is the only place between 7:1 and 23:15 where the words **my son** occur.

19:28. **A corrupt witness** deliberately distorts and **mocks at justice.** The word "corrupt" is literally, *belial*, "worthless and wicked" (see comments on 6:12). A false witness (see comments on 14:5) associates with **the wicked** who gulp **down evil,** that is, pursue sin with an insatiable appetite.

19:29. **Penalties . . . and beatings** (cf. 10:3b; 14:3a; 26:3), designed to correct wayward behavior, do no good for **mockers** and **fools.** This again points up the incorrigible ways of mockers (cf. 19:25).

20:1. **Wine** and **beer** are personified as people of degraded character: **a mocker** (cf. 19:25, 29) and **a brawler.** The idea is that wine mocks the one who drinks it and beer makes him aggressive. *Yayin,* the most common word for wine, usually referred to fermented grape juice but sometimes was unfermented. Beer (*šēḵār,* rendered "strong drink" in the KJV) referred to drinks made from barley, dates, or pomegranates. It was intoxicating (Isa. 28:7) and was forbidden for priests (Lev. 10:9), Nazirites (Num. 6:1-3), and others (Isa. 5:11). Intoxicating drinks can lead people **astray,** causing them to do foolish things. Other passages in Proverbs that condemn drunkenness are 23:20-21, 29-35; 31:4-5.

20:2. Kings are mentioned in verses 2, 8, 26. A **king's wrath** (cf. 14:35; 16:14) **is like the roar of a lion** (cf. 19:12; 28:15). It is dangerous to anger a ruler because he has power to take an offender's **life.** In fact making *any* person angry may pose problems.

20:3. Avoiding **strife** is honorable, though the way some people are **quick to quarrel** would make one think they thought *quarreling* is honorable. Such people are fools. Arguments can be avoided by overlooking insults (12:16), by dropping issues that are potentially volatile (17:14), and by getting rid of mockers (22:10).

20:4. In the Middle East the **season** for plowing and planting is the winter, the rainy season. **A sluggard** avoids the discomfort and work of plowing a mud-dy field in the cold, **so at harvesttime he looks** for a crop from his field **but he has nothing.** Without effort and advance planning there are few results; lack of work leads to lack of benefits.

20:5. A person's plans are like **deep waters** (cf. 18:4) which a wise person can draw **out.** That is, a discerning person can help another bring to the surface his true thoughts, intentions, or motives. Often a wise counselor can help a person examine his true motives—thoughts he may not fully understand otherwise.

20:6. Loyalty (*ḥeseḏ,* **unfailing love**) and faithfulness are desirable qualities (cf. 3:3; 19:22), but not everyone who **claims to have** them actually does. In fact faithfulness is usually missing. Keeping one's word and being loyal to one's commitments are important.

20:7. Verses 7-11 refer to various kinds of conduct. Usually a **righteous man,** a person who consistently behaves aright and is **blameless** (morally whole; cf. 2:7; 10:9), has **children** who are **blessed.** His children, seeing his example of integrity, are encouraged to be the same kind of people.

20:8. Kings often served as chief judges (e.g., Solomon, 1 Kings 3:16-28). By carefully examining (**with his eyes**) a case, a just **king** could detect (winnow or sift **out;** cf. Prov. 20:26) **evil** motives and actions. He could not easily be fooled.

20:9. Some people may claim to be perfect and **without sin,** but such a claim is false. What they claim (cf. v. 6) does not match what they are. All have sinned (Rom. 3:9-12, 23; cf. 1 Kings 8:46; Ecc. 7:20).

20:10. One evidence of a person's impure motives and depraved actions (v. 9) is his dishonesty in business dealings (cf. v. 23). God hates (see comments on 6:16; 11:20) **differing weights and . . . measures** used in selling or buying merchandise to get more money dishonestly (see comments on 11:1; cf. 16:11).

20:11-12. As already indicated (v. 6), what a person says does not always indicate what he is. This is true of children as well. Their **actions** and **conduct** reveal what they are like, whether they are **pure** (cf. v. 9) **and right** (cf. v. 7). One's behavior reflects his character. Therefore it is important not only to listen with one's **ears** to what people say but also to observe with ones **eyes** what people do (v.

12). **Both** senses should be used to see if people are consistent.

20:13. Laziness, here spoken of as **sleep** (cf. 6:9-10; 19:15a), leads to poverty (cf. 6:11; 10:4a; 19:15b), but diligence, referred to here as staying **awake,** leads to abundance of **food** (cf. 10:4b). Sleeping when one ought to be working results in lack of food (cf. 10:5).

20:14. Sometimes a shrewd **buyer** will downplay to a seller the value of a product in order to get its price lowered. **Then** having bought it, the buyer brags about the "deal" he got. Though merely stated as a fact, the verse implies that this action is wrong and that a person who sells products needs to be on guard against dishonest bargain hunters.

20:15. Gold and **rubies,** though rare and valuable (cf. 3:13-15), are **in abundance** compared with the **rare** and valuable ability to **speak knowledge,** to speak wise, appropriate words that fit the occasion.

20:16. This verse is repeated verbatim in 27:13. A debtor's outer garment could be taken by a creditor as collateral to guarantee that the debtor would pay (Ex. 22:26). Here a creditor is commanded to **take the garment of** a person who cosigns **for a stranger,** especially if the stranger is **a wayward woman.** Obviously without the garment as a pledge the creditor is taking a big risk that he may never be paid by the debtor *or* the cosigner! Other Proverbs passages that refer to the danger of cosigning for debts are 6:1-5 (see comments there); 11:15; 17:18; 22:26-27.

20:17. The taste of **food gained** dishonestly (cf. dishonest dealings in vv. 10, 14) may at first seem **sweet** (cf. "Stolen water is sweet; food eaten in secret is delicious," 9:17) but eventually it is as unpleasant as eating **gravel.** This contrasts the short-range pleasure of sin with its long-range consequences. Sin, usually attractive in its immediate payoff, ultimately turns on its host (cf. 7:14-23).

20:18. Getting **advice** from others when making **plans** (cf. 15:22), particularly in warfare (cf. 11:14; 24:6; Luke 14:31), is important.

20:19. Since gossiping **betrays a confidence** (also stated in 11:13a), a person ought to be careful with whom he shares secrets. Gossiping is also denounced in 16:28; 18:8; 26:20, 22. So people who talk **too much** should be avoided because they will probably divulge information that should be kept confidential.

20:20. In the Old Testament a person who cursed his parents violated the fifth commandment (Ex. 20:12) and committed a capital offense. Death was the penalty for cursing (and rebelling against) parents (Ex. 21:17; Lev. 20:9). To have one's **lamp . . . snuffed out** was a picturesque way of referring to death (see comments on Prov. 13:9; cf. 24:20; Job 18:5-6; 21:17). **Pitch darkness** is literally, "pupil (of the eye) of darkness," referring to the darkest part of the night (see comments on "apple" in 7:2).

20:21. An inheritance quickly gained may refer to getting one's inheritance prematurely by request, as in the Parable of the Prodigal Son (Luke 15:11-20) or by dishonesty (as in Prov. 19:26). Such wealth may be squandered and often squelches initiative and work. As a result, the recipient is **not . . . blessed at the end,** or later.

20:22. Verses 22-24 each refer to the Lord's involvement with man's actions. To take vengeance in one's hands is **wrong** (cf. 17:13; 24:29; Deut. 32:35; Rom. 12:19). It is far better to leave the punishment of injustice in the Lord's hands, for in time **He will deliver.**

20:23. This verse is similar to verse 10, except that in verse 10 dishonest weights and measures are referred to, whereas here dishonest **weights** and **scales** are mentioned. See the comments on 11:1.

20:24. The LORD guides **a man's steps** (cf. David's similar statement in Ps. 37:23), that is, God directs his decisions and conduct (cf. Prov. 16:1, 9; 19:21). Since God has the ultimate "say" in one's life, it is often difficult for a person to **understand** fully **his own way.**

20:25. Making rash promises without thinking them through is dangerous (cf. Deut. 23:21-23; Ecc. 5:4-5). Making a vow **rashly** and *then* considering what he did can get a person in as much trouble as if he stepped into an animal **trap.** It is better to think before acting.

20:26. Kings are responsible to separate **the wicked** from the righteous and to try to correct the behavior of the wicked by inflicting punishment. The first of these responsibilities is suggested by winnowing (cf. v. 8) and the second by

threshing. In farming, grain is threshed before it is winnowed. In threshing, a sledge with spikes is pulled **over** the stalks of grain to separate the grain from the stalks and to free the seeds from the seed coverings (the chaff). In winnowing the farmer tosses up the grain so that the wind can carry away the unwanted chaff. A **king** (or other ruler) should see that the wicked are detected and punished. This is important in maintaining order and justice.

20:27. A king ferrets out sinners (v. 26) and **the LORD** ferrets out one's inner heart. Just as a **lamp** shows up what is in the darkness, so God reveals what is in man's **spirit** and **searches out his inmost being** (cf. v. 30).

20:28. Love (*ḥesed*, "loyal love"; cf. v. 6) **and faithfulness** (cf. 3:3; 14:22; 16:6) are necessary requirements for an effective ruler. Loyalty (**love**) keeps him on the **throne** (cf. 16:12); disloyalty and unreliability could cause people to replace him with a different ruler.

20:29. In Hebrew culture the **young** and **the old** each had a particular excellence not possessed by the other. The young took pride in **their** physical **strength**, the older in their wisdom, revealed by their **gray hair** (cf. 16:31).

20:30. The purpose of corporal punishment (**blows . . . wounds . . . beatings**) is not to inflict pain but to veer one's conduct from sin. Such punishment, however, is not merely to change a person's conduct out of fear of physical pain but to help him mature (to **purge** his **inmost being;** cf. v. 27).

21:1. Chapter 21 begins (vv. 1-3) and ends (vv. 30-31) with references to the Lord. Verses 2, 8, 26, 28 of chapter 20 referred to kings. Now again the king is mentioned. The heart of the king is **in** God's **hand** (cf. Ecc. 9:1) as are the plans of all people (cf. Prov. 16:1, 9). A farmer directs water by digging canals. Similarly **the LORD** directs the hearts of kings, as, for example, Pharaoh (Ex. 10:1-2), Tiglath-Pileser (Isa. 10:5-7), Cyrus (Isa. 45:1-6), and Artaxerxes (Ezra 7:21; Neh. 2:1-8). God is sovereign (cf. Prov. 21:30).

21:2. Divine involvement in man's heart is not limited to kings (v. 1). This verse is almost the same as 16:2. A person may think nothing is wrong with his **ways** (conduct; cf. 12:15), **but the LORD** knows what is in his **heart.** "Man

looks at the outward appearance, but the LORD looks at the heart" (1 Sam. 16:7). The Lord accurately evaluates (**weighs;** cf. Prov. 16:2; 24:12) one's motives and tests them (17:3). God is sovereign (21:1) and also omniscient (v. 2).

21:3. God prefers people's obedience—their doing **what is right** (cf. v. 7) **and just**—over their **sacrifice.** In Israel involvement in the sacrificial system was no substitute for the "sacrifice" of righteous living (cf. 1 Sam. 15:22). **The LORD** detested the hypocrisy in a wicked person who brought an animal sacrifice to Him (cf. Prov. 15:8; 21:27).

21:4. Eight times in this chapter the wicked are referred to (vv. 4, 7, 10, 12 [twice], 18, 27, 29). Arrogance (cf. **haughty eyes** in 6:17) and pride (cf. 21:24), as well as hypocrisy (v. 3), is what the wicked thrive on. But pride is **sin.** Pride is **the lamp of the wicked,** that is, it is their very life (see comments on 13:9; cf. 20:20; 24:20).

21:5. Verses 5 and 6 refer to wealth. A person who diligently and carefully **plans** his work and works his plans contrasts with a careless one who makes hasty decisions and actions without thinking them through. The one results in **profit** and the other in **poverty** (cf. 14:23). As in 10:4, **diligent** work is associated with wealth. Diligence and laziness are contrasted in 12:24, 27; 13:4, and being hasty is also mentioned in 19:2; 29:20.

21:6. Verses 6-8 refer to the wicked—their lying, violence, and devious actions. Wealth (**a fortune**) acquired in dishonest ways (by **lying**) will not last (cf. 10:2; 13:11); it will fade quickly like a **vapor** (cf. 23:4-5; 27:24). **And a deadly snare** is the way some Hebrew manuscripts, the Septuagint, and the Vulgate read, but most Hebrew manuscripts read "seekers of death" or "for those who seek death." The thought is either that money gained dishonestly will ensnare rather than bless a person, ultimately bringing him to his death, or that seeking money dishonestly is like seeking or pursuing death.

21:7. People who are guilty of **violence** to others will find that it will boomerang (just as evil talk does, 12:13); eventually they themselves will be dragged away like fish caught in a net. In Habakkuk 1:15 the verb *gārar* (**drag . . . away**) is used of catching and dragging fish in a net. **The wicked** will be punished because even though they know **what is right** they **refuse to do** it.

21:8. Devious and **upright** describe the conduct **of the guilty** and **the innocent,** respectively. The Hebrew words for "guilty" and "devious" occur only here in the Old Testament. This verse, in antithetical parallelism, contrasts the crookedness of guilty people with the uprightness (straightforwardness or "rightness") of godly people. In 20:11 "innocent" (*zak*) is translated "pure," and "upright" (*yāšār*) is translated "right." Interestingly in 21:8 the Hebrew for "guilty" is *wāzār* and immediately following it is the similar-sounding Hebrew word for "but . . . the innocent" (*wᵉzak*).

21:9. The statement about **a quarrelsome wife** is repeated in 25:24. Similar thoughts are stated in 19:13; 21:19; 27:15-16. Verses 9, 19 of chapter 21 are 2 of the 19 **better . . . than** verses in Proverbs (see comments on 12:9). The point made in 21:9, 19 is the preference of living in cramped quarters (**on a corner of** a flat **roof,** v. 9) or in a desolate area ("a desert," v. 19) where one can at least have peace and quiet rather than in a spacious **house with** an argumentative, contentious wife. A wife who causes strife makes a home unpleasant and undesirable.

21:10. The wicked person **craves evil** as if he were addicted to it (cf. 4:16). He is mean even to those near him (**his neighbor**).

21:11. As stated in 19:25 (a verse almost identical with 22:11) the public punishment of a scoffer may cause **the simple** (*petî*, "naive, openminded") to become wise.

21:12. The Righteous One refers to God, not man, because only He fully knows what **the wicked** do and can bring them **to ruin** (or, "calamity"). **Brings** is literally "overthrows or subverts" (cf. 13:6; 19:3, "ruins"; 22:12).

21:13. A person who heartlessly disregards the needs of **the poor** (*dal*, "feeble, weak, helpless"; see comments on 10:15) is wicked (21:10-12). **He** himself **will** be disregarded when he is in need.

21:14. Giving someone **a gift** may help calm his **anger** for the recipient senses that the gift evidences love or at least concern. Even a secret **bribe** works to alleviate **wrath** (cf. 17:8). This does not condone bribery (cf. Ex. 23:8; Deut. 16:19); it simply states a fact.

21:15. Verses 15 and 16 refer to punishment of evil. Only **the righteous** can welcome **justice** because **evildoers** are its victims. **Terror** translates *mᵉhittâh* ("dismay, ruin, undoing"), a word used more in Proverbs than in any other Bible book (cf. 10:14-15, 29; 13:3; 14:28; 18:7, "undoing").

21:16. Being unwise is pictured as straying **from the path of understanding** (*śākal*, "being prudent"). Deliberately turning one's back on wise, godly living results in death. **The dead** translates *rᵉpā'îm*, as in 2:18; 9:18 (see comments on Job 26:5). An unwise person leaves the company of the wise only to find himself **in the company of** dead people!

21:17. Loving **pleasure** (the word rendered "joy" in v. 15) results in poverty. *Mahsôr* is yet another word for being poor. It means "deficient, destitute, or in need." It is used in Proverbs more often than in any other Old Testament book (6:11; 11:24; 14:23; 21:5, 17; 22:16; 24:34; 28:27). Proverbs 21:17a does not argue for a dismal, stoic life, but against living *only* for pleasure and self. If a person continues to use up his **wine and oil,** he will not become rich.

21:18. This verse does not mean that **the wicked** redeem **the righteous.** Instead it may mean that the wicked who have caused the righteous to suffer will themselves suffer and will thereby "set free" (**become a ransom for**) the righteous, for the godly will no longer suffer at the hands of the wicked.

21:19. On the **quarrelsome . . . wife** see comments on verse 9 (also cf. 19:13; 25:24; 27:15).

21:20. A **wise** person **stores** up **food** like an ant preparing for winter (6:6-8), **but a foolish** person is shortsighted. Caring only for the pleasures of the present time, he does not save for the future; he consumes **all** his food and therefore has nothing to eat between harvests.

21:21. Being righteous and loyal (*hesed*, **love**) results in **life** (cf. 3:18, 22; 4:13, 22; 8:35), **prosperity** (cf. 3:2, 16; 8:18; 13:21; 15:6; 28:25), **and honor** (3:16, 35; 4:8; 8:18). All three of these blessings are also cited in 22:4 (cf. Matt. 6:33).

21:22. A **wise** person is able to conquer **the mighty** (cf. 24:5). One whose strength is his wise, godly character is pictured as conquering another who trusts in physical fortifications. Wisdom gives strength and safety (as well as the blessings mentioned in 21:21).

21:23. This verse is similar to 13:3. **Guards** and **keeps** translate the same Hebrew word. Being careful and wise in what one says is a way of keeping out of trouble (cf. 12:13; 14:3).

21:24. Three words for pride describe the **mocker** (cf. v. 11; 13:1; 14:6; 19:29; 22:10): **proud . . . arrogant . . . pride.** The first and third words are related (zēḏ and zāḏôn), and the Hebrew word for "arrogant" is yāhîr, used only here and in Habakkuk 2:5. The Hebrew uses even two other words for haughty and proud in Proverbs 21:4. Mocking shows that a person thinks he is superior to others. This attitude is detestable (cf. 16:5) to God and others!

21:25-26. Both of these verses speak of a lazy person, a sluggard (see comments on 6:6, 9). He longs for things, but by refusing **to work** he eventually starves. In contrast to the lazy who long for things but do not have them, **the righteous** have and willingly give.

21:27. As stated in 15:8 God detests sacrifices brought by **wicked** people, for they are hypocritical. Their hearts do not match their actions. But it is even worse when they intentionally have **evil** motives in bringing sacrifices, perhaps going to the priests with pride or deceit.

21:28. Repeatedly Proverbs speaks against perjury, giving **false witness** in court (6:19; 12:17; 14:5, 25; 19:5, 9; 25:18). Both the false witness and the judge or others who follow his line **will be destroyed.** God punishes dishonesty!

21:29. In his arrogance and hypocrisy a **wicked** person **puts up a bold front.** He tries to persuade people to believe him, often by deceit and lies. On the other hand a righteous (**upright**; cf. vv. 8, 18) person reflects on his conduct, seeking to be honest, nonhypocritical, and consistent in all he does. His desire to be sure (**gives thought to** is lit., "makes sure or establishes") that his actions are right contrasts sharply with the bullheaded bravado of a wicked person who exercises no caution.

21:30. Human wisdom is no match against God's wisdom. **No wisdom** or plans of any person can ultimately thwart

the Lord's plans, for He is sovereign (cf. vv. 1-2; Job 42:2) and all-wise.

21:31. Human effort, like human wisdom (v. 30), has its limitations. It is useless to fight against God (v. 30), or without Him (v. 31). Soldiers may use horses in **battle, but** the superiority of a cavalry unit against foot soldiers is no guarantee of **victory.** That comes only from **the LORD,** who can turn battles His way in spite of man's efforts (cf. Pss. 20:7; 33:17).

22:1. Having **a good name** (cf. 3:4; Ecc. 7:1), that is, an honorable reputation because of good character, is to be valued far above having much wealth. **Riches** are useless (cf. Prov. 1:19; 10:2, 13:11) if in gaining them one ruins his character.

22:2. The **poor** are mentioned several times in this chapter (vv. 2, 7, 9, 16, 22). A person may acquire wealth (v. 1) but that does not completely separate him from the poor, for both are creatures whose **Maker** (cf. 14:31) is **the LORD.** God therefore is concerned about everyone, regardless of their economic status.

22:3. This verse is repeated in 27:12, and a similar thought is stated in 14:16. This is another contrast between the **prudent** ('ārûm, "shrewd in a good sense"; see comments on 12:23) and **the simple** (peṯî, "naive, untaught"). The one is aware of **danger** and wisely avoids it (cf. 22:5); the other may see danger **but** puts forth no effort to avoid it, so he suffers **for it.** This is illustrated in 7:7-23.

22:4. Humility and the fear of the LORD go together (cf. 15:33). A person cannot be fearing God (worshiping, trusting, obeying, and serving Him) and be filled with selfish pride at the same time. **Wealth . . . honor, and life** result from fearing God, and as in 21:21 (see comments there) they also come from righteous living. So the fear of the Lord and righteousness are closely related.

22:5. The wicked have problems; **thorns** (cf. 15:19) **and snares** (cf. 21:6) are in their **paths.** Like thorns, their conduct keeps them from getting ahead, and like snares they are stopped like a trapped animal. A wise person, on the other hand, being aware of those consequences (cf. 22:3) is cautious and avoids the paths of the wicked.

22:6. This is perhaps the best-known verse in Proverbs on child training. The other verses on child-rearing (13:24;

19:18; 22:15; 23:13-14; 29:17) are all on discipline. The Hebrew word for **train** (*ḥānaḵ*) means to dedicate. It is used of dedicating a house (Deut. 20:5), the temple (1 Kings 8:63; 2 Chron. 7:5), and an image (Dan. 3:2). The noun *ḥānukkâh* speaks of the dedication of an altar (Num. 7:10; 2 Chron. 7:9) and of the walls of Jerusalem (Neh. 12:27). Only in Proverbs 22:6 is the verb translated "train." *Ḥānaḵ* seems to include the idea of setting aside, narrowing, or hedging in. The word is sometimes used in the sense of "start." Child-training involves "narrowing" a child's conduct away from evil and toward godliness and starting him in the right direction. Gleason L. Archer points out that this Hebrew verb is similar to the Egyptian *ḥ-n-k*, which means "to give to the gods" or "to set up something for divine service." He suggests that in verse 6 this gives "the following range of possible meanings: 'Dedicate the child to God,' 'Prepare the child for his future responsibilities,' 'Exercise or train the child for adulthood' " (*Encyclopedia of Bible Difficulties.* Grand Rapids: Zondervan Publishing House, 1982, p. 252).

In the way he should go is literally, "upon the mouth of his way." "Upon the mouth of" is a Hebrew idiom meaning "according to" or "in accord with." A servant would respond "upon the mouth of" or at the command of his superior. But what does "the way" mean? Scholars have interpreted this differently. Does it mean according to the way he *ought* to go (KJV, NASB, NIV) either vocationally or morally? Or does it mean, as others have suggested, according to the demands of his personality, conduct, or stage in life? Since "way" in Proverbs does not mean personality or stage in life, it is preferable to say that "way" means *proper* way, the path of wise, godly living, which is emphasized frequently in Proverbs—basically the way of wisdom. It is from this proper behavior pattern or godly lifestyle that he will not turn **when he is old,** that is, when he is grown (attains adulthood).

Some parents, however, have sought to follow this directive but without this result. Their children have strayed from the godly training the parents gave them. This illustrates the nature of a "proverb." A proverb is a literary device whereby a general truth is brought to bear on a specific situation. Many of the proverbs are not absolute guarantees for they express truths that are necessarily conditioned by prevailing circumstances. For example, verses 3-4, 9, 11, 16, 29 do not express promises that are *always* binding. Though the proverbs are generally and usually true, occasional exceptions may be noted. This may be because of the self-will or deliberate disobedience of an individual who chooses to go his own way—the way of folly instead of the way of wisdom (see v. 15 and comments there). For that he is held responsible. It *is* generally true, however, that most children who are brought up in Christian homes, under the influence of godly parents who teach and live God's standards (cf. Eph. 6:4), follow that training.

22:7. Unfortunately a **rich** person may "lord it over" a **poor** person, **and a lender** is master of **the borrower.** This suggests that a person should be careful before making a large loan. He may become like a slave, a poor, oppressed person.

22:8. A person **who sows** seeds of **wickedness** (*'awlâh,* "injustice") will reap a harvest of **trouble** (*'āwen,* "trouble or sorrow," rendered "harm" in 12:21). Trouble is the inevitable result of sin (cf. Hosea 10:13; Gal. 6:7). **Fury** renders a word that means "overflowing rage." What the wicked achieve through their fury or wrath **will** not last; their manipulative techniques will be exhausted. This thought is encouraging to the oppressed. The trouble the wicked bring on others will come on themselves.

22:9. A **generous man** is, literally, "a good eye." (In 23:6 and 28:22 "a stingy man" is, lit., "an evil eye.") Willingness to share **food with the poor** (*dal,* "feeble, weak, helpless") shows that a person is genuine; he looks at others with the desire to help them, not to take advantage of them (cf. generosity to the poor in Deut. 15:10; Prov. 14:21, 31; 28:27).

22:10. A **mocker** (cf. 9:7-8, 12; 13:1; 14:6; 15:12; 19:25, 29; 21:11, 24; 24:9) causes **strife** (contention), quarreling, **and insults** (*qālôn,* "disgrace"; used eight times in Prov. and only nine times elsewhere). So by removing a troublemaker, trouble also leaves.

22:11. Purity of motives and thought (**a pure heart**) and **gracious** words are appreciated by a **king** (cf. 14:35; 16:13). Naturally he wants to have people like that around him. So purity and graciousness are advantageous; they help give a person a friendship with leaders in high positions.

22:12. In His omniscience (cf. **eyes of the LORD** in 15:3) God guards **knowledge.** On the other hand **unfaithful** (lit., "treacherous") **words** will be overturned or subverted (*sālap*; cf. 13:6; 19:3; 21:12). To be wise, then, is to be under God's protection. To be unwise and treacherous, even in what one says, is to be on a path that will end in frustration.

22:13. The extreme excuses made by a lazy person to avoid work are ridiculous. (On the word **sluggard,** see comments on 6:6.) Most probably **a lion** (cf. 26:13) would not be roaming the streets of an Israelite town. And if a lazy person actually feared being **murdered** he would *never* go outside!

22:14. To listen to the words **of an adulteress** and be seductively led into sin by her (cf. 2:16-22; 5:3-6; 7:10-23) is like falling into a **pit** (cf. 23:27) from which there is no escape. The dire consequences of adultery are part of God's punishment in His **wrath** on sin.

22:15. Though **folly** (from *'ĕwîl*, an arrogant, flippant, hardened fool) **is . . . in the heart of a child . . . discipline** can help expel that kind of attitude and replace it with wisdom. "Discipline" (*mûsār*) is moral correction, which includes spankings (**the rod;** cf. 13:24; 23:13-14; 29:15), verbal correction, and other forms of discipline.

22:16. Buying influence or favoritism with **gifts** (cf. 17:23) for those who do not need them (**the rich**) while oppressing **the poor** (*dal*, "feeble, weak, helpless"; see comments on 10:15) to gain **wealth** will boomerang. Ironically such actions result *not* in wealth but in poverty!

IV. The Sayings of the Wise Men (22:17–24:34)

This section falls into two parts. The first part (22:17–24:22) is introduced as "the sayings of the wise" (22:17), and the second part (24:23-34) is introduced by the statement, "These also are the sayings of the wise" (24:23). In style this section includes at least 20 instances in which two verses express a complete thought, rather than one verse as in

10:1–22:16 (see, e.g., 22:17-18, 20-21; 23:1-2). Also seven verses have three lines rather than the normal two lines (22:29; 23:5, 29, 31; 24:14, 27, 31), and two verses each have four lines (23:7; 24:12). "My son" occurs 5 times (23:15, 19, 26; 24:13, 21) whereas it occurs 15 times in chapters 1–9 and only once (19:27) in 10:1–22:16 and twice (27:11; 31:2) in the remainder of the book. "A wise son" occurs once (23:24) in 22:17–24:34 compared with 5 times in 10:1–22:16.

Many of the sayings are warnings, using the words "do not" (see 22:22, 24, 26, 28; 23:3-4, 6, 9-10, 13, 17, 20, 22-23, 31; 24:1, 15, 17, 19, 21, 28-29). Interestingly each of the 30 sayings in 22:22–24:22 includes a reason for the warning or other advice and several of the sayings in 24:23-34 include reasons.

The sayings in 22:17–24:34 were written by wise men other than Solomon, and were compiled either in his lifetime or later. As stated in 22:20, the first portion (22:17–24:22) includes 30 sayings. The outline in the comments on 22:17–24:22 shows how this section may be divided into 30 sayings (e.g., 22:22-23, the first saying; 22:24-25, the second saying).

Many scholars have maintained that these wise men borrowed from the Egyptian work *The Instruction of Amen-em-Ope*, which has 30 sections. However, this seems unlikely for several reasons:

(1) The sayings in the Egyptian work are much longer than those in Proverbs. The 30 chapters in *Amen-em-Ope* range in length from 7 to 26 lines, whereas most of the sayings in Proverbs are 4 lines long with a few being shorter and a few a little longer.

(2) The date of *The Instruction of Amen-em-Ope* is disputed. John A. Wilson writes, "A date anywhere between the 10th and 6th centuries B.C. is possible, with some weight of evidence for the 7th–6th centuries" (*Ancient Near Eastern Texts Relating to the Old Testament,* ed. James B. Pritchard. Princeton, N.J.: Princeton University Press, 1955, p. 421). If this work were written 500 or 600 years before Christ, its date was then much later than Solomon's time (he reigned 971–931 B.C.) but later than Hezekiah's reign (715–686 B.C.). The latest time indication in Proverbs is Hezekiah's day (25:1). Proverbs then could not have copied from the Egyptian work.

(3) An unusually small number of verses in Proverbs 22:22–24:22 are similar to the work from Egypt. Pritchard quotes D.C. Simpson, who suggests the following parallels (*Ancient Near Eastern Texts Relating to the Old Testament*, p. 424, n. 46).

Proverbs	The Instruction of Amen-em-Ope
1st saying, 22:22-23	Chapter 2, 4:4-5
2nd saying, 22:24-25	Chapter 9, 11:13-14
3rd saying, 22:26-27	Chapter 9, 13:8-9
4th saying, 22:28	Chapter 6, 7:12-13
5th saying, 22:29	Chapter 30, 27:16-17
6th saying, 23:1-3	Chapter 23, 23:13-18
7th saying, 23:4-5	Chapter 7, 9:14–10:5
8th saying, 23:6-7	Chapter 11, 14:5-10
8th saying, 23:8	Chapter 11, 14:17-18
9th saying, 23:9	Chapter 21, 22:11-12
10th saying, 23:10-11	Chapter 6, 7:12-15; 8:9-10
25th saying, 24:11	Chapter 8, 11:6-7

Only 11 of the 30 Proverbs sayings have similarities to 9 of the *Amen-em-Ope* chapters. This can hardly be considered an extensive borrowing or dependence of Proverbs on the Egyptian work. Either *Amen-em-Ope* borrowed from Proverbs or each was written independently of the other. Using the number 30 may simply have been a common literary device. Any similarities between the secular Egyptian work and the Bible do not annul the Scriptures' verbal inspiration, for God the Holy Spirit guided wise men to write exactly what He wanted written in Proverbs, even if a few of those sayings were similar to proverbial sayings in Egypt.

A. Thirty sayings of the wise (22:17–24:22)

1. INTRODUCTION TO SAYINGS 1-10 (22:17-21)

22:17-19. The exhortations in verse 17 to **pay attention** (cf. 4:1, 20; 5:1; 7:24), **listen** (cf. 1:8; 4:1, 10, 20; 5:1, 7; 7:24; 8:32-33), and **apply your heart** (cf. "applying your heart," 2:2) are calls to pursue and obey what is presented in the 30 sayings. Reasons for the exhortation are given in verses 18-19: **it is pleasing** to memorize the sayings (**keep them in your heart**) and to be able to quote and talk about them (**have . . . them . . . on your lips**) because they encourage people to **trust . . . in the** LORD.

22:20-21. On the **30 sayings** see comments under the heading "IV. The Sayings of the Wise Men (22:17–24:34)." The **counsel** in these **sayings** comes from the **knowledge** of the wise men whose **words** were **true**. Again (cf. 22:18-19) a reason is stated: **so that** the learner **can give sound answers.** "Sound" translates "reliable." The same word, *ĕmet*, is rendered **reliable** in verse 21. The one who **sent you** may be the learner's teacher or employer.

2. SAYINGS 1-10 (22:22–23:11)

22:22-23. *The 1st saying.* These verses give a strong warning against taking advantage of the **poor** (cf. 14:31). **The poor** (*dal*, "feeble, weak, helpless") and **the needy** are easy prey for wicked people who can get their way **in court** by bribery and false accusations. But the defenseless are defended by **the** LORD who champions their cause and justly takes from those who unjustly take from the needy.

22:24-25. *The 2nd saying.* The warning here is against being a friend or even associating **with a hot-tempered man** (lit., "an owner or possessor of anger"; cf. 19:19) or **one easily angered** (lit., "a man of wrath") because such an association leads a person to take on wrathful **ways,** which are foolish (14:17, 29), divisive (15:18), and sinful (29:22), and become **ensnared** (cf. 29:6), caught up in a situation which is hard to get out of.

22:26-27. *The 3rd saying.* The high risks in putting **up security for debts** is mentioned several times in Proverbs (6:1-5; see comments there; 11:15; 17:18; 20:16; 27:13). Striking **hands in pledge** means to confirm an agreement, like the gesture of shaking hands (see comments on 6:1). If a debtor fails to pay, the creditor will hound the cosigner, and if the cosigner cannot **pay,** then his furniture may be taken as payment. This serious consequence results from becoming foolishly entangled in others' financial problems.

22:28. *The 4th saying.* Six times the Bible mentions the sin of moving **boundary** stones (Deut. 19:14; 27:17; Job 24:2; Prov. 22:28; 23:10; Hosea 5:10). A farmer could easily increase the extent of his own land and decrease his neighbor's by moving the stones at the boundary lines.

This form of stealing violated the eighth commandment (Ex. 20:15).

22:29. *The 5th saying.* Being diligent and **skilled** (*māhîr* can also mean "quick or prompt") in one's **work** is the best way to influence an employer. Diligence often results in a promotion (serving **before kings** and **not** just obscure people). Hearing about a good worker, a king (or other leader) will want to hire him.

23:1-3. *The 6th saying.* When invited to a banquet hosted by a prestigious host (e.g., **a ruler**), a person ought to be humble and restrained. He should be aware of **what is** around him, and **if** he is tempted to be gluttonous (cf. "gluttons" in v. 21; 28:7) he should restrain his appetite. Humorously the guest is advised to **put a knife to** his **throat** (rather than to his food)! This does not mean he should commit suicide but that he should cut back on his gorging. **Gluttony,** interestingly, translates the Hebrew *nepeš,* which has a variety of meanings including physical life (13:3, 8), oneself (19:8; 21:23), one's appetite (16:26) or craving (10:3), and the seat of those cravings (21:10 is lit., "the wicked soul craves"). From that stems the idea of gluttony in 23:2.

Foods that are **delicacies** in a royal banquet may be **deceptive.** A ruler-host may *seem* to be friendly by serving a sumptuous meal, but in reality he may be planning to betray his guest or do him an injustice (cf. v. 7). The banquet may be a "buttering-up" occasion.

23:4-5. *The 7th saying.* These verses warn against overwork for the sake of gaining **riches.** This speaks not against being industrious but against consuming oneself for money. Wise **restraint** in this area (as well as in what one eats at a banquet, vv. 1-2) is needed, especially in the present day when materialism drives many people to excessive work loads in order to accumulate more money. The reason for this advice is that riches are temporary and unstable (cf. 27:24). The first part of 23:5 is literally, "If you cause your eyes to fly after it" (i.e., wealth). Ironically, flying after wealth results in wealth flying away **like an eagle.**

23:6-8. *The 8th saying.* Verses 1-3 advised against greedily eating food served by a generous ruler. Verses 6-8 warn against eating **food** served by **a stingy man** (lit., "an evil eye," which occurs only here and in 28:22 in the OT; cf. comments on "a generous man," lit., "a good eye," in 22:9). Craving **his delicacies** is as wrong and dangerous as craving the delicious foods served by a ruler (23:3). When a guest realizes his host is **thinking** only of **the cost** of the food while hypocritically feigning generosity (**eat and drink**), the guest is repulsed. The guest wants to **vomit up** (or spit up) the food since it was not served honestly and since he finds that his **compliments** were **wasted.**

23:9. *The 9th saying.* Trying to teach **a fool** (*kesîl,* "dull, thickheaded, stubborn fool"; see comments on 1:7) is useless. He does **not** welcome what is said by a teacher who speaks prudently (**wisdom** renders *šēkel,* "prudence," also used in 12:8; 13:15; 16:22, "understanding"; 19:11).

23:10-11. *The 10th saying.* Verse 10a is identical with 22:28a, and 23:10b-11 is partially similar to 22:22-23. Stealing land from a neighbor by moving his **boundary stone** is bad enough but to take **fields** from children of widows is worse yet! The Lord, in His concern for **the fatherless** (Deut. 10:18; Pss. 10:14, 17-18; 68:5; 82:3; 146:9) opposes all who mistreat and steal from fatherless children. He is **their Defender** (*gōʾēl,* a person responsible for meeting the needs of a troubled or defenseless close relative).

3. INTRODUCTION TO SAYINGS 11-30 (23:12)

23:12. This verse serves as a break in the long string of sayings and introduces sayings 11-30 much as 22:17-21 introduced sayings 1-10. **Apply your heart** (cf. 22:17b) suggests diligence and desire for **instruction** (*mûsār,* often trans. "discipline," as it is in 23:13). Applying **your ears** is another way of saying "pay attention and listen" (cf. 22:17a).

4. SAYINGS 11-30 (23:13–24:22)

23:13-14. *The 11th saying.* Children need **discipline** (*mûsār,* "moral correction," both verbal and physical; cf. 1:2, 7). Physical punishment (by **the rod** or a stick; cf. 13:24; 22:15; 29:15) is approved in the Bible though "rod" may also be used figuratively for any form of discipline. The pain caused by spankings may make the parent and the child think the child will **die,** but that is **not** so. The punishment will actually *deliver* him **from**

physical **death** (*š⁺ʾôl*, the grave), not *cause* his death.

23:15-16. *The 12th saying.* This appeal to **my son** (cf. vv. 19, 26) illustrates that a wise child learns from parental discipline (vv. 13-14). The truth that a **wise** rather than a foolish son gladdens his father's **heart** is also stated in 10:1; 15:20; 23:24; 27:11; 29:3. Wisdom is to be internalized in one's **heart** (cf. 23:17, 19, 26; also note v. 12; 22:17). The father's heart and **inmost being** refer to his inner self, his intellectual and emotional being. A wise heart is revealed by speaking **what is right.**

23:17-18. *The 13th saying.* Envying **sinners** (cf. 3:31; 24:1, 19; Ps. 37:1), wanting to do what they do, is senseless because they have no **hope** (24:20) whereas the wise and godly do. The immediate pleasure of sin cannot be compared with the ultimate **hope** associated with **the fear of the** LORD (cf. 19:23; 24:21).

23:19-21. *The 14th saying.* By listening and heeding his father's instruction and desiring **the right path** (proper conduct), a **son is wise.** One way to stay on "the right path" is to avoid drunkenness (see comments on **wine** in 20:1) and gluttony (cf. 23:2). These two sins cause **drowsiness,** which results in laziness and poverty. Other evils of strong **drink** are discussed in verses 29-35.

23:22-23. *The 15th saying.* Verses 22, 24-25 each refer to one's **father** and/or **mother.** Heeding parental instruction and advice is again encouraged. This is repeated often in Proverbs, apparently because of children's tendency to go their own ways. Wise children respect their parents **when** they are **old.** To **despise** (*bûz,* "to hold in contempt," a verb used often in Prov.; see comments on 1:7) them is to disobey the fifth commandment (Ex. 20:12). Buying **the truth** suggests spending whatever energy or financial resources are necessary to acquire truth, along with **wisdom, discipline** (*mûsār,* see comments on Prov. 23:12-13), **and understanding** (cf. 1:2-6).

23:24-25. *The 16th saying.* Verse 24 is another evidence that in Proverbs being **wise** (cf. v. 15) in God's view means being godly or **righteous.** Interestingly the words **has great joy** and **rejoice** translate the same Hebrew word *gîl,* and **delights** and **be glad** translate *śāmaḥ.* **The father** is said to have given the **son** life (v. 22) and

the **mother** . . . **gave** the son **birth.** Wise, godly living, in obedience to the parents' discipline, not only benefits the child; it also benefits the parents.

23:26-28. *The 17th saying.* Again the son (**My son;** cf. vv. 15, 19; 24:13, 21) was exhorted to follow his father's teaching. The words **give me your heart** (cf. 23:15, 17, 19) appeal to the son's thoughts and values so that his lifestyle (**ways**) will follow that of his father. The son's **eyes** as well as his lips (22:18) and ears (23:12) are important. What one sees, says, and hears should be pleasing to the Lord. The urgency of the father's appeal is related to the dangers of sexual waywardness (cf. 5:20; 6:24; 7:5; 20:16). Two kinds of immoral women are in view, the unmarried (the **prostitute**) and the married (the **wayward wife**). (On the Heb. words for these terms see the comments on 2:16.) Immoral women are like **a deep pit** (cf. 22:14) or a **well** in that they confine and trap men (cf. 6:27-35; 7:21-27), making it impossible for them to escape the consequences. **Men** need to be on guard against wayward women who seek to seduce them, springing on them suddenly (cf. 7:7-10) **like a bandit,** adding to the number of their victims. Of course the Bible also warns against men seducing women.

23:29-35. *The 18th saying.* These verses present the longest and most articulate warning in Proverbs against drunkenness (cf. vv. 20-21; 20:1; 31:4-5). Six questions call attention to emotional problems (**woe** and **sorrow**), social problems (**strife** and **complaints**), and physical problems (**bruises**—from beatings or bumping into things while staggering—and **bloodshot eyes**) that stem from lingering long **over wine** and **mixed wine** (*mimsōk,* used only here and in Isa. 65:11). **Wine** seems attractive (Prov. 23:31); **it is red,** sparkling, and smooth—the senses of sight and taste. But eventually (**in the end;** cf. 5:4; 14:12; 16:25; 19:20; 25:8; 28:23; 29:21) it is as devastating and painful as **a snake** bite.

Drunkenness also leads to mental problems (23:33): hallucinations and imagining **confusing** ("perverse or abnormal"; see comments on 2:12) **things.** Physically a drunkard is off balance as he walks. In his stupor he may imagine himself moving like a sailor swaying at the **top** of a ship's **rigging.** Also a drunkard is insensitive to pain when people **hit** him (cf. "bruises," 23:29). Sensing his stupor he still longs to escape by having **another drink**. Alcohol controls him; he is a slave to wine.

24:1-2. *The 19th saying.* Three times in these 30 sayings a warning is given against being envious of the **wicked** (cf. 23:17; 24:19; also see 3:31). In 23:17-18 and 24:19-20 the reason for not envying sinners is that their future is bleak. Here the reason is that they plan **violence** (cf. v. 8) and **talk about** the **trouble** they will bring on others (cf. 1:10-19). What is in **their hearts** comes out in **their** talk (**lips**; cf. 4:23-24).

24:3-4. *The 20th saying.* Sayings 20-22 pertain to wisdom. Plotting evil is mentioned a number of times in Proverbs (3:29; 6:14; 12:20; 14:22; 16:27, 30; 24:2, 8). The best policy is to stay away from such people. **By wisdom . . . understanding,** and **knowledge** houses are **built . . . established,** and **filled with . . . treasures.** This may refer to constructing literal houses or, perhaps more likely, to the undertaking of any enterprise. Folly and sin do not contribute to security and prosperity, but wisdom does. This fact contrasts with the violence mentioned in verse 2.

24:5-6. *The 21st saying.* Besides giving security and prosperity (vv. 3-4) wisdom provides **strength** to accomplish various tasks (cf. 21:22). A **wise** person is not self-reliant; he looks to others for counsel on how to win a battle (cf. 11:14; 20:18; also note 15:22). On the word **guidance** see comments on 1:5.

24:7. *The 22nd saying.* A **fool** ('*ĕwîl,* "an arrogant, hardened fool"; see comments on 1:7) cannot appreciate, comprehend, or **say** anything wise. **Wisdom** (here in the pl., as in 1:20; 9:1, for emphasis) is beyond him. Therefore **at the gate,** where legal and judicial decisions were made by wise leaders, he was (or should have been) silent.

24:8-9. *The 23rd saying.* A person **who** continually thinks up (cf. v. 2) **evil** schemes becomes **known as a schemer** (lit., "an owner or possessor of evil plans"; cf. "crafty" in 12:2; 14:17). Such scheming is foolish because it is sinful and leads to mockery (see comments on a **mocker** in 13:1), which people **detest** (cf. "detest" in 8:7; 16:12; 29:27).

24:10. *The 24th saying.* Giving in to

the pressure of **trouble** (a different word for trouble in v. 2 means "sorrow or mischief") shows that a person's strength is limited. This may subtly suggest that person is not wise, because, as stated in verse 5, wisdom gives strength. The Hebrew includes a wordplay by placing the word for **small** (*ṣar,* "narrow, tight, restricted") immediately after the word for "trouble" (*ṣārâh*).

24:11-12. *The 25th saying.* Verse 10 referred to trouble that comes on a person; verses 11-12 refer to trouble that comes on others. People here who are **being** taken **to death** and **slaughter** probably are victims of unjust oppression rather than guilty people being condemned. Some people may claim they are ignorant of others' plights, but God knows who is guilty of willful ignorance and **He** will judge (**repay**) it (cf. Matt. 25:41-46). **He . . . weighs the heart** (cf. Prov. 21:2), that is, He knows and considers peoples' inner motives and thoughts. God is concerned about the plight of the poor and the helpless (cf. 22:22-23; 23:10-11).

24:13-14. *The 26th saying.* Much as **honey,** the sweetest substance known in the ancient Near East, **is good** and tastes **sweet,** so **wisdom is** beneficial and desirable to the soul because it gives a person **future hope** (cf. 23:18). **Honey** is mentioned six times in Proverbs (5:3; 24:13 [twice]; 25:16, 27; 27:7). **My son** occurs in the 30 sayings five times (23:15, 19, 26; 24:13, 21).

24:15-16. *The 27th saying.* Sayings 27-29 are warnings (**Do not**) like sayings 1-4, 6-11, 14, 18-19. Verses 15-16 warn that it is futile for the **wicked** to attempt to destroy the **righteous** and his possessions. Because of God's protection the **righteous** person recovers from robberies and attacks but the wicked who instigate such schemes (cf. vv. 2, 8) find that *they* are the ones who suffer (cf. 1:18-19). Examples of this kind of judicial boomeranging are seen in Daniel 3 and 6.

24:17-18. *The 28th saying.* God is disgusted with those who **gloat** over someone's failure. Gloating over the disasters experienced by the poor is condemned in 17:5; in 24:17 gloating is not even permitted when an *enemy* has a problem. Gloating may cause God to side with one's enemy and to withdraw His **wrath . . . from** that enemy. God hates gloating because it suggests a superior attitude over others.

24:19-20. *The 29th saying.* For the third time in the 30 sayings envy of sinners is condemned (cf. 23:17; 24:1). Fretting over what sinners have and do (cf. Ps. 37:1) and wanting to join them is wrong because they have **no future hope.** They will die (on **the lamp** being **snuffed out** see comments on 13:9). The righteous and wise, on the other hand, do have hope for the future (cf. 23:18; 24:14). **Evil** and **wicked** are used as synonyms in both verses 19 and 20.

24:21-22. *The 30th saying.* Fittingly, fearing **the LORD** (cf. comments on 1:7) is referred to in the last of the 30 sayings. The Lord **and the king**—**those two**—are the agents who punish **the rebellious** (cf. Rom. 13:1-7; 1 Peter 2:13-17). The **calamities they can bring** refer either to troubles the rebellious bring on others or, more likely, to the calamities God and the king can bring on rebels. The Hebrew word for "calamities" (*pîd*) is used only here in Proverbs and four times in Job.

B. Additional sayings of the wise (24:23-34)

These verses present an additional six sayings of the wise men (see comments on 22:17). These proverbs discuss justice and injustice in the courts, honesty, priorities, false witnessing, revenge, and laziness.

1. THE FIRST SAYING (24:23-25)

24:23-25. Partiality in judging is condemned in Deuteronomy 1:17; 16:19; Proverbs 17:15; 18:5; 28:21. Letting **the guilty** go free **is not good** either (cf. comments on 17:26); perverting justice results in leaders being cursed and denounced. On the other hand exercising justice against **the guilty** brings judges **rich blessing;** those judges are respected and appreciated.

2. THE SECOND SAYING (24:26)

24:26. An honest answer is literally, "upright or straight words." This may tie in with verses 24-25. How are honest words and kisses alike? As a sincere **kiss** shows affection and is desirable, so an honest (and perhaps straightforward) answer shows a person's concern and therefore is welcomed.

3. THE THIRD SAYING (24:27)

24:27. Israelites, most of whom farmed land, needed to plow and sow seed (to **get** their **fields ready;** cf. comments on vv. 30-31) before they attended to more immediate creature comforts. Whether **house** should be taken literally (constructing a house) or figuratively (getting married and having a family), the principle is the same: it is important to have one's priorities straight.

4. THE FOURTH SAYING (24:28)

24:28. Verses 23b-25 spoke of judges; verses 28-29 comment on the witnesses in court. Giving false testimony—and thereby harming someone's reputation or unjustly acquiring things from him, or even taking his life—is frequently forbidden in Proverbs (see comments on 6:19). It is prohibited by the ninth commandment (Ex. 20:16). Being deceptive in what one says in court is wrong (see comments on "deceit" in Prov. 12:20).

5. THE FIFTH SAYING (24:29)

24:29. If this verse relates to verse 28 (rather than being a separate saying), then it refers specifically to revenge gained through perjury. If it is a separate saying, then it is a more general warning against revenge (cf. Deut. 32:35; Ps. 94:1; Prov. 20:22; Rom. 12:19; Heb. 10:30).

6. THE SIXTH SAYING (24:30-34)

Some of these statements about the sluggard are similar to those in 6:6-11 (see comments there). The writer made some observations about laziness (24:30-31), reflected on it (v. 32), and drew some conclusions about its consequences which he addressed to the sluggard (vv. 33-34).

24:30-31. The sluggard, a word used 14 times in Proverbs, is here called a person **who lacks judgment** (see comments on 6:32; 10:13). The lazy person did not get his fields ready (cf. 24:27). He so neglected them that **thorns** and **weeds** grew up (cf. 15:19) leaving no room for crops. And **the stone wall** around **the field** had not been repaired.

24:32-34. As the writer of these verses reflected on what he **observed,** he **saw** the **lesson:** indolence—staying in bed and resting when it is time to work—leads to **poverty** (see comments on 6:11). With no crops to harvest, a lazy person has nothing to eat and nothing to sell to others for income. Suddenly he awakens to the reality of the plight; poverty comes on him surprisingly **like a bandit** or suddenly like an attacking soldier. Interestingly the 30 sayings begin with a reference to the poor (22:22; *dal*, "feeble, weak, helpless") and the additional 6 sayings end with a reference to poverty (*maḥsōr*; "lacking, being in need").

V. Proverbs of Solomon Collected by Hezekiah's Men (chaps. 25–29)

25:1. Hezekiah's **men,** perhaps royal scribes, **copied** (lit., "removed," i.e., from one book or scroll to another) more than 100 of Solomon's **proverbs.** This was about 250 years after **Solomon** wrote them. Hezekiah's men grouped many of these proverbs in units of similar thoughts.

25:2. Verses 2-7 are sayings about the king. Though the king probably was Solomon, these proverbs applied to all kings of Israel and Judah. **God** has chosen not to reveal everything about Himself and His plans (cf. Deut. 29:29). This means that **kings,** to make proper decisions, must investigate matters fully. Whereas God delights in concealing some things, kings delight in being investigative.

25:3. This verse is the first of many verses in chapters 25–26 that make comparisons, using the words "like" or **as;** 12 are in chapter 25 (vv. 3, 11-14, 18-20, 23, 25-26, 28) and 13 in chapter 26 (see comments on 26:1).

God hides some of His knowledge from kings, and **kings** hide some of their knowledge from their subjects. Rulers, responsible for knowing what is going on and for investigating issues fully (25:2), need not reveal everything they know. "Search out" in verse 2 and **unsearchable** in verse 3 connect these two verses.

25:4-5. Just as undesirable slag is removed **from . . . silver** (cf. 27:21), so **wicked** people are to be removed **from the** king. Getting rid of wicked assistants (cf. 20:8, 26) enables a king to have a righteous reign. The last line of 25:5 is nearly identical to that of 16:12.

25:6-7. It is wrong for a person to try to promote himself to a king, claiming to be **great** when he is not. **It is** far **better for** the king to promote him **than for** the king **to humiliate** him in front of a **noble-man** whose position the status seeker is desiring. Christ illustrated this in a parable (Luke 14:7-10).

25:8. In Hebrew the words **seen with your eyes** are the last words of verse 7 (cf. KJV, NASB). Some versions (e.g., NIV, RSV) put those words with verse 8. The phrase makes verse 7 long for a proverb and also makes far less sense there than with verse 8.

Verse 8 warns against **hastily** taking another person **to court** (cf. 24:28). The reason is that the plaintiff may lose the case and be ashamed, for what he thought he saw may not have been what actually took place.

25:9-10. In providing evidence against a neighbor in a court case a plaintiff may be forced to **betray** a friend's **confidence.** As a result the friend may shame him and the plaintiff may have an irretrievable loss of **reputation.** It is risky business to accuse others publicly in court.

25:11-12. An appropriate and properly timed **word** (cf. 15:23; 24:26)—which sometimes may be a **rebuke** (see comments on 1:23)—can be attractive and valuable, like **gold** apples set against a **silver** sculpture or carving, or like a **gold** earring **or** other **ornament.**

25:13. Snow in the mountains (not snow falling on the crops in the dry season) is refreshing during the heat of **harvesttime.** Similarly a **trustworthy messenger** is refreshing to one **who** sends **him** (cf. 13:17). An unreliable messenger is referred to in 10:26 and 26:6.

25:14. Clouds and wind usually give farmers promise of **rain.** But if no rain comes, the farmers are keenly disappointed. Similarly people who claim they will give presents but never keep their promises are frustrating to the supposed recipients. A person ought not promise something if he knows he cannot follow through.

25:15. Patience and a **gentle** (lit., "soft") **tongue** (cf. 15:1) **can be** unusually influential, accomplishing far more than loss of temper and harsh words. A soft tongue breaking a hard **bone** is an unusual figure of speech—how can a tongue break a bone? The idea is that softly spoken words can accomplish difficult things. Also persuading a **ruler** to follow some difficult course of action takes patience.

25:16-17. Just as eating **too** much **honey** can cause a problem (cf. v. 27; 27:7), so visiting a neighbor **too** often may cause him to **hate** the frequent visitor. Overdoing anything can be a problem. **Seldom** is literally, "make precious," that is, "make it valuable" by its rarity. A person should refrain from frequently visiting his neighbor, to avoid being a nuisance, but he should visit enough so that his visits are valued.

25:18. Giving **false testimony** in court **against** a **neighbor** (see comments on 6:19) can crush, divide, or pierce like **a club . . . sword, or . . . arrow.** Lying can wound a person's character and even destroy his life as effectively as weapons.

25:19. **A bad tooth** and **a lame foot** can be problems, especially because a person relys on them to eat and walk. Also relying on a person who turns out to be untrustworthy can be disappointing and troublesome. Job expressed this concern over his friends (Job 6:14-15). An example of an unreliable person is one who lies in court (Prov. 25:18).

25:20. Trying to perk up by **songs** a person who is discouraged or depressed (**a heavy heart**) is as cruel as stealing his **garment** in **cold** weather. It is also **like** pouring **vinegar . . . on soda;** it is useless and it causes a violent reaction. Being insensitive and unsympathetic does much harm.

25:21-22. Kindness to one's **enemy**— giving **him food** and **water**—is like heaping **burning coals on his head** (quoted by Paul in Rom. 12:20). Sometimes a person's fire went out and he needed to borrow some live coals to restart his fire. Giving a person coals in a pan to carry home "on his head" was a neighborly, kind act; it made friends, not enemies. Also the kindness shown in giving someone food and water makes him ashamed of being an enemy, and brings God's blessing on the benefactor. Compassion, not revenge, should characterize believers (cf. Prov. 24:29). Alternately, light on this passage may come from an Egyptian expiation ritual, in which a person guilty of some wrongdoing would carry a pan of burning coals on his head as a sign of his repentance. Thus treating one's enemy kindly may cause him to repent.

25:23. **As** surely as an Israelite could predict the consequences of **a north wind,** so one can predict the consequences of **a sly tongue** (lit., "a tongue of secrecy," i.e., a slanderous tongue). One **brings rain** and the other **angry looks.** Slander leads to anger. However, in Palestine rain does not normally come from the north. So perhaps this saying originated outside Palestine (Derek Kidner, *The Proverbs: An Introduction and Commentary,* p. 160).

25:24. Solitude in cramped quarters with peace is **better . . . than** (cf. comments on 12:9) living in a spacious **house** with a cantankerous, contentious **wife.** This verse is identical to 21:9 (also cf. 21:19).

25:25. The impact of receiving **good news** (cf. 15:30) **from a** friend or relative who lives far away is **like** a refreshing drink of **water to a** tired person. In Bible times news traveled slowly; thus long periods of anxious waiting usually followed the departure of a loved one or friend to **a distant land.**

25:26. **A righteous man who** lets his reputation be compromised is **like** pure water being tainted and ruined by mud or other pollutants. The value of a pure **spring** or well in an arid country lends force to the statement. Once a spring or well is contaminated it may never be pure again, and disappoints those who come to it for a drink. A righteous person who defects to sin disappoints others who look to him.

25:27. Seeking to exalt oneself (seeking **one's own honor;** cf. v. 6; 27:2) is as bad as overeating **honey** (cf. 25:16; 27:7). Both bring problems.

25:28. Without walls **a city** was vulnerable to enemy attacks. And an undisciplined person, **who lacks self-control** (cf. 14:17, 29; 16:32; 29:11), is also vulnerable to trouble.

26:1. Thirteen verses in this chapter are comparisons, using the words **like** or "as" (cf. comments on 25:3). Each of verses 1, 3-12 refers to a fool or fools. **Snow in summer or rain in harvest** is inappropriate, highly unusual, and potentially damaging to crops. Putting **a fool** in a position of **honor** (cf. 26:8) is inappropriate (cf. 19:10) and may injure others who follow him as a model.

26:2. The unpredictable, **fluttering** nature of a bird's flight demonstrates a person's inability to place a **curse** on another who does not deserve it. Balaam experienced that same inability (Num. 23:8).

26:3. Just as a **horse** is motivated by a **whip** and a **donkey** is controlled by a **halter** rather than by reason, so a fool needs to be controlled by **a rod** (physical punishment) because he does not respond to appeals to his intellect (cf. 10:13; 14:3; 19:29).

26:4-5. These two sayings belong together; they complement each other. Their point is that one should not be drawn down to a fool's level (v. 4) but at times he must use the fool's language to refute the **fool** so he does not become conceited (v. 5; cf. vv. 12, 16). Wisdom is needed to determine when to apply verse 4 and when to apply verse 5. The Jewish Talmud suggests that verse 4 pertains to foolish comments that can be ignored and that verse 5 refers to erroneous ideas that must be corrected. **You** in verse 4 is emphatic and may be translated "you, even you."

26:6. Sending . . . a message by . . . a fool is useless and potentially damaging. It is **like cutting off one's feet,** that is, the message does not get delivered; it is as if the sender tried to take it himself by walking the distance without feet. **Drinking violence** is self-damaging, just like relying on an unfaithful messenger.

26:7. A fool cannot be trusted with a message (v. 6); also a **proverb** in his **mouth** (cf. v. 9) is as useless as limp **legs** to a **lame** man (cf. 25:19). A fool does not know what to do with a proverb; he does not understand it or apply it. Feet (26:6) and legs (v. 7) tie these two verses together.

26:8. It is senseless and possibly harmful to tie **a stone** into **a sling.** The stone might slip out and damage the thrower. So bestowing **honor** on **a fool,** for whom honor is inappropriate (v. 1), is senseless and may damage the reputation of the one giving the honor. His wisdom will be questioned.

26:9. As seen in verse 7, **a proverb** spoken by **a fool** is useless. Here it is compared to **a thornbush in** the **hand** of a drunkard. This could mean one of several things: (1) The drunkard may inflict damage on others by waving a thornbush around dangerously. (2) He may be so insensitive to pain that he does not feel a thorn in his hand, much as a fool is insensitive to wisdom. (3) A man who is so

drunk that he cannot pull a thorn out of his hand is like a fool who cannot apply a proverb that he can quote (Robert L. Alden, *Proverbs: A Commentary on an Ancient Book of Timeless Advice,* p. 187). Perhaps the first meaning is to be preferred.

26:10. The absurdity of an employer hiring **a fool or any passer-by** is like a berserk **archer** (cf. v. 18) indiscriminately shooting without aiming. Hiring "just anybody" will actually harm the hirer.

26:11. As a dog eats **its vomit** (quoted in 2 Peter 2:22), **so a fool** cannot learn from experience. He **returns to** his habits even though they are disgusting.

26:12. Concluding the series of statements on the fool (vv. 1, 3-12) is this saying that even **a fool** is better off than one who is **wise in his own eyes** (cf. vv. 5, 16). Self-conceit or pride blinds a person to his sense of need; at least a fool may sense his need for correction.

The last part of verse 12 is repeated in 29:20b. Pride and being proud are addressed frequently in Proverbs (3:34; 8:13; 11:2; 13:10; 15:25; 16:5, 18-19; 18:12; 21:4, 24; 29:23; cf. 26:5, 12, 16).

26:13. Verses 13-16 speak about the sluggard (cf. 6:6-11). **The sluggard** goes to bizarre measures to avoid leaving his house, such as saying **a lion** is **roaming** loose (see comments on 22:13).

26:14. The **sluggard,** though tossing in **bed,** seems anchored to it **as a door** is joined to the jamb. He will not even exert the energy needed to get up.

26:15. This picture of a **lazy** person starving because he refuses to feed himself is also found in 19:24 (see comments there).

26:16. In his self-conceit (cf. vv. 5, 12) **the sluggard** thinks he is smarter **than** anyone (**seven men**). Yet his answers lack discretion (lit., "taste").

26:17. Verses 17-28 refer to quarrels (vv. 17, 20-21), deceit (vv. 18-19, 24-26), gossip (vv. 20, 22), and lying (vv. 23, 28). **One who** grabs **a dog by** its **ears** may expect to be bitten. **So is a passer-by,** someone not directly involved, **who meddles in** (lit., "excites himself over") another's **quarrel.** He causes trouble for himself by interfering in a situation he knows little about.

26:18-19. The berserk archer is again referred to (cf. v. 10) to picture a troublemaker. After deceiving **his neighbor** he tries to avoid being accused by saying he was only joking. But that is humor in bad taste. His deception, like a deadly arrow, has already done its damage.

26:20-21. Fire and strife relate these two verses. **A quarrel dies down** without **gossip** (cf. gossiping in 11:13; 16:28; 18:8; 20:19; 26:22) just as **a fire goes out** when its fuel is removed (v. 20). Conversely quarreling contributes to (**kindling** is lit., "heat up") **strife** (cf. 17:1; 18:6; 20:3; 22:10; 23:29; 30:33) just as **charcoal** and **wood** build up a **fire.**

26:22. See comments on 18:8, where the same statement is made. Here gossiping fits with 26:20-21.

26:23. **A coating of glaze** refers to an attractive coating **over** a piece of pottery. This is likened to **fervent** (*dālaq,* "to burn or kindle") **lips** and **an evil heart.** A person who tries to disguise his evil motives and character by zealous speech is like an attractive glazed-over jar. (Note Jesus' reference in Luke 11:39 to the clean outside of the cup and dish; also note Matt. 23:27.)

26:24. Verses 24-26 expand the idea in verse 23 (**lips . . . heart,** and "speech" tie verses 23-25 together). A **malicious** person plans **deceit** (cf. v. 19) but seeks to disguise it by his smooth talk ("lips").

26:25. This verse warns against being taken in by a malicious person whose words are **charming** (cf. vv. 23-24) but whose **heart** (cf. vv. 23-24) is filled with **seven** (i.e., numerous; cf. "seven men," v. 16) **abominations** (cf. 6:16-19).

26:26. **Malice** (*śin'âh*) is translated "hate" or "hatred" in 10:12, 18; 15:17 (cf. the verb *śānē',* "hates," in 26:28). Though a scoundrel can hide his feelings temporarily through deceit, they will eventually be known. **The assembly** refers to any group called together for some purpose. Perhaps this group is assembled to administer justice.

26:27. Destruction by one's own devices is the subject of this verse and of Psalms 7:15; 9:15; 35:8; 57:6. If Proverbs 26:27 is related to verses 23-26 the point is that attempts to trap or destroy others will eventually turn on the schemer (cf. 1:18-19; 28:10). Many times Proverbs affirms that sin boomerangs.

26:28. People who lie are actually hateful (see comments on malice in v. 26); they desire to harm others by slandering their reputations. And people who flatter to help achieve their selfishly deceptive ends (cf. vv. 23-26) bring **ruin** either to themselves, their victims, or both.

27:1. Sixteen of the 27 verses in this chapter deal with relationships with people (vv. 2-6, 9-11, 13-18, 21-22). This warning about tomorrow's uncertainty is repeated in James 4:13-16. The Hebrew word for **boast** is translated "praise" in verses 2 and 21. A person should not praise himself about what he will do the next **day** because he really has no way of knowing for sure **what** will happen.

27:2. Praising oneself is evidence of pride and therefore is wrong. Not only should a person refrain from boasting about what he will do (v. 1); he should also refrain from boasting about what he has done.

27:3. Verses 3-6 discuss various interpersonal relationships. The burden of being provoked **by a fool** is a **heavy** one indeed. In fact it **is heavier than** a large **stone** and more burdensome than **sand.** So a wise person should not react to a fool even when the fool's actions and words are irritating.

27:4. When a person is angry and furious he can be **cruel** toward others. His words and actions may cause others to cower in fear. But jealousy is even worse because it may include **anger** and **fury** and merciless revenge, as illustrated in 6:32-35. **Who can stand before jealousy?** is one of the few rhetorical questions in Proverbs.

27:5. If a person's love is genuine, he will not fear to tell his friend about a fault or correct him. Rebuking (see comments on 1:23) is to be preferred to **hidden** (lit., "closed up, withdrawn") **love.** In other words correcting a person's fault is an evidence of love, but failing to correct him shows one's love is withdrawn. This verse is one of 19 "better . . . than" verses in Proverbs (see comments on 12:9).

27:6. **An enemy** (lit., "one who hates") **may** seem to be a friend by his many **kisses,** and a true **friend** (lit., "one who loves") may seem to be an enemy by **the wounds** he inflicts (probably inner hurts that come from being rebuked or criticized; see v. 5). Yet, ironically, the rebukes may actually be more genuine expressions of friendship.

27:7. If a person is **full** of food then **honey,** which ordinarily he would crave, is no longer desirable. Conversely, **to a hungry** person **even** something **bitter** may seem **sweet** because it satisfies his need for food. This verse may be teaching that one's attitude toward material possessions is influenced by how much he possesses. Those who have much do not appreciate or value a gift as much as do those who have little.

27:8. This verse may speak against a person abandoning his responsibilities at **home** along with its comforts. Just as **a bird** wandering **from its nest** too early or too far brings hardship on itself, so a young person leaving home too soon may find himself unable to care for himself (e.g., the prodigal son, Luke 15:11-32).

27:9. A friend's **earnest counsel** is as sweet or pleasant as the fragrance emanating from **perfume and incense.** Genuine advice shows that a person cares.

27:10. This proverb is designed more to exalt long-term friendship than to denigrate family ties. Normally in times of adversity, **a brother** (relative) is helpful (17:17). But if the brother lives a great distance **away,** a **neighbor** may be far more helpful (cf. 18:24).

27:11. This is the only verse in chapters 25–29 that includes the term **my son** (see comments on 1:8). Again Proverbs affirms the fact that a wise son brings **joy to** his father (cf. 10:1; 15:20; 23:15, 24; 29:3). In fact having a son who is **wise** also means that a father **can answer** critics who may accuse him of being an incompetent father. The son who leads a life of wisdom is evidence of good child-rearing.

27:12. This verse is nearly identical to 22:3 (see comments there).

27:13. This proverb is the same as the one in 20:16 (see comments there and on 6:1-5).

27:14. Blessing (i.e., praising or commending) a **neighbor** is commendable, but not **early in the morning.** Timing and sensitivity to others who are sleeping are important. The wrong time for the right action causes it to be received **as a curse.**

27:15-16. **Dripping** water pictures the irritating nature of **a quarrelsome wife** (cf. 19:13 and comments there). Like water dripping **on a rainy day,** she is annoying and never stops quarreling. She is as impossible to restrain as **the wind.** Trying to constrain her conten-

tious spirit is as impossible as trying to pick up a handful of **oil.** She is both unsteady and slippery.

27:17. When **iron** is rubbed against another piece of **iron** it shapes and **sharpens** it. Similarly people can help each other improve by their discussions, criticisms, suggestions, and ideas. On the influence of companions, whether good or bad, on one's life see 13:20; 22:24-25. A nagging wife (27:15), however, stimulates a husband toward anger.

27:18. Nurturing and cultivating a **fig tree** are necessary if a farmer is to have a good crop of figs (cf. 12:11; 28:19); and a servant who attends to the needs of **his master will be honored.** In other words working well at one's job brings favorable results.

27:19. The Hebrew is obscure; literally it reads, "Like water face to face, so is the heart of man to a man." Just **as water,** like a mirror, **reflects a** person's **face, so a** person's **heart** or mind **reflects** what he is really like. Or as water reflects a face, so thoughts (expressed in words) reflect one's personality.

27:20. The grave (on **death and destruction** see comments on 15:11) is personified as having an appetite. Seemingly it always wants another live person dead. Likewise **the eyes of man** are **never satisfied.** People constantly want to see new things (cf. Ecc. 1:8) and to own new things.

27:21. Heat both tests and refines **silver** (cf. 25:4) and **gold,** showing what the metals are really like. (This first line of 27:21 is identical with 17:3.) **Praise** tests a person in a similar way in that his reaction to it shows what he is really like. If he gloats over it, he shows himself to be arrogant; he "knows" he is good. But if he accepts the praise modestly, he shows his humility.

27:22. **A fool** (*'ĕwîl,* "an arrogant, hardened fool"; see comments on 1:7) and **his folly** are so inseparable that if he is punished repeatedly, like **grinding . . . grain with a pestle,** he still remains foolish.

27:23-27. These five verses are a brief treatise on life in an agricultural society. Earlier a cluster of five verses discussed the consequences of laziness (24:30-34). A farmer should care for his **flocks** and **herds** because they are a better investment than many things. Flocks and herds multiply through their offspring, but money when it is spent is gone (cf. 23:5) and being a king (having a crown) does not last. Hay and grass provide food for livestock, which in turn supply people's needs for clothing (lambs' wool), money (from selling goats), and milk and food for one's family and servants. It is important to care for one's resources, to work hard, and to recognize God's provisions through nature.

28:1. Like chapters 10–15, chapters 28–29 have a number of antithetical verses, verses of contrast in which the second line is introduced by "but." Eighteen verses of contrast are in chapter 28 (vv. 1-2, 4-5, 7, 10-14, 16, 18-20, 25-28), and 12 are in chapter 29 (vv. 3-4, 6-8, 11, 15-16, 18, 23, 25-26). In these two chapters rulers, kings, and other people in power are mentioned frequently (28:2-3, 12, 15-16, 28; 29:2, 4, 12, 14, 26). Five of the six references in Proverbs to the Law are in these two chapters (28:4 [twice], 7, 9; 29:18; cf. 31:5). Other frequent subjects are the poor and poverty (28:3, 6, 8, 11, 19, 22, 27; 29:7, 13-14), and the wicked (28:1, 4, 12, 15, 28 [twice]; 29:2, 7, 12, 16, 27) and the righteous (28:1, 12, 28; 29:2, 6-7, 16, 27).

The guilty consciences of the wicked cause them to run from imagined pursuers (28:1). Knowing they have done wrong, they suspect they are being chased by lawmen. By contrast **the righteous are as bold** (i.e., self-confident; cf. "confidence" in 31:11) **as a** young **lion.** God gives them courage; they have no fear of reprisal from wrongdoing.

28:2. Unrest and rebellion in a nation results in turnover of leadership. For example, the Northern Kingdom had **many rulers,** 20 kings in nine dynasties. **Order,** however, is maintained in a nation by good rulers who have insight and **knowledge** about how to govern.

28:3. The Hebrew word for **ruler** in this verse differs from the word for "rulers" in verse 2. In fact "ruler" (v. 3) translates two words which are literally, "a strong man" (*geber*) who is destitute or hungry (*rāš*; cf. NIV marg.; vv. 6, 27). When a man in need **oppresses the poor** (*dal,* "feeble, helpless, weak"; see comments on 10:15), he opposes people who in some ways are like him, who could be his friends. Such cruelty and perversion of justice are **like a hard rain** which destroys rather than nourishes **crops.**

28:4. Oppressing the poor (v. 3) is an example of forsaking **the** Mosaic **Law** (cf. "Law" in vv. 7, 9). And when people turn from obeying God's commands, they usually begin to commend (**praise**) and side with **wicked** people. Lawkeepers (cf. v. 7), however, **resist** wicked lawbreakers, seeking to uphold justice (cf. 18:5; 24:25).

28:5. When people disobey the Law and the Lord, their sense of uprightness and morality is perverted. They find it difficult even to **understand** ("have insight into") **justice.** On the other hand the righteous, **those who seek the Lord,** have a keen sense of justice.

28:6. This verse is almost identical to 19:1, except that there a fool's "lips" (words) are perverse, whereas in 28:6 **a rich** man's **ways are** said to be **perverse** (*'iqqēš,* "twisted"; see comments on 2:15). Perhaps this suggests that a perverse rich man is a fool. It is better to be **poor** (*rāš,* "destitute"; cf. 28:3, 27) and honest (**blameless,** "morally whole"; cf. 2:7, 21; 11:5; 28:10, 18) than to be rich and wicked. This is the last of the 19 **better . . . than** proverbs (see comments on 12:9).

28:7. A **son** who obeys **the Law** (cf. v. 4) is wise; he has insight. The Hebrew word for **discerning** is translated "understanding" in verse 2. Associating with **gluttons** is foolish and shows lack of insight, for it can start a person on the path of drunkenness, laziness , and, ironically, even poverty (cf. 23:20-21). Furthermore, a gluttonous son brings disgrace to **his father.** This implies that a discerning son (28:7a) brings joy to his father.

28:8. A person who charged exorbitant interest of others and thus became rich would eventually lose **his wealth** which would be distributed **to the poor** (*dal,* "feeble, weak, helpless"; cf. vv. 3, 11, and see comments on 10:15). Justice eventually overtakes injustice.

28:9. Refusing to obey God's **Law** (cf. vv. 4, 7) has disastrous results. **Prayers** of such a person are hypocritical. Therefore those prayers, hated by God, are not answered (cf. 15:8; Ps. 66:18; Isa. 59:2). If a person does not listen to (obey) the Lord, the Lord will not listen to him.

28:10. One who causes the righteous to sin will be trapped by his own devices (cf. 1:18; 26:27). In contrast, **the blameless** (cf. 28:6, 18) will be enriched. The wicked who lead others astray are suddenly trapped and die, but the righteous live on and **receive** their parents' **inheritance.**

28:11. The **rich** and the **poor** (*dal*, "feeble, weak, helpless"; see comments on 10:15) are again contrasted (cf. v. 6). A discerning poor person can **see through** the pretentious facade of a conceited rich person who thinks he knows it all (cf. **wise[r] in his own eyes** in 26:5, 12, 16). Having money does not mean a person is wise. **Discernment** ("insight") is translated "understanding" in 28:2 and "discerning" in verse 7.

28:12. As in verses 1 and 28, the righteous and the wicked are contrasted. **When a righteous** leader rules a nation, the people are happy (cf. 11:10), for there is order (cf. 28:2) and justice. **But when . . . wicked** leaders are in charge, good people **go into hiding** (also stated in v. 28a) to get away from oppression (cf. vv. 15-16) which causes them to groan (29:2).

28:13. After a person **sins** he may try to conceal (trans. "covers over" in 17:9) that fact from God and others. But hiding sin does not pay off. Solomon's father David knew this from experience (Ps. 32:3-4). It is far better to deal with sin by confessing and renouncing it. As David found out, confession results in God's **mercy** and forgiveness (Pss. 34:5; 51:1-12).

28:14. The words **the LORD** are added in the NIV as they are not in the Hebrew. The word **fears** translates *pāḥaḏ*, "to be afraid," as in 1:33; 3:24-25. In 1:7; 3:7 the word for "fear" is *yārē'*, "to reverence." Probably, then, 28:14 is referring to the fear or dread of the consequences of sin (cf. v. 13). A person who has that kind of dread will be happy (**blessed;** cf. Ps. 1:1) and will not harden **his heart** and fall **into trouble** (cf. Prov. 29:1).

28:15-16. The danger of **a wicked man** rising to power, introduced in verse 12, is expanded here. A wicked ruler is cruel and devastating like a **lion** (cf. 19:12; 20:2) or a **bear.** The **helpless** are the weak (*dal*, often trans. "poor," as in 28:3, 8, 11). A **ruler** who tyrannizes **lacks judgment** or good sense (see comments on 6:32; 10:13). In contrast, a person who refuses to abuse his power for personal **gain** (cf. **ill-gotten** treasures in 1:19; 10:2) **will enjoy** the blessing of **a long life.**

This implies that a tyrannical leader will not live long.

28:17. A murderer's guilty conscience hounds him, tormenting him and causing him to try to escape punishment. His only escape is **death.** One who tries to console or rescue **him** is out of line; to aid a criminal is wrong. However, rescuing the innocent *is* encouraged (24:11-12).

28:18. A **blameless** (see comments on v. 6) life (**walk**) brings safety (cf. 1:33; 3:23; 18:10; 28:26), **but** a person **whose ways are perverse** (from '*āqaš*, "to twist"; cf. the adjective '*iqqēš* in v. 6; 2:15) **will suddenly fall.** Similar statements are given in 10:9; 28:10.

28:19. This verse is almost identical to 12:11 (see comments there). A farmer **who works** hard will have plenty to eat (cf. 27:18). In contrast with the diligent, the indolent **who** chase their **fantasies** will not get their work done and **will have** their **fill of poverty,** not food (cf. 14:23).

28:20. The way to become **richly blessed** is by being **faithful** ("trustworthy"), not by using get-rich-quick schemes. Being **eager to get rich** often leads to devious, dishonest ways (cf. 13:11; 20:21) resulting in the person being punished either by the courts or by poverty or both (cf. 28:22). Others who **will not go unpunished** are referred to in 6:29; 11:21; 16:5; 17:5; 19:5, 9.

28:21. Showing **partiality** (cf. 18:5; 24:23) **is not good.** This is the last of six "not good" sayings in Proverbs (17:26; 18:5; 19:2; 24:23; 25:27; 28:21). In court cases some judges show partiality to those who bribe them even with a small bribe such as **a piece of bread.** It is ironic that justice can be so easily perverted especially when bribery is so firmly denounced (see comments on 6:35).

28:22. A **stingy man** is literally, "a man with an evil eye" (see comments on 23:6). Ironically a person who greedily tries **to get rich** quickly (cf. 28:20) will end up in **poverty,** the opposite of his goal (cf. 11:24b).

28:23. Giving a needed rebuke rather than overlooking it or **flattering** a person (cf. 29:5) is difficult. But **in the end** (later) a wise person is grateful for it (cf. 27:5; see comments on 1:23). On the word **favor** see comments on 8:35.

28:24. A son who heartlessly says nothing is **wrong** in robbing his parents (cf. 19:26) is like a destroyer. Disgracing them (cf. 28:7), **he is** like a person **who destroys.** That is, he has destroyed their honorable reputation and peace of mind.

28:25. Greedy is literally, "large of soul" and refers to an uncontrolled, avaricious appetite for material things. Because greed is selfish it results in **dissension** or strife. In this way, greed is a companion to deceit (6:14), hatred (10:12), temper (15:18), perversity (16:28), and anger (29:22). The one **who trusts in the LORD** rather than in riches gained by greed **will prosper** (cf. 11:25).

28:26. In contrast with one who trusts in the Lord (v. 25) is a person **who trusts in himself** (cf. 14:12). He **is a fool** (kᵉsîl, "dull, thickheaded"; see comments on 1:7). A person who is wise, not trusting in himself, will be **safe** (cf. 3:5-6; 28:18; 29:25).

28:27. Being generous **to the poor** (rāš, "destitute, hungry," also used in vv. 3, 6; cf. 29:7) does not mean the giver will then have to "do without." Just the opposite is true; he **will lack nothing.** Generosity is rewarded (cf. 11:24-25; 14:21b, 31b; 19:17; 21:26; 22:9; Deut. 15:10). However, a person who ignores the needs of the poor **receives . . . curses** from them (cf. Prov. 11:24b, 26a).

28:28. The first part of this verse is like verse 12b. The second part of verse 28 adds another thought: **When the wicked perish** (cf. 11:10), as they will, **the righteous** can then **thrive** (lit., "become great"; cf. 29:2) without having to be in **hiding.**

29:1. A man who is **stiff-necked,** that is, hardened and refusing to repent or submit to repeated correction (**many rebukes**; see comments on 1:30), **will suddenly be destroyed** (cf 1:27; 6:15; 10:25a; 28:18) in death. No longer will a **remedy** be available.

29:2. When **righteous** leaders are in control (**thrive,** lit., "become great"; cf. 28:28, which may mean this meaning) of a government, **the people** are glad because they are more secure and prosperous. But **when . . . wicked** leaders are ruling, **the people groan** (cf. 28:12) under cruel oppression (cf. 28:15; 29:16).

29:3. The **joy** of a wise man's **father** (cf. 10:1; 15:20; 23:15, 24; 27:11) is contrasted with a father's **wealth** being squandered by a son who associates with **prostitutes.** According to 2:12, 16; 5:1-3,

7-11 wisdom keeps one from adultery.

29:4. Justice brings a nation **stability** and joy (cf. vv. 2, 7, 14; 14:34; 16:12; 20:8, 26; 21:15; 28:12), whereas a greedy leader contributes to the nation's downfall. **One who is greedy for bribes** is literally, "a man of offerings or contributions." The Hebrew word for "bribes" usually refers to sacred offerings; here it may refer to taxes. Rehoboam illustrated the truth of this proverb (1 Kings 12:1-19), which he might well have heard from his father Solomon.

29:5. Flatters is literally, "makes (a person) smooth." In 2:16 and 7:5 the word is rendered "seductive." This flattery in 29:5 is smooth talk that deceives because it intends to harm. A flatterer, however, suffers for it (cf. 26:28). He is caught in the very **net** he set for others (cf. 29:6; 1:18; 28:10).

29:6. An evil person is caught in his self-designed trap (cf. comments on v. 5), while the **righteous** live happy, carefree lives. They need not worry that their actions might boomerang on them.

29:7. Righteous people want to see **justice** rather than oppression extended to **the poor** (dal, "feeble, weak, helpless"; cf. v. 14 and see comments on 10:15). **But the wicked** do not care whether the poor get treated fairly or not. One's relationship to God shows up in his attitude toward the needy.

29:8. Verses 8-11 contrast angry fools with honest, wise people. **Mockers** (cf. 1:22) laugh at moral restrictions and **stir up** (lit., "fan or blow on" embers) trouble. Mockers keep things in an uproar. These troublemakers get others angry and incite rebellion. (Cf. "anger" and "angry" in 29:11, 22.) The **wise,** however, help calm **a city** by averting **anger** and its rebellious results.

29:9. The word "righteous" connects verses 6 and 7. Here **wise** links verses 8 and 9. Trying to win a **court** case **with a fool** (ʾĕwîl, "an arrogant, hardened fool") should be avoided because he follows his emotions rather than logic (cf. 27:3) as he keeps things in turmoil (**no peace**) with his angry (cf. 29:11) ranting (raging and scoffing).

29:10. Honest people are hated by fools, who would prefer killing the honest so they could not testify against the wicked in court. **Integrity** is often translated "blameless" (e.g., 28:6, 10, 18).

29:11. A fool (*kesîl*; see comments on 1:7) readily gives in to **anger** (cf. 15:1; 29:8, 22), **but a wise** person maintains self-control (cf. 14:29; 16:32). **Keeps himself under control** is literally, "calms it back" like stilling a storm. The verb is used only here and in Psalms 65:7; 89:9 where it refers to calming the sea's waves.

29:12. If a ruler takes the advice of liars, then he encourages wickedness in the people around him. But if he instead rewards honesty then it will be encouraged and falsehood will be punished (cf. 20:8, 28).

29:13. The poor man (*rāš*, "destitute, hungry"; cf. 28:3, 6, 27) **and the oppressor** are opposites morally. One thing poor victims **have . . . in common** with their persecutors is that they both were given **sight** by the Lord (cf. 22:2 and "Maker" in 14:31; 17:5). Each can see the other.

29:14. Fairness (cf. v. 7) toward those least able to care for themselves (**the poor,** *dal,* "feeble, weak, helpless"; see comments on 10:15) is a mark of a good **king** (cf. v. 4) whose **throne** is therefore **secure** (cf. 16:12; 20:28). God blesses rulers who are concerned about the poor, and people appreciate such rulers.

29:15. In Hebrew **the rod of correction** literally reads "the rod and correction." Either the rod is the instrument of correction (in which case a figure of speech called a hendiadys is used), or both the rod (physical punishment; cf. 13:24; 22:15; 23:13-14) and verbal correction (lit., "rebuke") are to be used. **A child** who is not disciplined and is **left to** himself (allowed to do as he pleases and have whatever he wants) will become an unruly person. He will disgrace (bring shame to; cf. 19:26; 28:7) **his mother.**

29:16. When . . . wicked leaders govern a nation (see comments on **thrive** in v. 2), **sin** is encouraged. But as stated many times in Proverbs, the wicked will eventually fall and **the righteous will** live to see it and will then rejoice (cf. 28:12, 28).

29:17. Disciplining one's **son** results in the parents having **peace** and joy later because their son will behave and grow wiser (cf. 10:1). The verb **discipline** (*yāsar*) is related to the noun "discipline" (*mûsār*; cf. 1:2, which means "moral disci-

pline or correction").

29:18. The familiar KJV "where there is no vision" is misleading. The word "vision" is the **revelation** (*ḥāzôn*) a prophet receives. Also the KJV translation "the people perish" does not refer to unsaved **people** dying in sin. The verb *pāraʿ* means **to cast off restraint.** So the verse is stating that without God's Word people abandon themselves to their own sinful ways. On the other hand keeping (obeying) God's **Law** (cf. 28:4, 7) brings happiness.

29:19. This verse, coupled with verse 21, seems to suggest that discipline is needed for one's servants as well as for his sons. Sometimes **words** are not enough; **a servant** may know the words but obstinately refuse to do as he is told. If so, other forms of correction are needed.

29:20. A man who speaks in haste is **a fool** because he blurts out thoughtless, insensitive remarks (cf. "gushes" folly and evil, 15:2, 28), sometimes answering before he listens (18:13). In fact he is worse than a fool. Speaking in haste and being conceited are two things for which there is less hope than for being a fool (cf. 26:12). This kind of person brings trouble on himself and others (cf. 17:19-20; 18:6-7).

29:21. The importance of disciplining, not pampering, servants is again touched on (cf. v. 19). Failure to discipline a **servant** and to require him to carry out his responsibilities will result in **grief** (a Heb. word used only here in the OT) **in the end** (later) to his master.

29:22. The effects of a volatile temperament warn against losing control of oneself. An **angry . . . hot-tempered** (lit., "owner of wrath"; see comments on 22:24) person causes strife (cf. 26:21; 30:33) and **commits many sins,** perhaps including cursing or insulting others, misusing God's name, being rude, lacking kindness, being cruel or oppressive, and being proud.

29:23. The reverse effects of **pride** and humility warn against the one and encourage the other. Ironically pride, by which a person seeks to elevate himself, actually results in his being brought **low** (*šāpal*) whereas one who is of **lowly** (*šāpal*) **spirit** is elevated by others to a position of **honor** (cf. 3:34; 15:33; 16:18-19; 18:12). God hates pride (see comments on 6:17) because it influences a person to live independently of Him.

29:24. The **accomplice of a thief** becomes **his own enemy** because his involvement in crime works against him. In court he takes an **oath** but then must either lie or say nothing. If he testifies he will implicate himself, and if he says nothing he is assumed guilty (Lev. 5:1).

29:25. To **fear** ("tremble," not the word for reverence before God; e.g., 1:7; 8:13; 9:10) **man** ensnares in the sense that one's actions are controlled or confined by the person who is dreaded. It is far better to trust **in the LORD** because that brings safety (cf. 18:10; 28:18, 26). The words **is kept safe** are from the verb *śāg̱ab̠,* "to be inaccessibly high or to be exalted." Security in the Lord removes intimidation by man.

29:26. People may **seek an audience with a ruler** (cf. 19:6) to curry his favor or influence or to gain justice, but they have no guarantee that justice will be done. The ruler might even "prove to be a snare" (29:25). True **justice** comes **from the LORD;** He will make things right in the end. Therefore trusting Him is more important than any dread of man.

29:27. The antagonism existing between **the righteous** and **the wicked** is given in surprisingly graphic terms. **Detest,** in both lines of the verse, is a strong verb that may be translated "to consider abominable or detestable, to abhor." It is used of God's attitude toward idolatry and of the sacrifice of children (Deut. 12:31) and of other abominable and unclean acts. The righteous are so concerned for honesty that they, like God, hate what is dishonest. And the distaste of the wicked for **the upright** reveals their perverse values. All of Proverbs, of course, contrasts the righteous and the wicked. Here they are seen as stark opposites.

VI. The Words of Agur (chap. 30)

A. Introduction (30:1)

30:1. The identity of **Agur** is unknown. He seems to have been humble (vv. 2-4) and observant and inquisitive (vv. 5-33). **An oracle** translates *maśśā',* which means a weighty message (see comments on Zech. 9:1). Agur's words were addressed **to Ithiel and to Ucal,** whose identities are also unknown.

B. Knowledge about God (30:2-9)

1. MAN'S IGNORANCE OF GOD (30:2-4)

30:2-3. In calling himself **the most ignorant of men,** Agur may have been writing in irony. If so, he was contrasting himself with someone who arrogantly claimed wisdom, a person he challenged to answer (v. 4). Or the statement in verse 2 may be Agur's sincere response to the reflections he recorded in verse 4. "Ignorant" translates the Hebrew word *ba'ar* which means "to be brutish or dull-minded" like an animal (cf. Ps. 73:22; Prov. 12:1, "stupid"). In the second clause in 30:2 Agur wrote that he had less than human intelligence. Agur sensed his lack of **wisdom** because he did not know the infinite God (**the Holy One;** cf. 9:10). Knowing God is the basis of true wisdom (1:7; 15:33).

30:4. The only answer to the five questions in this verse is God. Only He can go **up to heaven and come down,** reminding one of Christ, the Son of God. And only God can hold **the wind in . . . His hands** (i.e., control the wind), and figuratively wrap **the waters in His cloak** (perhaps referring to the clouds; cf. Job 26:8), and only He has fixed **the earth** in its place (cf. Job 38:4, 6; Prov. 8:29). The question, **What is His name?** asks what His true character is like. The inquiry, What is **the name of His son?** suggests the question, "Has He imparted His nature or attributes to any other who may in any sense be called His 'Son'?" (T.T. Perowne, *The Proverbs,* p. 180) **Tell me if you know** reflects Agur's desire to know the nature of God.

2. MAN'S KNOWLEDGE OF GOD THROUGH HIS WORD (30:5-6)

30:5-6. Verse 4 emphasized man's inability to know by himself the nature of God. Now verses 5-6 show how **God** may be known: through His **Word,** which **is flawless** (lit., "purified" like the smelting of silver; cf. Ps. 12:6). Man can know God only because He has revealed Himself through the written Word, the infallible Scriptures. Those who trust in God have a personal relationship with Him; they are shielded by **Him.** Proverbs 30:5 is almost identical to Psalm 18:30. The warning not to **add to His words** may refer to the danger of adding human speculation to divine revelation. Man should derive his understanding of God (his theology) not from human ideas but from God's Word. God rebukes those who think they can know more of God than what He has revealed about Himself. In fact they are often so far off base that God calls them liars.

3. MAN'S PRAYER TO GOD (30:7-9)

30:7-9. The words **two things** introduce a series of six numerical sayings in this chapter (vv. 7-9, 15b-16, 18-19, 21-23, 24-28, 29-31). This prayer for "two things" affirms the humility introduced in verses 2-3. Realizing his frailty, the writer asked **the Lord** for specific help in two areas of weakness **before** he died: protection from lying, and provision of **daily** sustenance (**bread**; cf. Matt. 6:11) without the temptations of wealth or **poverty.** Wealth might cause him to **disown** and forget **the Lord** (cf. Deut. 8:12-17) thinking he could care for himself; and poverty might cause him to **steal** and thus **dishonor** God's character.

C. Observations about life (30:10-33)

1. ADVICE (30:10)

30:10. This verse is a warning not to meddle in another person's domestic affairs. A **master** may **curse** the person who falsely accuses his **servant.** In contrast with the "undeserved curse" of 26:2, this curse will "hit its target" so to speak, because it is deserved. This saying may stand as a self-contained maxim or, perhaps more likely, it introduces 30:11-14.

2. FOUR KINDS OF UNDESIRABLE BEHAVIOR (30:11-14)

Though not introduced as a numerical series (see comments on v. 7) four kinds of people are mentioned: those who are disrespectful, hypocritical, arrogant, and oppressive.

30:11. The sin of cursing one's parents (cf. v. 17) is mentioned in 20:20 (see comments there).

30:12. People who think they **are pure** (morally clean) before God but who still **are not cleansed** of **their** moral **filth** of sin are hypocrites.

30:13. Haughtiness (cf. 6:16-17; 21:4; Pss. 18:27; 101:5; Isa. 10:12), which the Lord despises, contrasts with Agur's attitudes of humility and reverence (Prov. 30:2-3, 7-9). **Eyes** connects verse 13 with verse 12.

30:14. People who oppress **the poor** (*'ānî,* "afflicted, humbled") and **needy** (*'ebyôn,* "people needing help"; cf. 31:9, 20) are like voracious beasts whose sharp **teeth** tear their prey (cf. Ps. 14:4).

3. FOUR THINGS NEVER SATISFIED (30:15-16)

30:15-16. This numerical listing deals with insatiable desires. The **cry** of the **daughters** of a bloodsucking **leech (Give! Give!)** introduces the theme. Leeches graphically depict the attitude of greed, with its tenacious insistence on having more of what is desired. On the stylistic feature of **three** followed by **four** (x and x + 1), which is used in verses 15, 18, 21, 29, see comments on 6:16. Four **things** are personified as **never satisfied: the grave** (*šeʾôl*) wants to take in more of the dead (cf. 27:20), **the barren womb** longs to give birth to a child, the **land** always wants **water, and fire** wants to continue to consume. Death and fire are destructive, and the womb and water are life-giving. Greed always wants more.

4. WARNING (30:17)

30:17. This saying may have been placed here to point to the fact that disrespect for one's parents is as bad as the insatiable greed mentioned in verses 15-16. An arrogant child who **scorns** (*bûz,* "to hold in contempt or ridicule"; see comments on 1:7) his or her parents (cf. v. 11) will die, and his corpse will remain unburied and be food for the birds of prey.

5. FOUR AMAZING THINGS (30:18-19)

30:18-19. What do the ways **of an eagle in the sky . . . a snake on a rock . . . a ship** in the ocean, and **a man with a** woman have in common? Some writers say the ways of these four are mysterious; others say their ways are nontraceable; others suggest that they each easily master an element that is seemingly difficult. Another suggestion is that they each go where there are no paths. "The way of a man with a **maiden"** refers to a man's affectionate courting of a woman.

6. WARNING (30:20)

30:20. An adulteress contrasts with the woman in verse 19. Here it is not the man's way with a woman, but an immoral woman's **way** with men (cf. 2:16-19;

5:1-14; 7; 22:14; 23:27-28). She takes a casual approach to her sinful ways, treating them as lightly as eating a meal and asserting that **nothing** is **wrong** (cf. 28:24) with adultery.

7. FOUR UNBEARABLE, UNFAIR THINGS (30:21-23)

Verses 21-31 include three lists of people and creatures that pertain to leadership or a perversion of it. The word "king" occurs in each list (vv. 22, 27, 31).

30:21-23. The statements that **the earth trembles** and **cannot bear up** are hyperboles. Also by a figure of speech known as metonymy the earth represents the people who are on it. The people tremble because social turmoil follows the sudden elevation of inexperienced, unqualified people to positions of power and success. It is not appropriate (a) for **a servant** to become a **king** (the servant is unprepared), (b) for a **fool** (*nāḇāl*, "one who lacks spiritual perception and sensitivity"; cf. 17:7, 21) to be **full of food** (he might become bullheaded regarding the needs of others), (c) for **an unloved** (lit., "hated") **woman** to be **married** (she brings grief to the marriage), and (d) for **a maidservant** to become a **mistress** (for she, like the servant in 30:22, does not know how to direct others). Harmony in society is encouraged when people maintain their proper roles and do not assume positions they are incapable of handling.

8. FOUR SMALL, WISE THINGS (30:24-28)

These verses build on the thought in 21:22; 24:5, which refers to wisdom triumphing over physical strength.

30:24-26. One of the **small** but **wise** creatures are **ants.** Though they have **little strength** they survive because of their foresight (see comments on 6:6-8). **Conies** (or rock badgers; cf. NIV marg.) are about the size of rabbits. Because they are rather ineffective at defending themselves, they wisely live in **crags** (cf. Ps. 104:18) that give them natural safety.

30:27-28. **Locusts have no** apparent leader (**king**) but fly in an amazing order and can devastate miles of crops like an approaching army (cf. Joel 1:4-7). **A lizard,** so small that it **can** easily **be caught** by **hand,** may be seen even **in kings' palaces,** seemingly having the run of the place. Two ideas emerge from these two

insects and two animals: (a) physical limitations may be compensated for in other ways; (b) since God protects and provides for even the humblest and lowest of His creatures, He certainly will provide for His own people.

9. FOUR STATELY CREATURES (30:29-31)

30:29-31. In contrast with lowly creatures like the four in verses 25-28 are those that appear noble **in their** bearing and walk. These include the **lion,** from whom people and other animals retreat because of its strength, the **strutting rooster** (lit., "girded at the loins"), a male **goat** with its arrogant appearance, **and a king** who may strut with pride as he is seemingly invincible **with his army** in his presence. In God's order of things, some creatures are small and in humble positions and others are more prominent.

10. ADVICE (30:32-33)

30:32-33. In contrast with creatures who strut in pride (vv. 29-31) is a person who has **played the fool** (the verb *nāḇal,* "to be spiritually imperceptive and insensitive"; cf. the noun *nāḇāl* in v. 22; 17:7, 21). By exalting himself and planning **evil** (cf. 6:14) he causes trouble. To **clap** one's **hand over** his **mouth** (cf. Job 21:5; 40:4) was a way of saying he should stop being proud and making trouble. As sure **as churning . . . milk** makes **butter and** the **twisting** of a **nose** brings **blood,** so the agitation and **stirring up** of **anger produces** trouble. Churning, twisting, and stirring up translate the same Hebrew word *mîṣ,* "squeezing or wringing," which occurs only here in the Old Testament. In an interesting wordplay "nose" (*'ap*) and "anger" (*'appayim*) are similar Hebrew words. Pride and anger work against humility, which is commended and promoted in Proverbs 30.

VII. The Words of Lemuel (31:1-9)

A mother told her son about the dangers of wayward women (v. 3; cf. 23:26-28) and wine (31:4-7; cf. 23:29-35) and reminded him of his responsibility to champion the cause of justice.

31:1. Nothing is known about **Lemuel** except that he was a **king.** The instruction in verses 2-9 was addressed to him by **his mother.** This is unusual for elsewhere in Proverbs a father was addressing his son(s), though twice a mother's teaching is referred to by the father (cf. 1:8; 6:20). On the word **oracle** see comments on 30:1 and Zechariah 9:1.

31:2-3. Lemuel's mother addressed her **son,** which is the Aramaic word *bar.* Also **kings** in verse 3 is Aramaic. Her **vows** may mean that she made a vow, as Hannah did, before his conception (1 Sam. 1:11) or afterward. Either way she wanted him to know that he was special to her. She warned him that adultery has a debilitating effect on one's mind and body (cf. Solomon's warnings against adultery in Prov. 2:16-19; 5:1-14; 7; 22:14, and the wise men's warning in 23:27-28).

31:4-5. In verses 4-7, Lemuel's mother warned about the dangers of alcoholism. Her advice echoes 20:1; 23:20-21, 29-35. The particular danger of drunkenness to a king lies in its tendency to cloud his memory and judgment, resulting in injustice (18:5) to **the oppressed** (cf. 31:8).

31:6-7. Beer ("strong drink"; cf. comments on 20:1) and **wine** (mentioned in reverse order from the way they are mentioned in 31:4) may have been acceptable as anesthetics or drugs to deaden physical pain or deep emotional bitterness (and the pain of those who were dying). Or verses 6-7 may be saying that though others may have used drink as an escape, the king was not to do so.

31:8-9. This second reference to justice (cf. **rights** in v. 5) in such a short discourse speaks strongly for its importance. A king who defended those who could not defend **themselves** and who were of little threat and made little contribution to him would be noted as a just and gracious man. He was to **judge fairly,** regardless of a person's social status. The word for **destitute** (used only here in the OT) means people who are passing away; they are "on their last legs." **The poor** (*'ānî,* "afflicted, humbled") **and needy** (*'ebyôn,* "people needing help"; cf. 30:14; 31:20), who were easily oppressed, were also to be defended by the king.

VIII. The Noble Wife (31:10-31)

This final section of Proverbs is an acrostic poem exalting a noble wife. Each of the 22 verses begins with a consecutive letter of the Hebrew alphabet. These verses were written by Lemuel, Lemuel's mother, Solomon, or someone whose name is unknown. This last view is probably correct.

31:10. The **wife of noble character** (*ḥayil*) is also mentioned in 12:4 (cf. "noble" in 31:29). Ruth was called "a woman of noble character" (Ruth 3:11). The word for noble character is translated "capable" in Exodus 18:21. The question **who can find?** (cf. Prov. 20:6) does not suggest that such women are nonexistent but that they should be admired because they, like noble men, are rare. Also they are **more** valuable **than rubies** (cf. a similar statement about wisdom in 8:11).

31:11. The noble wife's **husband** is mentioned three times (vv. 11, 23, 28) and is referred to as "him" in verse 12. His **confidence in her** is complete. He trusts her. Her careful household management enhances their family's wealth. He **lacks nothing of value** by way of household goods.

31:12. This kind of woman is an asset, not a liability, to her husband. **Good** comes to **him** that can be directly attributed to her. She supports and encourages him. And she is faithful in helping him **all . . . her life.**

31:13. She is involved in weaving and sewing as indicated in verses 13, 19, 22, 24. She uses **wool and flax,** and linen (vv. 22, 24) made from flax. **With eager hands** is literally, "with the delight of her hands," suggesting that she enjoys her work.

31:14. The noble wife also does shopping. She is **like . . . merchant ships** that brought unusual and fascinating merchandise **from** other places. She too brought interesting and unusual items home from her shopping.

31:15. Though she has household help she herself **gets up** early, before daybreak, to help prepare breakfast and **food for** other meals, and to delegate work (**portions**) to **her** servants.

31:16. The wife's considering and buying **a field** have caused some to question the validity of this poem because women, it is argued, were not permitted to do that in those days. However, in this wealthy household she apparently had money to invest. Then **out of her earnings** from various investments (cf. "trading," v. 18, and "sells," v. 24) she plants **a vineyard.** She has a business mind and she works hard.

31:17. She works energetically (lit.,

"girds her loins with strength") and with vigor (cf. "works" in v. 13). She has a healthy attitude toward **work.**

31:18. Her wise business dealings are again referred to (cf. "earnings," v. 16, and "sells," v. 24). The fact that **her lamp does not go out** speaks of her planning ahead. The five virgins whose lamps did not go out were praised for their foresight (Matt. 25:4). The extinguishing of one's lamp pictured calamity (Job 18:6; Prov. 13:9; 20:20; 24:20).

31:19. Verses 13, 19, 22, 24 refer to her weaving and sewing. She makes cloth by spinning wool or flax (v. 13) on a **distaff,** using a **spindle.**

31:20. The noble wife is also selfless and generous. She sells some things for profit but she also gives **to the poor** and **the needy** (see comments on these words in 30:14; cf. 31:9; also note 11:25; 21:26). Possibly 31:20 refers to her giving cloth she has made (v. 19) to the poor who have none.

31:21. Cold weather does not cause this woman to panic **for her household** (cf. v. 25b); she is prepared for it. She has **clothed** them **in scarlet,** that is, she has provided expensive garments. She spares no cost in protecting her family from the cold.

31:22. She even **makes** her family's bed coverings. **She** clothes herself **in fine linen and purple.** Linen is made from flax (v. 13) and purple is a dye made from a shellfish. Her own clothes were evidences of her family's well-to-do position.

31:23. A noble woman enhances **her** husband's standing among those who transact legal and judicial affairs **at the city gate** (cf. v. 31) **among the elders.** Though she is obviously aggressive and competent, she functions in a way that honors her husband's leadership rather then denigrates it. She respects him and builds him up.

31:24. Again her clothing enterprise is mentioned. She makes linen clothes for herself (v. 22) but is such a good seamstress that she also **makes** enough to sell. **Linen garments** were expensive. Supplying **merchants with sashes** (belts) speaks of her productivity.

31:25. Clothing is here referred to metaphorically to indicate that her appearance is one of **strength and dignity.** She is no shameful weakling. Also **she**

can laugh at the future, that is, face it with confidence (cf. v. 21). Though 27:1 cautions against boasting "about tomorrow," that does not do away with preparing for it (as ants do, 6:6-8; 30:25).

31:26. In keeping with the theme of Proverbs, this woman is praised for her **wisdom and faithful instruction.** The instruction probably refers to her teaching her children and her servant girls.

31:27. She is involved in management (**she watches over . . . affairs of her household**). Yet she is also directly involved in various activities as a housewife. She is **not** idle (cf. vv. 13, 17).

31:28-29. Her children . . . call her blessed. She is positive and optimistic and enjoys her role in life. **Her husband . . . praises her** by telling others she is the greatest of the **noble** women (cf. v. 10).

31:30. Her secret is her godly character. She is physically charming and beautiful but those qualities may not last. **But** as **a woman who fears the LORD,** she is **praised** by her husband (v. 28) and others (v. 31). Appropriately here near the end of Proverbs, the book concludes the way it began, by referring to fearing the Lord (1:7).

31:31. The writer urged his readers to recognize and **reward** the faithful diligence and kindness of such a woman. She along with her husband (v. 23) should be honored publicly. Honoring a *woman* **at the . . .** *gate* was not normally done in Israel. But an unusual woman called for unusual recognition.

The virtues of a noble wife are those that are extolled throughout the Book of Proverbs: hard work, wise investments, good use of time, planning ahead, care for others, respect for one's spouse, ability to share godly values with others, wise counsel, and godly fear (worship, trust, service, obedience). As Proverbs has stated repeatedly, these are qualities that lead to honor, praise, success, personal dignity and worth, and enjoyment of life. In the face of the adulteress' temptations mentioned often in Proverbs, it is fitting that the book concludes by extolling a virtuous wife. Young men and others can learn from this noble woman. By fearing God, they can live wisely and righteously. *That* is the message of Proverbs.

BIBLIOGRAPHY

Alden, Robert L. *Proverbs: A Commentary on an Ancient Book of Timeless Advice.* Grand Rapids: Baker Book House, 1983.

Bullock, C. Hassell. *An Introduction to the Poetic Books of the Old Testament.* Chicago: Moody Press, 1979.

Cohen, A. *Proverbs.* London: Soncino Press, 1946.

Delitzsch, Franz. "Proverbs." In *Commentary on the Old Testament in Ten Volumes.* Vol 6. (25 vols. in 10). Grand Rapids: Wm. B. Eerdmans Publishing Co., 1982.

Draper, James T., Jr. *Proverbs: The Secret of Beautiful Living.* Wheaton, Ill.: Tyndale House Publishers, 1971.

Eims, LeRoy. *Wisdom from Above for Living Here Below.* Wheaton, Ill.: SP Publications, Victor Books, 1978.

Harris, R. Laird. "Proverbs." In *The Wycliffe Bible Commentary.* Chicago: Moody Press, 1962.

Jensen, Irving L. *Proverbs.* Everyman's Bible Commentary. Chicago: Moody Press, 1982.

Jones, W.A. Rees, and Walls, Andrew F.

"The Proverbs." In *The New Bible Commentary.* London: InterVarsity Press, 1953.

Kidner, Derek. *The Proverbs: An Introduction and Commentary.* The Tyndale Old Testament Commentaries. Downers Grove, Ill.: InterVarsity Press, 1964.

Lawson, George. *Exposition of Proverbs.* Reprint. Grand Rapids: Kregel Publications, 1980.

McKane, William. *Proverbs.* Philadelphia: Westminster Press, 1970.

Mouser, William E., Jr. *Walking in Wisdom.* Downers Grove, Ill.: InterVarsity Press, 1983.

Murphy, Roland E. *Wisdom Literature: Job, Proverbs, Ruth, Canticles, Ecclesiastes, Esther.* The Forms of the Old Testament Literature. Vol. 13. Grand Rapids: Wm. B. Eerdmans Publishing Co., 1981.

Oesterly, W.O.E. *The Book of Proverbs.* New York: E.P. Dutton & Co., 1929.

Perowne, T.T. *The Proverbs.* Cambridge: Cambridge University Press, 1916.

Toy, Crawford H. *A Critical and Exegetical Commentary on The Book of Proverbs.* The International Critical Commentary. Edinburgh: T. & T. Clark, 1899. Reprint. Greenwood, S.C.: Attic Press, 1977.

ECCLESIASTES

Donald R. Glenn

INTRODUCTION

Authorship and Date. The author of Ecclesiastes identified himself, in Hebrew, as *Qōhelet* (1:1-2; cf. 1:12; 7:27; 12:8-10). Though this is sometimes treated as a proper name and hence transliterated, the presence of the article on the Hebrew word in 12:8 (and probably also in 7:27) shows that it is a title. The Old Testament uses this title of no other person. Nor is the form of the verb from which the title is derived used elsewhere. Therefore the exact meaning of this term is in doubt. Suggestions for its significance are generally drawn from the related Hebrew noun "assembly." For example, the Septuagint entitles the book *Ekklēsiastēs* ("one who calls an assembly"), whence the English word "Ecclesiastes." Several English versions of the Bible translate *Qōhelet* in relation to the function he supposedly played in the assembly (e.g., "The Teacher," NIV; "The Preacher," KJV; "The Leader of the Assembly," NIV marg.).

The author also identified himself as a "son of David" (1:1), a "king in Jerusalem" (1:1), and "king over Israel in Jerusalem" (1:12). Moreover, in the autobiographical section (1:12–2:26) he said he was wiser "than anyone who [had] ruled over Jerusalem before" him (1:16); that he was a builder of great projects (2:4-6); and that he possessed numerous slaves (2:7), incomparable herds of sheep and cattle (2:7), great wealth (2:8), and a large harem (2:8). In short he claimed to be greater than anyone who lived in Jerusalem before him (2:9). These descriptions have led many Jewish and Christian interpreters to identify the author as Solomon though his name is never explicitly used in the book.

Solomonic authorship of Ecclesiastes was generally accepted until the Age of the Enlightenment (17th century) when the use of literary and historical criticism and linguistic analysis led to its general abandonment by scholars of all persuasions, including such noted conservative commentators as E.W. Hengstenberg, Franz Delitzsch, Edward J. Young, and H.C. Leupold. The primary reason for this denial of Solomonic authorship has been linguistic. Some scholars have pointed out that the Hebrew of Ecclesiastes differs in vocabulary and syntax from that of the period of Solomon and is much closer to a later stage of Hebrew reflected in the Mishnah (ca. A.D. 200). Also certain Aramaic and Persian words in the book have led scholars to date the book after Solomon. On the basis of those characteristics, Ecclesiastes is generally assigned to the late postexilic period (ca. 350–250 B.C.), though Hengstenberg, Delitzsch, Leupold, and Young all argue for the late Persian period (ca. 450–350 B.C.). The presence of fragments of manuscripts of Ecclesiastes at Qumran from the late second century B.C. and its acknowledged influence on the apocryphal Ecclesiasticus (ca. 190 B.C.) exclude any date later than 250–200 B.C.

Scholars who date the book late and deny Solomonic authorship generally explain the autobiographical references as literary devices to validate the author's arguments. It is said that such a literary device was used by the author of the pseudepigraphical Wisdom of Solomon (ca. 150–50 B.C.). However, some recent studies have shown that some of the features explained as characteristic of Aramaic and/or late Hebrew can also be shown in Canaanite-Phoenician literature of the pre-Solomonic era. Gleason L. Archer, who has summarized some of these features, has further argued that the Hebrew in Ecclesiastes is unique, unlike that of any Hebrew literary work from any preexilic or postexilic period (*Zondervan Pictorial Encyclopedia of the Bible*. Grand Rapids: Zondervan Publishing House,

1975, s.v. "Ecclesiastes," 2:184-7). Thus the linguistic argument against Solomonic authorship is somewhat inconclusive.

Alleged discrepancies between the social and political conditions reflected in the book and those in the time of Solomon—for example, oppression (4:1; 8:9), injustice (5:8), and corrupt government (5:8-9; 10:16-20)—are likewise not compelling arguments against Solomonic authorship. Though they may apply to the condition of the Jews under Persian or Greek domination (as those who deny Solomonic authorship claim), they could also refer to social evils in the latter years of Solomon's reign when his subjects chafed under his harsh rule (cf., e.g., 1 Kings 12:4, 9-11). Alleged discrepancies between the autobiographical allusions in Ecclesiastes 1:12, 16 and the history of Solomon are likewise unproved. Those who argue against Solomon as the author say that the verb "was" in 1:12 means "I . . . was [and am no longer] king." However, the verb could just as well be translated "I . . . have been [and still am] king." The reference to those who "ruled over Jerusalem before me" (1:16) may refer to non-Israelite rulers as well as Israelite rulers. Thus there are no compelling internal inconsistencies in identifying the author as Solomon.

In summary, though many scholars deny Solomonic authorship because of the supposed lateness of the language of Ecclesiastes, recent studies have called into question the validity of their linguistic evidence and reopened the possibility of identifying the unnamed author with Solomon. Since the evidence is inconclusive, the following commentary assumes the traditional view that Solomon was the human author. However, regardless of who wrote it, whether Solomon or a later Jewish sage, the presence of this book in the Bible indicates that it is God's Word.

Theme and Purpose. There can be little doubt about the theme of Ecclesiastes; it is announced both at the beginning (1:2) and the end (12:8) of the book and is often echoed throughout (e.g., 1:14; 2:11, 17, 26; etc.). The author ("the Teacher") declared that everything is "meaningless" (NIV) or "vanity" (KJV, RSV, NASB). This includes toil (1:14; 2:11, 17; 4:4, 7-8), wisdom (2:15), righteousness (8:14),

wealth (2:26; 5:10; 6:2), prestige (4:16), pleasure (2:1-2), youth and vigor (11:10), life (6:12; 7:15; 9:9), and even the future after death (11:8). The word *heḇel*, translated "meaningless," elsewhere refers concretely to a breath, a wind, or a vapor (e.g., Prov. 21:6; Isa. 57:13). In Ecclesiastes several phrases are used parallel to *heḇel*: "chasing after the wind" (Ecc. 1:14; 2:11, 17, 26; 4:4, 16; 6:9), "no advantage" (3:19; cf. 5:11; 6:8), "nothing . . . gained" (2:11; cf. 2:22; 3:9; 5:16; 6:11). Thus metaphorically this Hebrew word means what is unsubstantial or without real value. Occasionally it also refers metaphorically to some other characteristics of wind or vapor: (a) what is fleeting or transitory (cf. 6:12 where it is parallel to "few" [days] and "days he passes through like a shadow," 3:19; 7:15; 9:9; 11:10); (b) what is enigmatic or perplexing (cf. 6:2; 8:10, 14); or (c) what is unseen and obscure (cf. 11:8).

Why did Solomon pass this verdict on man's toil? Because work, he felt, produces nothing of lasting value. Also man's work is often prompted by motives which sow the seeds of their own discontent—for example, rivalry (4:4, 6) and an insatiable desire for added wealth (4:8; 5:10; 6:9). And toil brings no lasting pleasure (2:10-11) no matter how great one's accomplishments (2:4-6) or how much one is rewarded for it (2:7-8). Moreover, one always runs the risk of losing the fruit of his labor. It can be lost through oppression or injustice (5:8-9), through some unpredictable misfortune (5:14), or through the judgment of God (2:26; cf. 5:6). Even if a person manages to retain the fruit of his labor throughout his life, he "can't take it with him" but must leave it to someone else (2:18; 5:15). Moreover, since the beneficiary of the fruit of a man's labors has not toiled for it (2:21) and may even be a fool (2:19), all the results of a man's labor may be squandered and his efforts ultimately go for naught.

Solomon saw a similar deficiency in a man's wisdom and righteousness because they provide no absolute guarantee of success. Wisdom does have a decisive advantage over folly (2:13-14), wealth (7:11-12), and physical strength or military might (9:16, 18; 7:19). And wisdom does make it easier to succeed even in hazardous tasks (10:8-10, esp. v. 10b; cf.

8:1-6, esp. v. 5; 10:2-4, esp. v. 2). However, wisdom's results can be vitiated through a little sin (9:18; cf. 7:7-9), a little folly (10:1), improper timing (10:11), or even a lack of proper appreciation (9:15). Moreover, wisdom is not always rewarded (9:11); a wise man is subject to the same unpredictable misfortunes as a wicked person (9:1-2, 12). Finally, any ultimate advantage in wisdom is obliterated by death; a wise man dies and is forgotten just like a fool (2:14-16).

Righteousness too provides no sure reward. Though Solomon affirmed that righteousness is rewarded and wickedness is punished (8:12-13), he had sometimes seen just the opposite (8:14; cf. 7:15; 8:10), and had observed wickedness practiced even in the courts (3:16) and had seen justice and people's rights denied (5:8). Though some of these inequities could perhaps be explained from the fact that absolute righteousness is impossible (7:20, 28-29), the truth is that the righteous are subject to the same unpredictable misfortunes as the wicked (9:1-2) and ultimately die just as the wicked do (9:3).

These observed inequities in the distribution of justice and the unpredictability of fate make all of life chancy in Solomon's view. Though he believed that God is providentially in control of all things (3:11; 6:10; 7:14; 9:1) and that everything has its appropriate time (3:1-8), there is a certain inscrutability about God's providential dealings even for the wisest people (3:11; 8:17). Thus Solomon repeatedly affirmed the inability of people to predict the future (7:14; 8:7; 9:1; 10:14) and to pick the best courses of action (6:12; 11:6). Moreover, the inscrutability of providence is not confined to this life; even life after death, contrary to the statements of some expositors, held no guarantees for Solomon.

Though he did indeed believe that God would judge people's deeds (3:17; 11:9; 12:14), he nowhere explicitly stated or even implied that this would take place *after* a person dies. Solomon confined his discussion of rewards and opportunities to enjoy God's favor to this life (9:4-7, esp. v. 5, "the dead . . . have no . . . reward," and v. 7, "it is now that God favors what you do"). Thus life after death was obscure to Solomon (11:8) and held no promise of redressing all the inequities and enigmas he had pointed out.

His reluctance to speculate about life after death (cf. 3:19-22) was in keeping with his method of demonstrating his theme, the method of empirical testing (e.g., "I have seen/saw"; 1:14; 3:16; etc.). His purpose for doing this, though nowhere stated, may be inferred from his conclusion (12:13-14) and from other intimations in the book (2:24-26; 3:14; 7:18). He intended to demonstrate empirically to people the insecurity of all human effort to provide any real meaning, value, or significance to their lives "under the sun" and to drive them to trust in God alone.

Even the enjoyment theme (2:24-26; 3:12, 22; 5:18-20; 8:15; 9:7-9; 11:7-10), though often mistakenly interpreted as the Epicurean counsel of despair, is closely tied to this purpose. Thus the enjoyment of life—joy in one's labor, enjoyment of its fruits—comes only as a gift of God (2:24-26, esp. v. 25; 3:13; 5:19-20; cf. 9:7). And it comes only to those who please God (2:26), who fear Him (8:12), and whose enjoyment of life is tempered by the recognition that God will judge their deeds (11:9). Thus the dominant mood of the book is pessimism, but the author, Solomon, was no pessimist, cynic, or skeptic as some critics have claimed. He was a believer who sought to destroy people's confidence in their own efforts, their own abilities, their own righteousness and to direct them to faith in God as the only possible basis for meaning, value, and significance to life "under the sun."

However, Solomon did not say that a person's efforts had no value whatever. One's labor can accomplish great things and gain him some pleasure (2:10). Skill can make it easier to succeed (10:10). Righteousness can give more security than wickedness (8:12-13). But in the light of the Fall (7:29), the inscrutability of providence (6:12), the imminence of death (12:1-7), and the obscurity of life after death (3:19-21; 11:8), labor, skill, and righteousness hold little promise of security or ultimate value.

Though Solomon wrote to combat the growing secularization of religion in his own day, his words provide a valid critique of modern secular humanism. Life is indeed short; it is filled with many enigmas and inequities. Apart from the assurance of future judgment and life after death furnished by the historical facts of Christ's crucifixion and resurrection (cf., e.g., Acts 17:30-31), the future after death is dark and obscure. However, in spite of this, life should not be abandoned or filled with despair. Rather, life should be lived in complete trust in God, be received and enjoyed as a gift from His good hand, and be lived in the light of His future judgment.

Unity and Structure. The view that Ecclesiastes consists of a combination of the contradictory views of three men (a skeptic, a writer of wisdom, and a believer)—a view common among critics at the beginning of the 20th century—has been largely abandoned. And the unity of the book, at least its thematic unity, has been generally affirmed. However, there is still no general consensus that the book follows a logical development or argument. Many scholars see the book as a loose collection of wisdom sayings similar to the Book of Proverbs. Other scholars see a connected argument only in the first part of the book (Ecc. 1–6) and a collection of practical exhortations in the second part (chaps. 7–12).

Among the many attempts to demonstrate a detailed argument throughout the book, two have gained some popularity. One method of tracing the argument, long in vogue, sees the repetition of the enjoyment theme at 2:24-26; 5:18-20; 8:15-17; 11:7-10 as concluding the arguments of four major sections.

A second method of tracing the argument, suggested by the methods of rhetorical criticism and involving the repetition of set formulas, is gaining current popularity and forms the basis for the outline in this commentary. Thus the main body of the book may be divided into two sections: (a) 1:12–6:9 emphasizes the limitations of all human effort (it is "meaningless and a chasing after the wind"), and (b) 6:10–11:6 emphasizes the limitations of human wisdom (man does not/cannot know/discover). Of the material that stands outside this structure 1:3-11 is a poem in support of the theme announced in 1:2, the vanity or futility of human endeavor, and 11:7–12:14 contains a poem recommending that people enjoy life as stewards of God (11:7–12:7). This final poem is followed by a reitera-

tion of the theme (12:8) and a final conclusion (12:13-14) to "fear God and keep His commandments." As Robert K. Johnston has noted ("Confessions of a Workaholic: A Reappraisal of Qoheleth." *Catholic Biblical Quarterly.* 38 January-March 1976:18), this introductory and concluding material nicely summarizes Solomon's argument: *all human endeavors lack ultimate value; life should be enjoyed in the fear of God, as a gift from His hand.*

OUTLINE

I. Introduction: The Futility of All Human Endeavor (1:1-11)
   A. Title (1:1)
   B. Theme: The futility of human effort (1:2)
   C. General support: The futility of human effort demonstrated from nature (1:3-11)
      1. Thesis: No ultimate profit in human labor (1:3)
      2. Proof: Ceaseless, wearisome rounds (1:4-11)
II. The Futility of Human Achievement Empirically Demonstrated (1:12–6:9)
   A. Personal observations on the futility of human achievement (1:12–2:17)
      1. Futility of human achievement shown by personal investigation (1:12-15)
      2. Futility of human wisdom shown by personal reflection (1:16-18)
      3. Futility of pleasure-seeking shown by personal experience (2:1-11)
      4. Futility of a wise lifestyle shown by reflection on death (2:12-17)
   B. The futility of human labor empirically demonstrated (2:18–6:9)
      1. Labor's fruits may be squandered by someone else (2:18-26)
      2. Labor cannot alter God's immutable, inscrutable providence (3:1–4:3)
      3. Labor is often motivated by inappropriate incentives (4:4-16)

4. Labor's fruits may sometimes not be enjoyed (5:1–6:9)
III. The Limitations of Human Wisdom Empirically Demonstrated (6:10–11:6)
   A. Introduction: Everything is immutably and inscrutably foreordained (6:10-12)
   B. Man cannot fathom the plan of God (chaps. 7–8)
      1. Man's ignorance of the significance of adversity and prosperity (7:1-14)
      2. Man's ignorance of the significance of righteousness and wisdom (7:15-29)
      3. Man's ignorance of the enigma of divine retribution (chap. 8)
   C. Man does not know what will happen (9:1–11:6)
      1. No one knows what will happen to him (9:1-10)
      2. No one knows whether his wisdom will succeed (9:11–10:11)
      3. Criticism is risky in view of one's ignorance of the future (10:12-20)
      4. Work diligently despite ignorance of the future (11:1-6)
IV. Conclusion: Live Joyously and Responsibly in the Fear of God (11:7–12:14)
   A. Call to live joyously and responsibly (11:7–12:7)
      1. Enjoy life because the darkness of death is coming (11:7-8)
      2. Enjoy life in your youth, remembering that God will judge (11:9-10)
      3. Live responsibly in your youth for old age and death are coming (12:1-7)
   B. Final advice in view of the futility of all human endeavor (12:8-14)
      1. Reiteration of the theme: The futility of all human endeavor (12:8)
      2. The peculiar authority of this book (12:9-12)
      3. Final advice: Fear God and keep His commandments (12:13-14)

COMMENTARY

I. Introduction: The Futility of All Human Endeavor (1:1-11)

In this introductory section the author identified himself (v. 1), stated his theme (v. 2), and defended it in general terms (vv. 3-11).

A. Title (1:1)

1:1. As with other wisdom literature in the Old Testament (e.g., Prov. 30:1; 31:1; cf. Prov. 1:6; 22:17; 24:23) the author of Ecclesiastes identified this book as his own. Elsewhere (Ecc. 12:11), however, he also claimed divine authority for it. The author identified himself only by his titles: **the Teacher,** a **son of David,** the **king in Jerusalem.** As indicated in the *Introduction* under "Authorship and Date" these titles plus other information in the book (cf. 1:12, 16; 2:4-9) suggest that the author was Solomon.

B. Theme: The futility of human effort (1:2)

1:2. After identifying himself as the author, Solomon declared most emphatically that everything is futile or **meaningless.** Five times in this one verse he used *hebel,* the Hebrew word for "meaningless." Four of those times are in a twofold repetition of a Hebrew superlative construction which the KJV renders "Vanity of vanities" and the NIV renders **Meaningless! Meaningless!** and **Utterly meaningless!** As indicated in the *Introduction's* "Theme and Purpose," he used this metaphorical term throughout the book to refer to what is without real substance, value, permanence, significance, or meaning. Here at the outset he applied this to **everything,** by which he meant all human endeavors, as is obvious from verse 3 and his argument throughout the book.

C. General support: The futility of human effort demonstrated from nature (1:3-11)

In support of his theme, Solomon argued first in broad general terms that it is impossible for human efforts to have permanent value. He did this in a poem on the ceaseless rounds of generations (v. 4) and of nature (vv. 5-7), introduced by a rhetorical question (v. 3) and followed by a poetic conclusion (vv. 8-11).

1. THESIS: NO ULTIMATE PROFIT IN HUMAN LABOR (1:3)

1:3. Solomon followed the announcement of his theme (v. 2) with a rhetorical question which demanded a negative answer. By this device, a common feature in his argumentation (2:2; 3:9; 6:8, 11-12; etc.), he denied any profit or **gain** to a person's **labor.** The term "gain" (*yitrôn*), unique to the Book Ecclesiastes, occurs seven times (1:3; 2:11 ["gained"], 13 ["is better"]; 3:9; 5:9 ["profits"], 16; 10:10 [not trans. in NIV]). "Gain" refers literally to what is left over (a gain or a profit) or metaphorically to what is advantageous or of benefit. Though some things have relative advantage over others (e.g., light over darkness and wisdom over folly, 2:13), Solomon affirmed at the outset that people gain no ultimate advantage or profit from all their toil. By the phrase **under the sun** he meant "down here on the earth." He used this phrase repeatedly (29 times) throughout the book, often in connection with man's toil.

2. PROOF: CEASELESS, WEARISOME ROUNDS (1:4-11)

Solomon supported his thesis by referring to the ceaseless rounds of generations (v. 4) and of nature (vv. 5-7). From them he concluded that people's labor, like these ceaseless rounds, produces nothing permanent or satisfying (vv. 8-11).

a. The impermanence of man (1:4)

1:4. The first fact Solomon cited in support of his thesis is the impermanence of a person's existence. In contrast with **the earth,** the scene of one's labor, which **remains** (lit., "stands") **forever,** every person is a transitory being, a small part of the coming and going **generations.**

b. The ceaseless rounds of nature (1:5-7)

1:5-7. The second fact Solomon cited in support of his thesis is the ineffectiveness of labor, demonstrated by nature's ceaseless activity. Mere activity in and of itself produces nothing of ultimate value. **The sun** and **the wind** are in constant motion but never arrive at any fixed goal or lasting rest. The **streams** continually **flow** to **the sea, yet the sea is never full.** (NASB's "to the place where the rivers flow, there they flow again" is preferred to NIV's **to the place the streams come from, there they return again.**) Thus all the activity of nature is monotonous (**round and round . . . ever returning**) and wearisome (**hurries** in v. 5 means lit., "pants [from exhaustion]"; cf. Jer. 14:6), without effecting any progress or reaching any fixed goal.

c. The repetition of human endeavors (1:8-11)

1:8-11. Next Solomon argued that what is observable in the rounds of nature is also true of all human endeavor. **Nothing** happens or is done that is really **new** (v. 9). Things are only apparently **new** (v. 10a) because people do not recollect former actions, events, and accomplishments (vv. 10b-11). (NASB's "earlier things . . . later things" is preferred to NIV's **men of old . . . those who are yet to come** because the missing noun or antecedent is to be supplied for the Heb. adjectives "earlier" and "later" from **all things** in v. 8 and **anything** in v. 10.) As several commentators note, Solomon did not intend by this to deny human creativity but to deny the complete newness of people's accomplishments. For example, man's journey to the moon and the discovery of America, though different, were both explorations of distant places, involving adventure and risk. And the invention of dynamite and of the atomic bomb shared the element of discovering an "explosive." Thus what is true in the realm of nature—the constant repetition of previous accomplishments—is in essence true of the activity of people and is included in the observation that all things produce only indescribable weariness and lack of satisfaction (all things **are wearisome,** v. 8).

II. The Futility of Human Achievement Empirically Demonstrated (1:12–6:9)

This long section is united by the repetition of the phrase "meaningless, a chasing after the wind." Apart from its occurrence at 4:4 where it seems to introduce a new section, this formula stands near the end of each of several sections and announces Solomon's verdict on the value of human achievement (1:12-15), human wisdom (1:16-18; 2:12-17), pleasure-seeking (2:1-11), and toil or labor (2:18–6:9).

A. Personal observations on the futility of human achievement (1:12–2:17)

The four parts of this section, which contain Solomon's allusions to his own experiences, are clearly tied together in two pairs. Thus the repetition of the wisdom, madness, and folly motif (1:17; 2:12) is not redundant but deals with wisdom's relationship to his personal investigation into the value of human achievements (1:12-15) and to his personal experience of the futility of pleasure-seeking (2:1-11).

1. FUTILITY OF HUMAN ACHIEVEMENT SHOWN BY PERSONAL INVESTIGATION (1:12-15)

1:12-15. Solomon began his argument on the futility of human achievement by citing his own personal investigation into its value. Alluding to his wide opportunities for observation because of his position as the **King** of **Israel** (v. 12; cf. v. 16; 2:12), he stated that, aided by his surpassing **wisdom** and knowledge (1:13; cf. v. 16; 1 Kings 4:26-34), he had made a thorough (indicated by the use of the synonyms **study** and **explore** in Ecc. 1:13) and comprehensive investigation of all kinds of human activities (i.e., **all that is done under heaven**; cf. "under the sun," v. 14). He concluded that they are all **a heavy burden** (v. 13, 'inyan rā', "a bad or unpleasant task"; trans. "a miserable business" in 4:8 and "some misfortune" in 5:14) and thus futile or **meaningless.** In fact they are as useless as **chasing after the wind,** a graphic picture of effort expended with no results gained since no one can catch the wind by running after it. Solomon used this phrase nine times, all in the first half of the book (1:14, 17; 2:11, 17, 26; 4:4, 6, 16; 6:9).

Solomon based this verdict on his observations which had shown him that human achievements leave much to be desired. Human effort and action cannot remedy all the irregularities or counteract all the deficiencies observable in the nature of **things** (1:14-15; cf. 7:13).

2. FUTILITY OF HUMAN WISDOM SHOWN BY PERSONAL REFLECTION (1:16-18)

1:16-18. Solomon also argued that when he reflected (v. 17) on his surpassing **wisdom** and vast experience (v. 16) by means of which he had conducted the preceding investigation (cf. v. 13) and

had reached his somber conclusion, he realized that it held little real advantage over **madness and folly** (i.e., foolish ideas and pleasures; cf. 2:2, 13-14). His pursuit of **wisdom** was as frustrating as **chasing after the wind,** and its acquisition, far from alleviating the depression created by his somber verdict, merely increased his mental anguish (**sorrow**) and sadness of heart (**grief**).

3. FUTILITY OF PLEASURE-SEEKING SHOWN BY PERSONAL EXPERIENCE (2:1-11)

Turning from the report of his careful investigation into the value of human achievement in general (cf. 1:12-15), Solomon next described an experiment he conducted on the value of pleasure. Emphasizing the objective nature of his experiment under the guiding hand of wisdom (2:3, 9), he announced the goal and conclusion of his experiment (vv. 1-2), described the means by which he sought and found pleasure (vv. 3-10), and related them to the ultimate value of his accomplishments (v. 11).

a. The conclusion: Pleasure has little value (2:1-2)

2:1-2. Solomon stated that in his quest to find something worthwhile in life (**to find out what is good**; cf. v. 3, "to see what was worthwhile [same Heb. word as the word 'good'] for men to do"), he experimented **with pleasure.** But he concluded that it was futile or **meaningless** because it was foolish and accomplished little or nothing. Solomon's question, **And what does pleasure accomplish?** is again rhetorical, expecting a negative answer (cf. 1:3).

b. The experiment: Pleasure-seeking is futile (2:3-11)

2:3. In Solomon's quest to find something worthwhile to do, he even experimented—though deliberately and with restraint, not blindly or in uncontrolled excess (**my mind still guiding me with wisdom**; cf. v. 9b)—with sensual indulgence (e.g., **cheering myself with wine**) and with what he would otherwise have characterized as a foolish or frivolous lifestyle (**embracing folly**). He wanted to test the effects of pleasure-seeking and frivolity to **see** if they were really **worthwhile.**

2:4-10. In his inquiry into the value

of pleasure he denied himself no avenue through which pleasure might be gained. As the richest and most powerful man who had ever lived **in Jerusalem** (v. 9; cf. 1 Kings 10), he surrounded himself with pleasureful objects such as magnificent buildings and **vineyards** (Ecc. 2:4; cf. 1 Kings 7:1-11), luxuriant **gardens and parks** (Ecc. 2:5) filled with **trees** (vv. 5-6), a great retinue of **slaves** (v. 7; cf. 1 Kings 10:5) who were available to serve him, musicians to meet his aesthetic needs, and a large **harem** (Ecc. 2:8; cf. 1 Kings 11:1-3) to satisfy his physical desires. Moreover, with the wealth from his great **herds and flocks** (Ecc. 2:7) and his great treasures of **silver and gold** (v. 8; cf. 1 Kings 10:14-15, 27) he could buy anything his heart **desired** and indulge in every **pleasure** (Ecc. 2:10).

2:11. However, though he could gain some satisfaction from the joy of accomplishment and had indeed experienced pleasure from it all (cf. v. 10), when he reflected on the real value of what he had accomplished, he concluded that it **was meaningless** and **a chasing after the wind** (cf. 1:14, 17; 2:17, 26; 4:4, 6, 16; 6:9). There was no real or ultimate gain (cf. 1:3) from all his accomplishments **under the sun** (cf. comments on "under the sun" in 1:3).

4. FUTILITY OF A WISE LIFESTYLE SHOWN BY REFLECTION ON DEATH (2:12-17)

2:12-16. The reason Solomon passed this verdict on the ultimate value of his accomplishments was the sad fact of the universality of death. Pointing out that his experiment with the value of pleasure could perhaps be duplicated but not exceeded ("for what can the man do who comes after the king? Only what he has already done," v. 12b, RSV), Solomon reflected on the relationship between wisdom and folly, namely, that **wisdom** enabled him to enjoy pleasure and the fruits of his labor judiciously (cf. vv. 3, 9) as opposed to riotous hedonism (**madness and folly,** v. 12; cf. 1:17). He concluded that there was indeed some advantage to **wisdom.** (**Better** translates the word *yiṯrôn* rendered "gain" in 1:3 [see comments there]. It refers to something excelling over something else.)

A **wise man** has the foresight to avoid danger while a **fool** gets into trouble as though he stumbles around in the dark (2:14; cf. Prov. 4:18-19 for a similar metaphorical use of light and **darkness**).

However, because **both** the wise man and the fool share **the same fate** (Ecc. 2:14)—they both **die** and are ultimately **forgotten** (v. 16; cf. 9:5)—he concluded that there was no real advantage to being **wise,** that is, to living wisely as opposed to living foolishly (2:15).

2:17. This also led Solomon to view life as repugnant or distasteful. He said he **hated life, because the work . . . was** grievous" to him. (The word trans. "grievous" [*rāʿ*] is the antonym for the word trans. "good" or "worthwhile" in vv. 1, 3.) If, he concluded, it does not ultimately make any difference how one lives and if there is nothing ultimately worthwhile to do, then **all** of life and all its accomplishments are futile or **meaningless, a chasing after the wind** (cf. 1:14, 17; 2:11, 17, 26; 4:6, 16; 6:9).

B. The futility of human labor empirically demonstrated (2:18–6:9)

Having discussed the futility of human achievements in general (1:12-15) and the futility of his own achievements (2:1-11) in view of death (2:12-17), Solomon then turned to consider the value of the toil he had expended in accomplishing them (2:18-20) and the value of human toil in general (2:21–6:9). He shifted from using "I" and "my" in 2:1-18 to using "he," "a man," and "his" in 2:19-20. Twenty-three of the 34 occurrences of the Hebrew word for "toil" and "labor" in Ecclesiastes appear in this section, which may be divided into four paragraphs (2:18-26; 3:1–4:3; 4:4-16; 5:1–6:9) on the basis of the recurring formula "meaningless, a chasing after the wind."

1. LABOR'S FRUITS MAY BE SQUANDERED BY SOMEONE ELSE (2:18-26)

a. Labor's fruits may be squandered by one's heir (2:18-21)

2:18-21. Life was not the only thing Solomon found to be ultimately repugnant; he also viewed all his labor with distaste. **I hated all the things I had toiled for** is literally, "I hated all my toil." Thus he viewed his work **under the sun** (vv. 18-20; cf. comments on 1:3) with **despair** (2:20) because there was no permanence to its fruits, to the things he accomplished through it. Though what he accomplished (vv. 4-6) and accumulated (vv. 7-8) might survive him, he would have no **control** over how it would be used after his death (v. 19; cf. Ps. 49:10). A person who inherited it, who had **not** had to work **for it** (Ecc. 2:21), and who consequently had no real appreciation for it, might be a **fool** (v. 19) who would squander it. So Solomon declared toil to be futile or **meaningless** (vv. 19, 21) and the loss of its fruits **a great misfortune** (v. 21).

b. Thus labor is not worth the effort (2:22-23)

2:22-23. Viewed in the light of the impermanence of its fruits Solomon asked whether a man's labor in this life (**under the sun**; cf. comments on 1:3) was really worth it all. In the final analysis, he declared, all that really resulted from it was the expenditure of a lot of painful labor and restless activity which is futile or **meaningless.**

c. It is best to enjoy labor's fruits as God enables (2:24-26)

2:24-26. In view of the impermanence of the fruits of a man's toil, Solomon recommended that a man enjoy its fruits (eating and drinking are only metaphorical for partaking of all its fruits) **and find satisfaction in his work** (cf. 3:13; 5:18; 8:15) as he himself had done (2:10). However, he warned that this was possible only if **God** enabled one to do so: **without Him, who can eat or find enjoyment?** Moreover, he warned that **God** only enables those who please Him to do so. Often sinners amass **wealth** which ultimately is enjoyed by **one who pleases God,** a task he identified as futile or **meaningless, a chasing after the wind** (cf. 1:14, 17; 2:11, 17; 4:4, 6, 16; 6:9).

Two points from 2:24-26 should be noted. First, Solomon stated that God's disposition of wealth and the enjoyment of one's labors and its fruits are based on whether a man is pleasing to God or is a **sinner.** As is clear from the words "the man who pleases" God and "the sinner" elsewhere in Ecclesiastes (7:26; cf. 8:12), this implies that a person will be judged on the basis of his ethical behavior and his trust in **God** or lack of it. Second, Solomon wrote that this judgment would take place in this life (not in a life after death) and would involve temporal not eternal rewards. These two points (en-

joyment of life and judgment), which are brought together only here, are crucial in the development of the book. The enjoyment theme, mentioned at crucial times in the book (3:12-13, 22; 5:18-20; 8:15; 9:7-10), is here specifically related to the theme of judgment (11:9; 12:14), and to the advice to fear God and keep His commandments (12:13).

2. LABOR CANNOT ALTER GOD'S IMMUTABLE, INSCRUTABLE PROVIDENCE (3:1–4:3)

The argument in this section revolves around the repetition of the word "time" in 3:1-8, 11, 17 and other repeated phrases such as "I have seen" or "I saw" (3:10, 16; 4:1), "I know" (3:12, 14), and "I thought" (3:17-18). Solomon argued that God has appointed a time for everything (3:11), even for injustice (3:16-17) and oppression (4:1-3). All this is part of the eternal (3:14), immutable (3:14), inscrutable (3:11) providence of God which renders a person's toil profitless (3:9).

a. Thesis: Everything has its time (3:1-8)

(1) Thesis stated. **3:1.** Solomon said, **There is a time . . . for every activity under heaven** (cf. 8:6). By the word "activity" Solomon meant people's deliberate, willful acts. The Hebrew word for "activity," always used of people, literally means "desire," and then by metonymy "what one desires" (cf. Isa. 58:13). For these willful acts people are held accountable (cf. Ecc. 3:17). Each activity, wrote Solomon, has its proper "time" (point in time) and **season** (duration).

(2) Thesis illustrated (3:2-8). Solomon followed his general statement with a poem on 14 opposites, each of which happens in its time. The fact that Solomon utilized polar opposites in a multiple of seven and began his list with birth and death is highly significant. The number seven suggests the idea of completeness and the use of polar opposites—a well-known poetical device called merism—suggests totality (cf. Ps. 139:2-3). Though the exact meaning of some of these "activities" is uncertain, Solomon intended to affirm that *all* a person's activities, both constructive and destructive, and *all* his responses to people, objects, and events happen in their times.

3:2-3. The list begins with a reference to the beginning and end of a person's life, two events over which he really has no control. Solomon continued by referring to the deliberate acts of one who begins and ends vegetable life (**a time to plant and a time to uproot**), takes and saves human life, and constructs and destroys buildings. Perhaps all these are suggested by the concept of birth and death.

3:4. From the concept of death and destruction, Solomon wrote of the human responses to those events. People experience weeping and mourning, and their opposites, laughing and dancing, two activities by which joy is expressed.

3:5-6. How the two opposites in verse 5 are related to each other and to those in verses 2-4 is uncertain. Many interpretations have been suggested for the meaning of the phrases **a time to scatter** (or "cast away," KJV) **stones and a time to gather them.** Perhaps it is best to see them as referring to the gathering and rejecting of building materials. This relates these opposites both to the idea of building (v. 3) and to the thought of keeping and throwing away (v. 6).

Solomon then spoke of the display of affections (v. 5b), probably of a man to a woman and perhaps also of a woman to a man. He then wrote about searching for a thing or giving it up as lost and about keeping a thing or throwing it **away** (v. 6). All the opposites in verses 5-6 seem to involve man's interest in things or affection for persons.

3:7. This verse may refer to actions associated with mourning (tearing one's clothes and remaining silent; cf. Job 2:12-13), and its end (sewing one's clothes and speaking out). If so, it would relate to the mourning in Ecclesiastes 3:4.

3:8. Solomon closed his list of opposites by referring to life's two basic emotions, **love** and **hate,** and the most hostile expression of the latter, **war,** and its opposite, **peace.** It may be significant that the list closes, somewhat as it began, with a set of opposites (war and peace) over which a person has little control.

b. Significance: Toil is profitless (3:9)

3:9. Turning from the thesis that every activity has its time, Solomon again raised the question of the value of a person's work, expecting rhetorically the same somber answer as before (cf. 1:3; 2:11), that there is no profit (**gain,** *yiṭrôn;* cf. comments on 1:3) in one's **toil.**

c. Reason: God's design is inscrutable (3:10-11)

3:10-11. To support the implied negative answer to his question in verse 9, Solomon referred to three observations he had drawn from his reflection on all the human activity represented in the opposites, verses 2-8. This activity is suggested by the word **burden** (*'inyan*), which is translated "task" in the NASB. (1) Solomon observed that **God . . . has made everything beautiful** (or, "appropriate"; the same word is trans. "proper" in 5:18) **in its time,** that is, God in His providential plans and control has an appropriate time for every activity. (2) Solomon observed that God has put **eternity in the hearts of men.** People have a longing or desire to know the extratemporal significance of themselves and their deeds or activities. (3) Solomon added that people **cannot** know the works of **God . . . from beginning to end,** that is, they cannot know the sovereign, eternal plan of God. Human labor is without profit because people are ignorant of God's eternal plan, the basis by which He evaluates the appropriateness and eternal significance of all their activities. Because of this ignorance there is an uncertainty and latent temporality to the value of all one's labor.

d. Recommendation: Enjoy life as God enables (3:12-13)

3:12-13. Since man in his ignorance of God's plan cannot be sure of the appropriateness or lasting significance of his labor, Solomon again recommended the present enjoyment of life (cf. 2:24), stating that **there is nothing better for men than to be happy** as long as they **live** (cf. 5:18; 8:15). The words **do good** (in the NIV and NASB) should be rendered "enjoy themselves" (RSV). No moral qualification is suggested here as a requirement for receiving God's gift of enjoyment (as there is in 2:26). Most commentators are undoubtedly correct in pointing to the parallel words **find satisfaction** (lit., "see good") in 3:13. There "good" is used in a nonethical sense (cf. 2:24; 5:18 for the same idiom).

Again Solomon indicated that this ability to enjoy life comes as a **gift of God** (cf. 2:25). Christian D. Ginsburg properly renders 3:13 as a conditional sentence: "If any man eats and drinks and finds satisfaction in all his toil, it is a gift of God" (*The Song of Songs and Coheleth,* pp. 311-2).

e. Purpose: That man may fear God (3:14-15)

3:14-15. Anticipating that people who cannot understand God's plan might accuse Him of being arbitrary, Solomon described the nature of God's plan and the response it should elicit. Solomon said the work of God is eternal (**everything God does will endure forever**) and perfect and immutable (**nothing can be added to it and nothing taken from it;** cf. 7:13). In support of this last point Solomon referred as he did in 1:9 to the repetition of natural events: **Whatever is has already been, and what will be has been before.** He added that this is part of God's deliberate plan. **God will call the past to account** may also be rendered "God calls back the past" (NIV marg.) or "God seeks what has passed by" (NASB). Some commentators suggest the paraphrase, "God seeks to repeat what has passed." Franz Delitzsch summarizes the thought of this statement: "The government of God . . . does not change; His creative as well as His moral ordering of the world produces with the same laws the same phenomena. . . . His government remains always, and brings . . . up again that which hath been" ("Ecclesiastes" in *Commentary on the Old Testament in Ten Volumes,* 6:264). The response **God** wants people to have to His immutable, inscrutable plan is one of fear, reverence, and humble submission: **so men will revere Him.**

f. Application: The place of injustice in God's plan (3:16–4:3)

The most likely exception to the appropriateness of any activity and the perfection of God's plan is the problem of injustice and oppression in the world.

(1) Observation: Injustice in the world. **3:16.** Anticipating a possible objection to the perfection of God's plan (cf. comments on another anticipated problem in vv. 14-15), Solomon stated that he had not ignored the problem of injustice (cf. 4:1; 8:14). He himself had observed in this life (**under the sun;** cf. comments on 1:3) that injustice was often evident in a place where one should least expect it—in the courts, **the place of judgment** and **of justice.** The repetition of the phrase **wickedness was there** em-

phasizes his surprise and consternation. Moreover, he affirmed in 3:17 that God was not ignoring injustice; He has both a future disposition and a present purpose for it.

(2) Future disposition: God will judge. **3:17.** Solomon affirmed that **God will** judge **both the righteous and the wicked** (cf. 11:9; 12:14) but that this **judgment** will come only in His **time.** The time of this judgment is ambiguous; it is future and in God's time but the verse neither states nor implies that it will be in the afterlife. Solomon undoubtedly believed with the wisdom writers in general that the judgment would take place on earth (cf., e.g., Job 27:13-23; Pss. 37:2, 6, 9, 11, 13, 15, 17-40; 73:18-20, 27; Prov. 22:22-23).

(3) Present manifestation: To demonstrate human finitude (3:18-21). **3:18-20.** The connection of verses 18-21 with the preceding is not well reflected in most English translations. The phrase **as for men** means literally, "for the sake of/because of men" and is generally taken by commentators to refer back to the injustice mentioned in verse 16: "injustice is both for the sake of and because of men." Thus Solomon affirmed a second purpose for injustice, namely, that by it God shows people **that they are like the animals** (lit., "they are animals, they with respect to themselves"). This does not say that people are nothing more than animals, with no immortal souls. It does suggest that people, like **animals,** die (cf. Ps. 49:12, 20). They have a common mortality, as Ecclesiastes 3:19-20 indicates.

Both people and animals **come from** the same **dust** of the earth, are animated by **the same** life breath (cf. Job 34:14-15; Ps. 104:29), and **go to the same place,** that is, return **to the dust** (Ecc. 3:20). So Solomon argued that **man has no advantage over** an **animal,** for both are transitory (*hebel* can be rendered "transitory" here rather than **meaningless;** cf. 6:12, and *kōl* can be rendered "both" rather than **everything,** as in 2:14; 7:18).

3:21. Moreover, any possible advantage man might claim over an animal was, according to Solomon, beyond empirical demonstration. This is indicated by his rhetorical question, **Who knows if the spirit of man rises upward and if the spirit of the animal goes down into the earth?** No living person can *observe* or *demonstrate* a difference between people and animals by watching them as they die. Some commentators, it is true, say that Solomon is here affirming a difference in the destinies of men and animals. They see vestiges of a belief in man's immortality expressed here and point to the absence of an "if" in the Hebrew text before spirit (cf. KJV, NASB). However, this conflicts with several things: (a) the context where Solomon is emphasizing the sameness of man's fate with the animals (vv. 19-20); (b) the use of the word "spirit" in this passage which refers to the breath of life which man shares with the animals (v. 19); (c) the rhetorical question in verse 22, "Who can bring him to see what will happen after him?" which denies Solomon's knowledge of an afterlife; and (d) the uniform testimony of many Bible versions which do reflect an interrogative in verse 21. Solomon had earlier argued that death negates all differences between a wise person and a fool (2:14c-16). Here he argued that death negates all differences between people and animals. Though people are endowed with a sense of rationality and a sense of eternity (3:11), injustice demonstrates their finitude, mortality, and ignorance of God's plan.

(4) Recommendation: Enjoy life. **3:22.** Since people are mortal (vv. 19-21), Solomon recommended that **a man . . . enjoy his work** (and probably, by metonymy, the fruits of his work or labor; cf. 2:24; 3:12). This **is** man's **lot** (a word that means lit., "portion, share, or allotment"; NASB translates this wrongly in 5:18-19; 9:9). This was especially pertinent in view of the fact that, as he had shown, people are ignorant of God's plan and cannot know what the future, including life after death, holds for them. He summarized this point in the rhetorical question, **Who can bring him to see what will happen after him?**

(5) Alternative response: Gloomy despair. **4:1-3.** Solomon also supported his advice to enjoy life (cf. 3:22) by describing his further reflections on injustice: **Again I looked** at **all the** acts of **oppression** (cf. 3:16) that occur on the earth (**under the sun;** cf. comments on 1:3). Plaintively Solomon lamented the desperate and hopeless plight of **the oppressed** who cry out for help but find none because of the irresistible **power**

and authority **of their oppressors.** The repetition of the words **they have no comforter** emphasizes their plight. Therefore Solomon stated that a man is better off **dead** or, better still, never having been born than having to witness (and possibly experience—the verb "see" often means "experience," as in 8:16) **the evil** oppression that takes place on earth because of injustice. In other words the only alternative to enjoyment of life as a gift from God's hand is the gloomy despair caused, in part at least, by reflection on unchecked oppression.

3. LABOR IS OFTEN MOTIVATED BY INAPPROPRIATE INCENTIVES (4:4-16)

This section employs the characteristic refrain "meaningless, a chasing after the wind" as a bracketing introductory and concluding formula (vv. 4, 16). This device, called an *inclusio*, is a common rhetorical feature in biblical literature (cf., e.g., Ps. 8:1, 9). Ecclesiastes 4:4-16 is also characterized by the repeated use of the word "meaningless" (vv. 4, 7-8, 16) and the word "better" (vv. 6, 9, 13) by which Solomon characterized certain motivating incentives of labor as futile and inappropriate.

a. Labor is sometimes motivated by envy (4:4-6)

4:4-6. The first inappropriate incentive Solomon referred to was envy of others. He said that **all labor and all achievement** (undoubtedly hyperboles) **spring from man's envy of his neighbor** and that envy is futile or **meaningless** and **a chasing after the wind** (cf. 1:14, 17; 2:11, 17, 26; 4:6, 16; 6:9). Some uncertainty exists about the meaning of 4:5 because the metaphors **folds his hands** and "eats his meat" (lit. trans. for **ruins himself**) refer elsewhere to sloth and self-destruction (Prov. 6:10-11; 24:33-34; Isa. 49:26). However, the view that Ecclesiastes 4:5 refers to a commendation of contentment with the simple needs of life ("eats his meat"; cf. Ex. 16:8; Deut. 12:20) with a minimum of effort (i.e., folding his hands) fits in better with Solomon's recommendation in Ecclesiastes 4:6 to be content with **one handful** (i.e., a little) accompanied by **tranquillity** ("rest," NASB; "quietness," KJV; the same Heb. word is rendered "rest" in 6:5 and the related Heb. verb is rendered "rested" in

Ex. 20:11) rather than a lot (**two hand-fuls**) accompanied by **toil** and anxious striving, which he characterized as **chasing after the wind** (cf. Ecc. 4:4).

b. Labor is sometimes motivated by selfish greed (4:7-12)

4:7-8. Selfish greed is another inappropriate incentive that Solomon said is futile or **meaningless** (that word, occurring at the beginning of v. 7 and the end of v. 8, points up another *inclusio*; cf. comments under "3. Labor is often motivated by inappropriate incentives [4:4-16])." On the words **under the sun** see comments on 1:3. Greed is the insatiable covetousness characterized by a man's having **no end to his toil, not** being **content with his wealth,** and not sharing with anyone, not even a **son** or **brother** (this refers to sharing in partnership, not to inheritance, as vv. 9-12 make clear). In the end, Solomon stated, such a greedy person would wake up and realize that it was futile or **meaningless** to toil incessantly to gather wealth which he neither shared nor enjoyed. Such a greedy person's questions, asked rhetorically, show his disparaging of his behavior. Solomon added that such futile or meaningless toil was **a miserable business** ('*inyan rā*', "a bad or unpleasant task"; trans. "a heavy burden" in 1:13 and "some misfortune" in 5:14; cf. '*inyan*, "burden," in 3:10).

4:9-12. In contrast with the futility of selfish greed, Solomon commended sharing with others by citing several advantages that come from companionship: better profit (**a good return**) from one's labor (v. 9), **help** in time of difficulty (v. 10), comfort in time of need (v. 11; one's body heat can keep another person from freezing), protection in time of danger (v. 12). The last three of these are illustrated by examples from the benefits of two persons traveling together. In the case of the second and third of these (vv. 10b, 11b) Solomon lamented the perils of isolation (characteristic of selfish greed; cf. "a man all alone," v. 8a).

Having set forth the advantages of joint effort and the mutual benefits of sharing one's toil and its fruit with another, Solomon stated climactically that if **two are better than one** (v. 9) then **three** are even better (v. 12). One's efforts and benefits should not be confined to merely two persons.

c. Labor is sometimes motivated by the desire for advancement and prestige (4:13-16)

4:13-16. The emphasis in these verses is on the transitory nature of fame and prestige. However, the precise interpretation and significance of these verses is somewhat unclear because of the ambiguity of the number of individuals involved and their relationship with each other. It is unclear whether there are two young men who in turn succeed to the throne of an old and foolish king or whether there is only one young man. It is also unclear whether the pronouns (in Heb.) in verse 15 refer to the poor yet wise young man (v. 13a) or to the old and foolish king (v. 13b). Though there are several ways to interpret these ambiguities, it seems best to follow the interpretation reflected in general in the NIV. Taken in this way the passage refers to **a poor but wise youth** who had advanced from poverty (**he** was **born in poverty within his** [i.e., the old king's] **kingdom**). The young person also lacked influence (he had **come from prison**; cf. Joseph's situation, Gen. 39:20—41:45). From this lowly position the youth advanced to great popularity and prestige: **all who lived and walked under the sun** (i.e., "on the earth"; cf. comments on "under the sun" in Ecc. 1:3) **followed the youth,** the king's successor. He also had great authority; he became the master of innumerable subjects (4:16; lit., "no end to all the people before whom [at whose head] he was"; cf. Num. 27:17). However, his prestige and authority were short-lived: **those who came later were not pleased with the successor.**

This passage illustrates the moral of Ecclesiastes 4:13: it is better to be poor (and without influence) than to be powerful and influential. Why? Because power, influence, and prestige are all transitory. Though the truth of verse 13 also commends wisdom over folly and commends responsiveness to criticism or counsel over unresponsiveness, these are not directly illustrated in the passage, which is confined to the futility of advancement. The point of the passage seems to be that the desire for prestige and advancement, two incentives which often motivate a person's labor, is, like envy and greed, futile or **meaningless** and **a chasing after the wind** (cf. 1:14, 17; 2:11, 17, 26; 4:4, 6; 6:9).

4. LABOR'S FRUITS MAY SOMETIMES NOT BE ENJOYED (5:1–6:9)

The argument of this passage has often been misunderstood. This is because of three things: (a) the use of the imperative mood in 5:1-7, (b) the absence of formal indications of divisions within 5:1–6:9, and (c) the failure of some commentators to make some connections between verses which Solomon apparently intended. This passsage concludes with the last of nine occurrences of the characteristic formula "meaningless, a chasing after the wind" (6:9).

a. Labor's fruits may be lost to God through a rash vow (5:1-7)

5:1-7. These verses are often wrongly interpreted as an interlude in Solomon's argument. They are assumed to give advice on proper worship, including the proper attitude for worship (v. 1), the proper practice of prayer (vv. 2-3), and the proper payment of vows (vv. 4-7). In reality, however, they are an important part of Solomon's argument, warning against the folly of rash vows which could cause a person to lose the fruits of his labor through God's destroying **the work** of his **hands** (v. 6). Thus Solomon warned against the folly of rash vows which he called **the sacrifice of fools** (v. 1) and **the speech of a fool** (v. 3). He warned against uttering a hasty and ill-considered **vow** to the Lord: **Do not be quick with your mouth; do not be hasty in your heart** (v. 2).

Solomon also warned that it would do no good to try to get out of fulfilling such a **vow** by pleading with the priest that it **was a mistake** (v. 6, something done inadvertently; cf. "error" in 10:5). **The temple messenger** probably refers to the priest as in Malachi 2:7. The basis for this warning was Deuteronomy 23:21-23, where vows were described as voluntary but binding once made, because failure to fulfill them was called sin and would result in God's punishment. Thus Solomon called foolish vows wrongdoing (**they do wrong,** Ecc. 5:1) and warned that a person's **mouth** could **lead** him **into sin** (v. 6), which could result in God's displeasure (v. 4) and anger (v. 6). Such a sin can ultimately lead to the loss of all a person worked for (v. 6).

Since a rash vow might result in the destruction of the fruits of one's labor

(and his labor might thus prove futile), Solomon compared rash vows to futile or **meaningless** dreams. This is the thought in verse 7a, which may be translated somewhat literally, "Through many dreams there is futility and also through many words." So Solomon exhorted his readers to fear **God** (v. 7b), being cautious not to make rash vows (vv. 1-2) and to **fulfill** the vows they had made (v. 4).

b. Labor's fruits may be lost to corrupt officials through extortion (5:8-9)

The point of these verses and their connection with Solomon's argument has often been misconstrued because of erroneous interpretations of some enigmatic expressions in verses 8b-9. Though many other interpretations are possible, as is obvious from the diversity in various translations (e.g., KJV, NASB, NIV), these verses probably refer to a hierarchy of corruption. This view, reflected in the NIV, seems to fit Solomon's overall argument in 5:1–6:9 best.

5:8-9. Having shown that the fruits of labor could be lost through a rash vow to God (vv. 1-7), Solomon added that one should **not be surprised** if the result of his labor were lost to the next highest authority, the king and his officials. In terms much briefer than but similar to Samuel's view of some typical evils of kingship (1 Sam. 8:10-18), Solomon described the oppressive exactions of officials at all levels. They were watching not to protect **the poor** and **oppressed** (cf. Ecc. 4:1) but to find ways to squeeze revenue out of the officials under them. At the head of this whole corrupt system was **the king** who **himself** profited **from the fields** of the oppressed. The potential of all a man worked for, **the increase from the land,** could be **taken** or extorted **by all** these corrupt officials.

Many commentators, arguing that Solomon would scarcely have depicted his own government in such poor light, have seen this passage as evidence that he did not write this book. But there is no evidence that Solomon was referring to any specific government. Like the other references in 2:18–6:9 (e.g., the hypothetical case in 4:13-16), Solomon was generalizing. Moreover, Israel's demand that Rehoboam, Solomon's successor (1 Kings 12:1-10), reduce his oppression suggests that the provincial governors under Solomon had made financial demands to support his opulence (1 Kings 4:7, 22-23). Solomon's government could scarcely be excluded from the truth in Ecclesiastes 5:8-9.

c. Labor's fruits may not be enjoyed because of one's own covetousness (5:10-12)

5:10-12. Having shown that the fruits of one's labors might not be enjoyed because they might be lost to God (vv. 1-7) or to governing officials (vv. 8-9), Solomon next argued that a person's own covetousness might keep him from enjoying them. Calling covetousness or the love of **money** futile or **meaningless,** Solomon argued that a covetous person **never** derives enjoyment from his **wealth** (v. 10) because his increased wealth merely brings him increased anxiety (v. 12b). While **a laborer** might rest content with **little or much,** a covetous person cannot sleep (his **abundance permits . . . no sleep,** v. 12). He has to be constantly on guard to protect his riches from the ever-growing number of people who would try to **consume them.** Thus Solomon asked satirically **what benefit** a covetous person gets from increased riches **except to** keep an eye on them (v. 11, lit., "to look at them with his eyes"). In summary, Solomon argued that the only results of increased wealth for a covetous person are increased anxiety and increased vigilance, not increased enjoyment.

d. Toiling to accumulate the fruits of labor may result in misery (5:13-17)

5:13-14. Solomon concluded his treatment of the futility of toil by showing how transitory its fruits really are and how striving to accumulate them brings only misery. Such striving and loss is **a grievous evil** (or, perhaps better, "a depressing misfortune"); the word for "grievous" (*ḥōlâh*) is literally, "sick"; and the word for "evil" (*rā'âh*) is often used for disaster or misfortune. Solomon emphasized this by referring to a person who had carefully treasured up or **hoarded** his **wealth** and then **lost** it all **through some misfortune** (not "bad investment" as in the NASB; this same expression, *'inyan rā',* refers in 1:13 to "a heavy burden" and in 4:8 to "a miserable business"). Such misfortunes would include the examples in 5:1-7, 8-9, experiences

such as those of Job (Job 1:13-19), *and* bad investments. As a result of such loss a man would have **nothing** to leave his **son** (Ecc. 5:14). Hoarding wealth may thus even bring **harm** (i.e., "misery") to **its owner** (v. 13). This is worse than accumulating wealth without knowing who will control it later (2:17-23).

5:15-17. Moreover, Solomon argued that even if wealth were not lost but kept throughout life, one could not "take it with him." Everyone enters the world with nothing, and leaves it with **nothing** (cf. Ps. 49:17). Since a person cannot take any fruits of his **labor** with him when he dies, he really gains nothing from his labor (Ecc. 5:16, **what does he gain?** [*yitrōn;* cf. 1:3] is again rhetorical; cf. 3:9). All his effort is as wasted as if he had toiled **for the wind.** Solomon called **this too . . . a grievous evil** ("a depressing misfortune"; cf. 5:13). He added that the misery that accompanies the windy or empty effort of toiling to accumulate wealth is like gloom (**he eats in darkness;** cf. **frustration, affliction, and anger**). The word "affliction" (*ḥōlî,* related to the word trans. "grievous" in vv. 13, 16) means literally, "sickness." Here as in verses 13, 16 it refers to psychological illness (cf. comments on v. 13).

e. Labor's fruits are to be enjoyed as God enables (5:18-6:9)

Having shown in some detail the futility of labor, climaxed graphically by setting forth the misery that often accompanies toiling to accumulate wealth, Solomon again recommended the enjoyment of life (cf. 2:24-26; 3:12-13, 22). But he warned that there are serious obstacles to such enjoyment.

(1) Recommendation: Enjoy labor's fruits as God enables (5:18-20). **5:18.** In contrast with the misery (*rā'âh,* "evil, disaster, misfortune") that accompanies toiling to accumulate wealth, Solomon declared that the only **good** (*ṭôḇ,* the antonym of *rā'âh* and what motivated Solomon's experiment in 2:1, 3) **and proper** (or "fitting" [NASB]; trans. "beautiful" in 3:11) thing is **for a man** to enjoy the fruits of and **to find satisfaction in his** hard **labor.** This is man's **lot** ("portion, share, allotment"; cf. 3:22; 5:19; 9:9).

5:19-20. The results of a man's labor (i.e., his **wealth and possessions;** cf. 6:2) and the ability **to enjoy them** and to **be**

happy (cf. 8:15) **in his work** are gifts of **God** (cf. 2:24; 3:13). (The NIV trans., "when God gives any man wealth and possessions and enables him to enjoy them," is preferable to the NASB which implies that everyone who is given wealth and possessions is also "empowered" to enjoy them, which is contradicted in 6:2.) However, the NIV phrase **to accept his lot** should be translated "to receive his lot"; it emphasizes enjoyment as a gift. This ability to enjoy life, this **gladness of heart** with which **God** occupies those thus gifted, keeps a person from brooding over life's brevity (**days of his life** in 5:20 refers back to "few days" in v. 18).

(2) Warning: Some people are not able to enjoy the fruits of their labor (6:1-9). **6:1-2.** However, Solomon warned that some men are given great **wealth**—so great that they lack **nothing** they desire—but they are not enabled by **God** to **enjoy** it. Someone else enjoys it **instead.** This problem **weighs heavily on men** (cf. 8:6; not "is prevalent among men," NASB). The fact that Solomon failed to specify the nature of this inability has led to a diversity of interpretations of 6:2 and its relationship to verses 3-6. It is difficult to decide whether verses 3-6 constitute a continuation of verses 1-2 or, as many interpreters suggest, a separate and contrasting case. Two factors speak in favor of seeing no break between verses 2 and 3: (1) No formal indicators of a break are given. (2) The interpretation that there is a break rests too heavily on the inappropriateness of the term **stranger** applying to an heir. (The Heb. word "stranger," which appears only here in Ecc., sometimes indicates only someone other than oneself, as in Prov. 27:2.) It is preferable to interpret the inability to enjoy one's possessions (Ecc. 6:2) as caused either by misfortune robbing a man of the fruits of his labor (5:13-14) or a miserly, lifelong hoarding of its fruits that rob him of the experience of enjoyment (5:15-17). Solomon called both of these **a grievous evil** (5:13, 16), a term similar to that applied in 6:2 to God's not enabling a man to enjoy his wealth. The terms, though translated the same, are similar but not identical. In 5:13, 16 *rāʿâh ḥôlâh* is lit., "sick evil" or "depressing misfortune"; the term in 6:2 is *ḥŏlî rāʿ* "evil sickness" or "a malignant disease."

6:3-6. The futility and grievousness of unenjoyed wealth is worse than the tragedy of being **stillborn.** A rich man is described in hyperbolic terms of extreme blessing: (a) great wealth ("he lacks nothing his heart desires," v. 2), (b) great progeny (**a hundred children**), and (c) a long life (he lives **many years, does not receive proper burial** [lit., "has no burial," i.e., even if he were to live forever; cf. Pss. 49:9; 89:48 for a similar concept], and **lives a thousand years twice over**). The stillborn is described in terms of ultimate futility: (a) **It** has no **meaning** (i.e., it does it no good to be born), (b) it disappears into **darkness,** (c) it is forgotten (**its name is shrouded** in **darkness**), (d) **it never saw the sun** ("the light of day"), and (e) it never **knew** what life is like. A wealthy person and a stillborn share the same fate; they **all** (*kōl* should be trans. "both"; cf. 2:14, 3:19; and comments on 7:18) **go to the same place** (i.e., the grave; cf. 3:20). And yet the lot of a stillborn is better because **it has more rest** (i.e., freedom from toil, anxiety, and misery; 6:5) than a richly blessed person whose soul is never satisfied.

6:7. Solomon concluded his description of the tragedy of unenjoyed wealth with a recommendation that one be content with what he has. With a word play on his earlier use of the word "heart" (lit., "soul") in verse 2, Solomon warned that there is always a danger of a man's desire (lit., "soul") outstripping his acquisitions. The soul of a man who "lacks nothing his heart [lit., 'soul'] desires" (v. 2) is not satisfied (cf. v. 3). Similarly though a man must indeed work to meet his basic needs, to fill his stomach (**all man's efforts are** [lit., "work is"] **for his mouth**), his desires (**appetite,** lit., "soul") may **never** be **satisfied.**

6:8-9. The **wise** and even the **poor** have no **advantage** over the **fool.** Though a poor person might know **how to** get along in the world (lit., "know how to walk before the living"), he is susceptible to desires that outstrip his acquisitions. So Solomon concluded his lengthy treatment of the futility of toil (2:18–6:9) by recommending that one be content with what he has rather than constantly longing for more. **Better what the eye sees than the roving of the appetite** (lit., "soul"; "heart" in v. 2 and "appetite" in v. 7 are also lit., "soul"). This clause is rendered in the NASB, "What the eyes see is better than what the soul desires." The reason for this wise advice is that constantly longing for more is futile or **meaningless, a chasing after the wind.** This is the last of nine occurrences in Ecclesiastes of the phrase "chasing after the wind" (cf. 1:14, 17; 2:11, 17, 26; 4:4, 6, 16). This phrase fittingly opens and concludes the first half of the book on the futility of human achievement.

III. The Limitations of Human Wisdom Empirically Demonstrated (6:10–11:6)

As indicated under "Unity and Structure" in the *Introduction*, this section is characterized by the repetition of the phrases "do(es) not/cannot know" (6:12; 9:1, 12; 10:14; 11:2, 6) and "do(es) not/cannot discover" (7:14, 24, 28; 8:17). As many commentators note, this section is characterized by many imperatives, recommendations, and commendations (e.g., "it is good," 7:18; or "X is better than Y"; 7:2, 5; 9:16, 18). This second half of the book thus contains much practical advice on how to live. However, this advice is given in the light of constant reminders of man's ignorance of the providence of God (i.e., "What God has done," 7:13; cf. 8:17) and what the future holds (e.g., 9:1; 10:14; 11:2). This advice is intended to encourage people to fear God (7:18; 8:12; 12:13) and lead lives that please Him (7:26; cf. 2:26).

A. Introduction: Everything is immutably and inscrutably foreordained (6:10-12)

6:10-12. Solomon introduced his discussion on the limitations of human wisdom by reverting to two themes he had used earlier to demonstrate the futility of human toil, namely, the immutability (1:15; 3:14; cf. 1:9) and inscrutability (3:11, 22) of divine providence. Solomon said that the nature and essence of everything that exists, including people, was foreordained long ago: **whatever exists has already been named** ("calling by name" parallels "creating," Isa. 40:26) **and what man is has been known** ("knowing" parallels "setting apart" and "appointing," Jer. 1:5). Furthermore Solomon said it was useless for a person to argue (**no man can contend**) about what is foreordained because God who had done it is

too powerful for man. **The more** man argues with **words** against God, **the less** he accomplishes (cf. Ecc. 10:12-15). Moreover, **man** is ignorant of what is best for him to do and of what the future holds (6:12). The questions are again rhetorical and call for negative answers.

Man is transitory in nature. His **days** are **few,** transitory (rather than **meaningless;** cf. comments on 3:19), and pass **like a shadow** (cf. comments on Job 14:2 for the meaning of this simile). As for man's future, he does not know **what will happen** (lit., "what will be after him") either before (Ecc. 7:14) or after death (3:22). Solomon thus stressed that man is ignorant of his place in God's foreordained plan of all things.

B. Man cannot fathom the plan of God (chaps. 7–8)

These chapters are characterized by the repetition of the phrase "cannot discover" (7:14; 8:17; in 7:28 the NIV translates the same Heb. verb "finding" and "found"), and "who can discover" (7:24), another rhetorical question. This section deals with human inability to discover or fathom the plan of God, called "what God has done" (7:13), "the scheme of things" (7:25), "all that God has done" (8:17), "what goes on under the sun" (8:17).

1. MAN'S IGNORANCE OF THE SIGNIFICANCE OF ADVERSITY AND PROSPERITY (7:1-14)

The key to this section is found in verse 14a where Solomon declared that God is the author of both adversity and prosperity and that He so mingles them together that man in his finite understanding cannot discover anything about his future. The ramifications of this for Solomon were that adversity might have positive benefits and prosperity might have ill effects. But the effects of either depend on how one responds to them, whether wisely or foolishly. Thus in verses 2-4 Solomon portrayed the positive benefits of the greatest adversity, death, if wisely considered, and in verses 11-12 he portrayed the benefits of prosperity if wisely used. In the verses between (vv. 5-10) he warned that both adversity and prosperity offer many temptations to abandon a wise lifestyle and live like a fool. Interestingly in pointing up preferences, he used the word "better" eight times (vv. 1 [twice], 2-3, 5, 8 [twice], 10).

a. How one lives matters (7:1)

7:1. The connection between the two halves of this verse are not as incidental or insignificant as some commentators claim. By using the Hebrew word for "oil" (**perfume**), which was both a symbol of joy (cf. 9:8) and prosperity (cf. Job 29:6) and a metaphor for reputation (cf. Song 1:3), Solomon combined the ideas of joy, prosperity, and reputation with the ideas of **birth** and **death**. So he suggested that it is **better** to come to the end of life with a good reputation (**good name**) than to have a joyful and auspicious beginning which, because of folly, might result in nothing.

This set the tone for the sayings which followed in which Solomon recommended how people should respond wisely to adversity and prosperity (cf. Ecc. 7:14) and warned them not to respond foolishly. Though Solomon had already demonstrated the limitations that death made on one's reputation (2:16; cf. 9:5) and though he would shortly demonstrate the limitations of wisdom (cf. 7:23-24; 9:11), he certainly did not advocate living foolishly (cf. his own example in 2:3, 9-11). After all, he did say that enjoyment of life was something God gave only to those who please Him (2:26), and he did warn that such enjoyment should be tempered by an awareness that God will judge everyone's deeds (11:9; 12:14).

b. It is wise to reflect on the brevity of life (7:2-4)

7:2-4. Solomon followed his comment about the value of maintaining a good reputation till death with a series of sayings about the wisdom of reflecting on the brevity of life. Reminding his readers that **death is the destiny of every man,** Solomon said that **the living should take this to heart,** or reflect on it. Continuing to comment on the "heart" (the seat of reflection and of moral decision and action; cf. Prov. 4:23), a word that occurs in each of these three verses, Solomon recommended (Ecc. 7:4) that people reflect soberly on the brevity of life (**the heart of the wise is in the house of mourning**) rather than be involved in foolish pleasure (**the heart of fools is in**

the house of pleasure). It is in this sense that Solomon said **a house of mourning** should be preferred to **a house of feasting,** that is, sober reflection should be preferred to levity. In the same vein he added that **sorrow is better than laughter.**

Such sober reflection can lead to moral improvement (**a sad face** [reflective of a serious mood; cf. Gen. 40:7] **is good for the heart**). Solomon's advice thus had in view wise moral behavior. This is similar to Psalm 90:12, where Moses, after lamenting the brevity of human life, said, "Teach us to number our days aright, that we may gain a heart of wisdom." Present-day society, which emphasizes self-centered hedonism, desperately needs to heed this reminder.

c. Foolish pleasure is vain and frivolous (7:5-6)

7:5-6. Comparing the frivolous pleasure **of fools**—their songs and their **laughter**—to **the crackling of** quick-burning **thorns under a pot** (cf. Ps. 118:12), Solomon said it was **meaningless,** vain, or useless. Thus it is more beneficial to live life wisely in light of the sober warning of life's brevity than to live as if life were one continual banquet (Ecc. 7:2-4). Also **it is better to** give **heed** to the warnings, corrections, and rebukes of the **wise** than to engage in foolish pleasure.

d. Adversity and prosperity bring temptations (7:7-10)

7:7. Having recommended that it was wise to live life in light of its brevity and to heed the warnings of the wise, Solomon then warned his readers that adversity and prosperity offer many temptations to abandon a wise lifestyle and to live like a fool. With a further wordplay on the word "heart" (cf. comments on vv. 3-4), Solomon said that the temptation to prosperity could even corrupt **the heart of** a **wise man**; he might give in to bribery. Moreover, he could succumb to the pressures of adversity. Oppression (the normal meaning of this word rather than **extortion**; cf. 4:1; 5:8) might turn him **into a fool.**

7:8-10. While suffering adversity a person might also be tempted in other ways to live like a fool. He might become impatient (v. 8) or be **provoked** to **anger** (v. 9), or complain about his lot, longing for **the** good **old days** (v. 10). Also in the light of an auspicious **beginning** he might become proud or haughty (v. 8). All these actions and attitudes are essentially contrary to the submissive attitude Solomon later implied in view of God's sovereignty (v. 13). Therefore they are foolish (v. 9b) and unwise (v. 10b).

e. Prosperity is beneficial if used wisely (7:11-12)

7:11-12. When accompanied by wisdom, prosperity can be beneficial. Solomon stated that wisdom is an added boon to prosperity. The translation, "Wisdom along with an inheritance is good" (NASB), is preferable to **Wisdom, like an inheritance, is a good thing** (NIV). The Hebrew preposition *'im* regularly means "with," and Solomon's purpose here was not to compare wisdom to prosperity but to show the value of prosperity *accompanied by* wisdom. **Wisdom,** in addition to providing **shelter** (lit., "shade") or protection (cf. Num. 14:9 for the metaphorical use of this word), **preserves the life of its possessor.** Other things being equal, a person who avoids a foolish lifestyle will live longer (cf. Ecc. 7:17; Prov. 13:14).

f. God's providence is immutable and inscrutable (7:13-14)

7:13-14. Solomon closed his treatment on the wise response to adversity and prosperity by reminding his readers that **God** sovereignly disposes of both and that His disposition of them is immutable (cf. 3:14) and inscrutable. Though people might find fault with God's ways (**what God has done**), no one can change what He thinks is wrong or unfair (**Who can straighten what He has made crooked?**). Moreover, God so mingles together adversity and prosperity that **man cannot discover anything about his future** (cf. 8:7; 10:14). In view of this, Solomon recommended submission to God's sovereignty, enjoying the **good** times (**be happy**) and remembering (**consider**) in **bad** times that adversity has inscrutable purposes beyond finite human understanding (cf. 8:17).

2. MAN'S IGNORANCE OF THE SIGNIFICANCE OF RIGHTEOUSNESS AND WISDOM (7:15-29)

The argument of this section has generally been misunderstood. This may be due to a failure to relate it to the preceding section (vv. 1-14) and the failure to recognize that Solomon was seeking to combat a false concept, namely, the rigid application of the doctrine of retribution by some of the wisdom teachers of his day. (Cf. Job 4:7-9; 8:20; 34:11-12; 36:6-7 for examples of overly rigid applications of this doctrine.)

Solomon argued that prosperity (cf. Ecc. 7:11-12) was no sure indication of God's pleasure, nor was adversity (cf. vv. 2-4) a sure sign of His anger. Solomon had seen the wicked prospering and the righteous perishing (v. 15). So a person should not depend on his righteousness as the means of guaranteeing reward (v. 16). Moreover, absolute righteousness is impossible because no one is so righteous that he always avoids sin (v. 20) or so wise that he is always able to avoid the snares of wickedness and folly (vv. 26-28). Besides, Solomon said, no one is wise enough to understand God's scheme of things (v. 24).

a. Avoid depending on your righteousness and living wickedly (7:15-18)

These verses contain advice on how to live in the light of God's enigmatic disposition of prosperity and adversity. In the light of the exceptions to the doctrine of retribution which Solomon had observed (v. 15), he advised against depending on one's own righteousness (v. 16). However, he continued to warn against indulging in wickedness because of its potential danger (v. 17).

7:15. Solomon said that in his brief or fleeting lifetime (not a **meaningless life** as in NIV; cf. comments on 3:19; 6:12) he had **seen** exceptions to the doctrine that God rewards the righteous and punishes the wicked. He had seen the **righteous . . . perishing** and the **wicked . . . living long.** The word "in" in the phrases **in his righteousness** and **in his wickedness** can here mean "in spite of." These phrases "in his righteousness" and "in his wickedness" argue against the common view that in 7:16 Solomon was warning against legalistic or Pharisaic self-righteousness. Such would have been a sin and would have been so acknowledged by Solomon who was concerned about *true* exceptions to the doctrine of retribution, not supposed ones (cf. 8:10-14 where this doctrine is discussed again).

7:16-18. These verses have generally been interpreted as teaching the "golden mean" or a moderate lifestyle, avoiding both overzealous righteousness and overindulgent sinfulness. And righteousness here is generally interpreted as referring to legalistic or Pharisaic self-righteousness. But this interpretation fails to relate these verses adequately to Solomon's argument against the rigid application of the doctrine of retribution in God's distributing adversity and prosperity. Moreover, the meaning of the verb *tiššômēm* (from *šāmēm*) must be correctly interpreted. Though almost universally interpreted in the sense of "to **destroy** or ruin oneself," the verb in this form never means this elsewhere. Instead it means "to be appalled or astounded" (cf. Dan. 8:27, "appalled"; Ps. 143:4, "dismayed"). This fits in nicely with Solomon's argument here. He urged his readers **not** to **be overrighteous** or **overwise** "lest they be confounded or astonished." He meant they should not depend on their righteousness or wisdom to guarantee God's blessing because *they* might be confounded, dismayed, or disappointed like the righteous people whom Solomon had seen perishing in spite of their righteousness (Ecc. 7:15).

Also the fact that God did not punish in some cases (cf. v. 15b) should not be taken as a license to sin (**do not be overwicked,** v. 17); God might judge them and they might die before they had to (**die before your time**; cf. Ps. 55:23). Solomon closed his argument in this section by noting that **it is good to** follow both warnings and by recommending that one who **fears God** (cf. Ecc. 3:14; 5:7; 8:12; 12:13) should **avoid all** (or better, "both") **extremes** (7:18). As in 2:14 and 3:19, the Hebrew word *kōl* can mean either "both" or "all." The two extremes to avoid are (a) depending on one's own righteousness and (b) becoming loose in one's living (being overly wicked).

It should be noted what Solomon *did not* say or imply in 7:16-18. Solomon's advice should not be taken to imply that he believed in halfhearted obedience to God's commands or advocated a little wickedness and a little folly. Though he believed that complete righteousness is unattainable (v. 20) and that some folly is unavoidable (see comments on vv. 26-29), he never advocated folly or wickedness. Instead he advocated living life in the light of God's judgment (11:9; 12:14). Though he had observed exceptions to the doctrine of retribution (7:15; 8:10-11), he nevertheless believed that God would judge (3:17; 8:12-13). Solomon's only uncertainty about God's judgment was its timing; like everything else, it would be in God's time (3:17; cf. 3:11). So people should avoid folly and wickedness as much as possible and live as wisely and as righteously as possible.

b. Wisdom though valuable gives inadequate protection (7:19-24)

Solomon had recognized the inadequacy of righteousness to provide protection because of a seemingly uneven application of the doctrine of retribution (v. 15). Moreover, he added, no person is truly righteous (vv. 20-22). Though he acknowledged wisdom's protective power (v. 19), Solomon also demonstrated from his own experience that complete wisdom is unattainable (vv. 23-24).

7:19. Since righteousness cannot always protect from adversity (as demonstrated in vv. 15-16), some other protective power—perhaps that of wisdom—is needed. Solomon affirmed that wisdom does give more protection than military strength: **Wisdom makes one wise man more powerful than 10 rulers in a city.** (See an example of this in 9:13-18; cf. Prov. 21:22.)

7:20-22. The need for wisdom is here made explicit by the Hebrew particle *kî* ("for," KJV; "indeed," NASB; not trans. in the NIV). Solomon noted that wisdom is needed "for" (or "because") righteousness is ineffective. No one is truly **righteous**; no one continually **does . . . right** ("good," NASB) **and never sins.** This absence of true righteousness is easily seen in the practice of one's servants (v. 21) and himself (v. 22); both had **cursed** ("reviled," JB) **others.**

7:23-24. However, Solomon immediately added that **wisdom** also has its limitations. Though he himself had applied all his great wisdom (1:16) to understand the enigmas in God's distribution of prosperity and adversity (7:1-18) and though he was **determined to be wise** (v. 23), he acknowledged that true wisdom was far **beyond** him. He also noted that nobody can comprehend or grasp what has happened (v. 24). The rendering, "Whatever has happened lies beyond our grasp, deep down, deeper than man can fathom" (NEB) gives the thought well. The NIV wrongly adds the word **wisdom** to verse 24 (the Heb. phrase *mah šᵉhāyâh* means "what has happened" or "what exists," as in 1:9; 3:15; 6:10).

c. True righteousness and true wisdom are nonexistent (7:25-29)

This passage is often misinterpreted because of the failure to understand the wisdom concepts being used here. Contrary to the views of many modern commentators the terms in these verses are used with moral and ethical connotations. Of course this is true of the phrases and terms one "who pleases God" (v. 26), "sinner" (v. 26), and "upright" (vv. 28-29). But also, as in Proverbs, the term "folly" is virtually synonymous with "wickedness" (v. 25); "wisdom" (v. 25) is virtually synonymous with "righteousness." Wisdom emphasizes moral skillfulness, while folly emphasizes moral indiscretion (cf. Prov. 1:3; 2:1-3 with Prov. 2:9-11).

Also a proper understanding of this section depends on recognizing that Solomon personified folly somewhat as he did in Proverbs 1-9. The woman who is a snare (Ecc. 7:26) is "Lady Folly," symbolized and epitomized in Proverbs by the adulteress (cf. Prov. 9:13-19 with Prov. 7; also cf. Zech. 5:7-8). Thus Solomon argued in this section that in his search to discover the place of wisdom in the scheme of things (Ecc. 7:25) he found that, though folly was a fate worse than death, only those pleasing to God escape folly's clutches (v. 26). He also discovered in this same search that such people are rare—in fact they are nearly nonexistent (v. 28). However, he noted that such a situation is not of divine but of human origin (v. 29).

7:25. The terminology in this verse is similar to Solomon's description of his earlier reflection on the relationship between wisdom and folly (2:12-17). He had already demonstrated the limitations of wisdom from his own experience (7:23-24). Now he reported on an investigation into the value of wisdom in relationship to wickedness and folly that further confirmed wisdom's limitations. The synonyms **to understand, to investigate, and to search** emphasize his diligence in seeking to comprehend **wisdom and the scheme of things.** ("And" should be rendered "in," pointing to "wisdom" and "scheme" as a hendiadys, a figure of speech in which two coordinated nouns form one concept. E.g., in Gen. 3:16 the literal Heb. phrase "pain and childbearing" refers to "pain in childbearing.") By this diligent search Solomon hoped **to understand** how stupid and insane **wickedness** and **folly** really are.

7:26. Solomon said that he made several discoveries in his investigation. First he discovered that "lady Folly" is worse **(more bitter) than death.** She **is a snare** and **a trap,** whose ways confine a person like **chains** (cf. Prov. 2:18-19; 5:3-6; 7:24-26). Second he discovered that only **the man who pleases God** (cf. Ecc. 2:26) can **escape her.**

7:27-28. Solomon also reported that in his continuing quest to **discover the scheme of things (still searching** modifies "scheme"), he made a third discovery: hardly anybody is **upright.** That this, however, is the nature of Solomon's third discovery may not be too clear because of (a) the elliptical nature of the wording in verse 28b, (b) the misunderstanding of the parallelism of the verse, and (c) the figures of speech employed in it. When Solomon said that he **found one . . . man among a thousand,** he did not define what he meant by "man." The Hebrew word is *'āḏām,* the generic word for man as well as the proper name Adam. Some commentators suggest that Solomon meant that nobody is as good as he was intended to be, that is, like Adam before the Fall. The NIV, on the other hand, adds the word "upright" to verse 28, understanding an ellipsis of this word which appears in verse 29. However, it is probably more in keeping with the argument of verses 26-29 to supply the ellipsis from verse 26, "a man who pleases [or, 'is pleasing to'] God." Using hyperbole, Solomon said that such men are extremely rare, that is, one in a thousand (cf. Job 9:3; 33:23 for the same figure).

Then Solomon added that **not one** such **woman** may be found. This does not mean that one out of every thousand males is pleasing to God and that no women at all please Him. Such a point hardly fits Solomon's argument. Instead, in the last line of Ecclesiastes 7:28 Solomon used (a) a kind of complementary parallelism in which the generic term *'āḏām* ("man") is explained as including also the feminine gender in the sense of "mankind," and (b) a kind of graded numerical sequence in which the second of two terms gives the climax or point (cf. Prov. 30:15, 18, 21). In this parallelism and numerical sequence his purpose was to say that such people—both men and women—are not only scarce but are nonexistent; there is "not one" **among them all.** This is also supported by the fact that "men" in Ecclesiastes 7:29 is "they" in Hebrew (i.e., both men and women).

7:29. Solomon, however, quickly noted that the reason for man's universal perversion was man's devising, not God's. **God made mankind** (*'āḏām*; cf. v. 28) **upright, but men** (lit., "they," i.e., men and women) **have gone in search of many schemes** (cf. "scheme" in vv. 25, 27 and "schemes" in 8:11). In other words, though people cannot know God's "scheme of things" they do follow their *own* schemes, which causes them to lack true uprightness, true righteousness, and true wisdom, and to fail to please God.

3. MAN'S IGNORANCE OF THE ENIGMA OF DIVINE RETRIBUTION (CHAP. 8)

The key to interpreting this chapter properly is seeing how its two parts are related. The chapter begins with a question and a statement that magnify the value of wisdom (v. 1) and closes with an acknowledgment of wisdom's limitations (v. 17). Wisdom enables a wise man to avoid the king's wrath (vv. 2-9), but not even a wise man can figure out the enigmas in God's distribution of justice (vv. 10-17).

a. *A wise man can avoid the king's wrath (8:1-9)*

The background for this section is the recognition of the absolute authority of the king (cf. Prov. 24:21-22) and the need for proper decorum to avert his wrath (cf. Prov. 14:35; 16:14; 20:2).

(1) A wise man knows the proper decorum. **8:1.** A **wise man** is able to practice proper decorum. In two rhetorical questions Solomon affirmed that only a wise man can size up situations properly and act accordingly. Only he **knows**

the explanation (*pēšer*) **of things.** The noun *pēšer* occurs only here in Hebrew. In the Aramaic in Daniel it refers to the interpretation of dreams (cf. Dan. 5:12). Here it is applied to the Hebrew word *dābār* ("matter, affair," trans. "things" in the NIV). Because of his wisdom a wise person knows how to act graciously and avoid brash behavior which would lead to his harm (cf. Prov. 14:35). For the two figures of speech (in the last two lines of Ecc. 8:1) where behavior is reflected in one's **face** or **appearance,** see Numbers 6:25 and Proverbs 7:13.

(2) Obedience to the king is of paramount importance. **8:2-4.** Solomon then set forth examples of proper decorum before a king. A king has great authority: he *can* (not **will** as in the NIV) **do whatever he pleases,** his **word is supreme,** and no one **can say to him, What are you doing?** (Cf. Job 9:12; Isa. 45:9 where the same idea is applied to God.) Therefore people should **obey** the king, maintain allegiance to him (**do not be in a hurry to leave** his **presence,** i.e., as suggested by the Heb. to resign from his service; cf. 10:4), and not be rebellious toward him by standing **up for a bad cause.**

(3) Proper decorum averts harm (8:5-9). **8:5-7.** Affirming that obedience to a king's **command** would avert **harm,** Solomon commended the value of wisdom, saying that **the wise** person would **know** the best course of action and when to apply it (**the proper time and procedure,** lit., "time and judgment"). Such wisdom is necessary, according to Solomon, because people (*'āḏām* is generic, referring to people in general) suffer harm (**a man's misery weighs heavily upon him**). The word for "misery" (*rā'âh*) is related to the word for "harm" (*rā'*) in verse 5. This misery comes because people are ignorant of "what will happen" and "when it will happen" (v. 7, NASB; not **what is to come** as in the NIV for the Heb. word means "when," not "what").

8:8-9. The reason for such misery is the inescapable consequences of wickedness that arise from such ignorance; just as **no man** can control **the wind** (cf. Prov. 27:16), postpone **the day of his death,** or be **discharged** while in the midst of battle, so **no** man can escape the consequences of his **wickedness.** The first three clauses in Ecclesiastes 8:8 are parallel in Hebrew and are comparative to the last clause. Solomon observed these things as he **applied** his **mind** (cf. 1:17; 8:16) to what was **done under the sun** (cf. comments on 1:3).

The consequences Solomon had in view here resulted from a ruler's anger (the harm a wise man can escape by proper decorum; cf. 8:1) as is clear from verse 9 where Solomon referred to a ruler lording **it over others to** their **hurt.** (The NIV marg., "to their hurt," is preferred to "to his own hurt." The pronoun refers back to "others," which is lit., 'ādām, "men.")

b. Even a wise man cannot understand God's judgment (8:10-17)

This section is often misunderstood because verses 16-17 are often separated from it and placed with 9:1–11:6 (cf., e.g., Christian D. Ginsburg, *The Song of Songs and Coheleth*, p. 406). However, the recurrence of the divider phrase "cannot discover" (8:17; cf. 7:14, 28) argues for the inclusion of verses 16-17 with verses 10-15. This is also supported by the bracketing effects of verse 1 ("the wise man . . . knows") and verse 17 ("man cannot discover" and "a wise man . . . cannot really comprehend"). Verses 16-17 thus refer in particular to the enigma of God's work of divine judgment.

(1) Failure to punish wickedness is a great enigma (8:10-14). **8:10-12a.** Solomon had noted that wickedness is not always punished (cf. 3:16; 4:1). He had seen that **the wicked** have access to **the holy place** (i.e., the temple), die, are **buried,** and even are praised **in the city where they** practiced wickedness. Affirming that such a contradiction of the doctrine of retribution was **meaningless** (*heḇel*; cf. 1:2) or enigmatic, Solomon lamented the fact that **a wicked man** could sin with impunity (i.e., commit **100 crimes and live a long time,** 8:12). According to Solomon, man's failure to carry out retribution (e.g., to punish **a crime . . . quickly,** v. 11) often leads to more wrongdoing: then **the hearts of the people are filled with schemes to do wrong** (cf. 7:29).

8:12b-14. These verses are one long sentence in the Hebrew. Verse 14 is the main clause of a subordinate clause consisting of verses 12b-13 and introduced by the Hebrew particle *gam* (meaning "though," not "still" or "yet" as in NASB, KJV; not trans. in NIV) before the words I

know. Solomon firmly believed in the doctrine of retribution: life is **better** for **God-fearing** people (cf. 3:14; 5:7; 7:18; 12:13) but does **not go well** for **the wicked** whose lives will be shortened (cf. Prov. 2:22; 10:27; 29:1). Yet Solomon had observed contradictions to retribution. He had seen the **righteous . . . get what the wicked deserve and** the **wicked . . . get what the righteous deserve.** Solomon affirmed emphatically that such a contradiction in the distributing of divine justice is enigmatic or **meaningless** (cf. Ecc. 8:10; "meaningless" occurs as a bracket at the beginning and the end of v. 14).

(2) Enjoy the life God gives. **8:15.** Having shown that there are enigmatic contradictions in the doctrine of retribution—righteousness is not always rewarded and wickedness is not always punished, and sometimes the wicked prosper and the righteous meet with disaster—Solomon again recommended **the enjoyment of life.** He said that life's best is to enjoy the fruits of one's labor (i.e., to **eat and drink;** cf. 2:24; 3:13; 5:18) **and** "to rejoice" or **be glad** (cf. 3:12; 5:19). Also he noted that this **joy** would enliven one's labor (i.e., it would **accompany him in his work**). As is obvious from earlier occurrences of this theme (cf. 2:24-26; 3:12, 22; 5:18-20), this is not Epicurean hedonism based on despair but is a note of submission. Man cannot control or predict adversity or prosperity; however, each day's joys should be received as gifts from God's hand and be savored as God permits (3:13; 5:19). All this is to be while one is **under the sun** (twice in 8:15; cf. comments on 1:3).

(3) No man can comprehend God's providence. **8:16-17.** Solomon closed his treatment of the enigma of contradictions in divine retribution much as he had concluded his discussions on the significance of adversity and prosperity (7:1-14) and on the significance of righteousness and wisdom (7:15-29), namely, by acknowledging man's ignorance of God's ways (cf. 7:14b, 28a). After searching diligently (**I applied my mind;** cf. 1:17; 8:9) **to** gain **wisdom** and observing **man's** many activities, he concluded that man is ignorant of God's work (the phrases **all that God has done** and **what goes on under the sun** are synonymous). In emphatic terms, repeating the negative three times

(v. 17) and the verb "comprehend" twice —**no one can comprehend . . . man cannot discover . . . he cannot really comprehend**—Solomon said that no one can understand God's ways (3:11; cf. Isa. 55:9; Rom. 11:33) **even if** he expended all his energies or were **wise** and claimed he could.

C. Man does not know what will happen (9:1–11:6)

This section is characterized by the repetition of the phrase "no man knows" (cf. 9:1, 12; 10:14) and "you do not know" (cf. 11:2, 6). It deals with man's inability to predict what will happen to him, whether good or bad (cf. 9:1), or whether his work will fail or succeed (cf. 9:11-12; 11:2, 6). Contrary to the writings of some, this formula ("no man knows" and "you do not know") serve to *introduce* the subsections, not *conclude* them, as is evident from their occurrences in 9:1 and 11:2.

1. NO ONE KNOWS WHAT WILL HAPPEN TO HIM (9:1-10)

a. Summary: No one knows what awaits him (9:1)

9:1. This verse closely relates verses 2-10 to the preceding section, as indicated in the NIV translation, **So I reflected on all this and concluded that the righteous and the wise and what they do are in God's hands.** The "all this" that Solomon "reflected on" is human ignorance of the significance of righteousness and wickedness in God's sovereign disposition of adversity and prosperity (chaps. 7–8). Solomon "concluded" (lit., "my heart saw") from his prior reflections "on all this" that people are not masters of their own fate; people and "what they do" are subject to God's sovereign will (i.e., they "are in God's hands"; cf. Prov. 21:1 for a similar use of this figure). Since one does not know God's providence, neither does he know whether he will experience prosperity or adversity, or **whether** he will be the object of **love** or **hate** (for a similar use of these two nouns; cf. Mal. 1:2-3).

b. All people are subject to the same fate (9:2-3)

9:2-3. Solomon supported the statement that nobody knows what awaits him (v. 1) by stating that **all** people **share**

the same fate or **common destiny.** However, there is some ambiguity as to the nature of that fate because of a common failure to relate the beginning of verse 2 to the end of verse 1. The same fate or destiny relates to the "love or hate," adversity or prosperity, referred to in verse 1. The Hebrew is literally, "whether it will be love or hate, no man knows"; both (i.e., love and hate—for this use of *kōl*; cf. 2:14; 3:19; 7:18) are before them (i.e., the righteous and the wise, 9:1). Both love and hate are experienced by everyone; there is one fate (or destiny) for **the righteous and the wicked.** This commonality of fate applies to **the good and the bad,** those who are ritually **clean** as well as those who are ritually **unclean, those who offer sacrifices** as well as **those who do not. . . . those who are afraid to take** God's **name** in **oaths** (cf. Ex. 20:7, "misuse the name of the LORD") as well as **those who** are not afraid to do so. **The same destiny** befalls **all** these. The bad part of all this (i.e., **the evil in everything that happens under the sun**), Solomon wrote, is that this common fate causes people to be rampant in sin (people's **hearts . . . are full of evil and . . . madness;** cf. Ecc. 8:11). Solomon added that not only does everybody (including the righteous and the wise, 9:1) share this same inscrutable distribution of adversity and prosperity *during* life, but they also share the same ultimate fate *after* life; **they** all **join the dead.**

c. Life is preferable to death (9:4-6)

9:4-6. However, despite the fact that all people, both righteous and wicked, are subject to the same inscrutable distribution of adversity and prosperity and ultimately join one another in death, they should not despair of life. Life has advantages over death. Comparing the lot of **a live dog** with that of **a dead lion,** Solomon affirmed that it is better to be alive and dishonored (cf. 1 Sam. 17:43; the dog was the most despised animal) than to be honored and dead (cf. Prov. 30:30; the lion was the most honored beast). **The living** at least have consciousness and **hope,** things they can look forward to enjoying. But **the dead** have no consciousness (they **know nothing**) or hope of **reward** or enjoyment. Moreover, their passions—**their love, their hate, and their jealousy**—are stilled. As Ginsburg has noted, the concepts of consciousness and unconsciousness here are not in their barest forms as though these verses taught soul sleep. Instead they should be understood in the context of enjoying life (Ecc. 9:7-9) and possessing the capacities for enjoyment; the living have those capabilities but the dead do not (*The Song of Songs and Coheleth*, pp. 414-5). Thus the living have opportunities and capacities for fruitful labor but the dead do not (v. 10). The living have opportunities for reward from that labor, but the dead do not (v. 5; the word trans. "reward" refers to wages or earnings). The living have capacities for enjoyment (vv. 7-9), but the dead do not (v. 6). Solomon was not describing what the state of the dead *is*; he was stating what it is *not*. He did this to emphasize the lost opportunities of this present life, opportunities for serving God and enjoying His gifts (cf. Isa. 38:11, 18-19 for similar ideas). Solomon added that the dead **never again . . . have a part in anything that happens under the sun** (cf. comments on Ecc. 1:3). The word for "part" (*ḥēleq*, "lot, portion, allotment") is the word he used elsewhere of life and its enjoyments (3:22; 5:18-19; 9:9).

Some commentators see a contradiction between 9:4-6 and 4:2-3 ("the dead . . . are happier than the living"). However, no real contradiction is here because Solomon was stating that a person who experiences the pressures of oppression (4:1) may feel that death is preferable. On the other hand in 9:4-6 (and in vv. 7-10) Solomon stressed that when a person is dead opportunities for enjoying life are gone. The two passages view life and death from different perspectives.

d. Enjoy life as God enables (9:7-9)

9:7-9. In view of the uncertainties of what the future may bring, whether adversity or prosperity (vv. 1-3), and in view of the certainty of death with the loss of all opportunity for enjoyment (vv. 4-6), Solomon again recommended enjoying life as God's good gift (cf. 2:24-26; 3:12-13, 22; 5:18-19). Solomon here spelled out in greater detail than elsewhere some of the aspects of life which should be enjoyed: **food** (lit., "bread") and **wine** which sustain life and make it merry (cf. Ps. 104:15), fine clothes and

pleasant lotions (cf. 2 Sam. 12:20 where they are the opposites of mournful grief), enjoyment of **life with** one's **wife** (cf. Prov. 18:22). In short, these include both the basic necessities of life and some luxuries God bestows as His gifts (cf. Ecc. 5:19). Solomon underlined the need to enjoy these gifts by emphasizing life's brevity. He did this by almost repeating a phrase, **all the days of this meaningless life** and **all your meaningless days.** "Meaningless" here (*hebel*) should be rendered "fleeting" (cf. comments on 3:19; 6:12; 7:15).

Affirming that **this is** one's **lot** (*ḥēleq*; cf. 3:22; 5:18-19 and contrast 9:6 where the same word is trans. "part") **in life** and **labor under the sun** (cf. comments on 1:3), Solomon encouraged his readers to enjoy life because it is God's will for them to do so. He stated, "God has already approved your works" (NASB; preferred over NIV's **God favors what you do**). By this he summarized what he had previously said about the enjoyment of life: (a) wealth and possessions, which stem from one's "labor," ultimately are gifts of God (5:18-19), (b) only God gives the ability to enjoy the fruits of one's labor (cf. 2:24; 3:13; 5:18), and (c) the ability to enjoy those things depends on whether one pleases God (2:26). So the statement "God has already approved your works" means that possessing God's gifts and the ability to enjoy them evidence God's prior approval that one can do so; if God had not so approved the gifts, one could not enjoy them.

e. Labor diligently while you can (9:10)

9:10. Besides encouraging his readers to enjoy life as God enabled them, Solomon also encouraged them to work diligently. The idiom **whatever your hand finds to do** means "whatever you are able to do" (cf. 1 Sam. 10:7). Whatever a person is able to do, he should **do it with all** his **might**, that is, expend all his energies. The reason for this advice is that when death comes all opportunities for work and service will cease. In death a person will have no further energies or abilities to work; there will be **neither working nor planning nor knowledge nor wisdom.** (This does not suggest soul sleep; see comments on Ecc. 9:5.)

2. NO ONE KNOWS WHETHER HIS WISDOM WILL SUCCEED (9:11–10:11)

The preceding section (9:1-10) began with a statement that the righteous and the wise are subject to the same uncertain future as anyone else (9:1). Then in 9:2-10 Solomon discussed this fact with regard to the *righteous* (in contrast with the wicked), and now (in 9:11–10:11) he showed that the wise are also subject to an uncertain future.

a. Introduction: Wisdom is subject to the uncertainty of the future (9:11-12)

9:11-12. The fact that wisdom is subject to the future's uncertainty is introduced by a series of five human abilities, each of which fails to succeed. The last three relate to a wise person: **the wise . . . the brilliant . . . the learned.** As a **race** is not always won by the swiftest runner, or a victory in a **battle** always won by the mightiest soldiers, so also the wise do not always earn a living (i.e., gain **food,** lit., ''bread''), get rich, or acquire a great reputation (gain **favor).**

The reason for such failures is that **all** people are subject to times of misfortune (**time and chance** is another example of a hendiadys; cf. comments on 7:25) which no man is able to predict (9:12, **no man knows . . . his hour**; lit., ''his time''). This refers back to times of misfortune (v. 11), not merely to death. Comparing such times of misfortune to a **net** and a **snare** by which **birds** and **fish** are **caught,** Solomon said that such **evil times** come suddenly and **unexpectedly upon them,** thus nullifying their abilities.

b. Wisdom may be unrewarded because of negligence (9:13-16)

9:13-16. An **example of wisdom** not being rewarded (v. 11) is a **poor wise man** who had delivered a **small,** poorly defended **city** from a siege by **a powerful king.** But the **poor man's wisdom** went unrewarded because **nobody remembered** him (also in 1 Sam. 25:31 ''remember'' conveys the idea of ''reward''). Solomon said this example **greatly impressed** him, that is, it was significant to him (lit., ''it was great to me'' in the light of his previous discussion, Ecc. 9:11-12). Though **wisdom** had proven **better than strength,** that is, military might (cf. 7:11-12; 9:18; Prov. 21:22), that **poor** wise man received no benefit from

his wisdom. His **wisdom** was **despised and his words** were not **heeded,** and he remained poor and unremembered (i.e., unrewarded with wealth or social esteem; cf. Ecc. 9:11).

c. Wisdom's value may be nullified by a little folly (9:17–10:1)

9:17–10:1. After giving the example of the poor wise man whose wisdom did not benefit him (9:13-16) Solomon warned that though wisdom deserves attention, its value can be nullified by a little folly. Alluding to his previous example, Solomon said **The quiet words of the wise are more to be heeded than the shouts of a ruler of fools** because **wisdom is better than weapons of war** (cf. 7:19; 9:16). Playing on the word ''good'' or ''better''—the same Hebrew word *ṭôḇâh*—and the contrast between ''one'' and ''much,'' Solomon said that **one sinner destroys much good.** In other words, **a little folly** can destroy the great value of **wisdom,** as **dead flies** in **perfume** ruin it by giving it **a bad smell.** The use of the Hebrew words for **outweighs** and **honor** is another interesting wordplay, for both words are used for weight or value and social esteem.

d. Wisdom's value may be nullified by a ruler's caprice (10:2-7)

Speaking of ''errors,'' literally ''sin'' (v. 4; cf. ''sinner,'' 9:18), ''fool,'' and ''fools'' (10:3, 6; cf. ''folly,'' v. 1), Solomon gave another example of how a little folly nullifies the great value of wisdom. Though wisdom suggests ways to maintain one's position at court (vv. 2-4), that position may be subverted by an error of some leader.

10:2-4. Solomon set forth the value of wisdom by stating that a **wise** person has the quality of **heart** and mind that will protect him from danger (cf. 7:12). This is stated in the words **inclines to the right,** which are literally ''is at his right hand'' (as in the KJV); as is well known, the right hand was the place of protection (cf. Pss. 16:8; 110:5; 121:5). Conversely a **fool** lacks such **sense** which is evidenced by his foolish behavior. Using a common figure for moral behavior—walking in the way (cf. 1 Sam. 8:3; 2 Kings 21:21)—Solomon said that **even as he walks along the road, the fool . . . shows everyone how stupid he is.**

Solomon then gave an example of how wisdom can protect one who possesses it. With a deliberate wordplay on the double sense of the Hebrew verb *nûaḥ*, meaning "to leave or abandon" or "to give rest to," Solomon advised that the wisest course when confronted with a king's **anger** is not to **leave** (*tannaḥ*) one's **post** (i.e., not to resign his office; cf. Ecc. 8:3) because calm and cool composure (cf. Prov. 14:30 for a somewhat similar use of the noun "calmness") could **lay great errors** (lit., "sins"; actually it is the anger caused by such sins, a metonymy of cause for effect) **to rest** (*yannîaḥ*; cf. Prov. 16:14 for a similar idea).

10:5-7. Though Solomon affirmed that a wise man's good sense might suggest ways to maintain his position before an angry king (v. 4), he also noted that one's position or job is not always awarded on the basis of merit. The Hebrew word for "errors" in verse 4 means sins, but the word for "error" is verse 5 means an inadvertent mistake, something done without proper consideration (cf. 5:6 where the same word is trans. "mistake"). The word for "ruler" in 10:5 differs from "ruler's" in verse 4. In verse 4 the word for ruler's (*môšēl*) emphasizes one's dominion or reign, whereas in verse 5 the word for ruler (*šallîṭ*) emphasizes one's sovereignty or domineering mastery (the same root is in 8:4 [*šilṭôn*, "supreme"] and 8:9 [*šallaṭ*, "lords it over"]). Solomon stated that he had seen **an evil** *rā'âh*; cf. 5:13, 16; 6:1) **under the sun** (cf. comments on 1:3), **the sort of error that arises from a ruler,** that is, the kind of reversal of roles that results from a ruler's caprice. Solomon had seen **fools** occupying **high positions while the rich** (who were supposedly therefore wise; cf. Prov. 14:24; 19:10) occupied **the low** positions. He also had **seen slaves** riding **on horseback,** a position of honor (cf. Jer. 17:25), **while princes** went **on foot like slaves.** Thus since position was not assigned on the basis of merit but on the basis of a ruler's caprice, the value of wisdom was often nullified.

e. Wisdom's value may be nullified by improper timing (10:8-11)

10:8-9. Verses 8-11, whose figurative language and proverbial character have occasioned a great variety of interpreta-

tions, are carefully related to one another. Thus the repetition of the words **snake** and **bitten** at the beginning (v. 8) and "snake bites" at the end (v. 11) forms a bracketing effect (an *inclusio*). Also Solomon repeated the Hebrew word *yitrôn* ("profit"; cf. comments on 1:3) in 10:10-11 (rendered "advantage" in v. 10 by NASB and not rendered at all in NIV). Though wisdom has advantages, that gain can be lost when wisdom is not applied or is applied too late.

Moreover, the reference to "ax" (v. 10) serves as a bridge between verse 9b, the last of four proverbs in verses 8-9, and the two contrasting proverbs in verses 10-11. Solomon strung together four proverbs that set forth the potential dangers inherent in representative daily tasks—digging **a pit,** tearing down **a wall,** quarrying **stones,** splitting **logs**—dangers which could only be averted by applying wisdom or prudence.

10:10-11. In log-splitting (v. 9) a man can either use wisdom and sharpen his **ax** or leave it **unsharpened** and **exert more** energy. Applying wisdom to using an ax makes it easier to succeed. "Wisdom has the advantage of giving success" (NASB).

However, in a contrasting proverb (v. 11) Solomon noted that a man's wisdom or skill has **no profit** if it is not applied at the proper time; **if a snake bites before it is charmed, the charmer** is in trouble. Thus Solomon showed in this series of proverbs that though wisdom is valuable in dangerous and difficult tasks, its value can be nullified by improper timing.

3. CRITICISM IS RISKY IN VIEW OF ONE'S IGNORANCE OF THE FUTURE (10:12-20)

Because there are few verbal links between the two parts (vv. 12-15 and vv. 16-20) in this section, it is crucial to see the link between Solomon's warning in verse 20 with the proverbial material in verses 12-15 and the link between his warning in verse 20 with the material in verses 16-19. Noting that multiplying words is foolish and self-destructive in view of one's ignorance of the future (vv. 12-15), Solomon warned against criticizing governmental officials (v. 20) even if their profligate leadership deserves such criticism (vv. 16-19). In this way Solomon counseled submission to governmental authority, a theme he had already broached in 8:2-3 and 10:4, which is well documented in other wisdom literature (e.g., Prov. 14:35; 24:21-22).

a. It is foolish to multiply words (10:12-15)

10:12-15. Solomon began this passage by contrasting the words of a wise man with those of a fool; **a wise man's words are gracious** (or, better, "win him favor"; Prov. 13:15 ["favor"]; 22:1 ["esteemed"] make similar use of this Heb. word *ḥēn*), **but** a fool's words are self-destructive (i.e., they consume him).

Using a merism, a figure of speech in which polar opposites are chosen to indicate totality (cf. examples in Ecc. 3:2-8), Solomon characterized a fool's speech as foolish and **wicked madness** both **at the beginning** and **at the end** (i.e., from start to finish). Though such is true of a fool's speech, he continues to multiply **words** (cf. 5:3; 6:11), oblivious to the fact that **no one knows** the future, **what is coming** in days ahead and **what will happen after** death. Besides being ignorant of the future, a fool is also ignorant of the most obvious; **he does not know the way to town** (cf. 10:3). This is a proverbial expression for extreme ignorance like the modern proverb, "He doesn't know enough to come in out of the rain." This is why a fool finds his **work** such a chore (it **wearies him**).

b. Criticism of profligate leadership is risky (10:16-20)

10:16-17. Solomon then strung together a series of proverbs describing the erosive effect of profligate leadership on a country and then warned against criticizing such bad leaders. In the first two of these proverbs, Solomon contrasted the sorry state of a nation whose leaders are incompetent and undisciplined (v. 16) with the fortunate (**blessed**) state of a nation whose leaders are competent and disciplined (v. 17). The former kind of leaders are childish (the "king is a child," NIV marg.; cf. Isa. 3:4 and 1 Kings 3:7 for the idea of incompetence and inexperience underlying this description). But the latter kind of leaders are well prepared by **noble birth** and training. Incompetent leaders are intemperate: they **feast in the morning** and are involved in revelry and **drunkenness** (Ecc. 10:17; see Isa. 5:11 and Acts 2:15 for similar ideas). But competent leaders are temperate: they **eat at a proper time—for strength and not for drunkenness.**

10:18-20. Solomon added that profligate, incompetent leaders are **lazy,** causing the ruin of the state and the loss of its protection, such as the sagging of **rafters** and the leaking of roofs. In their undisciplined lifestyle, they are involved in raucous feasting and merrymaking, which deplete state funds. The NEB renders this verse, "The table has its pleasures, and wine makes a cheerful life; and money is behind it all." The clause **money is the answer** (*ya' ăneh* from *'ānâh*) **for everything** means that the rulers *think* money can meet all their demands.

However, Solomon warned against criticizing such inadequate leaders. Aware that their hearts were the wellsprings of their thoughts and actions (Prov. 4:23), Solomon warned against reviling **the king even in** one's **thoughts** or cursing a **rich** man (i.e., a man in authority) in one's **bedroom.** The reason for such advice is that a report may get back to the king or rich person; **a bird** may tell them, that is, an unknown source may disclose one's secret criticisms.

4. WORK DILIGENTLY DESPITE IGNORANCE OF THE FUTURE (11:1-6)

Solomon closed his discussion on people's ignorance of the future (9:1–11:6) with some practical advice about their activities in view of such ignorance. To emphasize that man is ignorant of the future Solomon said, "You do not know" three times (11:2, 5-6); he also said, "You cannot understand" (v. 5). However, he counseled that ignorance of the future should lead not to inactivity or despair, but to diligent labor.

11:1-2. Solomon noted that people are as ignorant of God's providential dealings in human affairs (cf. 3:11; 8:17) as they are of "the path of the wind" and the formation of a baby in its "mother's womb" (11:5). Moreover, people do not know which of their ventures "will succeed" (v. 6) or what calamities might come on the earth (v. 2) and wipe out the results of their work. Even so, people should engage in diligent, active labor. Like the benefits that come from the seafaring trade of foodstuffs, so active involvement in business gives a promise of some return (v. 1; cf. 1 Kings 9:26-28;

10:22; Ps. 107:23 for references to maritime trade). But in view of the possibility of **disaster** a person should make prudent investments in numerous ventures (**to seven, yes to eight**) rather than put all his "eggs in one basket" (Ecc. 11:2; cf. Gen. 32:7-8 for a practical example of this advice). The NEB accurately reflects this interpretation of Ecclesiastes 11:1-2, "Send your grain across the seas, and in time you will get a return. Divide your merchandise among seven ventures, eight maybe, since you do not know what disasters may occur on earth."

11:3-4. Switching to an example of sowing seed and reaping a harvest, Solomon urged his readers not to sit around waiting for the most opportune moment to work but to be diligent constantly. The future is as beyond one's control as the acts of God in nature—the falling of **rain,** the uprooting of **a tree** by a gale. So waiting for just the right moment to **plant** (when there is no **wind** to blow away the seed) or to **reap** (when there is no rain in **the clouds** to threaten the ripened harvest) would result in inactivity.

11:5-6. In watching for **the wind** a farmer has no idea which **path** (direction) it will take. He is as ignorant of that as he is of something he cannot see such as a baby's **body** being **formed in** its **mother's womb.** Man cannot know the future or **the work of God** who has made and controls **all things** (cf. **Maker,** a title of God, in Job 4:17; 32:22; 35:10; Pss. 115:15; 121:2; Jer. 10:16). Using another merism (cf. Ecc. 10:13)—the polar opposites of **morning** and **evening** (11:6) to indicate total days—Solomon urged his readers to work diligently, sowing their **seed** all day long, because they could **not know which** sowing would **succeed, whether this or that, or whether both** would **do equally well.** Thus in two examples, one from maritime trade (vv. 1-2) and one from farming (vv. 3-4, 6) Solomon urged people toward constant, diligent effort and prudent diversified investment of their energies and resources, recognizing that all is in God's sovereign control.

IV. Conclusion: Live Joyously and Responsibly in the Fear of God (11:7–12:14)

Solomon has shown that human effort is futile because its results are not permanent and the prospect of enjoying those results is insecure (1:12–6:9). He has also shown that people cannot know which of their efforts will succeed because they are ignorant of God's plan and of what the future holds (6:10–11:6). Now Solomon returned to the theme of the enjoyment of life (cf. 2:24-26; 3:12, 22; 5:18-20; 8:15; 9:7-9) and explicitly related it to the idea of living acceptably before God. This is similar to what he had done at the first mention of this theme (2:24-26). The latter theme, that of living responsibly before God, is found at both the beginning (11:9; 12:1) and the end (12:13-14) of this section. The need for responsible living is further underlined by repeating the theme of the futility of all else (12:8) and by a brief treatment of the book's authority and value (12:9-12).

A. A call to live joyously and responsibly (11:7–12:7)

The three parts of this section are closely related. In the first part (11:7-8) Solomon called for enjoyment of life in view of the darkness of death. In the second (11:9-10) he urged that this enjoyment begin in one's youth because youth is fleeting; but he added that enjoyment should be tempered by responsible living because everyone is answerable to God. In the last part (12:1-7) Solomon underlined the urgency of this responsible enjoyment in one's youth because old age is a time of increasing gloom and of decay of one's powers, culminating in death.

1. ENJOY LIFE BECAUSE THE DARKNESS OF DEATH IS COMING (11:7-8)

11:7-8. Solomon wrote metaphorically of light and darkness as figures of life (cf. Job 3:20; 33:30) and death (cf. Ecc. 6:4-5; Job 10:20-22; 18:18). He characterized the future after death as obscure and enigmatic (**everything to come is meaningless;** cf. Ecc. 8:10, 14 for similar uses of the Heb. *hebel* referring to what is "meaningless" in the sense of being enigmatic). Solomon encouraged his readers to **enjoy** life as long as they **live** because life, like the pleasant **light** of **the sun,** should be enjoyed before the coming of the dark night of death which will last forever. The words, **the days of darkness . . . will be many,** is an intentional understatement (cf. 12:5 where the grave is called one's "eternal home"; also cf. Job 7:9; 14:10-12).

2. ENJOY LIFE IN YOUR YOUTH, REMEMBERING THAT GOD WILL JUDGE (11:9-10)

11:9-10. Solomon reiterated his advice to enjoy life (cf. v. 8), emphasizing that a person should do so in his **youth.** Elsewhere Solomon had said that enjoying life consists of eating and drinking (2:24; 3:13; 8:15; 9:7), wearing nice clothes and pleasant lotions (9:8), enjoying marital bliss (9:9), and finding satisfaction in one's work (2:24; 3:22; 5:18). Now Solomon encouraged his readers to do whatever their hearts desired ("follow the impulses of your heart and the desires of your eyes," 11:9, NASB). However, those desires should be tempered with an awareness that **God will** judge.

As previously noted (cf. comments on 2:24-26; 3:17; 7:15-18), there is no reason to believe from either explicit or implicit arguments in this book that Solomon believed this judgment would take place in the afterlife. Instead, like other wisdom writers of his era, he emphasized a temporal judgment within a man's lifetime (cf. comments on 2:24-26 and see 7:17). This may even be indicated in 11:10 where Solomon said a person should **banish anxiety from** his **heart** (psychological) and **cast off** the **troubles of** his **body** (physical). These imperatives are obviously the opposite side of the advice to **be happy** (v. 9) and contrast with the psychological gloom and declining physical vigor depicted in 12:2-5. Yet such passages as Proverbs 5:7-14 and Psalm 39 show that a means of avoiding these effects is a wise lifestyle lived in the fear of the Lord.

3. LIVE RESPONSIBLY IN YOUR YOUTH FOR OLD AGE AND DEATH ARE COMING (12:1-7)

Solomon underlined the thought of responsible living in one's youth by vividly depicting in a series of word pictures the increasing gloom and declining powers of old age which culminate in death. These word pictures are arranged in three groups, each introduced with "before" (vv. 1-2, 6) and modifying the basic imperative, "Remember your Creator in the days of your youth" (v. 1).

a. Live responsibly before the miseries of old age come (12:1)

12:1. The command **Remember your Creator** means to revere God, to keep His laws faithfully, to serve Him responsibly,

remembering that because He created people, everyone owes Him his life. This meaning is obvious (a) from the preceding verses (11:9-10) on living joyously but responsibly, (b) from the final advice at the end of the book to "fear God and keep His commandments" (12:13), and (c) from the meaning of the verb "remember" (in Deut. 8:18 and Ps. 119:55 "remember" is parallel to keeping the Law; in Jud. 8:34 it is contrasted with self-reliance and worship of other gods; in Ps. 63:6 it is parallel to meditating on and faithfully following God).

The epithet for God, "your Creator," emphasizes Him as the Author of life, who gives it and takes it away (cf. Ecc. 12:7; and the allusion to Gen. 2:7; 3:19).

Using a wordplay on the word "troubles" in Ecclesiastes 11:10 ("the troubles of your body"), Solomon advised responsible living in one's **youth, before the days of trouble come,** that is, the days of old age whose troubles he figuratively depicted in 12:2-5, **the years** in which he said they would find little or **no pleasure.**

b. Live responsibly before gloom and decay set in (12:2-5)

Using various figures to depict the declining joy and waning physical powers of old age, Solomon advised responsible living before old age sets in.

12:2. The miseries of old age ("the days of trouble," v. 1) and the approach of death (vv. 6-7) are likened to recurring rainstorms. As **clouds** often block out the light of **the sun, the moon, and the stars,** so old age is a period of diminishing joy (**light**) and increasing gloom (**dark**), heralding the approach of the long night of death. This obviously alludes to the earlier figurative use of light and darkness to depict life and death (11:7-8). This allusion would have been obvious to the ancient Hebrews who held a more dynamic view of death than people have today. Any decrease in the vitality of a person, even a young person, was viewed as the onset of death (cf., e.g., Pss. 18:4-5; 88:3-5).

12:3. Many diversified attempts have been made to interpret the highly figurative statements in verses 3-5. (For a brief, yet fairly comprehensive treatment of most views, cf. G.A. Barton, *A Critical and Exegetical Commentary on the Book of*

Ecclesiastes. Edinburgh: T. & T. Clark, 1908, pp. 186-91.) Though some interpreters have tried to explain this passage under a rigid adherence to one figure—either the decline of an estate or the gloom of a household after the death of its head—it seems that Solomon chose the various pictures to depict the declining physical and psychological powers of old age. Thus he referred to the days of misery (v. 1) and the days of decreasing joy and increasing gloom (v. 2) as a time **when the keepers of the house tremble** (the arms and hands grow weak). Also **the strong men stoop,** that is, the legs grow bent and feeble. **The grinders cease because they are few** refers to the teeth becoming fewer, and **those looking through the windows grow dim** refers to the eyesight beginning to fail.

12:4. The doors to the street are closed may picture the lips sinking in, due to the loss of teeth. **When men rise up at the sound of birds** suggests that old people get up early because of their inability to sleep. **All their songs grow faint** speaks of hearing that becomes impaired.

12:5. Being **afraid of heights and of dangers in the streets** points up lack of vigor and the fear that makes older people afraid to venture out. **The almond tree blossoms** refers to the hair turning gray and white (almond blossoms are white). **The grasshopper drags himself along** speaks of the body being bent and one's walk being slowed; the grasshopper, normally moving about quickly, is an apt figure of the past liveliness of one's childhood and youth. **Desire no longer is stirred** speaks of diminished appetites. The decline of physical powers culminates in death and **man goes to his eternal home** (i.e., the grave; cf. comments on 11:8-9) and people grieve (**mourners go about in the streets**).

c. Live responsibly before death comes (12:6-7)

12:6. Solomon urged people to live responsibly **before** death comes; the idea, **remember Him,** is repeated from verse 1. Solomon then referred to life under the two common figures of light ("golden lamp," JB) and water (cf. Ps. 36:8-9 for a similar use of these two figures of speech). The dissolution of the body is suggested by light being extinguished: **the silver cord** holding a **golden bowl** (in which the light burns) snaps and the bowl **is broken.** Death is also referred to by water being unavailable: **the pitcher** which holds water **is shattered** and **the wheel** by which it is drawn **from the well is broken.**

12:7. The final description of death, by which Solomon sought to motivate people toward responsible living, was that of the reversal of Creation. **The dust** of the body **returns to the ground it came from** and the breath of life (**spirit** and "breath" are translations of the same Heb. word *rûaḥ*) **to God who gave it.** This obviously alludes to part of the Creation account (Gen. 2:7; man was made from the dust of the ground and was given breath). This makes it evident that Solomon was not referring to the return of individual human spirits to God for judgment. Similar descriptions of death (as a dissolution of the body and the withdrawal of the breath of God) are referred to in Job 34:14-15 and Psalm 104:29-30 (cf. Job 10:9).

Moreover, a comparison of these passages with Ecclesiastes 12:7 makes it clear that the description of the return of the breath of life given here does not contradict 3:20. There Solomon, writing about the common destiny of people and animals, had denied the possibility of demonstrating a difference in the disposition of their life breaths, that is, whether a human's breath went upward to God and whether an animal's went down to the earth. A comparison of 12:7; Job 34:14-15; Psalm 104:29-30; and Genesis 1:30 shows that Solomon would have affirmed the same destiny for life in animals, that is, it also returns to God.

B. Final advice in view of the futility of all human endeavors (12:8-14)

Solomon closed this book by reiterating his theme of the futility of all human endeavor (v. 8; cf. 1:2) and by recommending that people fear God and keep His commandments (12:13-14). He underlined the validity of this summarization of his book by referring to the sources of its authority (vv. 9-12).

1. REITERATION OF THE THEME: THE FUTILITY OF ALL HUMAN ENDEAVOR (12:8)

12:8. Having demonstrated the limitations of all human efforts (1:12–6:9) and of all human wisdom (6:10–11:6), Solomon then reiterated the theme with which he opened his book (1:2): **Everything is meaningless** (*hebel*). As was stated in the comments on chapter 1, the immediately following context (1:3-11) shows that this statement applies to all human endeavor. Here (12:8) it applies to all that preceded, the futility of human efforts and human wisdom (1:12–11:6). Obviously, however, not included in this assessment is the advice to enjoy life as God enables, a course which Solomon repeatedly recommended (cf. 2:24-26; 3:12, 22; 5:18-20; 8:15; 9:7-9) and which he had just discussed explicitly in relationship to the fear of God (11:7–12:7). Apart from enjoying one's lot in life in the fear of God, life is indeed **meaningless**.

2. THE PECULIAR AUTHORITY OF THIS BOOK (12:9-12)

12:9-10. Solomon underlined the validity of the teaching in this book and the advice he offered in it by referring to its authority and by warning his readers about the futility of seeking answers from different kinds of books. Solomon first referred to his personal qualifications as a wisdom **Teacher**—one of the three kinds of leaders (prophets, priests, teachers) through whom God revealed His will to Israel (cf. Jer. 18:18; Ezek. 7:26). Solomon said he was . . . **wise** and **imparted knowledge to the people.** He took thoughtful care in producing this book; he said **he pondered** (i.e., carefully weighed in his mind) **and searched out and set in order** (i.e., carefully arranged) **many proverbs.**

Also Solomon said that he sought to give his book an aesthetically pleasing form without sacrificing the truth of what he wrote. He "sought to find delightful [or pleasing] words and to write words of truth correctly" (NASB).

12:11-12. Solomon related this book to the purpose and goal of other wisdom books (**the words of the wise** and **their collected sayings**) and to the ultimate source of their authority. Like ox **goads** and **firmly** planted **nails,** Solomon's teaching, like the words of other wise people, provides a guide and stimulus to godly living (cf. Acts 26:14 for an illustration of goads) and a secure basis for living (cf. Jer. 10:4 for a usage of nails). Moreover, like some other words of the wise these words have divine authority; they were **given by one Shepherd.** This refers to God and His care and concern (cf. Gen. 49:24; Ps. 80:1; in Ps. 95:6-7 the concepts of Shepherd and Creator are combined as they are in Ecc. 12:1, 11). Because of the peculiar value and authority of the words of the wise—of which this book was an example—Solomon warned his son (cf. "my son" in Prov. 1:8, 10, 15; 2:1; 3:1, 11, 21; 4:10, 20; 5:1, 20; 6:1, 3, 20; 7:1; 19:27; 23:15, 19; 23:26; 24:13, 21; 27:11) and all his readers not to seek answers beyond those God had given through the wise. If they would keep looking for answers in **many** other **books,** they would wear themselves out.

3. FINAL ADVICE: FEAR GOD AND KEEP HIS COMMANDMENTS (12:13-14)

12:13. The book concludes (**here is the conclusion of the matter**) with an explicit recommendation to **fear God and keep His commandments.** These words were not added by someone other than Solomon, as is often claimed, but are the culmination of many other implicit references in Ecclesiastes to fear God and serve Him acceptably (cf. comments on 2:24-26; 7:15-18; 11:9-10; 12:1). Here Solomon said such reverence and service are everyone's duty (NASB's "this applies to every person" is preferred to NIV's **this is the whole duty of man**).

12:14. The fact that revering God is every person's responsibility is underlined by the truth that **God will bring every deed** (every human act) **into judgment** (cf. 3:17; 11:9) **including every hidden thing** (cf. Matt. 10:26). Everyone is answerable to God for everything he does, whether obvious or concealed. Though this is often taken as referring to a future judgment after death, a comparison of Psalm 90:7-8 and a proper understanding of Ecclesiastes 2:24-26; 7:15-18; 11:9-10 show that this is doubtful. Though a future judgment after death is indeed the solution to the enigma Solomon had observed in the unequal distribution of justice in human history (cf. 7:15; 8:14), no evidence suggests that Solomon believed in such a judgment. Life after death was as enigmatic to him (cf. 11:8) as the unequal distribution of justice. His emphasis was on *this life* ("under the sun") and its opportunities for service (cf. 9:10; 12:1-7) and enjoyment (cf. 2:24-26; 3:12, 22; 5:18-20; 8:15; 9:7-9; 11:7-10); he thought life after death offered no such opportunities (cf. 9:5-6, 10). Therefore he did not comment on any differences *after* death between the righteous and the wicked, the wise and the fools, man and beast.

Many other Scripture passages, of course, do point up the eternal blessings of the righteous and the eternal punishment of the wicked. Solomon lived on the other side of the Cross and in the comparative darkness of the progress of revelation; nevertheless he affirmed belief in God and in His justice (cf. 3:17; 8:12b-13). He was content to leave judgment, along with everything else, to God's timing (3:17) for "He has made everything appropriate in its time" (3:11, NASB). So Solomon counseled his readers to enjoy life in the fear of God as God enables. Would that people who live on this side of the Cross would be as content as Solomon was to leave the enigmas of life in God's hands, to serve Him acceptably, and to enjoy life as He enables!

BIBLIOGRAPHY

Delitzsch, Franz. "Ecclesiastes." In *Commentary on the Old Testament in Ten Volumes.* Vol. 6. Reprint (25 vols. in 10). Grand Rapids: Wm. B. Eerdmans Publishing Co., 1982.

Eaton, Michael A. *Ecclesiastes.* The Tyndale Old Testament Commentaries. Downers Grove, Ill.: InterVarsity Press, 1983.

Ginsburg, Christian D. *The Song of Songs and Coheleth.* 1857. Reprint. New York: KTAV Publishing House, 1970.

Goldberg, Louis. *Ecclesiastes.* Bible Study Commentary. Grand Rapids: Zondervan Publishing House, 1983.

Gordis, Robert. *Koheleth—the Man and His World: A Study of Ecclesiastes.* 3rd ed. New York: Schocken Books, 1968.

Johnston, Robert K. "Confessions of a Workaholic: A Reappraisal of Qoheleth." *Catholic Biblical Quarterly* 38. January–March 1976:14-28.

Kaiser, Walter C., Jr. *Ecclesiastes: Total Life.* Everyman's Bible Commentary. Chicago: Moody Press, 1979.

Lange, John Peter, ed. "Ecclesiastes." In *Commentary on the Holy Scriptures.* Vol. 7. Reprint (25 vols. in 12). Grand Rapids: Zondervan Publishing House, 1960.

Laurin, Robert. "Ecclesiastes." In *The Wycliffe Bible Commentary.* Chicago: Moody Press, 1962.

Murphy, Roland E. *Wisdom Literature: Job, Proverbs, Ruth, Canticles, Ecclesiastes, Esther.* The Forms of the Old Testament Literature. Vol. 13. Grand Rapids: Wm. B. Eerdmans Publishing Co., 1981.

Reichert, Victor E., and Cohen, A. "Ecclesiastes." In *The Five Megilloth.* London: Soncino Press, 1946.

Wright, Addison G. "The Riddle of the Sphinx: The Structure of the Book of Qoheleth." *Catholic Biblical Quarterly* 30. October–December 1968:313-34.

Wright, J. Stafford. "The Interpretation of Ecclesiastes." *Evangelical Quarterly* 18. January–March 1946:18-34.

SONG OF SONGS

Jack S. Deere

INTRODUCTION

Interpretation and Purpose. The Song of Songs (called the Song of Solomon in some Bible versions, e.g., KJV, NASB) is perhaps the most difficult and mysterious book in the entire Bible. A cursory glance at the Song's history of interpretation reveals a diversity of opinion unequaled in the study of any other biblical work. The Song has been interpreted as: (a) an allegory, (b) an extended type, (c) a drama involving either two or three main characters, (d) a collection of Syrian wedding songs (a view held by E. Renan, J. Wetzstein, Umberto Cassuto, and others) in which the groom played the role of a king and the bride played the role of a queen, (e) a collection of pagan fertility cult liturgies (held by Theophile Meek), and (f) an anthology of disconnected songs extolling human love (held by Robert Gordis).

Viewed as an allegory, the details of the book are intended to convey hidden spiritual meanings, with little or no importance attached to the normal meanings of words. Jewish tradition (the Mishnah, the Talmud, and the Targum) viewed the book as an allegorical picture of the love of God for Israel. Church leaders, including Hyppolytus, Origen, Jerome, Athanasius, Augustine, and Bernard of Clairvaux, have viewed the book as an allegory of Christ's love for His bride, the church. Origen, for example, wrote that the beloved's reference to her being dark (Song 1:5-6) means the church is ugly with sin, but that her loveliness (1:5) refers to spiritual beauty after conversion. Others said the cooing of the doves (2:12) speaks of the preaching of the apostles, and some have suggested that 5:1 refers to the Lord's Supper. These examples show that the allegorical approach is subjective with no way to verify that any of the interpretations are correct. The Song of Songs nowhere gives an interpreter the suggestion that it should be understood as an allegory.

Some scholars view the book as an extended type, with Solomon typifying Christ and the beloved being a type of the church. This differs from the allegorical approach in that the typical view sees Solomon as a historical person and does not seek to discover a mystical meaning for every detail in the book. However, the Scriptures give no indication that various aspects of Solomon's life are divinely intended types of Christ.

Those who see the book as a drama (e.g., Franz Delitzsch, H. Ewald, and S.R. Driver) fail to note that the literary genre of a full-fledged drama was not known among the Israelites. Also the book cannot be analyzed into acts and scenes like a drama.

Scholars differ widely on the structure of the Song, its unity or lack of it, the nature of its metaphors, and the nature of the love extolled by the Song. In short, almost every verse has been the subject of lively debate by the Song's interpreters. Probably no other book of the Bible has such a variegated tapestry of interpretation.

Many evangelical scholars interpret the Song of Songs as a lyric poem which has both unity and logical progression. The major sections of the Song deal with courtship (1:2–3:5), a wedding (3:6–5:1), and maturation in marriage (5:2–8:4). The Song concludes with a climactic statement about the nature of love (8:5-7) and an epilogue explaining how the love of the couple in the Song began (8:8-14).

Some scholars say the book involves three characters, not two. Those three are the beloved, her shepherd-lover, and Solomon who wooed her away from the shepherd. No problem exists, however, with Solomon also being a shepherd (the two-character view) since he owned many flocks (Ecc. 2:7).

The purpose of the book is to extol

human love and marriage. Though at first this seems strange, on reflection it is not surprising for God to have included in the biblical canon a book endorsing the beauty and purity of marital love. God created man and woman (Gen. 1:27; 2:20-23) and established and sanctioned marriage (Gen. 2:24). Since the world views sex so sordidly and perverts and exploits it so persistently and since so many marriages are crumbling because of lack of love, commitment, and devotion, it is advantageous to have a book in the Bible that gives God's endorsement of marital love as wholesome and pure.

Author and Date. Song of Songs 1:1 attributes the authorship of this book to Solomon. Six other verses in the book refer to him by name (1:5; 3:7, 9, 11; 8:11-12). He is also referred to as the "king" (1:4, 12; 3:9, 11; 7:5). That a king is the lover referred to in the book is confirmed by references to his expensive carriage (3:7-10) and to the royal chariots (6:12). Solomon was a lover of nature (1 Kings 4:33), and the numerous references in the Song of Songs to flora, fauna, and other aspects of nature are consistent with his being its author. The book, then, was probably written sometime during Solomon's reign, between 971 and 931 B.C. Some wonder how Solomon could be the author of a book that extols faithfulness in marriage when he was so unfaithful, having 700 wives and 300 concubines (1 Kings 11:3). Perhaps the answer is that the "beloved" in the Song whom he married was his first wife. If so, then the book may have been written soon after his marriage, before he fell into the sin of polygamy.

Some interpreters have suggested that the maiden in the book was Pharaoh's daughter (1 Kings 3:1). But the beloved in the Song of Songs is never called a queen. She was probably from Lebanon (Song 4:8), not Egypt.

Unity. Many interpreters say that the book is an anthology, a collection of love songs that have no connections and that teach no lessons. However, several arguments speak for the book's unity: (1) The same characters are seen throughout the book (the beloved maiden, the lover, and the daughters of Jerusalem). (2) Similar expressions and figures of speech are used throughout the book. Examples are: love more delightful than wine (1:2; 4:10), fragrant perfumes (1:3, 12; 3:6; 4:10), the beloved's cheeks (1:10; 5:13), her eyes like doves (1:15; 4:1), her teeth like sheep (4:2; 6:6), her charge to the daughters of Jerusalem (2:7; 3:5; 8:4), the lover like a gazelle (2:9, 17; 8:14), Lebanon (3:9; 4:8, 11, 15; 7:4), and numerous references to nature. (3) Hebrew grammatical peculiarities found only in this book suggest a single author. (4) The progression in the subject matter points to a single work, not an anthology. As stated earlier, the book moves logically from the courtship (1:2–3:5) to the wedding night (3:6–5:1) to maturation in marriage (5:2–8:4).

OUTLINE

COMMENTARY

I. The Superscription (1:1)

1:1. This verse identifies the author of the Song as Solomon. As Israel's third king Solomon ruled from 971 to 931 B.C. Solomon was perhaps more gifted with literary skill than any other king of Israel for he wrote 3,000 proverbs and 1,005 songs (1 Kings 4:32). It is appropriate that a subject as wonderful as romantic love is described in sublime language by a competent human author, writing of course under the Holy Spirit's inspiration. Interestingly, of the more than 1,000 songs Solomon wrote, only this one was designed by God to be included in the biblical canon. Solomon is mentioned by name in six other verses: Song of Songs 1:5; 3:7, 9, 11; 8:11-12.

The title **Song of Songs** offers a clue to the interpretation of the work. It is *one* song out of many songs. The reader therefore is not to view the work as a collection of songs but rather as one unified song. The words "Song of Songs" suggest the superlative, as in "most holy" (Ex. 29:37) which is literally, "holy of holies." As a superlative the title may mean that this is the best of Solomon's 1,005 songs or, more likely, that this is the best of *all* songs. In either case the Song sets before its readers a paradigm

for romantic love in courtship and marriage.

II. The Courtship (1:2–3:5)

This section contrasts sharply with the other two major sections (3:5–5:1; 5:2–8:4). Though this section (1:2–3:5) abounds with expressions of sexual desire, great sexual restraint is exercised by the lovers. However, after the wedding procession (3:6-11) there is a notable absence of sexual restraint in the Song. So this section points up the fact that in romantic courtship restraint ought to be observed.

A. Introduction: The expressions of longing, insecurity, and praise (1:2-11)

1. THE THEME OF LONGING (1:2-4)

1:2-4a. As indicated in the margins, the NIV has indicated the male speaker as the "Lover" and the female speaker as the "Beloved." Other speakers are identified in the NIV as "Friends" in verse 4b and in 5:2, 9; 6:1, 13; 8:5, 8-9. In some instances the speakers are difficult to determine and are therefore debatable. Suggestions as to the speakers, with a few variations from the NIV margins, are summarized in the chart "Speakers in the Song of Songs."

The Song begins with a soliloquy by the beloved in which she first expressed her strong desire for her lover's (Solomon's) physical affection (**kisses,** 1:2). The rapid interchange between the third person (**him,** v. 2a, and **his,** vv. 2a, 4b) and the second person (**your** and **you,** vv. 2b-4a) is confusing to modern readers, but it was a regular feature of love poetry in the ancient Near East. This stylistic device gave a strong emotional quality to the poetry. When she spoke of his love (v. 2b) she was referring to the physical expressions of his **love** (the Heb. word for "love" is the pl. *dōḏîm*, also used in 4:10). The statement **your love is more delightful than wine** means that his physical affections were exhilirating, refreshing, and a great source of joy (cf. 1:4).

The **pleasing** aroma of his **perfumes** made him even more attractive to her. Mention of perfumes led her to compare his **name** to **perfume.** A person's name represented his character or reputation (cf. 2 Sam. 7:9). So comparing Solomon's

Speakers in the Song of Songs

The beloved	Friends of the beloved	Solomon (the lover)	God	The beloved's brothers
1:2-4a	1:4b			
1:4c-7	1:8*			
		1:9-10		
	1:11*			
1:12-14		1:15		
1:16-2:1*		2:2		
2:3-13		2:14		
2:15-3:11*		4:1-15		
4:16		5:1a-d	5:1e*	
5:2-8	5:9			
5:10-16	6:1			
6:2-3		6:4-9		
	6:10*			
6:11-12*	6:13a	6:13b-7:9a		
7:9b-8:4	8:5a			
8:5b-7				8:8-9
8:10-12		8:13		
8:14				

* In these verses the speakers suggested here differ from those designated in the NIV margins.

name to perfume meant that his *character* was pleasing and attractive to the beloved. For this reason, she said, many were attracted to him.

The statement **the king** (cf. Song 1:12; 3:9, 11; 7:5) **has brought me into his chambers** may be rendered as a request: "May the king bring me into his chambers." In this sense she was expressing her desire for intimacy and marriage with the lover. This matches the first part of 1:4, **Take me away with you.** In summary, this opening soliloquy suggests that physical desire is a characteristic of romantic love and that properly channeled the desire is good, not evil. One ought to be "intoxicated" with love for one's own mate (cf. Prov. 5:18-19), rather than with wine, drugs, or other people. However, the choice of a marriage partner should be based on far more than purely physical considerations. The beloved's speech indicates that the character ("name") of a person is vitally important in the selection of one's spouse.

1:4b. The beloved's "friends" (see NIV marg.), elsewhere referred to as the "daughters of Jerusalem" (v. 5; 3:10; 5:8,

16) and "daughters of Zion" (3:11), spoke in 1:4b. Many suggestions have been given concerning the identity of the "daughters of Jerusalem," such as female wedding guests, ladies of the royal court, concubines in the royal harem. Most likely they refer to the female inhabitants of Jerusalem. That city is frequently referred to as the "mother" of its inhabitants (cf. Isa. 51:18; 60:4; Ezek. 19:2, 10; Hosea 2:2, 5).

The chorus is a literary device in the Song whereby the beloved and her lover express their emotions and thoughts more fully. By praising Solomon (**you** is masc. sing.) in Song of Songs 1:4 the "daughters" seemed to be agreeing with one another that the couple had an ideal romance. The last line in verse 4 may be the words of the beloved (see NIV marg.) or, perhaps better, the words of the friends.

2. THE THEME OF INSECURITY (1:5-8)

1:5-6. The beloved's suntanned appearance (**dark am I**) revealed that she worked in the fields. This made her feel insecure (**do not stare at me**) among the city dwellers and in particular the women of Jerusalem. She compared her dark skin to **the tents of Kedar,** which were made of black goats' hair. The people of Kedar were nomads in northern Arabia who descended from Ishmael (Gen. 25:13). They were known for their archery (Isa. 21:16-17) and flocks (Isa. 60:7; Jer. 49:28-29; Ezek. 27:21; also see Ps. 120:5; Isa. 42:11; Jer. 2:10). Apparently **the tent curtains of Solomon** were also black.

Her explanation for her dark appearance was almost an apology. Because of hard outdoor work in **the vineyards,** required of her by her brothers, she was forced to neglect the cultivation of her **own vineyard,** that is, herself and her appearance (cf. Song 8:12).

1:7. The beloved's feelings of insecurity helped arouse in her a desire for her lover's presence. She addressed him as though he were a shepherd (a common epithet for a man in ancient Near Eastern love poetry). The verse is either a soliloquy (assuming the lover is absent) or, if he is present, a request for a meeting later in the day. If she could not be with him she said she would **be like a veiled woman.** This enigmatic expression means either that she would be mistaken for a prostitute (cf. Gen. 38:14-15) or, more likely, that without Solomon she would be as sad as a person in mourning (cf. Ezek. 24:17, 22).

1:8. The reply in this verse is usually credited to the lover since he was addressed in the preceding question (v. 7). If Solomon is the speaker then the verse is probably a playful or teasing response. However, the verse seems too cold and distant in tone for Solomon. So it may be a disdainful reply by the friends: **"If you,** of all people, **do not know** where he is, go to the other **shepherds** where you really belong anyway" (**graze your young goats**).

3. THE THEME OF PRAISE (1:9-11)

1:9-11. The answer to the beloved's feelings of insecurity (vv. 5-6) was the praise of her lover. Frequently he called her his **darling** (vv. 9, 15; 2:2, 10, 13; 4:1, 7; 5:2; 6:4). In ancient Arabic poetry, women were sometimes compared to horses as objects of beauty, but the reference in 1:9 is probably more specific. The words **a mare harnessed to one of the**

chariots of Pharaoh is literally, "a mare among the chariots of Pharaoh." Stallions, not mares, were used to pull chariots in antiquity. A mare, therefore, *among* the chariots might well start a chaotic experience. The point of the comparison is that in Solomon's opinion she was as beautiful and sought after as if she were the only woman in a world full of men. When he further stated that she was **beautiful** with jewelry (**earrings** and necklaces, v. 10), the daughters of Jerusalem (**we,** v. 11) were forced to change their attitude of disdain (v. 6) and to agree with royal opinion. They even agreed to make her **earrings.** Verse 10 includes the first of numerous times in the book where he said she is beautiful (cf. v. 15 [twice]; 2:10, 13; 4:1 [twice], 7; 6:4; 7:1, 6). In summary, since the beloved had felt self-conscious about her appearance, the lover praised her physical beauty so that her detractors were forced to agree with him.

B. The growth of love and its intensity (1:12–3:5)

This section consists of a series of units in the progression of the lovers' courtship. Their longing for and praise of each other expand and intensify, and the insecurity of the beloved is resolved. The first unit (1:12–2:6) records a growing intensity in desire, praise, and security. The refrain (2:7) is an appeal for patience since love cannot be forced. The second unit (2:8-17) records the reward of patience and a growth in intimacy. The third unit (3:1-4) records the most intense longing yet, and after an appropriate refrain, which is an appeal for patience (3:5), the longing is followed by the reward of marriage (3:6–5:1).

1. MUTUAL PRAISE (1:12–2:6)

1:12-14. The beloved praised **the king** for his pleasing and attractive characteristics which were like **perfume** (cf. comments on v. 3) whose function was to attract rather than repel. He was constantly in her thoughts just as the smell of the **myrrh** (in her **sachet** around her neck) was constantly in her nostrils. Myrrh was a pleasant-smelling gum that exudes from small trees in Arabia. It is mentioned frequently in the Song of Songs (v. 13; 3:6; 4:6, 14; 5:1, 5 [twice], 13). All other men, compared with him, were like the desert. Among them he stood out like a beautiful **cluster of** flowers in a desert oasis. **Henna** (cf. 4:13) **blossoms** were white, and **En Gedi** was an oasis on the west coast of the Dead Sea. Earlier David had fled to En Gedi while running away from Saul (1 Sam. 23:29; 24:1).

1:15. The lover returned her praise by commending not only her beauty (**beautiful** occurs twice in this v.) but also her tranquil character. In antiquity **doves** (cf. 2:12, 14; 4:1; 5:2, 12; 6:9) were noted for their cleanliness and tranquility. "According to Rabbinic teaching, a bride who has beautiful **eyes** possesses a beautiful character; they are an index to her character" (S.M. Lehrman, "The Song of Songs," in *The Five Megilloth,* p. 4).

1:16-17. Both of these verses may be seen as spoken by the beloved (rather than v. 16 by the beloved and v. 17 by the lover, as in the NIV). Though she recognized his physical good looks (**handsome**) she was more taken by the charm of his personality (**Oh, how charming!**). The word "charming" means "pleasant" or "lovely" and the combination, handsome and pleasant, was as rare then as it is now. This is the first of about two dozen times she referred to him as **my lover**. **The beams** of **cedars** and the **rafters** made of **firs** probably do not refer to a literal building but figuratively to the pastoral setting in which they first met. This is also suggested by the **verdant** (green) **bed** (couch). The field where they fell in love and sat talking was green.

2:1. Here the beloved spoke of herself as **a rose of Sharon,** the fertile coastal region of Israel from Caesarea to Joppa. The Hebrew word for rose is *ḥăḇaṣṣelet.* In Isaiah 35:1, its only other occurrence in the Old Testament, it is translated "crocus," which may be the meaning here. It was a common meadow flower. The **lily** too was a common flower mentioned often in the Song of Songs (2:1-2, 16; 4:5; 5:13; 6:2-3; 7:2). Though in her humility she likened herself to common flowers of the field, her statement (2:1) reflects a significant contrast with her earlier self-consciousness (1:5-6). Her improvement probably was because of her lover's praising her (1:9-10, 15).

2:2. The lover echoed his beloved's newfound sense of worth by comparing her to **a lily** and all other women to

thorns. He agreed that she was a lily (v. 1) but not just any lily! She was as unique among all others as a single lily would be **among** many **thorns.**

2:3-6. The beloved's reciprocal praise of her **lover** was also expressed metaphorically. As **an apple tree** would be a delightful surprise in a **forest** so Solomon was a delightful and rare "find" **among** all the other **men.** He was unique, sweet, and fragrant.

The beloved's praise of her lover reveals three aspects of romantic love that are important to women. First, she felt protected by him. Sitting **in his shade** was a metaphor for protection, not only in the Bible but also in the literature of the ancient Near East. She had worked in the sun (1:6) but now she enjoyed resting under his protection. Second, they cultivated the kind of relationship that allowed them to know each other intimately. The word **taste** expressed a knowledge of someone through intimate personal experience (cf. Ps. 34:8, "Taste and see that the LORD is good"). Third, the beloved appreciated the fact that Solomon let others see his love for her. As a **banner** (a military standard) was easily seen by the troops as they marched, so Solomon's **love** for his beloved was easily seen by anyone who observed their relationship. He was not ashamed of her; instead he delighted in her and it was evident to others. One way he showed this was by taking her to his **banquet hall** (cf. "table" in Song 1:12) in the palace.

These three things—protection by her lover, intimacy with him, and obvious displays and expressions of love from him—are crucial factors that enable a woman to develop a sense of security and self-worth and thereby to enjoy a stable marriage.

The beloved had begun to experience these three things with Solomon during their courtship so it is no wonder that she became **faint with love** (2:5; cf. 5:8). The theme of lovesickness was common in ancient Near Eastern love poetry. So she expressed her desire for his strengthening and his embrace. Physically weakened, she needed stimulation from food such as **raisins** and **apples.** Perhaps "raisins" should be translated "raisin cakes," a Near Eastern delicacy (1 Chron. 12:40; Isa. 16:7; Hosea 3:1).

Since Song of Songs 2:5 is a request,

verse 6 should probably be translated as a request also ("May **his left arm** be **under my head, and** may **his right arm embrace me**") rather than a declarative statement.

2. THE REFRAIN (2:7)

2:7. This refrain, spoken by the beloved to the **daughters** (inhabitants; cf. comments on 1:4b) **of Jerusalem,** appears again in 3:5 and part of it in 8:4. In these three verses the refrain serves as a structural indicator to mark the ending of one section and to introduce the next one. The meaning of the refrain is that **love** cannot be forced but must be patiently waited for. In other words the beloved reminded all those desiring a relationship like the one she and Solomon enjoyed to wait patiently for God to bring it into their lives. **Gazelles** (2:17; cf. v. 17; 3:5; 4:5; 7:3; 8:14) and **does** are graceful, agile animals. It was natural for a beloved one, thinking of the fields and forests (2:1, 3), to make an oath by mountain animals.

3. A VISIT TO THE COUNTRY (2:8-17)

The preceding sections (1:2–2:7) seem to have a royal setting (1:4; 2:4) though outdoor scenes were mentioned, (e.g., 1:14; 2:1-3). But the setting for 2:8–3:5 is the country, near the beloved's home. She probably lived in Lebanon, north of Israel (cf. 4:8, 15). More importantly, however, the intensity of the couples' longing for each other increased and their sense of intimacy grew.

2:8-9. As Solomon approached his beloved's home, she excitedly described him coming as **a gazelle or a young stag** (cf. v. 17; 8:14). This emphasized his attractive appearance, strength, and agility (cf. comments on gazelles in 2:7). He approached the **wall** around her parents' home and then peered **through the lattice.** He was anxious to see her.

2:10-13. Solomon, her **lover,** asked his **darling** to go for a walk in the countryside. At the beginning and ending of his invitation he said, **Come with me** (vv. 10, 13; cf. 8:14). The elaborate description of spring was probably meant to do more than simply emphasize the beauty of the setting. It is likely that he was also describing their relationship. In a sense when one falls in love the feeling is like spring for everything seems fresh and new. The world is seen from a different perspective, which is how Solomon felt when he was with his beloved. Several statements refer to the beauty of spring: (1) **The winter is past.** The word for winter ($s^e \underline{t} aw$, used only here in the OT) refers to the cloudy season of March and April with the "latter" **rains.** (2) **Flowers appear** in the spring, adding delightful colors to the landscape, causing people to sing for joy. (3) **Doves** coo, "announcing" spring's arrival. (4) **Fig** trees put forth their **early fruit** (cf. Nahum 3:12). The early figs were either those that had remained unripened on the trees from the previous summer and then ripened at the beginning of spring, or were small edible buds that appeared in March. (5) Grape **vines** blossom, giving off **their fragrance** just before the grapes appear. **Blossoming** translates $s^e m \bar{a} \underline{d} ar$ which occurs only here and in Song of Songs 2:15 ("in bloom"). So spring stimulates the senses of sight, sound, taste, and smell.

2:14. Another characteristic of genuine love is the desire to be alone with one's lover. This desire seems to be easily experienced during courtship, but unfortunately it often fades in marriage. Yet if love is to grow a couple must find time to be alone. Doves (cf. v. 12 and see comments on 1:15) hide in **rock** crevices, reluctant to leave. The lover likened his beloved to such a **dove,** hesitant to join him in the countryside. So again (cf. 2:10, 13) he urged her to leave her home and join him so he could enjoy her **sweet**-sounding **voice** and **lovely** face.

2:15. The beloved rather than the lover may well be the speaker here. She was probably speaking poetically about their relationship rather than about literal **foxes** and **vineyards. Foxes** were noted for their destructive tendencies in crop fields, so her reference to those animals probably suggested metaphorically some problems in their relationship. The beloved was asking her lover to take the initiative in solving the problems that were potentially harmful to their relationship. "The foxes represent as many obstacles or temptations as have plagued lovers throughout the centuries. Perhaps it is the fox of uncontrolled desire which drives a wedge of guilt between a couple. Perhaps it is the fox of mistrust and jealousy which breaks the bond of love. Or it may be the fox of selfishness and pride which refuses to let one acknowledge his fault to another. Or it may be an unforgiving spirit which will not accept the apology of the other. These foxes have been ruining vineyards for years and the end of their work is not in sight" (S. Craig Glickman, *A Song for Lovers*, pp. 49-50). Even in ideal courtships and marriages most couples encounter some potentially destructive problems. Their willingness to solve them together is an evidence of their maturity.

2:16-17. Though they had some problems in their relationship (see comments on v. 15), the beloved knew that her **lover** belonged to her and she belonged to him. They were committed to each other. She could rest in the shepherd-like quality of his love despite the struggles they shared. She said **he browses** (lit., "he pastures" his flock) **among the lilies** (cf. 6:3). Speaking to herself (using the personal pronouns **mine, his,** and **he**) in 2:16, it is likely that verse 17 is also a soliloquy. Her thoughts of their mutual possession of each other naturally led to her desire for physical intimacy. So in her mind she invited him to **turn** (i.e., to her) with the strength and agility of **a gazelle or . . . young stag** (cf. v. 9; 8:14). **Rugged hills** (*hārê bāṭer*) is literally, "hills or mountains of separation or cleavage." Some say this refers to actual mountains—perhaps "hills of Bether" (NIV marg.), though the location of such a site is unknown. In that case the hills separated the couple, but this seems unlikely since he was already at her wall and lattice (2:9). It seems preferable to take this as a subtle reference to her breasts (cf. 4:6), thus an inner longing that they consummate their marriage. If that is the meaning, then she wanted that intimacy to last during the night till **the day breaks** (lit., "breathes") at dawn and the night **shadows** vanish. When their marriage was consummated they did this (see 4:5-6). As already stated, in expressing their love in their courtship, the beloved and her **lover** used restraint. Yet because of their deep love and commitment to each other they longed for their wedding day to come.

4. THE BELOVED'S FEAR OF LOSING HER LOVER (3:1-4)

3:1-4. The king returned to Jerusalem, leaving his beloved at her home in the country. The phrase **All night long on my bed** indicates that the experience she was describing took place in a dream. When a person loves another person deeply, it is natural to fear losing him or her. In her dream she lost her lover and sought to **find him.** The repeated expression **the one my heart loves** (once in each of these four verses) revealed the depth of her love for Solomon.

In her dream she went to a **city** (either a town near her home or Jerusalem) to look **for him,** but she was unsuccessful. She even asked **the watchmen,** men who guarded **the city** at night, if they had **seen** him. Apparently they had not. When she **found** him in her dream, she took him **to** her **mother's house,** the most secure place she knew.

5. THE REFRAIN (3:5)

3:5. This refrain marks the end of the section on the courtship (1:2–3:5) and the beginning of the wedding section (3:6–5:1). Perhaps the wedding was to be seen as a reward for patience on the beloved's part. On the meaning of 3:5, see comments on 2:7.

III. The Wedding (3:6–5:1)

A. The wedding procession (3:6-11)

Marriages in the ancient Near East were usually sanctioned through civil contracts rather than through religious ceremonies. Except for Proverbs 2:17 and Malachi 2:14 marriage covenants or contracts are not mentioned in the Old Testament. However, examples of Jewish civil marriage contracts have been found in the remains of the Jewish colony at Elephantine, Egypt dating back to the fifth century B.C. The marriage of Ruth and Boaz before a court of elders rather than before priestly officials (cf. Ruth 4:10-11) also illustrates the "civil" rather than religious character of wedding ceremonies. It is not surprising, therefore, to find that weddings took place not in the temple (or later in the synagogue), but rather in the couples' homes.

A central feature of a wedding ceremony was a procession to the bride's home led by the groom, who then escorted her back to their new residence. Next a wedding feast was given which lasted up to a week or even longer. Though the feast was prolonged the couple consummated their marriage on the first night. The wedding feast is not described in the

Song of Songs but both the wedding procession (3:6-11) and the wedding night (4:1–5:1) are presented in some detail. Verse 11 of chapter 3 refers to the "wedding" and to "Solomon," who of course was the groom.

3:6. The author spoke as a narrator in this verse, as if he were a spectator watching the approaching wedding procession, which was elaborate. What at first appeared in the distance to be a great **column of smoke** was actually **incense** (lit., "frankincense"; see comments on 4:6) burning in front of the procession. The fact that the incense was **made from all the spices of the merchant** emphasizes the costly nature of this display. The **myrrh** (see comments on 1:13) added another fragrance to the procession.

The pomp and beauty of this procession were wholly appropriate in light of the event's significance. The Scriptures teach that marriage is one of the most important events in a person's life. Therefore it is fitting that the union of a couple be commemorated in a special way. The current practice of couples casually living together apart from the bonds of marriage demonstrates how unfashionable genuine commitment to another person has become in contemporary society. This violates the sanctity of marriage and is contrary to God's standards of purity.

3:7-8. The **60 warriors** accompanying **Solomon's carriage** (cf. v. 9) were friends of the groom. It was common for a groom's friends to go with him in the wedding procession. But they were also **the noblest** and most **experienced** soldiers in **Israel**, probably Solomon's royal bodyguard. David had a bodyguard (2 Sam. 23:23) and so possibly did Solomon. Since the caravan may have had to travel some distance (cf. "coming up from the desert," Song 3:6, and note also the mention of Lebanon in 4:8, 15), the king was taking no chances with the safety of his bride. If bandits would appear at **night** and terrorize the bride, the soldiers were ready for them. The lesson is valid today for a would-be husband. He should give proper thought and planning to protect his bride. One form this takes is providing economic security for her.

3:9-11. Solomon's **carriage** was **made** of the very best, that is, **wood from Lebanon** (possibly his bride's homeland; cf. 4:8, 15). The carriage was adorned with the most expensive materials, **silver . . . gold,** and **purple** (representing royalty) fabric. Solomon offered his bride the best he had. And his love for her brought out the best in him. Others shared the couple's joy by helping prepare for the procession (**the daughters**—female inhabitants—**of Jerusalem** helped make the interior of the carriage and did so gladly) and by watching it (**look at King Solomon**). In the procession he wore a **crown.** This was not his royal crown, but a **crown . . . his mother** (Bathsheba, 1 Kings 2:13) gave **him**; it probably depicted happiness more than royalty.

B. The wedding night (4:1–5:1)

1. THE BEAUTY OF THE BELOVED (4:1-7)

4:1. The first to speak on their wedding night was Solomon and his words praised his bride's beauty. Three times on the wedding night he told her she was **beautiful** (vv. 1 [twice], 7; cf. comments on 1:10). Women in the ancient Near East did not ordinarily wear a veil except at the time of their wedding, and then removed it in the wedding chamber. (This is why Rebekah immediately veiled herself when she learned the identity of Isaac, her husband-to-be, Gen. 24:65. It also explains why Laban was able to deceive Jacob with Leah on their wedding night, Gen. 29:19-25.) So Solomon, seeing her **eyes behind** her **veil** (cf. Song 4:3) said they were **doves.** Doves were known for their tranquility in the ancient world, and since one's eyes are "windows of his soul" reflecting his character, Solomon was praising her calm and innocent character (cf. 1:15).

To say that her **hair** was **like a flock of goats** coming down **Mount Gilead** (cf. 6:5) hardly sounds like a compliment, but it was. Seen from a distance the dark hair of Palestinian goats was beautiful in the sunset as a flock was **descending from** the mountains. The beloved's dark hair had the same beautiful quality. Mount Gilead was a mountain range east of the Jordan River in Gilead, known for its fertile pastures and many flocks (cf. Micah 7:14).

4:2-3. Her **teeth** were white (**like a flock of sheep just shorn**) and perfectly matched (**each has its twin**). Her **lips,** being red and thin, were like a **scarlet ribbon.** "Ribbon" is literally "thread," referring to the perfect outline and delicately formed shape of her lips. Her teeth and lips made her **mouth** beautiful. The beloved's **temples,** probably including her cheeks, were reddish and sweet **like pomegranate** fruit.

4:4. The **tower of David** may have been the tower (cf. Neh. 3:25) of the king's palace. This tower may have been built or used by David for military purposes, or it may have been built by Solomon and given David's name. The custom of hanging **shields** on the tower was symbolic of the warriors' allegiance to and valor for a particular king or country (cf. Ezek. 27:10-11). The **warriors** probably referred to David's elite corps of men (2 Sam. 23:8-39). By comparing her **neck** to the tower Solomon was emphasizing not so much her neck's symmetry and beauty as he was making a statement about her person. She had a queenly bearing and appearance as awesome and majestic as King David's tower.

4:5. When the groom said his bride's **breasts** were **like . . . fawns** he was comparing their softness, not their color or form. Looking on the soft coat of a little fawn makes a person want to stroke it. Solomon wanted his bride to know that her soft and gentle beauty had kindled his desire for her and he wished to express that desire with his caresses.

4:6. At this point Solomon was overcome with desire for his bride and resolved to fulfill her silent request (see comments on 2:17). **The mountain of myrrh** and **the hill of incense** refer to the beloved's breasts. The primary point of comparison was not in the visual area, but rather in the realms of function and value. Myrrh and incense were used to perfume the body as well as the bedroom in order to make a person and the surroundings more attractive (cf. 3:6). They would give their love to each other till the morning. Myrrh (see comments on 1:13) and incense (lit., "frankincense," a balsamic gum that exudes from the wood of shrubs and trees of the genus *Boswellia*) were not native to Palestine. Both were luxury items that had to be imported at considerable cost. A mountain of myrrh or a hill of frankincense would have been greatly valued. To Solomon, therefore, his bride's breasts were attractive and of great value to him.

4:7. Solomon summarized his praise by ascribing perfect beauty to his bride. She had **no flaw,** or physical defect. She was perfect in appearance. (Later she called him "my flawless one," 5:2.) Solomon praised eight parts of his bride's body: her eyes, hair, teeth, lips, mouth, temples, neck, and breasts.

Compared with this lavish praise of the beloved's beauty, some wives today may feel uncomfortable about their own appearance. However, one must remember that initially the daughters of Jerusalem did not seem to regard the beloved as a beautiful woman. Unlike the other royal ladies she was not fair-skinned, a preeminent sign of beauty in the ancient world (see comments on 1:5-6). Yet in her lover's eyes she was **beautiful,** even though she did not meet the objective standards of beauty in her society. In other words, though few people in any age meet their own particular culture's standard of beauty, a woman is beautiful in the eyes of her lover simply because he loves her. Every husband who genuinely loves his wife can say, "To me you are beautiful and there is no flaw in you."

Two features of 4:1-7 call for comment. First, these verses include one reference to the first person ("I" in v. 6). His total attention was focused on his bride and her beauty. The conclusion to be drawn from this is that sex, when enjoyed properly within marriage, draws attention from oneself to one's mate, to his or her needs and pleasures. Second, the metaphors and imagery which Solomon used in praising his beloved were drawn from a pastoral setting: doves, goats, sheep, pomegranates, fawns, gazelles, mountains, hills. Solomon's bride, having been raised in the country, understood and appreciated these images. Praise drawn from this well-known realm would have created a sense of peace and security in her on the anxious night when her new life began in new surroundings. Later (7:1-9) after she became accustomed to "royal" living, Solomon drew on royal imagery (as well as pastoral scenes) in praising her beauty.

2. THE KING'S REQUEST (4:8)

4:8. The beloved may have lived in **Lebanon** near the mountains mentioned in this verse. **Amana** is the eastern part of the Anti-Lebanon range facing Damascus, and **Senir** and **Hermon** are two peaks in the Hermon range (though Deut. 3:9 speaks of Senir as a synonym for Hermon). However, it is unlikely that she lived by **lions' dens** or **haunts of . . . leopards.** The lions and leopards may represent fearful places or circumstances. In other words Solomon was asking his bride to leave her thoughts of home and put her fears behind her in order to concentrate completely on him, as he had done for her. The fact that Solomon called her **my bride** five times (vv. 8-12) also confirms that chapter 4 depicts their wedding night.

3. THE KING'S PRAISE OF HIS BRIDE'S LOVE (4:9-11)

Apparently the bride granted Solomon's request (v. 8) to turn all her attention to him, for in this section he praised her physical expression of love and its effect on him.

4:9. The words **stolen my heart** mean to be robbed of either one's willpower or his ability to think clearly. The effect of his bride's love was so powerful that even a **glance** from her beautiful **eyes** (cf. v. 1; 1:15) or even seeing an article of jewelry or clothing associated with her was enchanting to Solomon. Five times he called her his **sister** (4:9-10, 12; 5:1-2) because in the ancient Near East "sister" was an affectionate term for one's wife.

4:10. The word rendered **love** (*dōḏîm*; cf. 1:2) was used for physical expressions of romantic love. The verse might be more accurately translated, "How delightful are your kisses. How much more pleasing are your caresses than wine." Her physical expressions of love had a more refreshing and intoxicating effect on him **than wine,** just as *his* expressions had earlier affected *her* (cf. 1:2). Even her **perfume** added to the excitement of their love. The senses of sight, touch, smell, and sound were involved in their lovemaking.

4:11. The beloved gave herself freely with joy. She was not at all passive in their lovemaking. Her kisses were as desirable as **milk** and as sweet as **honey.** Milk and honey are combined here probably to allude to the fact that Canaan was a land of milk and honey (see comments on Ex. 3:8). Just as the land, rich in agricultural prosperity, was a source of blessing and joy to the people, so her kisses were a source of joy to him. Besides ap-

plying perfume to herself she also applied it to her clothes. **Lebanon,** because of its cedar trees (1 Kings 5:6; Pss. 29:5; 92:12; 104:16; Isa. 2:13; 14:8; Hosea 14:5), was known for its **fragrance** (Hosea 14:6).

4. THE KING'S PRAISE OF HIS BRIDE'S PURITY (4:12-15)

4:12. The **garden locked up . . . spring enclosed,** and **sealed fountain** all suggest "inaccessibility." The king was obviously praising his bride's virginity. Gardens were walled to keep out intruders (cf. Isa. 5:5; cf. "wall" in Song 2:9). Springs were sometimes covered, and fountains were sealed on the sides with clay to indicate private ownership. Similarly, she had kept herself "sealed" from all others, thus preserving her purity for her husband.

4:13-14. By extending the metaphor of the garden (begun in v. 12) Solomon conveyed to his beloved how much he valued her purity. She was like a rich exotic garden, with rare and valuable plant life. Such a garden was therefore valuable, attractive, and desirable. Included were **fruits,** flowers, plants, trees, and **spices. Pomegranates** (cf. v. 3) were a delicacy in Bible times. **Henna** (see comments on 1:14) is a flower with white blossoms. **Nard** is a fragrant ointment from a plant native to India (cf. Mark 14:3; John 12:3), and **saffron** is a powder from the pistils of a plant in the crocus family (cf. comments on "rose" in Song 2:1). **Calamus** (also mentioned in Isa. 43:24; Jer. 6:20; Ezek. 27:19) is possibly sweet cane. Other perfumes were **cinnamon,** from the bark of a tall tree, **and myrrh** (see comments on Song 1:13), **and aloes,** a plant native to an island in the Red (Reed) Sea, whose partially decayed wood gives off a fragrance. These items would make an unusual garden, valuable for its pleasant tastes, sights, and smells. Similarly Solomon valued his bride for her pleasing attractiveness.

4:15. This part of the metaphor contrasts with her inaccessibility as a garden and water in verse 12. The water is pure and wholesome, like **flowing water streaming down from Lebanon** (cf. "Lebanon" in vv. 8, 11), and is now accessible to Solomon. When the bride surrendered her virginity to her husband, she was no less pure for doing so. The progression from **a garden fountain** to **a well** to "water streaming down" indicates that his beloved more than quenched Solomon's desire for her and fully satisfied him. As mountain streams are refreshing so she refreshed him.

5. THE CONSUMMATION OF THE MARRIAGE
(4:16–5:1)

4:16. The beloved's request that the winds **blow on** her **garden**, that is, herself (cf. vv. 12, 15) was a delicate, poetically beautiful invitation to her lover to fully possess her (**come into** her). She wished to be his with her charms as available as fruit on a tree (cf. v. 13).

5:1. With exhiliration Solomon declared that their marriage was complete. He had totally enjoyed his **garden** (cf. vv. 12, 15-16), that is, his **bride**. Possessing her was more delightful than gathering **myrrh** in a garden, as sweet as eating **honey**, as enjoyable as drinking the best **wine** and **milk** (cf. 4:11).

The NIV margin attributes the last part of the verse, **Eat, O friends, and drink; drink your fill, O lovers,** to the "friends" of the couple. However, it is unlikely that friends, wedding guests, or any other persons would have been present in the bedroom at the consummation of the couple's marriage. A more plausible suggestion is that the speaker was God Himself. Only their Creator would have been a "guest" on that occasion. Since their love was from Him it was fitting that He approve it. He invited them to enjoy sexual love in marriage as if it were a banquet ("eat . . . and drink"). This clearly indicates God's approval of marriage, which He designed in the Garden of Eden (cf. Gen. 2:24).

IV. The Maturation of the Marriage (5:2–8:4)

This section of the Song of Songs deals with the growth of the couple's marriage. The intimacy, joy, and physical desire of their wedding night did not fade as is often common in many marriages. They nourished their life together so that the joy of their married life increased rather than decreased. This does not suggest, however, that they did not encounter problems potentially harmful to their relationship. This section opens with the problem of indifference and offers a paradigm for the successful resolution of a serious marital problem.

A. Indifference and its resolution (5:2–6:13)

The bride's indifference is introduced by her dream (5:2-7). This problem caused the temporary absence of her husband-lover. Asking the daughters of Jerusalem to help her find him (5:8), she described his attractiveness. The conversation between the beloved and the daughters laid the foundation for the reconciliation of the husband and wife (6:4-13).

1. THE PROBLEM: THE WIFE'S INDIFFERENCE AND THE HUSBAND'S ABSENCE (5:2-8)

5:2. In a dream (**I slept but my heart was awake**; cf. another recorded dream, 3:1-4) the wife was approached by her husband, who said **Open to me** (cf. 5:6). The fact that the **lover** no longer addressed her as "my bride" indicates there is a time lapse between verse 1 (the wedding night) and verse 2. The couple should no longer be regarded as newlyweds. But he did address her by other affectionate terms: **my sister** (see comments on 4:9), **my darling** (cf. 1:9, 15; 2:2, 10, 13; 4:1, 7; 6:4), **my dove**, and **my flawless one** (cf. 4:7). This is the first record of his using all these terms of endearment. His **head** and **hair** were covered **with dew**, as he had been outside. Dew in Israel was often heavy.

5:3-4. She said in her dream that she had already gotten ready for bed. But this trivial excuse for not opening the door revealed her indifference or apathy toward her husband. Somehow she had grown cool toward his advances. But he did not accept her excuse. He tried to open the door but failed and then left. Then her compassion was aroused for him and she decided to open the door. The Hebrew expression translated **my heart began to pound for him** is used elsewhere to express pity or compassion (e.g., Isa. 16:11; Jer. 31:20). It was not used to express sexual arousal as some scholars have maintained.

5:5-7. When the beloved in her dream went to the door **to open** it for her husband (**my lover**; used of him six times in vv. 2, 4-6, 8), she found **myrrh** on the door **handles** and got some on her **hands**. **Myrrh** was sometimes associated with lovemaking (Prov. 7:17; Song 4:6; 5:13). Perhaps the **lover** had put liquid myrrh on the door handles as a token of affection for his beloved. He had wanted more than relief from the discomfort of the night air.

However, the beloved responded too late (vv. 6-7). When she set out to look for him she was **found** and beaten by the city **watchmen**. In her first dream the watchmen helped her look for her lover (3:3), but this time they mistook her for a criminal. In her dream this action by the watchmen may indicate that she was to blame for her separation from her lover. More importantly the dream symbolized the pain of separation brought about through her selfishness and the dream dramatized her need of the **lover** for her well-being and protection.

5:8. The beloved sought the daughters' (see comments on 1:5) help in finding her **lover.** The message they were to give him, **I am faint with love,** meant that she now wanted his embrace (cf. 2:5-6). Though she had been indifferent to him (5:2-3), her attitude changed so that now she was anxious for him.

2. THE ATTRACTIVENESS OF THE LOVER (5:9-16)

5:9. The daughters (v. 8) asked the beloved what was so special about her lover that they should help look for him. This question gave her an opportunity to praise her husband, which helped rekindle her former feelings of love.

5:10-16. In appearance his skin was **ruddy** and in character he was **outstanding.** The metaphors in verses 11-15 were not meant to be taken as visual comparisons for the most part. They indicate her husband's value and attractiveness. For instance, **his head** was not the color of **gold** (v. 11), but was as valuable as gold. (**His hair** was **wavy and black**; cf. his description of her hair, 4:1.) **His eyes** were not shaped **like doves** (5:12), but were peaceful and gentle like doves, reflecting his peaceful and gentle character (cf. his similar description of her eyes, 1:15; 4:1). Gray or black doves **washed in milk** pictured the dark pupils of his eyes set off by the whites of his eyes. **His cheeks** were delightful and desirable like **spice** or **perfume. His lips** were soft and beautiful **like lilies** to which had been applied flowing **myrrh** (5:13; cf. v. 5) to give an additional fragrance. **His arms** (lit., "his hands") were as attractive and valuable as **gold** (like his head, v. 11, and his legs, v. 15). **His body** (lit., "his abdo-

men") was as handsome as **ivory** and **sapphires** (v. 14). **Polished** or smooth ivory may have also referred to the hard muscular shape of his abdomen. **His legs** were strong, handsome, and valuable like **marble** and **gold** (cf. vv. 11, 14). **His overall appearance** was breathtaking; he was tall **like** the imposing **cedars** of **Lebanon** (v. 15; cf. Amos 2:9). **His mouth** (speech and kisses) was highly desirable. He was handsome in every way (Song 5:16).

3. THE LOVER IN HIS GARDEN (6:1-3)

6:1-3. The cause of the couple's separation (the indifference of the beloved) was overcome, as evidenced by her praise of her **lover** (5:10-16). Yet they were still separated at this point. So the question of the daughters (5:8) concerning his whereabouts (6:1) addressed the problem of their being apart. Having heard of his handsome appearance, the daughters were now anxious to help find him. **Which way did** he go? they wanted to know.

She answered that he was in **his garden** where **spices** and **lilies** were growing (6:2). This indicated that their separation was more in the emotional realm than in the spatial for she apparently had always known his whereabouts. Her statement of mutual possession (**I am my lover's and my lover is mine,** v. 3) is the inverse of her earlier passionate declaration (2:16a; cf. 7:10). This indicates that the emotional distance had been overcome on her part and she was confident that it had also been overcome on his part. All that was needed for a complete reconciliation was a statement of forgiveness or acceptance from the lover. **He browses** is, literally, "he pastures" his flock (cf. 2:16b).

4. THE RECONCILIATION: THE LOVER'S PRAISE OF HIS BELOVED (6:4-13)

6:4-10. In their reconciliation the first words of the lover to his beloved were words of praise. She was as **beautiful . . . as Tirzah,** a lovely city which later became the capital of four kings of the Northern Kingdom: Baasha, Elah, Zimri, and Omri (1 Kings 15:21, 33; 16:8, 15, 23). The beloved was also **lovely** like **Jerusalem,** which was called "the perfection of beauty" (Lam. 2:15). The beloved's beauty was so awesome that it "unnerved"

him as if he faced an army **with banners.**
Her **eyes** were so stunningly beautiful
(cf. Song. 1:15; 4:1) that they overwhelmed him. By repeating part of the
praise he had given her on their wedding
night (4:1-3) he was indirectly telling her
that his love for her had not diminished
since that first night. (For the meaning of
the metaphors on her **hair. . . . teeth,**
and **temples** in 6:5-7, see the comments
on 4:1-3). In fact his love and appreciation for her had grown since then. He
assured her that she was totally **unique**
(6:8-9a) as his **dove** (cf. 5:2), an opinion
shared by **her mother** (6:9b) and also **the
maidens** (lit., "daughters"), **queens, and
concubines** (v. 9c). On seeing the husband and wife reconciled, the women
were amazed at her beauty. They **praised
her** (v. 9), he said, by stating that she was
as fair as **the dawn . . . the moon . . . the
sun,** and **the stars.**

6:11-13. These verses tell the story of
the couple's reconciliation from the beloved's point of view. She knew that he
had "gone down to his garden" (v. 2). So
she **went** there **to see if** their love was
still **in bloom** (v. 11). As a person would
look in the spring for **new growth,** buds
on grape **vines,** and pomegranate blossoms, so she looked for fresh evidence of
their love. When she found him there his
first words were words of praise (vv. 4-
10), indicating that their love was in fact
flourishing.

One of the most difficult verses in
the Bible to interpret is verse 12 (see NIV
marg.). The Hebrew can be translated in
several ways. One translation which has
much to commend it is this: "I became
enraptured, for you placed me on the
chariots of the **people** of the prince."

When the husband's first words in
the garden were words of praise, she
"became enraptured"; she was beside
herself with joy. He then placed her on
his own chariot at the head of his entou-
rage. As they left, the inhabitants begged
her to stay (**come back**—stated four times
in v. 13) and the lover noted the intensity
of their desire to **gaze on** the **Shulam-
mite.** The Hebrew word rendered "Shu-
lammite" is actually the feminine form of
the name Solomon. Thus it means the
"Solomoness." "How you gaze. . . ?" (v.
13b) is better than **why would you
gaze. . . ?** They gazed at her and her
beauty, he said, as if they were viewing a

graceful **dance.** In some way the town of
Mahanaim is associated here with the
dance, though the point of the association is not clear. Mahanaim was east of
the Jordan River where David fled from
Absalom (2 Sam. 17:24).

B. Praise of the beloved and her love (7:1-10)

This section portrays the maturing of
the couple's marriage. The progress in
their love is revealed in two ways. First,
the imagery in these verses is much
bolder and more intimate than the imagery the lover used on the wedding night
(4:1-11). Such an increase in sexual freedom is a normal part of a healthy, maturing marriage. Second, the climactic nature of the refrain in 7:10 also speaks of
this maturation.

1. THE BELOVED'S CHARMS (7:1-6)

7:1. The beloved's **feet,** he said, were
beautiful and the shape of her **legs** reminded him of the exquisite **work** of a
master artisan.

7:2. The comparison of the beloved's
navel to **a rounded goblet** of **wine** would
be grotesque if taken as a visual comparison. The lover meant that her body was
as desirable and as intoxicating as wine
(cf. 4:10). Likewise the comparison of her
waist to **a mound of wheat** would be
absurd if interpreted visually. Wheat was
one of the main food sources in ancient
Palestine (Deut. 32:14; 2 Sam. 4:6; 17:28).
Thus his wife was both his "food"
(wheat) and "drink" (wine) in the sense
that her physical expressions of love
nourished and satisfied him.

7:3-4. On the comparison of her
breasts to **fawns** see the comments on
4:5. Her **neck** was beautiful and valuable
like an ivory tower (cf. 4:4). Her **eyes**
were beautiful and their effect on him
was as refreshing as **the pools of Heshbon,** a Moabite city (Num. 21:25) famous
for its fertility and water reservoirs. "The
soft glance of her eyes reflects the peace
and beauty of the Heshbon pools"
(Lehrman, "The Song of Songs," p. 26).
Those pools were near the city **gate of
Bath Rabbim,** whose location is unknown. Possibly Bath Rabbim was the
name of the gate. Her well-shaped **nose**
was like **the tower of Lebanon . . .
toward Damascus.** This strong tower
helped protect Damascus so her lovely

features reflected her strong character.

7:5. By comparing her **head** to **Mount Carmel,** he meant that she had a queenly bearing that was majestic and awesome. (On the majesty of Mount Carmel see Isa. 35:2; Jer. 46:18.) The beloved's **hair** (cf. Song 4:1; 6:5) was so beautiful that the powerful monarch Solomon was **held captive by its** beauty.

7:6. The lover concluded his praise of his beloved's charms with a summary statement of her perfect beauty, calling her **O love.**

2. THE LOVER'S DESIRE (7:7-9)

7:7-9a. In the remainder of the lover's speech he compared his wife's **stature** with the stately **palm** tree and her **breasts** to its **clusters of** dates. He also spoke of his desire for her **breasts,** comparing them to desirable and tasty **clusters** of grapes. He wanted to enjoy the sweet and intoxicating **fruit** of her love. Even her **breath** was sweet-smelling **like apples** and the kisses of her mouth were sweet **like . . . wine** (cf. 4:10).

7:9b. The beloved used the same image of wine (cf. v. 9a) to express her desire to satisfy her husband's wish for her. The rapid interchange of speakers (the beloved is not introduced as the speaker in v. 9b) reflected their excitement in giving and receiving kisses and caresses. The intermingling of their **lips** in kisses was stylistically reflected by the poem's intermingling of their voices.

3. THE REFRAIN OF MUTUAL POSSESSION (7:10)

7:10. The refrain of mutual possession was already given in 2:16 and 6:3. Here, however, the clause my lover "is mine" is replaced with **his desire is for me.** This is a more emphatic way of stating possession. How much more could a husband belong to his wife than for him to desire only her? She had so grown in the security of his love that she could now say that his only desire was for her. She had become so taken by his love for her that here she did not even mention her possession of him.

C. An invitation from the beloved (7:11-13)

7:11-13. In the preceding unit (vv. 1-10) the husband took the initiative in

their lovemaking; in this unit (vv. 11-13) she took the initiative. This is the first time in the Song where the beloved made a direct unambiguous request for sex. Previously her desire had been expressed in the third person (e.g., 1:2a; 2:6). Now, having grown more secure in the love of her husband, she felt free to initiate the lovemaking. So she asked him to **go to the countryside** where they could **spend the night** together.

Spring is a universal symbol for love. The beloved used the image of spring to ask whether there was still the same freshness and anticipation that had initially characterized their relationship (cf. 2:10-13). The answer, given by herself, was affirmative. Signs of spring were budding **vines** of grapes, blooming **pomegranates,** and fragrant **mandrakes.** Mandrakes, plants similar in size to apples and red in color, were supposedly aphrodisiacs (cf. Gen. 30:14-16).

D. The beloved's desire for a greater intimacy (8:1-4)

In these verses the beloved revealed a growing desire for greater intimacy with her husband-lover and rejoiced in the multifaceted nature of their relationship.

8:1. In the ancient Near East public displays of affection were frowned on except in the case of certain family members. Thus the beloved wished that her husband **were . . . like a brother** to her so that it would be acceptable to display her affection for him at any time.

8:2-4. The beloved playfully assumed the role of an older sister (**I would lead you**—the verb *nāhag* is always used of a superior leading an inferior) and even the role of the mother. The lady of the house **would give** special **wine** to the guests. So the beloved shared the characteristics of a sister, an older sister, and a mother in her relationship to her husband. The Song also portrays the lovers as friends (cf. 5:1, 16). Thus the lovers had a multifaceted relationship.

As his wife, she wished for his caresses. The Hebrew of 8:3 may be translated, "May **his left arm** be **under my head and** may **his right arm** embrace **me**" (cf. 2:6). But again she urged the **daughters of Jerusalem** (cf. comments on 1:5) not to force her expressions of **love** on her husband (cf. 2:7; 3:5).

V. The Conclusion: The Nature and Power of Love (8:5-7)

This section sums up the message of the Song of Songs with an enigmatic picture of love (v. 5) and a following explanation (vv. 6-7).

A. A picture of love (8:5)

8:5. No answer is given to the question **Who is this coming up from the desert leaning on her lover?** because none is needed. (In 3:6 the question was asked of the *groom*, "Who is this coming up from the desert?") A final picture of the Song's couple is presented here. The wilderness or desert had two symbolic associations in the Old Testament. First, the wilderness was associated with Israel's 40-year period of trial. In their love the couple had overcome trials which threatened their relationship (e.g., the insecurity of the beloved, 1:5-6; the foxes, 2:15; and indifference, 5:2-7). Second, the desert or wilderness was used as an image of God's curse (cf. Jer. 22:6; Joel 2:3). The couple's coming up out of the wilderness suggests that in a certain sense they had overcome the curse of disharmony pronounced on Adam and Eve (Gen. 3:16b; see comments there).

The image of the desert in Song of Songs 8:5a gives way to the image of **the apple tree** in verse 5b, in which the beloved speaks. The apple tree was sometimes used as a symbol of love and romance in the ancient world. The image here recalls the beginning of their love. The beloved **roused** (better, "awakened") her lover to love. The "awakening" is a metaphor for new life or rather a new way of perceiving life, which her love had brought to him. Much as he was the product of his parents' love and was brought into the world by physical **birth,** the lover had now received a second "birth" or "awakening" through the love of his beloved.

B. An explanation of love (8:6-7)

These verses may be divided into three parts: a request by the beloved (v. 6a), an explanation about the power of love (vv. 6b-7a), and a concluding practical application (v. 7b).

8:6a. In Old Testament times **a seal** was used to indicate ownership of a person's valued possessions. So the beloved asked to be her lover's most valued pos-

session, a possession that would influence his thoughts (**over your heart**) and his actions (**over your arm**). Such a demanding request required the explanation which she gave in verses 6b-7a.

8:6b-7a. These verses sum up the nature and power of the **love** depicted in the Song. It is as universal and irresistible as **death,** exclusive and possessive (in the sense of being genuinely concerned for the one loved) as **the grave,** passionate (as **blazing fire**) and as invincible and persevering as **many waters** and **rivers.** And all this is true because love is supported by the Creator who possesses all power. The words **like a mighty flame** are, literally, "like the very flame of the Lord" (cf. NIV marg.). Thus the Lord is portrayed as the Source of this powerful love.

8:7b. The final statement about the **love** depicted in the Song is that it is priceless. **All** one's **wealth** would be totally inadequate to purchase such love. In fact such money **would be . . . scorned,** because love cannot be bought. Any attempt to "buy" love depersonalizes it.

If love is priceless, how then can it be obtained? The answer is that it must be given. And ultimately love is a gift from God. The epilogue explains how the beloved received this priceless gift of love.

VI. The Epilogue: How Love Began (8:8-14)

Verses 8-12 are a flashback explaining (a) the protection of the beloved by her older brothers when she was young and (b) her subsequent initial meeting with Solomon. The Song concludes in verses 13-14 with statements that show the couple's love has not lost its intensity.

8:8-9. The beloved grew up in a home where her older brothers made definite plans to prepare for her marriage (**the day she is spoken for**). If she displayed good character and judgment and resisted temptation (**if she is a wall**) then they would allow her a large measure of freedom and reward her. **Towers of silver** may be translated "a turret (sing.) of silver," referring to a beautiful, much-valued head ornament, or it may simply refer figuratively to their adorning her as people adorned defense towers with silver. But if she were reckless and prone to immorality (**if she is** open to advances like **a door**) then they planned to restrict her freedom (figuratively spoken of as enclosing **her with** cedar **panels,** like barricading a door with planks).

8:10. The beloved's own testimony is that she was chaste (**I am a wall**). Therefore she did not need the restrictions her brothers suggested. Having grown up and matured physically, she was then pure for her husband which enabled her to give him (Solomon) **contentment.** The Hebrew word for contentment (*šālôm*) provides an interesting wordplay because it sounds much like Solomon's name (*šᵉlōmōh*).

8:11-12. Apparently they first met in **a vineyard** that **Solomon** had leased **out** to her brothers. (The location of **Baal Hamon** is unknown.) **Each** tenant was to grow enough grapes to make **1,000 shekels** (about 25 pounds) **of silver** for the landowner. And each tenant would receive **200 shekels** (about 5 pounds) **of silver** as his wages. As stated near the beginning of the book (1:6), the beloved worked in the vineyard, submitting to her brothers' discipline. While there she met Solomon and he fell in love with her. **My own vineyard** is a metaphor for the beloved's own person (cf. 1:6). Only she could give herself to another (she said her own vineyard was hers **to give**) and she freely chose to give herself to Solomon. Even her possessions (including her income, **1,000 shekels**) were his.

8:13-14. These words of the two lovers recall early passionate requests from their courtship days which show that their love had not lost its intensity. He said to her, **let me hear your voice** (cf. 2:14); and she requested that he (whom she again called **my lover**) **be like a gazelle or like a young stag** (cf. 2:17; also see 2:9). In their courtship she had longed for him to take her as his bride (see comments on 2:17). Now in their marriage she longed with the same intensity for his strength and agility. Like the "hills" in 2:17, the **mountains** in 8:14 may refer to her breasts. Being **spice-laden** means they were perfumed (see comments on some of the spices mentioned in 4:13-14).

The Song of Songs is a beautiful picture of God's "endorsement" of physical love between husband and wife. Marriage is to be a monogamous, permanent,

self-giving unit, in which the spouses are intensely devoted and committed to each other, and take delight in each other. "For this reason a man will leave his father and mother and be united to his wife, and they will become one flesh" (Gen. 2:24).

The Song of Songs shows that sex in marriage is not "dirty." The physical attractiveness of a man and woman for each other and the fulfillment of those longings in marriage are natural and honorable. But the book does more than extol physical attraction between the sexes. It also honors pleasing qualities in the lovers' personalities. Also moral purity before marriage is praised (e.g., Song 4:12). Premarital sex has no place in God's plans (2:7; 3:5). Faithfulness before and after marriage is expected and is honored (6:3; 7:10; 8:12). Such faithfulness in marital love beautifully pictures God's love for and commitment to His people.

BIBLIOGRAPHY

Carr, G. Lloyd. *The Song of Solomon: An Introduction and Commentary.* The Tyndale Old Testament Commentaries. Downers Grove, Ill.: InterVarsity Press, 1984.

Dillow, Joseph C. *Solomon on Sex.* Nashville: Thomas Nelson, 1977.

Ginsburg, Christian D. *The Song of Songs and Coheleth.* New York: KTAV Publishing House, 1970.

Glickman, S. Craig. *A Song for Lovers.* Downers Grove, Ill.: InterVarsity Press, 1976.

Gordis, Robert. *The Song of Songs and Lamentations.* Rev. ed. New York: KTAV Publishing House, 1974.

Harper, Andrew. *The Song of Solomon.* Cambridge: Cambridge University Press, 1907.

Lehrman, S.M. "The Song of Songs." In *The Five Megilloth.* London: Soncino Press, 1946.

Pope, Marvin H. *Song of Songs.* The Anchor Bible. Garden City, N.Y.: Doubleday & Co., 1977.

Rowley, H.H. "The Interpretation of the Song of Solomon." In *The Servant of the Lord and Other Essays on the Old Testament.* London: Lutterworth Press, 1952.

At David C Cook, we equip the local church around the corner and around the globe to make disciples. Come see how we are working together—go to **www.davidccook.com**. Thank you!